CHILDREN FROM THE SKY

Duncan Lunan

In the late 12th century, two very strange children came out of an ancient earthwork at the village of Woolpit in East Anglia. They wore clothes of a colour and material never seen before, spoke a language nobody recognised, and were coloured green all over. Later, when they had learned 'our manner of speaking', and lost their green colour, they described a homeland which was no place on Earth. The boy died within a year, but the girl grew up and married.

Is this a fairy story, or were the children runaways from some primitive tribe? In the 17th century Robert Burton included them in the astronomy section of *The Anatomy of Melancholy*, suggesting that they came from another world. Could it be true?

Duncan Lunan has located the places in the story and traced the people, who turn out to be real, though mysterious, and very highly connected. The incident at Woolpit was one of a series at linked sites, and seems to have been anticipated by the authorities of the time.

Lunan traces the green girl, traces her descendants to the present day, and investigates strange things happening in the sky and other events relating to her 'arrival'. It suggests that in mediaeval times there might have been mass abductions from Earth, by extraterrestrials, for experimental purposes, with the knowledge if not the agreement of some of the terrestrial authorities -if so, Lunan suggests, *"The X-Files* are set in the wrong century."

CW91425889

The Green Children

Artwork by Sydney Jordan

CHILDREN FROM THE SKY

A Speculative Treatment of a Mediaeval Mystery
- the Green Children of Woolpit

DUNCAN LUNAN

To Ajma, may thanks from Duncan and Linda

mutusliber

LONDON

First published in by Mutus Liber in 2012

BM Mutus Liber
London WC1N 3XX

A CIP catalogue record for this book is available from the British Library.

ISBN-13: 978-1-908097-05-7

www.mutusliber.com

DEDICATION

To Mr. A.R. Nicol, Principal Teacher of Latin, Marr College, but for whose efforts in the 1960's I would never have been able to research this book in the 70's, 80's and 90's.

CONTENTS

DRAMATIS PERSONAE

The people in this story were real: they had parents and descendants, uncles and cousins. They owned and exchanged property, fought in wars, appeared in court as plaintiffs, defenders and witnesses. Because real life is untidy, often their contacts have to be named, even if only once. Below the main players are listed by the reigns where they first appear; e.g. Richard de Calna under Henry I, though he also lived under Stephen and Henry II.

William the Conqueror, reigned 1066-87
His natural son **William Peverell**, lord of Nottingham.
His physician **Nigel the Doctor**, of Calne in Wiltshire.
Nigel's brother **Roger le Poer**, viceroy of England.

William Rufus, reigned 1087-1100

Henry I, reigned 1100-35
His heiress, the empress **Matilda**.
Stephen of Blois, next in succession, made king instead of her.
Matilda's son, the future **Henry II** of England.
Everard de Calna, bishop of Norwich.
His brother **Nigel de Calna**, bishop of Ely.
Nigel's son **Richard de Calna**, landowner in Suffolk, c. 1116-89.

King Stephen, reigned 1135-1154
His nephew **Hugh du Puiset**, bishop of Durham.
Gilbert Foliot, bishop of Hereford, later Bishop of London 1163-87.
William Peverell of Nottingham, son of the castle builder.
Hervey de Glanville, constable, leader of the English in the Second Crusade.
His priest **Raol**, chronicler of the fall of Lisbon.
William de Warenne, head of king Louis's personal guard on Crusade, d. 1148.
Richard Fitz-Neal, illegitimate son of Nigel de Calna, later treasurer of England and bishop of London (1190's).

Henry II, reigned 1154-1189
His queen, **Eleanor of Aquitaine**.
Their sons **Henry**, rebelled 1173, died 1183;
       Geoffrey, another rebel, died 1186;

> **Richard**, another rebel, later king Richard I;
> **John**, later king.

Thomas à Becket, archbishop of Canterbury; murdered 1170.

Pope Alexander III, elected 1159.

John of Oxford, dean of Salisbury, ambassador, later bishop of Norfolk.

Samson de Botington, monk of Bury St. Edmunds, abbot 1182-1210.

Geoffrey Ridell, archdeacon of Canterbury & acting Vice-Chancellor of England, 1163-73, bishop of Ely 1173-89.

Ranulf de Glanville, son of Hervey above, Sheriff of Yorkshire, future Chief Justice of England.

Richard de Hastings, Master of the Knights Templar in England, c.1155 to c.1180 or '85.

Walter de Coutances, joint Vice-Chancellor of England 1173-82, later archbishop of Rouen.

Ralph of Coggeshall, later abbot of Coggeshall 1207-18; compiler of the *Chronicon Anglicanum*.

Walter de Calna, magister of Norwich: son of Richard de Calna.

Walter's daughter **Sibylla**, later married to John Fitz-Bernard.

Her elder co-heiress **Agnes**.

Agnes's future husband **Richard Barre**, ambassador, later seal-bearer to prince Henry, later archdeacon of Lisieux and canon of Salisbury, still later a roving justice and archdeacon of Ely.

Their illegitimate son **Richard de Rushell**, aka Richard de Rowley.

Their legitimate son **William Barre**.

Richard I, reigned 1189-1199

William of Newburgh, compiler of *Historia Rerum Anglicarum*.

William de Longchamp, bishop of Ely, protector of England.

Walter Fitz-Bernard, son of John Fitz-Bernard and Sibylla de Calna.

King John, reigned 1199-1216

Richard Barre, grandson of Richard and Agnes.

William de Cantilupe, sheriff of Warwickshire.

His son **William**, second baron de Cantilupe.

His grandson **William**, third baron.

Henry III, reigned 1216-1272

Richard de Clare, seventh earl of Gloucester.

Matthew Paris, compiler of *Chronica Majora and Historia Anglorum*.

Hugh de Sherdilow, bought de Calna property in Suffolk.

<u>Edward I, reigned 1274-1307</u>
John Barre, knight, descendant of Richard and Agnes.

<u>Edward II, reigned 1307-1327</u>

<u>Edward III, reigned 1327-1377</u>
Anne, daughter of John Barre, married William Devereux.
John Bardwell, great-grandson of John Barre, inherited the former de Calna Suffolk property.

PART ONE - HISTORY AND MYSTERY

Chapter One - ABOUT THE GREEN CHILDREN

"'The historian, whatever be his subject, is as definitely bound as the chemist "to proclaim certainties as certain, falsehoods as false, and uncertainties as dubious"'. Those are the words, not of a modern scientist, but of the seventeenth century monk, Jean Mabillon; they sum up his literary profession of faith."

~ G.C. Coulton[1]

"We are all agreed that your theory is crazy. The question which divides us is whether it is crazy enough."

~ Niels Bohr to Wolfgang Pauli, 1958[2]

In the 12th century, two strange children appeared at the village of Woolpit in East Anglia. They spoke a language nobody recognised, wore clothing of unfamiliar colour and material, and were coloured green all over. When they learned 'our' speech, and lost their green colour, they said they came from a country of permanent twilight, though there was a brightly lit country in the distance, on the far side of a very broad river. Two 12th century chronicles, written separately, give the story in detail.

I discovered it in the 1621 *Anatomy of Melancholy* by Robert Burton, when I was a student. Burton was a 'Renaissance Man' and he packed his book with all fields of knowledge. In Part 2 Mem. 3, 'A Digression of the Air', on meteorology and astronomy, what most excited him was that astronomers such as Tycho Brahe, Johannes Kepler and Galileo, and theorists like Giordano Bruno, had proved the planets are actual worlds, moving around the Sun in ellipses, not crystalline shells. "Tycho Brahe and Jordanus Brunus... have one and the self-same opinion about the essence and matter of the heavens, that is not hard and impenetrable, as Peripatetics hold, transparent, of a *quinta essentia* [fifth essence], 'but that it is penetrable and soft as the air is, and that the planets move in it, as birds in the air, fishes in the sea'... as Mars among the

1

rest, which sometimes, as Kepler confirms by his own and Tycho's accurate observations, comes nearer the earth than the sun, and is again eftsoons aloft in Jupiter's orb; and other sufficient reasons, far above the moon ..."

In which case, space travel may be possible. "If the heavens then be permeable, as these men deliver, and no lets, it were not amiss in this aerial progress to make wings and fly up, which that Turk in Busbequius made his fellow-citizens in Constantinople believe he would perform: and some newfangled wits, methinks, should some time or other find out: or if that may not be, yet with a Galileo's glass, or Icaromenippus' wings in Lucian,* command the spheres and the heavens, and see what is done amongst them."[3]

And if we can go to them... "But *hoc posito*, to grant this their tenet of the earth's motion: if the earth move, it is a planet, and shines to them in the moon, and to the other planetary inhabitants, as the moon and they do to the earth: but shine she doth, as Galileo, Kepler and others prove, and then, *per consequens*, the rest of the planets are inhabited, as well as the moon... and those several planets have their several moons about them, as the Earth has hers, as Galileo hath already evinced through his glasses: four about Jupiter, two about Saturn [a blurred sighting of the rings]... and more about Mars, Venus [wrong]; and the rest they hope to find out, peradventure even amongst the fixed stars, which Brunus and Brutius have already averred. Then (I say) the Earth and they be planets alike, inhabited alike, moved about the sun, the common centre of the world alike, and it may be those two green children which Nubrigensis speaks of in his time, that fell from heaven, came from thence."

In Bishop Godwin's "The Man in the Moone" (1638), one of the first space-flight novels, the 'Lunars' exile their unpromising children to Earth, usually to North America. "Sometimes, though but seldom, they mistake their aim, and fall upon Europe, Asia or Africa. I remember some year since I read certain stories tending to confirm what is related by these Lunars, and especially one Chapter of Nubrigensis."[4]

'Nubrigensis' was Canon William of Newburgh Abbey in Yorkshire, whose *Historia Rerum Anglicarum* (History of English Affairs)[5], written in 1195-98, is considered reliable. After praising the Venerable Bede and the historian Gildas for their pains to be accurate, his preface denounces the fictional history of Geoffrey of Monmouth (see Chap. 4), particularly the story of king Arthur. He's been described as 'a humourless individual',[6] but that's not fair. To illustrate his scepticism about wonderful events, he tells how queen Margaret of Scotland tried to arrange for the sexual education of king Malcolm 'the Virgin'. A young woman of good family was asked to take the matter in hand, but on finding her in his chamber, Malcolm gave her his bed and spent the night in prayer: in the morning, she was found to be still *virgo intacta*. "Those who hold signs in awe... can say what they like; my emphatic view is that we should prefer the miracle of a young king's virginity, thus besieged but impregnable, not only to giving sight to the blind but even to raising the dead."

'Ghost-busters' were needed because miracles, which attracted pilgrims, were big business; Chaucer's *Canterbury Tales*, related by pilgrims to the shrine of Thomas à Becket, were later to be one of the first great works in the English language. Every town and village wanted a share of the new tourist industry: having the church confirm a miracle on your patch was the 12th century equivalent of having U.S. forces leave you with a runway which can take Jumbo Jets. William's unusual attitude is a reason to take the green children story seriously.

In Book One, chap. 27: *De Viridibus Pueris*, 'about the green children', he tells it reluctantly, because miracles are meant to be instructional, and he could draw no religious or moral lesson from this one. Unlike others of the time, it has no recognisable roots in folk-tales; in chap. 28, after attributing those to 'wicked angels', William adds, "However of those green children, who are said to have emerged from the earth, the explanation is so much more obscure, that the frailty of our perception is not adequate to unearth it."

It's not even connected with the 'Green Man' of the old pagan religion, featured in church carvings for 1700 years, commemorated on pub signs and by the Greene King brewery of Bury St. Edmunds, but named only by Lady Raglan in 1939. Kathleen Basford's *The Green Man* traces his origin to the 1st century AD and the more formal version to the century after, but includes no children nor other elements of the story, even though the Green Man is found at Bury, Southwell, Ely, Norwich and King's Lynn. The carvings at Ely and Norwich both date from the 14th century, two hundred years after William of Newburgh's time.[7]

3

Editing the 1884 edition of William's chronicle, Richard Howlett says there's no evidence that he ever left Yorkshire; yet he'd interviewed so many witnesses to this event that they overcame his disbelief. If he'd been to East Anglia in person, perhaps the longest journey of his life (Fig. 1.1), or even sent a representative, it suggests the case was important.

ENGLAND

Fig. 1.1. The counties of England.
Drawing by Dave Allen.

"And not to be omitted is a prodigy unheard of by the people of the age, which is known to have happened in England under King Stephen. And truly I was in doubt over this for a long time, even though this was known by many, and the matter seemed to me a joke, to admit either nothing or something very obscure of reckoning into the truth, until I was so overwhelmed by the weight of so many (and such) witnesses that I was forced to believe and wonder that by no force of mind could I attack or expose it.

"There is a village in East Anglia four or five miles (as they say) distant from the monastery of the noble and blessed king and martyr Edmund. Near this village certain very old ditches are visible: which in the English language are called Wulfpittes, that is [the] ditches of [the] wolves, and give their name to the village which they lie near. From these ditches at harvest time, and with the reapers occupied about the collection of the produce [plural] from the fields, there emerged two children, a male and a female, green of the entire body and dressed in clothing of extraordinary colour and unknown material. And when they blundered thunderstruck through the fields, captured by the reapers they were taken into the village, and many had crowded to a spectacle so novel: for several days they were kept without access to food. When therefore they had almost expired of fasting, nevertheless they would not consider any food which was offered; by chance it came to pass that beans were brought in from the fields; seizing upon which from that place, they sought the bean itself in the stalks; and finding nothing in the hollow of the stalks, they wept bitterly. Then one of those present held out to them the beans removed from the pods, which at once they accepted and ate up freely.

"They were fed by this food for several months, until they changed to the use of bread. At length with the nature of our foods prevailing, their own colour gradually changing, they were even 'completed' like us; they also distinguished the use of our speech. It appeared to the wise, that they might receive the sacrament of holy baptism, and that too [even that] was done. But the boy, who seemed to be younger by birth, living a short time after baptism died young, his sister remaining sound, and not in any way different from a woman of our race. Certainly it was afterwards said of her that she had taken a husband at/living at Lenna [modern King's Lynn], and was said to be surviving a few years ago.

"Naturally when now they had our habit of speaking, they were asked who and from whence they were, they are said to have replied: 'People of the land of Saint Martin, who of course in the land of our birth is held in the very

5

highest exceptional respect.' Consequently asked, wherever was that land, and by what means they had come from thence, 'Either of these', they said, 'we do not know. We remember this much: because on a certain day we were driving to pasture/adding to our father's animals in the fields, we heard a certain great sound which now we are accustomed to hear at St. Edmund's when they say the bells are ringing. And when we turned our minds to that sound which surprised us, suddenly/unawares, as if placed in some loss of mind, we found ourselves in the field where you were reaping.' Asked whether Christ was believed in and whether the Sun rose, they said that land was Christian, and had churches. 'But the sun', they said, 'of our countries does not rise; and our country is little lit by its rays, but is satisfied with that measure of light, which with you precedes sunrise or follows sunset. Moreover/far off a certain bright land is seen not far from our land, with a very broad river dividing the two'. These and many other things, *which it would be tedious to retell* [my italics!], they are said to have replied to those struck inquisitively. Let each one say what he wishes, and account for these things as best he can; but it does not grieve me to have set forth this strange and wonderful event."

Exact translation is important, even if it reads awkwardly. To quote a 12th century writer, commissioned by the Masters of the Knights Templar to translate the Book of Judges into French, "'Who wishes to translate such a book should not lose the truth of the sense in order to use beautiful words, nor so change the truth that his translation will be blamed, and neither sense nor words approach the truth any more' ...words which every translator may contemplate to his benefit."[8] Most published versions of the green children's story are inaccurate, and I've made my own translations, after comparing the 1988 William of Newburgh edition with the 1884 version, and the 1610 and 1719 ones in the National Library of Scotland, and the only suspect line with the British Library manuscript copy, made soon after William's death).

Ralph, sixth abbot of Coggeshall, 25 miles south of Woolpit, in Essex, west of Colchester (Fig. 1.2), told the later story in his *Chronicon Anglicanum*,[9] headlined *De quodam puero et puella de terra emergentibus* - 'of a certain boy and girl emerging from the earth'. He doesn't copy William - the few Latin words which they share seem significant, and his source is the family with whom the formerly green girl was living as an adult. By implication he places it not in

King Stephen's reign, which ended in 1154, but under Henry II between 1155 and 1189.

East Anglia and Essex

Fig. 1.2. Map of East Anglia.
Drawing by Dave Allen.

"Also another wonderful thing not unlike the first [a mermaid] happened in Suffolk at St. Maria of Wulpetes. A certain boy was found with his sister by the inhabitants of that place near the edge of the pitfall which it contains, who had a form in all parts similar to other men, but who differed in the colour of their skin from all mortals of our habitable world.   For the whole surface of their skin was dyed with the colour green.   No-one was able to understand their speech.   Therefore taken to the home, at Wikes, of the lord Richard de Calne, a sort of knight, to be wondered at, they wept inconsolably.   Bread and other common foods were offered to them, but they did not wish to be nourished by any food which was brought to them, so for a long time they were tormented by great hunger, because they believed all the food of that place to be 'undigestible', as the girl later stated in evidence.   At length when beans with newly cut stalks were brought into the house, they signed with great avidity for those beans to be given to them.   When these were freely brought to them, they opened the stalks, not the pods of the bean-plants, thinking that the beans were contained in the stalks.   But finding no beans in the stalks, again they began to weep.   When the bystanders realised this, they opened the pods, showing the beans uncovered; these were eaten with great joy, and for a long time they would take absolutely no other food.   Truly the boy, always seeming brought down by exhaustion/depression, died after a short time. Truly the girl enjoying a full recovery, and become accustomed to all kinds of food, put off that completely leek-green colour, and gradually regained a sanguine condition of the whole body.   Being later reborn by immersion of holy baptism, and remaining for many years on the staff of the aforesaid knight (as we frequently heard from the same knight and his family) she showed herself greatly wanton and lascivious/wilful and independent.   Truly asked often about the people of her country, she swore on oath that as many as all the inhabitants and all things that were held in that land/world were dyed with the colour green, and that they saw no sun, but were pleased with a certain light, as if happened after sunset.   But asked by what means she had come into this land with the aforesaid boy, she said, because when animals were being followed, they went down into a certain cave.   Having gone into it, they heard a certain delightful sound of bells; seized by that pleasant sound, they progressed by wandering through the cavern for a long time, until they arrived at the exit.   When they emerged from there, as if astonished and made breathless with fear by the excessive brightness of the sun and the unaccustomed temperature of the air, they stayed for a long time over the rim of the cavern.   When they were frightened by the strangeness of the men coming upon them, they wished to flee, but could by no means find the entrance of the cave, before they were captured by them."

8

Fig. 1.3. "Astonished and made breathless with fear by the brightness of the Sun".
Painting by Sydney Jordan.

Ralph's wonders are even more down-to-earth: a mermaid (a manatee?), a feral man (Chap.8) and giant fossil teeth. In the incident now called 'the Ghost Templars' (Chap.11), Ralph doesn't suggest that they were ghosts. His only supernatural incident is a talking poltergeist at Lavenham (Chap.10).

It's unusual to find a strange event in two chronicles written from different perspectives, in different vocabularies, yet agreeing on the main details. If we put the two versions together, it becomes even more interesting. For instance, the children didn't recognise the bean-plants - they didn't know which part was edible, but the colour was crucial. There's an elision in what the girl said later: not *everything* in her homeland was that colour, just everything that was safe to eat - a colour code so simple that even children knew it.

With permanent twilight in one place and bright sun in another, it sounds like an earthlike world, with a trapped rotation, keeping one face to its sun as the Moon does to us. Burton knew from astronomy that such conditions couldn't be found on Earth, so he thought the children might be from Mars or Venus. We know that for humans to exist on another world, it would have to be extensively modified to support them, and they must have come from here in the first place (Chap.8) – very interesting, if the children's story was literally true. And as William tells it, the children's arrival sounds like instantaneous transmission of matter - common in science fiction, but coming to seem possible, at least, in some versions of quantum theory (Chap.18). But first I have to show enough historical evidence for what happened here, to make it worth guessing what was going on elsewhere.

Chapter Two - THE VISITATION OF WOOLPIT

Bethan   I'm showing I'm just like her.

Sara   That's very kind,
        Except you didn't crawl from out a weed farm
        To gather all of Woolpit in a field
        For the amusement of the constellations.

~ Glyn Maxwell, *Wolfpit*

Woolpit is seven miles east of Bury St. Edmunds, just south of the A14 to Ipswich. In the 12th century it was on the pilgrim route from the coast to Bury St. Edmunds, and stood at its junction with two other roads. It achieved official market-town status in the 13th century.

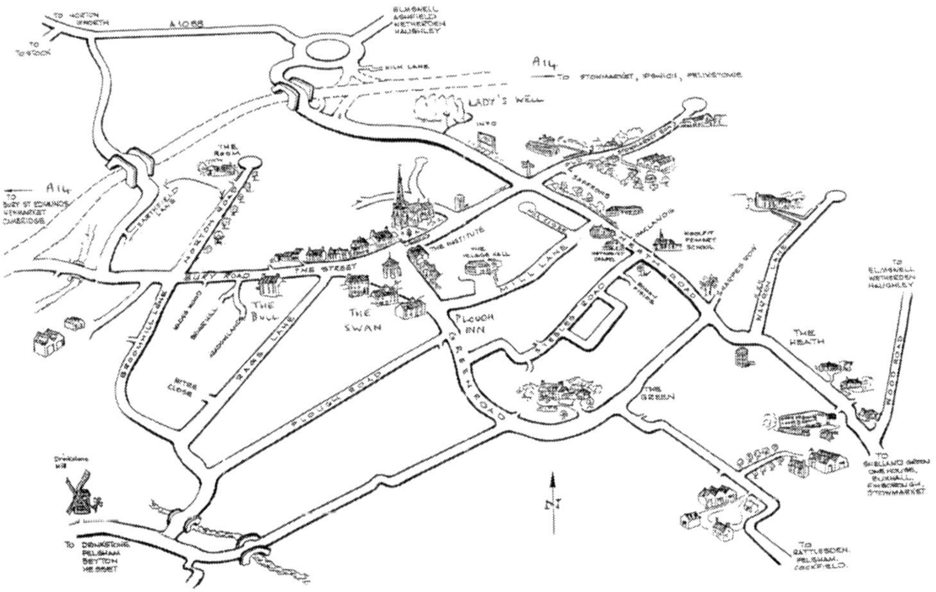

Fig. 2.1. Plan of Woolpit (Woolpit Bygones Museum) amended. Old Brickworks (top right), Swan Inn and Woolpit Bull captioned, Lady's Well and the former Plough Inn added.

Fig. 2.2. Woolpit centre and Swan Inn, 1993.
Photo by Duncan Lunan.

The village centre is a triangle, not a square, where the three roads converged (Fig. 2.1). Almost every building on the narrow main street is historic, the oldest from the 15th century.[1] The Swan Inn dates back to the 16th, (Fig. 2.2) and in 1993 it still had the old coach-yard and stables at the rear. At an 18th century fair a dancing bear proved so popular that both bear and owner became drunk, the owner thrown in the Lock-up and the bear taken to the Swan[2] - presumably chained up in the stable, but it's nice to picture it holding court at the bar, ordering rounds for its new friends.

Woolpit may have been Villa Faustini, home of a prosperous Roman in the area, perhaps the praetorium of the 14th Legion,[3] or a Roman settlement called Sitomagus (place of the Sitones, at the ford), though Blomefield's *History of Norfolk* says that's a mistake, confusing Norfolk miles with Roman ones.[4] The Woolpit Museum covers recent history, the brickworks and the school, but sells leaflets giving older details.

The village is called Wulfpettes, Vulpetes, Vulpites and Wulpetes - like *Quatermass and the Pit*, where 'Hob's Lane', named for the Devil, was changed to Hobbs Lane for the cricketer? But even in Anglo-Saxon 'Woolpit' means 'pit for catching wolves',[5] though this one may refer to Ulfcytel, Ulfketel or Alfketel, who donated the village to Bury St. Edmunds Abbey between 1005 and 1009 - hence 'Ulf's pits'. The base of the East Angles' kingdom was Dunwich, on the Suffolk coast, but some earls such as Ulfcytel were in Thetford, till he was driven out in 1011 by Danish raids. Bury St. Edmunds was attacked in 1013, but because the town wasn't fortified, the saint's relics had been removed to London. Ulfcytel was killed by the Danes in 1016. Another Edmund, king of the West Saxons, later gave Thetford to Bury St. Edmunds Abbey, starting a conflict between the abbots and the bishops of Norfolk (Chap.6).

Woolpit is listed in the Abbey's assets between 1045 and 1098. 'Wolves' pit' may be a *later* version, because the last wolves in East Anglia were caught nearby. The 1977 Jubilee sign commemorates the church, the green children and the wolves (Fig. 2.3).

Woolpit St. Mary church, named in Ralph's account, predates the Norman Conquest and is mentioned in the 1085 Domesday Book. The North and South Aisles are 14th century, the screen, chancel window, roof and benches from the 15th and the porch from 1473. There was once a Lady Chapel "in the churchyard", possibly where the vestry is now. The spire, destroyed by lightning in 1602, blown down in 1703 and hit by lightning again in 1852,[6] now dates from 1855 (Fig. 2.4).

Figs. 2.3. Woolpit village 1977 Jubilee sign.
Photo by Duncan Lunan.

Ralph of Coggeshall says the children reached Woolpit through caves, and Paul Harris suggested in the *Fortean Times* that there were underground passages to Woolpit, now filled in.[7] But Woolpit is on Pleistocene clay, broken by gravel deposits left by the glaciers; the water table is a foot or so below the surface, and Ralph's caves don't exist.[8] Steve Harvey, a local resident, told me that in the 1950s an underground room was found by children in a sandpit, and filled in by anxious parents;[9] but the County Record Office doesn't know about it, and it has a ring of urban myth. Maybe it began with genuine, man-

Fig. 2.4. St. Mary's Church, Woolpit, 2003.
Photo by Duncan Lunan.

made caves in Bury St. Edmunds, flint or chalk-mines for the town's lime-kilns: in the 1970s, a street of new houses disappeared into one.[10]

The pit from which Woolpit took its name isn't on record as such, and the County Archaeology Department had no aerial photographs because pits etc. had been filled in by farmers, and crop marks don't persist in clay soil.

15

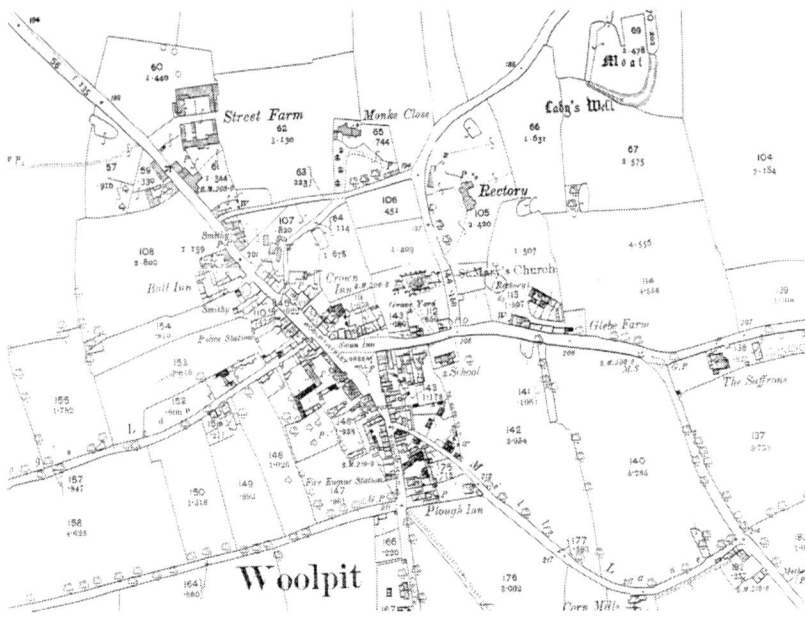

Fig. 2.5. Ordnance Survey Map of Woolpit, 1904.

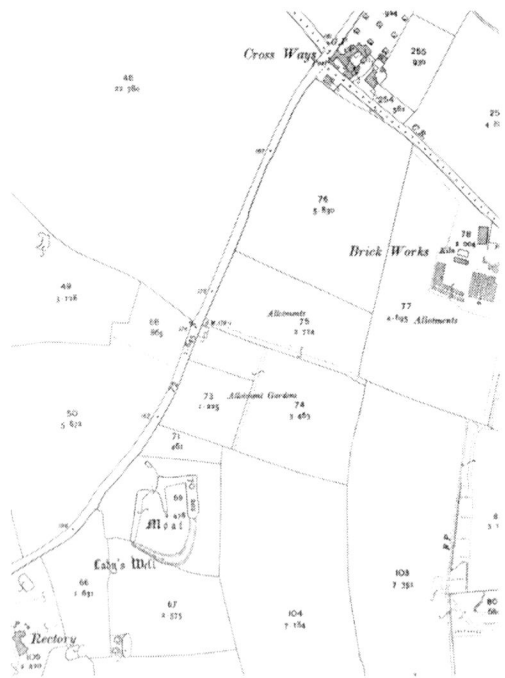

Fig. 2.6. Ordnance Survey detail of the Lady's Well.

16

There had been little excavation in or around the village, though a watch was kept on new foundations being dug. But the Woolpit streets are functionally named: Plough Lane to the former Plough Inn, Kiln Lane to the old brick-works, Green Street to Woolpit Green. In 1904, the main street, now just 'The Street', was 'Woolpit Street' (Fig. 2.5). Could it have led to the Wool-pit? There is a 'Street Farm' at the top, and the pit was near the village. There was a history exhibition in the church, including a feature near the farm, mentioned to me by the landlady at the Swan, and on the map as an antiquity.

Fig. 2.7. The Lady's Well copse in Autumn.
Photo by Lyndesay Birkmyre.

Just outside Woolpit, straight across the fields from the former buildings of Street Farm, is the Lady's Well (Fig. 2.6). Also known as Palgress, it's on the edge of a heart-shaped moated site northeast of the village, marked by a cresset on a pole outside the wood (Fig. 2.7). There's no evidence of a building in the central glade, but Mr. Pendleton, the County Archaeologist, told me that on the clay it was common to build on wooden sleepers, taken away when the building was demolished.

Fig. 2.8. Plan on D.o.E. plaque at the Lady's Well, 2003.
Photo by Tony Brown.

Large amounts of rubbish had filled in the moats before the site was restored by the Department of the Environment; only the eastern side had been cleared in 2003, but by 2011 it had all been done, though the well was now half buried and the D.o.E. sign had gone. The well is by the new entrance to the wood, diametrically across from the old one (Fig. 2.8), its brick casing is modern. The water's unusually high sulphate content is supposed to have curative powers for eyesight, and the surrounding trees were hung with votive offerings. According to the oldest inhabitants in 1826, it had then been there for at least ninety years, and there are records of pilgrimages to Woolpit for health reasons in the 15th century, even from Ireland; Blomefield's *Norfolk* records some even before the 12th century. (There was a 'John of the Welle' in Woolpit in 1346, but that could be any well, not necessarily the Lady's.)[11]

In August 2011, when I took part in a documentary for *The National Geographic Ancient X-Files*, the climax was filmed in Woolpit Wood, two miles away, at the suggestion of John Wiley of Woolpit Museum. I wasn't certain that we were in the right place for the ancient ditches he'd described, but the Wood seems too far from the village to fit the description and the Lady's Well seems a much better candidate. Its cleared moats are too large to be used as deadfall traps, and certainly deep and wide enough for the children to have hidden in - even though, according to Steve Harvey, the water level is twenty feet higher than in a gravel pit nearby, about the level of the dry floors I saw at the Lady's Well in 2011. "Creepy old ditch. Seen all sorts, I figure," says a character in Glyn Maxwell's play *Wolfpit*.[12] Although they're open to the sky in winter (fig. 2.9), in summer when they're overhung by trees (fig. 2.10), the moats are quite dark enough for the children to have been overcome by the brightness of the Sun when they emerged - especially if they had never seen it before.

"The home of lord Richard de Calne, at Wikes" took more finding, and I had to make a second trip to East Anglia before I felt confident about it. It's a long story, and to set the scene we have to start a century before the green children, at the time of the Norman Conquest.

Fig. 2.9.

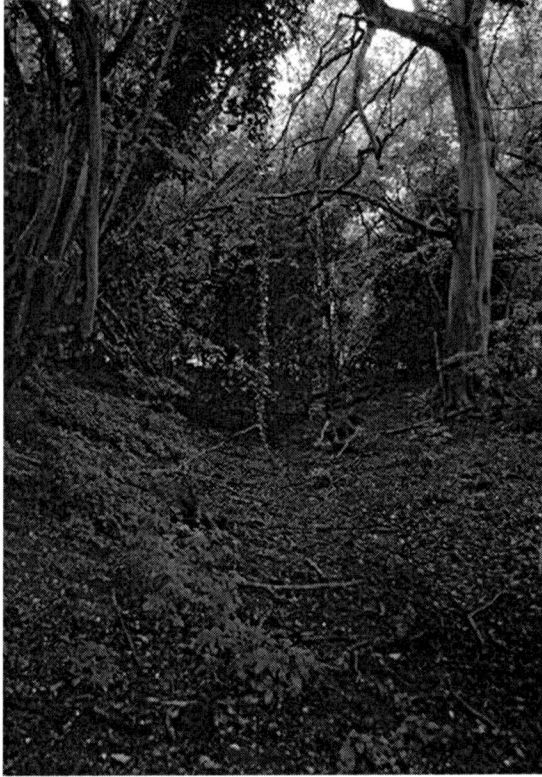

Figs. 2.9 & 2.10.
Eastern moat of the Lady's Well in winter 2003, western moat in summer 2009.
Photos by Tony Brown and Linda Lunan.

Chapter Three: 1066 AND AFTER

"...all the History that you can remember is in this book, which is the result of years of research in golf-clubs, gun-rooms, green-rooms, etc. For instance, two out of the four Dates originally included were eliminated at the last moment, a research done at the Eton and Harrow match having revealed that they are *not memorable*."

~ W.C. Sellar and R.J. Yeatman, *1066 and All That*

Sellar and Yeatman cite only two dates in English history - Julius Caesar's invasion of 55 BC, and the conquest of England by the Normans in 1066.[1] I can't be as cavalier about dates, but big events like the captivity of Richard I or John's signing of Magna Carta will be lightly touched on, or even ignored, if they have no bearing on our story.

Foucault's Pendulum (see Chap. 11) says that the mediaeval calendar year began at Easter: January was late in the year, not early. In Europe that was generally true, but in Britain there were several different New Years – Easter at some churches, but not until 1200 AD, apparently; some on January 1st (the Feast of the Lord's Circumcision), many at Christmas ('the 1179th year of Our Lord's birth', for what we'd call Christmas 1178 - see Chap. 12). The Venerable Bede used September 24th, and others adopted March 25th, the date of the Annunciation - each three days after the corresponding equinox, as Christmas Day is three days after the winter solstice, perhaps by analogy with the three days of Easter. Later March 25th began the civil year, till the Gregorian calendar was adopted in 1751 and dates jumped forward by eleven days. The British financial year has begun on April 5th ever since.[2]

Each way of telling this story has its problems, but I'll stick as closely as possible to simple chronological order, though it means that I can't bring the green children on stage until Chap. 9. Meanwhile a lot of background has to be introduced and carried forward. To help, the list of 'Dramatis Personae ' at the start identifies the participants in roughly the order they appear, and at the end the historical events are listed in *strict* chronological order.

1. Astronomy and the Conquest

Astronomically the 11th century was interesting.   At the start in 1000 AD there was a comet and two meteorites fell, one of them at Magdeburg.[3]   In 1018 a comet 'spouting flames' was seen in Northumberland for thirty nights. In 1054 light reached Earth from the supernova explosion which formed the present-day Crab Nebula.   The exploding star was recorded by Chinese astronomers, probably by native Americans and possibly in Constantinople, but in Europe, curiously, it drew little notice.   Perhaps the church refused to admit any change in the perfection of the heavens, but there are many astronomical events in the mediaeval chronicles, before and after the Norman Conquest, and the only European record of the Crab event comes from Dur-row Abbey in Ireland,[4] founded by St. Columba.

1066 was different: Halley's Comet was particularly spectacular, featured in the Bayeux Tapestry with the caption ISTI MIRANT STELLAM - these men are wondering at the star.   The Anglo-Saxons saw it as an omen of disaster (literally, misfortune from the stars) and William the Conqueror agreed: it did mean disaster for Harold of England and his army.   Harold had just defeated a Viking attack in the north of England, and got his troops back to Hastings in time, but victory was beyond them.

Mediaeval France was then separate from Normandy, which with England and Wales was nominally subject to the king of France, but in reality they were bitter rivals.   Border territory between Normandy and France, such as the Vexin, was fiercely contested (Chap. 6).   In the 12th century Henry II ruled not just England, Wales and Normandy but also Brittany, Maine, Anjou, Aquitaine, Gascony and large areas of Scotland and Ireland.   He was of the Plantagenets, who were Angevins, from Anjou, but they ruled Normandy and with it the rest.

The Norman Conquest and introduction of the full feudal system enormously affected social life in England.   Even in modern English we use the Anglo-Saxon cow, sheep and pig for living animals, and the French-derived beef, veal, mutton and pork for the cooked meats.   The earlier Roman occupation had far less effect, adding only about 400 'loan-words', mostly technical terms, to the Old English language.[5]

A new, French-speaking aristocracy displaced the Anglo-Saxons and the Welsh (see Chap.7). In Chap.5 we'll meet Ingelric, earl of Essex, who made a new life in holy orders after the Battle of Hastings; and the Peverells, well-connected with William before the Conquest and doing even better afterwards. They settled in Derbyshire, like the de Ferrars, from the ironworks of Ferrières-St.-Hilaire, near Bernay in Normandy. There was a Bernay in Norfolk, but there and in Suffolk the prominent newcomers were Roger Bigot, Robert Blunt (Blundus) and Peter de Valoines, whose descendants we'll meet later. de Valoines also had considerable property in Essex.[6]

Some altered their names: on my mother's side, Richard Le Fort, descended from the 9th century king of France,[7] was a shieldbearer baron at Hastings. He saved the Conqueror's life during the battle, was rewarded with English lands and titles, and took the name *Fort Escu*, a strong shield, a distinguished name for the next thousand years.

Many new barons and landholders took names and titles from English property they were given - in this story, Richard de Calne's ancestors (Chap. 4), Richard de Hastings, Richard de Barre and others. In 1085 William had to commission a major census to find who owned or occupied what. It was to be as final as verdicts at the Day of Judgement, so it was called the Domesday Book.[8]

2. Astronomy and the Crusades

Many people thought Doomsday itself was imminent, and that helped start the Crusades. Jerusalem was damaged by the Fatimite Caliphs of Egypt during the 11th century, with an earthquake in 1033 and more destruction by Kharis-mian Turks in 1077, but repairs were allowed by treaties of 1026 and 1037: the church of St. James the Elder was rebuilt between 1072 and 1088.[9] There was no western concern until the skies began to act up: a sharp rise in solar activity around 1087 (Chap. 20) increased global temperatures, shown by tree rings and other climatic indicators.[10] A lunar eclipse in 1093 was supposed to start the Apocalypse, more so when followed by a meteor shower, including one very bright fireball, in April 1094 or 1095.[11] 1095 saw meteor showers, auroral displays and comets over Europe: the *Anglo-Saxon Chronicle* says "At Easter, on the mass-night of St. Ambrose (April 4th) there were seen, nearly over all this land and nearly all the night, very many stars, as it were, to fall from heaven, not by one or two, but so thickly that no man could count them."[12]

In Brittany "the same year [as a comet, probably connected] it was seen by a great number of people that stars fell from heaven, so thick that no man could number them," as in Revelations 6.13, "the stars of heaven fell unto the earth, even as a fig tree casteth her untimely figs, when she is shaken of a mighty wind."[13] Peter the Hermit claimed to have a letter, fallen from Heaven, confirming that these were harbingers of Armageddon, so Jerusalem must be reclaimed before it was too late.[11] His followers' disorganised assault on the Holy Land followed in 1096, under a major comet in the evening sky that October.[14]

There were lunar eclipses over Paris in February and August 1096 or 1097, and soon after the first "stars seemed to fall from the skies, like a heavy rain". Another comet in October 1097[15] may have been the 'five-pointed star' which Aubrey de Vere, first earl of Oxford, incorporated into his coat of arms after it allegedly lit up the battlefield at Antioch.[16] Ralph of Coggeshall says there were two, in the east and south-east, and other stars apparently emitted from them, probably parts of a larger comet breaking up. The Abbot of Jerusalem's chronicle confirms at least three in late 1097.

That year, "One day during the summer, towards evening, such a great fire appeared in the northern sky [from Paris] that many people rushed from their homes to find out who was the enemy destroying their land with such flames." Three more auroral displays are recorded in November and December of 1097.[11] In late October or November, or in February 1098, or both, "a brilliant red light, like a fire, shone in the night above the army, and it also unmistakably took the form of the cross", over Antioch in Turkey.[13] Red aurora indicates powerful activity on the Sun, as indeed does any aurora as far south as France, let alone Turkey; but this was of the type later classified by Edmund Halley as 'coronal', marking still more violent disturbance.

On June 3rd 1098 there was white aurora over Antioch, and in September another coronal display all over Europe, in which "the heavens seemed to be on fire".[17] The red arcs meeting at the zenith were taken to represent

Christian armies converging on Jerusalem,[13] because by then the Crusades were official. Jerusalem had been taken back from the Turks by the Caliph of Egypt, but was captured with great brutality by the troops of the First Crusade on July 15th, 1099. The event was prefigured by a red coronal aurora over the city in February, by another display on the night of June 6/7th, and lastly by a lunar eclipse - but that was all right, the troops were told, because only solar eclipses were bad for Christians.[18] (That piece of flannel was to backfire 88 years later - Chap. 13.) The crown of Jerusalem was offered to Geoffrey de Bouillon but he refused, preferring to be 'Counsel of the Holy Sepulchre'[9] - see later.

Without the astronomical stimulus, it's not certain that the First Crusade and its successors would have happened at all: the purposes of the huge undertakings are more than a little obscure. The historian F.E. Peters writes, "From the beginning, Westerners have looked for the origins of the Crusades in the events and ideology of mediaeval Europe. That search continues, and still primarily within the West, though no longer with any great conviction that there was a singular or even a predominant reason why in the eleventh, twelfth and thirteenth centuries *hundreds of thousands* [my emphasis] of Europeans vowed themselves to the liberation of the Holy Land from Islam... a closer investigation of the Near Eastern milieu on the eve of the First Crusade has revealed little or nothing in the condition of Jerusalem to explain the rather remarkable outburst of European sentiment for its reconquest in the last decade of the eleventh century."[19] At Clermont in 1085 Pope Urban II stressed the safety of pilgrims to the holy places; but, Peters says, that could have been used to justify a Crusade at any time since the reign of Constantine. A vicious attack on a mass pilgrimage led by the bishop of Bamberg, near Jerusalem in 1046, provoked no European retaliation.

Another reason was to preserve the holy places; but again, destruction of the Holy Sepulchre in 1009 produced no calls for an invasion. "To put it as pointedly as possible", says Peters, "no one in Jerusalem summoned a Crusade, neither the local Christians nor the Latin visitors to the city, and nothing in the status or conditions of Jerusalem had so altered as to make an international expedition for the conquest of Jerusalem intelligible... It was then what it always had been, a provincial city with little or no commercial, strategic, or political value." Many participants were driven by faith, of course, but hitherto those needs had been met by pilgrimages, individual or collective.   Peter the Hermit claimed the end of the world was at hand, but that was expected in 1000 AD and 'millennium fever' was over; and crusading went on after 1100 passed without incident, except for an aurora reaching to Turkey on 25th October.

Even with Jerusalem regained, 'the skies were somewhat uneasy';[20] as another writer put it, "the 'signs' continued without mercy from the middle of the eleventh century to the middle of the twelfth".[13]   1099 saw a comet and a big meteor shower.[3]   In 1103 there was a 'comet with immense tail',[21] followed by a 'great diminution of light' recorded in Chinese annals on July 8.[22] Sundogs and parhelia, caused by ice crystals in the upper atmosphere, were seen in 1104.[23]   That wouldn't be strange in winter, but 1105 was a disastrous year, with destruction of crops, and with intersecting white halos round the Sun.   Two suns were reported, east and west,[3] on 23rd December 1105 - difficult to explain by high-altitude ice, but an Arab chronicle records a comet that month, visible in daylight, whose tail stretched "like a rainbow to the centre of the heavens" from the western sky after sunset.[15]   On February 4, 1106, a comet was seen near the Sun in daylight, and on February 12 there was another darkening of the Sun, accompanied by meteors, which was not an eclipse.[22]   The comet, or another one, was seen on February 13th,[24] perhaps also explaining 'two Full Moons, East and West',[25] reported again before Easter.   The comet, as bright as the Sun,[26] broke up after passing it and became the parent of at least 12 smaller ones, described as 'new stars'.[12]   The orbital periods of the fragments are between 600 and 1100 years,[25] so there's no connection with the 1178 event described in Chap. 12.   There was also a brilliant supernova in the south that year,[27] which complicates the record.

In 1107 there were "various tokens in the Moon, and its light waxing and waning contrary to nature."[12]   In 1109 there was a comet,[25] and a December comet near the Milky Way.[28]   In 1110, on May 5th there was a lunar eclipse lasting all night;[15] a comet, undated;[22] a bright comet moving northwest in June; tempests, a long winter, and frost damage accompanied by a strange Moon.[12]   In 1114 there was a comet,[25] and another in May 1115.   Solar activity returned to normal after 1106, but nevertheless two auroral displays were reported in 1117, the first on 4th January,[3] followed by lunar eclipses[29] on June 16th and December 11th, and another aurora on December 16th.   1118 had violent electrical storms in January, July and August, and in Epiphany week there was "very great lightning in the evening and a most immoderate thunderclap afterwards"[30] - we'll see another like that in 1172.   In 1128, two naked-eye sunspots were recorded by John of Worcester, and a big aurora was recorded in Korea five days later;[31] also in 1128 or soon after, a fireball from the sky exploded among the Egyptian ranks at Halin.[7]

So there are enough events, with multiple reports (even if some are copied) to show that mediaeval chroniclers *were* paying attention to the skies.   Maybe there are even enough to suggest that something odd was going on.

3. The Start of a New Order

Curious things happened in Jerusalem, meanwhile.   The Hospital of St. John of Jerusalem had been founded for Christian pilgrims in the 11th century, with a female hospice under a Dame Agnes, from Rome and of noble birth,[19] late in the century.   The organisers were arrested during the Crusader siege of June 1099, and after 1118 the Order was reorganised on a military basis by its leader Raymond du Pay.   Some say that the Hospitallers were the tutors of the second great military and religious order, the Knights Templar, and at first *they* were housed by the Augustinian Canons in the former Church of St. Mary Latin (Fig. 21.4), part of the Hospital due south of the Church of the Holy Sepulchre.[7]

It's generally said that the Templars were founded around 1118; in *The Holy Blood and the Holy Grail*, however, Baigent, Leigh and Lincoln cite a reference to the Order in 1114.[32]   The founder was Hugh de Payens, with eight other knights including an ancestor of Tostes de St. Omer, whom we'll meet later. They named themselves after the Dome of the Rock, on the site of Solomon's Temple and then known to Christians as the Temple of the Lord; but they were under the authority of the Pope, not of the Patriarch of Jerusalem. They swore to protect pilgrims in the Holy Land, and also assumed responsibility for protecting the Holy Sepulchre.   The king of Jerusalem gave them rooms in the so-called Palace of Solomon,[33] actually the El Aqsa/Aksa Mosque, 'the Remote' (from Mecca) south of the Temple.[34]

The Russian Prior Daniel, visiting Jerusalem in 1107, vividly described the dangers on the roads.[35]   Yet there seems to be no record of those knights sallying forth for them, supposedly what their Order was for (it did protect

27

pilgrims to the Jordan with regular patrols, later).[36]   Instead the Canons of
the Temple gave them precinct space around it for workshops, and they spent
a lot of time hollowing out storage chambers under the Rock.   It may be only
legend that there were so few of them - not enough to interest the king and the
Pope?   In Dante, nine was the holy cipher of the angels, and it has a mystical
connection with the Middle East: the Nine Men's Morris, the ritual maze cut
into the turf of English villages, was also known as 'Troy Town'.[37]

It's curious that almost all texts call the Templar chambers 'silos' - normally
vertical storage chambers, as in 'grain...' or 'missile silo'; like the one under the
Step Pyramid of Djoser, which *looks* as if it was designed to hold something
more interesting than a Pharaoh's corpse (Fig. 21.2).[38]   No photographs or
plans seem to be available showing those architectural marvels, supposedly
achieved by so few, though almost every book on the Templars refers to them;
access for archaeologists was limited even during the British occupation of
Palestine, and I've only turned up some references to a honeycomb of partly
explored, partly blocked 'extraordinary caverns or reservoirs' in the area
below the Aqsa Mosque,[9] and a 'peculiar structure... remains of steps leading
down to what seemed to be a tank or cistern', apparently pre-Moslem, below
the easternmost of its north doors.[39]   There were already many rock cisterns
for water below the Temple Mount, some fed by an aqueduct from Solomon's
Pools near Bethlehem, built by Pontius Pilate,[19] and twenty-five to fifty feet
deep.[35]

The Templars created a 300-foot tunnel under the palace, with no known purpose, but with two blocked-off tunnels running north from it towards the
Temple: one may lead to a blocked-off doorway facing south, below the Dome
of the Rock itself.[9]   They are said also to have created vast stables.   The
'Stables of Solomon' which still survive are considerably smaller,[36] but even
they suggest many more Templars than history records,[40] or that they
expected a big increase in numbers - as indeed there was.   In 1126 the
Templars were adopted by St. Bernard of the Cistercian Order, the Grey or
White Monks, who founded the monastery of Clairvaux in 1115.[7]   At the
Council of Troyes in 1128 he persuaded most of Christendom to back the
Templars,[41] after which they too assumed white habits.   They entered
England then, at the latest.[42]   Hugh de Payens went to Normandy and
England, "where he was received by all good men, and all gave him treasure,
and in Scotland also."[43]

Bernard de Clairvaux ordered the drafting of the Rule of the Templars, based on the Cistercians' (themselves founded only in 1098), including rejection of women, although in exceptional circumstances they admitted 'sisters'. However, internal evidence shows at least part of it was written before St. Bernard's time.[44]   Another rule forbade them to admit children,[42] perhaps giving our green children a better chance of a normal life, as we'll see.   Gérard de Sède, whose information isn't always reliable, says that St. Bernard announced the Rule under a great elm-tree outside Gisors, a traditional place of conferences between the French and English kings, and that when the Rule was announced a huge luminous cross appeared in the sky, as a result of which the Templars were allocated the right to wear it.[45]   But most writers say they weren't awarded that until the Second Crusade, twenty years later (Chap.4), and I can't find confirmation of an 1128 incident at Gisors - see Chap. 13.

From 1128 to 1138 the main growth of the Order was not in the Holy Land but in Languedoc, after a big public rally in Toulouse, and their first military experience was against the Moors in Spain.[44]   The first English site was in London, the Old Temple at Holborn Bar.[46]   By 1137 king Stephen's wife Maud had given them property at Cressing in Essex, the first grant to them outside London - renamed Cressing Temple.   The Master of a rural establishment of the Knights Templar was called a 'Preceptor' from the mandate issued to him, which began "*Precepimus tibi* - we instruct you".

In 1139 Louis of France assigned mills at La Rochelle to them,[47] and Eleanor of Aquitaine allowed them a 'freeport' there, a customs-free zone for their Atlantic shipping.   By 1140 they were established in Paris, where an entire quarter of the city came under their control.   The Order became an army of soldier monks, supported by a huge network of farms across Europe, so wealthy that their transactions foreshadowed modern banking, with royal treasuries entrusted to them.

As my friend Gerald Warner said, at mention of the Templars one's heart sinks, because so much nonsense has been written about them.   Most of the marvels attributed to them seem to be modern inventions.   the alchemy and mathematical skills made up in the 18th century,[48] in the 19th that they were guardians of the Holy Grail - first claimed by Rudolph Steiner,[49] apparently - and in the 20th that they guarded the Shroud of Turin.[50]   They did hold the supposed True Cross, miraculously 'rediscovered' under the Church of the

Holy Sepulchre, but they lost it in 1187 due to their habit of carrying it into battle (Chap.13).

In *The Trial of the Templars*, Malcolm Barber says that the story of an inner, secret Rule with links to eastern heresies didn't arise until the 19th century.[48] de Sède says it was compiled by a Master Roncelin, rediscovered in 1780, then found once more in 1877.[45] Gérard Serbanesco gives translations of two secret Rules 'rediscovered' by Roncelin, and attributes them to Robert de Samfort, provincial Master of the Order in England in 1235;[7] but if genuine, they're as tedious and unimaginative as the known Rule. In *La Vie des Templiers* Marion Melville argues that the idea of it arose because some parts of the Rule, 'the Respected', were more secret than others.[44]

In Michael Bentine's novel *The Templar*, the Rule blends Christianity with 'Wicca', Earth magic, and the banner is the circular, oriental yin/yang symbol.[51] But *Beauseant* or *Beaucent* was oblong and divided horizontally, white above and black below, for the triumph of good over evil;[43] and it's unlikely that a Templar logo incorporates a female principle. The red cross *pattée* which they wore was like the Hospitallers' Maltese Cross, but with the arms plain, not split; it could be imposed on the *Beaucent*[46] (Fig. 3.1). One Templar seal showed two knights on a single horse, usually taken to symbolise their poverty, but Melville says it shows their humility.[44] (When they had any: "King Richard I is reported, on his deathbed, to have bequeathed his pride to the Templars, as being the most fitting recipients."[52]) Another had the cross triumphant over the crescent of Islam, flanked on each side by the Star of Bethlehem (Fig. 3.1), and a third the *Agnus Dei*, the Lamb of God, with the cross *pattée* behind it on a pole, where the ones at the top of Fig. 3.1 have a pennon.

The head of the Order, the Grand Master in the Holy Land (*Outremer*), answered to the Pope, not the Patriarch of Jerusalem.[53] His badge of office was 'The Abacus', a round plate bearing the cross *patée*, on a baton.[9] In Europe (*cis mare*) each 'province', such as France, England and Ireland, was governed by a Master who had all the Grand Master's rights and powers in his absence, and wasn't subject to 'Visitations' by local bishops.[53]

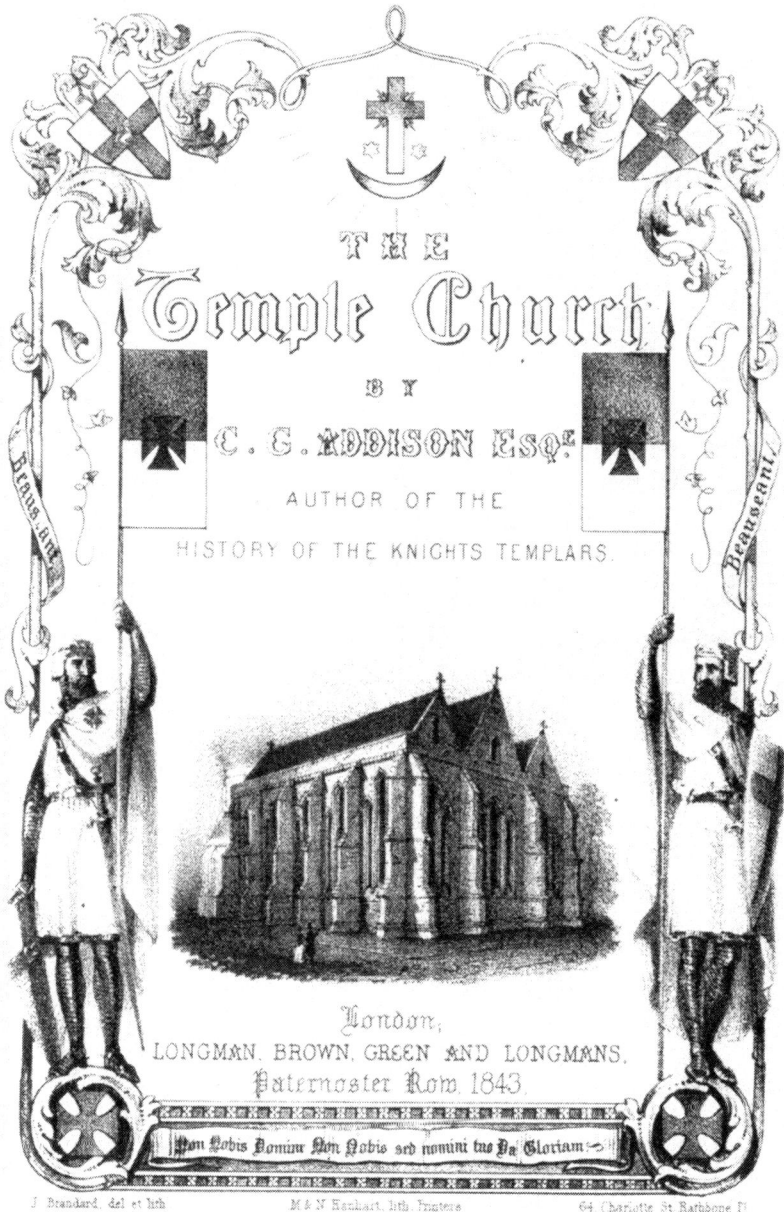

Fig. 3.1. Templar emblems on the title page of G.C. Addison, "The Temple Church", 1843. The Beaucent is drawn with black on top, possibly the Grand Master's variant.[57]

31

In 1128-36 Bernard de Clairvaux composed *De Laude Novae Militiae ad Milites Templi*, in praise of the Templars.[54]   "A new chivalry has appeared in the Land of the Incarnation... It is new, I say, and not yet proved in the world, where it wages a double conflict, equally against enemies of flesh and blood and against the spirit of evil in the heavens."   Interesting though that sounds, in his time comets and meteors were portents of evil, and he'd seen many examples.

To be blunt, I've found no esoteric knowledge in any 12th or 13th century account of the Templars.   They're often accused of greed for money, and of treachery - "beware the Templar's kiss" was proverbial,[55] as was "to drink like a Templar"; and with their fondness for corporal punishment, brothers under discipline were "on Fridays".   In the Holy Land, they would accept any wanted man into their ranks and many acted with brutality, provoking re-prisals by the Saracens.   Sophisticated they were not: allegedly, even the Grand Masters were mostly illiterate.[56]

Nevertheless, in the 12th century they were so prominent that if anything big was going on, it would be remarkable if the Order wasn't involved.   And with their European establishment in 1128, the stage is set for the appearance of 'lord Richard de Calne', in 1130.

Chapter Four: OF LORD RICHARD DE CALNA

"Therefore taken to the home, at Wikes, of the lord Richard de Calna, a sort of knight, to be wondered at, they wept inconsolably... "

~ Ralph of Coggeshall

1. Seeking Lord Richard

It took two visits to East Anglia to locate de Calna's property, because of false leads.   Ralph refers to him as *dominus*, 'lord' Richard de Calna, though he and his family never were barons - but I had to trace them to find out, and even old works like Sir William Dugdale's *The Baronage of England* told me nothing. Some modern writers translate it as 'Sir Richard...', but 'Sir' for knights came in with the Orders of Chivalry in 1344.[1] 'Lords' were masters of churches and manors till the 1370s, but by then it was coming to mean peers, above 'gentlemen'.[2]

Almost everyone assumes he was in charge at Woolpit, but there's no record of that - if he was, it was in secret, and my first attempts to locate 'Wikes' were no more successful.   For example, Antonia Gransden identifies Wakes Colne, nor-nor-east of Coggeshall, as de Calna's 'Wikes'.[3]   The river Colne gives its name to the four villages there, collectively called 'Calna' in the 12th century[4] , but they had different owners' names then.[5]   The Wakes Colne sign includes the family arms of Hereward the Wake, the 11th century Saxon partisan; but Baldwin Wake didn't acquire the village until 1280, and the name wasn't used till the 14th century.[6]   Before that it was Inglesthorp, after Ingelric, earl of Essex before the Norman Conquest.

'Wykes' simply means 'dwellings', usually with another word attached; that's why so many place-names end in '-wick'.   The church of Wykes next to Thetford in Norfolk belonged to Norwich Cathedral, and in 1096 Herbert de Losinga, first bishop of Norwich, assigned land there to Roger Bigot, earl of Norfolk, to support of a community of monks whom he intended to establish at Thetford.[7]   Bigot still had the land in 1119, but it eventually passed to the Thetford monks, and in 1231 Henry III confirmed the Priory's possession of

33

the whole manor. But the de Calnas' Wykes has a different history in the 1230s (Chap. 15), so the one next to Thetford can't be theirs.

Wykes (now Wix) in Essex, on the far side of Colchester from Wakes Colne, was owned by Walter the Deacon at the Domesday survey, and soon after 1100 his son, Walter Maskerell, and his siblings founded a Benedictine nunnery there in his memory.[8] The Maskerells owned the future Wakes Colne for part of the century, and their descendants, the de Hastings, appear in our story soon; but the Essex Wix/Wykes wasn't de Calna's, though a nunnery would be a logical place to take the children (see Chap. 10). Richard de Calna was more than willing to give them house-room in Suffolk, and we're going to have to think why, but first we have to locate him.

Births, marriages and deaths weren't listed systematically in parish registers until 1538. Before that births and christenings were seldom mentioned except for royal families, in the chronicles. Deaths are on record if property reverted to the crown and was reallocated to heirs or new holders. People of de Calna's status appear in the correspondence of bishops and abbots, as taxpayers (almost always on property), in court cases, or as witnesses to documents, mostly charters assigning property to churches or by churches to tenants. In the 19th century the government began to publish those mediaeval records, and in the 20th the task was taken over by groups such as the Camden Society (for texts), the Selden Society (for legal records), and many others for individual counties. That massive effort lets an armchair detective like me trace the life of someone like de Calna, and it's amazing how much there is to find, after eight hundred years.

Norman Scarfe correctly identifies de Calna's Wykes - after all that search in Essex, it's a manor north of Bardwell, back in Suffolk![9] My cousin Jill Bow-yer, in Norfolk, found the crucial lead: in the reign of Henry I, who died in 1135, Richard de Calna held six and a half knights' fees under the manor of Pakenham, north-west of Woolpit.[10] His feudal superior was Peter de Valoines, grandson of William the Conqueror's nephew, who settled in Suffolk after the Conquest (Chap.3). The first Peter 'encroached' on church land,[11] 'liberating' it as we say, including holdings of Bury St. Edmunds Abbey. Nevertheless, he and his wife Alfreda founded Binham Priory, with a Geoffrey Calna, whom I haven't traced, as a witness to the charter,[12] and de Calna connections with it continued.

Peter de Valoines died in 1166,[13] and Richard de Calna later renegotiated his feudal service with Peter's son Robert.[10]   Richard would have been quite young in 1135, and he doesn't appear in Suffolk before that.   Even so, he must have been in his seventies when he was visiting Coggeshall in the 1180s, before Ralph became Abbot, and that's an important clue to when the children arrived (Chap. 8).

That's well above average life expectancy at the time.   Ralph of Coggeshall lived to 68 or 70, and de Calna's granddaughter Sibylla at least to 64 – is this a mediaeval version of *Cocoon*?   But average life expectancies are misleading, skewed by high rates of infant mortality; in addition, older dating methods often underestimated the ages of skeletons by as much as 30 years, suggesting for instance that nobody in 11th century England lived beyond 55.[13]   But actually someone who survived infancy and childhood had a good chance of living out the Biblical 'three score years and ten', unless a serious accident or illness intervened.

2. Men of the Church

Now that I knew Richard's age, roughly, the search for his family turned to the reign of Henry I and earlier.   The only Calne in the Atlas is across England in Wiltshire.   A hamlet in 862 AD,[15] it may have had a castle and a palace of the West Saxon kings, but its fame was that in 977, at a council on the celibacy of the clergy, St. Dunstan was in dispute with some canons, backed by nobles, over rights to churches.   A row at Winchester had been resolved by a talking crucifix, but when they confronted him upstairs at Calne the floor collapsed, leaving him standing in safety on a beam.[16]

In Domesday Calne was called 'Caune', the *Britannica* gives 'Canna' and 'Kalne' as alternatives, and Calna and Calne are used interchangeably.   The Wiltshire de Calnas and Richard used them all, plus de Camne and de Kaunvill.[17]   Some book indexes read as if they also used de Cunte or de Cantilupe: de Cantilupe barons held Calne in the 13th century,[18] and the fourth of them to do so called himself "Sir William de Kalna alias de Cantilupo" at least once.[17] More widespread and powerful than the de Calnas, it seems they were connected by marriage (Chaps. 15 & 17).   I'm using Calne for the Wiltshire town and the Latin nominative 'Calna' for Richard and his kin.

Formerly Edward the Confessor's, Calne was held by William the Conqueror's physician 'Nigel',[19] one of at least seven he brought over[20] - maybe of humble origin, or a younger son of a prominent family, perhaps illegitimate. At any rate, he was 'Nigel the Doctor' in England. He never called himself 'de Calna', but he had no reason to, because William awarded him the use of royal estates in Gloucestershire, Hampshire, Herefordshire, Kent, Shropshire, Somerset, Worcestershire and five in Wiltshire as well as Calne. In Domesday he had 24 estates at least,[21] many taken from a Saxon priest called Spirtes, whom Nigel replaced as a canon of the royal college of Dover.[22]

Nigel was followed to England by his brother Roger, born around 1065-70,[23] a parish priest from Caen. During a private war between the future Henry I and William Rufus in 1091, prince Henry stopped by to hear Mass, and Roger hurried through it to oblige him. Henry's escort said he'd make an ideal chaplain; "And when the regal youth said 'Follow me', he stuck as closely to him as Peter once did to the Lord of Heaven when he uttered a similar invitation. Peter left his boat and followed the King of Kings, but this man left his chapel and followed the prince."[24] As the style suggests, the source is William of Newburgh, which is very interesting (Chaps.13 & 14).

William calls him *fere illiteratus*, 'almost unlettered', unlikely given his later career: 'literatus' may refer to classical studies rather than literacy.[25] Roger styled himself 'le Poer', in some texts 'pauper' or 'pauperus'. This may relate to his origins or be just a joke, because Henry gave him lands, churches, prebends (see below) and abbeys. He became Dean of St. Martin's-le-Grand, the great church next to St. Paul's, and in 1101 Henry made him bishop of Salisbury. Roger's election document calls him a priest of Avranches cathedral, a major centre of learning in western Normandy. He built himself a palace and a magistrate's house while enlarging the cathedral, 'Old Sarum', within an Iron Age hill-fort north of the present Salisbury Cathedral. A monument moved to the new church, begun in 1217, reads *de ducibus de nobilibus primordia duxit* - it could mean he too was a younger son of some noble family, but more likely 'he presided over the origins of dukes and nobles', being so close to the king.

Roger then became a justiciary, and Treasurer of England, initiating financial reforms and new procedures which reorganised the running of the country.[26] He was the most powerful man in England next to the king, in charge when

36

Henry was abroad, for up to three years at a time. But he made the most of it: the *Gesta Stephani*, an anonymous work of the time, says Le Poer was notorious for his 'wanton style of living'.[27] He built four castles, including one at Devizes for his mistress Matilda of Ramsbury, by whom he had at least one son, also Roger 'le Pauper' - see below. The stone castle replaced a wooden one, burned down in 1113, on a prehistoric site; there's virtually no record of it,[23] but there are prehistoric connections in our story throughout.

Confirming that he was brother to Nigel the Doctor, a century later Nigel's grandson said that his father was a nephew of Roger le Poer, bishop of Salisbury, whose precepts he was following now that he too was royal Treasurer.[28,29,30] Nigel held a 'prebendary' seat in the stalls of St. Paul's Cathedral, as well as at Dover. A prebend was a non-residential canon, but the position was hereditary; as the requirement of celibacy became more thorough they passed to nephews, rather than sons, and Nigel's was taken over by his nephew Everard, chaplain to Henry I; later it passed to *his* nephew William. (The next prebend, Henry de Sigillo 1141-50, was no relation.[29])

Nominally, a prebendary canon was responsible for the place represented by his seat in the cathedral stalls.   He drew an income from it (*singulorum canonicorum necessitatibus prebendae*, granted to the canons individually for their needs) and was supposed to live there, but often appointed a vicar (literally, someone to hold the place for him), for a share of the income.   Nigel the Doctor's seat was 'Mora', a manor owned by St. Paul's[31] in the parish of St. Giles, Cripplegate.[32] The gate was on the northwest of the city wall, north of St. Paul's, named for the beggars who traditionally gathered there; the parish includes Grub Street, the Barbican (originally a watchtower), Aldersgate Street and Cheapside.[33]

In the 1130's Cripplegate manor was owned by the canons of St. Martin's-le-Grand, where Roger le Poer was Dean. Aldersgate Street still runs south into the street of St. Martin's-le-Grand, where the church was demolished in 1542 and the headquarters of the Post Office were built in 1815. Near the top the Templars established their first UK headquarters at Holburn Bar, and the Hospitallers did the same nearby at Charterhouse in 1185, when the Templars moved to their New Temple in Fleet Street.[34] The Hospitaller St. John Street still runs north from the end of Charterhouse Street.

'Mora' is Hebrew for awe, fear or reverence, perhaps the origin of Moriah, the Jewish name for the Temple Mount in Jerusalem;[35] it's also the Latin name for Mourne in Ireland[36] and Irish Gaelic for the sea.[37] A Jerusalem connection or an Irish one would be interesting; but *mora* is also Latin for a delay or a hindrance, and in mediaeval Latin it meant a moor, or in this case a marsh.[38] Moor Lane, Moorgate and Moorfields are still there: the Moorgate was opened in 1415 after a road was driven across the marsh, which was drained a century later. In Shakespeare's time, Moorfields was used for military drills: the first London theatres, built there to draw on skilled extras, were often raided for conscripts in time of war. It's no coincidence that Macbeth meets the witches on a blasted heath: in Europe 'mora witches' were shape-changers, and the word derives from Indo-European *moros*, meaning death.[39]

Nigel the Doctor's son, also Nigel, and his kinsman Alexander, later archdeacon of Salisbury and bishop of Lincoln, studied at Laon - another centre of learning, particularly in mathematics - maybe returning to England because of rioting there in 1112. Nigel was definitely back by 1115.[23] They were Le Poer's nephews,[27,40] and Alexander's brother David was archdeacon of Buckinghamshire.[40] Nigel and Alexander could be brothers, sons of another brother of Roger's, Hubert, Humphrey or Herbert,[41] who appears only once, a witness to one of Roger's charters.[23] However, Calne and other Wiltshire property descended through the second Nigel, and we get a much simpler family tree, with continuity of Christian names, property and church connections (Fig. 4.1), if we take Alexander and David to be Humphrey's sons, cousins of Nigel (Fig. 4.2), and Nigel to be father of our Richard de Calna.

Nigel the Doctor died around 1123. On the deaths of the Conqueror or William Rufus, most royal estates had been reclaimed: three of Nigel's in Wiltshire,[42,43] but not Calne, or Henry I gave it back, because the next Nigel was 'de Calna'. He witnessed charters of Henry I's between 1107 and 1120,[44] was also a witness at Winchester in 1118,[45] and he and his nephew William were both witnesses in 1130.[46] (William de Calna earlier witnessed royal charters at Windsor and Woodstock.[34])

The Calne prebend, a good one worth 60 marks (pounds) per year,[47] was confirmed to Nigel de Calna and his successors in 1106 or 1107, and Nigel was canon till 1120, at least.[34] But he already had land in East Anglia, including some of his father's in Norfolk;[48] and in Huntingdon, later gifted to Ely Cathedral.[8] He was a chaplain to Henry I in France, 1111-20,[49,50] and travelled extensively with the king in the 1120s and '30s. He's frequently described as 'Nigel nephew of the bishop of Salisbury' between 1126 and 1131.[34]

He became the king's Treasurer in Normandy in 1130,[51] Treasurer in England, then bishop of Ely, 1133 to 1169.[8] His coat of arms as bishop featured three hands, supporting a crown, holding a key, and holding a bag of coins;[52] his election was forced on the monks of Ely, and he quickly returned to the Exchequer.[23] He had at least three brothers: Everard, who inherited the Mora prebend, Adam, and Arthur, all connected with Norwich. Everard de Calna was also a royal chaplain, witnessing a charter of Henry I's in 1101,[53] and others in 1112, 1113, two in 1120 (those last three in France)[34] and 1126; in 1120 he was a witness at Rouen to the king's agreement that the monk Eadmer of Canterbury should become bishop of St. Andrews. In the king's letter to the Archbishop of Canterbury, Everard was the only witness mentioned.[51]

Everard and Adam began at Salisbury, where Everard and Alexander were archdeacons,[26] and that puts Everard's birth no later than 1074;[54] he was a royal witness in Normandy in 1113 and 1120.[34] Adam was restored from illness by a holy relic, the left arm-bone of St. Aldhilm,[55] and went to Norwich as archdeacon of Norfolk and chaplain to Bishop Herbert de Losinga; Everard was archdeacon of Norwich in 1115 and was elected bishop in 1121.[56] A new bishop was expected to make large gifts to his church, so the de Calnas were doing well to afford four bishops in one generation.

Sir William Dugdale's great *Monasticon Anglicanum* says the bishop was Everard de Montgomery, another royal chaplain,[8,54] but that was disproved in 1872.[7,48] On election Everard de Calna received immediate royal assent and was consecrated in June 1121. He was a popular bishop, though he made enemies by opposing the cult of St. William, a boy allegedly murdered by the Jews in Norwich; perhaps why chronicler Henry de Huntingdon accuses him of cruelty,[57] not substantiated elsewhere. He continued the building programme at Norwich and Lynn, and in a letter of 1146, he says that he'd been at Windsor with William Rufus and at almost all royal and ecclesiastical councils since, till he retired.[58] Dugdale says he lost his see through supporting king Stephen in the civil war, below,[8] and he was with Stephen at Oxford and Westminster in 1136 - but so were all the bishops, and as Stephen was confirming the status of the church in England, with a separate declaration for Norwich,[34] he had little choice.   He retired to the Cistercian Abbey of Fontenay, in the Côte d'Or, where he sponsored completion of the great church and was buried in 1147.[58]

Tripping off the de Calna background may look like showing off, when other writers didn't find it - while mediaeval experts may say 'It's no big deal, everyone knows the surnames of the bishops'.   But if 'everybody knows' them, hardly anyone uses them: they're 'Nigel of Ely', 'Everard of Norwich', and so on.   It took me five years to learn that Richard de Calna was son of the bishop of Ely and nephew of the bishop of Norwich.   If my cousin hadn't found the first lead at Norwich Record Office and they hadn't supplied me with the last one, I wouldn't have known it yet.

Before I knew about the bishoprics, however, I'd drafted a tree for Richard's side of the family (Fig. 4.1); further research added the half-brother, Richard Fitz-Neal, and the cousins.   Bishop Everard's children are mentioned in prayers;   'Eudo son of the bishop' witnessed[58] a grant of land in Cambridgeshire to Bury St. Edmunds Abbey,[11] and a Eudo de Calna also appears, undated, probably in Essex.[59]   Everard and Adam surrounded themselves with nephews from Wiltshire, ten or more of whom – including another Everard and 'our' Richard[56] - are witnesses to Norwich cathedral charters in the twelfth century.   For example, somewhere between 1121 and 1135 Richard and another brother, Peter, witnessed a confirmation of rights to Roger de Valoines.[7]

By 1135 Richard was a tenant of the de Valoines, and the link between the families lasted over 120 years.   Richard was a clerk at Norwich in his youth, though he never took holy orders: contrary to 'the myth of lay illiteracy' in mediaeval times, there was no requirement for scholars at Paris to be in the church and they weren't even subject to canon law until the final year of their studies.   Samson de Botington (Chap. 6) studied in Paris and became a schoolteacher before he took holy orders.   Sons of good families normally had an education, especially if destined for knighthood.[25]

Cathedral staff were called the bishop's *familia*, and Everard took it literally. (Soon after, pope Alexander III said, "When God deprived the bishops of sons, the Devil gave them nephews".[60])   Adam was succeeded as archdeacon by another nephew, Roger, who gifted his mills of Ringelond to the monks in 1127.[61] William Turberville, the next bishop, followed with gifts of Beighton, near Norwich, Thornham, near Lynn, and Humbersfield - all held by Adam de Calna in life.[62]

William Stubbs wrote, "The office of archdeacon was no sinecure. Although a spiritual office, conferred by investiture of ring and book, it was concerned chiefly with matters of legal and secular interest, the judicial and pecuniary disputes which in the English Church never abounded more than at the period before us. It was this constant entanglement in temporal business which made

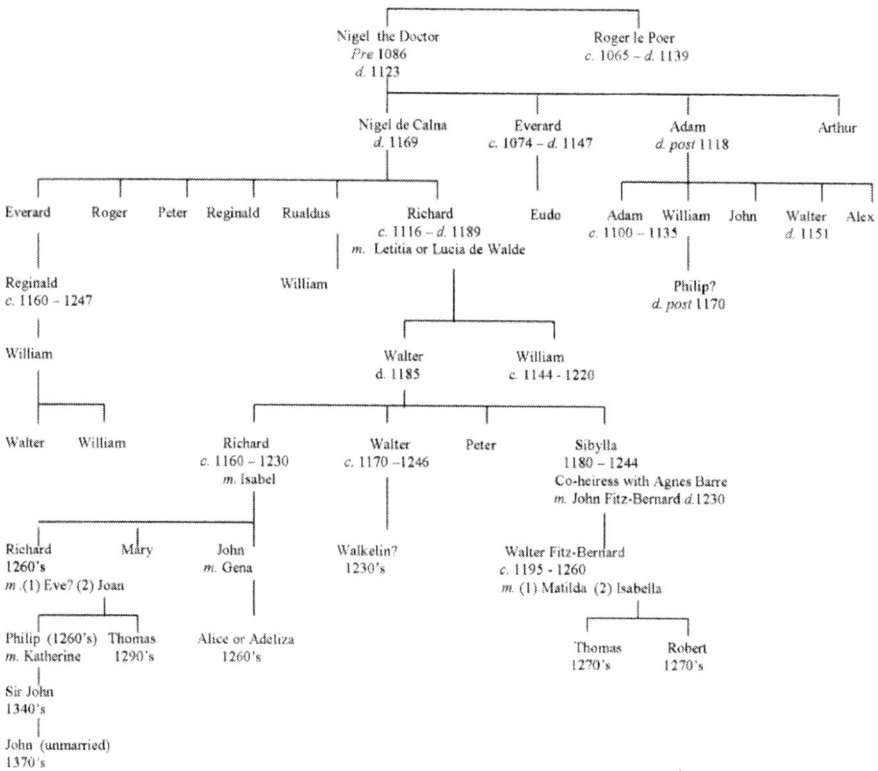

Nigel the Doctor
Pre 1086
d. 1123

Roger le Poer
c. 1065 – d. 1139

Nigel de Calna
d. 1169

Everard
c. 1074 – d. 1147

Adam
d. post 1118

Arthur

Everard   Roger   Peter   Reginald   Rualdus

Richard
c. 1116 – d. 1189
m. Letitia or Lucia de Walde

Eudo

Adam   William   John
c. 1100 – 1135

Walter   Alex
d. 1151

Reginald
c. 1160 – 1247

William

Philip?
d. post 1170

William

Walter
d. 1185

William
c. 1144 - 1220

Walter   William

Richard
c. 1160 – 1230
m. Isabel

Walter
c. 1170 –1246

Peter

Sibylla
1180 – 1244
Co-heiress with Agnes Barre
m. John Fitz-Bernard d. 1230

Richard
1260's
m. (1) Eve? (2) Joan

Mary
m. Gena

John

Walkelin?
1230's

Walter Fitz-Bernard
c. 1195 - 1260
m. (1) Matilda (2) Isabella

Philip (1260's)
m. Katherine

Thomas
1290's

Alice or Adeliza
1260's

Thomas
1270's

Robert
1270's

Sir John
1340's

John (unmarried)
1370's

Fig. 4.1. De Calna family tree.

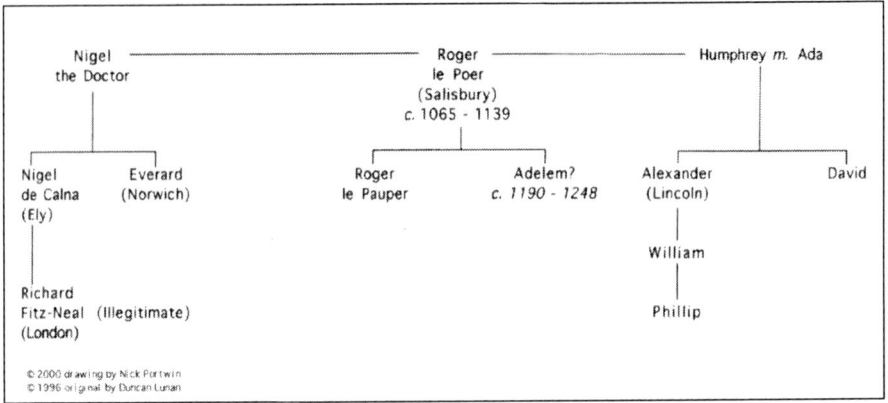

```
Nigel ————————————————— Roger ————————————————— Humphrey m. Ada
the Doctor                    le Poer
                              (Salisbury)
                              c. 1065 - 1139


Nigel        Everard        Roger        Adelem?        Alexander        David
de Calna     (Norwich)      le Pauper    c. 1190 - 1248 (Lincoln)
(Ely)


                                                        William


Richard                                                 Phillip
Fitz-Neal  (Illegitimate)
(London)

© 2000 drawing by Nick Portwin
© 1996 original by Duncan Lunan
```

Fig. 4.2. The bishops of the de Calna extended family.
By Duncan Lunan, layouts by Nick Portwin.

the archdeacon, of all clerical officers, the most unpopular with the laity, and which among the more religious of the clergy suggested an important doubt... Nicolas de Sigillo, a canon of St. Paul's, denied that it was possible for an archdeacon to be saved."[63]   Bishop Everard divided up his see between four archdeacons, with a total of 45 deacons under their control.[64]

Archdeacons could be laymen, so didn't have to be celibate, though it became compulsory for clergy in 1125: all must leave their wives or concubines by November 30th.   In a moment of inspiration, Henry I ruled that any who didn't should pay an annual fine, not to the church, but to himself - through Treasurer Roger, who kept his mistress at Devizes undisturbed.   (Three years later, Roger opposed the new doctrine of the Immaculate Conception, though advocated by his former tutor at Laon.[23])

William de Calna, another archdeacon, witnessed a letter of Henry I between 1100 and 1135, and one about Norwich between 1114 and 1129.[64]   Another Adam de Calna, a clerk, witnessed charters till 1161.[7]   They're not in Wiltshire records, so probably they're sons of archdeacon Adam; likewise John, Alexander and Walter.   Continuing the Mora inheritance, William was a canon of St. Paul's in 1108-38.

His brother or cousin Walter de Calna became archdeacon of Oxford,[30] an outstanding orator, a.k.a. Walter de Wallingford,[57] expert in 'various histories',

42

'well informed on the history of foreign countries'.[65]   He found the 'very ancient book in the Breton language' on which Geoffrey of Monmouth based *Historia Britonum*, the classic stories of Britain including king Arthur's and king Lear's.   Bishop Alexander of Lincoln, Walter's 'first cousin once removed', urged Geoffrey to include the prophecies of Merlin and the transportation of Stonehenge from Ireland.[66]   When Geoffrey wanted to leave out Guinevere's infidelity, Walter dissuaded him.[67]   De Calna support didn't protect Geoffrey's book from William of Newburgh's wrath, as we saw in Chap.1.

Oxford was under an archdeacon of Lincoln Cathedral, as was Leicester, each with.   Walter was Provost of St. George's College, Oxford, in 1129, witnessing next steps after the foundation of Oseney Abbey;[68]   apparently he was one of five secular canons of St. George's with Geoffrey of Monmouth and Robert de Chesney, bishop of Lincoln in 1148, after Alexander.   They were related to Gilbert Foliot, bishop of Hereford and later of London[70] - see Chap.10.

Walter de Calna was at Oxford at least until 1151,[67] and certainly knew the archdeacon of Leicester, Hugh Barre.   Hugh was from Staffordshire, though the nephew of Richard de Siffrevast, a baron of Buckinghamshire.   Richard and Robert de Siffrevast were barons of Berkshire,[70] after 1161, and held land there from the earls of Leicester under Henry II, Richard I, John and Henry III.[71]   But in the 1140s their feudal superior was Robert de Breteuil, called *le bossu*, 'crookbacked', because of his bookish habits rather than a deformity.   Favourites of king Henry I, he and his brother ('the Beaumont twins', from one of their castles in Normandy), were the most influential twins in British history.[72]

In Bucks they sublet four 'virgates' of land at Chesham to Hugh Barre.[73]   They were a much wealthier family than the Barres, from Chivrevast, near Valognes in Normandy, where they still had property.   It's not clear how the Barres were related to them - perhaps by marriage, like the future de Calnas and de Cantilupes.   But 'le Sire de Siffrewast' from Normandy served in the First Crusade, and 'Hugh Bar' of England was in the Holy Land in 1118,[74] so the connection may go back that far, at least.   Hugh Barre also had a link of some kind with the de Brocs (Chaps. 5 & 9), with two of whom he shared land in Missenden, Bucks., which they gave to the church there.[39]   But it seems the earl of Leicester was Hugh's patron: he witnessed eleven of the earl's charters over the next twenty years.[70]

Like Geoffrey of Monmouth and Walter de Calna, Hugh Barre was a man of learning. Richard de Siffrevast and his wife 'E.' gifted him the income from a mill, before he became archdeacon,[71] after which Hugh witnessed charters of Robert and William de Siffrevast's; in turn Robert donated part of the Chesham church to the abbey in Leicester, along with land which Hugh Barre had temporarily held from him.[73] A William 'Barred' later inspected a mill and watercourse which Richard de Siffrevast donated to the Abbey in 1148; and bishop Nigel de Calna witnessed a similar gift of his, so they were at least acquainted.[75]

As we'll see below, Richard de Calna may have been in the Second Crusade of 1147-50. He couldn't undertake it casually: Christopher Tyerman writes, "The departure of any crusader came at the end of a process whereby the *crucesignatus* obtained communal approval and frequently assistance for his pilgrimage. The consent of parish priest, landlord and family; the material help of those lay and clerical neighbours through whom the crusader con-verted assets into cash or pack animals; the religious ceremonies attendant on taking the cross; and, in many cases, the pious bequests and contracts with local monasteries were the familiar prerequisites of the journey to Jerusalem." For a knight, the commitment was usually between two and five times his annual income, raised by selling or pledging family land.[76] If Richard wasn't knighted yet, attached to a knight's retinue, for example, he wouldn't have to go so far into debt; but what he had to do was more complicated, as he'd have to go through it in East Anglia and in Wiltshire. He'd probably need the blessing of his learned older cousin at Oxford.

Perhaps Walter had introduced him to his friend Hugh and his infant son; by 1164 Richard Barre was legally adult, aged at least fourteen, so maybe born in 1146-50. Perhaps Richard de Calna was his godfather, and the boy was named after him? He could have been named after Hugh's uncle; either would be hard to prove, because christening details were seldom recorded - more's the pity, in the case of the green children. In general, though, at baptism children took the name of a godparent - so commonly so that parents who chose a different name could be asked for their reasons, and children couldn't marry godparents' offspring, as if they were related.[71]

Ralph V. Turner puts Richard Barre's birth earlier, in the 1130s.[70] I disagree (Chap. 6), but he became a royal ambassador in the late 1160s, and while he *might* achieve that in his teens, a few years would make a big difference. Whether Richard de Calna was godfather or not, the knight could later become the boy's patron. John Le Neve implies that Hugh Barre died in 1157 or 1159,[30] leaving Richard fatherless if not an orphan at eight or nine, and de Calna might have become his guardian - but actually Hugh lived at least nine years more,[73] enough to pass any inheritance on directly.

Meanwhile the Wiltshire de Calnas were now headed by Richard's elder brother Everard, who returned there and had holdings at Stokes up to 1144. Everard, Roger and Peter de Calna witnessed a charter there around 1155.[15] He was still there in 1160, and an 'Everard Wagepol' at Calne is mentioned twice in 1167-68,[17] though perhaps not the same man. Everard lived on in Wiltshire till 1194 at least,[18] and although he outlived Richard, his status and his son's there suggest that he was the eldest brother.

Other brothers of Everard, Roger, Richard and Peter, included Reginald, Rualdus   (Raoul), and possibly Randulfus, archdeacon of Berkshire.[44] Reginald was in trouble in 1147 for forcibly marrying his son to an under-age ward.[78]   Rualdus went to Wales,[79] though he was constable of Salisbury around 1170,[75] and his son William settled in Surrey, where his parents later founded a church and priory of black (Augustinian) canons.[80]   A Robert de Calna appears only twice[81,82] - perhaps by mistake for Roger?   I haven't shown him in the family tree, nor Walkelin, who appears only once[10] and might be a mistake for Walter - although there was another Walkelin de Calna in the 1230s (Chap.15).

Another Reginald, probably Everard's son, had a distinguished career in Wiltshire from 1180 to 1247.[83] He and his son William were knighted, and in Chaps.15 and 17 we'll meet others of that generation who went to Ireland. William had sons called Walter and William, 'the Scribe'.[84]

Between them, Everard and Reginald cover a span from c.1110 to 1247-51. It's not impossible: for instance, at age 60 Everard could have fathered Reginald on a woman half his age.   In the next chapter we'll meet the two William Peverells, father and son, who span the years 1066-1155 at least. But unless the 'Everard Wagepol' above is this Everard de Calna, neither he nor Reginald appears to have held Calne itself.

In addition to all those family members, Richard and Everard had an illegitimate half-brother, Richard Fitz-Neal or Fitz-Nigel, who was a prebendary canon of Chiswick.[32] He was taken hostage by king Stephen[51] in 1145 - and that brings us to the civil war.

Their father Nigel de Calna had become bishop of Ely in 1133; Alexander had been bishop of Lincoln since 1123 and after Nigel's consecration they appear together, often with Roger le Poer, as witnesses to many of Henry I's charters all over the realm. The *Gesta Stephani* calls them "men who loved display... they devoted themselves so utterly to warfare and the vanities of this world that whenever they attended court by appointment they too [like Le Poer] aroused general astonishment on account of the extraordinary concourse of knights by which they were surrounded on every side" - private armies, in effect.[27] Not surprisingly, there was trouble brewing.

3. War in England

On the death of Henry I in 1135 the throne should have passed to the Empress Matilda, but the barons in England didn't wish to be ruled by a woman, and chose Stephen de Blois, second in succession, whose queen was also called Matilda or Maud. Roger Le Poer had sworn fealty to the empress Matilda, at Henry I's insistence.[23] But Stephen seized the initiative while the empress was still in Normandy, and Roger handed over the royal treasury to him at Winchester, where Stephen's brother Henry was bishop. At his coronation by the archbishop of Canterbury, the only other churchmen were Roger of Salisbury and Henry of Winchester. The following year Stephen summoned all the bishops and barons to Winchester, where he guaranteed the rights of the church in an extended version of his coronation oath: Henry, Roger, Alexander and Nigel are the first four witnesses on the list, in that order. Stephen rewarded Roger by making Roger le Pauper chancellor, and Adelelm (who may have been another son) treasurer of England; Roger continued to run the country when Stephen was abroad, despite efforts by rival barons to displace him, and a false rumour that he was dead caused Stephen to cancel sailing to the continent in 1136. But he had enemies among the barons, there were justifiable doubts about his loyalty to Stephen, and the Beaumont twins were working up accusations against him.[72]

Dugdale's *Monasticon* says that both bishops Nigel and Everard supported Stephen, but that's only part of it. Nigel and Alexander were with him in York and Nottingham in 1136. Nigel joined him at Rouen in 1137,[34] and Alexander crossed the Channel to England with him that year.[85] In 1137, Nigel claimed he'd uncovered and scotched a conspiracy against Stephen at Ely, but meanwhile he was building a castle there and repaired another at Aldrey. In 1138 he witnessed a declaration of the empress Matilda's,[34] and the three bishops decided after all to support her. Growing concerned about their opposition, Stephen invited all three to a conference in June 1139.

He arrested Roger and Alexander, but Nigel escaped to Roger's castle at Devizes and laid waste the surrounding countryside, preparing for a long siege. Stephen's troops surrounded it, and Roger, imprisoned in a cowshed, 'voluntarily' swore not to eat or drink until the castle was surrendered. When that didn't work, after three days Stephen erected a gallows and brought out Roger's secretary, Chancellor of England, with a rope round his neck: Roger le Pauper, whose mother was inside and in charge.

She surrendered, but Nigel got away to Ely. (Bentham's *History of the Cathedral Church of Ely* says Nigel surrendered on condition that he was left at liberty.[86]) Roger le Pauper was banished from the kingdom; Alexander, who'd been given the cowshed treatment at Oxford, was told he'd be starved to death unless his castles were surrendered. In September, a hearing into the affront Stephen had given the church came to nothing - neither Alexander nor Nigel attended - but less than a fortnight later Matilda's invasion force landed at Arundel. She stopped at Calne, on her way across country,[15] and it's interesting to guess which family members might have been in residence. Not bishop Nigel, who was trapped at Ely - effectively an island, "always putrid because of the surrounding swamps", as a 12th century critic put it.[87]

The devastating civil war which followed is the setting of the 'Brother Cadfael' novels by Ellis Peters (Edith Pargeter), filmed for television starring Derek Jacobi. Nigel brought in mercenary knights and closed the causeway to Ely; it should have been impregnable, but Stephen took it in a surprise attack and Nigel fled to the empress at Gloucester. Around the same time, in December

1139 bishop Roger died in misery.[23]   Stephen may well have seized Calne then, since it was royal land - the de Calnas certainly lost it for a while, as we'll see below.

Stephen visited Everard de Calna at Norwich in 1140, and Alexander was there too.[34]   Nigel briefly rejoined Stephen's side in 1140, but was with Matilda in Reading in 1141.   He and Alexander accompanied her to Winchester, where she was acclaimed at the height of her success, expecting to be crowned in a few days.[85]

Peter de Valoines, to whom Richard de Calna owed feudal service, was at Winchester, and later at Bristol, witnessing Matilda's charter to the earl of Norfolk, Hugh Bigod, who was on her side.   They both witnessed another charter of Matilda's which comes up in Chap. 5.   His father Roger de Valoines had been with Stephen at Easter 1136, but Matilda made a grant to him in 1141, the year of his death.[85]

Since many of us are probably related to Richard de Calna, after 800 years, we might want to ask him, "What did you do in the war, daddy?" His brothers, churchmen, clerks, men of learning and lawyers, could stay out of the way in the *familia* of Norwich; only Nigel's illegitimate son, with him at Ely, was repeatedly seized as a hostage in the 1140s (see below).   But by 1139 Richard was already in his mid-twenties, at least.   If he had saved his father's life at Ely, say, we would expect an honourable mention for 'Richard son of the bishop' in the chronicles, but he's not there at all.

It raises the question of how Richard earned his spurs - especially when the rest of his family was non-military.   Normally the eldest son of a knight would follow suit, and fifty years later de Calna's clout was enough to make his grandson a knight, but his own family were all bishops or clerks.   He could be dubbed by a bishop, but that was unusual, and battlefield promotion by a king or a noble was more common.[88]   Glyn Maxwell's *Wolfpit* portrays him as a young knight, torn over which side to support,[89] but although Richard's elders were pretty certain, and it seems Peter de Valoines was also backing Matilda, apparently Richard wasn't a knight yet.

After Winchester, Stephen demanded Richard Fitz-Neal as a hostage.[51] Under that pressure, for the next two years Nigel shuttled between Stephen and Matilda, or simply said 'yes' to whoever was nearer as they used him to enhance their own status.   He orchestrated further risings at Ely in 1142 and 1143, but Stephen's earls re-took it[90] and Fitz-Neal was taken hostage again.[91] While holding him, Stephen forced Nigel to sign a lasting peace in 1144 or '45; Alexander died in February 1148,[85] and that ended the war for their generation of the family.   Nigel appears again in Stephen's documents several times between 1147 and 1153, but caused him no more trouble.

Around 1145, however, a man with the Saxon name of Brithstane, accused of an unnamed crime, took refuge at Ely but was hauled off to London and thrown into a dungeon in chains.   He was, supposedly, released by miraculous intervention of two of Ely's lesser saints, and returned to a big welcome at Ely. Bishop Nigel mounted his fetters beside the High Altar, and offerings to the saints were made there for three hundred years after.[92]   How he got loose with chains still attached isn't explained – but to this day, behind the altar, there's a chapel commemorating the trials of Christ with a realistic 3-D painting of the crown of thorns, the nails and a pair of fetters, which aren't in any Gospel that I have.   It's not the only strange story attached to the High Altar at Ely - see Chap.14.

We'll see how the civil war ended in Chap. 5.   It was agreed that Henry II should take the throne after Stephen's death, which was in 1154.   In land that he controlled or claimed, he was the most powerful king England ever had. He recognised Nigel de Calna's support by making him a Baron of the Exchequer.[8]   Nigel witnessed charters of Henry's in England and France between 1155 and '58, and Henry, Peter de Valoines and others confirmed Ely Cathedral's rights about the same time.[93]

But now we can turn back to Richard de Calna, who's been eclipsed by his father, uncle and relatives in the civil war, while we've heard nothing of Richard himself.

4. A Man of Property

In 1130 Richard held land in Wiltshire, Berkshire and Buckinghamshire,[94] where he was excused the Danegeld tax, so he was already in the king's service. Following his father, uncle and brothers to East Anglia, he and Robert de Calna witnessed a charter of Roger de Valoines to Binham Priory in Norfolk between 1121 and 1135,[8] and by 1135 Richard held land from the de Valoines in Suffolk, at Wykes and Knettishall. He aided another gift to Binham by Walter de Valoines in the 1140s,[81] and one where Peter de Valoines gave them Bernay church and half the nearby manor[8] – Richard's granddaughter lived there in the 1240s (Chap. 17), though others held it meantime.

Though seldom involved with Bury St. Edmunds, he witnessed one of the Abbey's charters in 1154.[11] By 1158-59 Richard had more land in Norfolk and Essex, with 15 knights under him in service to Peter de Valoines.[79] He married Letitia or Lucia de Valde, also spelled Walde, Walda, Wolde, Wade or Weald; perhaps as early as 1130, because in 1146 his son Walter was an adult and witnessing legal documents.

At Norwich under bishop Turbe, *magister*, a teacher, came to mean any man of learning. Recurring names are a problem: magister Walter de Calna fathered a daughter in 1180, who inherited all of Richard de Calna's property, so he must be the son Walter who appears with Richard in Wiltshire,[46] and not the Walter, nephew of bishop Everard, who became archdeacon of Oxford above. Likewise, he died in 1185, so he can't be the magister Walter de Calna signing Norwich charters 1190-1200.

My first source said Letitia de Calna's 'Walda' was in Oxfordshire,[17] but historian Jane Greatorex found it in Essex, near Chipping Ongar and now called North Weald Bassett.[95] In the Domesday Book it belonged to the de Valoines,[96] so probably that brought Richard and Letitia together. Her family still had it at the end of Henry I's reign,[46,97] and remained in the area till the 14th century,[98] though they lost Walda to the de Calnas early in the 1200s and it was renamed Canes Manor - see Chap. 15.[99]

Between 1186 and 1191 the Abbot of Bury St. Edmunds, Samson de Botington, compiled a 'Kalendar' of property owned by the Abbey, the rents and when due. In it, 'the heirs of Richard de Caune' held quarter of Bardwell, north-west of Woolpit.[100]   'Bardwell' may be broad-well (for Bradwell in Essex see Chap. 10), or property of a Beorda or Bearda, though it isn't a Norse proper name.[101]   Two knights there served William de Bardwell, whose family had been there since the Norman Conquest at least,[102] and owed service in turn to the Abbot;[103] but as we've seen Richard's was to the de Valoines, and through them to the bishops of Norfolk at Thetford, later Norwich.

In addition, most of Knettishall parish, on the river Waveney at the Norfolk-Suffolk border, was a fee-farm owned by Richard de Canne under the Abbot of Bury St. Edmunds,[104] though close to Thetford Priory.   Knettishall may have been 'Gnats-hall', or more likely Norse Knatter's-Hall.[101]   However, there were no knights of St. Edmund at Knettishall or Pakenham in the 1190s.[103]   Richard had other property in Norfolk, Essex, Hertfordshire and Staffordshire: as we'll see, de Calna's substantial estates lend a lot of weight to the green girl's status 'in ministerio' as part of his household.

They also bear on Ralph of Coggeshall's description of de Calna as 'a certain kind of knight'.   The first category of knight was a baron;[105]   then *milites mediae nobilitatis*, knights of middle nobility - 'active knights of good birth holding a manor or two... often younger sons or brothers of important men, and as a type in a minority'.[106]   Landed 'lawful knights' were eligible for jury service.   Thirdly, *militarii gregarii* or *stipenderii* were professionals hired by the two superior groups, little better off than the more well-to-do peasants,[105] some landless younger sons, hoping to be rewarded for military service.   Between contracts they were 'masterless knights', owning little more than a horse and a sword;   Richard de Calna was a younger son, but far from landless.   His properties made him a *vavasor*, a military tenant of a baron, intermediate between baron and ordinary knight - but there's probably more to Ralph's phrase than that.

Wlsius the nobleman gave 'Wiken and the adjacent wood' to the Abbey under Edward the Confessor.[8]   Held before the Conquest by two Saxons, Alan and Aki, in 1085 it was under the first Peter de Valoines, and occupied by Robert Blundus,[107] (Chap.3), whose family also had Wiltshire connections.[11]   Robert Blundus's descendant William still had a knight there[108] as a sub-tenant of de Calna's.   'Richard of Wyken' paid a third of a knight's fee to Bury St. Edmunds in 1166,[109] but that was a separate family in Bardwell.   Richard de

Wykes owned Wykes itself in 1264, with hunting rights, when the de Calnas were long gone.[104]

In Anglo-Saxon a wyken-place was 'hous<u>ed</u>' in the poetic sense, having houses, so Wykes and Wyken were equivalent.[110]   Bardwell later had two 'Wykes, Wiccen or Wyken' manors, and a note at the County Records Office says *The Manors of Suffolk* confuses them, treating them as one.   The first Wykes Manor, later Wick, dates to before 1066, while the present Wyken Hall first appears in 1742.[111]

A manor is an estate, not necessarily with a Hall, and Wykes/Wick Manor hasn't had one since the 18th century, when a map in the Records Office shows a stylised large house, near the north boundary of the manor, owned by the

Fig. 4.3 (a).

Figs. 4.3 (a) and (b).

18th century map of Wykes Manor; and detail showing remains of formal gardens (4.3b). (Suffolk County Records Office).

Fig. 4.4 (a).

Fig. 4.4 (b) & (c).

Fig. 4.4 (d). Tudor and Victorian buildings on the former site of Wykes
Manor House.
Photos by Lyndesay Birkmyre (1993) and Linda Lunan (2011).

Earl of Albemarle. A slightly later map shows only remains of formal gardens,
south of the new road across the estate from Sapiston to Barningham (Fig.
4.3). It seems Wykes Hall was demolished around 1800, when that part of
the manor was sold to the Duke of Grafton. The present-day farm is part
Elizabethan, part Victorian (Fig. 4.4), but when digging a septic tank the
1990s farmer found wooden posts from a large, very old building - perhaps the
hall to which the children were taken. William of Newburgh says the bean-
plants came from the fields, and in his time lords' gardens were mostly recrea-
tional, but garden beans, fruit and other vegetables balanced a diet heavy on
cooked meat,[104] so they may have been home-grown.

We haven't yet established *when* that happened, or why the children were
taken to Wykes and not to Bury St. Edmunds. As the Abbey owned Woolpit,
you'd expect the priest of St. Mary's to insist the children had to go there, or to
the Abbot's secular court at Cattishall, which was even closer. Bardwell
wasn't even in the same direction, and at eight miles nor-nor-west of Woolpit,
Wykes was actually further away. It wasn't that any noble would do: to
reach de Calna they had to cross land of at least two other families, the de
Bardwells and the de Valoines. But it wouldn't be conspicuous: contrary to

the impression that villagers rarely passed their manor boundaries, a tenant's duty to carry his lord's goods (using his own horses) could take him anywhere in England - especially if the manor was owned by a religious house.[105]

It suggests that de Calna expected something to happen at Woolpit, and there was a bag of silver in it for whoever brought the news. Already we know that Richard was not imaginary, not poor, nor the near-nobody suggested by Ralph's phrase which I first translated "a sort of knight". Literally it's 'a certain kind of knight', and though he was a vavasor, there may be more to it.

One of Roger le Poer's innovations was Treasury records on double parchments sewn together, a foot long by four feet wide. Bound at the top, rolled and tied for storage, they resembled pipes.[23] In the earliest surviving Pipe Rolls, from the end of Henry I's reign in 1130, Richard de Calna appears normally, as above.[46] There's a gap during the war, but when they restart in 1158-59 Richard is excused fees for his Essex land by mandate of Henry II,[114] and for his Norfolk and Suffolk lands below, except for sixteen shillings and eightpence which he cleared the following year.[115]

Thereafter he's hardly ever on record, so the arrangement was permanent. He must be doing major service for the new king - strange, so soon after the war, when there's no sign that he took part. His half-brother, Richard Fitz-Neal, was Treasurer then: after the Viking threat diminished he abolished the 'Danegeld', and exempted barons of the Exchequer, justices and sheriffs from ordinary taxes too. But not from *all* taxes, and de Calna wasn't a baron, justice or sheriff, otherwise we'd know a lot more about him. Many court *familiares* received concessions, but generally small ones.[116]

In 1155-59, Richard was a prebendary canon of Salisbury - a 'man of the church',[117] and as a member of the Chapter he had to be a prebend.[118] No canons of Calne are listed for a long time after Nigel de Calna, but it was assigned to him and his heirs, and Richard isn't listed in any other prebend. In 1158 Henry II reclaimed Calne manor from baron Hubert de Vaux,[119] present when he took knighthood vows nine years earlier,[120] and in 1159 Richard Fitz-Neal, Nigel of Ely's archdeacon by then,[121] witnessed Henry's confirmation of the Salisbury prebendary at Calne church.[117]

Prebendary canons often lived off-site. In the 1190s Stephan of Tournai (Chap.14) ordered canons in his see not to leave their charges, but within months he'd excepted chapter business, special service for the bishop, going to school or university, pilgrimage, seeing a specialist doctor or for a distant cure - all valid, but "some of them, provided with other benefices elsewhere, never set foot in the church to which they were attached and from which they were happy to receive an allowance."[122]

In 1130, Nigel de Calna appointed 'Sualfus, Presbyter of Calne', as his vicar who paid the taxes.[46] Richard wasn't in holy orders and lived in Suffolk in 1159, so perhaps Everard was *his* vicar. But if Richard was a 'man of the church' *as well as* a knight, was he a Templar or Hospitaller?

5. Earning his Spurs

In 1166 Robert de Valoines confirmed Richard de Calna's Suffolk holdings when he himself inherited Bernay;[9] Richard also had property in Wiltshire, and from the de Valoines in Hertfordshire and Essex.[123] Other than that, he disappears until he visits Ralph of Coggeshall in the 1180s. Whatever service he performed or still performed, it was out of the public eye: the only others I've found submerging so completely from view were the senior office-bearers in England of the Knights Templar.

The Templars had little property in Suffolk, but two of the three preceptories they had were near Richard de Calna: eight miles each from Bardwell and Woolpit.[124] The only one in Norfolk was within 15 miles of Knettishall.[10] But they were closely connected with the Cistercians, and their first pre-ceptory in England was Cressing Temple, near the Cistercian Coggeshall Abbey, at which de Calna was later a frequent visitor. If Hugh Barre was in the Holy Land in 1118,[74] perhaps he was at the formation of the Order and could have introduced de Calna to it.

Sure enough, in the same paragraph of the Pipe Roll of 1158-59, where Richard de Calna is excused taxes, there's the same entry for Richard de Hastings, the Master of the Templars in England, and he too disappears thereafter. Neither de Calna's property nor de Hastings's are identified, but their entries are only two lines apart.[114]

As a Templar, let alone a Master, de Hastings shouldn't have had individual property. But in 1236, the king's inspectors demanded a list of knights' fees paid annually to the Abbot of Bury St. Edmunds. Displeased, he supplied an old list, commenting on its accuracy, "God knows".[108] Several knights in it were dead, including Richard de Hastings, who retired and left England in 1185, and William Blundus, who first appeared in Suffolk in 1160,[115] and disappeared in 1172.[125]

It reveals that Richard de Hastings had property in Ixworth Thorpe (Saxon 'wealthy-farm village'[101]), next to Bardwell and Wykes, with William Blundus; half the fee of the knight in service to him as a sub-tenant in Wykes, was afterwards transferred to the de Hastings.[108] At least one of the Blundus family was himself a Templar.[126] In 1236 there were several de Hastings in Thorpe, so he owned it, not just a knight's service there; perhaps he owned Thorpe in his youth, and kept it for his relatives - presumably not direct descendants, unless from early in life, since he must have been a celibate Templar for a long time to be provincial Master. But as Richard de Calna grew older, the arrangements at Ixworth Thorpe and Wykes ensured a fast channel to Richard de Hastings and the king, if he had anything to report. There would have been plenty to exchange messages about, as we'll see.

Richard might be a doctor, like his grandfather, maybe physician to the East Anglian houses and Coggeshall Abbey, near Cressing Temple. In Henry II's time, it may explain why it was to him, rather than Bury St. Edmunds Abbey, that the children were taken to him when they were starving but wouldn't eat? The church was increasingly suspicious of medicine - "where three doctors, two atheists" - and by 1163 monks were banned from studying civil law and medicine, considered too worldly, although most monasteries had herb gardens.[127] (The *Cadfael* series, where he practises herbal medicine, are in Stephen's reign, pre-1155.) In 1215 Pope Innocent III forbade practising surgery, because monks must never shed blood.[38]

Ancient Greek medicine was taught at Canterbury from 570 AD, but Anglo-Saxon skills were mostly herbal, listing about 500 herbs with medicinal uses. The Crusades brought eastern knowledge including surgery into Europe and the first medical school was established in Salerno c.1090, followed by Montpellier, Bologna, Padua and Paris. Like 'Cadfael', de Calna could have learned medicine in the Holy Land.[20,128]

All Templars except chaplains were *conversi*, lay brothers,[129] so doctoring was allowed.   De Calna couldn't be a full Templar without separating from his wife, but there were two associate categories: *fratres coniugati, frères mariés* or *confrères*, married knights, and *fratres ad terminum* or *à terminé*, who joined for a time, perhaps for a Crusade or a pilgrimage.[130]   Associates buried in the Temple Church in London were depicted in armour, with their legs crossed.[131]   Either category could make de Calna 'a certain kind of knight', but it raises the question again of how he earned his spurs.   You couldn't just sign up for the Templars, even as an associate: you had to be of noble family and/or have a knightly track record.   Perhaps Richard was in the Holy Land, earning one, when his family were in the civil war at home.   One opportunity to distinguish himself would have been the Second Crusade, in 1147.

By then Jerusalem had been in Christian hands for nearly fifty years, and the Crusaders had set their stamp on the city.   At what's now the Aqsa Mosque the Templars built a new porch and other vaulted annexes, especially on the east.[132]   The Augustinian Order, founded 1059-61 on lines similar to the Benedictine, took over the Church of the Holy Sepulchre, holding the rock of Golgotha and the tomb of Christ, and around 1140 they extended it westward to enclose the Centre of the World, supposedly the burial-place of Adam and the rock on which Nicodemus and Joseph of Arimathea had washed the body of Christ; that was a 12th century confusion with another rock, the Stone of Unction - see Chap. 22.[133]   Dame Agnes (see Chap. 3) had the church facing the rock demolished and re-erected as Sancta Maria Maggiore, the new female hospice of the Hospitaller Order.

But dissension and chicanery among the Christian powers threatened the occupation, and again there were celestial omens.   Aurorae in 1122 and 1130[134] were followed by a comet in 1132,[135] but in 1133 there was a total solar eclipse in Jerusalem,[136] and an earthquake and tsunami two days later.[137]   After a lunar eclipse in 1135 and another solar one in 1140,[138] Halley's Comet returned conspicuously in 1145.[139]   The fall of Edessa in 1144 and a Moslem victory at Ba'albek showed the situation was becoming serious, but the decisive omen was in 1146, when both the Temple of the Lord and the Holy Sepulchre Church were struck by lightning.[140]   1146 was an interesting year (Chaps. 21 & 22), and electrical phenomena are important throughout this story.

St. Bernard of Clairvaux preached that the end of the world was at hand,[141] proven by a big eruption of Vesuvius in 1140, storms in 1141, famine in 1144 and another comet in 1147.[140] Clearly another Crusade was needed and was duly mounted by Louis of France. William de Warenne, related to the Beaumont twins, was one leader of the English force, and commanded Louis's guards.[142,143] The Knights Templar threw themselves into the campaign, and in 1148 the red cross was added to their white robes,[144] after which they were often called 'red friars' instead of white.[129] (In Sydney Jordan's drawing of the children's trial, Chap.10, he first drew de Calna with the cross on the wrong shoulder. The Templars would have had him 'on Fridays' for that.)

Louis of France and Konrad of Germany marched east in 1147. More German crusaders sailed from Cologne on 20th April, meeting Flemish and English ships at Dartmouth on 19th May; 146-200 ships sailed from there three days later[143] - not for the Holy Land, but to liberate Lisbon from the Moors for Bernard de Clairvaux. Exhausted by the civil war, England sent only eight ships, but there was a strong Norfolk and Suffolk contingent, and Hervey de Glanville led another from Hastings.[144] Is that how Richard de Calna and Richard de Hastings first met? Templars played big parts in the sieges of Lisbon and Tortosa, and the English contingent was vital because of their expertise with siege machines, which were new technology in Iberia. After storms in the Bay of Biscay, the fleet regrouped on the north coast of Spain, and anchored on June 28th at the Isle of the Phoenix (Peniche) before attacking Lisbon.[145] Raol, a priest with the de Glanvilles,[146] describes what happened next:

"In the forenamed island when we had passed the night, in the morning we began to make sail, making a prosperous journey from there almost to the Tagus river, a wind coming forth from the Suchtrium Mountains, the ships were then shaken by an amazing storm, which swallowed up part of the force with its men. Moreover the storm continued until the entry of the estuary of the Tagus river. Truly as we were entering the estuary a wonderful sign was seen in the sky. For behold! with great white clouds coming at us from the regions of the Gauls, and certain great black scattered clouds coming at us from the continent, they were seen to run together and in the form of hatchets arranged on the left horns, to contend between themselves with amazing force, and certain ones in the form of skirmishers, making an impact on the right and the left, sprang back into the battle-line, certain ones came to the entry to wheel round the rest, certain others penetrating them drained them of the form of vapour, certain ones raised on high, certain ones driven below, now almost touching the water, now borne from sight into heaven. When at last a great cloud, coming from our side, dragging all the impurity of the air with it, and was seen to have a kind of very pure blue around it, repelling all the others from the continent with its force, as if conquering, seizing the booty to itself, it alone held the mastery of the air, all the rest either drained away or if any little was left, it was seen to fly to the city, we exclaiming, "Behold our cloud has won! Behold God is with us! The power of our enemies is dispersed! They are thrown into confusion, because the Lord has dispersed them." And thus at last all turbulence of the storm ceased. Therefore after a short time, about the tenth hour of the day, we came to the town which was not far from the estuary of the Tagus river."

Raol does his best to describe something he doesn't understand - we'll see others, equally nonplussed, later. He doesn't mention lightning, but the "skirmishers'" behaviour and repulsion of the 'enemy' clouds suggest strong electrical forces. Everywhere the de Calnas and their associates went, they 'took the weather with them' – such strange weather, so often, that maybe they knew its causes and could control it.

In taking Lisbon, English-built siege towers proved crucial. The first was destroyed by fire, but the second, cut off by the tide, was heroically defended for 36 hours by 'seven youths from Suffolk' before it was moved up to the walls and the defenders surrendered on 24th October.[145] De Calna was now well in his thirties, but perhaps the youths were under his command and the action raised him to the Templar ranks.

Gilbert de Hastings became bishop of Lisbon and the task force split up, some going to Tortosa and on to the Holy Land in December. The others sailed on February 1st and arrived at Acre in April or May 1148.[147] The English under Constable Glanville then disappear from the record, absorbed in July into a force of 50,000, including the Army of the Kingdom of Jerusalem, commanded by the kings. But Louis's queen, Eleanor of Aquitaine, had disrupted the alliance en route by her all-too-public dallying with the count of Antioch.[140] William de Warenne was killed at the head of his troops, defending Louis against a Turkish attack in a mountain pass near Laodicea in January 1148.

61

The Templars then took command, and Louis said that alone saved the whole Crusade from catastrophe.[148]

When the crusaders assembled in Jerusalem, retaking Edessa was pointless, because the city was in ruins. They attacked Damascus, but failed, shifting the point of attack due to poor intelligence. There were no siege engines,[149] possibly because the English chief engineer was disablingly injured at Lisbon.[146]

An extremely bright aurora in 1150, when "all the sky turned red", must have seemed a fitting aftermath. Severe winter in England was marked by mock-suns and moons caused by high-altitude ice crystals, but the weather improved dramatically the following May.[151] It was the onset of the biggest solar disturbances since the Bronze Age, within which global temperatures rose markedly between 1158 and 1177. If it coincided with Richard de Calna's return to England, I don't think that was by chance.

I have no evidence that Richard de Calna was in the Second Crusade, but that's not 'evidence of absence'. Lists of 'English nobility and gentry', from chronicles and family records,[74] name only seven crusaders for Stephen's reign, including William de Warenne, who had many more with him, and only two for Henry II's, despite multiple defeats and the loss of the Holy Land in 1187. There was a Walrois de Valoines in the Third Crusade, under Richard I, probably was the 'Werris de Waloign' who had the family property in Kent in 1199. Richard de Calna died before the Third Crusade, but perhaps he was with an earlier de Valoines in the Second. (There was a John de Valences in Jerusalem in 1152 and 1171,[152] whose his tomb there was found in the 19th century,[132] but that's a different family, with another crusader under Richard I.)

After the Crusade, there was a popular myth about a white knight who app-eared to help people in trouble: he guided the army's retreat to Gadara in December 1147, riding ahead "on a white horse and with a vermilion banner". He was taken to be St. George, who was supposed to have led white knights from Heaven to the rescue at the siege of Antioch in the First Crusade.[153] If he could literally appear and disappear, Lone Ranger-style, it would be tempting to think the legend might be inspired by real-life exploits of Richard de Calna's! But at the end of his life (Chap.13), it'll become more likely that de Calna was a Templar, and in Jerusalem, at key dates.

Robert 'Beaumont' was now Justiciar of England. Nigel de Calna had purchased the Treasurership for Richard Fitz-Neal, who recorded frequent meetings between earl Robert and bishop Nigel - for example in 1166 and 1167.[72] Some sources say that Nigel was injured in an accident in 1164, and Richard Fitz-Neal took over the administration of the see. Nigel died in a frenzy, brought on by an ague, in 1169.[26]

The *Ely Book* says that in 1166 a local holy woman met the spirit of St. Ethelreda, who vowed to use the power of her sceptre against those who'd harmed the church. Stephen looted Ely's treasures, and Nigel entrusted others to Alexander at Lincoln, so he was blamed for both and for extravagance. A rash of strokes brought death or paralysis to Adam the constable, Alexander the cup-bearer, William de Scelford, Henry the Wanderer, Ralph Olof who had stolen a pall worth £40, Richard of St. Paul, William the archdeacon... many others, and finally the bishop. Stricken in church, in his chair, Nigel lingered for three years, sincerely repenting, so his death was bewept by the convent. William Turbe of Norwich conducted the funeral; Richard Fitz-Neal, "a long-standing enemy", persuaded the king to put the prior out of office and seized the cathedral income.[90] When Ely had no bishop, the revenues did go to the king; but the eventual successor was even closer to the green children story (Chap. 9).

In 1177 Fitz-Neal began a handbook for royal treasurers, in dialogue form.[28] He remained at Ely as archdeacon[5] till 1189, and was Dean of Lincoln from 1184 to 1189. Pope Alexander wrote that with his knowledge of letters and moral standing, his illegitimacy should be no bar to further advancement.[154] In September 1189 he was elected bishop of London, becoming deputy to the archbishop of Canterbury; he was a roving Justice in Essex in 1194, and remained Treasurer till his death in 1198.

His *Tricolumnus*, a tabular history, is lost,[51] despite his plea: "It this should by chance fall into your hands, beware not to lose it, for it may be useful to those of future times, and joyful to those anxious to know the state of the kingdom under the foresaid prince...", Henry II, who benefited by histories of previous kings.   But Benedict of Peterborough and Roger de Hoveden's chronicles may draw on it.[155]

As my friend John Braithwaite remarked, "When somebody makes up a story like this, they tend to do it out of whole cloth.   There might be names of real people and places, but it won't stand up to this kind of detailed examination." Whereas, by 1160 Richard de Calna was in Suffolk, a friend to the new king, excused all taxes, with family in high places and interesting neighbours, within eight miles of Woolpit - and something about Woolpit interested Henry II very much.

Before that, there was another incident - one almost as mysterious as the green children themselves.

Chapter Five – 1150s: THE 'ANTIPODES' INCIDENT

"... a neighbour, say, might've detected the change in the man and remarked off the back of her hand to a companion: 'Yon Paddy Cullen's fairly picked himself up since he got back from the swineherding!'... I'd no doubt whatsoever that Paddy's state of grace wouldn't outlast twelve-thirty p.m. when the Labour Club opened its doors and Auld Nick gave'm a crony's wink from the fiery pit of a whisky glass."

~ Jeff Torrington, *Swing Hammer Swing!*

Here, too, someone appears out of nowhere, at harvest time.   This time we know where he came from, and have to guess where he went.   You might expect many such incidents, in superstitious times;   but the multi-volume chronicles of Roger de Wendover, Matthew Paris and Gerald of Wales each have only one, though Gerald believed every tall tale in Wales and Ireland; Gervaise of Tilbury's collection of 143 marvels has only one, which Stevenson reprints with Ralph's Chronicle,[1] supposedly to show what absurd things 12th century readers believed.   But Gervaise and Ralph were friends: when I searched Stevenson's Index for references to Ralph's time at Barnwell Priory (Chap. 8), the founder's name led me straight to it.

In 1056 the church of St. Martin's-le-Grand, near St. Paul's, was re-founded after a fire, by Ingelric, earl of Essex.   He became Dean there in 1088, having lost his title,[2] taken holy orders, and served briefly as a canon of St. Paul's.[3] Here Kempe's 19th century history of St. Martin's-le-Grand cites "a manuscript which has been frequently resorted to in the course of these pages", held by the Chapter of Westminster.[4]   He doesn't identify it, maybe not allowed to; some he wasn't allowed even to see.

The sensitive issue was Ingelric's daughter, Ingelrica, married to Ranulph Peverell.   Well-connected before the Conquest, Ranulph's family did even better afterwards; among many places, in Essex for example, he held property at Thorpe in Suffolk (though not Ixworth Thorpe, near de Calna) from the Abbot of Bury St. Edmunds.   He also owned the church of St. Martin Vintry, in London, which he gave to St. Peter's Abbey-Church in Colchester, as well as making gifts to St. Paul's.[5]

Of Ingelrica's four sons, William Peverell was governor of Dover Castle; Pain Peverell founded Barnwell Priory[6] (where Ralph was a canon, before Coggeshall). Her last son, Lord of Nottingham, had great castles there and at Castleton, in the Peak District of Derbyshire. He too was William,[7] because he, at least, was fathered by William the Conqueror.[8] To atone for her sin Ingelrica founded the College of Mary Magdalene at Hatfield-Peverell in Essex, where she was buried.[9] For the Conqueror's 19th century admirers, this was an "uncertified and almost impossible scandal"[10] - quite funny since he himself was illegitimate.

As with de Calna, I've had to decide how to spell Peverell. Peverell and Peveril are most frequent versions, so I've used the former for the family and kept 'Peveril' for the castle, its modern spelling. 'William' was used in all branches of the family,[11] but I'm concentrating on the Conqueror's natural son and *his* son, also called William.

Most texts say William Peverell was made Constable of Nottingham[12] and given Nottingham Castle in 1068, just after the Conquest, which would mean he gained it (and over a hundred other estates in 'the Honour of William Peverell') at birth or even sooner, unless Ingelrica was already the Conqueror's mistress long before then. The Domesday Book does have a large Nottinghamshire entry under 'Land of William Peverell', plus others as far afield as south Essex.[13] But it doesn't say when he acquired it, and the survey was in 1086.[14] The 12th century Ordericus Vitalis says "The king now [1068] built a castle at Nottingham, which he committed to the custody of William Peverell", but that doesn't necessarily mean right away.[15]

In 1110 the bishop of Chester and others were ordered to return the bishop of Lincoln's churches in the Peak, which they'd wrongly taken over on the day when William Peverell was given Lordship of the Peak.[16] 24 years is a long time for that situation to persist, but 42 years would be very long. Modern dating shows that Peveril Castle was built between 1085 and '89, with additions in 1173-76,[17] so when Domesday lists William Peverell as the owner, the castle ('Pechefers')[18] was new.

'William Peverell of Nottingham' witnessed numerous grants, up to his death in February 1113.[19] His wife Adelina or Adeliza and his son William witnessed his grants to the church of Lenton in 1109; William the younger witnessed documents in 1121 and 1131,[16] and after 1135 he and his first wife Oddona, and his son Henry, established a Cluniac Priory at Lenton.[20]   He helped defeat the Scots at North Allerton in 1138, on king Stephen's side,[21] though he was holding Peveril Castle against him.[22]   By 1149 he was re-married to Avice de Lancaster, and around the same time he had an argument with the canons of St. Martins-le-Grand about land in the marshes of Maldon in Essex.[20]   The two Williams are frequently confused, but *The Itinerary of King Henry the First* pinpoints the father's death,[16,23] so all later references must be to the son.[24]

The younger William Peverell and Richard de Calna were contemporaries, and he knew the family: in 1131 he and bishop Nigel witnessed a charter at Northampton.[25]   In 1136 Roger le Poer, Roger le Pauper, Everard, Nigel, Alexander de Calna and he all witnessed Stephen's confirmation of the church's rights in England, at Oxford.   They were all at Westminster that Easter, and all at Bury St. Edmunds in November,[20] so he could have met Richard de Calna then, if not before.   Peverell lost the castle and his title in 1155 (see below), so the 'antipodes incident' can't have been any later.

Gervaise of Tilbury was born in the early 1150's, possibly 1152, in west Essex. In Italy, he studied at Bologna before practising canon law in Venice, in 1177.[26]   He then joined the household of prince Henry, the oldest son of Henry II, so he'd have known both Richard Barre and Richard de Calna's neighbour, William Blundus   (see Chap.9).   Gervaise wrote his Book of Wonders before the prince's death in 1183; if Richard Barre gave him the 'antipodes' story, it would suggest that Barre and Richard de Calna were doing something, involving both Peveril Castle and Woolpit, even before the children arrived.   The Norman churches of the Castle and the village are both dedicated to St. Edmund.[27,28]

Gervaise's source was Prior Robert of the Augustinian Priory of Kenilworth. A modern French writer puts him there in 1160 to 1180,[29] strangely vague since most documents about him are held in France.[30]   The earliest is no later than 1159, perhaps as early as 1155· the last one in English records is put at 1180, but nearer 1198.   When Robert took office, Hugh Barre witnessed confirmation of Kenilworth's properties in the Lincoln diocese,[31] so the story could have passed through them to Gervaise.

De Antipodibus et Eorum Terra - Of the Antipodes and their Land

"In Great Britain there is a castle sited between certain mountains, to which the people give the name Pech. Its fortification would be stormed with difficulty, and in the mountain there is the cave-mouth of a hole, which like a pipe emits air very strongly for a time. From it can come forth a great blast of air wondered at by the people; and among many things which are told of the same with wonder, I had this from there, from that most religious man Prior Robert of Kenilworth, who with the noble man William Peverell owned that castle with the adjacent barony of its borders, (a man indeed brave and capable, and well supplied with the various means of life). On one certain day a swineherd of his, who was lazy in the task entrusted to him, lost his pregnant, particularly well-bred sow of the breed. Therefore fearing on account of the harsh words hurled by the appointed lord whom he served, he thought if perhaps she had gone down into the drop of that Pech hole, famous but until that time unexplored. He put in his mind that he should make a search of the foresaid place. He entered the cave at a time when it was free from all wind, and made his way forward for a long time; at length from darkness he came out released in a bright place in a spacious flat land of fields. Entering that widely farmed land, he found reapers gathering ripe produce, and among the hanging ears of corn he recognised the sow, which had many wounds showing from the bites of her sucklings. Then the swineherd wondering and overjoyed with the loss made good, and with the way that had happened by the ruling of the steward of that land, took the sow and released with joy he led it forth from the pigs of the same. A wonderful thing: coming from the underground harvesters, he saw winter things frozen by cold persisting in our hemisphere, which verily I have thought can be ascribed to the Sun being absent in the presence of the edges [of the world]."

"'Yon Paddy Cullen's fair picked himself up since he got back from the swine-herding!'..."[32] Gervaise uses the word *hemisphaerium*: he knew the world was round,[33] with 'a circle of lands', surrounded by water, whose polar edges were far from the Sun. The 'Antipodes' weren't the children's home: it wasn't twilight, the people weren't green. They spoke English, though the swineherd emerged in flat countryside, very unlike Castleton's; so much for mutually incomprehensible dialects every few miles. An Englishman teleported to the Antipodes today would speak the language, but people wouldn't be casual about it.   Wherever this was, it's as if matter-transmission was routine.   "Is that your pig?   OK, the boss says just take it back..."

Flat, bright, well cultivated, at harvest time, where the reapers spoke his language, and knew what to do with people coming out of the ground... it could be Woolpit, Wykes or Cressing Temple.   The *praepositus*, a person appointed to be in charge (a bailiff or steward, in mediaeval Latin,[34] not *dominus* like de Calna), didn't exercise the right of 'waif' by which his master could have seized the pig (Chap. 14).   At Woolpit, pre-1160, that right was the Abbot of Bury St. Edmund's - so perhaps it was at Wykes.   The swine-herd wasn't green, and spoke English, so de Calna would know what had happened and send him and his beast back to Derbyshire.

After a distinguished career in Rheims, Sicily, Italy and Arles, Gervaise of Tilbury returned to Essex and became a canon, though we don't know where.[26]   If he told Ralph the Peveril story, maybe Ralph thought there was a connection with the green children.   The cave and harvest-time emergence are like his version of the girl's story - perhaps he or the de Calnas edited it to match, either because he was unhappy with instantaneous transmission or because the 'other side of the world' was a cover-up.   There's no mention of bells - and if there were any the swineherd wouldn't feel inclined to follow them.   Non-believer as I am, I'd hesitate to enter a cavern alleged to be the Devil's territory if I could hear bells ringing down there.   To quote John Lennon, "who would fight this wondrous beast?   I wouldn't for a kick off".[35]

In 1153, to gain Randulph of Chester's support against Stephen, the future Henry II promised him "the city and county of Stafford, Nottingham castle, Derby, and Mansfield, with many great baronies" - whose owners weren't pleased.   Some grants were absolute, others if the owners wouldn't support Henry; they included Nottingham, its castle, and all fees of William Peverell's "unless he can acquit himself in my court of his wickedness and treason".[36]   It's not known what that treason was, since Henry wasn't on the throne yet; Peverell hadn't behaved any worse in the civil war than the de Calnas, for instance.   His trial never happened, but it all looks like a cover-up.

Stephen's heir, Eustace, died suddenly while plundering the lands of Bury St. Edmunds.   The earls of Chester had a long connection with the Abbey: Randulph's great seal, showing him in armour on horseback, carrying a great sword, was hidden under the main aisle for safety and discovered in the early 19th century.[37]   The earl of Arundel had proposed the treaty which would end the war, making Henry king when Stephen died, but Chester opposed it because the terms cancelled Henry's promises to him.   Peverell lured the earl to his home and served poisoned wine, killing three others.   Chester drank little, but his health was broken and he died soon after.[38]   Gervase of Canterbury says Ranulph was poisoned by Peverell "as the story was";[39] Matthew Paris says many others were suspected of conspiracy in the murder.[40]

Peverell lost his land and titles, which came back to the family later, and even those he kept until after Stephen's death.   Henry embarked on a leisurely tour of his new realm, going all round Peverell's territory as if to give him as much time and warning as possible.   When he approached Nottingham in 1155, William supposedly was overcome with fear.   He took holy orders at Lenton Priory, founded by his father,[41] and is said then to have fled to the continent.[22]

Fig. 5.1.

Fig. 5.1. Peveril Castle, 2011, and Peak Cavern, 1994.
Photos by Duncan and Linda Lunan.

It all seems too convenient.   When Chester's death was so timely, Peverell
escaped with so much warning, and so many others were implicated, it
suggests that Peverell drew the short straw, acted on orders, and loyally took
the rap.   One way out might have been to 'take the cross', becoming a
crusader; many a wanted man did likewise.

And maybe the rap wasn't as bad as made out.   Peverell's lands left the family
only briefly, so it's even more likely that Henry and Peverell agreed on killing
Chester;   and if Peverell hadn't killed the earl, ownership would have
transferred to *him* in any case.   There was more activity at the castle
nevertheless.   Henry was there in 1157,[42] receiving the submission of Malcolm
king of Scots,[43] and again in 1158 and 1164; in 1173, he had the castle
strengthened and put in crack troops (see Chap.9).

The Peak Cavern is in a gorge below a 200-foot sheer drop on the castle's west
side, where an even more extended cave system has collapsed.   The show

cave entrance is the largest in Europe and second largest in the world. By the 16th century it held a village of rope-makers for the lead mines of the Peak.[43] One cottage on which "the sun never shone and the rain never fell" was still in use in the 1840s,[45] and the last rope-maker retired only in 1975. The spectacle is diminished by the ticket office, though the hoarding which used to block the entrance has gone (Fig. 5.1).

Off the entrance cavern there's a 'Swine Hole', not on the regular tour because it's wet and slippery. The river below the cave complex cuts across the end, flooding the Swine Hole when it rises, so its inner stretch is virtually cylindrical. The entrance cavern bends to the right beyond it, once ending 75 yards along in a water-filled passage. Only divers could go on (the first attempt was in 1777) except when there was a two-foot clearance for a boat. "It is said that Byron felt the liveliest emotions while yet he remained 'the unspoiled child of nature'... when crossing this dark pool with the object of his first love, Miss Chaworth."[45] In the 19th century a taller passage (aptly known as the Lumbago Walk, even so) was blasted out for a visit by Queen Victoria.

The Great Cave beyond has a hole in the roof, an oubliette for condemned prisoners from the castle - no way to find the exit in the dark, even when the water was low. There's no question of the swineherd getting so far. The cave system extends many miles beyond, not one cavern but a 'resurgence complex', in which water has carved multiple paths through the limestone.[46]

Richard de Torigni confirms the 12th century winds from the cave. "There are four wonders which are seen in England: first, that a wind comes out of the cavern in the earth on the mountain which is called Pec [Peak], with so much force that it repels torches thrown into it, and lifts them on high..." The second was Stonehenge, the third Cheddar Gorge, and the fourth mountain springs.[47] Ralph Diceto puts the first three at the head of a much longer list, with the Rollright Ring as the fourth.[48] But Henry de Huntingdon's gives the same four as de Torigni, and it's the oldest - the first known mention of Stonehenge. It had four editions, the last in 1154, the year Henry II came to the throne, so it places the winds during Peverell's time in charge.[49]

Domesday says "In Peak's Arse Arnberg and Hunding held the land of William Peveril's castle, in Pechefers."[22] In the 18th century the cave was 'Peake's Arse' or 'The Devil's Arse',[44] which the *Britannica* ambiguously tones down to 'The Devil's Hole'. Sir Walter Scott's *Peveril of the Peak* calls it 'The Devil's Cavern',[50] but Scott was bowdlerised by his editors, who were particularly sensitive to the word 'arse'.[51]

The Lumbago Walk is a siphon, 'Puttrell's Aven', with breezes through a 40-foot shaft to the surface, but the chronicles describe much stronger wind, the top natural wonder of England. The Peak District is used to wind: the road to Castleton from Chapel-en-le-Frith is still called 'Winnats', Wind-Gates,[52] but to hurl torches high in the air would take hurricane force, over 100 miles per hour (Chap.22). We're not told the torches were extinguished, so the wind was breathable, but the earliest record of the village is 1196;[28] perhaps it wasn't there until the winds stopped, blocked by rockfalls? The area's subject to minor earthquakes, even disasters when pent-up waters break out.[53] Conan Doyle wrote, "All this country is hollow. Could you strike it with some gigantic hammer, it would boom like a drum, or possibly cave in altogether and expose some huge subterranean sea."[54]

'Winter things frozen by cold' may be stalactites.[55] Nearby Treak Cliff Cavern has huge displays; Peak Cave has flowstone on the walls, but only one stalactite stub, now. There were three big ones in 1700:[56] before smoke from the rope-works cottages, they'd be gleaming white and too high to tell from ice. But when young Byron visited as 'an unspoiled child of nature', he produced a shotgun and blew them away.

They'd have to be large to resist the winds, or else the Devil would spit his teeth at you. Sir George Head wrote, "nor could a more characteristic vestibule of the pale Prince of Darkness be found than the lofty and ample vault, most properly denominated 'The Hall of Pluto'."[57] The swineherd must been sure the sow was ahead of him, following tracks or smelling it, for his fear of Peverell to drive him forward into that.

Henry II was interested in such incidents: he asked the king of Scotland for a cup, of unknown material and unusual colour, allegedly stolen from the fairies.[58] Yet Henry wasn't superstitious: he defied prophecy by crossing an accursed stone in Wales, though at popular wishes he wasn't crowned in Lincoln, believed to be unlucky.[21]

Crowned at Bury St. Edmunds in May 1157, he went on to Colchester, near Coggeshall, then met Malcolm of Scots at Peveril.[59]   He was back there in 1158,[60] just before he excused de Calna and de Hastings from taxes.   In May 1160, while out of England for two years, he signed a treaty with Louis of France; de Hastings was a witness,[59] so perhaps he was on hand when the swineherd report came up.   He had become Templar Master in England in 1155, when Henry took over Peveril Castle.   The only English bishop with them was Hugh du Puiset, bishop of Durham[61] - see Chap. 12.

When the story got out, it seems it rang alarm bells of some kind.   Because in 1160, acting from Normandy, Henry II annexed Woolpit.

Chapter Six – 1160s: CONCERNING SAMSON DE BOTINGTON

"Put it this way - if it's not Contact with Other Intelligence, you've got the political thriller of all time."

~ John Braithwaite

1. Samson Goes to Rome

Woolpit is peaceful now, and perhaps was even more so in the 12th century, when it had only 60 people.   But it's unlikely to have been untouched by the civil war, which raged through England with almost Bosnian ferocity: Essex, for example, was largely depopulated.   After Stephen's 18-year-old son Eustace wasted the property of Bury St. Edmunds Abbey in 1153, he promptly died of "a burning fever and a frenzy" - another miracle credited to the saint, because it made possible the peace plan under which Henry II became the next king.[1]

Then and after, Woolpit was at the eye of a hurricane.   Two steps away from it, in any direction, and we are in the big issues of the century; and no-one had more reason to know it than Samson de Botington, the future Abbot of Bury St. Edmunds.

Born in 1135, Samson had a boyhood vision that St. Edmund had picked him to do great things.[2]   Educated in Paris at the school of William of Diss, sponsored by a chaplain from the proceeds of selling holy water, by 1159 he was a schoolmaster in Bury.   Samson's biographer, Jocelin de Brakelond,[3] became a novice at Bury St. Edmunds in 1166[2] or 1173,[3] and was placed under Samson's tuition.   It seems that he and Samson were close for many years, and he was Samson's personal chaplain for a time, but there's an implied breach between them in Samson's later career.[4]

In 1160-61 Samson's life changed out of all recognition, and what did it was Henry II's annexation of Woolpit.   Previously the village was in 'soccage', paying feudal rents etc. to the Abbey, for about 150 years.   Suddenly Henry took control and assigned it to one of his people in 'frankalmoin', free alms, by which the Abbey no longer received anything; not even obligations of homage and military service.   The individual sums were trifling - a few pence here, a shilling or two there - and with only 60 inhabitants, the total was only ten pounds a year.[3]   Yet supposedly Samson went to Rome on his own initiative, accompanied by a monk named Roger of Hingham, to petition the Pope to tell Henry to give Woolpit back - a very odd thing to do.

In 1159 there were two candidates for the papacy, and though Alexander III had a large majority, Victor IV, supported by Emperor Barbarossa of Germany (nephew of the Second Crusade's Konrad III), refused to admit defeat.   In 1161 Henry II hadn't decided whom to support, and according to Lord Lyttelton, would better have backed Victor.[1]   Yet Samson went to Alexander, supposedly motivated by principle and a conviction that any letter from Rome would be enough.   His account is a classic.

"... I passed through Italy at a time when all clerks carrying letters for the Lord Pope Alexander were seized and some of them imprisoned, some hanged, and others sent to the Pope with their lips and noses lopped off, to his great dishonour and confusion.   But I pretended that I was a Scot, and putting on Scottish garb, and bearing myself after the fashion of a Scot, I often thrust out my staff as if it were a javelin against those that mocked me, uttering threatening words after the fashion of the Scots. Thus did I that I might disguise myself and my purpose and that 'in likeness of a Scot, I might more safely wend my way to Rome.'

And when I had obtained letters from the Lord Pope such as I desired, on my homeward way from Rome I passed by a certain castle, and behold!   the servants of the castle surrounded me, seizing me and saying, 'This fellow that wanders all alone, pretending that he is a Scot, is either a spy or carries letters of the false Pope Alexander'.   And while they searched my rags and boots and trews [*femoralia*, 'things of the thigh'], and even my old shoes, which I carried slung over my shoulders after the fashion of the Scots, I thrust my hand into the leathern wallet which contained the writing of the Lord Pope, placed beneath a small cup, from which I used to drink; and by the will of God and of St. Edmund, I pulled out the writing together with the cup, so that when I raised my arm on high, I held the letter under the cup.   The cup they saw, but not the letter.   And thus I escaped from their hands in the name of the Lord."

It's tempting to picture this scene as it would be played by Ronnie Corbett, Dudley Moore and John Cleese. But according to Jocelin, Samson was of average height, making Samson's tale even harder to believe. Why was Samson travelling alone through France, when he left England with Roger de Hingham, and came back with him? James Bentley, a conjuror among his many accomplishments, reckons it would be impossible to conceal a document the size of the papal letter in that way.[6]

The kilt and the tartan, as we know them, are primarily Victorian inventions; in mediaeval times 'tartan' was scarlet cloth from Tyre.[7] A typical Scot would have worn a saffron linen shirt, pleated at the back with a rough leather pouch on a belt at the front, both to preserve decency because the shirt was worn short. A semi-circular cloak - possibly with a check pattern - was often worn over the shirt, particularly in cold weather, with trews under it.[8] The Scots and French were backing Victor for Pope, but though his garb and 'threatening words' might convince non-Scots, since 800 AD there had been a network of hospices across Europe for Scottish pilgrims to Rome.[8] With his broad Norfolk accent (see Chap.13) Samson would have to avoid those, so giving himself away nonetheless.

The quotation is apparently from a song, maybe by Samson himself. He must never have heard the joke about the sparrow ending, "... and if you're in it up to the neck, for God's sake don't sing about it!" Because that's just where he had landed himself.

"Whatever coin I had they took from me, so that I had to beg from door to door, without any money to spend, until I came to England. But when I heard the church had been given to Geoffrey Ridell, my soul was filled with sorrow for that I had laboured all in vain. So when I came home, I hid myself secretly beneath the feretory of St. Edmund, fearing lest the Lord Abbot should seize me and put me in prison, though I had deserved no such thing; nor was there a monk dared speak with me nor any layman feed me, save by stealth. At length, after he had taken counsel, the Abbot sent me into exile at Acre, and there I remained for a long time." Roger of Hingham was gone even longer, for after 1173 Samson said he was recently returned from exile.

Not only did Samson go to Rome without the authority of Abbot Hugh, he didn't wait to see who'd take charge of Woolpit. It's frequently said that

Henry seized it to assign the living to one of his poor clerks; Geoffrey Ridell was indeed a *magister*,[9] but he was a great deal more, and didn't need the tiny income from Woolpit. His grandfather was a justiciar of Henry I's,[10] drowned with the heir to the throne and many others in the king's *White Ship*, in 1120. The king arranged for Ridell's daughter to marry Richard Basset, another justiciar, in 1123;[11] Basset wasn't particularly wealthy,[10] but as his son-in-law, in 1144 at Devizes empress Matilda restored all of Ridell's inheritance in England and Normandy - and there was a lot of it. When Henry II came to the throne, he confirmed the restoration of Ridell's land.[12]

It seems that from 1161 to 1173 Ridell was Acting Chancellor of England; for example he was signing documents as Chancellor in 1162. He became archdeacon of Canterbury before March 1163 in 'a rather mysterious event'.[13] At the least he was Acting Vice-Chancellor in 1170, which required a large private income. When he became bishop of Ely in 1173, his long list of gifts to the Cathedral included five thousand silver marks and corresponding sums in gold and rubies, plus large gifts in kind.[14] He was also a patron of the Knights Templar,[15] and still had plenty of money left for Henry II to seize by when the king's supply ran out (Chap.13). At death he left 3200 gold marks, a large string of horses and many other treasures.[9] Putting someone like that in charge of Woolpit would show just about anyone except Samson that something serious was at stake - the way he tells it. But maybe Samson was playing a more subtle rôle than his friends at Bury supposed.

For all his claimed satisfaction with the Pope's letter, it wasn't to the king but to Abbot Hugh, covering many issues, including, "We have ordered the church of Woolpit to return to the use of the brothers *when it shall become vacant* [my emphasis]" - in other words, when the king had finished with it.[2] It suggests that Woolpit was annexed with his knowledge, or even on his instructions - perhaps through Richard de Hastings - and dated 2nd January, 1161, so Woolpit was annexed no later than 1160.

I haven't found another case of Henry taking property from a church, much less from Bury St. Edmunds, for which he asserted the deepest reverence. Perhaps pope Alexander didn't want to annoy him; it would be strange to side with the Abbey on so small an issue, when Henry had yet to side with him. In 1161 Alexander canonised king Edward the Confessor, legitimising Henry's new Plantagenet dynasty.[16]

2. Samson Goes to 'Acre'

Meanwhile, Samson was exiled to the Holy Land - he said.   In *Memoirs of St. Edmund's Abbey*, without giving a source, the editor says he became a preceptor to the de Warenne family, in their great baronial castle at Acre, where his skills would have been valuable.   The Index says he served the Earl himself,[2] and that's impossible.

William de Warenne (1030-1088) was the first earl of Surrey.   The next two were also called William: the second took over Rouen in 1130, the third supported Stephen and Matilda in the civil war.   Half-brother of the Beaumont twins, in 1140-41 he was at the battle of Lincoln with one, [17] either the earl of Leicester, Robert, or his elder twin, Waleran.   de Warenne and his troops fled, contributing to Stephen's defeat and capture, but his reputation was undiminished.   He held Rouen for Stephen against Waleran after the count had changed sides; held Neufchâtel-en-Brai in 1144, until defeated by the earls of Anjou and Flanders plus the king of France in person; and was acclaimed in 1146 for taking the cross, for the Second Crusade.   He and Waleran led the Anglo-Norman contingent to the Holy Land, with Arnulf, bishop of Lisieux.

Killed there in 1148 (Chap.4), with no male heir, he was succeeded by his daughter Isabel.   In 1153 she married William de Blois, son of Stephen and Matilda, who received the title.   In 1157 Henry II returned Surrey to him, and knighted him at Carlisle in 1158,[17] but he died, childless, in 1159[18] or '60,[19] and she didn't remarry till 1163 or '64.   Samson couldn't serve the *earl* from 1161, because there wasn't one.   In 1139 Stephen had awarded Isabels's father the advowson of churches at Thetford,[20] so Samson could have known them; but it all makes the Acre story suspect.

The port of Acre is mentioned in the records of Tuthmosis (1479 BC), later of Akhenaten, Seti I, Ramesses II and still later Assurbanipal in 700 BC.   In 39 BC Herod landed at Acre (then called Ptolemais, after Ptolemy II c.281 BC) to retake Palestine; its true Arabic name of Akka was restored in 636 AD. After capturing Jerusalem, king Baldwin took Acre in 1104; the Templars were well established there by 1172.[21]

But I can't find any de Warenne holdings in Acre, in plans from the middles of the 12th and 13th centuries and the end of the 13th.[21-23] The second husband of William de Warenne's widow was murdered in 1168 by Guy de Lusignan, who then fled from England *to* the Holy Land, so it's unlikely that they had a stronghold there in 1161.[24]

But the de Warennes held Castle-Acre in *Norfolk*. They founded a priory under William the Conqueror,[20] given to the Cluniac Order in the reign of William Rufus,[25] but the monks took residence only in 1090, and its church wasn't dedicated until the third baron left for the Crusade in late spring 1147.[26] Bury St. Edmunds Abbey was Benedictine; but Samson wasn't yet in holy orders, and in Everard de Calna's Norwich charters, Castle-Acre is simply 'Acra', as in the Holy Land, and the prior there in 1161 was named Jordan.[26] It's as if the 19th century editor read something saying 'Samson went to Jordan at the de Warenne's Acre', and thought 'that can't be right'. However you look at it, Samson's self-portrait as a 'holy fool' in 1160-61 is at odds with the shrewdness of his future career, and suggests that his 'exile' to Acre was misdirection.

A preceptor was a teacher, literally, like Samson - especially an individual tutor to a prince.[27] He could have tutored Isabel de Warenne, though she was in her mid-teens at least. But 'Preceptor' was also the title of a Master of a rural establishment of the Knights Templar (Chap.3).[28] That could make Samson and Roger de Hingham's rôle very different, considering the wording of Samson's letter. Did they separate in France for Roger to get a similar letter from the *other* Pope? If he was working on the king's behalf, Samson may have known why Woolpit was important. Under the Abbey the priest would have been in charge, collecting the income and passing it on; whoever Ridell appointed as vicar would have to pay taxes on it, since it was now royal land, unless exempted from them; and the annexation of Woolpit was within two years after de Calna and de Hastings were excused from paying taxes. Perhaps the Abbot 'took counsel' with *them* before moving Samson for the good of his health. Castle-Acre was linked by river to Lynn, where the green girl was later to marry, and that was linked by canal to Ely, where Nigel de Calna was bishop.

Gérard de Sède says that in 1161 the Templars were in disagreement over the election of the Grand Master, and the English branch anticipated the break-up of the Order.[29]   If Samson was involved, his tracks are well covered, but when he became Abbot in 1182, he adopted a Templar emblem on the reverse of his seal.   Personal seals of abbots and bishops were oval, and on them a bishop would have his pastoral staff in his left hand, an abbot have it in his right. Sure enough, Samson is shown with a mitre on his head, staff in right hand and a book in his left.[30]   But on the reverse is an Agnus Dei, and on the staff behind the lamb is a cross *pattée* or *formée*,[31] not the Maltese cross of the Knights Hospitallers but the Templar version[32] (Fig. 6.1).   The Hospitallers used the Agnus Dei as an emblem, but with the lamb looking backwards.[33]

The Templars' Agnus Dei was second only to the emblem of two knights on a horse[34] (Chap.3).   Maybe that's why the lamb symbol for Christ was banned in the later Middle Ages, though the prayer remains part of 'the ordinary of the Mass', recited every day: "Lamb of God, who taketh away the sins of the world, grant us peace", or "grant them eternal rest".   The only seal like it in the catalogue of the British Library (formerly British Museum), has that wording, used by the Bishop of Norwich in the early 13th century, but Samson's has SECRETUM SAMPSONIS ABBATIS.   *Secretum* was a personal seal, but the alternative translation - 'The Secret of Abbot Samson' - makes the Templar emblem more intriguing, especially on a Benedictine seal.   The Banner of St. Edmund bears the Agnus with a more conventional cross *botonné* or *preflée*[35] (Fig. 6.2): when Henry III visited in the 1240's he forbade the bakers to impress the Agnus on loaves for public sale, because he thought that disrespectful.[30]

Samson's tomb, opened in 1903, held a similar lead cross *pattée*, like the insignia of Templar Grand Masters.[36]   Provincial Masters had the same rights as the Grand Master, and each province had add different logo: for England it was the Agnus Dei, and from c.1155 to 1185 it was used by Richard de Hastings, next door to Richard de Calna.   Samson's emblem implies a connection with de Hastings, if not both of them;   though a later abbot, Edmund de Walpole, had a similar cross in his coffin, perhaps because in 1250 he signed up for the next Crusade in defiance of his monastic vows.[37]

Between 1186 and 1197, Samson founded the hospital of St. Saviour in Bury. On the charter seal he has an orb, surmounted by a plain cross, in his left hand,[30] in his right "a sceptre fleur-de-lizé" (Fig. 6.3).   Neither he nor the Abbey had any known connection with French royalty, though he was educated in Paris; but the fleur-de-lis might show a link with the de Cantilupes and de Calnas (Chaps. 14 & 15). One book says the cross floriated, with arms ending in fleurs-de-lis, was a Templar logo, but if so it was minor, not mentioned elsewhere - not in Fig. 3.1, for example.

Fig. 6.1. Seal of Abbot Samson in the Camden edition of Jocelin's Chronicle.

Fig. 6.2. Bury St. Edmunds banner in the Camden edition of Jocelin's Chronicle.

Fig. 6.3. Reverse of Abbot Samson's St. Saviour seal. Richard Yates, "History and Antiquities of the Abbey of St. Edmund's, Bury", 1843.

In 1163 Henry II annexed Hagenet Castle, four miles from Woolpit,[38] and he visited Peveril Castle again the following year.[39] But if Samson knew the background to all this, from whom was it hidden? Richard Fitz-Neal, the Treasurer, set up his half-brother's tax exemption, so it wasn't to hide Woolpit from him. The only other person with access to those records was the Chancellor, Thomas à Becket.

In 1162 Henry made Becket Archbishop of Canterbury, though till then he was a layman. Henry obtained a special dispensation from Pope Alexander to do it, and in return supported Alexander against his rival.[1] But Alexander believed the papacy had supreme power, and Becket considered himself bound to support that. He resigned as Chancellor, and by 1163 the situation was deteriorating rapidly. In 1164 Henry tried to contain it by the 16 Constitutions of Clarendon, backed by Gilbert Foliot, the new bishop of London, although only six of the new laws were acceptable to the Pope. Three others related to Samson's Woolpit intervention: no appeals to the Pope without the king's permission, no cleric to leave the country without it, and all secular offences by clerics to be tried in secular courts.

3. Samson in the Church

If as ingenuous as he claimed, Samson thought Henry was after him; in 1164-65 he took holy orders, becoming novice-master, guest-master, pittancer, then third prior at Bury St. Edmunds.[40]   (Training *pueri*, minors, ended around 1150 and Jocelin doesn't mention them; otherwise Samson would have been 'childmaster' before novice-master.)   But Woolpit was never forgotten, though the Abbey had 70 churches in Suffolk.

In 1163 Geoffrey Ridell became archdeacon of Canterbury, Becket's own launch-pad, at Henry's request.[41]   Becket soon regretted it, because Ridell was Henry's man: in February 1164 he was one of Henry's ambassadors to the Pope, after the Constitutions of Clarendon.   Becket called him the "arch-demon of Canterbury", excommunicating him in 1167, renewing it in 1170. Ridell made "a saucy answer" when Becket offered him reinstatement in a peace package, nearly losing the king's favour as a result.[24]

The Clarendon committee was chaired by John of Oxford,[42] chief ambassador to Rome in 1164.   Rural dean of Oxfordshire by 1160, he was excused paying the Danegeld, so already in royal service.   He was in Wiltshire in 1161-62,[41] and in 1165 became Dean of Salisbury, against the wishes of Becket and the Pope.[43]   He swore never to recognise Alexander III as Pope, and Becket ex-communicated him in 1166.[44]

In 1160, Henry II engaged Prince Henry, at six years old, to the even younger Margaret of France.   The treaty was negotiated by Richard de Hastings,[45] already Templar Master in England.   Margaret's dowry was to include the castles of Gisors, Neusle and Neuchatel in the Vexin, with Templars Richard de Hastings, Robert de Pirou and Tostes de St. Omer as custodians.   The castles weren't to be handed over until the wedding, but they were delivered to Henry immediately,   Louis expelled the custodians from France, to a warm welcome in England.

Richard de Hastings's predecessor, Oto or Osto, used to be so mysterious that even his surname was uncertain. He signed the 1153 treaty between Stephen and Matilda simply as 'Oto knight of the Temple'.[32] Marion Melville identifies him as Tostes de St. Omer, originally from Flanders,[46] as do Gérard de Sède[29] and Malcolm Barber.[23] He was younger brother of Godfrey de St. Omer, one of the nine founders of the Templars,[46] chronicled by another St. Omer in 1137. Tostes witnessed a donation by the count of Flanders to the Templars in 1128; he joined the Order in the 1140s, serving in northwest Europe and Catalonia, in the kingdom of Jerusalem in 1145, and at a war council in Acre in 1148. He was Templar Master in England from 1153 to 1155, but stepped down for de Hastings, whom he served as *compagnon de rang*, an inseparable second-in-command. Tostes was still active in 1174 (Chap.9).

The de Hastings family's land in Essex lay between the river Stour and the mouth of the Colne, on the east of Great and Little Horkesley[47] - later connected with the de Calnas (Chap.17). Little Horkesley Priory belonged to Thetford Priory, near the de Calnas at Knettishall. Walter de Hastings was eldest son of Walter the Deacon, father of the Maskerells of Earl's Colne, who founded Wix Nunnery (Chap.4). William de Hastings was steward to Henry I, and held land in Norfolk, not far from Thetford.[20] His son William was steward to Henry II, and had hereditary stewardship of the Liberty of Bury St. Edmunds.[3] In 1166 William de Hastings was a major landowner in the area.[15] In 1182, when Samson became Abbot, Thomas de Hastings demanded the post for his nephew Henry, but he wasn't yet a knight, so had to appoint a deputy.[48] Henry died in the Third Crusade, but the family retained the stewardship until 1389. Curiously, though, *Richard* de Hastings isn't in the family tree at all.

Richard de Hastings and Tostes de St.Omer urged Becket to comply with Henry at the Council of Clarendon. In 1169 Becket excommunicated a clerk Richard de Hastings, nephew or brother of William, who'd occupied the archbishop's church of Manech.[24] In one of Becket's letters, however, Richard the clerk is identified as also a nephew of Richard de Hastings.[43] Elsewhere he warned of two Templars spreading lies on the king's behalf; but if they were de Hastings and Tostes, Becket didn't act against them.

On Christmas night (December 24th) 1167, "appeared in the west two stars of the colour of fire; one great, and the other small; at first joined together, but afterwards they were separated from one another by a long space." It was the birth-night of the future king John, and inevitably seen as an omen, though an eminent 19th century editor described the two stars as 'meteors'.[49] It sounds like a comet nucleus breaking in two, and it's a fitting moment to reintroduce Richard Barre.

4. New Stars

Barre was the king's envoy to Pope Alexander in 1169, with John of Oxford. Both had been there before, separately; this time they were to arrange the crowning of prince Henry, but they also brought back a papal commission requested by John of Oxford, authorising them to negotiate between Henry II and Becket. This was very prestigious work for such a young man: the first record I've found of Richard Barre has him witnessing charters in Lincoln in 1160-66, probably 1164-66 - as Richard Barred or Baretto, but almost certainly our man because Richard's father, archdeacon Hugh Barre of Lincoln, also used the alternative spelling 'Barret' (Chap.4).[50] One charter was also witnessed by Nicholas de Sigillo, archdeacon of Huntingdon in 1164-66 (not the Nicholas in Chap.4, claiming that an archdeacon could not be saved?).

Barre held land in Harbury, Warwickshire, which he gave to Nuneaton Priory in 1163-68.[51] If he could afford that, he had to have more, and he's listed in Lincolnshire in 1166.[52] With his first firm date in the records as an adult around 1164, it could mean he was only 17 on his first trip to Rome, but more likely he was older.[4]

Ralph V. Turner says in his essay on Barre, "Anyone seeking a position in the middle ages needed a patron if he did not have a powerful family to support him. Second-rank royal officials often served in households of some influential *familiaris regis* [a member of the king's inner circle] before joining the king's service. A number of them came to the *curia regis* [the royal justicial court] by way of the justiciar's or chancellor's staffs. This cannot be demonstrated for [Barre] however. Richard Barre's first post seems to have been with Nicholas, archdeacon of Huntingdon [Nicholas de Sigillo above], or with Robert de Chesney, bishop of Lincoln, [whom Hugh Barre succeeded as archdeacon of Leicester.[50]]   How he got from England's ecclesiastical circles to the royal court of Normandy can never be known."[53]

First there's the question of his age.   Turner suggests that Richard Barre was at law school in Bologna before 1150, but as far as I can tell, his only evidence is a letter to Barre in the early 1190s from Stephan or Étienne de Tournai.[54] Stephan was born at Orléans in 1128, studied at Bologna and returned c.1155, joining the convent of Orléans and later abbot; in 1176 he became abbot of Saint-Geneviève in Paris, then bishop of Tournai early in 1192.[55] The full text of the letter is in Chap.14: it does refer to Barre's popularity at Bologna, but it doesn't say that he and Richard Barre were students there *together*.   There are several reasons why he might not have been.

(1) Turner suggests that Hugh Barre and Richard were kinsmen.   But they died about forty years apart, c.1169 and in 1209, as we'll see, and if Hugh was the 'Hugh Bar' in the Holy Land in 1118 (Chap.4), then it seems they were father and son.

(2) Stephan went to Bologna in 1150 at latest, but probably was there from 1145 to 1150.   If Barre was at Bologna before 1150, that leaves Turner's question - what prompted his meteoric rise more than 15 years after he graduated?

(3)   The canon law course at Bologna took six years, usually preceded by several years of general study; Bologna and Paris were not just the best law schools but the best schools of any kind, before the rise of Oxford and Cambridge, with seventeen 'nations' of overseas students.[56]   If Barre was born in the 1130's or earlier, he'd have been in his 40's when he fathered his two children (Chaps.11-13), 52 or over when he took the (reportedly) longest journey of his life (Chap.13), between 60 and 70 when he was most active in his career (Chap.14), and up to 79 when he died (Chap. 15).   None of that is impossible, but it would all be more likely if he was 15 to 20 years younger. In that case Richard was born in 1145-1150, around when (I think) Richard de Calna, newly knighted, left for or returned from the Second Crusade - but if he became Barre's godfather, and if he returned from the Crusade as a Templar, as I suggested in Chap.4, then the christening must have been before he went, because the Templars' Rule 72 forbade them to be godparents.[56]

88

John Le Neve's *Fasti* implies that Hugh Barre died in 1157 or '59. I thought that if Richard de Calna became Richard's guardian, he probably sponsored his education. However, research published in 1986 showed that Hugh Barre lived at least nine years longer.[17] He resigned his posts at Lincoln no later than 1163, but having been archdeacon of Leicester, he became chaplain to Robert *le bossu*, earl of Leicester, and witnessed at least eleven of his charters between 1154 and the earl's death in 1168. In 1164 Beaumont made a charter to the priory of Le Desert, for the souls of his family and of 'Hugh my chaplain', an unusual act showing a close relationship between Hugh Barre and the Beaumonts. He became tutor and later chaplain to the next earl of Leicester, also called Robert, who has a big part in Chap.9. Hugh witnessed another eleven of his charters, but we don't have any firm dates after 1168 and meanwhile his Buckinghamshire property, particularly Chesham, passed to Richard. It's possible that they were brothers or kinsmen, but father-and-son is more likely.

Whether or not Richard de Calna was Richard Barre's godfather, and sponsored his education, as a canon of Salisbury he was in a good position to influence John of Oxford, who was Dean of Salisbury (though still comparatively young[13]), and even to influence the king, to give the young Barre ambassadorial responsibility.

Henry II introduced him to the Pope as 'our clerk and member of our household', giving him authority to negotiate *viva voce* on behalf of his king as well as carrying letters. Obviously that came from a personal appreciation of Barre's talents, not just the say-so of Richard de Calna and John of Oxford. The bishop of Paris and the future archbishop of Canterbury both called him 'magister', so he might have studied at Paris rather than Bologna. Turner suggests that he might have written the *Summa de multiplici iuris divisione*,[57] a legal treatise of the 1160s (borrowing from Stephan de Tournai) on whether cases involving clerics should be heard by royal courts if they involved the King's Peace - an English legal concept, in the Constitutions of Clarendon. The archbishop and his followers called him 'foremost of the false prophets', ally of the archdemon Geoffrey Ridell,[44] and 'Goliath in the court of Achitophel', which even as a negative is pretty impressive for such a young man.

Henry II charged Ridell in 1169 to assemble the kingdom's bishops and abbots for a showdown in London, but they refused to come. Richard Barre and other envoys tried unsuccessfully to see the Pope in early 1170, and when they returned, allegedly Ridell's intrigues prevented a peace with Becket.[58] Ridell's excommunication continued after peace was supposedly made between Henry and Becket, lasting into 1171. Meanwhile Becket had returned to England, escorted by John of Oxford.

But he refused to lift the excommunications of the bishop of York and Jocelin bishop of Salisbury - the latter for making John of Oxford his dean.[43] When this was reported to Henry II, his outburst of rage prompted four of his knights to cross the Channel and kill Becket at Canterbury. They stopped to confer at Saltwood Castle with Ranulf de Broc, Usher and Chief Marshal of Henry's household:[59,60] Becket had excommunicated him in 1166 and repeated the sentence in 1169.[24] After the murder, the knights gave Becket's papers to de Broc, to pass on to Henry.[2] We'll meet both de Broc and his wife again, in Chaps.9 and 13.

At the very moment of the murder, there was a flashback to the mystery of Samson and the de Warennes. When first widowed, when Samson was allegedly in her service, Isabel de Warenne wanted to marry William, third son of the empress Matilda. Thomas à Becket prevented it; William de Blois died in 1164, and one of the killers is said to have struck with the words, *"Hoc habeas pro amore domini mei Willelmi fratris regis* - take that for the love of my lord William, brother of the king".[60] It needs less breath control in Latin, but it's still a lot to say while killing with a mediaeval sword - those were not the duelling rapiers of Shakespeare's time, 'One, two, and the third in your bosom'. And the witness who quoted it was a kinsman of Geoffrey Fitz-Stephen, Richard de Hastings's successor as English Master of the Templars.

In January 1171 the Archbishop of Sens carried out the Pope's threat to put England under interdict, forbidding all church activity, and asked Alexander to ratify the sentence. Richard Barre and others who were there appealed it,[44] causing it to be suspended while they went to the Pope at Frascati. Barre left France on January 25th and got ahead of the party, delayed by bad weather and the frailty of the archbishop of Rouen, who had to turn back.[61] An unnamed Knight Templar also disappeared from the party, yet managed to arrive with them. The pope was refusing to see Barre, and at first granted audience only to two of the delegates whom he considered innocent, or at least less involved.[1]   One was an archdeacon of Lisieux, as Barre soon afterwards was himself (Chap.10).   Some books say that Barre was taken ill at Tusculum on the way home, but that's not in the sources cited.[45,61]

On reflection, however, pope Alexander was impressed with Barre's performance as Henry's ambassador.   He wrote to Henry in 1171 and 1172 praising him as "our beloved son Richard Barre", and urged Henry not to forget the service he had rendered.[44]   Alexander's approval stood Barre in good stead later   (Chap.11).   In other letters he spoke well of David of London, another envoy and a protégé of Gilbert Foliot's, but never called him 'our beloved son'.[62]

For Alexander to speak of Barre in such terms, there must be more to it.   In 1171, Barre had also delivered a secret commission from Henry II to the Pope.[42]   We don't know what that was about, but most historians believe it was Henry's invasion of Ireland, which by then had been going on for two years, and where still another extraordinary event had just taken place.

Chapter Seven - 1170: GHOSTS IN THE NIGHT

Deazil	Sir Richard, you are a wise
	and dutiful good man. And you will inform me
	Of any riders strange to you at Woolpit.
	For these must be reported to the Abbey
	Without delay.
Calne	I'll take that liberty.
Deazil	That would be best, sir. This is a testing time.
	I'm off to Cugford village, where they say
	They saw black riders higher than their black houses.

~ Glyn Maxwell, *Wolfpit*

Despite his fondness for tall tales (Chap.5) Giraldus Cambrensis (Gerald Barry of Wales), relates only one case of people appearing or disappearing, during the English and Welsh invasion of Ireland.[1]   The invasion was in support of Dermod MacMurrough, who had been given the kingdom of Leinster in 1161.[2]   Banished in 1166 or '68,[3] he went first to Bristol, where he gained the help of Richard 'Strongbow' de Clare, earl of Pembroke, then, crossing to St. David's, he enlisted the Welsh half-brothers Maurice Fitz-Gerald and Robert Fitz-Stephen, son of the former king.

The Fitz-Stephens and du Barrys were 'Geraldines', descended from Henry I's favourite Gerald of Windsor, and dispossessed of their Welsh holdings, which Henry II had returned to the former owners.[4]   Dermod promised them Wexford.   He returned to Ireland in 1167[5] or '68, with a small force; Fitz-Stephen followed in May 1169, with an army including two of his nephews, Robert du Barry and his cousin Meiler, still in their teens.   Du Barry, Giraldus's brother, was the first knight wounded in the invasion, and narrowly escaped with his life in the assault on Wexford.[1]   Later that year, they were joined by a force headed by Richard Strongbow.

In late 1169 or early '70 Dermod and Fitz-Stephen entered Ossory, to avenge the blinding of Dermod's son by Doncahd, the king there.[5]   They overcame defensive cuttings, ditches and palisades on the Pass of Gowran, the ancient route through the bogs and forests of Ossory.   At a favourite spot of the

Ossorians for ambushes, Fitz-Stephen lured them on to the plain and won a decisive victory.

But when the army camped "in a certain ancient fortification", by night, "a force of infinite thousands of men burst in on them everywhere, as if devouring them all together in the force of their fury, with the sound of their arms, and the immoderate clashing of their axes, and filling the heavens with terrible shouting. Such phantoms used to appear often in Ireland around hostile expeditions." The army scattered, taking cover in the woods and marshes, except Meiler and du Barry: "these two men only, at once leaping to arms, valiantly presented themselves at Fitz-Stephen's tents, fiercely calling back and rallying their dispersed colleagues. Indeed Robert du Barry was so greatly calm, among the great confusion of all, that to the great admiration of the ashamed majority, he pled anxiously the case for his sparrowhawk, which he himself had tamed by his will, not to be lost."

du Barry had just introduced hawking into Ireland (so he wasn't a Templar: they were forbidden hawking, and to hunt anything except lions.[6]) Giraldus told the story to prove his brother's courage, but it seems excessively cool - unless he knew the attack was phoney. "But the marvel of this phantasm was such, that as the next day cleared, in the place where that army was seen to break upon them, the grasses and nettles, which before were high and erect, lay wasted, flat and levelled" - like another Irish event, in 1236 (Chap. 16). It makes du Barry's calmness even more remarkable: if he knew the attack wouldn't be pressed home, perhaps his search was for something else, or he had to plant something. Or perhaps the army had to be dispersed so he could receive unusual visitors, with no witnesses.

The alarm was raised by Ranulph Fitz-Ralph, Captain of the Watch - related to the holder of Peveril Castle at the time.[7] Troops from Wexford, camped separately, were attacked simultaneously.[8] Maurice Regan, Dermod's interpreter,[7] gives the site as Fethard, though the army was marching west from Ferns into Ossory. The two Fethards in Tipperaray and Wexford are too far off, in the wrong direction.[8]

Regan's 18th century editor thought it might have been at Burtin or Athy in County Kildare, north of Kilkenny. The attack was before a river crossing, and Rev. Shearman puts it at an old castle at Hy Bairrehi, maybe Dinn Reigh,

south of Leighlinbridge on the River Barrow.[5]   The Rev. William Carrigan
also suggested that, since the army came from Ferns and its target was Fresh-
ford.[9]   If so, that puts it north of Gowran: Dinn Reigh is the Ballyknockan
Mote, an ancient ring-shaped bank.   But a *mote*, from Icelandic 'mot', is not a
motte, a fortification, but a place of meeting, for judgment, usually a high
spot.[10]   For a Norman writer, the difference between a mote and a motte
would be, literally, a moot point - but not for us.

Giraldus set the attack in 'an ancient earthwork'.   The motte at Gowran itself
was built later by the Normans, and is west of the Barrow, as is Ballyknockan
Mote.   But in County Laois (Leix), formerly Queen's County, Upper Ossory,
the Mote of Skirk, east of the river Nore - *before* the crossing, as the army
marched west - had a central stone six to seven feet high, with others in a disc-
shaped amphitheatre 240 feet across.

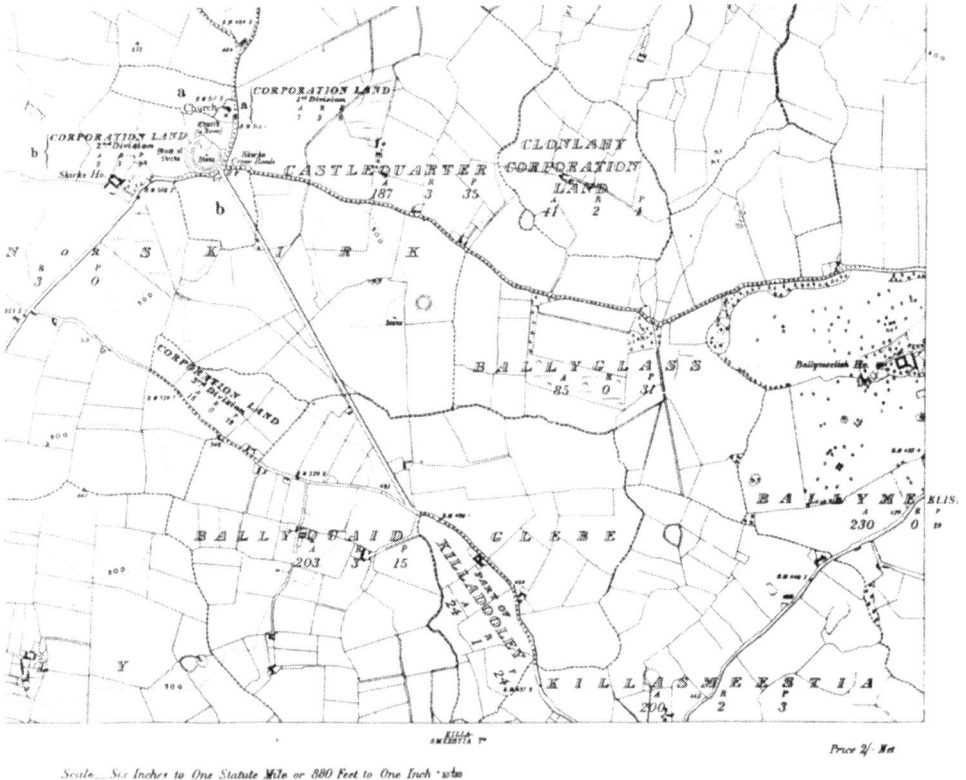

Fig. 7.1.

.SKIRK.

Figs. 7.1 & 7.2. 1909 Ordnance Survey map of the Mote of Skirk (top left), 18th century woodcut of the Mote of Skirk.

Fig. 7.3.

Figs. 7.3 & 7.4.   Mote of Skirk stone and Skirk Church.
Photos by Duncan and Linda Lunan.

Figs. 7.5 & 7.6. Photo by John Braithwaite,
Aerial view of Mote and Church by Archaeology Ireland.

(Fig. 7.1).   With a high bank, and a cromlech (remains of a Neolithic tomb)
on the east, it later had a 13th century motte-and-bailey fort inside[11,12]   (Fig.
7.2).   The central stone is Neolithic, with no inscriptions in the Ogham alpha-
bet (Fig. 7.3).[13]

The nearby churchyard, from 1216 or earlier[14] (Fig. 7.4), had a pre-Christian Lady's Well,[9] like Woolpit's, which "survived all efforts to destroy it. It was filled in over a century ago, but emerged as a fount of spring water rising to a height of three feet in the bole of a spreading sycamore tree which was planted over the original well. This well is held in great veneration by the people of the neighbourhood, and a pilgrimage was made there on 15 August each year until 1964, when it was discontinued".[12]

In the 1990s John Braithwaite visited Skirk, but couldn't get in and took photos over the hedge from the top of his van (Fig. 7.5). In 2011 it was still more overgrown and I lost my bearings inside, coming out on the east (Fig. 7.6) when I thought I'd turned north. Fig. 7.1 shows the north of the circle sliced off, but it's intact and impassable.

12th century Ossory was mostly forest or bog, so armies kept to river valleys, but Skirk is only four and a half miles from the monastery of Aghaboe, (Ag-had-bou, the field of the cow), "close to the Great Pass of Ossory... a haven of hospitality for weary travellers",[12] founded c.577 AD by St. Canice, a friend of St. Columba and St. Brendan, under patronage of the prince of Ossory. An 8th century abbot, 'Virgil the Geometer', maintained "in defiance of God and his own soul" that the world was round, with people at the antipodes.[15] The bishop of Ossory was at Aghaboe in 1052-1110 or 1111, and back in 1178-1202 after Kilkenny cathedral was destroyed in 1175.[16]

In 1172 or '73, Strongbow gave half the town of Aghaboe and the surrounding land to Adam de Hereford.[17] Young Adam had come over with him in 1170; in 1173 he defeated a fleet of ships from Cork. The same year, the lid came off at Woolpit, and twelve years later, Adam de Hereford married someone directly concerned. But before we come to that, some other issues have to be resolved.

Chapter Eight - GREEN CHILDREN AND RED HERRINGS

"I found myself constantly falling back to the cry of 'coincidence!' Now coincidence may be invoked once or even twice, but when several divergent elements coincide and coincide again, coincidence becomes conformity rather than chance."

~ Dr. John Wilson[1]

"'Coincidence' isn't a refutation of an argument, it's a refusal to have one."

~Brian Finch, poet, Glasgow

1. When Was it?

There are two discrepancies between William of Newburgh's story and Ralph of Coggeshall's. One is the caves; the other, more significant, that Ralph puts it in the reign of Henry II, where William's definite that it was under king Stephen, before 1155.

For children who came out of the ground, didn't speak English and were green, they were treated surprisingly well   (appearing at a holy well would help, if I'm right about that) though it was established quickly that they were green all over.   In Burton's time, it would have been much worse in the era of the witch trials, which makes his recognition of their possible origin more striking.   Nevertheless, at first the children weren't taken to be human. Nobody thought to feed them for the first few days, probably longer - as witness the boy's death, though the way it's worded, psychological factors had more to do with it.

Compare Ralph's account of a 'wild man of the woods', captured by fishermen and taken to Bartholomew Glanville, custodian of Henry II's castle at Orford. To us it's obvious that the man had a feral childhood, in the wild without human contact (but he didn't refuse food).   He was completely mute, maybe why he'd been abandoned in infancy.   Bartholomew had him hung up by the feet and severely tortured - and at that word 'severely', the blood runs cold. For all his praised good nature, Ralph approves the slow burning of Gervaise's young woman heretic,[2] and the regular beating of recalcitrant servants at other abbeys "on the Lord's days and Sabbath days, after dinner".   William of Newburgh how in 1165-66 thirty Cathar heretics from Germany, men and women, were whipped, branded and exiled from Oxford.   Forbidden all help by order of the king, they died of hunger and exposure.

Had the children been taken to Abbot Hugo of Bury St. Edmunds, 1157-80, they might have been all right: to the anger of Samson and his Boswell,[3] "The Jews, I say... had free entrance and exit, and went everywhere through the monastery... *and more unseemly still,* in the days of the war their wives and children took refuge in our pittancery." [My italics].   A 'pittance' was a grant or tax paid to the Abbey in food, and Samson was pittancer for part of this time, so that particularly annoyed him.   If Hugo had given shelter to the green children, Samson would surely have had something to say about it - unless he was pretending ignorance, as I've suggested.

It might have been around 1182, when Samson was in a heated election campaign for the Abbacy.   Jocelin says "at this time... many signs and wonders were performed among the common folk, as I have set down elsewhere".   That doesn't survive, but probably was the martyrdom of St. Robert, a boy allegedly murdered by Jews in Bury in 1181.   One modern commentator bluntly accuses Samson of inventing it.[4]

Once Abbot, he encouraged the Jews' eviction from Bury, which cost 57 lives (one text actually uses the Latin for 'cleansed'), imitating a massacre at Richard I's coronation in 1190.   In his secular court he had a sheriff's powers of imprisonment and hanging, at Cattishall, between Bury and Woolpit, and later as a roving justiciary.   The Cattishall court retained trial by fire and water after the rest of England abolished it, only ended by special charter in 1232.[5]

Samson had a straightforward view of his duty: when his servants' friendly Christmas boxing match degenerated into a brawl, he excommunicated them all and didn't readmit them to the fold until 'smartly scourged', much as it grieved him.   Unless he was in the secret, it's unlikely that he'd give the children time to learn English or French; burning them might have upset him, but the villagers wouldn't take them elsewhere just to spare his feelings.   They probably didn't care too much for Samson, with his super-efficient 'Kalendar' of rents due to him.

But Ralph heard about the girl's behaviour as an *adult* on Richard de Calna's visits. "Being later reborn by immersion of holy baptism, and remaining for many years on the staff of the aforesaid knight (as we frequently heard from the same knight and his family) she showed herself greatly wilful and independent/ wanton and lascivious." Richard died by 1189, as we'll see, so arrival after 1182 is too late.

Coggeshall Abbey was founded in 1140 and dedicated in 1167 by the bishop of London, Gilbert Foliot,[6] (Chap. 6). Its name derives from Cock's Hall or Cocks' Hall, with three cockerels on the Abbey seal. Ralph, 1207-1216, was preceded by Simon de Toni, Abbot Odo, of whom little is known; Abbot Peter, 1176-1194, and Thomas, 1194-1207. A 16th century farmhouse incorporates parts of the Abbey with its distinctive brickwork (Fig. 8.1), including the cloisters and the Abbot's quarters. The current owner, Roger Hadlee, is restoring the Abbey's guest house; the Grange Barn was erected between 1090 and 1180, probably before 1167 because the abbeys often put up agricultural buildings first for financial support; and the Chapel of St. Nicholas at the old gatehouse was built around 1223.

Fig. 8.1.

Figs. 8.1 & 8.2. Coggeshall Abbey farm, Abbot's Quarters and Guesthouse. Photos by Duncan Lunan, 1993, and Linda Lunan, 2011.

Ralph died in 1228 or 1230: even if he lived to near 70, he was born around 1160. Before coming to Coggeshall he was a canon at the Augustinian Priory of Barnwell in Cambridge,[7] (not *Bardwell*, to which Wykes manor was attached). In those days one could be a bishop at 20, but Ralph couldn't have been a canon before his late teens, say 1175. In 1179, a Council at Rome ruled that bishops had to be at least 30 and legitimate, and all other officers, including archdeacons and deacons, had to be at least 25.[8]

In 1175 the new Prior at Barnwell, Robert Joel, set up a harsh regime. Maybe that decided young Ralph, an intellectual, to move on, and the 1296 history of the Priory's first 200 years includes a standard dismissal for a brother moving to another monastery[9] (the only example I've come across). It would take time to apply, for the Prior to give permission, and for *his* superior to approve it (the bishop of Ely, then Geoffrey Ridell, promoted and relieved of responsibility for Woolpit). So Ralph probably reached Coggeshall around 1179; Richard de Calna died in 1189, so his visits to Ralph must have been in the 1180's.

Between 1160 and 1182 Woolpit wasn't controlled by Bury St. Edmunds. In 1160- 61, and in 1173-74, Samson was out of England, and there was no priest at Woolpit to take charge of the children, or make the villagers take them to the Abbey. If the girl was ten when she arrived, to speak so well at her trial (Chap.10), 1161 would put her in her 30s during de Calna's Coggeshall visits, very late to find out, supposedly, that her behaviour in his household wasn't satisfactory.   Jocelin came to Bury in 1165 or 1173, a very active year (Chap.9), so he could have missed the arrival.   Ralph described it along with the wild man of Orford: Orford Castle was new in 1173.

Maybe the wild man's mistreatment prompted de Calna to advertise for the children, saying two of his family were missing.   But when such unusual ones turned up, he'd have to offer a substantial reward, even if the village wasn't then under Bury St. Edmunds, to make it worth displeasing the Abbot. Maybe sudden prosperity in Woolpit set tongues wagging, leading to William of Newburgh's investigation.   Any of this would imply that de Calna knew the children were in the area; at the very least, he had made arrangements that any strange arrivals were to be brought to him, and from the arguments here and the facts in Chap.9, I think it was in 1173.

2. A Catch of Red Herrings

Misconceptions about the story are mainly 'natural explanations', and modern versions which don't match the original texts.   Many claim the children were refugees from some primitive tribe, raised on a poor diet, or wandering, eating only berries,.   In the *Fortean Times* in 1991,[10] Paul Harris stressed 'Chlorosis', an iron deficiency which supposedly turns people green, particularly adolescent girls.[11]   Chlorosis was treated with ferrous sulphate, which Richard de Calna might not have to hand.

But the children were well when they arrived, because they *then* survived prolonged starvation; "...healthy, though, of that I'm sure," de Calna says of them in Glyn Maxwell's play.[12]   Nowadays, when children are seldom lost for long, we tend to underestimate their resilience.   In 1994, two children aged six and four survived in the Andes for three weeks on apples, berries and stream water, wandering over 100 km..   Not only did they not turn green, they were "in good shape... They're playing with toys with the other kids and are obviously happy",[13] not like the green children at all.

Even in children otherwise well, iron deficiency immediately affects mental health, especially attention span; it extends into adulthood, even if not nearly bad enough to change a child's colour;[14] yet the green girl had nothing wrong with her brain, as we'll see.   Girls at puberty have higher red cell counts than boys do, so the odds were doubly stacked against her if she had Chlorosis. Yet she survived and the boy died.

The whole existence of Chlorosis is suspect. Though allegedly described by Aristotle, I couldn't find it, even in his section on the causes of skin colours.[15] *The Anatomy of Melancholy* is a medical textbook, but under *Symptoms of Maids', Nuns' and Widows' Melancholy*, followed by *Immediate Causes of these Precedent Symptoms*, Burton doesn't mention Chlorosis or anything like it, despite many classical references. That's because, in his time, doctors hadn't invented it yet! First described by Johannes Lange in 1554, long after the advent of the green children, it was an urban 'condition', rarely found in Europe after 1910, most noted in factory workers and unknown in rural areas, which excludes the 'unknown tribe' explanations.

In fact, few if any young women diagnosed with Chlorosis in the late 18th and 19th centuries turned green. The colour has been used as a metaphor for sexual inexperience or innocence throughout folklore, and in *The Go-Between*, for example. 'The green sickness', also called 'the virgin's disease', with marriage bluntly prescribed as the cure, was probably a catch-all for adolescent problems which we understand better nowadays, such as *anorexia nervosa*.[16] Prof. Helen King, an studies Open University expert in ancient medicine and classical studies, backed that view in the *National Geographic* documentary filmed with me at Woolpit.

Introducing less nutritious, polished rice brought on beri-beri in the South Pacific, and similar dietary changes caused pellagra elsewhere. Scurvy broke out in Ireland in 1846 because grain sent from Britain, during the potato famine, contained no vitamin C; it also happened in the California Gold Rush in 1848, and again in the 1870-71 siege of Paris.[17] But over-refined food doesn't explain the green colour, it doesn't tie in with the 'primitive tribe' explanation; and even if Chlorosis were real and the children had it, why not eat the food they were offered?

Might they have come from Grime's Graves, near Brandon in Norfolk: a Neolithic flint-mine complex of 254 shafts, 20 to 60 feet deep, with radiating galleries?[18] Paul Harris suggested underground passages linking them to Woolpit and now filled in, and the first-floor clerestory windows of St. Mary's are surrounded by intricate patterns of flint.[19] But the caves don't exist, and although Paul says they're within walking distance of Woolpit, Grime's Graves are 24 miles away, beyond Thetford. On the surface, going the wrong way, it would be strange not to see the Sun - it's very bright at harvest time, in that flat country, and was a big shock to the children.

A smattering of Bronze Age, Iron Age and Roman objects were found in Grime's Graves, so they were raided for flints after working stopped, until the shafts collapsed.[20] Flint-knapping continued locally till modern times, but the pits were sealed for around 2000 years with no mediaeval intrusion; the first one reopened was in 1870. Grim (Norse 'Grimr') was another name for Odin,[21] and the surface depressions were thought to mark a Danish encampment even in 1805. But it all shows that a community couldn't hide there in such isolation that they spoke a different language. Even if it did exist, with a diet as restricted as Paul Harris suggested, I can't believe that children from it would refuse *all* food - even the Wild Man of Orford didn't have that problem. Paul has now withdrawn the Grime's Graves suggestion, and thinks, as I do, that Ralph put in the caves to match his friend Gervaise's swineherd story.

Paul also suggested that the children came from the small village of Fornham St. Martin, nor-nor-west of Bury St. Edmunds; "a non-local dialect could well be unintelligible to the insular 12th century farmers of Woolpit." But Woolpit was far from isolated, on the pilgrim route to Bury and evolving into a market-town. Travel round Europe was easier than today: describing Gervase's travels, H.G. Richardson wrote, "...the narrow seas were a means of communication rather than obstacles to travel. So much of Western Europe, so much of the Mediterranean, was, as it were, one vast country, where clerks and knights and merchants passed freely over great distances, however toilsome the roads, however hazardous the sea-passages. There were many difficulties to be overcome, but language never seems to present itself as one."[2] For a 12th century critic of England's cathedral cities, the worst thing about Durham, Norwich and Lincoln was that one would hardly hear Latin spoken there.[22] Even peasants moved more than we suppose: the Abbot of Bury could require Woolpit's villagers to take farm produce anywhere in the country, and as bishop of Norfolk, Everard de Calna decreed that everyone in his see must visit Norwich Cathedral at least once a year.[23]

The villagers would recognise a wide range of dialects and most European languages, from traders and pilgrims to Bury; they would know the sounds of

Latin and Greek from church services, and of Yiddish from the large Jewish community in town. And if the children were from just a few villages off, it's incredible that even after days of starvation, they would refuse perfectly normal food. As Glyn Maxwell's character 'Sara' says, "If I was green with hunger I'd eat earth".[12]

Many people believe that the children were abandoned in Wayland Wood in Norfolk, after being poisoned with arsenic compounds by their guardian.[24] Arsenic itself is relatively inert;[25] copper arsenite (Scheele's green) was used in green wallpapers and fabrics, and might have killed Napoleon Bonaparte, but he didn't turn green. Arsenic may turn people white, or blue-gray, as does an overdose of silver (argyria),[26] but doctors consulted wouldn't confirm it because they'd never seen arsenic poisoning, and Prof. King was definite that green doesn't happen. A 1998 article seemed to show victims with green hair and skin patches,[27] but it was an artefact of printing and the author hadn't seen any green people in India, where arsenic pollution is serious.[28]

Again, the children were otherwise healthy when found; and Wayland Wood is even further away from Woolpit, near Swaffham. Paul Harris suggests that the green children have been mixed up with 'the Babes in the Wood' (as in the pantomime), first published by Thomas Millington of Norwich in 1595.[29]

Milarepa, a Tibetan saint who ate only nettles for twelve years, is alleged to have turned greenish - but even modern versions say only 'greenish', not bright green.[30] Nettles are very nutritious, the whole plant is edible (even stalks) and it's almost possible to live on them alone. The Roman nettle was introduced to Britain as vegetables and is still common in eastern England. But in Tibet green was the colour of spirits (Milarepa appeared green in a vision of him, earlier in life), and I can't find a way for him to turn green on nutritious vegetables. The Romans also introduced the leek, and Ralph calls the children 'leek-green' in Latin. The ornamental 'houseleek' or 'housegreen' is often planted on roofs to secure tiles, and Romans believed it was a gift from Jupiter, protecting against lightning[31] - of which this story has odd cases.

The children's clothes were of "a colour and material never seen before". Most people then wore 'tabby-woven' woollen broadcloth in drab browns and greys[32] because they could afford no better, but in a market town on a pilgrim route, in the pedlars' packs there would be linen, silk, goatskin, woven goat, weasel and stoat hair - red, yellow and blue, but seldom green.[33]

Red dyes came from madder and brazilwood, and the expensive scarlet (originally a kind of finish, not a colour) from a European insect, a big secret, imported as 'grain'. Woad and indigo were blue dyes; purple came from lichens in northwest England, Scotland, Norway, and another variety from the Mediterranean; yellow was made from weld and brazilwood. (Weld has been regrown from mediaeval seeds at Mount Grace Priory, Yorkshire.[34]) Iron and other mordants made black. Sanguine, vermilion, crimson, violet, azure, murrey, russet and perse (dark blue) were all produced, and mixed colours, checks and stripes. A light blue cloth called 'plunket' was popular; treated madder could give peach, yellow, brown and tan, and turn weld golden. With other yellow die it made orange, and *could* make green by mixing with woad; probably difficult or unreliable, because only one example is known - but perhaps mastered in Ireland, where woad and madder were plentiful in the north.[35]

Robin Hood's Merry Men allegedly wore 'Lincoln green' in the 1190's. In *The White Goddess*, Robert Graves suggests who *they* might have been[36] (Chap.15); but in the 13th century Lincoln was actually known for scarlet cloth. 'Kendal green', in the north of England, was more famous,[37] but the community of Flemish weavers in Kendal, who had the secret, wasn't founded until 1331.[38]

Graves reveals that secret: fast green dyes were made from alder-flowers.[36] The alder/elder's wood and leaves are water-resistant: the oldest European houses were built on alder-pilings, like Roman causeways in the Ravenna marches, and the Rialto in Venice. Virgil says the first boats were alder-trunks, and they reinforced the waterfront at King's Lynn, but around 1250,[39] long after the green children.

Alder bark gives red and brown dyes; it was banned in Solomon's Temple and replaced with pomegranate, which gives a similar red dye. It was one of the trees of resurrection in Calypso's grove on the island of Pharos, in the *Aeneid*, and the fairies used alder-dye to colour their clothes green. It was the tree on which Christ was nailed;[40] the thirteenth tree of the Druidic calendar, it was unlucky to cut it down without asking its permission;[41] and alder-lotion was used for eye problems - a link with the Lady's Well?   The street from Cripple-gate Manor   (Chap. 4)   to St. Martin's-le-Grand was Aldersgate;   but according to John Stow and John Strype's survey of London, it was originally 'elder-gate', older, to distinguish it from Aldgate = Old Gate, to the east.[42.]

(Yellow Dyer's Greenwood could also combine with woad to make green dye, found in quantity at King's Lynn later,[39] when the secret was out.   Richard Hakluyt wrote in the late 16th century that "yellows and greens are colours of small price in this realm, by reason that Alder and Greenwood with which they be dyed be natural here".[43])

Woolpit villagers would have seen clergy and nobles in their finery at Bury - especially at the king's crowning there in 1157.   Buttons or pockets would be extraordinary, since neither came in till the 1330s,[44] but to impress nobles as well as peasants, the clothes must have been really unusual - fluorescent, reflective, water-repelling?   My friend Irene Gordon gave me a coloured pen-cil drawing, by Sue Jones, who wrote, "I was intrigued by the idea of the Green Children, which stuck out as something out of the ordinary run of hauntings, murders, drownings and the other staples of 'local legends'... I intended to make them rather more elfin than human.   Once I'd got going on the picture, though, it seemed to take on a life of its own.   I didn't intend the children to be well-dressed, but the clothes came of their own accord."[45] Rightly so, I think - along with the jewellery (Chap.20).

The writer Montse Stanley suggested that the strange clothes might have been *knitted*.   One early example, already advanced, was buried with a 13th century Spanish prince at the Cistercian Las Huelgas monastery,[46] founded in 1187 on the pilgrim road to Santiago de Compostela, near Finisterre (Land's End), the northwest point of Spain.   Its design includes the fleur-de-lis (Chaps. 6 & 15); we have a Compostela connection   (Chap. 13);   'Compostela' may mean 'graveyard'   (there was a Roman one there), but the likely translation is 'Starfield'.[47]

Allegedly the headless body of St. James (Santiago), the cousin of Christ, put to sea at Jaffa in the Holy Land, floated along the Mediterranean by boat and was carried by 'mystic oxen' to the hill tomb where they were rediscovered by a local bishop, or a hermit, led to them by a star in 813 AD.[48]   The saint's body came ashore at Padron, claimed to produce the best green peppers in the world.   There's no suggestion that the children confused them with green beans, but there were many green foods in the English diet; dishes were often coloured with 'food-paints' boiled out of chopped-up leaves or petals.[49]   Rose-petals gave red, saffron or dandelion yellow, heliotrope or turnsole blue, violets indigo; but mint, parsley, spinach or hazel could all be used to turn food green, especially for May Day feasts (Chap.15).   Had the children arrived near May Day, rather than harvest-time, they might not have starved so long.

Still more recently Paul Harris suggested the children might be from a Flemish community in the Romney Marshes, near Dover, or from the continent and originally bound there.[50]   There was a 'Court of Wyke' in the area, though as 'wyke' means 'house' that's not very striking.   When Geoffrey Ridell was archdeacon of Canterbury, 1160-73, his official residence was at Lympne, on the north end of the Marshes.   But Ridell would have given up the residence when he was promoted in May 1173 – before the children's arrival, if I have that right (Chap. 9).

Stone for St. Mary Woolpit was brought from Caen in Normandy, in 1097, and taken up the River Gipping from Ipswich as far as Rattlesden, only four miles south.[51]   From there a ridge runs north, then east through Woolpit to Haughley Park, near Hagenet Castle, which Henry II annexed soon after Woolpit (Chaps. 6 & 9).   Ron Jones, a local historian in Woolpit, suggested that the children were stowaways on a North Sea crossing, staying on the boat up to Rattlesden, so slow that they developed Chlorosis *en route*.   Waterway traffic was extensive, especially in East Anglia: in Matthew Paris's 13th century map of Britain and the Gough map of 1280 (redrawn 1355-66) the width of rivers is exaggerated, showing them as traffic routes, not mere lines as on modern maps.   Cambridge was listed as a seaport till the end of the 13th century.[53]

But could the children get so ill on so short a trip?   Mediaeval seamen could sail the length of the Mediterranean, from Acre to Marseilles, in just fifteen days,[54] and generally had a better and more varied diet than land-dwellers.[55]   Paul Harris suggested that the children, confused by illness and malnourishment (to the point of brain damage, though he doesn't say so), thought they were in Romney Marshes and asked to go to the Court of Wyke, so went to 'the home of lord Richard de Calna, at Wikes'.[50]   He hasn't a reason why they should ask for the Court of Wyke in particular; nor why someone of Ridell's status was in charge of tiny Woolpit in the first place. There was a St. Martin's Hundred in the Romney area, but I have a much better candidate for 'the Land of St. Martin' (Chap.10).

The Flemish element of the thesis has caught on: in 2011 several people in Woolpit told me it's proven fact. The new version is that the children were the last survivors of a Flemish community wiped out in a local dispute. But why were they immersed in green dye; if people saw enough of the Flemings to hate them so much, why didn't they know the sound of the language; and above all, why would people like de Calna and the king that the case was important?

The usual reply, to that and other awkward questions, goes, "Of course, we can ignore that part of the story". If I discarded all the parts that I've been told I could discard, there'd be no story left. But as WAG-TV producer Isobel Tang said to me at the end of the *National Geographic* documentary filming, "Everybody has an explanation for *part* of the story - you're the only one trying to explain all of it."

Everyone imposes their own ideas on the text, and that's what I'm doing, but at least I'm doing it to the *actual* text. Some authors, really surprising ones, make no attempt at that. William Camden's *Britannia* says both children were male, and were *satyrs*, an't please you! Even his 19th century editor couldn't resist an annoyed note at having to correct that.[56] It's a mish-mash of William's account and Ralph's, and it's as if when Camden wrote it up, he looked only at the headline *De Viridibus Pueris* and did the rest from memory. (*Pueri* is plural of *puer*, a boy, but more generally means 'children'.) But he mentions the Antipodes *and* St. Martin's Land (Chap. 5 & Chap. 10), and compares the story to Lucian's *True History* (150 AD), the oldest interplanetary voyage we know. Lucian's second one, *Icaromenippus*, was also quoted by Burton in the astronomy section of *The Anatomy of Melancholy* (Chap.1). It's as if Camden indirectly agrees that the children came from another world.

Most modern writers make it a children's story, changing the details as required. In *Tom's Tale* by Judith Stinton, they're found in woods, by other children, and adopted by peasants.[57] *The Green Children*, by Kevin Crossley-Holland and Alan Marks, starts as in Ralph's version, and they're adopted by a well-to-do family, but they don't lose their colour;[44] it includes a song from an opera by Nicola LeFanu, where the children speak backwards to show their strangeness.[45]

In another semi-fictional version, *The Enchanted World - Fabled Lands*, the children are found by a shepherd, watching the harvest from a hill overlooking the fields, with the wolf-pit "a bowl of hard, red earth, rimmed with brambles", still higher up-slope. There isn't any such hill near Woolpit. The shepherd himself escorts the children to Richard de Calne, but he's "the master" of Woolpit and the journey is a short one.[60]

The Enchanted World assumes they're from Fairyland. Giraldus Cambrensis, Gerald of Wales, gives a detailed, contemporary description of it by a monk who supposedly went there as a boy. There's virtually no match with the children's account: Fairyland is without Sun, but that's because its sky is always cloudy, making its nights unpleasant with no stars or moon. The fairies are all yellow-haired, with the stature of pygmies and horses the size of hares. They have no overt religion but are devoutly truthful: when his mother persuades their guest to steal a golden ball from the son of their king, they ban him from their land with contempt. He looks in vain for the way back, as Ralph has the children do, but takes nearly a year to give up. The fairy language is a variant of Greek, and the examples are easy for Giraldus to understand.[61]

The tunnel to Fairyland is near water, behind a fall or hidden in a riverbank. The river itself is the gateway in Sir Herbert Read's *The Green Child*, which moves the story to the 19th century,[62] with children both about four years old, where the girl, at least, had to be ten or over, as we'll see. Read's character returns with her to a troglodyte world, portrayed lyrically like *The Crystal World* of J.G. Ballard,[63] except that the undercurrents, the questioning, seem altogether lacking.

One possibly supernatural element is the emphasis on beans, traditionally the food of the dead.[36] In Greece and Rome, to defend against ghosts you spat beans at them. Pliny's *Natural History* said souls of the dead reside in beans, so Pythagoreans wouldn't eat beans (or fish). Montgomerie wrote that 17th century Scots witches rode to their Sabbaths on bean-stalks. But these were *black* beans, thrown backwards at the Roman feast of Lemuria to placate spirits - "With these I redeem myself and my family" - and green is the colour of life, in Egypt the colour of Osiris, whose myth was an allegory of death and rebirth, the vital annual sequence of the Nile floods.[64]

In *The Girl Green as Elderflower*, Randolph Stow uses Ralph's wonders as a frame for his character's recovery from a nervous breakdown.[65]   Glyn Maxwell's *Wolfpit* alludes to Stow's version, Read's and Judith Stinton's: Tom Parch, a villager, says at the end, "I'll be the man who found 'em in the Tale, the Tale, it'll be, of Tom".   The boy's body turns to stone after his death, like the characters in Read's novel.   Maxwell follows William of Newburgh by setting it in Stephen's reign, with 'Richard de Calne' as a young knight, unsure which side to back in the civil war.   But again, de Calne is the master of Woolpit itself, living close by;[12] the truth is more interesting.

A semi-fictional account by John Crowley changes how they were discovered, the language they spoke and the place they came from (underground, he says, with one-way entrances and exits).   "If there were children, and children of such children, so that in some way that green land elsewhere... entered our plain human race, it must surely be so diluted now, so bound up and drowned in daylight and red blood, as not to be present in us at all".[66]   We'll see in Chap.17 how true *that* is.

Since Burton, I know only two writers who suggested that the green children story *as told* might be factual, and they got it all wrong.   Peter Kolosimo cites "the scholarly writer John Macklin" in the magazine *Grit*, December 1966. I've been unable to obtain it, but US friends tell me it's an unlikely place for a scholarly writer, and Kolosimo's judgment is patchy: he rejects the UFO fantasies of George Adamski and Robert Charroux, but is impressed by Raymond Drake and Serge Hutin.[67]

"One afternoon in August, 1887, two children came out of a cave near the Spanish village of Banjos..."   From there Macklin follows the 1884 edition of William of Newburgh, including the footnote about Ralph and Richard de Calna.   The children "were brought to the house of Ricardo da Calno, a magistrate who was also the largest landowner in the village".   Macklin and Kolosimo have the boy die only a month later.   The girl became a servant in da Calno's house; the green colour faded, and eventually she was able to say a

112

few words in Spanish and describe her home - where there was no sun, a country of eternal twilight.

Saying the girl ended in service, rather than marrying and leaving the area, Macklin follows Ralph rather than William. The supposed date is only three years after the 1884 edition of William's *De Rerum*, but Macklin contradicts himself, suggesting it could be a story handed down from generation to generation - hardly so, if he had interviewed eyewitnesses still alive in 1966. A 1992 book, *The Unexplained*, adds that there's no such place as Banjos.[68] It suggests the Spanish version was coined by British UFO writer H.T. Wilkins, who seems also to have originated a spurious UFO at Byland Abbey - attributed to William of Newburgh but set in 1290, nearly 100 years too late![69]

The green children are in various compendia of folklore and mysteries:[70,71] one adds a giant wolf emerging from the pit, then vanishing before the onlookers' eyes. But I couldn't find that in either the village museum or the Suffolk County Records Office.

Green colour, or wearing green, traditionally identifies someone special or different; *Sir Gawain and the Green Knight* is an example. In ancient Mesopotamia it was the most-used colour in makeup.[72] In ancient Egypt, the pharaoh's funerary boats at Dahshur were coloured or striped in green.[73] Michael Bentine's novel *The Templar* mentions an anonymous green knight from Spain in the Holy Land,[74] but I didn't find him, only the white one (Chap. 4). However, a knight who contracted leprosy there could be transferred to the Order of St. Lazarus, who wore a green cross instead of red.[75] In von Eschenbach's *Parzival*, written in 1200-1220, the Holy Grail is a stone from Heaven carried on a green cushion.[76] In *The Discovery of the Grail* Andrew Sinclair insists that the Grail itself is green,[77] like the green goblet which Mohammed saw in Heaven, and in reconstructions of the Last Supper, during Passover, at the Church of the Holy Sepulchre. Green was also the colour of the Abyssinian royal family, who claimed descent from Solomon, and a green umbrella symbolised their presence at the Abyssinian mass and 'Search for the Body of Christ' at Easter.[78]

Green is the holy colour of Islam: the archangel Michael, greatest of all, is "of the colour of green emerald" (in Christian imagery, his wings are). A green turban signifies descent from the Prophet, and in 1119 the Moslem victory at

Sarmada near Aleppo was said to have been assisted by Mohammed or his emissary, wearing a green robe and riding a green horse. A green slab from the Garden of Eden was set in the floor of the Dome of the Rock, and the Dome of the Great Mosque of Acre was green.[79] The cenotaphs of Abraham, Isaac and Jacob in the Hebron Mosque are covered with green cloths, as is the cenotaph of Aaron at Petra.[78] During the Crusades and earlier, green was holy for both sides: *Maryam-al-Khadra*, the church of St. Mary the Green in Ascalon, became the Green Mosque in 937 and later *Sancta Maria Viridis* once again.[80] The Mughal Emperor at Agra and the Persian Shahs had verses from the Koran engraved on emeralds and sewn into their clothes.[81]

El Khidr, the 'unseen guide' of the Sufi, is 'the green one', symbolising the holiness he imbued from the waters of the Well of Life.[82] Identified with Elijah and Elias, he was reincarnated as St. George, who has particular care for sailors and the sea, and when the Khidr becomes visible he wears a robe of 'shimmering, luminous green' which rejects water; sometimes it can be seen shining beneath his everyday clothes. There's a prayer station devoted to him in Jerusalem, near the Dome of the Rock.[83]

In the afterword to C.S. Lewis's *Out of the Silent Planet*, he cites a space voyage described by Bernardus Silvestris, a 12th century Platonist, implying that the sect might have had Contact with beings from other worlds. "More than this it would be unwise to say." In the sequel, *Perelandra* (aka *Voyage to Venus*), the heroine is green (all over).[84] Silvestris also wrote on the cosmic egg as a metaphor for Creation, and free-will versus determinism.[85] He came from St. Martin's city of Tours, and calls it 'Martinopolis':[86] "The Loire shimmers where the city of St. Martin lies between starry waters and brightly tinted fields." The journey between worlds is in the *Cosmographia*, read before Pope Eugenius II in 1147;[87] but the astronomy is all wrong. The voyage begins in the outer heavens, made of the crystalline 'fifth essence' (see Chap. 1). The Earth is spherical, with climatic zones, and the apparent movements of the planets are quite accurate, but Earth is the centre of the Universe and the natures of the planets are fanciful. From Mars, for example, a river of fire pours continuously on to the Earth.

Supposedly the Hebrew *Cabbala* (also spelled Kabbala, Qabbala, etc) describes seven inhabited worlds, with human or non-human occupants. The principal book, the *Zohar*, 'Splendour', written by Moses de León in the 13th

114

century as 'Simeon ben Yohai', a 2nd century mystic,[88] actually says there are seven 'nether earths', under the world: their number coincides with the naked-eye planets (as moving objects in the heavens - Mercury, Venus, Mars, Jupiter, Saturn, Sun and Moon), the number of levels in the firmament (hence 'in seventh heaven') and the days of the week.

They get little attention in the text, and don't even rate entries in some books on the *Cabbala*.[89] Rappoport's *Myth and Legend of Ancient Israel* says they're layers beneath the earth.[90] But in the *Zohar* three are names for Earth itself: one for Israel and one for the rest, though either can be used for Earth as a whole, and another the Earth even more generally, so the inhabitants of all three are "descendants of Adam". Another is a level of non-existence reserved for those who have no children on Earth.[91]

The last of the seven, Arqa, is divided into zones of perpetual day and perman-ent night, with "mountains of darkness" as well as a "great sea", but it's the same sea as ours. Its seed-time and harvest differ from ours, and a journey from it and back takes many years. But Arqa too is underground, adjoining the limbo world; it has nightfall, though the Sun goes round from west to east; and the rest is mythological.

The *Cabbala* compilers knew that the world was round, that temperatures and racial types were related to latitude, and that when one pole has Midnight Sun the other is in darkness.[92] Whether the Sun rises east or west in the southern hemisphere is a matter of convention, if you think the Sun goes round the Earth, but if Arqa is the legendary southern continent, then of course its seed-time and harvest are different from ours, it shares the same ocean with us, and to get there and back takes a long time.

The *Zohar* rabbis' meeting with the man from Arqa[93] makes delightful reading but actually introduces a sermon about unleavened bread, because the bread of Arqa is not kosher. Not a lot of post-contact trauma there! That's the closest I've found to Contact with non-terrestrial beings, in the 12th century - there are no sustainable, realistic details of other life-forms. But it is important to shed the idea that the children might have been alien, which somebody persists in adding to my Wikipedia page.

It rests on 'convergent evolution', getting to similar destinations by different routes. For example the eye has been invented separately by animals, molluscs and insects. It's argued that other intelligent beings will be bipeds, like us, with erect stance, one head, binocular vision, etc., and it may be true. However, that's far from saying that they'll *look* like us, (even leaving knees, elbows and the Gogo fish to Chap.23). On a generally earthlike world evolution might select for faceted eyes and external armour, producing intelligent, warm-blooded beings who nevertheless *look* like giant insects.[94]

At the other extreme, the historian Martin Jenkins urged me to consider convergent DNA, very strong convergent evolution in which extraterrestrials would not only look just like us but be able to reproduce with us. I have to say that I don't believe that for a second. Humans and chimpanzees have a most of our DNA in common, but we don't look alike, can't reproduce together and aren't sexually attracted to one another. Even if we and aliens *did* look alike enough for mutual attraction, fruitful unions would be out of the question: eyes that function similarly don't allow squid to mate with houseflies. In Edgar Rice Burroughs's Mars novels, John Carter marries Dejah Thoris,[95] who lays a fertile egg which he has fathered - as Carl Sagan said, "as likely as a successful mating of a human being with a petunia".[96] In the next few chapters, we'll see that whoever the green children were, they were unquestionably human.

And having cleared those red herrings from the path, now we can look at what really happened in 1173.

PART TWO - ENTER THE GREEN CHILDREN

Chapter Nine - 1173: THE OVERTHROW OF LEICESTER

"Heralds tell us that the shield of the traitorous knight is to be reversed. Had this law of chivalry been observed... would not the beautiful stained-glass glowing in the rich church windows have looked oddly? the majority of the emblazonments turned upside down, unless a double infidelity authorised Sir Knight to turn his shield right [way] up again."

~ Sir Francis Palgrave, "Normandy and England"[1]

1173 was the peak of the 12th century's solar activity, the most violent since the Bronze Age. In our time, aurora borealis (northern lights) are seldom seen south of the Highlands of Scotland, coloured ones still more rarely. In the 1170s, bright red aurorae reached far into France, and it was easy to see them as the blood of Thomas à Becket streaming in the firmament. During a display at Christmas 1172, a single, deafening clap of thunder was heard over France, England and Ireland; in February 1173, during another, there was something like a high-altitude nuclear explosion over Derry, seen as far south as Canterbury. (More on both in Chap.20.)

There was extraordinarily fine weather over winter and spring, breaking with a violent electrical storm in May.[2] In summer 1173, in Scotland an extraordinary star was seen, motionless in the west by both day and night; at night, many other stars could be seen about it. In September, also in Scotland, there was a two-hour solar obscuration, at noon and with no clouds or eclipse.[3] In England, reported for 1172 but a year out, by other events listed, "two moons were seen in the sky that year."[4] Whatever the star, solar obscuration and moons may be, in Chaps.20 and 22 I'll suggest that the auroral events at this key point are far from coincidental.

In Suffolk, Henry II's control of Woolpit was a continuing issue for Samson and his associates. In 1173 it blew up, sparked by a bigger one: Henry's refusal to abdicate in favour of his eldest son, prince Henry. Though crowned heir to the throne in 1170, he was no nearer power three years later. Backed by his mother, Eleanor of Aquitaine, and his brothers Geoffrey and Richard, while king Henry was in Ireland he'd formed alliances with Louis, king of France, William the Lion, king of Scots, and English nobles including the earl of Leicester, 'chief incendiary' of the trouble in France, now gathering support in Flanders.[5] That was serious, because the Flemish were well established in Scotland,[6] and had strong settlements in Wales and Ireland.

But Henry returned unexpectedly to inspect and prepare his castles in France and Normandy. The speed of his reaction amazed Louis, who said "The king of England neither rides nor sails. He flies with the rapidity of a bird. One moment transports him from Ireland to England: another from England to France."[7] This was when couriers were called *volants*, fliers, but it took three months for a letter from the pope to reach the bishop of Paris.[8] In October and November 1172 Henry was in Normandy, and spent Christmas at Chinon. In March 1173 Geoffrey and Richard went to Paris; queen Eleanor tried to follow, dressed as a man, but was arrested and imprisoned. In April Louis attacked Henry's territory, and the war was on.

The see of Ely had been vacant since Nigel de Calna's death in 1169, its income going to the king, through Richard Fitz-Neal as archdeacon. But such an important bishopric now had to be filled. Geoffrey Ridell was in charge of Ely property,[9] and in the reorganisation to meet the crisis, he became Bishop of Ely on May 1st.[6] And, despite Samson's letter from Rome in 1161, *Henry didn't give Woolpit back*.

The bishops of Norfolk had been trying to assert authority over Bury for over a century, when Herbert de Losinga was ordered by the Pope to move his see from Thetford, in penance for buying the bishopric from William Rufus. He tried to move to the new Abbey at Bury, but was frustrated by the Abbot, who went to Rome to have it declared independent. William I ruled in 1081 that the Abbey wasn't under the bishop,[10] but in 1107 de Losinga left for Rome to buy control of the Abbey and its property; taken prisoner in France, he had to use the money for his ransom.[11] Samson probably thought that very funny, in view of his own misadventures in France. But in 1173, the sudden vacancy at Woolpit was the pretext for another bid for authority by William Turberville of Norwich[12] - not what Samson had in mind at all, and if he knew why Woolpit was important, maybe he alerted the Pope to the new situation.

Alexander III's position had changed greatly since 1161. He won the papacy outright in 1165, he was at odds with Henry on the Constitutions of Clarendon and now had him dead to rights on the murder of Becket. This time he made Woolpit subject of an entire papal Bull; and as we say in Scotland, he didn't miss and hit the wall.

"Bull of Pope Alexander, that it may be allowed to the abbot and convention to present suitable clerics for the church of Woolpit, who will take entire possession of the same church... 11th June.

"Alexander the servant of the servants of God, greeting and blessing to Abbot Hugh of St. Edmund... the church of Woolpit is for the use of your monastery... none from all mankind shall be allowed to break this page of our decree, or to go against it in any way. However if anyone dares to attempt this, let him be aware that he incurs the wrath of almighty God and of his blessed apostles Peter and Paul..."

In the let's-annoy-the-king competition, this supposedly was the tie-breaker which won Samson another holiday at the far end of the Mediterranean. From how he talked about Acre later, editors Butler and Arnold[12] thought Samson had been there again - probably in 1173-74. If so he'd have missed both the children's arrival, and the extraordinary coincidences which followed. But if he was in the Woolpit secret - whatever it was - if he was an agent of the king or of Richard de Hastings, then Acre could be a cover-up for Samson's disappearance from Bury St. Edmunds at a crucial time.

Henry II hadn't yet replaced Ridell in charge of Woolpit because he had bigger things on his mind. But Richard Barre was on Geoffrey Ridell's staff: he had been a royal justice briefly in 1172, but appeared in only one case, in Oxford,[13] before being assigned as seal-bearer to prince Henry - almost certainly as a 'mole', because he remained the king's man. When the prince rebelled in March 1173, Barre brought the seal back to the king, and to his embarrassment the prince had to have another cut in Paris.[14]

Richard de Calna's former neighbour William Blundus, who left Suffolk in 1172, was prince Henry's usher. His family was closely linked to Geoffrey Ridell.[15] Blundus and other clerks left young Henry's service "bringing with them carts and pack-horses with the property of the king, which they had withdrawn, as luggage." Henry sent some back to his son, including Blundus, with bag and baggage including silver cups and other gifts which he added to the load.[14]   The prince demanded that they swear allegiance to himself; Blundus refused to do it and was finally dismissed.

Barre remained with the king, so maybe he became acting custodian of Woolpit that May - especially if the auroral events led de Calna to expect something was going to happen.   It seems Barre was assigned to some confidential task, because although he was so prominent in 1167-73, he almost disappears for the next fourteen years.   The events surrounding Woolpit, below, do look to have Barre's distinctive style.

From April to July Henry was at Rouen, but after July 15 he made a surprise visit to England.   He didn't go to London, Winchester or any seats of power; nor to any of the war zones, or potential rebel areas.[5]   But he was financed for at least four days by the sheriff of Northamptonshire, fifty miles from Woolpit; he could be there, or at Wykes, in a few hours' hard riding from the boundary. He wouldn't apply to the Norfolk or Suffolk sheriffs for funds, especially if the visit was secret, because the earl of Norfolk and Suffolk was backing the rebels - see below.

If I'm right, the reason for this mystery journey was the finding of the green children.   When I was at Woolpit in late September the crops had been lifted and ploughing was under way; but the children arrived when harvest was in progress.   If it was in late July, hay-cutting would be ending, because Lammas (August 1st) marked the start of the corn-harvest;[16] but it explains why fresh beans weren't immediately available.   I once worked at a cold store in Lincolnshire: the fresh vegetable harvest began in July, but our throughput changed from peas to beans in August.

Thirteen years after Woolpit's seizure, the children arrived just when Geoffrey Ridell had moved on and the church was vacant.   Had Henry II been in the area just before they did, it would be remarkable coincidence; but just *after* they arrived (see below), I can't accept it as coincidence at all.   The children were 'taken to *the home*' of Richard de Calna, rather than himself; he could have been in the war, could even have been in Scotland at the end of July (see below), but he would make backup arrangements, if he was expecting something to happen at Woolpit.

120

Once he'd taken steps in response to the green children's arrival, Henry had to get back to the war at once. In September 1173 he was at Le Mans, then Gisors;[5] but in East Anglia, a fresh emergency was about to break.

Robert, earl of Leicester, was one of Henry's biggest problems. Robert 'Beaumont', *le bossu*, was made Grand Justiciary in 1155 (Chap.6), but by 1167 he was dying.   As his son Robert expected to take over, but the post wasn't normally for a layman. He became joint Seneschal, High Steward, but that wasn't enough for him, and by 1173 he had broken up a peace conference between Henry and his sons by 'laying his hand on his sword', threatening the king himself.

William the Lion invaded Northumberland in May. Hugh du Puiset, bishop of Durham, gave the Scots army free passage through the north of England[17] - treason, since William the Conqueror gave the Prince Bishops of Durham 'Palatine' (from the palace) hereditary powers of self-government, to keep the Scots at bay. Maybe Hugh took belated revenge for the death of his co-ruler, the late earl of Chester. Richard de Lucy, now Chief Justiciary of England, was besieging Leicester city with Reginald earl of Cornwall; after victory at the end of July they marched north to oppose the Scots, joining Humphrey de Bohun, Lord High Constable of England, en route.

Louis and William had made their moves: now it was Leicester's turn.   On October 3rd he crossed from Flanders with more than 3000 troops, supplemented by France, landing at Walton-on-the-Naze, at the mouth of the Orwell in the extreme south of Suffolk[5] - territory of Hugh Bigot, lord of Norfolk and Suffolk, on the rebel side.

Leicester marched north to Hagenet Castle, taking the garrison by surprise. He took and burned it in only four days, seizing 300 soldiers for ransom, then marched east to Bigot's Framlingham Castle. However, Blomefield's history of Norfolk has Leicester landing on 21st September. At Framlingham he was reinforced by a second Flemish contingent, then marched to Ipswich, where Bigot's troops joined him.   He took Hagenet Castle in early October, then *returned* to Framlingham.[18]   For his hopes and his followers' lives the Hagenet detour was fatal. Why did it seem so important?

Hagenet was a motte-and-bailey castle, big enough to supply the principal guard at Dover.[19] Its *motte* was a conical mound 120 feet across with a flat top, 80 feet high, surrounded by a ditch three to six feet wide; it had two *bailey* courtyards side by side, one moated and the other protected by a bank.[20] On the mound summit there was a wooden tower or house, and other wooden buildings, surrounded by a fence or palisade and reached by a sloping bridge across the ditch.[21] In 1173 Hagenet was held for the king by his Usher and Chief Marshal Ranulf de Broc,[22] indirectly involved in the Becket's murder (Chap.6). We aren't told whether he or his wife were among the prisoners taken at Hagenet, but it wasn't their main home (that was Saltwood in Kent) and it wasn't expected to become a war zone. Damietta or Dametta de Gorram, from Shropshire, had married Ranulf by 1166, after Henry II's annexation of Woolpit and Hagenet. She gave Ranulf five daughters, but he was dead by 1185; some sources say 1187,[22] but Damietta had remarried and her second husband was in charge of de Broc land by then.[23] He was Adam de Hereford, (Chap.7) - lord of Aghaboe and the Mote of Skirk. The link between Woolpit and Aghaboe highlights the troops captured at Hagenet.

Feudal military service was normally for 40 days, so 300 is a large force to be doing nothing in the middle of Suffolk; but to take them all for ransom is extraordinary. Leicester had only 80 knights and horsemen, with 4-5000 infantry plus archers and light horse,[5] and what became of *them* we'll see in a moment. It seems Henry had put crack troops into Hagenet, by Woolpit - *after* the children arrived, since they were taken eight miles to de Calna rather than four miles to the castle. Diceto, copied by later chroniclers, calls them a *mora*,[24] originally a division of 300 in the Spartan army - not a feudal rabble but an organised unit which Leicester captured intact, surprised and outnumbered by fourteen to one - perhaps they surrendered because there wasn't time to build up the castle's stores. They might have been mercenaries: Henry hired 10,000 on the continent, and 300 could be sent to England without being missed. But the comparison with the Spartans makes it more likely that they were Templars. As Dean of St. Paul's, Diceto knew the de Calna connection with the Mora prebend (Chap.4). If the troops were Templars under Richard de Calna, or even Tostes de St. Omer and Richard de Hastings, it would put the whole scenario on a new footing.

I was expecting something like it, even before I had a possible date for the children's arrival. The whole episode was too casually described: in an age of superstition, anyone in power would think that a gateway had opened from Hell, or Fairyland at least. They would put in troops, in case anyone or anything came after the children.

Strangely, the Itinerary of Henry II has no entries in October 1173. In September, he was in Le Mans, then Gisors; in November, Anjou.[5] In October he signed no charters, incurred no bills, and did nothing to interest the chroniclers. It would be too much to suggest that he was back at Hagenet, disguised as a Templar (as his son, Richard I, was later), and like king Arthur in *A Connecticut Yankee*, he was captured and couldn't reveal himself. He would need a very good disguise to fool Leicester, his sworn enemy, when assessing the prisoners' value for ransom.

Leicester's welcome back at Framlingham wasn't what he expected. The countess of Norfolk disliked having Leicester's force and prisoners camped on her household;[17] she "did not well agree with the countess of Leicester",[5] who dressed as a man and bore arms. Asked to leave, Leicester's only option was to strike across country to his city, now in the king's hands. Blomefield says Leicester's wife now had a second Flemish army; they joined up and decided to relieve their allies in Leicestershire.[18] What became of his captives isn't recorded, but as professionals, already paroled, he probably had them swear not to pursue him.

If he had known what was coming, he might have asked them for protection. "Secret intelligence" of the invasion had already reached de Lucy, the earl of Cornwall and de Bohun, all the way up in Lothian - we might wonder how, because William the Lion didn't know it. But if Henry put crack troops in Woolpit, he would also arranged for word to reach his senior officers if anything happened. They didn't even need to get a messenger out: the Hagenet motte could be seen from the tower of Ely Cathedral, 30 miles away.[25] Even if they didn't exchange signals, the burning castle would alert Geoffrey Ridell, and we may guess that he rapidly sent a messenger north. Even so, he reached de Lucy and de Bohun very fast indeed. They gave William the Lion a truce until the feast of St. Hilary (14th January), and marched south. Such delay for religious festivals was common; that's how they ended the conflict at Leicester. But William would never have agreed if he knew about the Flemish invasion.

123

By October 17th, fourteen to 28 days after the landing, they'd marched south more than 400 miles - when the first 120, down to Durham, had been savagely plundered by the Scots. A remarkable achievement, to say the least. In East Anglia, they met the earls of Arundel and Gloucester, at the head of armies from Ireland and Cornwall.[18] Instead of bottling up Leicester's force at Framlingham, they secured Bury St. Edmunds, which didn't even have a castle - officially, on Henry's orders because of his reverence for the saint[6] - from whose Abbey he'd annexed Woolpit, which he was now disobeying a direct order from the Pope to give back. But any uncaptured elements of his force in Woolpit were probably very glad to see the cavalry arrive.

The Wild West analogy doesn't end there. Marching west, Leicester got word of what lay ahead of him and tried at the last moment to slip past Bury to the north (Fig. 9.1). His force was trapped between the marshes at Fornham St. Genevieve and cut to pieces; had Leicester not been taken alive, his last words might have been the counterpart of Custer's apocryphal "Where the **** did all those Indians come from?"

His Flemish followers were much less fortunate. As Jordan Fantosme tells it:

"If God had been their help the Flemings would have been very brave;
But they had not deserved it for their great robberies.
The earl of Leicester in an evil hour saw their company,
Nor will lord Hugh de Chastel rejoice in it:
They are in the midst of the crowd, feebly, helplessly.
My lady the countess has taken the road,
And has met with a ditch where she almost drowned herself.
In the midst of the mud she forgets her rings;
Never in all her life will they be found.
The earl's wife wished to drown herself
When Simon de Wahull caught her to pull her up.
'Lady come hence with me, let that alone.
'Thus it goes with war: losing and gaining.'
Then earl Robert began to be greatly dismayed:
When he saw his wife captured, he had good reason to be sad,
And saw his comrades slain by hundreds and thousands...
There was not in the country a villein or clown
Who did not go to kill Flemings with fork and flail.

124

The armed knights intermeddled with nothing
Except the knocking down, by hundreds and by thousands
They made them by main force tumble into the ditches."[26]

The casual reaction of the nobles, who can expect to live, is in total contrast to the slaughter of the foot soldiers. If you weren't impressed by the value of the Hagenet garrison, listen to Matthew Paris on what happened to Leicester's expendable army:

"... And so at the beginning of the contest, driven together by blows and the constant pressure of blows, after various chances of war the earl and countess, the Flemish, Normans and Franks, who also had come with them, all were taken on the 17th of October. Truly the countess having on her finger a ring of great value, she threw it into the river nearby, not wishing his armies to have such proof of her capture. At length the greater part of the Flemish were massacred, a certain proportion of them drowned, the smaller part dragged to be put in fetters, which were allotted by the guardians of the prison."[27]

How many fetters do you suppose they had in Bury, which didn't have a castle with dungeons? Furthermore, Roger de Hoveden says those prisoners were not ransomed and starved to death.[28] "And deservedly so," says Gervase of Canterbury. "For the Flemish wolves, long envying the plenty of England, and in particular by nature avoiding the art of weaving, boasted that they would seize England for themselves. But, massacred before any warfare, they rotted in the land they thought to overwhelm. Indeed others, whom count Hugo Bigot had received into his castles, were given permission to leave and returned to Flanders with nothing more than their lives."[29]

The countess's ring, gold with a ruby stone, was found "in the bed of the river in the adjoining parish of Fornham St. Martin",[30] on the land of a Mrs. Orde, and taken to a schoolmaster whose son, Charles Blomfield, had it altered to fit himself;[31] he wore it as a signet ring when bishop of London, 1828-1856.

GREAT BRITAIN
THE 1173 RESPONSE TO LEICESTER'S INVASION

Main English Army

Irish Army

Cornish Troops

Bury St. Edmunds

Framlingham

(ALL THREE MET LEICESTER'S ARMY NORTH OF BURY ST. EDMUND'S)

Fig. 9.1. Map of the 1173 campaigns.
Drawing by Dave Allen.

Richard of Torigni says of the defeat, "perhaps it was because they had carried out pillage in the land of St. Edmund, king and martyr, which could not be allowed unpunished to anyone."[32]   If you believe that, there's a bridge I'd like to sell you.

"…human bones, fragments of weapons, and other relics of war, beside pennies of King Henry II, have been occasionally found upon the spot.   In particular, in felling, in 1826, an ancient pollard ash that stood upon a low mound of earth, about fifteen feet in diameter, near the church of Fornham St. Genevieve,   (the ground being within the Duke of Norfolk's park, but apparently part of the churchyard at some former time) a heap of skeletons, not less than forty, was discovered, in good preservation, piled in order, tier above tier, with their faces upward, and their feet pointing to the centre. Several of the skulls exhibited extreme marks of violence, as if they had been pierced with arrows, or cleft with the sword."[30]   Most of the Flemings were buried at Seven Hills, on the Bury-Thetford road, six miles north of Bury[33] - only five-and-a-half miles from Wykes, which must have been close enough to be worrying.   The tumuli are on the Ordnance Survey Map to this day.   But was Hugh Barre still Leicester's chaplain; was he at Fornham St. Genevieve, and is he too lying at Seven Hills?   With Richard Barre in Prince Henry's entourage, were they both 'moles' - how *did* word of the invasion get to de Lucy so fast?

Another version of the Flemish 'explanation' is that the green children were refugees, from some important family, and their story is a fantasy which happens to look science-fictional to us.   But there's no hint that the earl and countess, or other nobles, lost children in the battle; and it was long after harvest-time.

Although the Irish trade in English slaves through Bristol had been stamped out in 1095, it continued elsewhere.[32]   It was so fashionable to have English slaves that children were being sold across the Irish Sea 'even though their parents were not in need'.   In 1169 the Synod of Armagh concluded, somewhat ironically, that the English Invasion was a divine punishment for encouraging the wicked English to sell their children, and ordered all English slaves released.[33]

There were Irish troops at Fornham under Robert Fitz-Bernard,[34] whose young relative later married Richard de Calna's granddaughter (Chap. 13). There were Maskerells and de Hastings in the invasion of Ireland; Waterford was assigned to Robert Fitz-Bernard in 1172, and his troops would have embarked from Crook, which had been given to the Templars. They also had large holdings at Bristol,[37] from where their own ships traded with La Rochelle (Chap.3). The de Calnas wouldn't sell their children, but a boy and girl could have been abducted and brought back from Ireland, in view of the later links between the Fitz-Bernards and the de Calnas. But why not claim a reward from a de Calna representative in Bristol, or from Everard de Calna in Wiltshire, rather than take the children across the country to Suffolk?

The refugee idea might fit 1190, when there were massacres of Jews in London, Bury and Lynn (Chap.14). But nobody would think finding Jewish children in the fields was extraordinary, then. I still think Henry II's cross-Channel dash in 1173 marks the children's arrival; and if it doesn't, the recently arrived, ransom-worthy troops at Hagenet Castle in October need some explaining.

The same year, the garrison at Peveril Castle was beefed up to twenty knights and their servants, whom Henry paid the very high rate of £20 for twenty days, a shilling per man per day. It supports the idea that he sent mercenaries - the very best of them - to both sites. In 1175-76 he strengthened the castle with a chamber and a large keep, as well as a north-east gateway, as if expecting *something* to happen there.[38]

Officially, the castle was to protect the mines in the area, for the value of their lead and the silver extracted from it. The explanation for the new building is that Henry was expecting trouble from Robert de Ferrars, now earl of Derby and Nottingham,[39] and there was: the earl supported the rebels against Henry, sacking Nottingham, but was pardoned when the war was over.[5] He'd fought beside the younger William Peverell at Northallerton,[40] and married William's daughter Margaret[41] - so putting the family back in charge of the Castle some time later, and connecting the Peverells to modern descendants of the green girl (Chap.17).

Henry was informed rapidly about the children's arrival, but it seems Eleanor of Aquitaine missed it, luckily for all concerned. If Leicester had known that was why there were special troops at Hagenet, the children and anyone else in the Woolpit area could have become pawns in the conflict. What *did* happen probably convinced Henry that the children had been sent by God - but for them, he might no longer be on the throne. If he hadn't already done so, he would arrange for their upbringing (Chap.10).

Maybe it persuaded Henry to humble himself at the new shrine of Thomas à Becket. In July 1174 Henry had himself scourged by the monks of Canterbury and the "several bishops and abbots there present", sufficiently to give him a fever for which he had to be bled. This bothered his biographer Lyttelton, unable to decide whether the miracles attributed to Becket had convinced Henry, or whether the exercise was "an impious hypocrisy and mockery of God, which no policy could excuse."[7]

Henry had recently survived a risky crossing of the English Channel,[41] but vagaries of weather were unlikely to move him. At any rate, the penance paid off: he had barely recovered when a messenger arrived in the dead of night. His attendants refused to admit him, but the argument woke Henry and he demanded to know why.

"My lord," said he, "I bring greetings from your kinsman, lord Ranulph de Glanville."

It's on record that Henry, who was probably sizing up the messenger for the Iron Maiden, replied politely, "He is well, I trust?"

"Very well," was the reply, "and he has captured the king of Scots for you. He holds him in Yorkshire, awaiting your pleasure."

Ranulph was Sheriff of Yorkshire, son of the Second Crusade leader, and a future Chief Justice of England. He'd surprised William the Lion in fog, with only six knights about him. Henry made the messenger repeat it; after which, it was party time. He could pick off the other rebels at leisure, and they sued for peace; the revolt went down like a stack of dominoes.[7] Hugh du Puiset's Flemish allies landed in the north of England just after William's capture, and were hastily sent back, after which Puiset had to surrender Durham and two other castles to the king.[16]

In July 1174 Henry marched on Framlingham; the earl of Norfolk surrendered and was pardoned. But while Henry was receiving the surrender, he was kicked severely on the thigh by Tostes de St. Omer's horse; in 1177 the wound broke out again, suggesting the bone had been damaged.[5] But for that accident, we wouldn't know that a senior Templar was helping the king to secure East Anglia, even though the Templars had virtually no interests there. It suggests again that the 'mora' at Hagenet Castle might have been Templars. The St. Omers were in the area afterwards: they held Grimeshoe Hundred in Norfolk (including Grimes Graves) under Edward I.[18]

If Henry was in doubt over the children, the collapse of the rebellion must surely have removed it. But to keep control of Woolpit, there was the Pope's Bull to deal with, though the Bishop of Norfolk was no longer a problem (Chap. 10). The answer was an early example of the 'typically British compromise'.

The Allocation of the Said Church Confirmed by the King

"Henry, by the grace of God king of England and Duke of Normandy and Aquitaine, and count of Angevin, greets the archbishops, bishops, abbots, counts, barons, justices, viscounts, and all of his ministers and the faithful of England. Know ye that on my prayer and petition abbot Hugo of St. Edmund and his convent have conceded and given the church of St. Mary Woolpit in permanent alms to my clerk magister Walter de Coutances, with all that belongs to it, and I have conceded, and I have confirmed by my charter here present, that the said church, after the death or resignation of my clerk aforesaid, shall return forever to the use of sick monks of St. Edmund, just as was confirmed by the bill of the lord pope. Witnessed by R(ichard Toclive), bishop of Winchester."[12]

Richard Toclive wasn't just a bystander. Before bishop of Winchester, he was archdeacon of Poitiers. Committed to Henry II, he was sent by Richard de Lucy and the other supporters in England to convince him to come in person, to secure the kingdom against the insurgents. As Henry was crossing the Channel a severe storm arose, which he and his followers were lucky to survive:[42] Henry then went to Canterbury, and the rest you know. It might be that his 'miraculous' delivery at sea changed Henry's heart - but this is the king who was supposed to fly, rather than ride or sail, between Ireland, England and France. He crossed the Channel 28 times, and I doubt if he could be shaken by a natural storm, however severe - which makes it odder, though interesting later, that according to Serbanesco Henry was afraid of lightning.[43]

Walter de Coutances, supposedly a poor clerk who needed the money, was from the same mould as Ridell: his forbears were barons in Somerset,[44] and Giraldus Cambrensis gave him a fake pedigree, from a 'Trojan prince who settled in Cornwall'.[34]   He began in Henry's chancery, became archdeacon of Oxford,[45] and in 1173, once Ridell rose to bishop of Ely, Walter became Vice-Chancellor of England because the new Chancellor, Ralph de Warneville (Chap.13)   couldn't afford to entertain foreign dignitaries as the post required.[46]   de Coutances was 'archisigillarius', keeper of the Great Seal,[43] and in 1175 treasurer of Rouen Cathedral.[47]   He didn't need ten pounds a year from Woolpit to keep body and soul together, any more than Ridell had.

Henry took Leicester and William the Lion to France in August 1174, and Walter de Coutances witnessed the peace with Scotland at Falaise in December.[5]   In 1175, he oversaw moving the king's treasure across the Channel, and he filled ever higher posts into the 13th century.   He and Ridell were chaplains to Henry, later; he, Richard Toclive and John of Oxford witnessed Henry's charters, confirming the independence of Bury St. Edmunds in 1182[46] - the year he gave Woolpit back (Chap.13).   So, once again, why was a man of this calibre in charge of a tiny village in East Anglia?

It could only be because Woolpit was part of something much bigger: the arrival of the green children begins to look like an accident.   But they were here now, and too valuable to ignore.   Arrangements had to be made for them.

Chapter Ten - 1174: 'THE LAND OF ST. MARTIN'

"If someone invents a story like this, they tend to do it out of whole cloth. There might be a few real names, but it won't stand up to this kind of detailed investigation."

~ John Braithwaite

If Richard de Calna was a doctor (Chap. 4), he successfully nursed the green girl back to health and (to him) a normal colour. But the children weren't safe yet.

"... they believed all the food of that place to be 'undigestible', as the girl later *stated in evidence*... Truly the boy, always seeming brought down by exhaustion/ depression, died after a short time. Truly the girl enjoying a full recovery, and become accustomed to all kinds of food, put off that completely leek-green colour, and gradually regained a sanguine condition of the whole body. Being later reborn by immersion of holy baptism, and remaining for many years on the staff of the aforesaid knight (as we frequently heard from the same knight and his family) she showed herself greatly wanton and lascivious/wilful and independent. Truly asked often about the people of her country, she *swore on oath* that as many as all the inhabitants and all plants that were held in that land/world were dyed with the colour green..." (RC, my emphases)

"It appeared to the wise, that they might receive the sacrament of holy baptism, and *even that* [my emphasis] was done. But the boy, who seemed to be younger by birth, living a short time after baptism died young, his sister remaining sound... asked who and from whence they were, they are said to have replied: 'People of the land of Saint Martin, who of course in the land of our birth is held in the very highest exceptional respect'. Asked whether Christ was believed in, in that place... they said that land was Christian, and had churches ..." (WN)

While they were spared the Inquisition of a century later, what was at stake (literally) was whether they had souls. We glimpse the seriousness of it in Ralph's *asserebat*, 'swore under oath'. *Asserere* is the origin of our verb 'to assert', but its Latin meaning was like the English 'to attest': to give evidence, but also to claim someone as a slave or proclaim their liberation - as if liberating someone from a false impression. Ralph's other verb, *confessa est*, means 'formally stated'. Like the *Inquisitio* of a suspected heretic, if there was any doubt about the legitimacy of a christening it required at least the authority of a bishop,[1] and would still, even today. In the 12th century, there was no doubt about the outcome if the bishop decided against them.

"We are people of the land of St. Martin." "And do they believe in our Saviour there, my dear?" "Oh yes. You can't see the place for churches, we've got so many." Either she'd learned more English or French than they knew, or she'd been coached in those answers; neither way was she an outcast from some primitive tribe, intelligence stunted by malnutrition. To be an envoy to Rome, Richard Barre had to be expert in church law and would be the ideal tutor - and if he was in charge of Woolpit for Geoffrey Ridell, he would be free when de Coutances was appointed. He might have volunteered or been assigned to help lord Richard, now in his 50s, with the strange children he had to care for – indeed, it's more likely that the king would entrust the case to de Calna, if his sponsorship of the young Richard Barre brought about his early success. Barre also knew civil law: in 1172 he was a justice in the court of Richard de Lucy,[2] and if Barre was her coach, the de Lucy link would be significant - see below.

To defend herself at this level, she must have been highly intelligent, highly motivated and a real survivor. If she was an undernourished troglodyte, put in front of a bishop and asked to prove she had a soul, the girl would have curled up in a corner and whimpered. Fortunately she was old enough to be adaptable. The boy couldn't do it, too old to adapt instinctively and too young to do it by willpower; like a modern 8-year-old, hauled away from his computer games and set down in a rice-field in communist China. Even a 10 to 12-year-old couldn't do it without help, and I picture Richard Barre at the back of the hall wiping his brow as she gave the right answers. De Calna would be there, as the children's guardian: Ralph's terminology implies that de Calna described the hearing to him, or the Coggeshall records included it.

My friend Bill Ramsay remarked that the children are asked if Christ is believed in where they come from, *after* they've said the place is named after a saint, and that shows the questions were following a pre-set order. And it's odd not to know the sound of bells, if they really came from a land filled with

133

churches.   However, 'people of the land of St. Martin' wasn't the answer to *where* they were from – see below.

1. Who conducted the hearing?

Samson de Botington had the knowledge (he was later accused of being a "Norfolk lawyer"), but not the authority, especially before he was Abbot.   If he had done it, Jocelin de Brakelond would have written it up, but Samson would give the children a much harder time.   Abbot Hugo might have been imprisoned them till a Bishop's visit;   hence perhaps the "great sound when *they say* the bells are ringing" [my ital.ics].   It might have been the bishop of Norwich, in theory, but William de Turberville was dead by 1173, and the see was vacant: John of Oxford became bishop in November 1175.   The Abbot wouldn't ask Turberville anyway, when he was using Woolpit to try to assert control over Bury.

If the children *had* arrived in Stephen's reign, it would have been easy for Nigel de Calna to take the hearing, since he was bishop of Ely throughout. Geoffrey Ridell was appointed in 1173, but not yet consecrated due to an argument about it: as archdeacon Richard Fitz-Neal wanted to present him for the ceremony, but was over-ruled in favour of the Prior.   Ridell wasn't consecrated till October 6th, 1174.   Unlike Nigel's (Chap.4), Ridell's coat of arms at Ely was uninformative - a dark square at upper left on a field of dots[3] - unless it represents a land in shadow among the stars!   But his appointment wasn't final for more than a year after the children arrived, so he wasn't authorised to hold an *Inquisitio*.

Abbot Odo of Coggeshall didn't have the authority, but his superior was Gilbert Foliot, Bishop of London from 1163 to 1187.   The emphasis on St. Martin is a clue - not because he was the patron saint of drinkers and reformed drunkards!   Bishop of Tours in the late fourth century,[4] there's little or nothing to connect him to our story.[5]   In the window overlooking his altar in Bury St. Edmunds Abbey, he was felling a pine tree sacred to a pagan god, causing it to fall on peasants who protested;   before Dissolution of the Monasteries, the Abbey library had a book, *The Miracle of the Translation of St. Martin*,[6] about moving his body into a special church built for it.   But that was the usual healing of bodies and souls in the area,[7] the sort of miracles about which William of Newburgh was sceptical (Chap.1).

Nevertheless, in County Londonderry there was a Cave of St. Martin, in country where he was highly regarded. A woman named Cantighern used to distribute milk and meat to the poor there and also, at the same time, in Tours, so the Irish alms would be blessed by the saint. 19th century editors found three historical candidates for the lady, in 622, 728 and 1054, but as she appears in the Irish version of the Chronicle of Nennius,[8] she could be 12th century. So it might have some bearing on the overhead explosion at Derry in 1173 (Chap. 20).

There was a village, Fornham St. Martin, north of Bury St. Edmunds; there was a chapel of St. Martin in St. Edmunds Abbey, from the time of abbot Anselm (1119-1148),[6] but it was much smaller than St. Edmund's shrine and most of the other saints' chapels.[9] Samson built a window in the lavatorium, depicting the Sun, Moon, stars and the twelve months of the year, both astrologically and in relation to rural tasks, and its light was "pale yellow like the Sun's, but like the Sun's of late evening" - just before twilight, which was permanent where the children came from; and the Abbey's water-clock helped to extinguish a fire in 1198.[10]

None of these is the link to St. Martin that we're looking for. But the Templars' Cressing Temple preceptory, near Coggeshall Abbey (near enough to have used Coggeshall bricks), was established in 1137 by a grant from king Stephen and his queen Matilda or Maud. First or at most second Templar site outside London, listed first in an Inquest of their assets in 1185,[11] it has moats like the Lady's Well's, though narrower and more extensive in the past.[12] Two barns from the Templar period barns survive and it continues as a farm, now under Essex County Council. In a confirming charter to the Templars in 1147, however, Stephen excluded the local church and its lands, "which I have given to the church of St. Martin in London and its canons".

St. Martin's-le-Grand was probably the oldest abbey in Britain, refounded in 1056 by Ingelric, Earl of Essex (Chap. 3 & 5). Its secular canons were second only to those of the original St. Paul's (before the Great Fire of London), the Bishop's own church between St. Martin's and the river, and the two were closely linked. When Ingelric became Dean in 1068,[13] several Essex properties were returned to the Abbey, and in the Domesday Book they're listed under the heading, in block capitals, TERRA SANCTI MARTINI - the Land of St. Martin.[14]

Surely William of Newburgh stressed it to reveal the Bishop of London's involvement. In his see, St. Martin definitely was "held in the very highest exceptional respect": no fewer than five parish churches in London were dedicated to him,[15] including one belonging to Ranulph Peverell. And St. Martin's was the principal sanctuary in England. At others sanctuary could be claimed for 30 to 40 days, but at St. Martin's it was permanent - a powerful reason to have the children christened under its name. "Who are you?" "People of the Land of St. Martin, who have been given sanctuary." With that, the formalities were just for the record.

They suggest that someone needed to be convinced - from Bury St. Edmunds, perhaps, since the arrival happened on their territory. But there was a general direction that all wondrous events were to be reported to Rome, through the church: "You were charged, sir, to apprise me of all things unnatural," the parson says sternly to de Calna in Glyn Maxwell's *Wolfpit*.[16] There was no priest at Woolpit in 1173, but by the time of the trial word had almost certainly reached Rome. The Black Monks in Sydney Jordan's woodcut-style drawing (Fig. 10.1) could be Benedictine, from Bury St. Edmunds, or they could be from further away and more dangerous. He's dramatized the situation: a night setting, a minimum of witnesses, the girl watching anxiously as the boy replies to the bishop, de Calna with his hand resting casually on his sword. It's theatrical - de Calna wouldn't be allowed to bear arms in church - but he catches the tensions we may imagine at the hearing.

To get ahead in the 12th century needed a strong personality, and Gilbert Foliot was no exception. As a monk of Cluny, in 1136, he pled empress Matilda's cause at the court of Rome. Soon after he became Prior of Cluny, then of Abbéville, and in 1139 Abbot of Gloucester - confirmed by king Stephen in spite of siding with Matilda. He was in the Second Crusade,[17] in 1148 the Pope made him Bishop of Hereford, and in 1155 he prevented a new civil war by dissuading the earl of Hereford from rebellion over yielding Gloucester and Hereford castles to the crown.[18]

The Green Children

Fig. 10.1. Trial scene drawing by Sydney Jordan.

Though Henry II's confessor, he was the only bishop to oppose Becket's election in 1162, even under threat of banishment; he stood for Archbishop of Canterbury himself, in the interests of the church, not personal ambition. Becket still made him bishop of London in 1163 - so making Foliot *ex officio* Dean of Canterbury, and he backed the king through the subsequent quarrel.[19] He evaded swearing obedience to Becket; tried to make the London see independent, despite excommunication; and partly estranged Becket from the Pope, saving Henry from head-on conflict with Rome. Facing Henry's knights, Becket's refusal to reinstate Foliot was what provoked them to strike; he stayed excommunicated until he showed, in 1173, "that he had not knowingly brought about the death of saint Thomas either by word, deed or writing".[20]

Nigel the Doctor was a canon of St. Martin's (Chap.4), and Roger le Poer was Dean of St. Martin's and all its property in 1139, since 1108 or earlier,[21] perhaps since the 1070's.[22] After he died, empress Matilda assigned it in 1141 to king Stephen's brother, Henry de Blois, Dean till 1171. His successor Geoffrey de Lucy was Dean of St. Paul's but not yet a bishop, so if the children were under his protection he would pass the *Inquisitio* to Gilbert Foliot. Geoffrey was educated at Paris or Bologna, a royal civil servant since 1169,[23] so he may have known Richard Barre as a student; surely he knew him as a young man on the fast track to preferment, and probably knew that Richard Barre had been a justice in his father's court. During the civil war, Roger le Poer might have set up a 'safe house' on the Land of St. Martin in Essex, where de Lucy could let Barre coach the children for the hearing.

In 1141, Gilbert Foliot was present with Nigel and Alexander de Calna when empress Matilda was acclaimed at Winchester.[24] In 1146 or soon after, when Roger de Calna was his archdeacon, Bishop Turberville of Norwich let the canons of St. Martin's-le-Grand preach in his churches for aid in rebuilding it.[25] One of the largest of those was at Thetford, next to Knettishall manor.

Now it seems that in 1174, Gilbert Foliot investigated the green children and passed them as human - probably on Henry II's instructions. The hearing couldn't be in Coggeshall Abbey, because women[26] and boys under 16 were barred from Cistercian grounds,[27] so the monks weren't allowed to give baptism. The Gatehouse Chapel wasn't built for visitors till the following century, and it wouldn't have a font until much later, because for 300 years after Dissolution of the Monasteries the chapel was used as a barn. It might have been at Cogges-hall itself, the manor house, which was Abbey property, held by lord Thomas Coggeshall in 1149 and by his son of the same name in 1188 and 1194. They probably knew Richard de Calna and his family, since they were frequent visitors to the area. Thomas's seal was four cockle shells, the badge of a crusader, and he might have known de Calna in the Holy Land.[28]

Jane Greatorex suggests that the most likely place nearby is Bradwell, formerly Bradwell-juxta-Coggeshale,[29] with connections to Wix nunnery, so to the Mascerells and de Hastings (Chap.4), as well as an estate gifted to the Templars. Its manor hall no longer exists, but its Norman church has curious brick archways, facing each other, high enough to let a man on horseback ride straight through (note Cistercian arches and Coggeshall brickwork in Sydney Jordan's drawing). The hearing could have been at the church or the hall (perhaps with the children temporarily in care of nuns from Wix, as my mother suggested), and the boy need be taken only a mile to the Abbey infirmary - suggesting that his condition was the reason to christen them then.

As its Bishop, Foliot could hear the testimony nearby, baptise the children, and order the boy buried at the Abbey. It would need his authority, because usually Cistercian cemeteries were restricted to their own dead;[30] hence Ralph's emphasis on 'the cemetery of the brothers' in Chap.11, where we'll see reason to think the boy *was* buried there. Jane pointed out that even Hildegard von Bingen, one of the most holy abbesses of the time, had her church interdicted (deprived of the Mass, the sacraments, music etc.) because she buried an excommunicated noble revolutionary in its cemetery, and refused to have him exhumed. Burying the boy at Coggeshall could explain why the bishop isn't named by Ralph, and why he refers to "a certain boy and his sister", even though she was the older, and did all the talking in his account.

If St. Martin was interpolated into the story after the boy's death, it could tell us something about the burial. The saint famously divided his cloak with a beggar: maybe the girl gave her brother some clothing "of extraordinary colour and unknown material" in which she arrived, or his own clothes might be at hand, if they were evidence at the hearing. It would be nice to find it, but I don't believe we shall (Chap.11).

James Bentley suggested she wouldn't let him be buried at Coggeshall, because she couldn't visit the grave; that assumes that her people's customs resembled ours, but they might - even Neanderthals buried their dead. But at the age of ten or so she'd have no say, especially if it was high summer, a year after they arrived, and he had to be buried quickly. She might be able to do something about it later - see Chap.12.

Of course, St. Martin's-le-Grand had property elsewhere, e.g. Cripplegate manor outside the walls of London; and there were many St. Martin churches in England, like Paul Harris's 'St. Martin's Hundred', belonging to the priory of St. Martin in Dover.[31] That in turn was Canterbury Cathedral's, and magister William de Calna (Chap.13) was a witness to the inspection and

139

confirmation of its rights in 1195/98.[32]   But it was one of many which he witnessed at that time, and 'St. Martin's Hundred' is less convincing than the
TERRA SANCTI MARTINI capitalised in the Domesday Book.   It has no
Cistercian abbey to justify Gilbert Foliot's presence, and no connection with
Coggeshall or Richard de Hastings (though Hastings itself isn't far).   I think
the children were christened near Coggeshall, probably at Bradwell as Jane
suggests.

I found another 'Land of St. Martin' myself: the enclosed fields outside Paris
of the monastery of St. Martin des Champs, linked to the Templars.   The
Templar complex in Paris was a sanctuary, from 1200 at least, and included *la
Rue des Enfants-Rouges*, Street of the Red Children!   But they were orphans,
Enfants-Dieu - God's children, dressed in red, the colour of charity; the monastery isn't on record till 1279, and the Paris Land of St. Martin is 14th century.[33]   And if from there, the children would speak French and it's inconceiv-
able that nobody would understand them.

Later, I'm going speculate in detail on where the children came from and how
they got here.   The girl adapted to the 12th century, and that's important: as
Spock says more than once in *Star Trek*, it's easy for us to act as primitives or
barbarians, but much harder to pass oneself off as *more* cultured or sophisticated.

The de Calnas were prosperous, and Wykes Manor Hall would be comfortable
for its day.   Standards of hygiene then were higher than we think: cities had
public baths, and manor house records include cloths that lined bathtubs to
protect users from splinters.[34]   White linen was a status symbol, carefully kept
clean: the de Calnas would employ a professional laundress.[35]   But even royalty, in silks, furs and linen, lived among dogs, horses and other animals in
what we'd often call squalor, as *The Lion in Winter* portrays.[36]   The dislocation
of the family in *The 1900 House* would be minor by comparison.   To be
stripped, exhibited, perhaps worse, and starved, then find that 12th century
manor life was as much better as it would get, would hit civilised children
much harder than primitives.   "You would cry too, if it happened to you".

It seems the boy died of it - and as James Bentley pointed out, dietary
treatment for melancholia excludes broad beans (and cheese) which have a
high tyramine content.   (Tyramine in red wine causes severe headaches in

140

susceptible people, over and above the congeners which supply flavour, colouring and hangovers.[37]) There's also *favism*, a genetic flaw whereby broad beans can cause fatal anaemia, with liver and spleen damage, and only male carriers are affected.[38] But the first attack is usually severe enough for victims to avoid eating beans in future - even inhaling pollen from bean plants can trigger an attack, so it's unlikely that the boy would sign for them to be brought to him. But if high-tyramine food was all the boy would eat while suffering culture shock, the odds were against him all the way. Sydney Jordan suggested that the girl survived because she was older and more adventurous: perhaps she developed a taste for a more balanced diet before he did, and that saved her while the boy's stubbornness doomed him.

Despite the culture shock, the girl carved out a niche for herself. Ralph says she was *in ministerio praedicti militis...commorata*, 'remaining in the service of the foresaid knight'. Almost everyone thinks she was a domestic servant: in Glyn Maxwell's play, 'Master' Richard has her scrubbing floors because she shares her favours among the villagers, not with him.[16] But in noble houses all domestic servants were male: "the mediaeval serving wench is a Hollywood invention".[39] The only exceptions were laundresses and brew-wives, out-siders who threatened the order of a well-run household. Among the categ-ories of feudal service, *ministerium* means *administrative* service, the origin of our word 'Ministry' for a government department, the church or a career within it. In mediaeval France, Seneschals and other royal officers with exec-utive power were the 'Ministrie', and in Germany a knight in administrative service of a lord was called *ministerialis*.[40]

'In ministerio' the girl wouldn't be the female equivalent of a villein, bondsman or serf, but a manor housekeeper or estate manager, *praeposita*, as in Chap.5: put in charge of something or somewhere. It should at least be translated 'on the staff of...', as above: however she was of service to de Calne, she was skilled and valuable, making the 'undernourished primitive' theory even less likely. It suggests that the children's experience on de Calna's manor was at least analogous to the life they had left, though not close enough for the boy to make the connections.

That brings us to the language she learned - perhaps with Samson as her 'pre-ceptor'. By the late 12th century English was gaining ground: when Ralph of Coggeshall wrote about the talking poltergeist in the 1190s, the spirit spoke to the family in English and argued with the priest in Latin.[41]   De Calna, born no later than 1116 to be legally adult by 1130, would grow up with Norman French and still use it at home.   Maybe the girl was on his staff because she spoke better English than he did: she'd need it in later life, as we'll see.   The *Inquisitio* would of course be conducted in Latin, and maybe, like the spirit, she spoke that too.   That word *incomestibilia* in her evidence, which I translated by the made-up word 'unedible', is very specific in meaning (Chap.23).   English, perhaps French and possibly Latin - at least one in the first year, despite the trauma and culture shock she'd undergone.   If you say her green colour *must* have been due to iron deficiency, sufficient to cause permanent brain damage, what do you think her IQ would be if it *wasn't* cut back?

And after marrying, and a mysterious further delay, in the 1190s she built a whole new life, which we'll glimpse below and later trace in detail.   The children deserve our sympathy, at this distance in time, but the girl in particular also merits our respect.

But once she was older, no longer green-coloured, and out of immediate danger, it seems she dropped the Christian aspect of the story, and gave her hosts some problems.   "…remaining for many years on the staff of the aforesaid knight (as we frequently heard from the same knight and his family), she showed herself greatly wilful and independent..." (RC)

Ralph's words are *lasciva et petulans*, whose primary meaning is 'lascivious and wanton'.   Jim Campbell suggested that after being stripped, maybe girl was raped, and if promiscuous later, she was psychologically disturbed.   While all too likely, it doesn't fit her long stay with the de Calnas, in that unforgiving time.   It might explain marrying her off at a distance, in William of Newburgh's account - Lynn was 40 miles off, a long way for a commoner, unless on a lord's business.   If true, it makes her special – as if de Calna did his best for her.   It made me opt first for the non-sexual meanings of 'wilful and independent', though both meanings are possible, as we shall see.

If Henry II made her de Calna's ward, she made herself useful *in ministerio*, and the king issued no fresh orders, by the late 1170s Richard had a problem. As his ward, he would have to arrange her marriage at age 14; so she *had* to be christened, if she wasn't already.   If she refused the husband arranged, her guardian could extend his wardship to the age of 23, "as a mark of displeasure

142

at the contradiction and disobedience". But if she married, he'd have to provide a dowry, usually land. Even if he stalled because no-one knew her age,
in time the problem would be obvious. He could escape that obligation only if
she was unchaste,[42] and blackening her reputation would prevent her receiving any de Calna property the king had assigned to her.

For comparison, when de Calna's granddaughter Sibylla was orphaned in
1185 by the death of his son, Walter, she was made a royal ward. Henry II
arranged a marriage for her and gave her North Fambridge in Essex as part of
her dowry (Chap.15).[43] But the manor was part of her brother's holdings,
and the knight from whom he held it later took Sibylla and her husband to
court to make sure they gave none of it away.[44] The green girl might have
been in a similar position, to the family's annoyance.

2. *What* was she christened?

I couldn't resolve such conjectures unless I found find the green girl, and what
became of her. In Sir Herbert Read's *The Green Child* she's called 'Siloën',
anglicised to Sally;[46] in *The Girl Green as Elderflower* Ralph Stow's monks
suggest Barbara and Peregrine, both meaning 'stranger', but eventually
christen them Mirabel and Michael;[47] and Glyn Maxwell's *Wolfpit* calls the
girl 'Adela',[16] an alternative for Alicia or Alice - another literary allusion, apt
for a girl who comes out of a hole in the ground - and not the only link to
Lewis Carroll (Chap.12). James Bentley said I too should invent names to
personalise the children, proposing 'Selena' and 'Edwin' for his own family
reasons. Even before I found the girl's likely identity I'd decided not to, for
the same reason that I haven't told the story as fiction. If I make things up,
how can anybody tell conjecture from historical fact? Made-up names would
have to be in quotation marks throughout, as above, which would defeat the
object.

I thought the answer might be staring us in the face, because for a while the
research was dominated by Sibylla de Calna, who sold Wykes and Knettishall
in 1235. Sibylla, "seeress, prophetess, or woman inspired by the gods" was
fostered, a royal ward. A seeress called Sibylla featured with the Old
Testament prophets in the 'New-Town' plays of mediaeval East Anglia.[48] But

Sibylla really was de Calna's granddaughter, whose life we'll look at in Chaps. 13-17.

But there was a lead to follow, apparently minor: an entry in the 1190s property records that Sibylla's husband, John Fitz-Bernard, was farming at Reed in Essex with the daughters, plural, of Walter de Calna - lord Richard's eldest son, through whom the family property descended. He witnessed Norwich Priory charters in 1168[49], 1155[50] and c.1175;[51] he held land in Wiltshire, Essex and Hertfordshire in 1177-78, but by 1185 he was dead. So far, the only daughter was Sibylla, and indeed she seems to be - the Pipe Rolls editor thinks the plural's a mistake.[43]

By 1195 her son, Walter Fitz-Bernard, had land in Reed, "with the daughter [singular] of Walter de Calna".[52] Sibylla was only fifteen in 1195, so it must be very soon after his birth. Like other clues in the story, it's been added to the record later, in a different hand, and it's an odd way to indicate Walter's mother. Perhaps 'Walter' is a mistake and should read 'John'; or perhaps 'daughters' should read 'heiresses'. It was a long shot, but enough to keep me looking for another woman with a claim on de Calna property. And eventually, just two volumes from the end of the nine cases of mediaeval records in Glasgow University Library, I found what I was looking for: an older woman sharing an inheritance with Sibylla de Calna.

The breakthrough was in a collection of Fines paid between 1195 and 1214.[53] Since all property belonged to the king or the church, Fines were paid by heirs claiming their inheritance.[54] In September 1197 "Richard and Agnes his wife, and John and Sibylla his wife" petitioned in Bedford for Prior Walter of Merton to yield up their joint inheritance from Richard de Calna's son, Walter, of land in Eyton, also spelled Eiton or Eston. In final settlement the women paid one silver mark to the prior and were given the land, plus duties to the king which went with it (Chap.14).[43] Nevertheless, in 1202 Richard and Agnes had to bring another case in Nottingham about it.

Richard and Agnes are listed first: Richard was older than John Fitz-Bernard, and if Agnes was the green girl, she'd be older than Sibylla, adult by 1185. Perhaps Agnes was named after Walter de Calna's wife, whose name we don't know; but it was apt to name her after the patron saint of young girls, if she'd escaped burning at the stake, at age 13, like the saint. St. Agnes was martyred in 304 or 305 AD, by the emperor Diocletian, but she was beheaded because the faggots piled around her stake refused to light. Picture the old and young Richards, de Calna and Barre: "By God, it was a close thing! After that, we'll have to call her Agnes." St. Agnes's fate was shared by her 'milk sister', daughter of a servant who wet-nursed both girls as infants,[55] and that was prophetic for Agnes Barre a few years later (Chap.13). If de Calna *was* in the Second Crusade, she could be named after the Hospitallers' Dame Agnes - or Agnes de Courtenay, mother of the king of Jerusalem and lover of Heraclius, the city's patriarch. In 1180 her daughter Sibylla married Guy de Lusignan, who 'took the cross' in 1168 after murdering the Earl of Salisbury. They became queen and king of Jerusalem in 1185, backed by the Templars, but so unlikely that his elder brother remarked, "If Guy is king, I must be God."[56] Sibylla de Calna was christened in 1180 (Chap.14), and she and Agnes were joint heiresses. To anyone who knew the Holy Land, the names would be as significant as a regimental tie: "You were in Jerusalem, then - whose outfit were *you* with?"

(They could be named after Agnes de Valoines, wife of Roger, mother of Peter, to whom Richard de Calna successively owed feudal service; and Sibylla de Valoines,[57] born about the same time as Sibylla de Calna. But if de Calna followed one or more of the de Valoines to the Holy Land, [Chap.4], the Jerusalem connection is the same.)

Agnes isn't identified as Sibylla's sister, in 1197 or in 1202. When Agnes was widowed, she didn't revert to de Calna or any other maiden name (Chap.15). It implies that she wasn't one of the family; if she was the green girl, perhaps she was never formally adopted. Bill Ramsay doubted very much that she would be, and suggested that instead she might be illegitimate; but if so, she couldn't have inherited from Walter de Calna or anyone else. She could be given property, but not inherit it.[42] The 1835 edition Index reads as if Richard was a clerk of Stafford and John a chaplain in Buckinghamshire, but that's misleading. The Pipe Rolls Society identifies them correctly: Agnes's husband was Richard Barri or Barre, archdeacon of Ely and royal justice in the 1190s.[58] There are a number of Estons, etc., and this one is Aston Clinton, in Buckinghamshire,[59] but it's connected with Aston (Estone) in Warwickshire, now part of Handsworth in Birmingham (Chap.14).[60]

Ralph Turner suggests that Richard and Hugh Barre's family who took their name from the Norman village of La Barre.   Everard des Barres became Templar Master in France in 1143, and is often said to have been Grand Master in the Second Crusade; actually that was Robert de Craon.[61]   But it's virtually certain that they really hailed from the Barr north of Aston-juxta-Birmingham in Staffordshire, just over the boundary from the Aston there today (the sheriffs had to relocate the boundary several times in the early 13th century).   Nowadays, the parishes are Great Barr and Perry Barr, which was originally Perry Barr and Parva Barra (Little Barr).   Some say Great and Little Barr were one parish till 1232,[62] but they're separate even in Domesday, held by 'Robert and Drogo'.   Robert likely had Great Barr, because Drogo's land went to the Birmingham family, holders of Little Barr later.[63,64]

Robert du Barry defied the phantoms in Ossory, and Agnes's husband used de Barri as an alternative spelling, but Robert and Gerald du Barry took their name from Barry island, near Cardiff.[65]   Richard Barre's is from the Welsh *bar* meaning 'top or summit', here the 700-foot Barr Beacon hill in Aston.[66] Edricus de la Barre, in Staffordshire in 1169,[64] might be Richard's father; however, he was in Northumberland in 1180-85 and 1200,[66] so he couldn't be the father unless he gave Little Barr to his sons and lived to a very good age. The best candidate for Richard Barre's father remains Hugh Barre or Barred, archdeacon of Leicester, a learned man who donated his personal collection of books to his church.[67]   Richard's mother might be Margaret de la Barre, with Alexander de Barre in 1186-87, in Worcestershire,[68] but probably not: Alexander de Barre was in Yorkshire,[2] Wiltshire[69] and elsewhere from 1170, but never associated with Richard except once by a clerical error (Chap.14).

In 1175 lands in Barr were given to Robert de Barr and his wife Petronilla.[70] They applied for the use of common pasture soon afterwards.[71]   Robert shared or split Little Barre with Richard while remaining the principal tax-payer, but continued in Little Barre until 1208 at least,[71] and was a juror in nearby Handsworth in 1212 when Richard was dead,[72] so probably he was Richard's older brother, as I've shown him in the suggested family tree (Chap.17).   Roger, brother of Robert, is listed in Dudley between 1176 and 1189, so presumably he was youngest of the three.

My bet is that Agnes was the formerly green girl herself, and Agnes's husband is the Richard Barre of Chaps.4 and 6: Henry II's trusted ambassador, expert in church and civil law, on Geoffrey Ridell's staff, in the right position at the right time to have been in charge of Woolpit when the green children arrived; available and with the necessary skill to coach them before the trial; and strangely almost absent from the records for the next fourteen years, as we'll see. It helps to explain why Walter de Calna had property next door to Richard Barre and his brother, before his own death in 1185. Before Agnes and Sibylla claimed them, Aston Clinton and the Staffordshire Aston were held by Walter de Coutances, probably since he was responsible for Woolpit.

3. Secretum Abbatis Samsonis

On the reverse of Abbot Samson's seal with the Templar version of the Agnus Dei (Fig. 6.1), those words could mean 'the Secret of Abbot Samson' - a lamb - Agnes? Such visual puns were common in mediaeval heraldry. On the royal coat of arms the first of the three lions was Henry I's, the second was brought to it by Henry I's queen Adeliza, whose father, Godfrey de Louvain, wore it on his shield as a pun on *leo*. (The third was Eleanor of Aquitaine's, so the three were first used by her sons Richard and John.)[73] Godfrey de Lucy's seal included a pike-fish (*lucius*) as a pun, and Thomas de Cantilupe, 13th century chancellor of England and Oxford, included an enraged wolf (*lupus*).[74] Punning shields or emblems are called 'canting arms' or *armes parlantes*;[75] Agnus/Agnes as Samson's secret is not out of the question.

A Norwich seal of John de Grey, John of Oxford's successor, also has the Agnus Dei with the Templar cross, like Samson's. Having the same Christian name, they may have used the same seal, which identifies the bearer simply as 'John', so another with a similar front may also have been John of Oxford's and may have had the same symbols on the other side. On John de Grey's, the words surrounding that Lamb are from the prayer, *Agnus Dei Qui Tollis Peccata M[undi]*, 'Lamb of God who taketh away the sins of the world', but as he had no connection with the Templars, it continues to suggest that Samson had unpublicised links with the Order.

Among 3265 ecclesiastical and monastic seals catalogued in the British Museum (now British Library), there are only sixteen other examples of the Agnus Dei, none with the cross *pattée* or presented in the same way as Samson's and John de Gray's (identical, except for the surrounding words), and almost all from later centuries.   Some face the other way, mostly Hospit-aller versions on a shield held by John the Baptist.   In his book on *Seals*, the compiler doesn't mention the Agnus in either the Glossary or Index and men-tions lambs only as farm animals.[74]

In John Lydgate's illuminated manuscript, the Banner of St. Edmund carried by loyal troops at Fornham St.Genevieve[18] has the Agnus with a more conventional cross,[76] but the Lamb and cross are surrounded by upturned crescents (Fig. 6.2), on a field of stars - *woolly* stars, remarkably enough.   The crescent and star may be St. Edmund's because he made a pilgrimage to the Holy Land – the cross-crosslet on the banner is a pilgrim symbol.[77]   Maybe the banner suggested they call the girl Agnes, because she came from the stars?   The upturned crescent and stars became de Calna emblems, as we'll see in Chaps.13 & 15.

Richard Barre was an archdeacon of Lisieux in France until 1188.   Henry II married Eleanor of Aquitaine at Lisieux, and the 1170s bishop was Arnulf, who was in the Second Crusade;[17]   having given sanctuary to Thomas à Becket, he was out of favour with Henry and in 1178 Walter de Coutances tried to displace him.[78]   de Coutances was still against him in 1180, which may help to explain why there's hardly any record of Barre at Lisieux itself.

The appointment probably was in 1173, to give him an income; if born in 1148, he'd now be 25, qualified for an important church position.   Arnulf was a friend of Gilbert Foliot's,[78] and the first record of the post is in a letter of Gil-bert Foliot's,[79] the next in a charter of Foliot's, both between 1173 and 1178.[80] He didn't do much for it: unlike other archdeacons, he's never mentioned in Arnulf's correspondence;[78] in the few cases where he worked for Lisieux, the earliest was in 1179.[61]

Since Richard de Calna was a prebendary canon of Salisbury in the 1150s, and probably arranged for Barre to join John of Oxford's staff when he was Dean of Salisbury (Chap.6), we might guess that they arranged the canon appoint-ment as well.   In 1177 Richard Barre was also a 'cherished' canon of Salis-bury, and also drawing income from the church of Husseburn in Hampshire, now Hurstbourne Priors, near Andover - near the de Calnas' home base, though even nearer to Winchester (10 miles) and Stonehenge (20 miles). With it came the income from the church of Burbage, near the east boundary of Wiltshire, between Hurstbourne Priors and Calne. The Husseburn and Burbage canonry was prebendary, set up by charters of Henry I and II and assigned to Barre no later than November 1175;[81] it didn't stop him marrying Agnes five years later. The income was only five marks a year, but there was a top-up from land dedicated to Salisbury by king Stephen, and when Barre was challenged for it, his rights were confirmed by Pope Alexander III, not once but twice (Chap.11).[82]

It wasn't to provide for the girl, because in 1173-87 it seems she was with de Calna, much of it *in ministerio*. De Calna was rich enough to support her, even if he meanly wouldn't provide her with a dowry. Perhaps Walter de Calna tried to help by taking property in Staffordshire, next door to the Barre family, and leaving her the rights; they had no other de Calna property recorded in Staffordshire or Warwickshire. We can guess that any the king assigned her were in Essex, and 'the daughters [heiresses?] of Walter de Calna' there could mean she wasn't completely dispossessed.

So what was Richard Barre doing, off the record, to justify the allocation of the Lisieux archdeaconry and prebendary income through Salisbury? The de Calnas and the Barres were engaged in something big, and whatever it was, clearly the green children were part of it, if only by accident.

But if Agnes was the green girl, then she not only carved out a niche for herself, perhaps running one or more of de Calna's estates, but she went on to a long and successful marriage with a very important man, albeit a commoner. In his later career as a justiciary, Richard Barre would need to be fluent in English as well as French; as an archdeacon, he had to be fluent in Latin and he wrote a book in it, as we'll see. Herself bilingual or trilingual, Agnes would be a real asset to him. She was a survivor *par excellence*. As I said before, she really deserves our respect.

But it was to be a bumpy ride for her in the meantime; and more strange things were about to happen at Coggeshall.

"The lunatic is all *idée fixe*, and whatever he comes across confirms his lunacy. You can tell him by the liberties he takes with common sense, by his flashes of inspiration, and by the fact that sooner or later he brings up the Templars."

~ Umberto Eco, *Foucault's Pendulum*

Figs. 11.1, 11.2. Coggeshall Abbey Barn, Bury St. Edmunds Abbey. Photos by Linda Lunan, 2011, and Duncan Lunan, 1993.

The 12th century Coggeshall Abbey barn (Fig. 11.1) wasn't open when I got there in 1993, but John Gunson, the Administrator, kindly gave me access. That morning the St. Edmunds Abbey ruins were misty and atmospheric (Fig. 11.2), but in Essex it was a fine summer afternoon. As I studied the exhibition, John asked if I'd like to see an old photocopy he'd just received from the Essex Archaeological Society, typed under the pen-name 'Beaumont',[1] after an 18th century Coggeshall historian.[2]

The first page described the Abbey's founding and listed the early Abbots, including Ralph, saying (wrongly, as I learned afterwards) that he was a crusader. But when I turned the page, to say 'my jaw dropped to the table' is a cliché, but that was how it felt; one of the few times that I've had such a jolt.

There's no general translation of Ralph's Chronicle, and the incident isn't headlined,[3] so I'd missed it in the Latin text. It seems no-one's connected it with the green children before, taking it to be supernatural, but I don't think it is. In Chap. 10 I said the boy might have been buried at Coggeshall Abbey, soon after his christening, and it would be good to find his body, perhaps in the clothes he arrived in; but, referring ahead to this chapter, "I don't think we shall". This is why.

"In the time of lord Peter the fourth abbot of Coggeshall it happened that brother Robert, a convert of that place, who had responsibility for the guests, on a certain day before the dinner hour entered the hall of guests in a routine way.   Having entered however, he met with certain persons of reverend/ frightening countenance and dress sitting in the halls, who used what seemed to be the mantle of the Templars, having only caps on their heads. But they were in number about nine or more, because that brother did not observe accurately enough how many had gathered. Thinking the aforesaid men to be Templars in truth, the brother greeted them kindly.   One of them, who seemed to be superior to the others, said to him, "Where now are we to eat?" And he said, "You will eat in chambers, with the lord Abbot." He immediately responded, "It is not our custom to eat in private chambers, but in the halls with our hosts." After that going out from the [guest] hall, the brother advised the Abbot, who ordered the table to be prepared and insisted on dining with them himself in private. Therefore with the Abbot about to come to the table, he instructed the foresaid brother to bring in the guests themselves. The brother verily entering the [guest] hall, those same guests whom he had left a little before, were not at all to be found. Entering however the inner bed-chambers and other lodgings, he found no one of them at all. And he soon emerging and reporting that through the Hall and to this place [the Abbot's quarters], it was asked what harm [could come] from such men. And one bore witness that he had seen men of this kind going to the church, and hastening to the cemetery of the brothers. When a messenger was sent there quickly, the messenger saw nobody. When however the gatekeepers were asked about such visitors, they avowed that no such men had been through the gate that day. Who indeed these men might have been, or by what means they might have come there, or by what way they might have departed, even today remains unknown. But of the account of the aforesaid brother that indeed he saw them and was spoken to, we do not doubt his experience and we long knew his integrity, because he frequently narrated these same things to us, and also in his final illness, by which he was removed from this light, when spoken to upon these matters he simply restated them. For he was an honest relater of things, using few words, holding forth no ostentation in words or deeds." (RC)

Fig. 11.3.

Figs. 11.3 & 11.4 Coggeshall Abbey Guest House (two storeys).
Photos by Linda Lunan, 2011, and Duncan Lunan, 1993, before restoration.

This story is called 'the Ghost Templars', only because of their rush to the cemetery. Ralph never says they were anything but men, and big men at that; the guest house is small (Figs. 11.3, 11.4), and with the rear partitioned off, nine unexpected men big enough to pass for Templars would be intimidating - especially if it was dark. And sending Robert on a fools' errand about their dinner isn't exactly spectral behaviour.

The cemetery was on the north of the church,[4] reached by a special door, the *porte de morts*, opened only for the monks' burials.[5] 1990s owners turned it a garden with a swimming pool, to local resentment: supposedly the bones were re-interred, but even that's uncertain. The graves were shallow, and if the boy was there, he could quickly have been exhumed. Taking in boy entrants died out well before this incident, so even among recent burials his shorter grave would stand out.

But the guest house is on the *south* of the Abbey, next to the Abbot's quarters, and to get to the church they had to pass those, then through the Cloister, between the kitchen and refectory. In Fig. 11.5 the way runs north from the Abbot's lodgings past the kitchen, extending eastward to the river Blackwater, redirected to power the mill (Fig. 11.6).[6] Another plan puts the infirmary there, with the warming room, refectory and kitchen on the west;[4] if so the knights had to go through the parlour and chapter house before the church, and were almost certain to be intercepted at dinner-time.

Going round the church on the west would bring them dangerously close to the watchman there, though the western gatehouse wasn't completed until c.1220.[5]

Surprised by Robert, the knights were now in much more hurry, though their fast thinking had gained them some time. With only 24 monks at the Abbey, nine or more unexpected guests would strain the night's catering, and it would take time to prepare more food or reallocate what they had: perhaps they could only dilute broth and stew, bringing them back to the boil. But the visitors didn't expect to be surprised at all, and already they had made a mistake, giving away their true status.

Off the battlefield, the Templars were governed by The Rule - supposedly filled with arcane knowledge, but actually full of mind-numbing trivia such as when a brother could borrow a horse or wear a second-hand habit.[7] I sympathise with the knight who, interrogated as to why the Rule was secret, replied, "because it's so stupid!" - or, as a more formal version has it, "through folly".[8] Nevertheless, it sheds light on the Coggeshall incident. The Templars

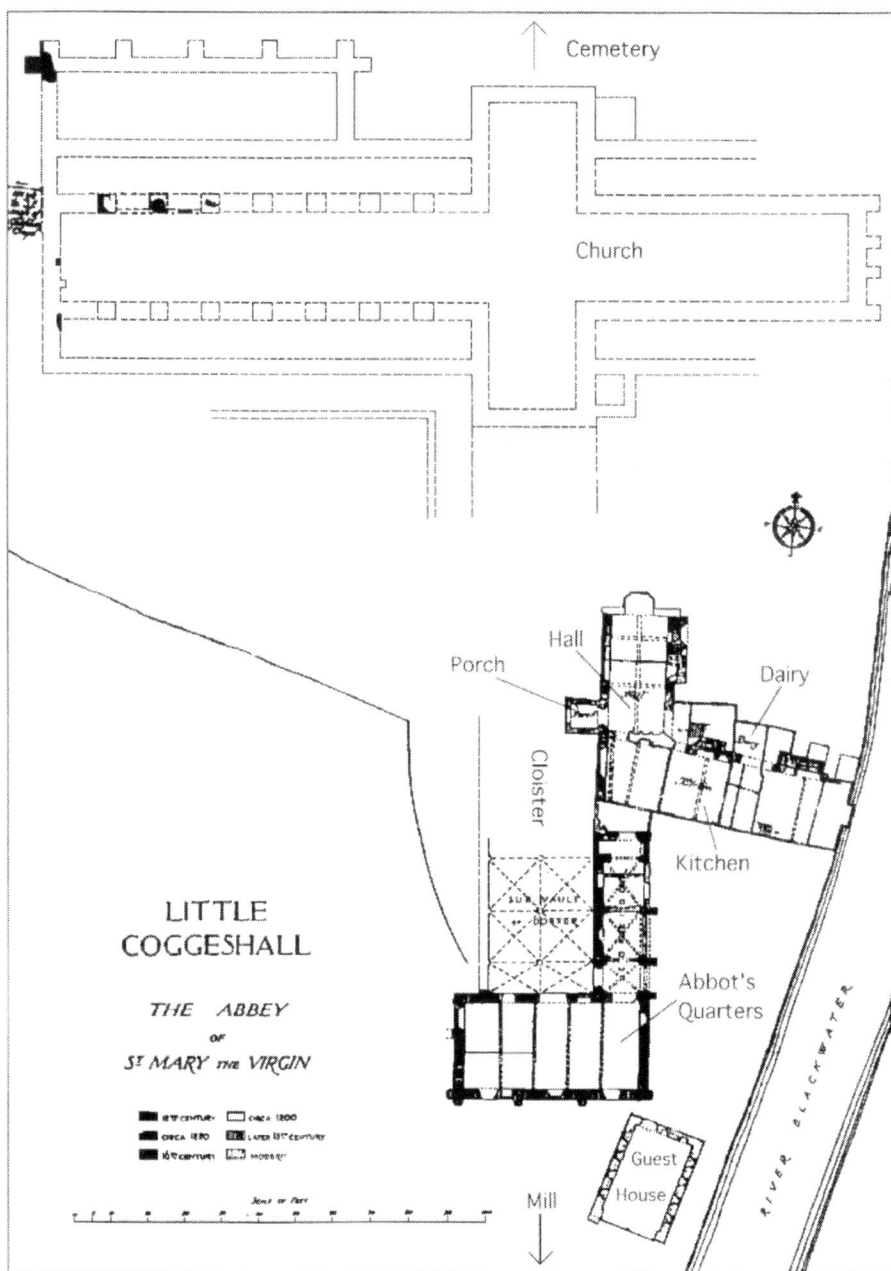

Fig. 11.5. Plan of Coggeshall Abbey.
Drawing by Nick Portwin, after Royal Commission on Ancient Monuments.

155

Figs. 11.6, 11.7. Coggeshall Abbey Mill and Abbey Bridge over the 'Back Ditch'.
Photos by Jane Greatorex, 1990s.

normally went bearded, and except when in war helmets, wore a red cap, as described by brother Robert. ("No brother may wear a hood on his head", Clause 324.) Forbidden all social contact, even with their own families, they needed a Master's permission to enter any building within fifty miles of a Templar house. Cressing Temple was closer than that, so they were acting with authorisation: in fact, the leader's words imply he was a Master. (Clause 182, "The Master and all other strong and healthy brothers should eat at the convent's table and hear the blessing.") So it's interesting that they went on to break Clause 228, "The fifth thing [justifying expulsion] is whoever leaves a castle or fortified house by any other way except by the pre-scribed gate." With all the restrictions on their lives, a Templar climbing through a window or over a wall was assumed to be up to no good, and the Abbey was surrounded by a high wall except on the east along the river.

James Bentley suggested tunnels or secret passages, but Coggeshall is on the same type of clay as Woolpit,[2] and next to the river, so the water table is close to the surface- that's why the graves were so shallow. In 1993 the eastern approaches were unusable, beyond a sea of mud. The guest house is only yards from the river, and its brick walls are too thin for secret passages. James suggested the Templars came upriver by boat, but the mill was in the way, even then; or they crawled in through drains, but below such a small Abbey, drains (if any) wouldn't be big enough. Below the *lavatorium* there was no drain, only a sand-filled soak-away.[4]

As James said, when discovered they'd have done better to dine with the Abbot, not to attract attention - though he'd ask how they got in, unless they were expected. Ralph doesn't say who the gatekeepers were, but probably they were monks, rather than men from the village. The Cistercian Rule, on which the Templars' was based, states: "At the gate of the monastery a wise old man is to be posted, one capable of receiving a message and giving a reply, and whose maturity guarantees that he will not wander around. This door-keeper should have a cell near the gate, so that persons who arrive may always find someone at hand to give them a reply... If the doorkeeper needs it, he should have a younger brother to help him... nor should any living quarters be placed outside the gates of the monastery... because of the need to protect people from dangers..."[5] Though the Abbey had only 24 monks, Ralph says there were gatekeepers, plural. They could be bribed, but that would be hard to hide; and so many knights would be hard to smuggle in, even if not in armour.

Jane Greatorex came up with plans, descriptions, and an aerial photograph showing the Abbey grounds in full. The approach from the east was discontinued because of the waterlogged ground, and a new gatehouse was established on the west. A chapel was built there in 1225 for the use of guests, who couldn't worship in the Abbey. The monks dug a new course for the Blackwater, hard against the Abbey with a deeper, faster channel to power the mill - it isn't clear when, but could be in the 1200s.[6] The original course of the river is 'the Back Ditch', with an Abbey Bridge giving access straight to the Guest House (Fig. 11.7), and something like it was there even in the 1170's because the Abbey gardens were east of the river. They were known as 'paradisus', and each monk was responsible for his own plot within them.

The Templars might come in by that route, unobserved, if the eastern gate was no longer in official use. Jane suggests that it was used in 1216 by king John's mercenaries, who stole 22 horses of the bishop of London's and others. But as we'll see the Templars' visit was in the late 1170's, not a time of major unrest, yet 'gatekeepers', plural, implies that both gates were manned – if not, why would Robert, Abbot Peter or later Ralph himself, think there was anything odd about the knights getting in? But even if there was access from the east, to get to the graveyard unseen the Templars would have had to pass the kitchens. If they extended all the way to the river, as they did when it was redirected, the knights would have had to go north through the gardens and ford the river higher up. The next bridge, Shortlands, is well upstream.

If Brother Robert hadn't happened to check the guest house on his way to dinner, they wouldn't have been discovered: there was only one meal per day, served at the same time in all Cistercian abbeys, so waiting in there until then, the Templars would expect to come and go unobserved, but the risk was obvious and apparently they were prepared for it. When Robert told him they were there, Abbot Peter would know that Templars wouldn't ordinarily eat with him in private, but would realise that these were leaders of the Order in England and their visit must be important. Preparing extra food for so many might take up to an hour, time to confer with them in the Guest House, so close to his own quarters, and for them to do what they came to do. Since places had meantime been laid for them in the Abbot's rooms, that would be

158

the best place for them to hide during the search - nobody would think to look there. However, it would mean that Abbot Peter was in the secret; that he knew why the knights were there, so presumably the significance of the hearing and the christening. It seems more likely that the knights did what they came for, and left - over the wall, over the river or by some more interesting method.

Eventually, I'm going to suggest that there was extraterrestrial Contact at the time, and there were matter-transmitters in human hands. If so, what happened to the green children, and the Peverell swineherd, were accidents – consistent with the disturbances of the Earth's magnetic field at the time. But with the 'phantom army' in Ireland, and now the 'Ghost Templars' in Essex, perhaps we see matter-transmitters being used under control. I hinted in Chap.7 that du Barry could have planted some kind of device: the de Calnas could have done it in the guest house, on one of their visits. Maybe the aim was to retrieve one that the green boy was carrying - buried with him, if Agnes had persuaded de Calna, Abbot Peter and Bishop Foliot to let her brother wear the clothes he arrived in. It might have seemed a nice gesture, but it would be highly dangerous (Chap.20).

Peter was Abbot of Coggeshall from 1176 to '94; so the Templars' visit was after the children arrived, after their christening, after the boy was buried - yet before Ralph arrived at Coggeshall, around 1180. Brother Robert was *conversus*, a convert: originally, a monk on manual work because he was too old or too stubborn to learn to read.[9] The Cistercians used the word for lay brothers, who led separate lives from the *monachi*, choir monks, remaining untaught and devoted to manual labour.[10]

James also suggested the incident never happened at all – that brother Robert was syphilitic and had hallucinated the encounter. Until recently the first known record of syphilis was at the siege of Naples in 1494, and supposedly it came from the New World with sailors in Columbus's fleet. Yet the West Indies claim that Europeans brought the disease to them, and the 1950 *Britannica* says, "During the middle ages there had smouldered in various districts an obscure disease known most frequently as *lepra*. Towards the end of the 15th century this disease broke out in epidemic form all over Europe... In 1530, on the suggestion of Fracastoro, it received the cognomen *syphilis*." In 2000 mild cases, regarded as a form of leprosy, were discovered in mediaeval corpses - particularly an isolated colony at a 14th century priory in Hull.[11]

Hull is far from Coggeshall and the Templar incident was 200 years earlier, so to assume that monks had the condition everywhere is unwarranted. Syphilis was found in a girl's bones at Rivenhall, on the main road from Colchester to London, south of Coggeshall and Cressing Temple - but even those were dated between 1295 and 1445.[11] There's no suggestion that brother Robert was subject to visions, let alone hallucinations - quite the contrary, according to Ralph.

But the Cistercians at Coggeshall ran fishponds, a mill and brickworks, as well as introducing sheep to Essex, taking over the wool trade, digging a new course for the river - all this with just 50 or so monks and servants. As the Order became more intellectual, manual work was done by servants and *conversi*, but instead time was spent in study, copying manuscripts, and each monk still had to tend his own vegetable garden. When Ralph resigned the abbacy due to illness, the reluctance of the monks to accept it must have been at least partly due to their inability to carry passengers - as witness the small size of the infirmary. If brother Robert became too ill to pull his weight, as a mere *conversus* he'd soon be packed off to a caring facility in Colchester - especially if he had a 'notifiable condition' believed to be a form of leprosy.

Ralph was an early intellectual of the new order;[12] so the Templars' visit was probably between 1176 and 1179 - unless the knights of the search party were disguised, presumably Richard de Hastings and Tostes de St. Omer, the leaders in England, were in personal charge. The number available for a search might be surprisingly low, when the Order had between 5000 and 20,000 members throughout Europe. At the end (Chap. 24), there were only 144 Templars in England and only 15-20 of these were knights; 8-16 were priests and the rest sergeants and serving brothers, who wore brown or black, not white.[8] A *frère marié* like de Calna should have worn the brown mantle of a sergeant rather than white, but in the smaller Templar houses in the west, little such distinction was made.[13] Ralph doesn't say what robes the visitors wore, but their leader spoke as a Master, and was dressed like the rest. Though Cressing Temple was nearby, its knights would be sick or retired, with the neighbouring farms managed by procurators or stewards under the preceptor's direction.[14] The search party at Coggeshall could have contained

160

most if not all the active knights in the country; hence James's suggestion that the Abbot would realise who they were.

Tostes de St. Omer, Richard de Hastings and Richard de Calna largely avoided the limelight. It's the hallmark of a well-run, low-key operation, which could be a perfect cover for another. At Templar holdings - safe houses for pilgrims - you would *expect* to see strange people come and go.   One imagines the accidents generating some very stiff memos - to this day Military Intelligence issues them in green ink.   In 1163, the same year that Henry annexed Hagenet Castle, the Templars were granted   (or confirmed) permission from the Pope to appoint their own chaplains.[15,16]   In 1173 that was confirmed by Alexander III,[17] and they were exhorted to confess *only* to their own chaplains - as John Braithwaite remarked, extraordinary in a fighting order.

In March or May 1176, a charter of Henry II's to the bishop of Winchester was witnessed, at Westminster, by Gilbert Foliot, Geoffrey Ridell, John of Oxford, Hugh du Puiset and Walter de Coutances, among others.[18]   March is probable because de Coutances was ambassador to Flanders in May and John of Oxford went to Sicily that year,[19] and March 1177 is another possible date for this event.[18]   They only needed Richard de Calna, Richard de Hastings and Richard Barre for a full set of the players - and since they were in London, they could all meet at the New Temple to confer.

In August 1176, Geoffrey Ridell as bishop of Ely made a deal with Richard de Hastings, resolving a long-standing quarrel between the cathedral and the Templars about ownership of six cathedral properties, including two key preceptories in Cambridgeshire and another in Lincolnshire – sufficiently important for the agreement to be endorsed in a backup charter from the king at Westminster, witnessed by Gilbert Foliot, probably in March the following year.   Richard Barre might have been at those discussions - and any behind the scenes - though not listed among the witnesses at Westminster.[19]   He could have been one of those listed at Ely as 'et alii',[21] because he later became archdeacon of Ely, in 1189, probably on Ridell's recommendation (Chap.13). Maybe the raid on Coggeshall was agreed at one of those meetings.

In January 1177, problems at Waltham Abbey were the reason for meetings between Henry II and Geoffrey Ridell, Gilbert Foliot, and the archbishop of

Canterbury; in June, with Foliot, John of Oxford and Hugh du Puiset. Richard Barre may have been involved, because he was presented with a pre-bendary income by the monks of Waltham soon afterwards (Chap.13). In 1177, Walter de Coutances and Ridell were appointed ambassadors to Louis of France, along with the bishop of Bayeux; John of Oxford, now bishop of Norwich, sat at the exchequer with Ridell in 1178. But Barre had by now disappeared almost entirely from the records, apart from his Lisieux and Salisbury rôles, ever since he brought prince Henry's seal back to Henry II in 1173.

Ralph Turner writes, "Like other cathedral canons in the king's service, Richard Barre probably resided at Lisieux only during those periods when Henry II's court was nearby in Normandy [never at Lisieux itself, in the key years - D.L.]. A few surviving documents locate him at Lisieux or Rouen [see Chaps.12 & 13], involved in ecclesiastical matters, in the 1170's and 1180's. There is little to indicate, however, that he visited England during the years that he was Henry's clerk."[22]

But in 1175, Barre was challenged over the Burbage church in Hampshire,[23] from which, as part of the Hussburn (Hurstbourne Priors) prebend, he drew income as "our cherished Richard Barre, canon of the church of Salisbury... the archdeacon", in the bishop's words. The previous holder was William Giffard, canon of Salisbury, who died no later than November 1175, and a local man, Alan de Hussburn, was already making an issue of it by then.[24]

At the time of Domesday the manor belonged to the Priory of St. Swithun in Winchester.[25] It was called 'Hussebourn Prioris' manor by 1167. King Stephen confirmed the status of Hurst and Burbage in 1139, but also confirmed the prebend. When the chapelry of St. Mary Bourne was established there, it was dependent on the Hurstbourne Priors church.[26] Henry I established a prebend of Salisbury drawing five marks per year from the church, plus the income from the land it was on.[27] Stephen and Henry II confirmed the incomes, and Stephen added income from other land (left blank in the charter) to be divided among the prebendary canons.[23]

The Hurstbourne package was assigned to Richard Barre after William Giffard, and when Alan de Husseborne challenged him for it, Barre appealed directly to the Pope, who confirmed his position, three years after

162

commending him as "our beloved son" (Chap.6). Alan de Hussburn wasn't satisfied and got a ruling in his favour from other judges, after which Barre appealed to the Pope again. Not surprisingly Alexander III wasn't pleased, and the case was referred to Roger, bishop of Worcester, for impartial judgement, with instructions from the Pope to settle the matter.[25]

Roger conducted a thorough, if somewhat leisurely enquiry, and convened a hearing at Leigh, near Worcester, in November 1187, which Richard Barre attended. Alan de Hussburn didn't appear and the bishop ruled that he had the facts wrong: in particular, he claimed against Barre for the whole church, which Barre didn't have, and for the prebendary rights the two letters from the Pope were decisive. The bishop ruled that if Alan had misled the judges who ruled for him by concealing the first of them, he should meet Barre's expenses in obtaining the second. And because of that one's strong wording, his ruling was like Alexander III's on Woolpit: "... by force of our episcopal authority, we have imposed upon the same Alan perpetual silence concerning the same church. Let nobody therefore have the bold presumption to cancel or in any way disturb what is ruled to be established with such solemnity and such authority of the see, which we have decisively laid down with our seal attached."

The ruling was attended and backed by two other bishops, one of them Robert Foliot, brother of Gilbert, formerly archdeacon of Oxford (succeeding Walter de Calna and preceding Walter de Coutances!), now bishop of Hereford.[28] Perhaps the hearing was delayed until Barre was available, hinting that he wasn't normally based at Salisbury. (The bishop of Salisbury reissued the ruling a month later in his own name.[23]) Although Leigh and Worcester aren't far from Little Barr, on the far side of Birmingham, Richard wasn't living there yet. The bishop told Alan to meet Barre's expenses in coming to the hearing; Alan appealed because he had been sick, and had sent a priest and a deacon to speak for him, though they didn't appear.[24] It was agreed that if that was verified the expenses would be waived; but wherever Barre was based, it was at some distance. There's no evidence that he was at Lisieux either (Chap.13).

Richard needed money now, because in 1178 Agnes had an illegitimate son - perhaps unwillingly, because it seems she rejected the child. Richard Barre had the boy christened Richard, as if he was his own son, and he was fostered with his family's neighbours in Staffordshire. The truth didn't come to light until 1220, and even then there's no evidence that the son was ever reunited with Agnes. Meanwhile Barre remained almost invisible through the rest of the 1170s and most of the 1180s. Gerald Warner remarked that if Agnes was a royal ward and Barre made her pregnant, he might well leave the country for the good of his health... But instead, when he suddenly reappeared he was a more important ambassador than before.

Perhaps Agnes now looked fourteen, and de Calna planned a marriage for her which was frustrated by the pregnancy. Children could be pledged at twelve years old, but for royal wards it required the permission of the king.[5] Sometimes Henry broke the rules and pledged children, including his own, as young as five and six. If that was done with Agnes, I can't find a record of it, and if not, de Calna had a problem (Chap.10). If her pregnancy was to make de Calna marry her to Barre, and release any property assigned to her, it failed: the child went to Staffordshire to be raised by the Barre family's neighbours, and Agnes lost touch with him for many years.

Richard Barre acquired property in Nottingham or Derbyshire in 1178-79, on which he had to pay half a mark to compensate for an unjust 'disassiesin'[29] (seizure),[30] and it seems that he assigned that property to Agnes's bastard son. In Chap.15 we'll see other arrangements made for the boy. Jane Greatorex found a charter in central Nottinghamshire witnessed by a Richard Barre, which might also be related to it, but unfortunately could be any time between 1175 and 1184. Nottinghamshire records include a Thomas de Barra, chaplain, Robert de Barra and Sir Geoffrey Barre, all in the 1240's but not descended from Richard and Agnes.[30]

However, a Geoffrey Barre - perhaps an uncle or an older cousin - was a landholder in Nottinghamshire, with two knights in service to him, in 1166. In 1176-77 he was fined five marks for offences under the forest laws.[31] Did he ask his kinsman the lawyer for help or advice? If our Richard Barre did have Notts. relatives, he could have been up there making arrangements for the boy in 1178 or '79 - perhaps very late in '78 or early '79 (Chap.12). Apparently he then married Agnes, no later than 1180, because their second son, William, became legally adult aged 14, in 1194.

164

Among the common people, sexual relations usually began after the secular plighting of their troth. Later at the church door, the man endowed the woman with land which would be hers at his death, and at a subsequent Mass any children they already had were made legitimate under a pall known as the 'care-cloth'[32] ('born on the wrong side of the blanket'.) So it's possible that William too was born illegitimate, further explaining de Calna's 'wanton and lascivious' complaints in the 1180s, and in that case Richard and Agnes might not have married till after de Calna's death in 1189. If Agnes was judged to be ten years old in 1173, she wouldn't be 25 until 1188, and if the alternative was to surrender family property, de Calna could spin out the question of her true age and keep her on his staff in the 1180s, as Ralph of Coggeshall says.

But if William was legitimised that way, why not reclaim the first son when they married, whenever it was? Richard didn't even tell Agnes where he was (Chap.15). If William too was illegitimate, why was he not fostered out in the same way? Whatever motivated Barre, it wasn't shame: with his contacts he could have had young Richard sent anywhere, but he took care to provide for the boy, as we've begun to see.

Previously, James Bentley suggested that the whole green children case was faked by Henry II: the children were dyed green at birth, perhaps in Ireland, where St. Martin was popular; allowed to see only people similarly dyed, taught an esoteric language, and eventually drugged and planted at Woolpit dressed in Oriental silk (or knitted clothes, as Montse Stanley suggested). Silk was known in England since Roman times, however, and never lost: the Anglo-Saxons had a luxury fabric, *purpura*, maybe been silk taffeta. Early mediaeval silks were routinely imported from central Asia, silk clothing was made in England from the 10th century onwards and gold and silver threads were woven into it by the 12th.[33] There was an even more advanced silk workshop in Spain; Chinese silks and dyestuffs were traded in Flanders by the late 12th century, and were in England by the 13th at the latest. Even *green* silk was imported to Western and Central Europe from Syria by the 1190s,[34] though still special, fit even for carrying the Holy Grail.[35] Satin might be a better mystery fabric, apparently not in England until 1275, though it then became very popular. But in Ireland, "satins and silken clothes... both scarlet and green" had been carried off by the Irish from a Viking stronghold in Limerick as early as 968,[33] and a more esoteric fabric seems to be indicated for the green children.

Henry's plan could be to found a new dynasty, anticipating his existing family's rebellion. Supernatural origins were *de rigeur* for royalty, like having a convict ancestor in modern Australia: Henry himself, Eleanor of Aquitaine and Guy de Lusignan all claimed fairy ancestors.[36,37] Guy de Lusignan's was so popular in folklore that several families, including the Counts of Luxembourg, falsified pedigrees to lay claim to her;[38] while the Merovingian kings of the Franks claimed descent from a horned sea-creature in the 5th century. Baigent, Leigh and Lincoln suggest that the story commemorated a dynastic marriage.[39] The proverb about the Plantagenets was "From the Devil they came, to the Devil they will return", though another version says that 'Henry-le-Diable', ancestor of the dukes of Normandy, was a bad person rather than actually diabolic; and that Eleanor of Aquitaine's demon/fairy grandmother was invented by her first husband, Louis VII of France, as an excuse for divorcing her.[40] However it also says that her parents were baptised to put them beyond the grandmother's power, so why would it matter?

Henry II was interested in the supernatural and esoteric (Chap.5), and James's suggestion is in keeping with the *X-Files* world of plot and counterplot in which Henry operated. In 1190, suspiciously timely, what were claimed to be king Arthur's remains were 'discovered' at Glastonbury Abbey, in restoration ordered by Henry and continued by Richard I. Historians still argue over how much of that was faked.[41]

In James's view, Henry's plan was frustrated by the unexpected death of the green boy. Ralph's 'a certain boy and his sister' could mean he was more important, but in Latin it was not unusual to put the second subject of the verb first, though more often when writing in the first person. Centuries later when Cardinal Wolseley wrote *ego et meus rex*, 'I and my king', "he made a good scholar but a poor courtier".

Bill Ramsay suggested that Henry, not Richard Barre, made Agnes pregnant when she looked old enough, and Barre passed the child off as his own. If Agnes was not of this world, Henry might wanted to find out how human she was. It would be quite in character for him - whether she wished it or not. Jane Greatorex suggested that if the children's greenness was sexually symbolic, maybe they were to be joint victims of a Beltane ritual, before May Day, when the Lord of the Forest would ceremonially deflower a virgin - and the ultimate lord of the forest was the king. He owned them all, and under the Normans, many forests which had been communally owned under the Anglo-Saxons were now exclusive royal hunting-grounds.

It still seemed far-fetched, till I checked Henry's movements. In April 1177, Henry II was at 'Wick' - and we can be pretty sure which 'wikes' that was, because on May 1st, at the end of Easter, he was in Bury St. Edmunds. If he knew of a Beltane ritual in the woods near Wykes, he could demand to attend, with himself in the lead rôle and Agnes involuntarily cast as the ceremonial 'bride'. Carers' protests could be brushed aside: he would find out once and for all whether she was human.

Usually, Henry was generous to his bastards, rather than isolating them as Agnes's son was. Most sources say Geoffrey Clifford was Henry's natural son by his great love Rosamond de Clifford, Rosamond the Fair:[42] Henry's relationship with her became open in 1174, a year after Eleanor of Aquitaine's imprisonment. The story has been challenged: Rev. R.W. Eyton calls Geoffrey 'FitzRoy', the son of a common harlot, confused with William Longespée, Henry's son by Rosamond fifteen years later.[19] Whoever his mother was, by the time he was 20 Geoffrey was about to be bishop of Lincoln. When the 1173 rebellion broke out he postponed his consecration and allied himself with Ranulph de Glanville; in 1174, after de Glanville had captured the king of Scots, Geoffrey joined mopping-up operations with 140 knights and a force of men-at-arms, causing Henry to say "that his other sons by their conduct had proved themselves bastards, but this alone had shown himself to be his true and legitimate son".[41] Geoffrey was at Henry's side when he died in July 1189, and accompanied his body on foot from Chinon to Fontevrault;[19] he then became bishop of York, by Henry's deathbed wish,[37] with consequences which we'll see in Chap.14.

Leaving Richard Barre to make provision for the king's child by Agnes would be less handsome, but in the next chapter we'll see why Henry might want it that way; while if Agnes was made pregnant against her will, and she rejected the baby, that might explain why Barre fostered out the child and never told Agnes where he was. It makes it more remarkable that she had the resilience to marry, have a legitimate son, work *in ministerio* for de Calna and eventually settle to a full married life. But if it's true, it helps to explains why Barre was in obscurity and yet his fortunes steadily continued to improve. In 1180, the monks of Waltham Abbey assigned him the income from a church in

'Bradburgham', which hasn't been identified.   In August that year he also became a prebendary canon of Hereford, drawing income from Moreton and
Whadon churches in Gloucestershire.[43]   Although the appointment was made
by bishop Baldwin of Worcester,[44] the bishop of Hereford was Robert Foliot,
Gilbert's brother;   Gilbert himself was bishop there between 1148 and
1162/63, and Thomas Foliot had been Treasurer in 1160.[28]   Barre also drew
income from farmland belonging to the Siffrevast family (Chap.12).[22]

Before 1184 he received a charter from the archbishop of Rouen,[22] Walter de
Coutances's predecessor.   All this was just as well, because in 1180 he was
fined with other bettors on a mock battle fought at night in Lisieux.   Penalties
on the cathedral staff were particularly heavy, and Barre had to pay no less
than £20 - four years' income from Hurstbourne Priors.   He was doing well,
however, because he paid in a lump sum,[45] even though it seems he and Agnes
married in 1179 or 80 and de Calna provided no dowry.   To help explain that,
de Calna had the ear of the new, educated young monk at Coggeshall, lately
transferred from Barnwell Priory.   Ralph befriended the ailing Brother
Robert, from whom he heard the story of the Templar visitors at first hand;
but he also formed a rapport with de Calna, and legend has it that Ralph
burned one of his first manuscripts because it was too influenced by eastern
lore.[46]

De Calna's *Lasciva et petulans*, 'wanton and lascivious', also implies 'wilful and
independent' – we might describe her as 'liberated', suggesting again that she
came from a more advanced society than de Calna's.   Blackening her name
freed him of dowry obligations, and she was under his thumb for nine more
years, at least.   If that seems selfish or unreasonable, remember the difference
between them in age and the expectations which someone like de Calna would
have of young people, especially young women, under his care.   He had taken
the children into his home, saved Agnes's life and done his best for her
brother, and he had groomed her for a responsible position within his
household *familia*.   He probably felt that she owed him a return on that
investment, rather than being entitled to an independent life on a piece of his
property.

Meanwhile bigger things started happening in the year of the illegitimate son's
birth: the skies, and the king, were once again more than a little uneasy.

Chapter Twelve - 1178: MAKING AN IMPACT WITH KING HENRY

"I could more easily believe that two Yankee professors would lie than that stones could fall from heaven."

~ Thomas Jefferson

Early in the enquiry, the late Danny Kane asked me, 'What astronomical events were happening at the time?' I found a lot, including the auroral displays of 1172 and 1173, and the odd motionless 'star' in summer 1173. In 1178 there was an even stranger one, simulated in Prof. Carl Sagan's book and series *Cosmos*.[1] Gervase of Canterbury, who carefully recorded events such as aurorae and mock-suns, wrote:

"In this year, on the Lord's day before the nativity of John the Baptist [June 18th – but see below], after sunset, on the first day of the new Moon, there appeared a wonderful sign, five or more men witnessing it. For the new Moon was bright, extending the horns of its new form to the east, and behold suddenly the upper horn was divided in two. From the middle of this division there rose up a burning torch, hurling flame, burning coals and sparks for a long way. Meanwhile the body of the Moon which was below it was twisted as if anxiously, and as it is borne by the words of those who retold it to me and saw it with their own eyes, the Moon waved like a wounded snake. After this it returned to its normal state."[2]

The 'doubling' would be caused by a fountain of dust in vacuum and low gravity, like the plumes on Io, Jupiter's volcanic moon Io (Fig. 12.1). As described, debris was thrown over 1200 km, so the impacting body was travelling at 20 km per second or more; about 1% of material ejected would have escaped from the Moon altogether.[3]

But Prof. Sagan omitted details which didn't make sense till March 1993. "It repeated this change *twelve times* and more - [my emphasis] - namely the various torments of fire, as if it endured again what had already happened, and returned to its former state. And after these and such changes, it was made as

Fig. 12.1.　Impact on the lunar Farside, 1178 AD.　Painting by Sydney Jordan.

if darkened from one horn all the way to the other.　The very men who saw these things with their own eyes retold them to myself who writes them, willing to give their oath or to swear to it, that to the above they have added nothing false."

In 2001 the account was challenged by Paul Withers, [4] who noted that the Moon wasn't visible on June 18th.　But Graeme Waddington argued that the text should be read as June 19th, when the very thin crescent was visible even in the Holy Land, marking the start of the Moslem month. [5]　In June, the event could be caused by the Beta Taurid meteor stream, an intense shower of daylight meteors first detected by radar in W.W.2.　Seismometers left by

Apollo astronauts detected several large impacts in June, and the Tunguska impact in Siberia, June 1908, may have been one.

In September, Gervase records a partial solar eclipse - "Moreover elsewhere the eclipse was total, and the shadow of night was seen in the middle of the day, and one friend could not see another standing next to him.   The same eclipse was also seen in France" - and is in the chronicles of Melrose Abbey[6] and Ralph Diceto.[7]   Curiously, none mention the *corona*, the extended upper atmosphere of the Sun: during strong solar activity it should have been bright around the rim of the Moon.   In fact, there are no definite descriptions of the corona in the mediaeval chronicles,[8] though in 1185 solar prominences 'the colour of fire' were reported at another eclipse,[9] and one at Verona in 1187 was 'red-hot'.[10]   Diceto's chronicle adds the date, September 13th, and a previous one on 21st January (Matthew Paris says 8th January), but that's not possible: the only UK eclipse that year was on September 13th.[8]

Eclipses can occur only near the nodes where the Moon's orbital plane crosses the *Ecliptic*, the plane of the Earth's orbit around the Sun, around which they cycle in 18.61 years due to the pulls on the Moon from the Sun and the Earth's equatorial bulge; so between June and September 1178 they moved very little, and the Moon was close to the Ecliptic when one day old in June. Precise calculations put the Moon's setting at Canterbury only 45 minutes after sunset.[11]   So the twelve impacts were in rapid succession - and we know now what sort of event that was.

As Comet Shoemaker-Levy (SL-9) passed Jupiter in July 1992 it split into 22 fragments, discovered in March 1993.   They hit Jupiter in July 1994, on the far side from Earth, but the flares were seen by the Galileo space probe and over the rim of Jupiter by the Hubble Space Telescope.   As the impact points came into view, optical and infra-red telescopes saw scars the size of the Earth forming in Jupiter's cloud layers.

Two of Jupiter's moons, Callisto and Ganymede, have crater chains with no identified 'parents', probably due to SL-9-type events.[10]   Callisto has 12 or 13 and Ganymede three (Fig.12.2) - the active surfaces of the other large moons (Io and Europa) erase impact marks.   Our Moon has secondary chains, where debris from impacts fell back, but they begin next to 'parents' such as craters Davy and Humboldt.[13]   There are at least two 'parentless' crater chains on the Farside, north of crater Tsiolkovsky but not pointing to it: one on the equator,[13] the other at 5° Lunar North,[14] but they look old, not bright.   The 1178 impacts apparently formed the 20-km crater Giordano Bruno on the lunar Farside, discovered by the USSR's Luna III in 1959, but predicted from its rays of impact debris on the hemisphere facing Earth   (Fig. 12.3).[15]   A bright feature there was named 'the Soviet Mountains',[16] but it's composed of rays from Bruno crossing another ray system, confirmed by the Apollo 8 mission.[17]   The Bruno rays are as extensive as the larger crater Tycho's, around 60 million years old, and ray systems fade with time, so Giordano Bruno is much more recent.   If the flare divided the upper horn of the Moon as described, the impacts were around 45° North, which fits.[11]

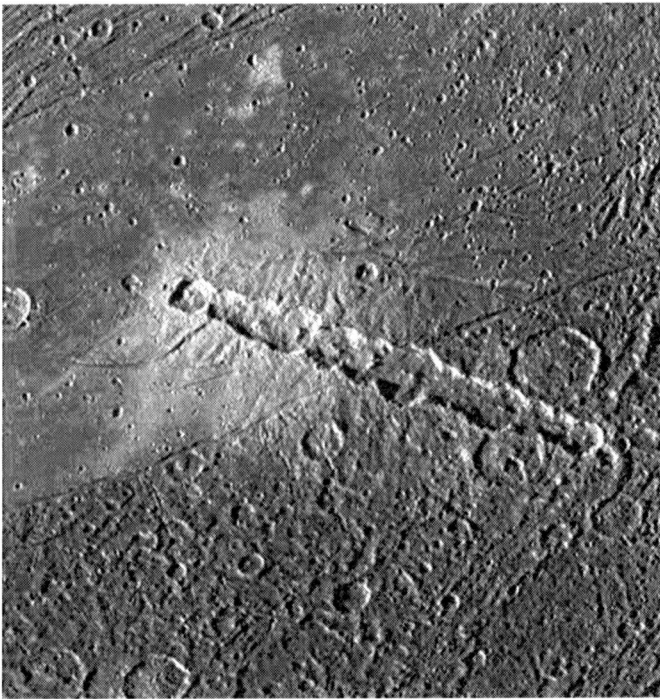

Fig. 12.2. Galileo spacecraft image of Enki Catena crater chain on Ganymede (NASA).

Giordano Bruno is the 'Jordanus Brunus' cited by Burton, speculating that the green children came from another planet (Chap.1).   A Dominican monk, he was burned at the stake in 1600 for holding that the Sun was the centre of the Solar System, and that there were many inhabited worlds; but he had also adopted the traditions of Neo-Platonism (Greek, but claiming Egyptian origins[18]) and challenged the Church on transubstantiation and the Immaculate Conception.

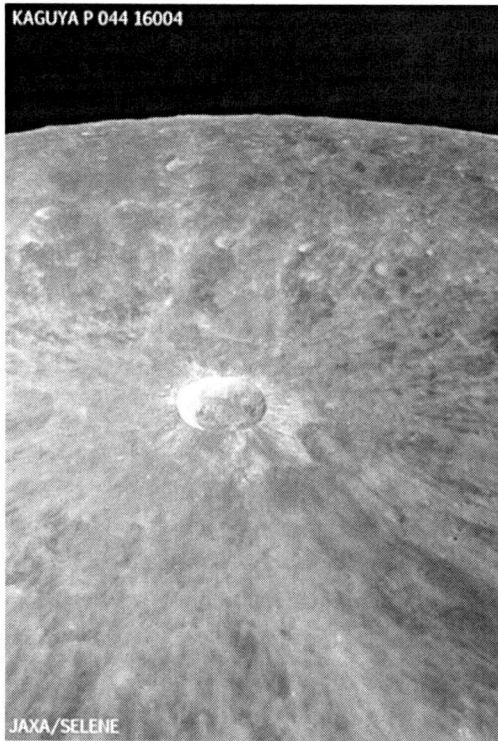

KAGUYA P 044 16004

JAXA/SELENE

Fig. 12.3. Selene image of crater Giordano Bruno (JAXA).

Laser retroreflectors, placed by Apollo astronauts and Soviet Lunokhods, show that the Moon is still oscillating in its orbit by 15 metres, from one or more big impact(s) in the last thousand years.[19] Such effects were sought in the 19th century but were too small to measure, proving that the Moon had not been struck by anything with more than one 100,000[th] of the Earth's mass.[20] Now we know how low comet masses are, that's true, although the energy released was around 100,000 megatons.

The Moon's crust lacks 'volatiles', such as carbon, hydrogen and nitrogen compounds. To give the Moon a lasting artificial earthlike atmosphere would require a comet-like body 80 km. in diameter,[21] or 400 comets the size of the

Shoemaker-Levy parent, with impacts at much lower velocity than the violent Gervase event.   Smaller impacts might create a temporary atmosphere, and released volatiles could collect in 'cold traps' on the permanently shadowed floors of craters near the lunar poles.[22]

The Clementine probe in 1994 found signs of ice at the south pole, in small craters within the Aitken basin, which is 2500 km. across and at least 12 km. deep.[23]   In 1998 Lunar Prospector results suggested larger deposits at both poles, very thinly mixed with dust[24] - an effective insulator, explaining why ice grains could survive even in sunlight.   Arguments about its existence continued till 2009, when the L-Cross probe impacted near the south pole and raised a plume of water vapour whose isotopic composition showed it was definitely from comets;   at the same time India's Chandrayaan-1 orbiter discovered at least 600 million metric tons of water ice in shadowed craters at the north pole.[25]

The date of Bruno crater isn't entirely certain: one estimate of four million years would still make it one of the newest large craters on the Moon.   It turns on whether small craters on the surrounding ejecta blanket are due to the ongoing 'sweeping-up' of Solar system debris, or were formed by fragments thrown to high altitudes and falling back.[26]   The other, more serious challenge is that the impacts never happened at all - that the monks saw a bright meteor which happened to come from the direction of the Moon - and "Of course, we can discount the claim that it happened twelve times".   When filming at Cambridge for the *National Geographic Ancient X-Files*, I discussed the sighting briefly with Dr. Alan Chapman, who agrees: he thinks that there was only event, and "the Moon throbbed like a wounded snake" describes the meteor's trail twisting in high-altitude winds.   I'd politely counter that we *shouldn't* discount eyewitness testimony so readily.   Perhaps Gervase compared the Moon's appearance to a snake lying still, with pulses rippling down its wounded body - as the thin crescent Moon might look with plumes of ejecta falling back, and waves of temporary atmosphere carrying dust with them. Paul Withers doubted the impact because he'd found no records of debris falling to Earth.[4]   But there's a further detail in Ralph of Coggeshall's chronicle, though not in his handwriting.   He describes the finding of St. Alban's relics that year, and another hand has added '*et lapides pluebant* - and stones rained down'.[27]

174

About 1% of ejecta from the surface would exceed the Moon's escape veloc-ity.[3] The 'sparks' flying off into space must have been big, and there are two asteroids which could be from lunar impacts: 1991 VG, about ten metres across, and 1999 CG9, 220-380 metres in diameter.[28] Some ejecta would have less than the combined escape velocity for Earth and Moon,[3] and coming from the Moon's trailing hemisphere, could fall on Earth as secondary impacts. With the Moon near the Ecliptic, in June, its *declination* (terrestrial latitude, projected on to the sky) would be 23 - 24° North. Debris from Giordano Bruno, at 37°.7 Lunar North, *could* fall in England, depending on the angle of ejection from the lunar surface. Around 1200, there was a big meteorite fall in Nebraska,[29] 10 degrees south of southern England; perhaps one in New Zea-land,[30] near the Antipodes; and major disruptions of population in Polynesia and South America, which Emilio Spedieato, of the University of Bergamo, suggests were due to impacts,[4] tying in with the legendary origin of the Incas (Chap.22).

In later years the Psalm to be read daily in the Calne stall at Salisbury Cathedral was Number 18.[31] In it, after David calls to God for help - "Then the earth shook and trembled; the foundations also of the hills moved and were shaken, because he was wroth. There went up a smoke out of his nostrils, and fire out of his mouth devoured: coals were kindled by it. He bowed the heavens also, and came down: and darkness was under his feet. And he rode upon a cherub, and did fly: yea, he did fly upon the wings of the wind. He made darkness his secret place; his pavilion round about him were dark waters and thick clouds of the skies. At the brightness that was before him his thick clouds passed, hail stones and coals of fire. The Lord also thundered in the heavens, and the Highest gave his voice: hail stones and coals of fire. Yea, he sent out his arrows, and scattered them; and he shot out lightnings, and discomfited them. Then the channels of waters were seen, and the foundations of the world were discovered at thy rebuke, O Lord, at the blast of the breath from thy nostrils."

We've seen episodes like those in *Deep Impact* and *Armageddon* much more recently, and Prof. Mike Baillie suggests in his book *Exodus to Arthur* that similar imagery in Psalm 74 and the book of Isaiah relates to impact events.[32] The Psalmist may have called on pre-Biblical Sumerian, Hittite and Egyptian accounts of the Flood, which have the characteristics of an impact[33] - probably in the Tigris marshes around 2350 BC.[32] But the same imagery in 2 Samuel 22

175

is thought to be contemporary with I Chronicles 21:16: "When David looked up and saw the angel of the Lord standing between earth and heaven, and in his hand a drawn sword stretched out over Jerusalem, he and the elders, clothed in sackcloth, fell prostrate to the ground" - probably a comet in Chinese annals for the 970s or 960s BC. [34]

Carl Sagan found it striking that even one impact with the Moon should occur within the span of recorded history. [1] Many comets passing Jupiter later approach the Earth and Moon, so perhaps an SL-9-type chain could get here before it dispersed, but it's very unlikely that they'd all strike within an hour, in precisely the same spot, in the 1170s of all decades. The Moon's slow rotation would allow multiple impacts to form a single crater in that time - but only if all were aimed dead centre at the lunar disc. It suggests that they were under control – that the crater is artificial.

And it happened just when Agnes gave birth to, and then gave away, her illegitimate son, probably fathered by Henry II? It's unlikely to have been a firework display to celebrate the event, but it seems to have made a big impact with Henry. In June 1178 he was in Normandy, [35] but on 15th July, less than a month later, he sailed for England and made an immediate pilgrimage to Becket's shrine at Canterbury - or perhaps his priority was to interview the witnesses there.

Henry would have to see the impacts to believe them. So close to Moonset, and on the far side of the Moon, with only ejecta plumes visible from here, they wouldn't blind or even terrify witnesses. To impress as tough a king as Henry II, as the plumes rose one by one, he would have to be shown in real-time what was happening round there: colossal detonations, creating a huge fire-pit and hurling debris far over the lunar surface and into space (Fig. 12.1). Bill Ramsay argued that Henry wouldn't think of the Moon as a world, but as a disc a few hundred feet up. But Henry had an excellent education, [36] and probably knew classical estimates of the Moon's size and distance, some surprisingly accurate. If he could see the plumes coming up over the Moon in the sky, and what was happening simultaneously in the moving picture, he could make the connection. Even today, though we know intellectually that the Moon has craters and Saturn has rings, first sight of them through a telescope makes a big impression.

If the event wasn't a message to leave Agnes alone, perhaps Henry thought it was, and had Richard Barre sort out a solution.   There was another scare to come: at Christmas that year, Henry was at Winchester, with queen Eleanor under house arrest at Old Sarum and his sons Geoffrey and John with him, probably with an itchy feeling between his shoulder-blades because princes Henry and Richard were out of the country.   Hugh du Puiset, bishop of Durham,[35] was there, so word would come quickly.

"At the 1179'th incarnation of the Lord Henry king of England held court at Winchester, Geoffrey and John his sons being with him. Truly Henry his son tarried in Normandy, and Richard his son in Poitou.   Truly on the same Lord's natal day there happened, at Oxenhall, something wonderful... because, in the very farmland of Lord Hugh, Bishop of Darlington, the ground itself rose so violently on high that its top was made level to the peaks of the hills, and it loomed over the spires of the churches: and it maintained this height from the ninth hour of the day until sunset.   Truly the Sun having set, it followed it to earth with such a horrible sound, that it terrified all seeing that heap, and hearing that sound; whereby many died from that fear; for the earth swallowed it, and made the same a deep pit, which lies there to this very day."

~ Johannes Brompton, *Chronicon.*[37]

It recalls the million-pound mine detonated under the German trenches at the Messines Ridge, in 1917;[38,39] but in a conventional explosion earth and rock don't remain suspended for any time.   A plume of dust might, on a windless day, in which case the horrible sound after sunset would be just the collapse of the ground.   Lord Lyttelton comments, "Camden supposes three deep pits in a field near Darlington... called the *Hell-kettles*, to be the remains of this very extraordinary rising and sinking of the earth... This hill, probably, was pushed up by subterranean fires"[40] - a volcanic eruption in 12th century Yorkshire: to which we can only reply, in the words of Glasgow poet alburt plethora, "Eh? Naw!"[41]   It's been a very long time since we had anything like that in the British Isles.   Underground nuclear explosions raise a hemisphere of rock and earth, which slumps into a crater;[42] if the fireball breaks out to the air, it carries radioactive gas and dust, which makes one wonder about those deaths 'from fear of the sound'.   But the deaths suggest this may really have happened: in the 1980s psychiatrist George Engel investigated nearly 50 cases of

177

people '"scared to death", during or immediately after a disaster such as an earthquake or explosion.[43]

Daniel Defoe,[44] and later John Braithwaite, suggested it was a gas explosion in a Durham coal-field; but the Hell-kettles are in the alluvial plain, which on that stretch of the Tees overlies Permian limestone,[45] capped by a 'thin' layer of red sandstone.[46]   But when the current owners of the Hell-kettles had a new well drilled at their farm, only half-a-mile from the pits, the sandstone was found to be 200 feet thick.

The Hell Kettles are almost circular, with gently sloping sides, punched with startling beauty into a field by the Croft road, south of Darlington, a quarter-mile north of the Tees.   The farm is 'North Oxen le Fields', to this day.   The Double Kettle is a dumb-bell 34 yards across (Fig. 12.4), and the South Kettle 25 yards across;   another, shallow one was filled in the 1950's.[47]   The water level is independent of the height of the Tees:[48]   the Double Kettle, fed by drainage from the fields, was three feet below ground level when I was there in 1995, but is often higher, and a contour round the Double Kettle shows it's been higher still in the past.[49]   In 1958 divers found unbroken bottom of mud and weed 15 to 22 feet down, confirming 18th century soundings[50] - though a Dr. Jabez Kay had earlier found 90 feet.   Intriguingly, bores by the Biology & Archaeology Departments of Durham University held pollen up to 5000 years old;   the most likely candidate for the 1178 event is the South Kettle (Fig. 12.5), which hasn't been dated, but is fed from below by calcareous spring water, rich in carbonates and sulphates,[51] though the divers couldn't find the entry point.

Brompton's chronicle was compiled around 1328.[37]   The original version was written by Roger de Hoveden, secretary to Henry II,[49,50] who says only that the earth "rose on high, in the likeness of a high tower", collapsing after sunset. Perhaps the event was release of hydrostatic pressure in limestone, though it's hard to imagine through 200 feet of sandstone.   If the Hell-kettles overlie sink-holes in it, they're unique in Britain;[51] yet drilling nearby in 1739 released a spring with a similar sulphur content, "with such force that the workmen were fain to escape for their lives, and even left their shovels and picks behind them.   (Another report says that they never saw their wheelbarrows again)."[52]   There could be other reasons for that.

178

Figs. 12.4 & 12.5. Double Kettles and Single Kettle.
Photos by Matt Ewart, 1995, and Linda Lunan, 2011.

Almost everyone takes "the 1179th incarnation of the Lord" to be Christmas 1179. But Henry spent Christmas 1179 at Nottingham, and didn't reach Winchester till the following April.[35] It was Christmas 1178 when he was at Winchester with Geoffrey, while princes Henry and Richard were in Poitou, where Richard was Count: it was 'the 1179th year of the Lord' in the reckoning where the new year began at Christmas.

'None' wasn't nine in the morning but the ninth hour of daylight, under the Benedictine Rule. The day began with Matins at midnight or 2 a.m. in winter;

Prime service was at 6 a.m., Mass at 9 and 11 a.m., dinner at noon, None at 2 or 3 p.m. and Vespers at 4; supper at 6 p.m. and Compline service at seven.[53] So there wouldn't be more than an hour between the explosion and sunset, at Christmas in Durham.   None was the hour of Christ's death on the cross, of the expulsion from Eden, and when Satan's power on Earth was greatest. (Maurizio Cattelan's controversial sculpture of the Pope struck by a meteorite is titled *The Ninth Hour*.)[54]   If something ominous happened soon after, the chronicler might say it was None on the dot.

The bishop of Durham then was Hugh du Puiset or Pudsey (Puteaco), nephew of king Stephen, ordained in 1153. He rebuilt a castle on the River Tweed destroyed by the Scots, and improved Durham Castle, the Cathedral and several churches including the one at Darlington, after the 1178 event.[55] A contemporary poem describes Durham as "half house of God, half castle 'gainst the Scot."[56] Although on Stephen's side in the civil war and the wrong side in 1173, he was twice forgiven by Henry II. du Puiset was with Henry II and Richard de Hastings in Normandy in 1160, probably there when Henry annexed Woolpit (Chaps. 5 & 6). He may have been a royal justice in 1179-80,[57] but he definitely was one in 1188, before Henry's death, and he'd have been in touch with Richard Barre soon after that (Chap.14). His arms were a Templar cross pattée in blue, on a gold and white background.[57]

Darlington with surrounding land was given to the cathedral of St. Cuthbert in Durham between 1002 and 1016,[52] and was its best farmland.[51]   At least twelve farmers there, plus mills and a smith, etc, were subject to the bishop,[59] and in 1164 Puiset built a manor house there for his own use.[60]   He established a college of secular canons in the town,[58] likewise a leper hospital at Badele (later Battlefield) nearby,[61] and a distinctive church there in 1192, despite Richard I's demands for his crusade and his ransom.[62]   The decorations featured his emblems, eagles and St. Cuthbert's griffins.[55]

In 1183 Hugh ordered a survey of his holdings, and the Oxenhall entry is a good example of feudal service. "William holds Oxenhall, to wit one carucate [about 120 acres, also called a hide - enough to support a family, with one plough][63] and two cultures of the territory of Darlington, which Osbert de Selby used to hold to farm, in exchange for two carucates of land at Ketton, which his father and he used to hold in drengage [as a freeman, not a villein or serf],[64] which he has quit-claimed for ever to the bishop and his successors for himself and his heirs; he ought also to have the horse-mill, and he and his family are free from multure [tax on mill products] and work at the mills, and he renders 60 shillings per year; moreover he does the service of a fourth part of one drengage, to wit, he ploughs four acres, and sows it with the bishop's seed, and harrows it, and makes four precations [work for the bishop] in Autumn, to wit, three with all his men with the whole house, except the house-wife, and a fourth with one man for each house, except his own house, which shall be free, and he keeps a dog and a horse for the fourth part of the year, and carts wine with four oxen, and makes utware [military service] when it shall be laid on the bishopric."[59]

In other words, not much happened at Oxenhall without the bishop getting a share, in cash or in kind. It's interesting too that William ran a mill (see Chap.22), though it wasn't one of the powerful new wind or water mills.

Lyttelton quotes William Camden, whose *Britannia* states, "Cuthbert Tunstall first discovered that these pits had subterranean passages and discharges, having found in the Tees a goose which he had marked and put into one of them for an experiment."[65] Camden cites John Stow,[66] who in turn cites Tudor historian John Leyland, chaplain to Henry VIII when Tunstall was Bishop of Durham, 1530-59. "... a duck, with the customary markings of ducks in the bishopric of Durham, was placed in one of the pools between Darlington and the banks of the Tees, which are called Hell Kettles; and this duck was subsequently found at [Croft] Bridge on the Tees... So that local people came to the conclusion that an underground passage connected these two places."[67] Tunstall's records don't mention that or anything unusual for Darlington.[68]

If the water was high in Tudor times, and the pits "of surprising depth", the goose would just have paddled about and honked occasionally. Either the level was then much lower, or the story has to be dismissed; but, for comparison, a 36-metre sink-hole which opened in Florida in 1994 was initially 54 metres deep.[69] A similar one in Ripon, North Yorkshire, in 1997, was over 30 feet wide and 120 feet deep. The legend that the Hell-Kettles were bottomless may have inspired Lewis Carroll, who lived at Croft until 1852, although Alice Lidell lived in Ripon and collapses there in 1796 and 1834 probably had more to do with the rabbit-hole to Wonderland.[70]

"As recently as 1935 a fishing rod dropped into the largest and deepest pond was found at the Croft Bridge over the Tees".[50]   Like the disappearing wheel-barrows, it's not beyond the wit of man to explain that.   The divers saw no fish, though the Kettles used to have the largest pike in England, last seen (but not caught) in 1942.   Maybe an earlier link with the river had been sealed off by then; but even when there were fish they were trapped there, judging by the fat in their tissues when cooked.[44]

If the king expected a sign at Christmas, perhaps he'd gathered his allies. Gilbert Foliot, Geoffrey Ridell and Walter de Coutances were at Winchester, plus John of Oxford,[35] now bishop of Norwich, recently with Ridell on the exchequer and about to become one of the king's justices.   Hurstbourne Priors was only ten miles away: if Richard Barre was there, perhaps he was sent to Darlington to investigate.   It would underline any message about not harassing Agnes; perhaps it gave her enough influence to have her brother's body moved from Coggeshall, where she couldn't visit him, and if so the Templar raid on Coggeshall Abbey might have been as late as 1179 - it can't be much later, as it was before Ralph moved there in the 1180's.

A trip north would let Richard Barre do business in Nottinghamshire (Chap.11); and in 1178 or '79, he witnessed a charter of Robert de Siffrevast's to Missenden Abbey in Buckinghamshire, excepting a piece of land belonging to himself and his heirs - perhaps the same property Robert's father had assigned to Hugh Barre more than thirty years before (Chap.4), or perhaps a present for his impending marriage, because several of the de Siffrevasts and their personal chaplains were also witnesses.[70]

Raphaell Holinshed linked the two 1178 events but wasn't impressed ("Touching these celestial apparitions, the common doctrine of philosophy is, that they be mere natural, and therefore of no great admiration"), like eclipses, whose cause he knew.[71]   If they *were* natural, it's remarkable that the sequence between 1172 and 1178 began and ended on Christmas Day (Table.12.1).

But in 1179, "The 19th day of August at night, the Moon was eclipsed, which was seen of king Henry and his company, as he rode all night, to meet the king of France, coming into England, to visit the tomb of Thomas Becket the arch-bishop."[71]   Henry knew lunar eclipses were natural, but that one would give him a fresh scare, if his sudden trip to Canterbury the previous year was made in alarm.

Table 12.1. SEVEN YEARS OF INCIDENTS

1172: December 25th, airburst explosion or sonic boom during auroral storm.
1173: February 18th, apparent high-altitude explosion during auroral storm.
1173: July, green children arrive?
1174: November 4th, auroral storm.
1177: November 29th, auroral storm.
1178: June 19th, impacts on Farside of Moon; fall of stones in England.
1178: December 25th, underground explosion at Darlington.

For details of the 1172, February 1173, 1174 and 1177 events see Chap.21.

Chapter Thirteen - THE 1180'S: IN MINISTERIO

"Despite all the theoretical gallantries of the poets, the Middle Ages, at the end of the twelfth century, were still very hard for a woman, however noble she was; and the precepts of chivalry, which commanded total deference to the weaker sex, were not put into practise nearly as much as the *chansons des gestes* would have us believe."

~ Joseph Warichez, "Étienne de Tournai et Son Temps"[1]

Sara	She's ours, she is our servant, vagabond.
	She's Richard's property.
Juxon	I do not think
	She's even earth's, and as for what you think
	Young spitting thing, I care not the least izzard.

~ Glyn Maxwell, *Wolfpit*

1. Living at Lynn

In 1180, when de Calna's granddaughter Sibylla was born, it seems Richard Barre and Agnes were married: their legitimate second son, William, was legally adult by 1194 (Chap.14). Richard was archdeacon of Lisieux, but probably not there: when archdeacon of Ely in the 1190s, apparently he lived in Staffordshire (Chap.14). Lisieux had at least six more archdeacons, two of them bishop Arnulf's nephews,[2] all conspicuous: John of Alençon, 182-95, was vice-chancellor to Richard I and a witness with Richard Barre at Ely in 1191.[3] Gilbert de Glanville, 1151-85, became bishop of Rochester and was a justice with Barre in the 1190's.[4] Hugh de Nonant, one of the nephews, was Henry II's ambassador to the emperor Frederick in November 1184.[5] But despite his expertise and standing with the Pope, Barre first *acts* as archdeacon in June 1179, viewing St. Romanus's body in Rouen,[4] and seldom otherwise.

Being an archdeacon was no barrier to marriage: one controversy over Becket's appointment as Archbishop of Canterbury was that, although an archdeacon, he wasn't in holy orders. Geoffrey Ridell married in 1163 when archdeacon of Canterbury: he had to take an oath of celibacy when he became bishop of Ely ten years later.[6]

There's no record of Barre in 1173-1187, except one-offs like the Worcester hearing in 1177. A charter that he witnessed in Yorkshire could be as early as 1185, or any time between then and his death in 1209.[7] He wouldn't be a 'house-husband', bringing up young William while Agnes went out to work as de Calna's business manager! From 1188 on we know just where he was, till the end of his life, but between 1177 and 1188, there's a strand still to unravel, a mystery within a mystery.

William of Newburgh says the girl married a man *apud Lennam* - living at Lynn. Founded by bishop Herbert de Losinga of Norfolk, the port was 'Bishop's Lynn' until the reign of Henry VIII, when it became 'King's Lynn' as it is today. The original name was 'Len', an estuarial lake.[8] The Lynn church was dedicated to St. Nicholas, the patron saint of sailors,[9] and de Losinga built the church of Mary Magdalene, St. Margaret and all the Virgins for visiting 'sailors and all others from ships'. Lynn was under John of Oxford from 1175: Magister Walter de Calna witnessed a grant to the Lynn monks in the 1160s;[10] young Walter, Sibylla's older brother, witnessed a grant by John of Oxford to Lynn church, in 1186-1200.[11]

Had Richard Barre rejoined John of Oxford's staff? For East Anglia and London, Lynn was the principal port for the Baltic, especially Norway, also Holland, Flanders and other places. In the 14th century Lynn exported Kendal green cloth, first made at Norwich, but earlier the main exports were grain, wood and salt.[12] Timber, pitch and fur were imported from Norway, fish from Denmark and Iceland, and wine from Gascony, especially Bordeaux.[8] John of Oxford had seagoing experience: after his trips to Rome and Sicily, in 1173 he shipped Henry II's treasury across the English Channel in the royal yacht. (Rev. Eyton calls it *Esneccia*[13], but that was a type of ship, not a name [Chap.23].) There was contact between Lynn and Lisieux: between 1170 and 1220 at least one charter at Lynn was signed by a man from there.[11] It would be very interesting if that was Richard as Lisieux archdeacon.

If Barre was away on national business a lot, perhaps he had no property of his own yet and that's why Agnes was still *in ministerio* for Richard de Calna.

185

Mediaeval lords moved constantly between properties, seldom spending more than two weeks in each; estates were run by stewards, almost always men, but women sometimes took over when their husbands died, especially if the mistress was herself a widow.[14]

If Agnes was running Knettishall or even Wykes, they're not that far from Lynn; if it was de Calna's property at Bernay, that's much closer. But there's no trace of Barre's doing anything to justify his status at the end of this chapter. He wasn't one of John of Oxford's archdeacons: we have a full list - Thomas of Norwich, Geoffrey the chaplain, magister Reiner, Roger (possibly a doctor), John in 1189, Geoffrey de Buckland 1197-98; finally Geoffrey de Burgh, when John of Oxford died. But no sign of Richard Barre, good though it would be to place him at Lynn or Norwich.

The chief port of West Lynn belonged to the bishop of Ely, who was Geoffrey Ridell from 1173 to 1189. Ridell and John of Oxford were in constant touch in the 1170's and in the 1180's, when they were both justices[7] - as Richard Barre had been and would be again. Corn was shipped from Cambridge and Huntingdon to Lynn by way of Ely, along fenland waterways, and Ely was connected by a man-made channel to the river Ouse by 1250, if not sooner.[11] The Little Ouse links it to Woolpit and Ixworth, joining the main river below Ely, though it flowed into the sea at Wisbech ('Ouse-beach' - probably where King John lost his treasure, shortly before his death)[15] until the time of Henry III. The river Larke connects Lynn to Bury St. Edmunds and the port's water-links stretched inland to Bedford and Northampton; vessels with fifteen tuns of cargo could reach Bedford from Lynn. The mediaeval town was also laid out for freight going by road: it was on the Roman Peddar's Way, through Castle Acre and Bardwell to Colchester, while the prehistoric Icknield trackway led to Bury St. Edmunds through Ixworth, crossing the Ouse by the Nuns' Bridges at Thetford.[11]

Ridell shared the port with the prior of Castle-Acre (Chap.6), linked to Lynn by the river Nar,[16] and the North Lynn church belonged to the Abbot of Bury St. Edmunds,[13] now Samson de Botington himself. The shield of Lynn, under its pelican crest, bore the heads of three dragons - perhaps originally conger eels - each pierced with the cross-crosslet of the Banner of St. Edmund, sharpened to a point (*fitché*).[18]

John of Oxford, Samson or Ridell could marry Richard and Agnes at Lynn; maybe at the church of Mary Magdalene, because of the *lasciva et petulans* as well as because she was a stranger to the town. Either the bishops or the de Calnas could give them a home. Most Lynn houses were built of oak or hazel,[19] but Barre's status probably required stone. By 1187 John of Oxford had a house built for his visits: a 'fine' stone-built house excavated on modern King Street, dating from c.1180 when it was 'Stockfish Row', could be the bishop's house, or the 'Boyland Hall' in a lost text of 1173.[11]

We have to think for whom William of Newburgh was writing. Ralph of Coggeshall's account of the children was for people who'd know they had to be examined by a bishop, and could guess which; anyone hearing that de Calna had an Agnes and a Sibylla in his family would think 'Jerusalem'; William would expect anyone reading *his* account to know that 'the Land of St. Martin' implicated the bishop of London and that Lynn was shared by Norwich, Ely, Castle-Acre and Bury St. Edmunds, perhaps hinting at who his high-class witnesses were - and William is our source for the family anecdote about how Roger Le Poer came to the notice of prince Henry (Chap.4).

Another William de Calna first appears in 1160, gifting two thousand herrings to the church of St. Mary in Binham;[20] the de Calnas were connected to Binham Priory because they held land in nearby Bernay. Before 1181, William witnessed a gift to the canons of St. Paul's.[21] He witnessed a grant of John of Oxford's in 1188[22] and one by the bishop of Hereford in 1191;[23] and another, requested by Abbot Samson, to Samson's new St. Saviour's Hospital at Bury St. Edmunds. (In 1326 the Abbey's income from Woolpit was donated to St. Saviour's.)[24]

In 1193/95 he was prior of Codeham or Cotheham, and by then he too was a 'magister', witnessing numerous charters at Canterbury. He witnessed many more at Norwich in the 1200's, and in 1202 he was a 'Commissary' of the bishop of Northamptonshire, opposing Gerald of Wales (Chap.7) in his claim to the see of St. David's.[23] He could be a distant cousin, since both Everard and Rualdus de Calna had sons called William; perhaps William son of Rualdus, listed in Surrey in the Pipe Roll for 1185.[16] But the Binham connection suggests that he was one of our de Calnas, and in 1186 he witnessed a Canterbury charter with another 'W. de Calna', probably lord Richard's grandson Walter (see below).[25] He could be a younger son of the

187

second Richard's (Fig. 4.1), or William de Caune, a monk at St. Albans in 1216.[26]

So far we haven't seen any de Calna land near the Wash or the Norfolk coast. He could pay a coastal merchant to provide the herring; there was a well-run distribution, with fresh sea-fish sold as far inland as Coventry. But probably the de Calnas had property or even a boat at Lynn itself. A visit to King's Lynn makes clear how important fishing was, and herring was a major food. 'Stockfish' were cod, beaten with sticks before cooking, and haddock, plaice and ling were all in the regular Lynn diet.[19]

Herring came up again around 1205, when bishop John de Gray of Norwich discovered that John of Oxford had claimed twenty marks' worth of the fish per year from the monks of Norwich Cathedral Priory, and excused them the payment in future.[10] Binham belonged to St. Albans, not to Norwich; but one witness to the new agreement was magister William de Len', William of Lynn. He's a witness with Walter de Calna from 1188 onwards, and in many charters and agreements until 1205. But although charters are witnessed by Walter and William de Calna, and others by Walter de Calna and William of Lynn, it seems he and William de Calna never appear together. Were they the same man? In Glyn Maxwell's *Wolfpit*, the girl's rescued from her degradation by a fishmonger from Lynn,[27] and fish from Lynn may be important.

If Richard de Calna had property at Lynn, not on record because he paid no taxes, held by his younger son William, maybe he gave Richard and Agnes use of it, and the legitimate son was named after him. If William reclaimed it in 1188 (we'll see below why he might), then perhaps he was 'William of Lynn' from then on. William de Len was Prior of St. Margaret's Church and the Chapel of St. Nicholas at Lynn in 1199.[11] 'William son of William of Lynn' first appears in 1185-86;[28] if he was a son, before William took holy orders, that too could explain taking such property back.

William of Lynn was a canon of Salisbury from 1222, prebendary of Yetminster Prima in Dorset.[29] He answered a summons to the first ceremony in the new cathedral, in 1225, suggesting he wasn't resident there, and several canons had other affiliations - one was dean of St. Martin's, for example. In 1226 he witnessed an agreement assigning the income of the Calne prebendary

188

to the cathedral treasurer.   He was there for the election of a new bishop in 1228 and still a member of the cathedral chapter in 1231.[30]   Though not proof, the Wiltshire rôle supports the idea that he might be William de Calna.   [In 1237, a major agreement about lands in Calne was witnessed by 'lord William de Calna', canon of Salisbury,[31] but that's the knighted son of Reginald de Calna, and Calne was in other hands by then (Chap.15).]

A William of Lynn was Sheriff of Dublin in the 1230's, with son Walter in the 1240s and '50s,[32] but unlikely to be the same man unless *very* long-lived and active.   In a charter of John de Gray's to Lynn, magister William de Len is identified as the brother of another witness: Geoffrey, archdeacon of Norfolk,[33] who could be Geoffrey de Buckland, Geoffrey de Burgh or Geoffrey 'the chaplain' of Norwich, later put to death by king John for talking out of turn.[34]   de Buckland had connections to the de Calnas, but wasn't related;[35] de Burgh was no relation either, so only the unlucky Geoffrey of Norwich could be the brother - unless Geoffrey and William were more distantly related and 'brother' should read 'kinsman'.

2. Samson Reclaims Woolpit

Geoffrey Ridell ceased to be responsible for Woolpit in 1173, Walter de Coutances took charge of it in 1174, and both were ambassadors to Louis of France in 1177 (Chaps.9 & 11).   By 1180 Louis had been succeeded by Philip, and Henry II feared an attack on Normandy; de Coutances was among ambassadors sent to Paris.   He was Henry's personal chaplain,[36] as was Ridell at another time, but presumably later because de Coutances didn't take holy orders until elected bishop of Lincoln in 1182-83).   Henry was displeased,[37] perhaps because now he had to hand back Woolpit.   As if Woolpit held back Walter's career, two years later he was Archbishop of Rouen.

Butler's notes to Jocelin's Chronicle can give a false impression here: "Geoffrey probably vacated [Woolpit] in 1173 (on his appointment as Bishop of Ely) or in 1174 (after his consecration).   In his place Walter of Coutances received it in frankalmoin [free alms] at the request of the King.   But it is laid down in the Charter that, after the death or resignation of Walter, the church shall return to the use of the monks.   Walter had now been made Bishop of Lincoln and had resigned the living, which now at last was free."[37]

It reads as if de Coutances became Bishop of Lincoln before put in charge of Woolpit, so it reverted to St. Edmunds Abbey on a technicality; it's an easy mistake to make, because there *was* a new Bishop of Lincoln in 1173. But Butler means now in the *text* - 1182, when Woolpit at last reverted to the Abbey. And the same year - surely no coincidence - Henry let Samson become Abbot.

Abbot Hugo died in 1180, and the election campaign was vigorous. Samson was sub-sacrist then, responsible for the Abbey buildings, and was adding two great towers. Asked how the materials had been paid for, he claimed secret donations from the burgesses of the town, but William the Sacrist accused him of misappropriating public donations.[37] The knights in charge of Abbey property, on behalf of the king, halted the work and insisted the money be used to reduce the Abbey's debts.[36] Under Hugo the finances were a shambles, and when the whistle was blown there were 33 copies of the Abbey seal in circulation, some being used like a license to print money. The Jews of Bury, to whom William the Sacrist was a friend, supported him against Samson - which didn't do them any good later, as we'll see in Chap.14.

So for new Abbot, Samson wasn't everyone's choice. "Some there were," says Jocelin, "who, if they had known who was to be our Abbot, would not have prayed [for a successor to Hugo] so devoutly." He quotes lively speeches on both sides: Samson was called "a Norfolk lawyer" (*barrator*, enough like 'barrack-room lawyer' to give the sense), and there were dreams of him as a wolf, perhaps because of his preoccupation with wolf-pit village. In the end a delegation went to the king to decide, but he had a reputation as protector of St. Edmunds to maintain and wouldn't be responsible for a bad choice. The delegation had to go next door and choose, and Henry replied, "You have pre-sented Samson to me: I do not know him. If you had presented your Prior, I should have accepted him; for I have seen him and know him. But, as it is, I will do what you desire. But have a care; for by the very eyes of God, if you do ill, I will be at you!" Yet Henry knew Samson perfectly well: Samson and another monk crossed the Channel two years before to tell him of Abbot Hugo's death. The denial suggests that Samson's 'interference' on Woolpit was on the king's behalf all along.

Samson called together his brethren, telling them (as if they didn't know) about his adventures in 1161, with Roger de Hingham and on his own in

France. And then: "Behold! the church for which I have endured so many ills, has been given into my hands; and now, since it is vacant, I have power to bestow it as I will. And I restore it to the Convent, and assign to its proper use the ancient custom or pension of ten marks, which you have lost for more than *sixty years* [my emphasis]" - the first indication, now it was all over, that the Woolpit issue went back so far. Butler takes it to be true, that Woolpit had been in royal hands, given in frankalmoin to royal clerks, since 1123 at least: Samson would have been sent to Rome in 1160 by the monks, for whose comfort in sickness the ten marks had been allocated, not because the king had just seized it but because Abbot Hugo was going to let it continue.

For all my insistence on trusting the texts, I doubt this one. There's no sign from the Pope, the king, the Abbot, the monks or the bishop of Norwich that the issue was so old; those last two 'clerks' were vice-chancellors of England, much more than mere pen-pushers; and Samson says he rushed off to Rome in 1160 without waiting to see to whom Henry II would allocate Woolpit; so it must only just have happened. But in the text the number is a Latin figure, '*plus quam lx. annis*' - maybe a mistake for 'ix. annis'. 'More than nine years' would mean the nine years that de Coutances had it, plus Ridell's years in charge before the 1173-74 break.

Samson wasn't one to forgive an old wrong, as witness his treatment of the Jews when the chance came. He quarrelled with Ridell over land rights, and took great delight in depriving him of prime timber, which Ridell wanted for Ely Cathedral. Like Samson, Ridell had an extensive building programme for his church, including turrets and a great west tower.[38] Samson didn't forget old friends either: he made Roger Cellarer of the Abbey, but he was a disaster in the post, and had to be removed.[36] He put Hugh, Roger's brother, in Woolpit, adding, "I would gladly give you [monks] the church in its entirety; but I know that the bishop of Norwich would say me nay, or, if he permitted it, he would avail himself of the opportunity to claim submission and obedience from you, which it is unwise and unbecoming for us to give."[37] The village was now the pivot of the century-long argument over whether Bury St. Edmunds was independent or subject to the bishops. With all St Edmund's property, it's obvious why they kept trying, but were there other reasons to want control of Woolpit?

From 1181 onwards John of Oxford was frequently at Westminster, where he had a town-house (Chap.14). In 1182, Henry II named Ridell as one of his executors, perhaps when he was Henry's chaplain. In 1184, Ridell and John of Oxford were once again at the exchequer. Meanwhile in July 1183 the new pope, Lucius III, instructed Richard Barre and others to resolve a dispute between two churches; he and Hugh de Nonant, as archdeacons of Lisieux, were asked to deal with another in January 1184,[39] and a papal document later that year noted it had been done. In 1184 he was back in England, however, because he witnessed another charter to Missenden Abbey.[40]

In the larger frame, Eleanor of Aquitaine continued her intrigues. The earl and countess of Leicester were reinstated in 1176, with their property restored in early '77, but re-arrested in 1183 in case they sided with princes Henry and Geoffrey, who'd expelled Richard from Aquitaine. After prince Henry's death they were released, likewise Eleanor the following year. Aquitaine was returned to her in 1185 after king Henry fell out with Richard; but she kept causing trouble, and in 1186 she was arrested again[41] and imprisoned until Richard became king - hence *The Lion in Winter*.

3. Agnes and Sibylla

In the early 1180s, de Calna's son Walter witnessed a decree of John of Oxford's,[41] but by 1185, both he and his wife were dead. His lands in Suffolk and Essex changed hands in 1187-88, with the words *exitu terre*, 'upon his leaving the earth'.[42] *Terre* is underlined, both times, as if there was something strange about it - leaving *this* Earth.

Sibylla became a royal ward. In 1185, "The lord king gave the daughter of Walter de Calna to the son of Thomas Fitz-Bernard, with North Fambridge manor, which is worth £20 per year with its attachments; and she herself is five years old, and is in the care of the wife who was Thomas Fitz-Bernard's, after the death of Thomas himself." A fee years later identifies the unnamed daughter as Sibylla.[43] The Fitz-Bernards were very wealthy: Thomas Fitz-Bernard, who died in 1184, was master and chief justice of the king's forests[5] and had property in at least seventeen counties. His widow held land in Oxfordshire, to which Sibylla may have gone. Sibylla's dowry, North Fambridge manor, was in east Essex, but linked to Reed in Hertfordshire, south-west of

Cambridge - almost certainly lord Richard's.   North and South Fambridge ('Foul-bridge'), divided by the Crouch estuary, were given to Ely Cathedral by Canute and Godiva.[44]   South Fambridge was still the bishop's under Geoffrey Ridell,[45] so perhaps Nigel de Calna gave North Fambridge to Richard between 1133 and 1158-59.   If it was still the church's, the king couldn't assign it to Sibylla.

At five years old in 1185, Sibylla was too young to be the green girl.   But John Fitz-Bernard later held Reed with the daughters, plural, of Walter de Calna   (Chap.10);   the modern editor takes that to be a mistake, and I suggested that perhaps it should read 'heiresses'.   We can even guess why: Walter was already an adult in 1146, so he was born no later than 1132 and was 47, at least, when he fathered Sibylla.   His sons were already adult, so Sibylla was an after-thought.   If Walter's wife died in childbed, the same year that Agnes gave birth to her legitimate son, perhaps Agnes wet-nursed Sibylla. That could explain her name: as we saw in Chap.10, in 1180 Sibylla de Courtenay married Guy de Lusignan in Jerusalem, and *her* mother was Agnes. Knowing the story of St. Agnes and her 'milk-sister' (Chap.10) the two families might have felt that this closer relationship was foreordained.   But if Sibylla got her name because Agnes was her surrogate mother, the family was keeping in close touch with events in the Holy Land.   Just how close, we'll see below.

Perhaps Agnes was also assigned to look after Sibylla's inheritance: Richard de Calna might frequently visit Coggeshall, as an old man, going to check the management of North Fambridge.   Walter de Calna might have left land in Aston Clinton to Agnes, as well as Sibylla, out of gratitude, and it all could be why Richard and Agnes were finally allowed to marry, making the infant William legitimate in retrospect; and when Sibylla was fostered, perhaps then they moved to de Calna property in Lynn.

The connection with Aston in *Warwickshire*, so close to Little Barre, remains mysterious: why did Walter de Calna have property next door to the Barres in the first place?   Were the de Calnas frequent visitors to Staffordshire, as well as to Essex?   The missing link could be at Merton Priory in Surrey, from whose Prior Walter Agnes and Sibylla reclaimed Aston in September 1197. Since it was a relatively small (though influential) house, we have only the first names of Priors at the time: Dugdale lists William who died in 1177,

Stephen 1177-78,[46] Robert who died in 1186, Richard (supposedly) 1190-98, supported in some modern versions[47,48] - but the Prior in 1197 was Walter, as above. It appears that Walter was really appointed in August or September of 1197 and was Prior from then until 1217.[49]

Any of them might be a Barre, or a de Calna, of whom we've no other record. The 1197 prior might even be the younger Walter de Calna, but that's unlikely because he was still in the *familia* of Norwich, and witnessing charters there as 'magister', not as a prior. Walter senior might have been a friend of the prior in office when he made his will, and made him executor of the Aston part to be sure that Agnes wasn't 'disasseisined' by Sibylla's guardians; but the overall executor of the will was Walter de Coutances, at a still higher level and in charge of Woolpit until 1182.

Meanwhile in Ireland, in 1185 Robert du Barry, who defied the phantom army in Ossory, was killed at Lismore, by chiefs whom prince John had insulted.[50] The same year Adam de Hereford married Damietta de Gorram, widow of Ranulf de Broc, establishing the connection between Aghaboe and Woolpit which we saw in Chap.9.

There had been changes in the Blundus family, by 1185, with the death of William Blundus. His widow now styled herself Alice de Hemeford' (Hainford, Norfolk), given to her by Gilbert Blundus as a wedding present; her son was called after her own father, however. Hubert Blundus was born in 1175, and by 1185, when William was dead, he was a ward of the bishop of Ely[51] - Geoffrey Ridell – who received income on his behalf from Ixworth and two other manors. In 1188 Hubert was a landholder in his own right; he married Cecilia de Vere, no less, but by 1189 he was dead, 'exitu terre', like Walter de Calna four years before, but without any strange emphasis. The family still had their connection with Wykes, while in London from the 1170s they were knights, goldsmiths, sheriffs, clerks, aldermen, and even Lord Mayor.[52] At least one was a Templar: Robert Blundus, in Berkshire in 1189.

4. Loss of the Holy Land

In 1185, the Templars were very active in England. Their first site in London, the Old Temple at Holborn Bar, was built of Caen stone like many great

English churches,[53] named for a tributary of the river Fleet, and rented to the Bishop of Lincoln in 1161. The Order moved downstream, near the Thames, on Fleet Street, to Temple Bar at the junction of Fleet Street and the Strand. The New Temple was consecrated in 1185 by Heraclius, the Patriarch of Jerusalem, partly because of its resemblance to the Church of the Holy Sepulchre. The Rotunda of their Paris church was modelled on the Holy Sepulchre, and the New Temple matched the Paris one in all but secondary features - very much like the Old Temple, which was slightly smaller.[54]

On his arrival at Dover, Heraclius was met by John of Oxford.[10] While in England he reminded Henry of his vows to mount a crusade, to atone for the murder of Becket. "He even went as far as to recognise him as heir and lord of Palestine. (The importance of this point appears greater when it is remembered that the kingdom of Jerusalem was looked upon as a fief of the Holy Sepulchre.) But this bribe had no charms for Henry: any little town in France would have been more inviting."[55]

I'm not so sure about that, given the significance of Jerusalem and the Holy Sepulchre which we'll see in Chap.22. But the situation in the Holy Land was so bad that its crown was a poisoned chalice, especially as Henry's exchequer was in trouble. The military Orders were seriously disappointed: the Templar Grand Master and the Prior of the Hospitallers came with Heraclius to back up the request, but the Grand Master died at Verona, after seeing the Pope.[56] Leaving the Holy Land unattended was a mistake, and his successor was Gerard de Ridefort, under whom the Templars had to back Sibylla and Guy de Lusignan for the throne, against the wishes of the Hospitallers and the barons of Palestine.[57] Those choices were disastrous, as we'll see.

74 years later, in 1258, a new bishop of Ely sued the Master of the Templars in England for restoration of rights in New Temple facilities. Two previous bishops *and other predecessors* [my italics] had the use of the Great Hall, the Chapel at its entrance, chambers, a kitchen, pantry, buttery, cellar for wine throughout the year, stable 'and other easements' (TV room, photocopier, phone and fax machine... and I'm only half-joking). When the Ely rights were confirmed, the Master paid £200 compensation for temporary loss of them, a great deal since Ely was deprived of them for more than four years at most.[6] When the Temple was assigned to the Hospitallers in 1337 Ely paid for lamps to burn permanently on the altars, and the Bishop of Ely's Chamber remained

part of it until the Dissolution of the Monasteries. But the 13th century bishop's London palace was in Holborn, close to the Old Temple. If Geoffrey Ridell had such valuable privileges when bishop, perhaps he brought them to the post, and if so, his working relationship with Richard de Hastings was a very strong one.

1185 was also when Richard de Hastings retired and left England. He left with pilgrims for the Holy Land,[58] so he may have travelled with Heraclius. Some suggest that Richard de Mallebeench or Malbank succeeded him as early as 1164, but probably he was a locum, when de Hastings was abroad on royal business,[59] the year of the Constitutions of Clarendon. 1185 is the last possible date for de Hastings's resignation, because later that year the Inquisition into the Templars' property in England was commissioned by the new Master, Geoffrey Fitz-Stephen, whose relatives were in the invasion of Ireland and helped defeat the Flemish in Suffolk.[60]

Sibylla de Lusignan was crowned in Jerusalem in 1186, arranged by the Templars so she could crown her husband, Guy, their supporter[61] - but the end of Christian rule was at hand. A truce with Saladin was broken by Renaud de Châtillon, custodian of the stronghold of Kerak, who attacked a caravan bound for Mecca and captured Saladin's sister. An Arab chronicler wrote, with astronomical metaphors, that Saladin "marshalled his gallant knights and his battalions who swept like a cloud over the face of the earth, making the dust fly up from the earth to the Pleiades and sending the crows, to escape the dust, flying as far as Vega".[62] In Arab lore the Pleiades are the wellspring of life and immortality, the celestial counterpart of the Well of Life whose waters gave the Khidr his green colour (Chap.8). The Koran says the days when they're behind the Sun are "the occasion of great harm to mankind".[63] Vega was still more ominous because in ancient Egypt it was *Ma'at*, the vulture-star, and 'Vega' derives from Arabic *Waki*, as in *al-nasr-al-waki*, the plunging vulture. If the crows flew to the star of the 'carrion king',[64] they would soon be back to feed.

De Châtillon declared himself independent of Guy de Lusignan and refused to return prisoners or booty, but he was with the king and the Masters of the military Orders at the final battle on July 4th, 1187 - the Feast of St. Martin, ironically. Hattin or Hittin, traditionally the site of the Sermon on the Mount, is an ancient volcanic crater near the Sea of Galilee, overlooked by two hills

196

('the Horns of Hattin') and fortified in the past; there are remains of walls on the rim and in it a cistern for catching rainwater[65] - but when the Christians were cut off and made their stand there, no water was to be had. "The Dog-star [Sirius, the scorching] shed its beams on the men clad in iron, and the rage did not go down in their hearts..." In Egypt the 'Dog-days' in July, when Sirius was invisible behind the Sun, brought the Nile floods, but they meant heat and drought elsewhere, worsened by brush fires which the Moslems kindled upwind. Many collapsed from thirst and heat exhaustion before the battle; even so, at one stage the fighting reached Saladin's camp, only to be forced back uphill.

The mounted knights made a charge, led by Raymond III, prince of Galilee; but the Saracens parted before them and closed in behind, cutting them off from the Christians on foot on the hill. Lightly armoured, the Moslems would have paid heavily if they had tried to halt a downhill charge. Instead, using greater manoeuvrability, they had split the Christian force and with numerical superiority, could have dealt with the knights if they turned back to give battle on the flat. Lacking the kamikaze temperament of the Templars (which had led them to disaster shortly before), the knights who found themselves outside the death-trap made good their escape. Raymond was accused of collusion with Saladin, and died, broken-hearted, within the year.[58]

Some say that the Master of the Hospitallers fought his way out of the ensuing mêlée; others that he fell, but the Preceptor of the Templars in Jerusalem, Terric, got clear with two others,[5] to become acting commander in the city.[66] Guy de Lusignan and Renaud de Châtillon were taken alive, and after refusing water to de Châtillon, lest he be bound by Moslem rules of hospitality, Saladin killed him with his own hands, sparing de Lusignan because "kings do not kill kings". 200 Templars, given the choice between death and conversion to Islam, unanimously refused. de Lusignan and de Ridefort were held for ransom: de Ridefort gained release by promising to surrender the Templar castle at Gaza, adding disgrace to blame for mismanaging the battle.

Gérard de Sède claims *documents certains* show de Hastings and Toutes de St.Omer were with the Templars wiped out at Hattin. Since the context is different presumably these aren't the notorious '*documents secrets*' which de Sède, Plantard and others allegedly fabricated for the claimed descent of France's Merovingian kings from Jesus Christ and Mary Magdalene. But de

Sède doesn't name them, so this claim too must be treated with caution. The list of English crusaders (Chap.4) has only one 'Hastings' of uncertain date. Marion Melville says de Hastings *may* have been at Hattin, but gives no evidence for it. If the two former Masters were there, at their age it's not unlikely that they survived to confront Saladin, but there was *another* Otto de St. Omer at Hattin, Otto of Tiberias,[67] so de Sède may have confused them.

"It was believed by the Christians in accordance with the superstitious ideas of those times, that heaven testified its approbation by a visible sign, and that for three nights, during which time the bodies of the Templars remained unburied on the field, celestial rays of light played around the corpses of these holy martyrs." An Arab Christian also recorded it: "a light from heaven spread itself upon the dead for three days, to the shame and blame of the infidels and the glory of the faithful".[68] Similar tales were told about the shrine of St. Edmund, and crusader graves at Lisbon (Chap.4). But if Richard de Hastings fell in battle there, we might wonder what he was carrying.

The Templars were carrying the supposedly True Cross. The Turks boasted of capturing it, but a knight who claimed to have survived the battle said he buried it beforehand. He led a party to recover it, but it couldn't be found. Marion Melville says it's probably still buried there, but later that it was back in Christian hands in 1249.[58]

Although it took only fifteen days to sail from Acre to Marseilles, word of the disaster at Hattin was delayed and didn't reach France and England until October,[68] when Jerusalem was already lost. Hans E. Meyer suggests that the money which Henry II had been putting by for his much-postponed crusade, now at least 30,000 silver marks, was mostly kept in Jerusalem, in care of the Templars, with orders that it wasn't to be used.[69] When Henry wouldn't have the crown of Jerusalem, Heraclius asked in desperation asked for prince John instead. Not wanting that to happen either, Henry packed John off to Ireland, with unfortunate consequences for du Barry and others.

Meyer suggests that before Hattin the money was spent without permission, to meet the new threat from Saladin, and now the campaign had turned to chaos, the main reason for delaying the news was that nobody wanted to carry it. Henry lost the power of speech for several days when the news did reach him, perhaps more due to the loss of his money than the loss of the city.

On September 4th there was an eclipse of the Sun, partial in the UK, total and 'red-hot' at Verona. The path of totality passed just north of Ascalon,[69] and after the claim in 1099 that only solar eclipses that were harmful to Christians (Chap.3), it did nothing to encourage Jerusalem's occupants. The siege began on the 21st, and is described in the *Chronicon Sanctae Terra* - once ascribed to Ralph of Coggeshall, because it was bound with it in one edition, but in the 19th century the two authors were shown to be different, with differences in style and factual contradictions.[70] Its true author is unknown, but in it there's an eye-witness account apparently supplied by still another writer. "Moreover the arrows fell like drops of rain, so that nobody could put up a finger to the defences without risking injury. Truly there was so great a throng of wounded, that all the doctors of the town and the Hospital were scarcely able to remove what was embedded from their bodies. For even the narrator of these things was wounded by an arrow embedded in the middle of the nose, and with the wood removed the iron remains to this day."

We might have known who he really was, because at the foot of the page, below the account of the sacking of the Church of the Holy Sepulchre, there's a damaged inscription *Ricardus...explicit*, "Richard... stated this". If the missing word said Richard *who*, it's gone for good. But also in the 19th century, a man's body was found in the cloister at Coggeshall Abbey, with the tip of an arrow-head still embedded in his nose.[71] It's natural to suppose he's the author of the *Sanctae Terrae* interpolation, since its unknown author reveals he had connections with the Colchester area.

He was striking in his day, over six feet tall when that was unusual. Jane Greatorex suggested he might be Richard de Calna, fascinating, especially if he and de Hastings were in the Holy Land together. Did he sail with de Hastings in 1185, after the untimely death of his elder son, leaving Agnes in charge of his estates? Favourable references to the military orders imply that the writer was Templar or Hospitaller; and since the burial wasn't in the Coggeshall cemetery, presumably *he* wasn't Cistercian.

But if Jane's right, it raises new questions. The defence of Jerusalem was organised by Balian, who took over from the Templar preceptor Terric, but the only knights in the city were two survivors of the break-out at Hattin, like himself. He knighted all suitable males over the age of sixteen, but what about Richard de Calna? In 1187 he was been an old man, 71 at least. Was he discounted because of his age, or did he survive Hattin in spite of it? Perhaps his status was secret, because he was undercover (Chap.22). He'd be lucky to survive a head wound and captivity before he was ransomed - but it could explain his death within two years thereafter.

Perhaps he died at Coggeshall; Templar practice was to be buried anonymously.[72] Jane sent me a copy of a tile, found near the burial, bearing a star, crescent, and dagger whose hilt is a cross, arms not bifurcated, so it's definitely Templar (Fig.13.1).[73] The same cross is on Samson's seal (Chap.6), and upturned crescents and stars on the Banner of St. Edmund (Chap.10). In the late 12th century those were crusader emblems, flanking Richard I on a royal seal.[74] But the de Calnas made them a family logo, and in Chap.15 we'll find the upturned crescent and star on Sibylla's seal in later life. They're also on the seal of William de Cantilupe (Chap.15), to whom the de Calnas were related – the family took over Calne itself in 1222. There was a really bright 'star' that year: Halley's Comet, brighter than the Moon and very red, passed through Boötes, Virgo, Libra and Scorpius, disappearing near Antares.[75]

The tile with its Templar cross, crescent and star strongly suggest that the body in Coggeshall Abbey is Richard's, despite his age in 1187; not being royal Treasurer or the eldest son, he wouldn't be entitled to the arms of his father bishop Nigel but as a knight would have earned his own - perhaps in the Second Crusade. (He wouldn't wear them on his shield, that didn't begin till Richard I's reign.)[76]

The body was surrounded by cockle-shells, the sign of a crusader or of a pilgrim to Santiago de Compostela. It's often said that they mark a pilgrim to the Holy Land, and there was confusion even at the time - Thomas de Coggeshall wore cockle-shells on his crest because he'd been to the Holy Land - but correctly a pilgrim to the Holy Land carried a cross. In mediaeval illustrations pilgrims carry crosses or shells to distinguish where they've been.[77]

After Jerusalem was lost Santiago became a major pilgrim site: the kings of León and Castile, and the monastic house of Cluny, levied tribute on the Moors and brought in French monks, priests and craftsmen to build Burgos and León cathedrals, with hospitals, hospices, monasteries and convents to

Fig. 13.1. Tiles in Coggeshall Abbey cloister near unmarked grave.
Reconstruction by Jane Greatorex, in "Coggeshall Abbey and Abbey Mill".

support pilgrims on the route through northern Spain.   In Spanish the Milky
Way is *El Camino de Santiago*, 'St. James's Way', because there were as many
pilgrims on the road as stars in the sky,[78] and cockleshells and scallops were
emblems of Santiago for centuries.[79]   If Richard de Calna was injured at the
siege of Jerusalem, perhaps he paused at Compostela to recuperate on his
journey home.

After excavations in Yorkshire, forensic scientists reconstructed the face of a
soldier killed at the Palm Sunday battle of 1461, in the Wars of the Roses.   To
their surprise, he'd recovered without infection from a previous facial injury
which severed the roots of a molar and the tongue, 'using instructions handed
down from the Arabs'.[80]   If de Calna had such medical knowledge (Chap.4),
perhaps he applied it to himself.

5. After the Fall

Jerusalem fell in October 1187, and word reached Henry II and prince Richard in France in late October or early November. Richard immediately took the cross, to his father's annoyance, since as heir to the throne he should have asked permission. Between 13th and 21st January 1188 Henry met Philip of France at Gisors, under the great elm, and heard an impassioned plea from the Archbishop of Tyre to mount a new crusade. "In that same hour that the foresaid kings received the cross, the sign of the cross appeared over them in the sky. And when they saw it all were seized with great joy, both clerics and laymen, and rushed in bands to the hanging cross".[5]

It's just like what de Sède says happened there in 1128. For it to happen twice in the same place sixty years apart would be fascinating - but as I can't confirm the first, likely the two have been mixed up, deliberately or accidentally. The 1188 incident is in Benedict of Peterborough above, and Roger de Hoveden in less detail. Apparently it was a coronal aurora, because in England "on the 14th of January, around the last watch of the night, a certain light broke out, of unparalleled brightness and terrible to see, which completely shattered the darkness of the night... as if in the form of a dragon", a common mediaeval description of aurora.[5]

Henry II immediately wrote to Frederick Barbarossa, king of Germany; Bela, king of Hungary; and Isaac Angelus, emperor of Constantinople, seeking safe conduct over their territory for the English and French armies of the Third Crusade.[5] The ambassador he sent with the letter was Richard Barre, Agnes's husband, who reappears out of nowhere in the chronicles. He now had property in Staffordshire, which he'd recently inherited or been renting, because until then he wasn't paying taxes on it in his own name. But at Michaelmas 1187, at the end of September, he was listed as *fugitivus* - missing, if not actually on the run.[81] The county sheriff seized his chattels to pay his annual dues to the crown, but that was obviously a mix-up, implying that Barre had been called away urgently - probably to Henry in Normandy, in response to the disaster at Hattin. And that may be why John of Oxford had turned over his house in Lynn to his nephew, in 1187, with Walter de Calna as witness.[81]

The bishop of Lisieux was now Ralph de Warneville, Treasurer of Rouen Cathedral in the 1160's, and of York in the 1170's, as well as being Henry II's

Chancellor 1173-80.[3]   In April 1181 he succeeded bishop Arnulf.[12]   Ralph and Richard Barre would almost certainly have met previously, during the 1173 rebellion.   Barre's Lisieux duties may have grown in October 1185, when Gilbert de Glanville became bishop of Rochester,[4] but there's no evidence that he was ever active in running the cathedral.   However, the Paris law school (one of the top two) was overseen by monks of Lisieux,[82] and if Barre did that, it would explain how he was known and trusted by the king of France.

My friend Andy Nimmo remarked that what we aren't told here gives us information.   After fourteen years in supposed oblivion, Richard Barre suddenly reappears with enough status to represent the kings of England and France at the same time, though normally they were rivals; and to negotiate, on their behalf, with kings and emperors.   Andy argued that he must have been at the courts of Germany, Hungary and Constantinople, meantime, and perhaps in that order of increasing precedence.   Diceto gives Henry's letters to the three rulers, and in each he's described as *clericus noster familiaris et fidelis*, 'our faithful household clerk', much closer to the royal staff than to Lynn, Salisbury or Lisieux on a regular basis.   It makes him a member of the *privata familia regis*, the inner circle of the king, yet he hadn't been signing royal charters.   Of 160 witnesses to Henry II's charters between 1179 and 1189, only ten, including de Coutances and Ridell, signed fifteen or more of them.[4] Richard Barre didn't sign any.

His near-anonymity till 1187 suggested to Andy that he was on intelligence work - more the province of traders than ambassadors, then, but Barre was clearly a 'mole' in prince Henry's household over the winter of 1172-73. Whatever his main job between 1173 and '87, it was extremely confidential and well rewarded.   Indeed, Jane Greatorex noted that 'familiaris et fidelis' isn't Henry's usual turn of phrase.   He gave no such praise to Walter de Coutances, when he assigned Woolpit to him, calling him simply "my clerk". Perhaps the stress on Barre's faithfulness was because he covered up a big mistake with Agnes, as Bill Ramsay suggested.

Jane suggested that he also stayed loyal to Henry while not being paid (it could be why he missed paying taxes that year).   Henry was under pressure to honour the vows he'd been forced to make after the death of Becket, to support the Templars in Cyprus and to organise a third Crusade.   In 1188 he had to send 300 knights and a naval force, carrying all available Templars from Genoa, Pisa and Venice, and he had still to support another 200 Templars and lead a crusade. In 1189 he had to seize property from supporters, including Richard Toclive (Chap.9) and Geoffrey Ridell, soon before he and Henry both died.[82] The deal for Richard Barre might have be that if he undertook that major trip, he'd be promoted on his return - and indeed he was.

If Barre was preparing to move back to the Justiciary, as he did in 1190, then in 1187 he might have been in Paris or Bologna, the principal law schools of the time. He was resident in Paris for a time in the late 1180s or early 1190s.[83] He could already have been involved in running the Paris school, as above, and the Bishop of Paris described him as 'magister', implying that he'd been there before; and as he wasn't a royal justice in 1176 or 1179,[55] maybe it was time for an update. But there was no chair of civil law in Paris in the 12th century,[1] and he might have been at Bologna when the crisis broke (Chap.14). If so it would be with Henry's approval, and with his previous diplomatic track record he'd be known at the French court as well.

The 1187 events also tell us about Agnes's status then. She wasn't yet lady of Barre's manor, or she could have told the sheriff where her husband was. Presumably, she was still with the de Calnas. Her husband's non-appearance otherwise, 1173-87, in the English records, could mean he was being excused taxes because of service to the crown, like Richard de Calna.

But if de Calna was in Jerusalem, although 71 years old at least - was Agnes with him? He could have left England with de Hastings in 1185, the year that Sibylla was fostered with the Fitz-Bernards, by royal command; no doubt Agnes missed her greatly, but so would young William Barre, and Agnes would rather continue her duties on the de Calna manors, than leave her son or take him to the Holy Land. If she and William were captive in Jerusalem, Richard Barre would want to focus on their ransom, rather than resume his duties as ambassador: although Saladin allowed many Christians in Jerusalem to be ransomed, those who couldn't pay were badly treated and many (men, women and children) were enslaved in Egypt and elsewhere.[57]

Diceto prints the replies of Frederick, Bela and Isaac to Henry II regarding the Crusade, so it seems that Barre completed his mission. However the German records I've traced don't mention his visit, only the papal envoy who came to preach the Crusade about the same time, meeting Frederick in Strasbourg in December 1187. In February Frederick was in Nuremberg, and he took the cross before the end of April.[84]

Reaching Byzantine territory in August 1189, he met trouble - *"autre surprise!"* as a French historian puts it.[85] Isaac Angelus and Frederick were not friends, both claiming to be 'emperor of the Romans', heirs of the Roman empire. Isaac, a close friend of Saladin's, had made alliance with him, imprisoned Frederick's ambassador in Constantinople and demanded, among other things, half of any territory which the crusaders might take back from the Saracens.[86] He claimed the kings of France and England had told him Frederick intended to occupy Constantinople: it would make Richard Barre responsible for the double-cross, or so Isaac wanted Frederick to believe. Frederick swept the Byzantine advance guard aside and continued on his way, only to die in a swimming accident the following June before he reached the Holy Land. We can only guess whether he'd complained about Barre meantime: if so it fell on deaf ears, because Henry II died in July 1189, before trouble with Isaac arose. But when Barre returned to England then, he gave up diplomacy and resumed his legal career.

His Lisieux appointment continued until 1188, at least, until he got back from the Middle East. Perhaps he brought Richard de Calna home to die; we may even glimpse that in 1189, when "two English gentlemen, belonging to the king of England's own household, who were passing through Toulouse, on their return from a pilgrimage to St. James of Compostela" were seized by the earl of Toulouse as hostages.[87] One went to prince Richard, to propose an exchange of prisoners, but Richard refused, with the backing of Philip of France, because pilgrims should pass unmolested. He attacked the Toulouse region, putting him at odds once again with his father.

Between September 30th and October 2nd 1188 Henry II and Philip had been at Gisors again, and this time they disagreed seriously. Some say that the English worsened the incident by hogging the shade of the elm, leaving the French in the hot sunshine; at any rate, the French destroyed it. The incident's called 'the cutting of the elm' but others say Henry encased the tree in iron, then the French then burned it down.[13] De Sède jokes that English anger was due to love of Nature, but more seriously suggests that it marked the breakaway of some English Templars from the Order. He says the Gaelic

205

for 'elm' and 'fire' are the same word, *ullw*, (more accurately, Welsh for ashes; Scots Gaelic doesn't have a 'w') and he invokes 'St. Elmo's fire', coronal displays of static electricity. Casing the tree in iron would earth it, perhaps attracting lightning, but iron imprisons evil spirits - strange after the cross apparition earlier in the year.

In the sky there was another 'grand aurora' on December 20th that year,[88] and a 'night-time illumination after sunset' in spring 1189.[89] By then Henry II's truce with Phillip had folded, and French troops had invaded the disputed territories, joined again by prince Richard's. They gathered on June 9th at Nogent-le-Rotrou (see Chap.24), and after several feints, on July 3rd they attacked Tours, which was exposed because the Loire was unseasonably low. The defenders fired the outskirts, but wind blew the flames into the city and large parts were burned for the second time that century.

Henry was ill: next day he came in a litter to parlay at a Templar house, Colombières, between Tours and Azuay-le-Rideau, but met Phillip on horse-back.[90] "And when the foresaid kings were speaking mouth to ear, the Lord thundered over them, and hurled a lightning bolt between the two, but caused them no injury; and many fled in terror from the place, and all who remained were awed, because the thunder was heard so suddenly, when the shade from no cloud preceded it. Again after a short interval, the two kings met as if to speak, and again thunder was heard greater and more terrible than before, the day remaining pristinely clear. Greatly shaken by that the king of England plunged to the ground from the horse on which he sat, and could not support himself in his surroundings except with his hands. And from then he placed himself wholly in the hands of the king of France, and conceded the above peace, stipulating that the names of those who, on his death, would follow the king of France and count Richard, should be committed to writing and revealed to him. And when that was done, he found the name of his son John written at the head of that list.

"And wondering at that he came to Chinon, and touched inwardly with grief he cursed the day that he was born, and gave the curse of God and his own to his sons, which he wished never to lift, although the bishops and other relig-ious men admonished him wisely to lift it. And being sick unto death, he had himself carried into church before the altar, and there received the communion of the Body and Blood of the Lord, confessing his sins, and he died absolved by the bishops and clergy, in the 35th year of his reign, on the eighth day of the apostles Peter and Paul [6th July, 1189].[91]

Most historians ignore the lightning or play it down, stressing the heartbreak of John's betrayal, but with the emphasis I've put on electrical phenomena, it would be too easy to say it was coincidence or never happened. Richard Barre was at the elm when the cross appeared in 1188, so perhaps he and de Calna were watching from the wings this time. They didn't witness charters Henry issued immediately before and after, though Geoffrey Ridell had returned to England from Henry in March and was back with him near Le Mans at the beginning of June.[13] Hoveden and the other chroniclers say only that the kings met accompanied by 'bishops, archbishops, barons and counts', and that there were bishops and clergy with Henry when he died.[92] But Ridell himself died within weeks, and Richard de Calna died no later than 1189.

Ridell went to Winchester to meet the new king Richard, and died there in August while waiting for him. In September his archdeacon, Richard Fitz-Neal - de Calna's half-brother - became bishop of London, leaving the archdeacon's post vacant.[60] Ely had only one archdeacon at a time, and Richard Barre was appointed in his place the same year.[5] So Barre was never archdeacon under Ridell, despite the connection between them from 1173 at least. Agnes would be about 26 years old, but even if Barre was only 16 in 1166, when he was listed with property in Lincolnshire, (Chap. 6), he would now be 39. (If he really was born c.1130 he would be pushing 60, but I've given reasons to doubt that.) If de Calna died soon after Barre returned to England, perhaps it let Barre take Agnes to Staffordshire at last, to sort out the problems with family property during his absence.

Up in Derbyshire, the Honour of Peverell remained in crown hands and in 1189, soon before his coronation, Richard I gave it to prince John as a present with its surrounding land and titles.[26] Richard may have owed him a favour for joining the list of rebel princes, supposedly bringing on Henry II's death. Nevertheless, if he let John, of all people, have Peveril Castle, perhaps its importance to us was over, or Richard didn't know what it was It was a momentous gift: the resulting unholy alliance between prince John and the Sheriff of Nottingham hardly needs to be retold here, but there was plenty more happening in the 1190s to hold our attention.

One that belongs in this chapter, however, was that in 1192, "In that same year on 14th May at Nogent in Perche lines of soldiers were seen descending to earth from the air, [the modern translation has 'from the sky', but the Latin is *ex aere* - out of thin air, again, as in Chap.16] and there having made extraordinary battles among themselves they suddenly disappeared."[93] 'Nogent' in Perche is Nogent-le-Rotrou, on the river Huisne, where Richard and Philip gathered their armies in 1189 before attacking Tours; the towns took turns to be capital of the region in mediaeval times. It may be coincidence that Richard and Philip followed that route, but it does lend more weight to the tenuous connections with Tours which have previously turned up - see the end of Chap.17.

Chapter Fourteen - THE 1190s: LADY OF THE MANOR

Juxon   Say your goodbyes
(to 'Adela')   To Woolpit, for it's gone, and history
                          Will have it for a pit that once had a village.

~ Glyn Maxwell, *Wolfpit*

1. Letter from Tournai

With the deaths of de Calna, Henry II and Geoffrey Ridell, all in 1189, life
changed out of all recognition for Richard and Agnes.   Richard I now became
king, but his priority was the Holy Land: his coronation was amid prepar-
ations for the Third Crusade.   Foreseeing trouble, Richard ordered that no
Jews attend, but a group demanded to swear fealty to the new king, and were
massacred in the ensuing fighting.   Richard ordered no copycat killings, but
that held only until he left for the Crusade.[1]   Abbot Samson promptly staged
his purge of Bury St. Edmunds, at cost of 57 Jewish lives.   Lynn had a massacre of Jews the same year, fuelled by foreign seamen seeking loot, but though
Lynn was a major port,[2] the 'foreigners' could be from Ely, Wisbech and
Boston.[3] "A man may commit murder in Lynn without fear of the gallows".[4]

Soon after becoming archdeacon of Ely in 1189, Richard Barre received a
letter from his friend Stephan, aka Étienne, abbot of Saint-Geneviève in Paris[6]
and soon to be bishop of Tournai in Belgium.   He linked Bologna to the new
law schools in France,[7] especially Paris, but was also an explicator of natural
law.[8]   He knew Walter de Coutances and Hugh du Puiset, for whose natural
son he obtained holy orders.[9]

"To Richard, archdeacon of Ely.   On your translation from Lisieux to the city
of Ely, it is uncertain to me whether I ought to rejoice or to grieve.   If you
should turn your attention to the principles of oratory, you are translated from
the planet of the Cyprian to the Sun, from the shadows into the light, from
gliding motions to the stability of splendour: this change should be pleasing, if
your move did not mutually separate us.   I beseech it, that you beware in this
transfer, that you do not, as you once said to me jokingly about certain
neighbours in these parts, begin to err in reckoning and wish to celebrate

Pentecost around Easter. I believe that if at any time you should fall into that error, you are made the companion of those about whom the Apostle says: 'But you have been purified, but you have been sanctified, but you have been justified.' [I Corinthians vi, 11.] For what else is to be presumed of an archdeacon, unless that he should be solicitous first of his own salvation, second of those subject to him?

"I wish you so to be moderate between the concerns of the court and merry conversations of colleagues after work, that neither should the former press you down with a heavy burden/great honour, nor should the latter dissipate you with speedier [easy] leisure. You who were beloved by your fellow scholars will now be admired by your fellow curialists. May I say that *curiales* is not from *cruor* [blood], but from *curia* [the court], where sometimes the foolish is held serious, the serious is held foolish, where it is rare for anyone to wish to have an equal, never a superior. Remember a couplet of that poem, which rather in a poetic than prophetic, but nevertheless in a true spirit, was spoken to you by a certain man in your Bolognese hideaway:

> 'You will handle the causes of bishops and the business of kings,
>   Who prepare you for riches and pleasures.'

"Greet for me your lord bishop, legate, chancellor [William de Longchamp], and frequently admonish him that, in this triple position, he acknowledge himself to be the servant of the Trinity, and if he should recognise that he is above men, let him confess that he is below his Creator. I love him because he loves you, although with him the value and joyousness of his reputation and the sublimity of his life commend him as deserving in his own right." [10] [What he deserved will become obvious below.]

Perhaps due to printers' errors, there are several mistakes and missing words in the version attached to Ralph V. Turner's essay on Richard Barre. [11] In particular it omits 'from darkness into the light', mistranslates *lubricis motibus* (smooth or gliding motions) as 'whirring orbits', and introduces a double negative, 'do not... begin to err in reckoning and *not* wish to celebrate Pentecost around Easter', which is wrong.

Stephan's biographer believed that Stephan composed the verse lines in the letter himself, at a farewell *soirée* in Bologna. [9] Apparently it's the only

210

evidence that Richard Barre was at Bologna with Stephan before 1150,[11] 15-20 years older than my idea that he was born in 1147-50. It doesn't even say that Barre *studied* at Bologna - a 'hideaway' sounds more like a teaching post or a sabbatical to me. The school at Bologna was no place for a quiet retreat: all subjects were taught together, with languages, philology, writing, drawing, dialectics, maths, music, astronomy, botany, physiology and medicine taught in the same rooms to pupils of all ages.[9]

Nor does it say Stephan and Richard were students together as young men. Before we even knew about it, Jane Greatorex suggested that Barre was at Bologna, preparing for his return to the judiciary, when recalled to diplomatic service in 1187. If so, Stephan was referring to Barre's recent popularity there. But he was writing from Paris, and his references to 'mutually separating us' and 'joking about certain neighbours in these parts' show Barre had been in Paris recently.

William de Longchamp was not only a bishop but also chancellor of England and a papal legate, hence the bizarre comparison to the Holy Trinity.[12] Stephan uses 'translated' in its literal sense, 'carried from one place to another', but overall he's writing according to the principles of oratory - 'figuratively speaking', in other words.

'The planet of the Cyprian' is Venus. The cult of Aphrodite spread from Phoenicia and her principal shrines were at Cythera and Pathos on Cyprus, which is why Homer calls her 'Cytherean' and 'Cyprian'.[13] Some astronomers still prefer 'Cytherean' to the ungrammatical 'Venusian' or the correct 'venereal', which is used for other things. Stephan knew the classical rôles and symbolism of the planets, which he invoked in sermons and in poetry.[9] Although Venus can be seen in daylight if you know just where to look, it's the morning and evening star, generally seen in twilight. Reading between the lines, as Stephan bids us, 'it's as if you have moved from the planet of twilight to the Sun, from the shadows into the light'. We're hardly likely to find more explicit reference to the green children - but see the chapter end.

'From gliding motions to the stability of splendour'. In Ptolemaic astronomy the planets moved around the Earth in circular paths on crystalline spheres, but to account for their observed motions they had to follow epicycles, circles superimposed on circles. The longer observations continued, the more epicycles

had to be added – whirring orbits, indeed. But grammatically, 'the stability of splendour' refers not to Earth but to the Sun - more than 300 years before Copernicus put the Sun at the centre of the Solar System. Neoplatonism put the Sun at the centre, but Giordano Bruno went to the stake for that in 1600.[14] It's remarkable to find it openly expressed in 1190, though the idea that Mercury and Venus circled the Sun, which circled the Earth, was widely discussed – by John of Oxford among others.[15]

"... do not, as you once said to me jokingly about certain neighbours in these parts, begin to err in reckoning and wish to celebrate Pentecost around Easter". In a footnote J. Desilve writes, 'The canon law removed the danger of impromtu Lents by requiring every priest to learn the system of ecclesiastical calculation',[10] but that's not very helpful, especially since Barre wasn't a priest. Stephan was interested in the calendar and the motions of the planets - he wrote a poem about them as a young man - but Tournai clerics were often uncertain of dates, even which days were Sundays.[9]

Pentecost began as a Jewish harvest festival, fifty days after the Passover; the dates of Easter and Whitsun are set by a complex formula starting with the first Full Moon after the Vernal Equinox, with a nineteen-year cycle of modifications explained in the Preface to the Book of Common Prayer, approximating to the 18.61 year cycle of the lunar nodes (Chap.12.) Different formulae in Christian churches varied by up to eight days, but fifty days would take some doing. English practise was standardised in 669 AD, and by 1190 even Irish churches had fallen into line with it. On the continent the new year normally began at Easter, but in Britain it generally was at Christmas or January 1st; neither explains a difference of fifty days, nor why it would interest jurists like Richard Barre or Stephan.

The Julian calendar then in use had too many leap years, and was gradually moving out of phase with the seasons. By 1190 it was about a week ahead of the true date; Roger Bacon highlighted the problem in an impassioned letter to the Pope in 1267, but was ignored.[16] But, although he exaggerates the difference, Stephan apparently knows about it and warns Barre to take it into account in any calculations he makes.

The Biblical quotation is even stranger, unless Stephan deliberately uses it out of context. The full text reads, "Know ye not that the unrighteous shall not inherit the kingdom of God?   Be not deceived: neither fornicators, nor idolaters, nor adulterers, nor effeminate, nor abusers of themselves with mankind, nor thieves, nor covetous, nor drunkards, nor revilers, nor extortioners, shall inherit the kingdom of God.   And such were some of you: but ye are washed, but ye are sanctified, but ye are justified in the name of the Lord Jesus, and by the Spirit of our God." Stephan appears to be saying that if Barre falls into error in his reckoning of the calendar, he will put himself *into* the company of those who have renounced the sins of the flesh - the clergy. The hidden message seems to be, 'Stick to true astronomical dates, keep track of the Moon and don't take holy orders'.   It's consistent with Stephan's *Summa Decreti*, published at Orléans in the 1160s, which opposes divorce for any reason including taking holy orders.[10]   But the movements of the Moon could be relevant to our story (Chap. 22), and it looks as if he was in Richard Barre's confidence.

(Stephan was no stranger to secrecy. In 1181 Philip of France sent him on a mystery mission to Toulouse, during the crusade against Cathar heretics ordered by pope Alexander.   In a letter he described the ruin of the countryside, adding that he was under orders to seek out a certain individual in the city, and "I am here for still another reason besides what I've told you; but keep the same silence on that too." Whatever he did was so important that the marshal of the palace, "a very influential person in the court of France", was in charge of Saint-Geneviève meantime.)

Moving from Lisieux to Ely would put Barre *closer* to Tournai, but Stephan was writing from Paris, and he didn't know in 1190 that he would be bishop of Tournai in 1192.   Presumably he forgave Barre's support of Henry II , though he met Becket in 1166 and was incensed by his death till 1175 at least.

2. New Trouble in England

Having returned to England in 1189, Barre was a roving justice by 1190: "you will be admired by your fellow curialists".   Though required to do little at Lisieux, at Ely he was the only archdeacon (salary £100 per annum), mainly responsible for the upkeep of church property and collection of tithes, but he also appointed the prior of Barnwell and various vicars, and dealt with lay people affected by canon laws: matrimonial (degrees of affinity, accusations

213

of incest and adultery) and testamentary, mostly probate of wills. He also heard cases of defamation, and theft, if sacrilegious, and the archdeacon's court had power of excommunication. His successors appointed the Master of Glomery, overseer of grammar schools linked to the University.[17] But much of the work was assigned to a deputy, 'the Official', and Barre must have been away from Ely for much of the time.

Shortly after Richard took the post in 1189, William de Longchamp was consecrated as bishop of Ely on December 31st, enthroned before many other bishops soon after. "It then came to his and the bishops' notice, that the tomb of his predecessor Geoffrey [Ridell] had been violated, because the episcopal ring, which he had on his finger in the shelter of the tomb, had secretly been removed. Therefore mounting the pulpit the bishops placed the violators, whether doing it or consenting to it, under anathema."[18] The theft came to light as Ridell was being reinterred by the High Altar, on the far side from 'le Boiis', the miraculous fetters of Brithwald (Chap.4). If Longchamp knew who did it, he wasn't saying; but it's very interesting (Chap.22).

In 1190 Longchamp was at Winchester when Barre was challenged again over the income from Hurstbourne Priors. Alan de Husseborn had obeyed the injunction to 'perpetual silence' concerning the church, but now the case was renewed by Thomas de Husseborn, a justice who may also have been a prebend of Salisbury.[19] He first appears as a justice in 1185, when he heard two cases involving Abbot Samson.

The case was heard by Geoffrey de Lucy (Chap.10), now bishop of Winchester. Dean of St. Martin's-le-Grand in 1174, when the green children were 'people of the Land of St. Martin', he'd been a justice since 1179 and an ambassador twice,[20] to an unknown destination in 1179 and to Normandy in 1184, so he and Richard Barre now had still more in common. Geoffrey agreed that Thomas had a claim on the church, but the charters of Henry I and II were again inspected and Barre's prebend was confirmed. The papal letters weren't cited explicitly, but William de Longchamp was present not only as bishop of Ely but as papal legate, appointed for England, Scotland, Ireland and Wales, at the request of Richard I the previous year.[21,22]

The other primate at the hearing was Peter de Leia, bishop of St. David's 1176-1198, whom Giraldus Cambrensis considered "a poor creature without

an atom of spirit".[23]   If so, he was well out of his league that day, but it's
curious that his surname was sometimes attached to land of Richard Barre's,
as we'll see in Chap.15.   But Barre and Thomas de Husseborn sat together in
many royal courts in 1996-98,[24] including a dispute of Barre's relative, Richard
de Siffrevast, with the Templars over land in Berkshire.   Barre was now
better off: though he kept the Hurstbourne rights through the 1190s, he
restored the Badburghe church to Waltham with Longchamp's permission,
and gave Hurstbourne back to Salisbury later.

Back in Bury, Samson can't have disliked the Holy Land all that much, if he
actually went there in exile: as we've seen, there's doubt about that.   He'd
volunteered to go on Crusade with Henry II,[22] and repeated the offer to
Richard I in 1190.[25]   Richard refused it, because John of Oxford already had
his name down, as bishop of Norwich, and they shouldn't be out of the
country at the same time.[26]   This was well thought on, but John of Oxford
wasn't gone long.   Having raised a substantial contribution for the Crusade,
he was robbed in Burgundy, had to appeal to the Pope for relief from his vow
and returned to England in temporary poverty.[22]

But William de Longchamp was made Lord Protector of England, and within
the year had overstepped his powers.   Even in 1190, according to Benedict of
Peterborough, "He came to abbeys and priories, and other religious houses
entertaining visitors, with so great a surplus of men and horses and dogs and
birds, that a house in which he was billeted for one night could scarcely regain
its former condition in less than three years afterwards.   Truly he carried off
the churches, lands and possessions of laymen and clerics alike, which he
either distributed to his nephews, clerks and servants, or more blameworthily
kept for himself, or squandered in bizarre ways."[27]

He was allegedly of peasant stock, and of him Walter Map quoted Claudian,
"Nothing is harder than the lowly whenever he riseth to high degree".[28]   He
arrested Geoffrey Clifford, when he came to take up his archbishopric in York
(Chap.13);   that gave prince John an excuse to intervene, as Clifford's half-
brother.   Longchamp's excesses in the Protector's rôle caused the citizens of
London and the barons to depose him and appoint John instead.   John was
made chief Justice, and Longchamp had a fit when he heard about it.[22]   In
October 1191 Richard sent Walter de Coutances back to take over the
justiciary and restore order, though John remained Lord Protector.[29]   de

Coutances excommunicated Longchamp, who then got a hostile reception at Ely and suspended all church activity in the diocese. When Eleanor of Aquitaine visited property of hers in 1192, she found the people in misery, the dead lying unburied, etc., and successfully appealed for all excommunications to be lifted.[22]

Richard Barre witnessed a declaration of Longchamp's in April 1191, as did John de Alençon, archdeacon of Lisieux.[30] He was at trials in Northamptonshire in January 1191, Ipswich in July, Norwich in September, Cattishall in October, then Cambridge and Huntingdon;[31] nevertheless, a Richard Barre of England was in the Holy Land in 1191, as was William de Birmingham,[32] of Barre's feudal superiors. If ours, he did well to get there so late in the year, because the Mediterranean was dangerous to shipping from mid-September, closed from 10th November to 10th March, due to storms.[33]

Richard I marched on Jerusalem in summer 1192, but had to sign a truce with Saladin in early September. Small parties of crusaders were allowed to visit the sacred sites, including the Holy Sepulchre; but if Richard Barre was among them, following up whatever Richard de Calna was doing in 1187, then he got home *very* quickly, because he held trials at Ipswich at Michaelmas, September 29th.[34] Richard I sailed for home in October, and soon afterwards was reported missing (actually in captivity in Austria). It didn't take John long to bid for power, trying to convince the justices, nobles and church that Richard was dead. But Walter de Coutances repelled a French and Flemish invasion fleet supporting John, and the arrival of the bishop of Salisbury with word from Richard in captivity settled the question.[35]

Meanwhile, after the mystery of his whereabouts in the 1170's and '80's, for the rest of his life Richard Barre was highly visible, starting with trials at Huntingdon again in 1193.[36] He would be involved in the struggle for power: with Eleanor's backing, the justices remained loyal to Richard, and having ousted Longchamp, blocked John's moves to seize the throne. The bishops turned against de Longchamp, with the single exception of Geoffrey de Lucy; Hugh du Puiset, briefly chief justice before ousting by Longchamp in March 1190,[37] had received custody of Windsor Castle in 1191 and reluctantly passed it to John in 1192; John's Welsh mercenaries were besieged there in 1193 by the justices, who also took Peveril Castle and Wallingford,[31] while du Puiset besieged Tickhill.[38]   So he would have been in touch with Barre then, if not before (Chap.12), though I haven't found Barre by name in the conflict.

Abbot Samson played a big part in raising the money for Richard I's release, while refusing to let the shrine of St. Edmund be touched.   When Richard returned in 1194 he went straight to Bury to express his thanks,[25] spending 'scarcely a day' in London beforehand.   (The next priority was to appoint a new sheriff of Nottingham, William de Briwerre, who farmed the Honour of Peverell for the next six years.[39])

Meanwhile, "the heirs of Richard de Caune" held part of Bardwell, near Wykes, in the early 1190's.[40]   Although Sibylla's father died in 1185, another Walter de Calna, presumably his son, witnessed many of John of Oxford's grants between 1186 and 1198, e.g. to the Priories of Blythburgh and Eye.[41-45] In 1186 he witnessed the founding of Leiston Abbey[46] and grants by John de Gray, the new bishop of Norwich, in 1200-14.   He may have been clerk to John de Gray in 1218;[47] as a clerk to the king he paid various royal grants and expenses[48] in 1242-43 but he has no direct part in our story.

He was one of lord Richard's heirs, though, and another was his brother Richard, who later fell out with his grandmother Letitia, over land in North Weald which his father had returned to her.[49]   This Richard de Calna was knighted: he and his wife Isabel settled in Oxfordshire.[50]   Peter de Calna was sacristan of Norwich in 1236,[51] and if he was another heir, their careers probably give their order of birth: Richard the knight, Walter the clerk, Peter the churchman.   Their five-year-old sister may have gone to the Fitz Bernards in 1185 because the first Richard and his wife were growing old, while her elder brothers were making their way in the world and couldn't yet provide a suitable home for Sibylla as an orphan.

After lord Richard's death, the heirs in Bardwell didn't stay there long: though there were mills at Wykes, the de Calnas weren't named in a 1204/5 action against mill-owners there.[52]   Knettishall had always been rented out, and Wykes was too, soon after William of Newburgh's investigation into the green children.

I've said why I believe Ralph of Coggeshall, rather than William of Newburgh's statement that the children arrived in the reign of Stephen, who died in 1154. We don't know whether William visited Woolpit, but his enquiry has to be after word about the children spread, perhaps in the late 1180s or early 1190s. Perhaps the lid of secrecy came off when Gilbert Foliot died in 1187; maybe getting the girl talked about at Coggeshall worked too well, because the de Calnas underestimated Ralph's contacts. He gave away the abbey's land in London, near another St. Martin's church, to St. Peter's monastery in Gloucester, where Gilbert Foliot previously was Abbot.[53] St. Peter's was Augustinian, like Barnwell, where Ralph began his career, and Newburgh Abbey, which now sent an investigator to Suffolk from North Yorkshire - maybe not William himself, but a representative.

William wrote in 1195, "And truly I was in doubt over this for a long time ... until I was so overwhelmed by the weight of so many witnesses (and of such quality) that I was forced to believe." Odd that there were so many, to an event supposedly over 40 years before. The historian Martin Jenkins suggested to me that in village memory the bad times had run together, so the children arrived "during the troubles", "when the army was here" - and William took it for the razing of the area in the civil war, not the 1173 Flemish invasion. James Bentley agreed, because he recalls old Londoners running together the Blitz and the Zeppelin raids of the First World War.

Within three years of his own death, perhaps William himself was confused; but he was right on the ball in other respects, as we've seen, so I suspect confusion (deliberate or accidental) by his sources. If told of the boy's burial at Coggeshall Abbey and a connection with Cressing Temple, both founded by Stephen and Matilda, he might assume it all happened in their time. But if told it was more recent, and he didn't believe it, maybe he was misled by the witnesses - and since they had details of the bishop's hearing, presumably those witnesses included the de Calnas themselves.

They also told him that the girl married a man *apud Lennam*, 'living at Lynn', and last was heard of some years before. The best lies contain a large part of the truth - and William describes the 1190 Lynn riots in detail. If he or his agent went there looking for (as they thought) an old woman, but couldn't find her, no doubt she was caught in the fighting and killed.

Because she was no longer green, and William didn't know her true age, Agnes might have misled him herself, if they met. But she and Richard were in Staffordshire by then, at Little Barr manor, near Handsworth.   In 1199 there was an assize to decide whether their (legitimate) son William had unjustly uprooted a fence or hedge 'to the harm of the freehold of Henry de Perry'.   The jury found the fence had blocked a path by which Henry accessed his woods, and Henry was happy with the demolition.[54]   But it was "after the second coronation of king Richard", following his return from captivity in 1194.[55]   William was legally adult, at least fourteen then - and Richard and Agnes were in residence, though sub-tenants of Richard's elder brother Robert.

The son's name, William de Barre, was abridged to 'William Dare'.   A long search turned up only one other possible use of it: in 1201, William Darri or Derri was a witness twice in Northamptonshire.[49]   Two similar names, Darre (short for de Arra) and Daire, are obviously different families.   So 'Dare' for de Barre was shorthand, or a version William affected as a young man and then abandoned.

In 1194 Richard Barre was with Richard I in Normandy, and by then he was a senior justice, holding his own court with other justices in support at Norwich,[56] and chairing courts in Berkshire, Cambridge and Huntingdon, Northamptonshire, Sussex, Devon, Dorset, Somerset, and many other places,[57-59] including Westminster itself in 1199-1200.[60]   If he was in any secret which required moving about the country, he was in the ideal job to do it without arousing suspicion.   In 1197 he was again with Richard in Normandy, and as archdeacon of Ely he was sent back to sort out a delay in electing a new bishop.[61]   He also had land in Cambridgeshire, rented to Jewish holders.[62]   The same year, he was in East Anglia investigating sale of corn to Flanders in defiance of a royal embargo; sometime after that, the Pope appointed him a mediator along with new bishop Eustace of Ely and the prior of Barnwell[63] - whom Barre appointed, as archdeacon.[17]   In spring 1198 Eustace made him attorney for all pleas concerning Ely, especially those involving abbot Samson - with whom he may have had a special under-standing, as we'll see.   In his essay Ralph Turner says that he left the judiciary after 1198,[11] but that's not the case.

3. Sibylla and Agnes

Meanwhile, the orphaned Sibylla de Calna was growing up. Her husband John Fitz-Bernard, also a minor when Henry II arranged their marriage, is first listed in Essex and Hertfordshire in 1194,[64] taking over family property in Surrey in 1196. When she was 17, in 1197, the Barres and the Fitz-Bernards reclaimed the two women's inheritance in Aston. The exact date is uncertain, due to vagueness about prior Walter's dates.[65] But in 1197, '98 or even '99, there was more to it than meets the eye.

Near Little Barre there was more than one Aston/Easton/Estone, and another northeast of Peveril Castle. But Aston Clinton in Buckinghamshire was 'escheated' to Richard Barre on the death of William de Clinton in 1193 or 1194,[66] with the estate's duty of 'sergeanty', service to the crown which couldn't be delegated,[67] in this case supplying the royal larder.[56] Normally when a property was escheated the holder had died childless or been convicted of treason; in this case the heir was a minor till 1219.[68]

Richard Barre was put in charge of Aston Clinton by Walter de Coutances, now archbishop of Rouen. The rights which Walter de Calna left to Agnes and Sibylla were similarly entrusted to the prior of Merton; and their claim seemed to bypass Bucks entirely and segue into rows about the Aston on the Staffordshire/Warwickshire border, though neither woman seems ever to have lived there. The two Astons were connected, because the church in the Warwickshire one was donated to the priory of Newport Pagnell in Bucks more than sixty years before.[26,69] William de Calna witnessed the inspection and confirmation of the presentation in the 1190's,[65] and a subsequent dispute about it was won by the prior of Newport in 1220.[70]

There were constant disputes over the Warwickshire Aston, held for a time by Adam de Cocefeld.[71] There is a Suffolk Cockfield near Thorpe Morieux, south of Bury St. Edmunds, and another Cocefield/ Cockfield next door to Aston on the north,[72] and as with the two or more Astons, legal actions about the two Cockfields are mixed up. The Warwickshire land passed eventually to Adam's widow and then back to the crown.[73] Adam was the son of Robert, who died in 1191, great-grandson of a previous Adam de Cockfield.[74] Richard Barre was Adam's guardian and Abbot Samson challenged him for custody in 1198, before the bishop of Ely, who ruled for Barre.[49] If the previous disputes between Samson and Ridell were a cover, it must have been effective for Samson still to be keeping up the act nine years after Ridell's death.

Earl's Hall Manor, in Cockfield, was held in 1167 by Aubrey de Vere, who married Euphesia, the daughter of William de Cantilupe;[71] and Samson had a seal at the time on which he holds a fleur-de-lis (Chap.6), a de Cantilupe emblem (Chap.15). Were Adam and Samson both related to the de Cantilupes, hence Samson's challenge? When Adam died, before 1209, his daughter Nesta was made Samson's ward; he assigned her care to Thomas de Burgh, whom she later married.[71] But if Samson was related to the de Cantilupes, that connects him with the de Calnas, and Sibylla de Calna used the fleur-de-lis in the same way (Chap.15).

I found that seal of Samson's described in Birch's "Catalogue of Seals in the British Museum", as it then was, referring to a reproduction in Richard Yates's "History and Antiquities of the Abbey of St. Edmund's, Bury".[74] The major Glasgow libraries didn't have it, and in the copy at the National Library of Scotland, the plate of seals was missing! It didn't seem to have been removed, rather not bound into the book in the first place. Bury St. Edmunds Record Office sent me a copy (Fig. 6.3).

But in the British Library catalogue (as it is now) the seal is 'lxxi.90', and the impression they have of it doesn't match the plate in Yates's book. It's more complete, with more of the surrounding lettering visible. Samson's face-on instead of angled right, so both arms of his low-backed chair are visible, likewise its feet; he holds the sceptre between finger and thumb, instead of clasped in his hand; there are no stripes on the orb in his other hand. The inscription begins SIGILLUM SANCTI EAD... (EADMUNDI, presumably). But on Yates's version there are only three letters, 'RIS' (Fig. 6.3), which could be part of *Christus* or *Christi*, as on the damaged reverse of one Templar Grand Master's seal.[74] But on the BL copy those letters are either RIS or RUS, at the end of a word, but on Yates's they seem to begin one. Latin dictionaries offer only *risus*, laughter, and other words derived from it, or else *riscus*, 'a window within a wall', a trunk or a clothes-press.

If Samson had a seal inscribed RISUS ABBATIS SAMSONIS you'd expect it to be for 'Friends and Family', not official documents. On the BL seal

221

impression the two heads on the chair's arms look canine, and the feet could be paws, but in Yates's drawing it's definitely a duck's head behind him, with a cheerful expression as if inviting a visual pun, like the ones with pikes, wolves and (possibly) lambs. *Anas*, a duck; *anus*, an old woman; *agnus*, a lamb... surely not! 'Duck of God, who taketh away the sins of the world', seems far too irreverent. But this was long before Henry III clamped down on the Bury bakers putting the *Agnus Dei* on their loaves ... and the word 'anus' was used by the poet Horace to designate one very special old woman, the seeress of Cumae, whose books of prophecy were kept in the temple of Jupiter Capitolinus in Rome and consulted in national emergencies by command of the Senate. Her proper name and title was Sibylla, the Sibyl. Agnes and Sibylla, Sibylla and Agnes... And Yates's version of the orb may be significant too (Chap.22).

With her experience 'in ministerio' Agnes would have been a competent lady of the manor, and it seems that Robert Barr increasingly turned over Little Barr to Richard and Agnes. Though the parish remained in Robert's name, as time went on court cases about it were increasingly directed to Richard; eventually it passed to Richard's son and grandson (Chap.15), suggesting that Robert and his wife were childless.

Such a lady's duties were spelled out by Christine de Pisan, over a century later.[75] "A slightly different manner of life from that of the baronesses is suitable for ladies and demoiselles living in fortified places or on their lands outside of towns. Nevertheless, since, like barons, knights, squires, and gentlemen must also travel and follow the wars, their wives, when they are wise and capable, should be able to manage their families' affairs. The women spend much of their lives in households without husbands. The men are usually at court or in distant countries. So the ladies will have responsibilities for managing their property, their revenues and their lands. In order for such a woman to act with good judgement, she must know the yearly income from her estate. She must manage it so well that by conferring with her husband, her gentle words and good counsel will lead to their agreement to follow a plan for the estate that their revenues permit. This plan must not be so ambitious that at year's end they find themselves in debt to their retainers or other creditors. Surely there is no disgrace in living within one's income, however small it may be. But it is shameful to live so extravagantly that creditors daily shout and bellow outside the door, some even raising clubs and threatening violence. It is also terrible to have to resort to extortion from one's own men and tenants. The lady or demoiselle must be well informed about the rights of domain of fiefs and secondary fiefs, about contributions, the lord's rights of harvest, shared crops, and all other rights of possession, and the customs both local and foreign. The world is full of governors of lords' lands and jurisdictions who are intentionally dishonest. Aware of this, the lady must be knowledgeable enough to protect her interests so that she cannot be deceived. She should know how to manage her accounts and should attend to them often, also superintending her agents' treatment of her tenants and men. If they are being deceived or harassed beyond reasonable bounds, both she and her husband would suffer. As for penalties against poor people, she should be more compassionate than rigorous.

"Farming also is this good housekeeper's domain. In what weather and in what season the fields should be fertilised; whether the land is moist or dry; the best way to have furrows run according to the lay of the land; their proper depth, straightness and parallel layout; and the favourable time for sowing with seed suited to the land - all these she must know. Likewise, she must know about vineyards if the land lies in a region where there are grapes [as there were in England, during those years of heightened solar activity]. She requires good labourers and supervisors in these activities, and she should not hire people who change masters from season to season. It is a bad sign if workers are always on the move. Nor should she hire workers who are too old, for they will be lazy and feeble, nor too young, for they will be frivolous.

"She will insist that her labourers get up early. If she is a good manager she won't depend on anyone else to see to this but will arise early herself, put on a cloak, go to the window, and watch there until she sees them go out, for labourers usually are inclined to laziness. She should often take her recreation in the fields to see just how they are working, for many willingly stop raking the ground beyond scratching the surface if they think nobody notices. There are plenty of workers capable of sleeping in the shade of a willow tree in the field, leaving the workhorses or the oxen to graze by themselves, caring only that by evening they can say they have put in their day. And for that the good housekeeper will be alert."

(Or as 'Tom Parch' says in *Wolfpit*, dropping out of a line of reapers, "Let's have no quarrel. God's an elevener, and opens up his box of lunch when I do.")

"With that, when the grain is ripening in the month of May, she won't wait for the season, but will prepare for August by engaging good, strong, diligent fellows, to be paid in money or in grain. And when it comes to the time when they're so employed, she will take care or have care taken that they leave nothing behind them, or work any other deceptions which such people well know how to practise and don't find beneath them. As with other labourers she will willingly rise early in the morning [to supervise], because in the household where the mistress spends morning in bed it's hard to get anything done. Keeping an eye on her entire domestic enterprise will give her plenty to oversee, for indifference reigns where supervision won't be bothered.

"Sheep must be put to pasture on schedule, paying attention to how the shepherd governs them and that he's a good master, and that he's not spiteful, because those will let the sheep die to spite the master and mistress. Therefore, she must make sure that the sheep are kept clean, protected from too much sun and rain, protected from mange and wild beasts. And she herself will often go to the roof, if she is wise, or send one of her women to see how the sheep are managed, and thus the shepherd will be more attentive than if all he had to do was report.

"She will think on lambing time well in advance, and take great care of the lambs, because they often die for lack of forethought. She will take care of their feeding, and be present at the shearing, when the right time comes.

"If her lands are in a warm, humid country with abundant meadows, she will keep many horned animals; and if she harvests more oats than she can sell, she will feed them to the cattle in byre to sell them later at great profit. If she has woods, she will have a breeding stable there which can turn a tidy profit if well run. During the winter when labour is cheap, she will have her workers cut her willow and hazel groves, to make vineyard stakes for sale in season, and then she will set them to woodcutting for heating the house, or to clear some field. And if the weather is too bad out of doors she will make them thrash in the granary, and thus never leave them idle, because there's nothing worse in a household than lazy staff.

224

"Likewise she will instruct her chambermaids to take care of the animals, of preparing food for the labourers, and of the dairy, and to weed the gardens and hunt for herbs even if it soils them to the knees; that's their job. She, her daughters and attendants, will make cloth, separating the wool, sorting it out, and putting the finer yarn aside to make clothes for her husband and herself, or to sell; thicker yarn will be used for small children, serving women and workmen. She will stuff bedclothes with large balls of wool, and she will have hemp grown by the farmers so that her maids can spin it in the evenings and work it into coarse linen. And all these and similar tasks, which it would take too long to describe, are the business of management in the lowlands, and she who is more diligent in them, however great she is, will be more than wise and will be highly praised. The wise manageress sometimes brings in more profit than the rents and incomes of the land itself... Of such a woman one might well repeat the praise with which the Book of Solomon describes the wise woman."

All this and motherhood as well!   Admittedly, with young William legally adult in 1194 he might become less of a burden, and they don't seem to have had any other children - though she and Richard had young Adam de Cockfield to raise, and his early death as a young father must have been a blow to them.

Agnes would have extra duties if she was in charge of the mill at Aston[72] - and she and Richard might have had unusual uses for it (Chap.22). But she and Richard also had responsibilities above their social station, which came to light in 1293, when their descendant lord John de Barre was asked by what right he held a major court on Little Barr manor, likewise a fair and market, and how he came to exercise the rights of 'gallows and waif'.[72] (Waif was the right to seize stray animals and lost property, not people.[76])   John replied that he had those rights by virtue of a rent of 20 pence a year, which he paid to the Prior of the Knights Hospitallers, the head of that Order in England. On the strength of that John de Barre held two courts a year, and the family had done so since the reign of king John, i.e. since the time of Richard and Agnes.

One of their neighbours had given the 'advowson' of St Mary church, Handsworth, to the Hospitallers, who appointed a new priest there in 1200. Around 1212 the Order gave half those rights back, and the other half to Lenton Priory, founded by the first William Peverell. But the rights at issue in 1293 could only have gone with land, and in 1242-43 the neighbours held Handsworth from the Prior of the Hospitallers.[49]

Major courts were held by either the feudal lord of the county or the sheriff ('shire-reeve', the king's representative).[76]   Perhaps, because of Richard Barre's status as a justice, in the 1200s the Prior let Barre exercise his legal rights in the area.   When Richard Barre died, William should have relinquished the court, market, fair and waif rights, because he wasn't qualified to hold courts and it had been only an ad hoc arrangement.   But he didn't, and the family kept their control of events on the manor until 1293, when a jury returned the rights to the crown.[72]

But it wasn't all work and no play, since they included the right to hold markets and fairs, particularly cheerful when they coincided with the major festivals of Christmas, Twelfth Night, Valentine's Day, Easter, All Fools' Day, May Day, Midsummer Eve, Saint Swithun's Day, Lammas, Michaelmas, Halloween and St. Catherine's Day.   Many still included pre-Christian traditions, and the colour green featured prominently.   At Christmas, when the hall was decked with evergreens including holly and mistletoe, the First Foot was dressed in green, carried a green bough and had to be the first to cross a green line on the floor.   On May Day the hall would be decked with 'The May', greenery and flowers.[77]   As well as Maypole and Morris dancing there would be backgammon, chess, billiards and Nine Men's Morris, played as a board game or in a maze (also known as Troy Town).

On May Day all food and drink was green: parsley, lettuce, spinach, peas, endive, fennel and green gage plums were served with fruited beef and green peppermint rice, washed down by green cider with 'lamb's wool' apple and cream floating on it.   Apple slices in minted green whipped cream, in a leaf-shaped bowl, were followed by Jack-in-the-Green gingerbread figures decorated with wreaths of parsley or lime icing.   If they had arrived at Maytime instead of harvest the children might not have starved for so long. But the annual feast must have aroused memories for Agnes; and she must have thought of her brother when the King and Queen of the Bean were picked to head the revels on Twelfth Night.   The Feast of St. Agnes on January 21st, which was an annual holiday for women in England, would also have special meaning for her.

Some of Richard Barre's court cases are also revealing. In 1199, he judged a woman named Galiena, accused of sorcery by another Agnes, the daughter of a Norwich merchant. He was disturbed by the case, or feelings were running high in Norwich, because he adjourned it first to Thetford, then to Westminster, where Galiena 'proved' herself innocent through trial by ordeal with a hot iron.[60] (I did say that the green children were relatively well treated.) The accuser's name would draw Barre's attention to dangers his Agnes could be in, even now, and explain his misgivings.

In the Hertfordshire Court Rolls for 1200, one Agnes of Torlee in Oxfordshire accuses Richard Barre of breaking into her bed chamber to steal ten silver marks and a coffer. Richard says it's all malice on Agnes's part, aimed at Alexander Barre (Chap.10). At that point, the record is struck out and a new version substituted, in which the accused is not Richard Barre but Richard Lefrere,[49] and everything to do with Alexander Barre is sweetness and light. Maybe it made sense if you were there at the time. Richard's clerk John appears in the record this year, though not in the same context - luckily for him, if the original naming of Richard Barre was, literally, a clerical error. As a senior justice he would not be amused to be wrongly named as the accused.

In later chapters, we'll look at some other things which Agnes Barre could be running at home in Staffordshire. Unfortunately the whole area of Great and Little Barr was extensively developed during the industrial revolution, and there are few traces if any of its mediaeval past. The older Ordnance Survey maps have an 'Old Hall Farm', south-south-west of Barr Beacon, and a moat to the north of it, but I couldn't trace the farm back beyond the late 17th century, when it was owned by the Lord of the Manor of Barr - Great Barr, apparently.[78] Older maps showed nothing in the area except the Handsworth Church of St. Margaret, which does go back to the mediaeval period.[79]

A map drawn between 1769 and 1775 made things a lot clearer.[80] The two Astons in the area were north-east of Barr Beacon and to the south. Little Barr later merged with Perry Barr, so if Agnes's land was adjacent to it her rights would have been in Aston-juxta-Birmingham, to the south of the Barr manors. The moat is on the wrong side of Great Barr to have been on Richard and Agnes's property. 'The old moated mansion' of Perry Hall was the manor-house of the earls of Warwick in the 15th century, after Little Barr merged with Perry (Chap.17), so it might have been Richard and Agnes's.[81]

227

By 1473 it was a private house separate from the manor, apparently rebuilt in 1576, but the 1798 owner wouldn't let antiquarians inspect it, nor tell them its history.[82]   Its grounds became a park in 1929, the house was demolished and the moat became a boating pond.   In the other Aston, the Hall survives but dates only from the third quarter of the 17th century.[72]

4. Fire over London

I haven't found any mysterious appearances or disappearances connected with Barr and Aston, although the Sun was extremely active through the 1190's.   William of Newburgh recorded two big aurorae, in 1192 and '93, though they don't seem to have been accompanied by strange events.   The next of those was in 1195, and could be natural, but it was certainly spectacular, according to Gervase of Canterbury.

On June 7th, about the sixth hour, "there appeared a wonderful sign at London.   For a very dense and most hideous cloud formed in the air, growing exceedingly, and surrounding the Sun which was shining clearly.   In the middle of this aperture, as if from the outlet of a water-mill, an unknown white substance ['I know not what'] flowed down.   This, growing into a globe below the black cloud, was suspended over the Thames and the guest-house of the bishop of Norwich [John of Oxford].   From it what seemed to be a globe of fire descended on the river, and forming a cone-shape it descended within the walls of the courtyard of the foresaid bishop."[83]

John of Oxford had a town-house because he was often required at Westminster - he didn't share the privileges which the bishops of Ely, perhaps as early as Geoffrey Ridell, had at the New Temple.   It was on the south-west corner of the parish of Westminster, not far from the Ivy-Bridge, and in 1365 the bishop of Durham built another town-house next to it.   (Did Hugh du Puiset, on whose land the Hells-Kettles event occurred, previously have one there?)   It was demolished by the Duke of Buckingham after 1556 and the site is now York Buildings.[84]

If the conical shape assumed by 'I know not what' was pointing downward, perhaps it was just a tornado.   Was its brilliance merely due to sunlight refracting through it?   But ordinary tornadoes don't come out of single clouds, don't make holes in them, don't form globes and aren't white. ("Of course, we can discount ...") If it really was incandescent and this is another electrically charged vortex, then given the previous de Calna connections with Salisbury, where John of Oxford was first based, and the uncle, brother, son and possible grandson of lord Richard at various times at Norwich, we may well wonder why whatever came out of the sky happened to land in John of Oxford's courtyard, with all of London to choose from.

5. Richard Barre's Compendium

There is one possible source for the answers - but it would be a mammoth task, well beyond my abilities. During his first eight years as archdeacon of Ely, Richard Barre began the creation of a 234-page Compendium of the Old and New Testament, dedicated to bishop Longchamp. Although now held by the British Library,[85] it's omitted by most catalogues of early manuscripts, suggesting that it was in private hands until relatively late: there's at least one personal dedication on the flyleaf, though the ink of the later inscriptions has faded too much to make out.

I had already made a preliminary study, when I found it was attributed to the 15th century in the catalogue of the British Library's Harleian Collection.[86] Another copy, supposedly, was held by Lambeth Palace Library and was attributed by M.R. James to the 13th century when he compiled its manuscript catalogue.[87] But on inspection, though titled *Liber Ricardi barre super bibliam*, 'Richard Barre's Book on the Bible', the Lambeth Palace book is quite different and a great deal shorter.[88] Barre laid out his texts working through the Bible, but the unknown author of the Lambeth MS has them "treated in no order", as M.R. James put it, "though roughly grouped in subjects: each of which is shortly explained in the allegorical sense. It is very likely that most of this matter is extracted from the *Moralia* of Gregory and from other equally well known books."[87] In other words, it's not Richard Barre's book at all.

Having examined both, what most puzzled me was how similar they looked - both written on lined vellum in similar styles, similarly bound in the original - even both perforated with strange holes caused by hot wax dripping from candles or tapers, though in both cases, great care had been taken not to let it burn through the text on either side of the page. I'm a novice when it comes

229

to mediaeval manuscripts, and M.R. James hadn't given reasons for a 13th century date, but after re-examining the British Library MS I asked how it had been dated. Dr. M.C. Breay replied, "I have checked this volume and can confirm that there is an error in the Harley catalogue, since this manuscript definitely was not written in the fifteenth century... Although it is not possible to assign precise dates to manuscripts solely on paleographical grounds, there are several features of this manuscript which suggest that it was written in the early thirteenth century.

"The text of this manuscript is written on the top ruled line. This is a dating feature because it has been shown that between 1220 and 1240 scribes altered their earlier practise of writing on the top line and afterwards always began each page on the second ruled line. Another dating feature is the use of the abbreviation [today's division sign] for the word *est*, which did not continue after the early thirteenth century. Also, the letter 's' at the end of words is written in both the tall and short forms in this manuscript: the use of the tall form at the ends of words did not continue after the early thirteenth century, while the short form began to be used from the early thirteenth century onwards. In addition, the abbreviation for *et* was written as [a British figure 7] until the end of the twelfth century, but [like a continental seven], as in this manuscript, from the beginning of the thirteenth century."[89] So the British Library MS may be in Richard Barre's own hand, or if not, copied soon after his death in 1209.

The dedication is addressed to Longchamp in glowing terms. "Your generosity especially commends you and shines forth from your earliest youth with the brightness of a fire..." Chroniclers say Longchamp's fund-raising tour of England for Richard I was ruinous for his hosts because he took "a court of clerks... singing his praises as a liberal and munificent patron".[90] But Richard Barre didn't need such patronage, and anyway his itinerary as a justice shows that he wasn't part of de Longchamp's train.

The justices of England including Barre had been united in ousting Longchamp from his position as Chancellor and Lord Protector. Longchamp was still Richard Barre's boss as bishop of Ely, but Barre wasn't living there and wasn't dependent on it for his livelihood. It remains to be seen whether the dedication is purely formal, sarcastic, or has some hidden meaning in relation to the text.

The text itself is a lot less 'user-friendly' than the dedication. As Dr. Breay mentions it's handwritten in mediaeval Latin shorthand, in what seems to be a vocabulary of Barre's own, and it's colour-coded, numerically coded, and full of underlinings, footnotes, and comments plus symbols in the margins. Some of these, according to the preface, identify topics "as do the experts in Roman law" - but there are further comments in at least two neater hands, so small that on a first attempt I couldn't read them at all. Barre himself wrote with a broad pen, and the ink has spread, especially where he used colours: for example the title can only be read by angling the page so that the scratch left by the pen catches the light. Even to transliterate the text would take an experienced mediaeval scholar many months of work, and to produce a full translation would take at least as long again; then it would need correlation of the colour codings, number codes, footnotes and cross-references, to decrypt the book in full.

As a very preliminary start, I tried to transliterate the underlined words in the excerpts from the Books of Genesis and Exodus, on the first page. This is how they read:

"The earth was without form, and void...
"and darkness...
"was on the face of the deep...
"Let the earth bring forth grass, the herb yielding seed, and the fruit tree yielding fruit after his kind...
"And he rested on the seventh day from all the aforesaid work...
"He drew them forth from the earth...
"He watered the whole face of the land...
"A River...
"went out from that pleasant place, which is called the watering of paradise...
"And the Lord said to Moses, 'Put your hand into your bosom'...
"as for him, so for many: at last he drew it out as white as snow...
"And the Lord said to Moses, 'Certainly I will go with thee'."

It could be the start of the green children's story, including the great river running through the land from which they were 'drawn out'. Barre's text divides it into the four heads which mediaeval texts identified with the Ganges, Nile, Tigris and Euphrates,[91] but he doesn't underline them. The words 'as for him, so for many: at last' have been added to the Biblical text, in which

231

God shows Moses his power by striking his hand with leprosy and then removing it. Barre is talking about more than one hand - perhaps, more than one body - turning white over time, as the children's did.

So far I haven't made sense of the next sets of underlinings, in Judges and Isaiah, though Judges was one of the Old Testament books which Richard de Hastings had translated into contemporary French (Chap.16). But the decorations of mediaeval manuscripts were very carefully chosen. The text of Richard Barre's book begins with the capital 'O' of *Ovate*, 'Rejoice'. It's drawn as a dragon, green on top, with red below, like the oxygen and nitrogen in a deeply penetrating auroral arc (Chap.20) - perhaps a hint of more information, encoded in the Biblical texts which follow. There may be a great deal more to find.

Chapter Fifteen - THE 1200s: AGNES AND SIBYLLA

"[The crossbow] had been introduced into England by William the Conqueror, who greatly availed himself of it at the battle of Hastings: but the second Lateran Council having forbidden it in wars between Christian nations, it was laid aside in this country, during the reigns of King Stephen and King Henry the Second. Nevertheless Richard the First, at his return out of Palestine, brought it again into France, very fatally for himself, as he was killed soon afterwards by an arrow shot out of that engine."

~ George Lord Lyttelton, "The History of the Life of King Henry the Second"

1. The Lost Son Returns

Richard I was killed in 1199, and that year 'Richard son of Agnes' first appears in Staffordshire.[1] We're going to see more of him, though his return didn't cause a stir at the time. Richard and Agnes Barre continued at Little Barr; Ralph Turner says Richard was no longer a justice,[2] but he held courts in Rutland in 1201, Canterbury 1202, Essex 1203,[3] Canterbury again in 1204, and Leicester in 1207.[4] By 1204, he held the farm of Reileia, acquired from Gerald Fitz-Peter of Essex;[5] in 1208 it's given as Raigl', in the Liberty of the Bishop of Ely,[6] where Barre was still archdeacon.

It's not in Ely's assets at its dissolution by Henry VIII.[7] The Pipe Rolls editors put it in the Honour of Rayleigh in Essex, which included Great Horkesley and could be linked to our story through Richard de Hastings - or through Sibylla de Calna, below. But the Barre property was Rowley Regis in Staffordshire, also spelled Roelegia, Rolegia, Rulegh, and Ruggeley, confused with the modern town. But in Domesday it was Rouueleia, and Barre's link with it was becoming complicated - see below.

In 1197, when Sibylla de Calna and Agnes reclaimed their land in Aston, Sibylla was seventeen. Soon her husband, John Fitz-Bernard, claimed his own inheritance: in Hampshire and Northamptonshire, 1201, Sussex 1206, (where he called Radulph de Calna as a witness in the king's court); Norfolk and Suffolk in 1207, likewise Hertfordshire and Essex; Buckingham and Bedfordshire in 1211, Derbyshire, in the Peak District - near Peveril Castle? -

in 1212,[8] and Berkshire in 1220.   The arranged marriage worked: their son, Walter Fitz-Bernard, later farmed Reed with "the daughter of Walter de Calna".   That comment in a different hand could be a cross-reference to the entry with 'daughters'[9] plural, which perhaps should read 'heiresses', but led me to Agnes as candidate for the green girl.   Walter and Sibylla's rights at Reed excluded the church, given by king Stephen to the monastery of St. Pancras in Devon c.1136.[10]

Meanwhile the de Calna connection to the wealthy and powerful de Cantilupes now came to the fore.   Walter de Cantilupe held land in Wiltshire in the 1170s,[11] and Engelisia de Calna had land in Calne in the 1190s.[12]   But king John disliked royal land in female hands[13] and by 1205 he'd allocated Calne to Fulk de Cantilupe,[14] whom Matthew Paris calls one of his 'evil counsellors':[15] John sent him to expel the monks of Canterbury and take charge of the see when they elected an archbishop he didn't like.

In 1203, a Richard de Rushale (Rushell, near Great Barr) lodged a claim for land in Staffordshire held by his father Richard under a charter of Henry II's, confirmed by king John in 1201.[16]   Nothing came of it at the time, but a time-bomb was ticking.

In Ireland, Damietta de Hereford (formerly de Broc) died about 1204.   The bishop of Ossory had by then moved back to Kilkenny, where the cathedral church was rebuilt by 1202.   However, the Irish connection was far from over - see Chap.16.   Also in 1204-05, Richard de Calna (Sibylla's older brother) again laid claim to his grandmother's North Weald manor in Essex.   This time he succeeded, giving part to his brother Walter; it passed to Richard's sons Richard and John around 1230, to that Richard's son Thomas in 1295, to his son Sir John by 1343, and to his son John before 1371 (Fig. 4.1.)   On his death it passed out of the family, but as it was now Canes or Cawnes, the son of the new occupant, John de Rous, called himself 'Thomas de Caune' and the surname was reborn.[17]

In the early 1200s solar activity was declining, though still high, and rose briefly around 1204-05.   On April 1st 1204 bright red aurora was seen over England, "such that truly all believed it to be a fire.   And what was to be wondered at, in the same very strong redness flashing stars appeared. Moreover this vision lasted until the middle of the night."[18]   It may have been a meteor shower, but it's too early for the annual Lyrid display. Then, says Ralph of Coggeshall: "In the year 1205 the winter caused great problems, and rivers were frozen, so that the Thames could be crossed on foot. Indeed the earth was so solid with the cold, that from the Circumcision of the Lord to the Annunciation of our Lady it was not possible to plough. Indeed the winter caused seeds in such ground as could be shifted to be made dead of coldness; also many living plants died when planted. Also from this came a great famine, so much so that in many parts of England products were sold for whole marks, which many times in the reign of Henry II could be had for 12 pence... On the night of St. John the Baptist [June 24], there were heard horrible thunders throughout the night, and frightening lightnings, incessantly produced from the clouds, were seen throughout England. A certain monster was found struck by lightning in Kent, near Maidstone, where the most frightful crash was heard, which was seen to have the head pertaining to an ass, a human belly, and other monstrous limbs truly dissimilar from any kind of animal; to which very black corpse one could scarcely approach nearer, than the burning's smoke, because of the intolerable odour (Chap.22).

"Specifically on the night of St. Felix [July 29] after the feast of St. James, so great a crash of frightening thunders, and of crashing thunderbolts ceaselessly flashing from the collisions of the clouds appeared throughout all England at the same time, that the day of Judgement was thought to have begun, making men and animals dead with fear and the fear of being cast out which filled the whole kingdom. Also likewise animals were struck, homes thrown down and consumed, cornfields wasted by stones of hail, which in some places were said to be as large as goose eggs, everywhere sharp. Certain trees were overturned by the roots, and transplanted, as if distorted by a certain deadly rain, some cut through the middle. Also next day certain monstrous footprints were seen in many places, the like of which were never seen anywhere, which men said were the footprints of demons, who long to escape from the terrible blows of the Angels, hither and thither, according to St. Jerome in his *Ethics*."

No auroral storms this time: winters severe enough to freeze the Thames are usually during prolonged decreases in solar activity (Chap.20). The detailed plot in Fig. 20.2 shows a brief dip around 1200 AD, but not enough for Thames ice. The footprints in the July storm are not easy to account for (crop circles, perhaps?), but the monster is our first and only glimpse of a non-human being in the entire story – revealed by yet another accident associated with a violent electrical discharge.

1209 sees Richard Barre's last Pipe Roll entry, in Huntingdon,[19] and his last appearance as a justice, in Canterbury.[20]   In 1210 Richard was replaced by someone with the initial 'W',[21] then by Stephen Ridell, Geoffrey's nephew.   In 1212 Richard de Siffrevast reclaimed land in Buckinghamshire, formerly held by Hugh and Richard Barre.[19]   Barre gave his Wiltshire church rights to the dean of Salisbury in 1200: Henry III ruled on them in 1232, 'with consent and by concession' of Richard Barre,[22] but that meant only that his earlier wishes were being respected.   Were he still alive, then if he was sixteen in 1166, when he had land in Lincolnshire, he would be 86 in 1232 - but there are no records of him after 1209, and it's clear below that he was no longer head of the family. But Agnes was still alive, and if who I think she was, she'd be around 13 years younger than Richard.   And that fits what happened next.

In 1208 and 1209 William de Barre was sued by William de Rushell, "concerning a wrongful theft of rights to land".[4]   de Rushell's witnesses didn't appear; the case was adjourned, but the clock was still ticking.   In 1210 William de Barre defended another case, over woodland in Handsworth and land in Parva Barra itself, brought by William de Parles, who'd previously tried to claim land left on the death of William de Rushell.[4]   de Parles said his father Pagan de Parles secured the land in trial by combat under Henry II; it had been taken by force, said de Parles, when he himself was in prison.   William Barre said de Parles was claiming the wrong land: he still held Parva Barra in 1212, and the case continued until 1214.

Prince John was not been pleased when Abbot Samson helped to raise Richard I's ransom, and now he was king, he could harass Bury St. Edmunds Abbey in revenge.   When Samson died in 1211 John refused to fill the vacancy, seizing the Abbey's revenues until pressured by the Pope in 1215.   That year, the earls and barons of the area assembled at a pillar in the Abbey, marked today by a plaque, and swore jointly to enforce John's signature of the Magna Carta.   There were no de Calnas - the other heirs had left the area, giving Wykes to Sibylla, who had just returned in dramatic fashion.

In 1206 Peter de Valoines and his son Roger donated all of Binham manor and its church, plus half of Bernay manor and *its* church, to Binham Priory.[23]   The other half was held by John and Sibylla Fitz-Bernard.   In 1210 John was among the 'knights of the army in Ireland',[24] but he was back in England by 1214, because that year, in concert with his neighbours, including one John de Stanton, he forcibly evicted Adam de Wikes, who had given up his tenancy in favour of his natural son, Peter.[4]   On the latter's death Adam wanted to pass the tenancy to another son, William, but on hearing of Peter's illegitimacy Fitz-Bernard wouldn't entertain it.   It sounds like an excuse, as if he (or Sibylla) had some other reason to want Wykes back, because he didn't object to Peter's tenancy while he was alive. Adam took the case to a royal court, who let John de Stanton remain in the manor and to keep anything of Adam's which he found there, "by reason of his age, for his sustenance and honourable entertainment".

This highlights an oddity.   Henry II gave Reed and North Fambridge to Sibylla as her dowry; with Agnes she inherited a share of Aston from her father, and she also got Bernay. Now she had Wykes and Knettishall too: the family's major property, and the last of lord Richard's holdings that I've been able to trace.   Although the youngest de Calna in her generation, she now apparently had all the property of her branch of the family, and her elder brothers didn't care: there's no record that they challenged her for it.   For some reason it was important for Sibylla to have those sites, perhaps because of their locations (Chap.17); was it because of her connection with Agnes?

In 1215 John and Sibylla granted their rights in the Bernay church, and some of their land, to Binham Priory.[25] She'd kept up the de Calna connection with the de Valoines, who'd already given other parts of the estate to the Priory, with Richard de Calna as a witness to the first gifts (Chap.4), but this act of piety caused her trouble later.

1220 was another disturbed year, with a great wind throwing down houses and church towers, while "dragons of fire and evil spirits were seen flying in the air".[26]   Things were fraught in Staffordshire, too.   In 1211, William de Rushell had renewed the contest with William Barre over land. The case was again adjourned because Barre was ill, and by 1212 William's son Richard Barre, Agnes's grandson, was involved.[27]   In 1215 he had land in Buckingham,[28] but by 1221-22 he was back in Warwickshire, listed as the son of William. The Nottinghamshire property was still in the family name, and in 1220 he had to pay a fine on it, in his father's absence.[29]

He had a big shock coming, which he brought upon himself: he laid claim to the manor of Rowley, now held by Richard de Rushell/de Rulegh. The case was going well, and young de Barre probably thought he'd won, when de Rushell revealed that he was Richard's uncle - William de Barre was his brother and he was the illegitimate son of the first Richard Barre and Agnes.[30] It came as such a surprise that the court set up an assize to determine whether William had ever held the land at all. Clearly it was a bigger surprise to young Richard Barre, that the neighbour and participant in the long-standing dispute with the de Rushells and de Parles was such a close relative.

Knowing whom to look for, Richard de Rushell can be traced from 1195, when he took up former property of Nottingham Castle,[31] presumably the land in the area which Richard Barre assigned to Agnes's illegitimate son had 17 years earlier. Older than William Barre, he had his supposed father's Christian name, and perhaps the deal was that, if he later got the Rowley manor, he wouldn't reveal his true identity while either Richard Barre or William was still alive.

So he was fostered out with the de Rushells, the Barres' neighbours. Normally, wardship went to the nearest of kin to whom the inheritance couldn't descend – usually on the mother's side of the family,[32] but if Agnes was indeed the green girl, that wouldn't be possible. If a man fostered his son with another man, normally he gave land for the favour - presumably the land now disputed between the two families - and Barre had also acquired land in Notts/Derbyshire and assigned it to young Richard. But the boy had taken his guardian's surname; the land assigned to de Rushell had now come to him; he hadn't claimed any other inheritance, and he'd kept his identity secret from Agnes, all those years. All this confirms that he was illegitimate: in common law, bastards couldn't inherit land.

Richard de Rushell was still in Notts/Derbyshire in 1196, but in 1201 he gave ten marks and a palfrey for a royal charter in Rowley, repeated in 1202 and 1203.[33] In 1212 he took passage to Ireland,[34] so he could have been there at the same time as John Fitz-Bernard. But he was back in 1215, now calling himself Richard de Rualeia[35] (Rowley) where he was living in 1218.[36] Literally, he was making a name for himself. And now it had all come home to roost for Agnes, still alive in 1222.

The revelation must have caused some stress between Agnes and her grandson, but however she reacted to being put back in touch with her illegitimate son, it wasn't to be for long. In 1224 Phillip, son of Richard de Rulegh, paid the Fine to gain his inheritance on his father's death.[37] It would be interesting to know who his mother was. But his wife was Alice Barre! They obviously didn't know they were first cousins when they married - see Chap.17.

In 1228, Phillip was at odds with the earl of Chester about rights to the church of Rowley, this time spelled Rudeley.[38] He was sharing the place with the sheriff of Staffordshire[39] and the bishop of Coventry and Lichfield, who have multiple entries in the Pipe Rolls and elsewhere from 1195 onwards; but they don't seem to have been caught up in the quarrels, even when the grandson Richard Barre renewed them.

2. de Calnas and de Cantilupes

In 1228 there were more electrical phenomena on the Thames. "As the bishop of London was celebrating [Mass] in the church of St. Paul, the density of the clouds was so great, and the obscuration of the Sun with thunder and lightning and unbearable stench, that it made the people evacuate, leaving the bishop with his charge."[26] Bearing in mind how Robert du Barri kept his cool in the phantom attack in Ossory, one wonders what that signified.

Around 1219, Henry III reclaimed Calne from Fulk de Cantilupe and in 1220 or 1221, crucially, he assigned it to William de Cantilupe.[40] Steward and Justiciar to king John and sheriff of Warwickshire several times,[40,41] governor of Kenilworth Castle 1215-23,[42] he also had land in Somerset, Hereford, Northamptonshire, Devon, Bedfordshire, Leicestershire, Lincolnshire, Kent, Shropshire, Suffolk, Essex and Buckinghamshire; he was a justice in Nottingham, Glamorgan, Hereford and Bucks, and had served 'faithfully' in Poitou. Others in the family had equally large holdings.[4]

He was another 'evil counsellor' of John's, and when the minor Henry III inherited the throne he was one of the barons who opposed him. Calne was one of the first sites to be seized when the king moved against them, but de Cantilupe quickly changed sides, and got his Wiltshire property back in hereditary right. "Had there, perhaps, been gatherings and conjurations in the area?" asks one writer.[40] But 'conjurations' just means 'swearing together' and nothing more exotic was intended - though there are curious things about the de Calna and de Cantilupe seals, below. William was the first baron de Cantilupe, whose son and grandson were also William; the son was guardian of Eve de Braose of Kilkenny, who married the grandson[43] (Chap.16).

In 1225 still another Richard de Calna was a servant to Gilbert Livet of Dublin, with a ship he captured in a raid on La Rochelle,[44] lost by Henry III the previous year. He could be from another branch of the family, in Wiltshire, the West Country or Wales, but he might be lord Richard's great-grandson. Presumably, he's the same Richard de Calna who witnessed undated grants of land in Drogheda to St. Mary's Abbey, Dublin, and made one with his wife Eve.[45]

Also in 1225 'Sibyll the widow' was listed in Suffolk,[46] but not our Sibylla, because John Fitz-Bernard was still alive in 1228.[4] In 1229 she and John gave evidence for the great-grandson, 'Richard de Calna son of Richard de Calna', confirming his claim to the North Weald manor.[47] Nevertheless, in May 1229 our Sibylla paid a Fine of five marks, as 'Sibylla who was the wife of John Fitz-Bernard', to regain part of her inheritance from Walter de Calna, held by the Sheriff of Hertfordshire - presumably Reed. By 1230 her Essex holdings as 'Sibylla de Calna' were listed separately from John's;[48] widows often reverted to their maiden names.[49] She applied for permission to remarry, which was granted "without impediment",[37] but she didn't do it.

In 1225 a Walkelin de Calna was sued by the abbot of Bury St. Edmunds, in a case going back to Samson's time. In 1227 he was in one before the abbot of Coggeshall,[4] and in 1231, when Sibylla was in financial difficulties, as her lawyer he tried to regain various estates, with mixed success: in most the court refused to oust the sitting tenants. She regained North Fambridge, where her claim was incontestable, and with it land in Reed rented to the abbot of Coggeshall. Did that go back to Ralph's abbacy, or even to lord Richard's days? Ralph himself had just died; that may have prompted Sibylla to reclaim possession, though once she had it, she made an arrangement with the new abbot. Walkelin went to Westminster to collect payment for her.

Not all the cases went well: in the North Fambridge one, her son Walter was called as a witness against her, and trying to claim 100 acres in Stowe, nearby, she had a humiliating defeat. Bayngard the defendant called Walter de Horkesley to 'warrant' his status as a sitting tenant. de Horkesley first refused, and when summonsed, tried to brazen it out, but Bayngard had a contract with him and Sibylla. They claimed that it was no longer binding, because of her husband's death, but Bayngard produced another which Sibylla had given him since.[4] The business relationship between Sibylla and Walter de Horkesley continued for at least fourteen years, because de Horkesley was in dispute with the Prior of Binham about land in Bernay in 1233, and he and Sibylla were there together in 1234-44.

Great and Little Horkesley are adjacent in Essex, originally combined as 'Nayland', five miles east of Wakes Colne, adjacent to land of the de Hastings and the Mascerells. Walter de Horkesley was lord of Little Horkesley Manor until his death in 1266;[50] his wife was Alicia,[4] so Sibylla de Calna couldn't have married into the de Horkesley family. Whether she hoped to, 'without impediment', is another matter.

Sibylla tried to reclaim her land at Bernay from Binham Priory,[4] but couldn't prove at the time that she and John had given the land. Richard de Parco, prior of Binham since 1225, said it came from his predecessor - which didn't stop him subsequently accepting the whole manor as a gift from Christiana de Valoines. In 1232 Sibylla was still in difficulties, and the sheriffs of Huntingdon, Canterbury and Essex were ordered to help with her finances.[51]

3. Seals of Approval

Sibylla now adopted a seal, "SIGILL'.SIBILLE:DE. CALNA", showing her in a tight dress and cloak, with her left hand on her breast and a fleur-de-lis topping a wand or sceptre in her right (Fig. 15.1) - very much like the one Abbot Samson had at the opening of St. Saviour's Hospital, and possibly a Templar logo (Chap.14).

The fleur-de-lis was linked to the French monarchy since 1147 at least and first used on a royal seal in 1180. (The 1950 *Britannica* contradicts itself here: the 'Heraldry' entry says it wasn't used until 1223-1226). But the de Calnas had no connections with them, except that maybe Roger le Poer and Nigel the Doctor were of noble birth (Chap.4). By 1250-75, when the motif is on the knitted cushions of the Spanish royal family at Las Huelgas (Chap.8), it was used by royal families throughout Europe. Traditionally it goes back to Clovis, the fifth-century founder of the Frankish royal dynasty, given a lily by an angel at his baptism.[52] According to Dürer it was a stylised toad, whose secretions were psychedelic drugs. Toads are found with the Cross in the catacombs of Alexandria and elsewhere in Egypt;[53] there are still 'toad-licking' cults in the US south and west, and in Mexico the toad is a symbol for 'magic mushrooms'. We still call some fungi 'toadstools'; and Santa Claus's flying reindeer, and dress of red and white, may represent fly agaric mushrooms used by Lapp shamans.[54]

Fig. 15.1. Sibylla de Calna's seal.
Photo by the British Library.

Jane Greatorex suggested that if you received a document bearing Sibylla's seal, the message was 'Barbecue with a difference at Woolpit, don't miss it, details to follow', and maybe 'Clothing optional, green if any'. If it bore Samson's personal seal with the duck's head and the fleur-de-lis, an interesting time might be in prospect, but it would have to be in the 1190s or early 1200s when Samson was still alive. If John Fitz-Bernard formally returned her dowry land to her, she might have used her maiden name in dealing with it: at Reed she was 'the daughter of Walter de Calna', and one document with the seal on it relates to Fambridge.[55] But Walkelin de Calna is on it as a witness, and Walter Fitz-Bernard is on another,[56] so the seals which have come down to us are from the 1230s.

In the British Museum catalogue, she's 'standing on a carved corbel',[57] but on the master seal it looks very like a fish.[58] It could mean that Sibylla was a priestess, a *parfaite*, of the Cathar sect: if so she'd practise strict celibacy and reverence for all forms of life, with a strict vegetarian diet *except for fish*.[59] But any hint of Catharism was extremely dangerous (Chap.8): there were 12th century campaigns against them in southern France (Chap.14), and by the 1230s there had been three major Crusades and the Inquisition created specifically to identify and wipe them out. If Sibylla thought that anyone would take her for a Cathar, she certainly wouldn't have a fish on her seal. It could refer to family business at Lynn (Chap.13) - now using the ship that young Richard de Calna captured at La Rochelle? In 1238 the herring harvest from East Anglia was very good, because the Mongols had broken into Russia and eastern Europe, and the usual fishing boats from Gotland and Friesland didn't compete with the locals.[60] 'Sometimes a fish is just a fish.'

But what's most extraordinary is that she's depicted with a crescent Moon on her head, with a star above it. In Islam it's usually turned ninety degrees, but the crescent was upturned, the way Sibylla wears it, on a metal column surmounting the Dome of the Rock in Jerusalem.[61] It was replaced in 1115 by a cross, which Saladin pulled down in 1187 and had beaten through the streets; a felt and leather hood protected the gilt of the new crescent in winter,[62] and if it turned in the wind, that was an evil omen[61] It wasn't replaced when the Christians regained Jerusalem in 1229-39, because the Dome remained Moslem under the treaty. The present-day one extends the horns of the Moon to a ring,[62] as the Earth would look in crescent phase, or the Moon would if it had an atmosphere. A Star of David was briefly substituted in 1967 after the Six Days' War, but the crescent was replaced by order of General Moshe Dayan.

Fig. 15.2. Ishtar seal, c.2700 BC, with crescent and star at top left. Photo: Henri Frankfort, "Cylinder Seals".

In the form Sibylla used them, the crescent and star were the symbols of Ishtar, the Mesopotamian and Hittite Venus-goddess, later known as Astarte, the counterpart of the Greek Aphrodite. For example, Ishtar's emblems appear on a cylinder seal c.2700 BC (Fig.15.2), where she's breaking a drought, sending down rain and calling on the Thunder-god, who bears a whip representing lightning.[63] For Sibylla to be presented as Ishtar is very interesting, because the Church of the Holy Sepulchre in Jerusalem replaced a temple of Venus (Chap.22) - and it was struck by lightning immediately before the Second Crusade (Chap.4).

In *The Holy Blood and the Holy Grail*, Baigent, Leigh and Lincoln suggest that the early Merovingian kings secretly worshipped Ishtar, and they reproduce a Templar seal of 1303 with the cross *pattée* supported by an upturned crescent, flanked by a star on each side, which they say is the emblem of the Mother Goddess, Isis of Egypt - identified with Astarte as 'the Queen of Heaven', a name annexed for the Virgin Mary.[52] But like Osiris, 'Isis' is a Greek name, imposed on Egyptian culture c.600 BC. Her original name was 'Ast';[64] probably for that reason Isis was confused with Aphrodite in later times in Greece, and adopted in that guise as the Star of the Sea, but she was distinct from Astarte, from whom she retrieved the body of Osiris in Phoenicia.[65] There are descriptions of her 'wearing the Moon upon her head',[66] but it was actually the horns of a cow, linking her to Nut, the goddess of the sky.[65] Aphrodite/Astarte/ Ishtar was normally identified with Venus, whereas Isis was Sirius, the brightest star in the sky.[67]   Given the importance of the crescent in Islam, I'd think the 1303 seal represents the emblems of Islam being surmounted by the Templars', as in Fig. 3.1, even if that was optimistic when they'd been thrown out of the Holy Land.

The authors suggest that the Merovingian kings descended from Jesus and Mary Magdalene, and their fleur-de-lis was the Jewish symbol of circumcision, while before their marriage - at Cana, in St. John's Gospel, where neither bride nor groom is named - Mary of Magdala was a priestess of Astarte.   In St. Mark, "he appeared first to Mary Magdalene, out of whom he had cast seven devils", which they say was a seven-stage initiation into the rites of Astarte, adding that doves, emblems of Astarte, may have been bred at Magdala.   It may sound good coming from me, but I have to say that I find the thesis shaky.

But the crescent and star also appear, with the Templar cross, on the tile at Coggeshall which is very probably Richard de Calna's (chap.13).   And the setting Sun, Moon and stars were portrayed on a window which Samson installed at Bury St. Abbey (Chap.10); was it sponsored by Richard de Calna or his heirs, and was a *sonitus* rung for him (Chap.)?   Then there's that intriguing sentence of Stephan de Tournai's in Chap.14, "You are translated from the planet of the Cyprian [Venus] to the sun".

Do the fleur-de-lis, crescent and star relate to the name Sibylla, 'the seeress' or 'prophetess'?   According to Classical writers there were ten Sibyls: the Persian Sibyl, Libyan, Delphian, Cimmerian etc.   One of them was called Sabbe,[68] and is thought to have lent her name to the Biblical Queen of Sheba - and Solomon's Temple may originally have been Phoenician and dedicated to Astarte.[69]   But is there any reason to think that a cult of Venus/Astarte had survived into mediaeval England?

In *The White Goddess* Robert Graves suggested that Robin Hood, Maid Marian and the Merry Men personify the cult of Mary of Egypt, a sea and corn goddess who became diminished in popular culture to the mermaid.[70]   (Before I told him, the poet Brian Finch predicted that if a pagan goddess had a cult in mediaeval Europe, it would be camouflaged with a name like the Virgin Mary's.)   In Asia Minor she was Marian or Ay-Mari, a Moon goddess corresponding to Athene, and she lent her name to the cities of Myrine and Smyrna.[71]   It was because of her sea-goddess aspect that she was fish-tailed: the mermaid's mirror is either a representation of the Moon in her hand[72] or a corruption of 'myrrh', because her name was originally *Stilla Maris*, Myrrh of the Sea, aka *Stella Maris*, Venus/Aphrodite   (also annexed for the Virgin Mary).[71]

According to Graves, Aphrodite's cockle-shells were the emblems of Compostela because that's where Marian's cult took hold in mainland Europe, as its name implies; the Merry Men were Morris-men = Mary's Men, while 'Robin' was a demon, the Lord of Misrule, disguised as a gold-crest wren (ritually hunted at the midwinter festival),[73] while 'The Hood' was the log at the back of the Yuletide fire. (The Oxford English Dictionary has *hode* as an old verb meaning 'to consecrate'.)   Robin's demonic aspect was toned down to 'Robin Goodfellow', the Hobgoblin, alternative name for Puck.   (Last lines of *A Midsummer Night's Dream*:

> "Give me your hands, if we be friends,
> And Robin shall restore amends.")

In *The Temple and the Lodge* Baigent and Leigh identify Robin Hood not only with Robin Goodfellow but also the 'Green Man' of mediaeval churches (Chap.1).[69] "To shoot at an apple poised upon the head, or at a penny set in the cap, of one own son was a test of marksmanship prescribed to mediaeval archers, whose guild (as appeared in the *Malleus Maleficarum* and in the *Little Geste of Robin Hood*) belonged to the pagan witch cult both in England and in Celtic Germany. [Robin Hood's merry men, like the German archers, shot at silver pennies, because these were marked with a cross; the archer-guilds being defiantly anti-Christian.]   In England this test was, it seems, designed to choose a 'gudeman' for Maid Marian, by marriage to whom he became Robin Hood, Lord of the Greenwood."[70]   *Robin Hood and Little John* was performed by strolling gypsy players, particularly at May Day celebrations; hence "Robin Hood and Little John have both gone to the fair" in the ritual song *Hal an' Toe*. The play included a Venus-like Queen of the May, and play and festival were frequently denounced for their sexual content,[74] which takes us back to green food and, below, to green children.

'Let each man say of this what he will'; but if the body in the cloister with its cockle-shells is Richard de Calna's, this could explain why his grand-daughter had Ishtar's crescent and star above her head and a fish below her feet. There is a possible link between the Knights Templar and the cult of Aphrodite (Chap.24). The scallop-shell was an emblem of Venus in late Roman Britain, symbolising rebirth,[75] and there were temples of Venus at Shingham and Caldecott, both near Lynn.[76] As recently as the 1820's, prostitutes in Dublin were known collectively as 'the Cyprian tribe';[77] and in the popular mediaeval legend of Seth, son of Adam, the harlot character is introduced as 'Sibylla', though her name later changes to 'Susanna'.[68]

In *The Girl Green as Elderflower* Randolph Stow conjectures that the green children's 'St. Martin' was Merddin, another name for Satan, or Merlin, according to Graves.[70] The Merry Men wore green, the colour of the sea and of sexual inexperience. Were the children dyed green to show they were too young for some adult ritual - or to prepare them for one which they were lucky to escape? It might seem a 'natural' explanation, but there's a great deal which it doesn't explain - see the end of Chap.17.

More prosaically, with the fleur-de-lis Sibylla was advertising her relationship to the de Cantilupes. After Everard de Calna, the next member of the family at Calne was Reginald, in 1180,[78] and he had the church and manor house of Calne in 1199, at least.[79] The Pipe Rolls show him with land in Wiltshire until 1221, when he became a justice and was excused taxes on it. He was a justice in 1223 and 1225; took joint charge of Salisbury church in 1236;[38] became escheator of the county in 1232, and was knighted by 1233,[14] if not before; he was collector of feudal aid in Wiltshire in 1235, based at Salisbury Castle;[39] collector and joint keeper of royal funds at Devizes Castle, 1238;[38] mandated by the king to release various prisoners in 1241 and arrest various defaulters in 1242; witnessed an agreement on lands near Calne in 1240-45, and was still in harness 1247-51.[39] His son William was knighted and is too often in the records to list, and *he* had sons Walter and William, 'the scribe' (Chap.4).

But Calne and district remained royal land, given to Fulk de Cantilupe no later than 1205 and to the first William de Cantilupe in 1220,[80] as above. Henry III threatened to take it back soon after, but de Cantilupe kept it in return for a 'donation' to the royal Treasury. After the upsets of 1224 he finally retrieved it for good in 1233, along with his other lands including his hereditary rights in

Warwickshire.[40]   In the 1230s he was a steward in Henry III's household, before his death in 1239, and he used a family seal of three fleurs-de-lis, along with the star and crescent.[57]   He may even have used it in the young king's name, as several of the government and royal household did with their seals when Henry was still a minor.[40]   In particular the Public Record Office holds a document in which William de Cantilupe orders flour from the bailiffs of Winchester "on the part of the lord king".   The seal is missing, and it may even be a de Cantilupe seal from early in Henry's reign held by the British Library.[81]

The Catalogue of Seals says it has a star with a crescent over it on the left and a star enclosed by a crescent on the right, but in fact the left-hand side is obscured by wax.   The upturned crescent on the right has its horns extended, like the ring on the Dome of the Rock, but elongated to enclose the star like an Egyptian royal cartouche.[82]   Henry III later adopted the crescent and star for himself: it's on both sides of the royal seal of 1243 (Fig. 15.3).   In the Temple Church he was depicted 'on an azure background semé with stars', like Henry II and Richard I, but with the addition above his head of 'a crescent and star as displayed on the great seal of king Henry III'.

Fig. 15.3. 1243 seal of Henry III.
Walter de Grace Birch, ed., "Catalogue of Seals in the Deparment of Manuscripts in the British Museum", 1887.

But Richard de Calna's grandson was a knight, and presumably bore the same arms as his; if the crescent and star on the Coggeshall tile were Richard's, earned in the Holy Land, then they would be used by his children and might well be adopted as the arms of Calne when he was its prebendary canon.

Reginald de Calna and his son William were also knighted, as above; William witnesses a document in 1251-52 along with Walter de Calna and William, the scribe; and the crescent and star appear on a round seal (green-coloured!) of a document which clerk William witnessed at Calne in 1250-60.[83] The king could give Calne to anyone he liked, but if William de Cantilupe put the de Calna crescent and star in his seal when he gained the estate from John in 1219, and Reginald and William used it too, it suggests that an earlier de Cantilupe had married a de Calna. And that suggestion is strengthened by a document of the third William de Cantilupe, in 1266, which he signed 'William de Kalna alias Cantilupo'.

The first William's wife was called Mazilia or Mascilia,[4] but I don't know her surname. His father was Walter de Cantilupe,[84] son of Walter and Emecina.[85] The family was from Canteleu on the lower Seine near Dieppe, but Walter was in England by 1166, in service to baron Geoffrey de Mandeville.[86] He still had land in France in 1189, where he owed his feudal service to William de Roumara, a knight of La Chapelle in Manche.[87] Walter could have the fleur-de-lis on his arms if *he* was related to the French royal family - though earlier Cantilupe seals use different emblems.[57] 'Roumara' was a forest south of Rouen, where Walter de Coutances was archbishop since 1182, another link to the de Calnas; and from 1175 on, if not sooner, Walter de Cantilupe held land in Wiltshire, including forest near Southampton.[11]

I don't have his wife's name, but if she was the Engelisia de Calna who had land in Calne itself in 1193, and she used lord Richard de Calna's crescent and star on her own seal, passing it down to William de Cantilupe, then presumably she was Richard's daughter. Walter de Cantilupe last appears in the 1195 Pipe Rolls, but he could already have transferred Calne back to her under her maiden name. If William de Cantilupe were her elder son, and Reginald de Calna was the younger, that would explain how William acquired the property from the king and the way he combined the emblems of the two families - as in the provisional, altered version of the family tree shown here (Fig. 15.4). Calne passed through William's son and grandson to Milicent, daughter of the third William and Eve de Braose.[43] She married Roger de la Zouche, and when widowed and calling herself Milicent de Monto Alto, on her seal she holds the de Cantilupe shield with inverted leopards and fleurs-de-lis. It's on a document which William de Calna the clerk witnessed for her in 1280-81.[88]

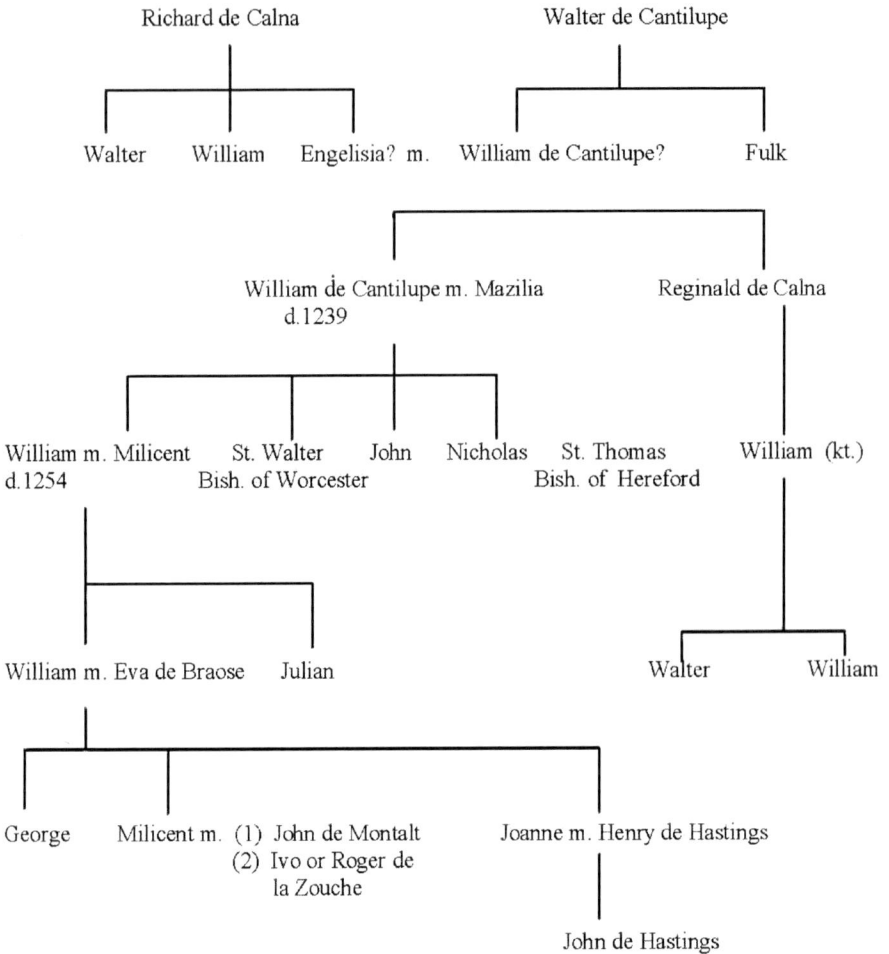

```
      Richard de Calna                    Walter de Cantilupe

   Walter  William  Engelisia? m.  William de Cantilupe?   Fulk

              William de Cantilupe m. Mazilia        Reginald de Calna
                      d.1239

William m. Milicent   St. Walter    John   Nicholas   St. Thomas      William (kt.)
d.1254                Bish. of Worcester               Bish. of Hereford

William m. Eva de Braose    Julian                      Walter      William

George   Milicent m. (1) John de Montalt    Joanne m. Henry de Hastings
                     (2) Ivo or Roger de
                         la Zouche
                                                        John de Hastings
```

Fig. 15.4. Tentative de Calna/de Cantilupe family tree.
Layout by Nick Portwin.

The Warwickshire de Cantilupes didn't retain it: they used the three fleurs-de-lis supported by inverted heads of leopards, without the crescent and star.[42] Thomas de Cantilupe used that seal as bishop of Hereford 1275-1282, and after he was canonised it became the arms of the cathedral in perpetuity.[7]

4. Meanwhile, in Suffolk and Staffordshire...

Sibylla's son, Walter Fitz-Bernard, was a royal clerk, posted around: 1214 in Cumberland,[89] 1223 in Huntingdon, where perhaps he settled, as he was there again in 1237,[4] 1241 and 1243.[90] In 1232 he held an inquisition into the property of Bury St. Edmunds Abbey, causing all kinds of trouble, with the Abbots of St. Edmunds and Ramsay taking his villeins prisoner and driving off livestock from his Hertfordshire property in 1234.[91] (Villeins were peasants on a lord's manor.[92]) So he'd have little time for his mother's business, and next year Wykes, Knettishall and part of Bardwell were sold by 'Lady Sibila de Calna and her son Walter'.[49]

In 1234 Sibylla arranged with the prior of Binham to take over part of Bernay held by Walter de Horkesley and his wife Alice.[93] She and Walter sold Wykes and Knettishall before 1236.[94] The British Museum bought the charter in 1861 from A.F. Bernard - coincidence, or had it stayed in the family all those years? John Bernard was rector of Reed in 1361, so maybe it passed down through him. The sale price was £200, including a water-mill in the middle of the land. There also was a windmill,[95] soon after 1200 (see Chap.20) but the one now in Bardwell dates from 1823.[96]

The charter exempted some rights which Sibylla had assigned to Walter for his wife Matilda, and he still had those in 1242,[39] though everything else was sold to a Hugh de Sherdilow, from Shardlow, between Derby and Nottingham. Hugh had two brother knights, Robert and Edward, based in Norfolk;[97] Robert witnessed the purchase; he was a 'magister', a junior justice in 1229, sheriff of Surrey, constable of Guildford and a justice in Strafford, all in 1231, and a roving justice in Ireland 1245-53.[98]

In 1236 a Nicholas of St. Edmund took Hugh de Sherdilow to court, demanding use of Wykes manor which he'd been promised. Walter Fitz-Bernard was dragged in, to his anger,[4] insisting that Nicholas's contract didn't concern him, nor Hugh for that matter; neither case was proved, Nicholas lost. But by 1238, 'the justiciaries with responsibility for Jewish affairs' took over Robert and Hugh de Sherdilow's land in Nottingham, Derbyshire, Leicestershire and Suffolk, to settle the brothers' debts to four moneylenders, spread from York to London.[39] In 1239 the guardian of the bishopric of

Norwich appointed a bailiff to look after Wykes.[99]   Hugh doesn't appear again; if he 'went missing' in 1236 that would be interesting (Chap.16).

Around 1230 a Richard de Barre had land in Nottinghamshire, thought to be near the Cistercian priory of Southwell.[100]   Robert de Barre was a witness there, as was lord Geoffrey Barre, and Thomas de Barre canon of Southwell. Lord John Barry and his wife, possibly called Maud, had a son called Hugh, parson of Ruddington.[101]   All the names are in our Barre family tree, but so common that they may not be in 'our' family.   They might be related to the Alexander Barre in the 1200s.   But the first Richard Barre acquired property in Nottinghamshire or Derbyshire for Richard de Rushell, and perhaps by 1230 the grandson Richard wrested it from Phillip de Rulegh - and lord John Barry may also have had a daughter named Agnes.   Southwell is 40 miles from Peveril Castle, and 25 miles from Roche Abbey, where the action goes next.

Chapter Sixteen - 1236: YORKSHIRE AND IRELAND

"Ah but in Kilkenny, it is reported,
On marble stones there, as black as ink:
With gold and silver, I did support her –
But I'll sing no more now, till I get a drink."

~ 'Carrickfergus' (traditional)

When prince John fell out with the Justices in 1193, they assigned Peveril Castle to Eleanor of Aquitaine,[1] who was on Richard I's side. Henry II would have turned in his grave at that. The castle came back to John when he was king, but one of the barons who forced him to sign Magna Carta in 1215 was Hugh de Neville, whom John had made governor of the castle (then called Hope). It was seized back for John by William de Ferrars,[2] great-great-grandson of the original William Peverell through Margaret.[3] He took part in the Fifth Crusade, 1218-21,[4] and married Sibylla, daughter of William Marshal; their daughter turns up later in this chapter, and more recent descendants in Chap.17. Henry III was there in 1235,[5] about when Sibylla de Calna sold Wykes to Hugh de Sherdilowe. Soon afterwards, Hugh died or disappeared - interesting, because some very curious things happened east of the Castle in 1236.

Once again, indirectly, Ralph of Coggeshall provided the lead. Although he wasn't the author of the *Chronicon Sanctae Terrae*, Ralph had other works which haven't survived. One was *Super Quibusdem Visionibus*, 'Upon Certain Visions' (of the afterlife), experienced by a monk of Evesham and described by the 13th century chronicler Matthew Paris, of St.Albans, whose *Chronica Majora*[6] incorporates and continues the *Flores Historiarum* of Roger de Wendover. His chronicle spans the history of the world from the Creation up to 1235, and the *Encyclopedia Britannica* dryly says that "it is of original value from 1202". It was Roger who wrote up the Evesham visions, but in the 19th century, his work was ascribed to Matthew Paris. So when I started looking for it in more recent editions of Paris, I couldn't find it at first.

But under 1236, the year of Henry III's coronation, I found another part of our story:

Of a Certain Prodigy of Men Appearing

"Also under this same time, in the month of May, not far from the abbey which is called Rupe (Roche), located in the north part of England, there appeared a battle-line of finely armed knights, mounted on horses of great value, with standards and shields, coats of mail and helmets, and furnished with the other protective coverings of knights: but they came out of the earth, as it appeared, and again they vanished, swallowed by the earth. And this vision through many days held the eyes of the beholders as if [they saw] illusions. Moreover they rode in arrayed ranks, and at times having made a meeting they fought fiercely, sometimes as if in tournament they shivered their spears into very small fragments with a crash. The inhabitants saw them, and more from a distance than close, wondering beyond measure, because they never remembered themselves having seen such things..."[6]

Paris adds more in the margin - two notes, in fact. The first reads, "A noted prognostic like that which is read in the beginning of the Maccabees. [Ed. note: 2 Macc. iii, 25-28]", and the second: "These more plainly arrived in Ireland and in its confines, so that sometimes as if coming from battle and defeated they dragged their horses after them wounded and broken down, without rider, but also themselves were badly wounded and bloodstained. And what was more wonderful, their tracks appeared plainly impressed on the earth, and the plants flattened and trampled down. And many seeing these things, fleeing before them eagerly took shelter in churches and castles out of fear, because they thought these things not to be of the fantastic. These things *came to our notice* [Paris's emphasis, underlined in red] from the account and most true formal declaration of the earl of Gloucester several years after this event, and from the evidence of many other people."

After completing the *Chronica Majora*, in 1250 Matthew Paris went on to the *Historia Anglorum*, and retold the Roche event:

Of Certain Fantastic Apparitions

"At almost the same time, in the month of May, in the parts of England bordering Wales there appeared in the air visions of men elegantly armed, gathering as if in combat. This seemed unbelievable to all who heard it, unless they had read the like in the prince of the Maccabees."[7]

And in the margin: "Moreover similar things happened in Ireland, of which apparition we were later informed by the faithful account of the count of Gloucester. For Richard count of Gloucester related this to me, who writes it, upon his oath."

This means that when Paris got the Irish information, he went back and amended both manuscripts. It's not obvious why, since like the green children's story, this one has no religious significance. It's even stranger that he puts so much stress on the Maccabees tie-in, in both chronicles, when it's not Christian but Jewish. The Maccabees, priest-kings of Palestine, 161-40 BC, came close to holding off the Romans. In 40 BC the title was held by Herod, who went to Rome to be recognised king of the Jews.
Two steps away from Woolpit, in any direction...

The 2 Maccabees incident has no direct link to our story. During the Asian occupation of Jerusalem, 187-185 BC, allegedly Heliodorus, Treasurer of king Seleuchus IV, came to seize money from the Temple of Solomon, giving plenty of warning.[8] As he entered he was set upon by a rider and two attendants, who came out of nowhere and left him likely to die but for medical aid from his intended victims.[9] It's not hard to explain by secret passages and trapdoors, especially as there are caves, artificial chambers and passages below the Dome of the Rock,[8] e.g. below the previous Temple's Altar of Burnt Sacrifice,[10] and below the Aqsa mosque (Chap.3).

But the Templars rejoiced in the title of 'Second Maccabees', bestowed by St. Bernard de Clairvaux.[11] Richard de Hastings and either Tostes de St. Omer, or the provincial Master in France, commissioned a book in French of abridged versions of Genesis, Joshua, Kings and Judges, also the Apocryphal Tobias, Judith and Maccabees. Ralph of Coggeshall says that at Hattin, Grand Master de Ridefort urged the Templars to "be mindful of your fathers the Maccabees". So yet again the mystery knights were Templars. They 'appeared in the air', not in the clouds but out of thin air.

Matthew Paris had a Londoner's attitude to Britain, and when he said Roche Abbey was in the north, it's actually in South Yorkshire - and only 24 miles from Peveril Castle, closer than Coggeshall is to Woolpit. 'The parts of England bordering Wales' seem to contradict that, but in his own map of Britain, he made Wales too large and too far north, with the Peak District and Yorkshire to the east.[12]

Roche Abbey was founded in 1147 by two barons, who gave the banks of the Maltby Dike stream to the Cistercians. "Charter of Richard Fitz-Turgis, concerning the foundation of the Abbey de Rupe.

Figs 16.1 & 16.2. Roche Abbey ruins.
Photos by Linda Lunan, August 2011.

Be it known to all seeing or hearing this charter, that I Richard son of Turgis, with the consent of my wife, and of my heirs, have given to God and St. Mary, for the good of my soul and those of all my forbears, the whole land of the parish of Eilrichetorp, as far as the brow of the hill at the stream which runs from Fogswelle, and so to the heap of stones which lies in the *sart* of Elsi, and so past the road *as far as the Wlvepit* [my emphasis]..."[13]

Allowed to choose either bank, the Cistercians changed the design and built on both (Fig. 16.2).[14]   Eilrichetorp is on the north-west corner of the wall; Elsi was a pre-Conquest Saxon, and a sart (usually an assart) was a piece of land appropriated for someone's use, given the rights or paying an annual rent[15] - in this case a clearing, so the ground was wooded on the west, as it is today.   The stones were still there in the 19th century,[16] so the Wlvepit was near the Ladies' Well (originally Lady's, as at Woolpit?). 'Capability' Brown, who ruined the Abbey further to make it more picturesque (Fig. 16.1), made the stream a lake:[17] the 1854 Ordnance Survey shows its former line, and on the 1930 edition the lake is 'Laughton Pond'. The upper southwest corner fits Turgis's directions to the Wlvepit (Fig. 16.2), and there are remains of the wall by the footpath.   Between path and lake a stagnant pool is presumably the Wlvepit, though much smaller than the Suffolk moats. Since the lake didn't exist in the 12th and 13th centuries, the pit may then have been dry.

To the west there's a long field, ideal for a tournament if clear of trees then: the few oaks there now are a good age.   Blythe Castle, three and a half miles off, was licensed by Richard I for tournaments,[18] banned by the church but reintroduced in 1194; after 42 years people should be used to them, though not to Templars taking part - banned from the mid-twelfth century "unless no spears were thrown".[19]   "The inhabitants... never remembered having seen such things," so the 1236 events were unusual.

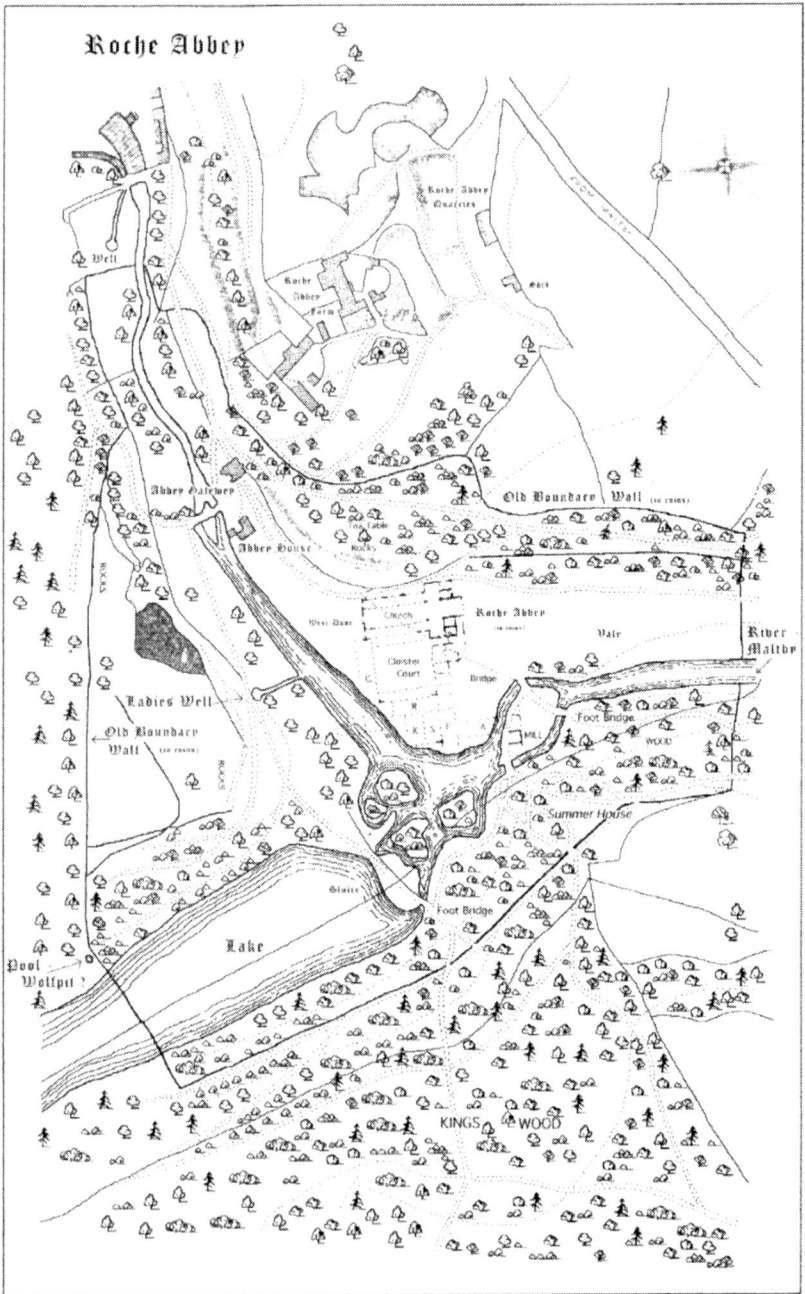

Fig. 16.3. Roche Abbey plan showing Wolfpit and Lady's Well. Drawing by Nick Portwin, after Aveling.

Fig. 16.4. SIGILLUM ABBATIS DE RUPE.
Personal seal of the Abbot of Roche.

The Abbey was called 'Roche' because of a miraculous sculpture of a crucifix on a rock.[20] But the abbot's seal has the crescent and star on it (Fig. 16.4): the upturned crescent 'signifies the increase of the Gospel', while the star is the symbol of the Epiphany.[16] Although the crescent and star aren't together as on Sibylla de Calna's seal and Henry III's, the star is accompanied by five-petalled Dog Roses. As a Christian symbol the Dog Rose stands for the Resurrection and the Virgin Birth, because the flower is self-pollinating; but it also represents Venus, or Ishtar,[21] and the knights were appearing and disappearing at Roche Abbey while Sibylla was still alive.

Strangely, in the "Catalogue of Seals in the British Museum" the seal is described with the crescent and stars and the reader is referred to the plate in Avelling's history of Roche Abbey (Fig. 16.4). But as with Abbot Samson's seal (Chap.14), the one under the catalogue number has no crescent, stars or roses - no match at all.[22]

259

Roche Abbey was finished in 1170-80;[14] Reginald was Abbot 1223-38, when the knights appeared.[13] But the Templars' Yorkshire holdings were all in the north, east and west, not in south Yorkshire.[23] As in Derbyshire and Suffolk, where they owned very little, it's as if they wanted to keep unusual activity away from their own land.

In the 1230's solar activity was far below late 12th century levels, and weather was correspondingly poor. In April and June 1233 Roger de Wendover noted parhelia, caused by high-altitude ice, as 'snakes' in the sky. Nevertheless, in July that year Matthew Paris records two huge dragons fighting in the sky over the south coast of England - presumably an auroral storm. The eye-witness accounts so impressed him that he referred back to it in 1250, among major events of the first half of the century.[24] He then describes a major meteor shower, unfortunately without giving the year. "One night an infinite number of stars were seen to fall from the sky, so that at one and the same time ten or twelve could be seen flying at the same time, some in the east, some in the west, in the south, in the north and in the middle of the firmament. If these had been the real stars, not a single one would have been left in the sky. No apparent reason for this can be found in [Aristotle's] *Book of Meteors*; [25] but Christ's menace was threatening mankind, 'and there shall be signs in the sun' [Luke 21:25]." Some editors put it in 1239, but that was one meteor, at dusk before the stars came out, coming from the south and disappearing in the northern sky.[6,24]

In March 1233 England had storms and floods, and thunderstorms in November. There was severe frost and famine in 1234, heavy rain and floods in February 1236, followed by a dry summer, with mock-suns and tempest in December.[6,26] In Ireland there were "heavy rains, harsh weather and much war", though between Irish chieftains, not concerning English barons or the Templars.[26]

The history of Roche Abbey[16] cites other phantom knights, including "the spectre horsemen" of Southerfell in Cumberland, who left no marks on the ground;[27] and near Bury St. Edmunds, between Fornham St. Martin and Pakenham, "on Christmas Eve, at midnight, a coach drawn by four headless horses, and driven by a headless coachman, might be seen to come from the parish of Great Barton, across the fields, regardless of fences..." A 19th century ghost-buster found nothing at the appointed time except a local who didn't believe it.[27]   But the 1236 knights had their heads screwed on, and appeared in daylight, marking the ground and flattening plants - like the 'phantom army' of 1170 (Chap.7) - according to the earl of Gloucester. Looking into his background, I found another fascinating character.

Richard de Clare succeeded to the title in 1230, at eight years old.   His guardian was Hubert de Burgh, earl of Kent and Justiciar of England,[28] and in 1236, aged 14, he was still a royal ward.[29]   His family property was in Wales, southwest England and Suffolk, including the village there from which they took their name: County Clare in Ireland was then outside the English holdings.[30]   The de Clares built the first Norman castles there, but not until the 1270s.[31]   The rest of his life was interesting, to say the least, but not necessarily related to our story.   For now it's his ancestry that counts.

He was descended from Richard 'Strongbow' de Clare, earl of Pembroke, leader of the invasion of Ireland in 1170.   Strongbow became lord of Leinster (except Dublin and the coastal cities), and was given custody of the conquered part of Ireland in 1173.   After his death in 1176 prince John held Leinster in wardship for Strongbow's daughter, Isabel de Clare, till in 1189 she married William Marshal, later regent for young Henry III until his own death in 1219. On his death-bed Marshal became a Templar - not suddenly, for he'd ordered his mantle years earlier.[32]   The next William Marshal, his son, was lord of Leinster, justiciar of Ireland in 1224, in London in 1231 for the second marriage of his sister Isabel, mother of 'our' Richard de Clare; he died soon after and was buried with his father in the New Temple.[33]

William Marshal the younger died childless, succeeded by his brother Richard, who found himself at odds with the king.   In April 1234 the Templars arranged a parley at the Curragh in which this third Earl Marshal was treacherously attacked, wounded and captured, to be killed by the prison doctor.   His sons also died in strange circumstances: Gilbert at a prohibited tournament in 1241, Walter in 1245 and Anselm just eleven days later. Leinster was divided among the daughters of the first William Marshal and their heirs, including Eve de Braose, who married William de Cantilupe aka de Calna, and took possession of Aghaboe in 1247 as part of her inheritance. Through Isabel, Richard de Clare inherited Kilkenny, now capital of the Pale, where his grandfather had built a castle in 1192.   Other holdings with it gave him most of the old kingdom of Ossory, and probably he learned there about the 1236 knights' appearance - hence Matthew Paris's post-1250 margin notes 'some years afterwards'.

If the event was in Ossory, maybe it was at the site of the 1170 'phantom attack' – the Mote of Skirk near Aghaboe! We should look for Cistercians or Templars nearby.

The Templars entered Ireland with the later wave of Strongbow's invasion, and in 1234 the new Master there was Ralph de Southwark, who promptly "abandoned his habit"; the Justiciar was ordered to arrest him if he showed face in Ireland again – perhaps because of the earl Marshal affair, but maybe he didn't care for whatever the Order was going to risk in 1236. His replacement Roger le Waleis was in charge till 1250, but little else is known about him.[34]

In 1236, a Templar force in the Holy Land was wiped out at Antioch. Matthew Paris describes Hospitallers' reinforcements leaving in response, but not Templars'.[6] Others have Templars at Antioch redeemed later that year,[35] maybe 20 survivors out of 120. Some say that although they were commanded by the preceptor of Antioch, the Templars' defeat was at Aleppo.[6] But many put it in 1237, even if quoting Paris[36] - did Richard de Clare have the date wrong?

In 1174 Richard Strongbow gave the Templars a preceptory at Gowran,[36] "the place of steeds"[38] - strategically important, with a commanding position on the Pass of Gowran, which the English army penetrated in 1170. In 1255 Henry III resolved a dispute between Richard de Clare and the Irish Templar Master, over ownership of the Honour of Gowran.[39] One witness was Eve de Braose, widow of the William de Cantilupe who had Calne from 1222 onwards (see Chap.15); royal business often took de Cantilupe into Ireland, and Eve was also Eve Fitz-Thomas, of Thomastown, between Gowran and Jerpoint, south of Kilkenny. Around then a William de Calna married the seneschal of Ossory's widow, and from 1283 onwards a William de Calne and his wife Roesia were moving between Ireland and in England; "there was then quite a little colony of people from Calne and the neighbourhood settled in Ireland."[40] The king of South Ossory, 1113-46, founded an abbey at Jerpoint, and the Cistercians took over around 1158, under the Abbot of Ossory.[41] Clay from the site "was considered to have miraculous powers, especially for those afflicted with eye trouble", like the Lady's Well at Woolpit. Until 1252 Newtown-Jerpoint was held under de Clare by Matilda de Bohun,[42] daughter of William de Ferrars - the same one, descended from William Peverell, who was in charge of Peveril Castle 1208-14,[43] and whose descendants later linked up with Richard Barre's (Chap.17).

So by 1236 we have links between Jerpoint and Peveril Castle, Gowran and the de Calnas, Aghaboe and Woolpit; and an earlier link between Peveril Castle and the phantom attack of 1170, through Ranulph Fitz-Ralph (Chap.7), and William Fitz-Ralph, in charge of Peveril Castle six years later.[44] As the layers of records are peeled back, a pattern begins to appear. But we still have to trace what happened to the major characters, and more links will come to light as we do.

Chapter Seventeen - 1240'S AND AFTER: SIBYLLA, AGNES AND BEYOND

"We do not wish anything to happen.
Seven years we have lived quietly,
Succeeding in avoiding notice...
We have seen births, deaths and marriages,
We have had various scandals,
We have been afflicted with taxes,
We have had laughter and gossip,
Several girls have disappeared
Unaccountably, and some not able to..."

~ T.S. Eliot, *Murder in the Cathedral*

1. Sibylla and Son

Walter Fitz-Bernard took over Sibylla's dowry manor of North Fambridge and is listed there in 1239-41.[2]   Coincidentally (or perhaps not) the sky lit up again, with the large meteor recorded by Matthew Paris in 1239, red aurora on St. Lucius' Day in 1241, and a major meteor shower in 1243.[3]

In 1239 Sibylla made a final concord with the prior of Binham, dropping her claims to Bernay manor in return for a payment of 20 silver marks, followed by a charter from Walter dropping any future claim of his.[4]   But in 1244, 'Sibila de Calna and Walter de Horkele' were sued for rent of Bernay, now called Binham-Priory manor, because Christiana de Valoines gave it to the priory before her death in 1236.[5]   It was one of several actions brought by the Prior before moving on to Tinmouth, and apparently that's why it's in the *Chronica Majora* though it wasn't exactly a major event.[6]

The manor extended into Thursford from the next parish;[5] "in which pleasant place [Sibylla] keeps the whole, certainly one carucate of land (about 120 acres, enough to support one family) with appurtenances, viz. the wood, fold, and all other things belonging to the said manor".[6]   Prior Richard de Parco had set up a grange, a hall, a vault, a byre, a fishpond and other buildings there; his complaint was that Walter de Horkesley was deducting ten pounds a year from the rent. The hall's not on a 1790 map of the area,[7] but there's an Old Hall Farm in modern Barney, and three moats on the Ordnance Survey map, east of the road. The northern one appears to have enclosed a mediaeval garden or building, the middle one's likely to have been a dwelling, and the southern one's function is unclear.[8] As with the Templars in 1236, Paris adds a margin note, saying that the case was resolved by "a secret predisposition" that the manor drew nine marks from other sources including "the mill of Winkeneye", donated to the Priory in king John's reign,[5] so they were no worse off.

After that Sibylla disappears from the records. Walter Fitz-Bernard continued in royal service.[9] By 1251, he had made a gift of land at Thorunden (Thorndon, north-east of Woolpit?) to Coggeshall Abbey.[10] He was now married to Isabella, (presumably his second wife, after Matilda, and not to be confused with Richard de Calna jnr's wife Isabel) and in 1253 she had to bring a legal action herself, because Walter was with the king in Gascony.[11] In 1254, perhaps because of that, Walter was excused all further royal service for life,[12] and retired to Reed. In 1247, Eve de Braose had taken over her inheritance of the manor of Aghaboe, and she married William de Cantilupe, aka de Calna, whose seal incorporated the de Calna crescent and star. Around the same time Richard de Clare inherited his holdings in Ossory.

2. 1250s: A New Sequence of Strange Events

In early March, 1253, supposedly the New Moon was three days early.[3,6] If true, it might be caused by more impacts or similar events on the Farside of the Moon, generating another temporary atmosphere. Shortly afterwards on March 18th there was a red obscuration of the sky, in which the Sun, Moon and stars were immersed in a kind of mist or smoke.[3] Volcanic dust might explain it: in the spring of 939 a Scottish report of 'the colour of blood on the sun from the break of day until the middle of the next day' has been used to date an eruption of Eldgja in Iceland.[13] But I don't have a candidate eruption for 1253: the extremely destructive one of El Chichón in Mexico, associated with the end of the Maya civilisation and accelerating the first 'mini-ice-age' in Europe, linked to the 'Wolf Minimum' (see below), wasn't until 1259.[14] Wind-borne dust from the Sahara is the most likely explanation, but perhaps it was meteoritic, like the stones which 'rained down' in 1178. In 200 BC a rain of stones in Europe was accompanied by a 'diminished Sun',[15] and Chinese astronomers reported massive fireball activity, suggesting that the Earth was passing through denser than usual meteor showers. In 1861, when Earth passed through the tail of a comet, there was a yellow obscuration over the sky, with the Sun barely visible and candles needed at 7 p.m. in midsummer.[6]

It would have interested Robert Grosseteste, the bishop of Lincoln, whose interest in physics, optics and astronomy was taken up by Roger Bacon. Grosseteste's *Compendium Spherae*, 1232, has the first account outside the Arab world of the precession of the equinoxes (Chap.21);[16] but he died on 9th October, 1253. Supposedly bells were heard in the air in two places at the time;[6] despite the bells in the children's story, I wouldn't mention that if it weren't among so many other phenomena. But in many cases aurorae, meteors and even comets allegedly produce sounds, possibly by electromagnetic disturbances affecting the nervous system.[17] There surely were disturbances in 1253:

"In the same year on 15th October, when the sky was clear, about the hour of vespers [4 p.m.], at the manor which is called Alvaston near Derby, there was seen, by the knight Sir Thomas Hanselin, lord of that manor, weakened by old age, and by his son and heir Geoffrey, and many others from his own family, as well as others from the same manor, among whom was a certain freeholder called Nicholas de Findern, who saw this and told it to us; suddenly, in a certain great, thick cloud there appeared a certain great, bright star shining like the Sun, and behold, beside it two small red stars sparkling like tapers, which immediately made a violent assault against the great star, upon which it can be said that they were attacking it, and rushing upon it, and strongly fighting with it; to the extent that it was seen by those who were present there at this spectacle, that sparks of fire fell from them. And the battle continued in this form *until late in the evening* [my italics], so that those who were watching it, dazed with fear and wonder, not knowing what it might portend, withdrew from it."[18]

The margin and Index of the 13th century Burton Chronicle, Rolls edition (not to be confused with Robert Burton's 17th century *Anatomy of Melancholy*), caption this 'Remarkable meteor', in the sense of 'phenomenon in the atmosphere'. A meteor slowed by a previous pass through the atmosphere, might take a minute or so to cross the sky - but whatever this was, it lasted for hours, so

266

long that the witnesses gave up on it.   We aren't told where in the sky it was, but Alvaston is 35 miles south-west of Peveril Castle and a similar distance SSE of Roche Abbey.   It's another like the event over John of Oxford's house in 1195 (Chap.20).

For December 14th, 1253, Matthew Paris used the heading 'Of an unnatural perturbation of the air and sea'.   "That same year, on the night before Saint Lucia's Day, with heavy snow falling from the clouds, winter thunder announced dire things to come".[6]   As solar activity headed down into the 'Wolf Minimum', 1252 had seen drought in May, June and July followed by a murrain of livestock, dogs and crows, worst in Norfolk and south, causing famine.   1253 had heavy rain and floods, with tsunamis on the coasts of Estonia and Jutland following creation of a new island, and in 1254 continual storms from May to November caused great hardship.[19]   But other events were strange enough for Matthew Paris to list in both his chronicles and his extended version of Roger de Wendover's *Flores Historiarum*.[3,6]

On January 1st, 1254, the day after the First Quarter Moon, there was 'a wondrous fantastic apparition'.   "In the very night of the Lord's Cirumcision, when the air was very serene in the middle of the night, and the starry firmament was being watched on the eighth day of the Moon, there appeared in the air, wonderful to relate, a certain large ship very elegantly constructed, of wonderful design and colour.   As certain monks of St. Albans were considering it, commemorating the feast of Saint Amphibalus and inspecting the stars to see if it was the hour to sing matins, they called together all of the *familia* and their dependents who were in the court to see the wonders.   And for a long time there appeared as many sheets and planks as would make up a true ship;   but the same gradually began to dissolve and disappear;   whence it is believed to have been made of clouds, but wonderful and miraculous."[6]

The monks were "inspecting the stars to see if it was the hour to sing matins", more than eighty years before Abbot Richard of Wallingford built his great clock at St. Albans to tell the hours of prayer as well as showing the movements of the Sun and Moon.[20]   Perhaps it was just an imaginative interpretation of an auroral display - though more static than the usual mediaeval account of 'fighting dragons'.   In his *Meteorological Chronology*, C.E. Britton quotes an account of 1115, mixing up moon-dogs and sun-dogs (which might happen consecutively)   "...as if there had been two suns, somewhat less bright than the larger sun: and on the top of each of these two narrower ones appeared two imperfect circles, *in the shape of a ship* [my emphasis]."[14] Moon-dogs are rare, and complete circles round the Moon are more common: the same chronicle records those in February 1115. The detailed description is hard to pare down to a single arc of a lunar halo, when the Moon was just past First Quarter. It might be a more purposeful signal, in view of what happened next.

"In the same year, to be precise at Septuagesima [February 8th], when furious winds were stirred up, certain barbarian ships were made to put in by their masters; the like of which had not been seen by us, so large and elegant, stoutly armed with weapons of naval warfare and furnished with the best of supplies. They landed in the northern part of England, not far from Berwick. When the guardians of the coast heard that, at once they seized the men that were in them, as if they were barbarians or spies or even enemies. And on examining everything, they found the holds of the ships filled with very many weapons, and filled with coats of mail, helmets, shields, and provisions, which were enough for an army. And when they were asked who they were, they didn't wish to indicate to the bailiffs who, why, from whence, or how they had come. *Nor could any of them understand the speech of the bailiffs* [my emphasis]; other similar ships were seen upon the sea. And since all believed them to be distressed [sailors], they were allowed to depart in peace, so that [the bailiffs] were not found to be more cruel than the storm, and the matter was pursued no further."[6]

Berwick-upon-Tweed grew important during the thirteenth century, as the Tweed came to be the Border between Scotland and England. For neither the type of ship nor the sailors' language to be recognised there is almost as strange as it was for the language and clothing of the green children at Woolpit. James Bentley suggested they might be Genoese or Arabs, carrying weapons to the Hanseatic League in Germany, taking shape at the time - Lynn was a contact port, and it seems the Templars traded with the League out of Bristol.[21] But Templar ships would have been recognised, and I'd expect Genoese or Arabs to be recognised even if not understood.

In 1258 Walter Fitz-Bernard leased North Fambridge to Richard de Clare,[12] source of the 1236 Irish report, who held court at Fambridge in 1258-59.[2] de Clare had led an interesting life meanwhile: Henry III wanted him to marry the earl of Marsh's daughter, but he secretly married his guardian's instead: Henry divorced them and made him marry the daughter of the earl of Lincoln. He and Margaret de Burgh remarried later.   In 1240 he was in the Holy Land; in 1244 fought in Wales; was knighted in 1245; in 1246, with other peers, complained about the king to the Pope.[22]   In 1247 Henry III twice had to prohibit him from tournaments with the king's half-brothers.   In 1249, he angered the English nobles by fighting against them in a tournament, on the foreign side.   In 1250, he and other barons went abroad for unknown reasons, and he was received with honour by the queen of France and the Pope.[23]

Notorious for his avarice, in 1253 he was bribed by Henry to marry his eldest son to the underage daughter of the count of Angoulême, causing a royal row with the abbots of England, the Templars and Hospitallers, all of whom refused to put up the money.[23]   In 1258 he quarrelled with the Abbot of Bury St. Edmunds over rights at Mildenhall, and in retaliation he introduced the Franciscan Order into Bury against the Abbey's wishes.   He led the barons' resistance to Henry III in 1258.   After a poisoning attempt at Winchester, in 1262 he succumbed to another "at the table of Peter de Savoy, the uncle of the queen, along with Baldwin earl of Devon and other persons of note",[24] including the earl of Bedford;[25] so ending what Sir William Dugdale accurately called 'an active career'.[22]

Walter kept six and a half knights' fees at North Fambridge for himself, so this manor too was big.   It later reverted in full to the Fitz-Bernards, because it's not among de Clare's holdings in 1263, after his death.[26]   Lord Robert Fitz-Bernard rented it out again in 1276,[27] and a John Bernard was Rector of Reed in 1361.[28]   Did the sale charter of Wykes and Knettishall (Chap.15) pass through his hands?   Walter Fitz-Bernard's son Thomas stayed on at Knettishall as a tenant for at least part of the late thirteenth century.[29]   It was among land seized by Edward I in dispute with the abbot of Leyston in 1302,[30] but goings-on of that sort were common: that trail goes cold.

In 1261 Richard de Calna (grandson or great-grandson) was receiving a pension from Walter de Horkesley, under the auspices of Binham Priory. Subsequently Robert de Waltham, prior of Binham, allocated 24 acres of arable land in Bernay to Philip, the son of Richard de Calna, and Richard's niece Alice or Adeliza.[31]   Prior Robert took office after 1264, was there in

1279 and '89, and had left by 1296.[32]   So Philip and Alice's time at Bernay didn't overlap with Richard de Clare's at North Fambridge, interesting though it would have been if they had; that it didn't, raises other possibilities which we'll see at the end of the chapter.

3. The Barre Inheritance

We saw in Chap.14 that Agnes Barre's neighbour Pagan de Parles gifted the church in Handsworth to the Hospitallers, whose Prior passed on his court and market rights to Richard Barre; but he assigned the church itself to one Walter de Hereford, perhaps giving Agnes a link to the de Herefords in Aghaboe.[33]   Agnes had now outlived her husband and elder son, but William and his wife Christiana were still alive (Fig.17.2). In 1238-39, Christiana de Barre, Richard her son, Agnes de Parva Barra, and Thomas de Acton brought an action about common pasture in Parva Barra itself.[34]   This Richard is the grandson   (Chap.15); as Ricardus de Parva Barra he had ten fees there in 1242-43.[29]   If Agnes was about ten in 1173, she'd be 81 in 1238 - old, but not impossible.   Unlike Sibylla, she didn't revert to 'de Calna' when widowed, as if never allowed or never wanting to use it.

In the previous generation, there was a Christiana de Ruili with a son in Chelmsford, Essex, who appears again in Leia in 1202,[35] and a daughter called Isabel.[36]   Editors identify this 'Leia' with Great or Little Leigh in Essex, but if 'Ruili' was still another spelling of the Staffordshire Rowley, 'Leia' could be a short version of Rouueleia, Rowley's Domesday spelling.   Could Christiana have a third child, named after her, who married William Barre, son of her former neighbour?   And if she was a de Rulegh, the name Richard de Rushell had now switched to, did she know that he was the illegitimate son of Richard and Agnes Barre?   Was her marriage to William part of the deal with the de Rushells/Ruleghs to keep it quiet?   It would be very interesting to be 'a fly on the wall' that day in 1222 when the grandson Richard Barre got back from court, having learned Richard de Rulegh's identity.   Many questions might be answered if we knew what he, Agnes, William and Christiana had to say to one another.

Hugh Barre (c.1100 – 1166 or 1168)

Robert de Barr
m. Petronilla
pre 1150 – 1212

Richard Barre
1140? – 1209
m. Agnes *c.* 1180 *d. c.* 1238
Co-heiress with Sibylla de Calna

Roger
1170's – 1180's

Richard de Rushell *aka* de Rowley
(illegitimate)
c. 1178 – 1224

William Barre
m. Christiana (de Rowley?)
1180 – 1255

Phillip de Rowley
d. 1272. *m.* ?

Alice

Richard *d.* 1284
m. Felicia

Guy
(Geoffrey?)

Robert

Jordan

Richard

Robert
(rebel,
beheaded 1272)

Richard

Phillip

Giles

Walter

Alice
m.
Bartholomew de Swinnerton

Robert *d.* 1290
m. Cecilia

Felicia
m. Roger Hillary *d.* 1327

(Sir?) John de Barre
c. 1270 – 1348
m. Margaret

William

Roger

John
m. Joan

Geoffrey

Anne
m.. Sir William Devereux
1351

Henry

William

Roger

Richard
m. Joan

Nicholas
m. Felicia

1290 – 1360

Thomas de Bardwell
m. Isobel
1348

Sir Walter Devereux

William   John

John   Elyas   Agnes

William de Bardwell

William Washington (USA)

Robert Washington Shirley (Earl Ferrars) *b.* 1929

1990's

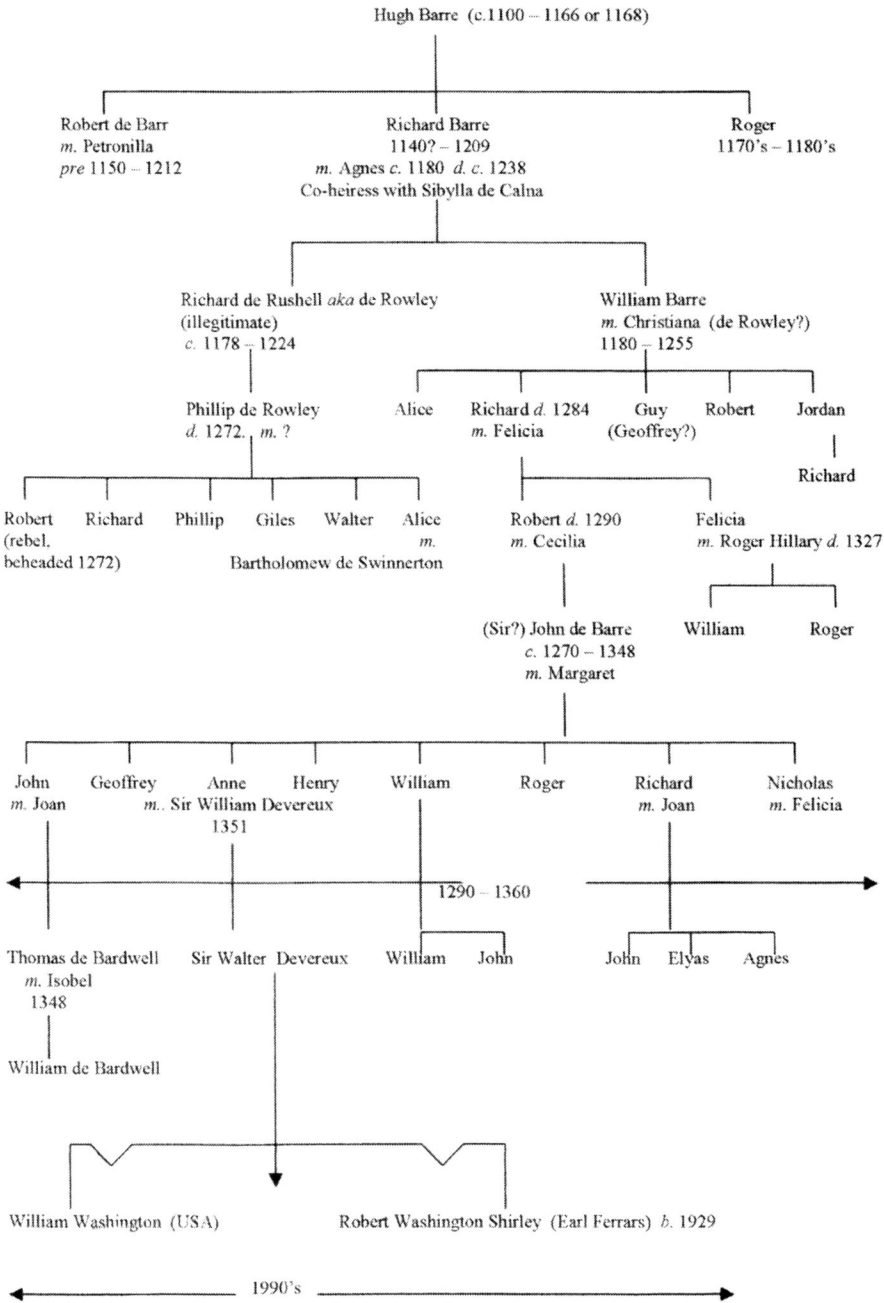

Fig. 17.1. Barre family tree.

By Duncan Lunan, layout devised by Nick Portwin.

271

1238-39 is the last I've found of Agnes. But in 1238 Henry III was at Erdington, part of Aston![11] If her arrival on Earth justified the personal attention of Henry II, it seems her departure from it - 'exitu *terre*', like Walter de Calna? - merited the presence of his grandson. If so, she really must have been something special.

In 1240 the quarrel with Richard de Rowley's heirs flared up again.[37] This time, Phillip de Rulegh's rights were challenged by Roger de Somery, whose family took over most of the area later. Phillip cited king John's charter to Richard de Rushell, which still survives;[38] Richard de Barre put in a counter-claim, according to a note in the margin in a different hand - without which the multiplicity of 'Richards' would make the case impossible to follow, as it tries to make out who was father of whom.

Now the old grudges came out. Richard de Rushell would never have had the land, Roger alleged, if Richard his father (Agnes's husband) hadn't been allowed to seize it while the rightful heirs, his own ancestors, were minors. Another note, again in different handwriting, adds that the case was referred to Westminster for judgment. Richard de Barre was awarded the Rowley manor, at last, but he had to pay a cash settlement to Phillip de Rulegh (this time spelled Rughel) in 1242. Perhaps out of pique, he tried to wrest Rushell itself from the occupants, the same year, without success.[37]

In 1226 'Robert Barry' was listed at Winchester,[9] and 1248 saw Richard de Barre suing 'Robert, son of Christiana' (apparently his brother, though an odd way to put it) and sixty others for entering his land at Barr by night and throwing down a fence.[39] In 1250 he witnessed a grant of lands in Great Barr to Richard Tyrell and Felicia Barr;[40] this is an even odder way of putting things, because Felicia was Richard de Barre's wife. Presumably the Great Barr land was her dowry, and Richard was returning ownership to her: in which case Richard Tyrell may have been her brother.

Meanwhile, William de Barre was having a sprightly old age: in 1253 he and 37 others were accused of trespass and damage.[39] He and Christiana were sued over Aston, in 1254-55, when William would have been 74 years old at least; no doubt that's why the judgement was binding on their heirs.[41]

Richard Barre appears in a dispute about a mill in 1262,[39] and again as 'Richard Barry' in 1266.[30] Guy de Barre had free tenement in Parva Barra in 1272, as a sub-tenant;[41] in the same year there was an Alice Barre, with a married daughter of the same name - but Alice herself was the widow of Phillip de Rulegh[39] (Chap.15)! If they knew they were first cousins when they married, they would have needed special dispensation from the Church. Phillip must have died very recently, because in the same year he had won a case about a fence wrongfully erected on the land he held in Barre (probably the first Alice's dowry.) His daughter married Bartholomew de Swynnerton, of a prosperous local family; but they either died or left the area, because they don't appear elsewhere in the records or in the Swynnerton family tree.[42]

Perhaps they left to escape a continuing quarrel with the de Barres, because there was a sad day coming for both families. In 1265-66 one Robert de Rowley, along with his brothers Richard, Philip, Giles and Walter, was in trouble because he'd backed the rebellion led by Simon de Montford.[43] In 1272 Robert was pursued as a thief and beheaded without trial by a posse including Richard, son of Jordan de Barre. Robert's widow Matilda tried to get compensation but failed to turn up for the court case, so a warrant was issued for her arrest and Richard and his companions got away with it. If he was who I take him to be, in the family tree (Fig. 17.1), then just 99 years after Agnes arrived at Woolpit, one of her great-grandchildren had helped to kill another.

In 1272 a Felicia de Barre is described as the wife of Roger Illari, with land in Little Barr as her dowry;[39] this must be a daughter of the Richard and Felicia above, because Richard de Barre was still alive. Roger Hillary, the more familiar spelling, was a chief justice, and at his death in 1327 he was holding land in Great and Little Barr - the latter from still another Richard de Barre, below.[44] His son of the same name had hunting rights ('Free Warren') in Handsworth, Great, Little and Perry Barr, in 1344,[45] but in 1374 he and his wife Margery were sued for wasteful damage to the property.[46]

Felicia senior had problems in Great Barr in 1275, when one of her tenants was a felon,[47] and again in 1277, when her tenant Geoffrey de Terhull (son of Richard Tyrell? her nephew?) was outlawed for felony. In 1279 and 1280 she was at odds with Robert de Barre and his wife Cecilia, over one-third of Great Barr manor which they held from her.[48] However, this isn't 'Robert

273

son of Christiana', her brother-in-law above: this Robert is her son, with whom she shared property until 1302 at least.[49]

In 1280 Robert de Barre witnessed a grant of the advowson of Handsworth Church by Lenton Priory;[50] presumably he kept quiet about the associated rights of court, market, fair etc. which the Barres were still exercising instead of returning (Chap.14). Robert stood surety for a deer-poacher in 1286,[51] under the oppressive laws relating to royal forests; one Hugh de Barre, whom I haven't otherwise traced except for one appearance as a witness,[47] was in a crowd who attacked the Staffordshire Court of Forest Pleas in 1289. In 1289 Felicia's hedges and ditches were vandalised, and her son Robert stood surety for Richard Tyrel in 1293;[52] Geoffrey de Terhull's rented land came up for investigation again in 1295 after he was hanged.[30]

Richard de Barre kept up the family longevity, still in Little Barr from 1276 to 1284. Robert de Barre had it in 1285-90, however,[53] and there were court cases later about land in Great Barr which he and Felicia were alleged to have given away.[54] John, son of Robert and Cecilia, took over in 1290, holding the parish from William de Birmingham.[55] He was a witness regarding the ownership of Handsworth and Mere manors in 1291.[48] As John of Little Barr, in 1316 he was elected to parliament with Thomas le Rous, who was knighted that year, fought in all wars from 1300 to 1345, was sheriff of War-wickshire 1321-22 and Commissioner for the Army in 1325.

In his parliamentary history of Staffordshire, Josiah Wedgewood found John inadequate by comparison: "He was never knighted, bore no Arms, and seems altogether a most inconsiderable man to send to parliament for the country".[56] Wedgewood suggests John went to Westminster with Thomas le Rous as Thomas's squire. But perhaps he was a little harsh: John de Barre apparently was a chaplain in 1306, so he might not be eligible for knighthood (but see below). He held not only Little Barr but also Great Barr in 1316;[48] he was a juror in 1322,[56] when he still had Little Barr;[48] he had had Little Barr and land in Lichfield, with Nicholas de Barre, in 1327;[57] he had Wilton manor in 1340;[58] so he was of some consequence. He also had a large family: John, Geoffrey, Henry, William, Roger, Richard, Nicholas - and Anne, see below - though I'm guessing at the sons' order, based on their court appearances and apparent priority in the records, and Nicholas might perhaps have been a

274

grandson.   John de Barre's last appearance seems to be in 1348,[58] so he too lived into his seventies.

In the 1300's, with the property divided among such a large family, inevitably confusions arise.   Richard de Barre (misprinted de Bane) is listed as holding Little Barre from William de Birmingham in 1310, for example,[59] but if so he must have been a sub-tenant because John still had it in 1327.[57]   But by 1339 Little Barr passed to Henry Barre, previously listed in Hammerswich in 1327; in 1339 he was living in Coventry and renting out Little Barre.[60]   The latest Richard and his wife Joan were then living in Lichfield,[54] but he had land at Little Barre in 1340.   His brother Geoffrey appeared as a witness in 1333, likewise Roger in 1347.[44]

Nicholas de Barre is listed with wife Felicia and son Nicholas in Lichfield, in 1358.[46]   Elyas and Agnes Barry appear as Richard's children in Warwickshire in the 14th century, otherwise undated,[61] and Richard appears again in 1356 and 1365.[62]   Their uncle Henry is in Lichfield still later, in 1369 and 1387, while still another John Barre was excused military service in 1374.[64]   By then, the taxpayers of Perry Barr and Parva Barra were being listed together. Parva Barra was later held in dower by the Countess of Woodstock; after her death in 1407, the two became a single manor.[41]

As for the de Rowleys, despite the loss of his elder brother, 'Richard son of Richard son of Phillip de Rowley' (starting with the son of the illegitimate Richard, but not disinheriting   Phillip as the product of a first-cousin marriage) was still on the Rowley manor in 1307[65] and in 1309.[55]   So if Agnes was the green girl, she not only had children but continuing lines of descendants, many of them.

When my *Analog* article[66] went to press in 1996 it seemed I'd reached the end of the trail, which petered out before full parish records.   I'd traced the family virtually to the end of the odd events in mediaeval times (the last in Chap.24) and it seems their connection with those events died with Agnes.   It was amazing that I'd managed to identify Agnes at all, let alone trace her descendants so far, but that seemed to be it.

After the article came out in September 1996, I was contacted by Bill Washington, an American reader.   He had traced his family tree back to the de Ferrars family, whom we met in Chap.5 in the Peak District and again in Kilkenny above. In the 15th century they intermarried with a branch of the Devereux family, from Évreux in France, and their pedigree included Anne, daughter of Sir John Barre, who married Sir William Devereux in 1351.[66] Could she be descended from the green girl?

The answer was yes. The mid-14th century de Ferrars' history contained Staffordshire place-names and people whom I recognised, e.g. Thomas de Aston and Thomas de Erdington, frequently in the Aston records.[67] In the Staffordshire records, the connection was obvious: the Devereux family had been in the area since 1223, at least, and Felicia Barre and Matilda Devereux both had land in Cannock Forest in 1286; Felicia and Walter Devereux, (who lived in West Bromwich and fought in the wars against the Scots and at Crécy), were both tenants of the Dudley Barony in 1290 and the manor of Seggesley in 1291, along with John de Barre, William de Birmingham and other familiar names. Anne Barre was indeed the daughter of John de Barre, son of Robert, as above.

Through the marriage the Devereux family acquired rights in Barr including the advowson of the church.[68] The de Ferrars connection was also telegraphed well ahead, with many entries for the Derbyshire family in Staffordshire and in the Handsworth area; in particular, the Staffordshire estate of Chartley which was famous for its wild cattle. Robert de Barre witnessed a charter of the sixth earl, Robert de Ferrars, in 1262.[69] In 1450 when the last Lord Ferrers of Chartley died without a male heir, the title passed through his daughter to the Devereux family, and later to the Shirleys who still hold it today. In 1598/9, presumably as a further consequence of the 1350 marriage, Sir William Devereux had land in Great Barr.[70]

Apparently John de Barre was never knighted: in the 1300's he was described several times as 'lord', *dominus*, of Little Barre,[58] but by then the term was coming to mean just 'landowner' (Chap.4). If the compilers of the Devereux family tree knew he was a member of parliament, maybe they took knighthood for granted, because almost all county MPs of that time were 'knights of the shire'.[71] When William Devereux is listed in Bromwich in 1356, he's not identified as a knight either.[44]

I did wonder if John de Barre's son of the same name might be the knight, but it's not likely, even though he may have been eldest son, because he surrendered his claim on Little Barre to his mother in 1342.[72]   Even before then he had given management of the manor and part of its ownership to his brother Geoffrey, listed with his father in 1330, only to be sued by him in 1335 for not keeping adequate accounts as bailiff, and again for theft from the fish-ponds in 1338.   In 1340 Geoffrey and John junior were charged with beating, wounding and illtreating their father.[54]   John de Barre junior had an active criminal career which included breaking into a close with others, armed with bows and arrows, to steal sparrowhawks;[72] cattle theft;[73] assault, as above, and who knows what else.   Whatever else he achieved, including marriage to Joan, it's not likely to include a knighthood; and he died before his father, in 1342 or '43.[72]

Bill Washington wasn't the only descendant in the present day.   Shortly after I heard from him, my cousin Jill Bowyer took me to visit Norwich Cathedral. My hope was to find some more information about the de Calna archdeacons, but instead I learned that since 1979 the High Steward of the Cathedral had been the current Earl Ferrers, as the family now spells the name.[74]

When I got back to Glasgow, it didn't take long to find him in *Who's Who*[75] and other references.   The Right Honourable Robert Washington Shirley is the 13th Earl Ferrers and 19th baronet; he was Deputy Leader of the House of Lords 1979-83 and from 1988; in 1996 he was Minister of State for the Environment and the Countryside, ending when the Tory party was defeated in the 1997 General Election.

The story broke in the Scottish press on April 26th, five days before the poll: to my relief the Earl took it in good part, declaring "It sounds bizarre.   The Shirley family have a colourful history, but not *that* colourful."[76]   He's not wrong about the history: the founder of the title died in a feud before the Norman Conquest, in which his son took part.   The third earl was on the rebel side in 1173, as we've seen, and died at the siege of Acre in 1190; the thirteenth century earls rebelled twice against Henry III   In 1423 they acquired Staunton Harold Hall, near the Leicestershire-Derbyshire border, by marriage, and not sold until after World War II.   In 1653 Sir Robert Shirley built a chapel there in defiance of Cromwell and was thrown into the Tower, where he died "not without suspicion of poison".   When the title was revived in the 17th century the first of the new earls Ferrars married Elizabeth, daughter of Laurence Washington of Wiltshire, through whom he briefly owned Stonehenge (Chap.21). The later Shirleys were therefore related by marriage to George Washington, first President of the United States, but he wasn't descended from Richard and Agnes. Meanwhile they livened up their history with the "Wicked Lady Ferrers", Katherine, who was shot as a highwaywoman in 1660.[77]

But Laurence Shirley, the fourth of the new earls, was a direct descendant of theirs. The *Encyclopedia Britannica* says he was "the last nobleman in England to suffer a felon's death... In 1758 his wife obtained a separation from him for cruelty. The Ferrers estates were then vested in trustees, an old family servant, Johnson, being appointed receiver of rents. On Jan. 18, 1760, Johnson called at the earl's mansion at Staunton Harold, Leicestershire, when Lord Ferrers shot him. Ferrers was tried for murder by his peers in Westminster Hall. He pleaded insanity, but was found guilty. On May 5, 1760, dressed in a light-coloured suit, embossed with silver [his wedding suit, according to other sources], he was taken in his own carriage from the Tower of London to Tyburn and there hanged. It has been said that as a concession to his order the rope used was of silk."

Not only is the present earl Ferrers (with an 'e') descended from Richard and Agnes Barre, but also from William Peverell: the William de Ferrars who seized Peveril Castle for King John in 1215 was the great-grandson of Peverell's daughter Margaret. He'd previously claimed part of the Peak District on the strength of it, but dropped that in exchange for Higham Ferrers after John's coronation.[78]

Numerous relatives were listed in the present day: an aunt, daughter of the 11th earl; a cousin, daughter of the 11th earl's younger son; two sisters; a son, three daughters, four grandchildren. There is indeed blood of the green children spread through the human race, as John Crowley poetically supposed in his half-fictional version of the story[79] - through the Devereux family, the Barres, the Shirleys, the Washingtons, and uncounted other family marriages over the last 800 years. Most of us are probably carrying some of Agnes's genes by now, and they would be hard to identify, as Crowley said, especially if Agnes's forbears came from here in the first place.

It's even surprising that the link between the Barre descendants and the de Ferrars wasn't forged until the 15th century, when they would have been in touch in the early 13th, if not before. In 1246-47 a grant of Free Warren in Shirley itself was witnessed by - wait for it! - Richard de Clare, William de Cantilupe, Roger Bigod (count of Norfolk, descendant of Leicester's ally), Henry de Hastings and Panulph Peverell.[66]   Undoubtedly, another conversation where one would love to be a fly on the wall.

4. ET Contact or Politics?

Continuing research into North Fambridge turned up two further oddities. In 1296 the manor was in the hands of a knight named William Avenell;[80] Robert, William and Gervase Avenell were among the builders commissioned by Henry II to upgrade Peveril Castle in 1175-76.[81]   In the 14th century a descendant of Richard and Agnes Barre had rights in Wykes and possibly Woolpit (see below and Chap.24), and in the 16th century the Devereux family, by then fully descended from Richard and Agnes,[66] took over North Fambridge when they became the new earls of Essex.

Listing the connections between the sites and the people, it's clear that they form some sort of a web (Fig. 17.2); and although it seems as if the sites are changing hands in the general Brownian movement of property, in the days before commercial banking, what's actually happening in the 12th and 13th centuries is a shuffling of the key sites between just a few hands.

Twelve families feature in the grid, but only three major bloodlines. It's not clear whether the de Valoines were involved, though they owned Wykes, Knettishall, Thorpe and Bernay. They held land in so many places that they might be unaware what was going on in those few. Similarly, when the Fitz-Bernards were in at least seventeen counties, John Fitz-Bernard's property in the Peak District may not be part of the Peveril Castle operation. As for Richard de Clare, if he was involved, he broke the rules by making himself so conspicuous; but although his family had Crepping manor, on the Horkesley side of Wakes Colne, and had been there since the Domesday survey,[27] I haven't found any sign that his ancestors were involved.

Fig. 17.2. ET CONTACT OR POLITICS?

A POSSIBLE CONSPIRACY OF GREAT FAMILIES.

Peter de Valoines
(Knettishall, Wykes, Thorpe, Bernay etc.)

William Peverel
(Peveril Castle)

Richard de Calna
(Knettishall, Wykes)

Robert, William and Gervase Avenel
(Peveril Castle)

Richard de Calna's heirs
(Knettishall, Wykes)

William de Ferrars
(Peveril Castle)

John Fitz-Bernard > Sibylla de Calna
(in Peak District)   (North Fambridge)
                       (later Bernay)

Matilda de Bohun
(Jerpoint)

Ranulf le Broc/Damietta de Gorram
(Hagenet Castle)

Richard de Clare (Strongbow)
(Kilkenny, inc. Jerpoint, Gowran)

Adam de Hereford/Damietta
(Aghaboe)

Richard de Clare (Gloucester)
(Aghaboe)
(later North Fambridge)

Walter Fitz-Bernard
(Knettishall, Wykes, North Fambridge)

Eve de Cantilupe
(Gowran)

Thomas Fitz-Bernard
(Knettishall)

William de Calna
(Kilkenny)

John Bardwell (descended from Richard and Agnes Barre)
(Wykes)

William de Bardwell
Sir William Avenell
(Bardwell - including Wykes?)
(North Fambridge)

Walter Devereux, Earl of Essex
(North Fambridge)

For the same reason, I haven't shown in Fig. 17.2 that Richard de Clare and Christiana de Valoines were both married to de Burghs. Richard de Clare married Margaret de Burgh and Christiana de Valoines married Raymond. The family were very powerful - during the minority of Henry III, Hubert de Burgh ruled England from 1219 to 1232 as Justiciar and regent after the death of William Marshal, and was also guardian of the young Richard de Clare. He had the Honour of Rayleigh, including Nayland and within it Great Horkesley, and the Honour of Haughley (Hagenet), though the castle was gone. In Ireland the de Burghs were in Limerick, Connaught and Munster, earls of Ulster from 1255. Hubert may have been a friend of Ralph of Coggeshall's, and definitely was of Matthew Paris, later:[82] he might have influenced what they wrote and the clues they planted for us, but there's no actual evidence that he and his descendants were involved.

None of the families owned Woolpit, but the distances from Woolpit to Hagenet, Cressing Temple to Coggeshall, and Skirk to Aghaboe are all between four and five miles, which may prove significant. None of them were connected to Darlington, or Roche Abbey, but William de Ferrars was, at least by a grant of land,[83] and he was William Peverell's great-great-grandson.

At the beginning of Chap.5, I said there were very few possible cases of matter-transmission, in the many mediaeval chronicles I've looked at. The list we have now is:

Before 1155:	Peak Cavern (to Suffolk?) swineherd incident.
Late 1170:	'phantom army' in Ossory (Aghaboe?)
July 1173:	green children arrive at Woolpit?
After 1176:	Templars at Coggeshall Abbey.
1192:	knights appearing out of the air at Nogent-le-Rotrou.
1236:	Templar incidents at Roche Abbey and in Ireland (Aghaboc?)

along with astronomical and meteorological events which may not be coincidental:

1095:	auroral and meteor storms.
1146:	electrical storm over Jerusalem followed by onset of severe auroral disturbances.

1147:	electrically charged vortex over the sea off Lisbon.
1172 Dec. 24:	atmospheric explosion during auroral storm.
1173 Feb. 18:	upper atmosphere explosion over Derry during auroral storm.
1173 Summer:	mystery 'stars' stationary in west.
1178 June 19:	lunar Farside explosions.
1178 Dec. 24:	underground explosion at Darlington.
1189:	Henry II struck twice by lightning out of clear sky.
1195:	mystery event over John of Oxford's London house during electrical storm.
1205:	monster in electrical storm at Maidstone.
1228:	electrical storm envelops St. Paul's.
1253, early March:	supposedly the New Moon seen three days early.
- March 18th:	red obscuration of the sky, in which the Sun, Moon and stars were immersed in a kind of mist or smoke.
- October 15th:	thick cloud with bright star shining like the Sun, 'attacked' by two sparkling red stars over many hours.
1254, January 1st:	'wondrous fantastic apparition' of 'a certain large ship' in the air at St. Albans.

and along with those, the historical events which might also be related to them:

1096:	Peter the Hermit's crusade.
1155:	Henry takes control of Peveril Castle.
1158/59:	Richard de Calna excused payment of taxes by royal mandate.
1160:	Henry annexes Woolpit.
1163:	Henry takes control of Hagenet Castle, near Woolpit.
1173, May:	Geoffrey Ridell becomes Bishop of Ely. Richard Barre temporarily in charge of Woolpit?
1177-78:	Birth of Richard de Rushell, natural son of Richard Barre and Agnes.
1180:	Richard Barre marries Agnes?
1180s:	Ralph of Coggeshall a monk there; Richard de Calna's visits to him.
1182:	Walter de Coutances becomes Bishop of Lincoln. Henry lets Woolpit revert to Bury St. Edmunds Abbey, and allows Samson to become Abbot.

1196:	First records of Castleton village; because wind from Devil's Cavern had ceased?
1214:	John Fitz-Bernard, Sibylla de Calna's husband, reclaims Wykes & Knettishall.
1217:	Earl of Derby (descendant of William Peverell) gains Peveril Castle.
1236:	Hugh de Sherdilowe refuses tenant access to Wykes.
1254:	February 8th, mystery ships put in at Berwick.

We'll see more events in Chap. 24, and Appendix 1 gives a longer historical list, but there's enough here to suggest that something's going on. Critics may argue that I've selected incidents which back up the idea of extraterrestrial Contact. In a sense that's true, just as I've trawled the historical record for evidence that there was more to the green children story than just a fairy-tale, more even than a political conspiracy of Henry II's. But for comparison, I've compiled a very long list of comparable phenomena over the history of humanity: supernovae, eclipses, aurorae, meteors, comets, earthquakes, pestilences and the like - so many that I'm thinking of making another book out of them. But although there are lots of them, in each category, there's nothing odd about them: the strange ones are within the green children list, either in time (above) or in space - because the events above are also related geographically.

Walter de Horkesley's Nayland lay south of Woolpit, itself south of Thursford; while North Fambridge is almost due south of Coggeshall. Whatever else you say about Sibylla, she was a straight-up-and-down sort of girl. All the key sites in East Anglia lie within a 'corridor' just ten miles wide, extending 120 miles from north to the south of the region. Maidstone's not within it, if it's extended into Kent; but if it's extended into France it takes in Nogent-le-Rotrou, where knights appeared 'out of the air' in 1192 (Chap.13). Nogent never appears in Henry II's Itinerary,[84] nor on the long list of Templar 'Commanderies' in France.[85] But as the Huisne is a tributary of the Loire, the corridor leads straight on to Tours, 'the City of St. Martin' (Chap.8).

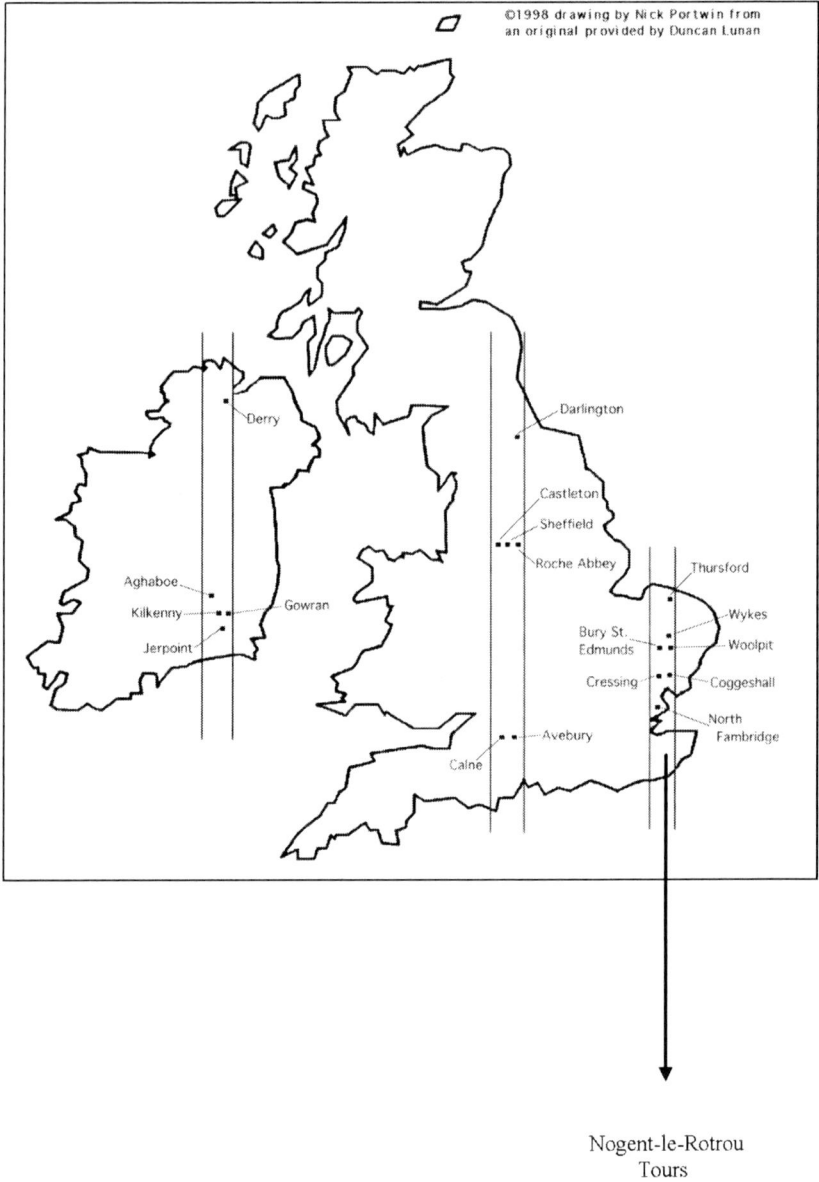

Darlington

Castleton
Sheffield
Roche Abbey

Derry

Aghaboe
Kilkenny
Jerpoint

Gowran

Thursford
Wykes
Bury St.
Edmunds
Woolpit
Cressing
Coggeshall
North
Fambridge

Avebury
Calne

Nogent-le-Rotrou
Tours

Fig. 17.3 'Corridors' drawing.

East Anglia 'corridor' continued into France

Drawing by Nick Portwin, extended by DL.

284

In Ireland the apparent high-altitude explosion of February 1173 (not the first of its kind, as we'll see) was over Derry, north of the sites in Ossory (Fig. 17.4). Similarly, Darlington, Peveril Castle and Roche Abbey, Little Barre, and Calne, together form a corridor 225 miles long and 25 miles wide, north to south through central England, taking in Avebury and Stonehenge, which may be significant (Chap. 21). The de Barres were in that middle 'corridor' throughout, and the de Calnas had a presence in Kilkenny after the death of Adam de Hereford. Sibylla and her husband repossessed Wykes when she rented out North Fambridge, and she moved to Bernay when she sold Wykes; when she died Richard de Clare took over North Fambridge, and when he died the de Calnas moved back into Bernay as a family.

It's as if one of the key families had to occupy at least one site on each corridor, at any given time, and what happened later at Wykes was striking. There's a record of the running of Wykes manor in the late 13th century, but there's nothing odd about it.[86] There was a row in 1275 when Robert de Valoines abducted the underage heir to Wykes,[87] but meanwhile the de Bardwell family remained, holding their land from the Abbot of Bury St. Edmunds, and associated with the de Pakenham family who had rights in Bardwell, Thorpe and even in Woolpit.[11] John Bardwell, lord there in 1348, married Isabel, the daughter of Sir Thomas Barra - probably the one at the bottom left of Fig. 17.2, a descendant of Richard and Agnes. His son William had free warren in Bardwell and Thorpe in the 1360's, perhaps including Wykes, which later passed on to a younger cousin of the same name.[24]

But as we'll see in Chap.24, no sooner was William established in the Wykes area in the 1360's than the strange events restarted, with people appearing and disappearing in broad daylight and with violent events in the upper atmosphere and on the far side of the Moon. Before adding those, it's time to look for an *overall* explanation. I've reviewed other people's explanations for the green children in Chap.8, and given my reasons for finding them inadequate. In Chap.13 I looked at the idea that the children might be pawns in a political plot, and in Chap.15, at whether they and the de Calnas might have been part of a secret sex-cult. Either is possible, but only if we say that the strange astronomical events and the alignments of the English and Irish sites are all merely coincidental. As a writer of science fact and science fiction, I'd rather speculate on what it could mean if they weren't coincidental; on Robert Burton's conjecture, which first drew me to the case, that the children's home and the Earth "be planets alike, inhabited alike...and it may be those two green children which Nubrigensis speaks of in his time, that fell from heaven, came from thence."

PART THREE – SPECULATION

Chapter Eighteen - A DIGRESSION OF MATTER TRANSMITTERS

"The king of England neither rides nor sails.   He flies with the rapidity of a bird.   One moment transports him from Ireland to England: another from England to France."

~ Louis VII of France, 1172

To work out what may have been happening, it's time to look at the details. Even if the green children incident was relatively minor, it's the one to begin with.   Although not first-hand, relying on William of Newburgh and Ralph of Coggeshall, it is said to be the children's own testimony.   Many bend over backwards to avoid that ("Of course, we can dismiss…") especially how they got here.   Glyn Maxwell's *Wolfpit* avoids it for dramatic reasons,[1] but others go to remarkable lengths: they were caught up by a whirlwind, snatched by a spirit - anything but what they said themselves.

"Consequently asked, wherever was that land, and by what means they had come from thence, 'Either of these,' they said, 'we do not know.   We remember this much: because on a certain day we were driving to pasture/adding to our father's herd/flock in the fields, we heard a certain great sound such as now we are accustomed to hear at St. Edmund's when they say the bells are ringing.   And when we turned our minds to that sound which surprised us, suddenly/unawares, *as if* placed in some loss of mind, we found ourselves in the field where you were reaping'" (WN, my emphasis).   Agnes, at least, not only has the concept of amnesia, but knows it isn't what happened to her.   For me, that rules out the primitives from some underground tribe, with iron deficiency beyond the level of brain damage.   But in tracing her story, we've seen there was much more to her than that.

Ralph too says there was a sound of bells.   "Asked by what means she had come into this land with the aforesaid boy, she said, because when animals were being followed, they went down into a certain cave.   Having gone into it,

they heard a certain delightful sound of bells; seized by that pleasant sound, they progressed by wandering through the cavern for a long time, until they arrived at the exit... When they were frightened by the strangeness of the men coming upon them, they wished to flee, but could by no means find the entrance of the cave, before they were captured by them."
As we've seen, there are no caves under Woolpit.

William and Ralph both use causative Latin *quia* for 'because', and their vocabularies are so different that when they use the same word it's striking. This happened to the children *because* they were with the animals on a particular day, as if they brought the misfortune on themselves, and shouldn't have been out there that day - or were sent out deliberately, as James Bentley suggested. *Pascere*, to pasture, can mean 'to enlarge a flock or herd': perhaps a livestock transfer was scheduled, and people at the other end were supposed to be out of the way for safety (Chap.20).

But can there be instantaneous movement from one place to another - 'matter transmission' - as science fiction writers have imagined for decades? In October 1998 it was announced that a combined team of scientists from the USA, UK and Denmark had achieved a form of teleportation, using 'quantum entanglement'; but it couldn't strictly be called 'matter transmission', as we'll see below, because nothing with mass was transported (see below). For something like the green children's transportation, a much higher level of technology is required.

Star Trek has made matter transmission well-known: "Beam me up, Scotty," is a catch-phrase, though like "Play it again, Sam," with Bogart, William Shatner never said it. The 'transporter' was devised to avoid landing the *Enterprise* on a planet almost every week, and get stories under way more rapidly.[2] There's lots of talk about 'coordinates', three groups of three digits, but we're never told what they measure. They're fixed, whatever the target's motion with respect to the *Enterprise*, so they relate to the reference frame of the planet or other space vessel, not the transporter's own location. It can locate people or objects without any tracking device - even within solid rock. It's limited to small objects, the size of a human body. Its range too is limited, though James Blish had an interstellar version in the first *Trek* novel[3] - not developed, because it would dispense with the ship which was central to the series.

The *Enterprise* itself travels faster than light, which most physicists believe to be impossible, so many SF writers imagine a matter-transmitter system which moves whole ships, as in my own 'Interface' series (*Galaxy*, 1970-71).[4] There are more story possibilities if the device has limitations, so I stipulated that the area of congruency was a disc half-a-mile in diameter, which mustn't touch a planetary surface; the Interface relay by which a transfer was set up was, therefore, normally a satellite; an Interface could only be created within 10,000 miles of it and needed two-way radio contact. Moreover the relays had to be carried to the target star systems, by idealistic members of a civilisation who called the task 'Furtherance'.

In *Man and the Stars* I suggested that if matter-transmission happens in nature, the place to look for it would be around the Sun, and I quoted a possible example where matter seemed to materialise over the Sun and cascade back.[5] I also looked at whether black holes could be 'Star Gates': the scientific view then was that even if they could, no object or message could get through in recognisable form, so preserving relativity theory, in which information can't be exchanged faster than light-speed. If you could do that, you could violate causality, acting on events which were still in the future at your destination. And there's the problem of getting to the black hole first, not to mention where you'd emerge. In *The Iron Sun* Adrian Berry suggested that interstellar dust and gas could be swept up to create a black hole 'gate' one light-year from the Solar System.[6] In *Man and the Planets* I argued that the exit 'gate' might form in the closest concentration of mass, the core of the Sun, with disastrous effects.[7] Also, entry to the 'gate' must be at a high fraction of light-speed, to cross the event horizon (the point of no return) at a tangent. In Berry's first book the velocity quoted was at first far too low, but corrected in later editions.

In 1981 the late John Fadum gave a paper called 'Black Holes, Stargates and Starships' to ASTRA, the Association in Scotland to Research into Astronautics, showing that in theory a ship could pass through a black hole 'gate' without being destroyed.[8] The circumstances were rather special: in his analysis, it seemed that the ship had to approach the black hole from all directions at once. The ship could be compressible, to be crushed in the gravity well near the event horizon. I suggested making it a telescopic structure, or a ring folding into a pleated ruff. (Gordon Ross of ASTRA has designed a parabolic solar sail, 'Solaris', stored that way for launch.) Water ice can be compressed into higher-density forms; another idea was to build the ship of graphite and have it emerge as diamond. Occupants must be protected from crushing, but Dr. Robert Forward had suggested ways of 'flattening spacetime' with large surrounding masses,[9] which might keep conditions bearable in life-support sections. Stresses would be enormous, requiring large scale engineering, but it might be done. But how to control where the ship emerges? The favoured answer is to create a matched pair of black holes, linked from the outset, and send one of them off into space.[10] That could allow instantaneous exchanges, violating causality; [11] at relativistic speeds it could allow travel back in time, though not to before the 'gate' was created. That would allow classic paradoxes: what if you go back in time and kill your grandfather, so preventing yourself from being born and going back to do it?

In recent years, quantum physics has begun to favour more robust views of causality. Even Prof. Stephen Hawking, who long held that time-travel is impossible, came to say it might be achieved. If you go back and kill your grandfather, you don't prevent your own existence: your parents just don't visit you in prison. You create a new history in which you live out your span as a parentless anomaly, but nothing prevents you from doing it if you have the technology and are that way inclined.

Does it require a stellar black hole, many times the mass of the Sun, to create a gateway through which a human being could pass? Often it's called a 'wormhole', linking two locations in space (Fig. 18.1). In the 1970's it was suggested that wormholes could be kept open by electric fields, letting solid objects pass through,[12] and then they might not require such huge masses to open them in the first place.

'Through' isn't really the word, because the sides of the wormhole in the diagram represent space-time itself (despite the odd scene in Sagan's novel *Contact*, where a vehicle bounces off them.[13] The movie version and others have fixed the image of a wormhole as an actual tunnel, but transfer would really be instantaneous.) It's hard to find a better word to use.

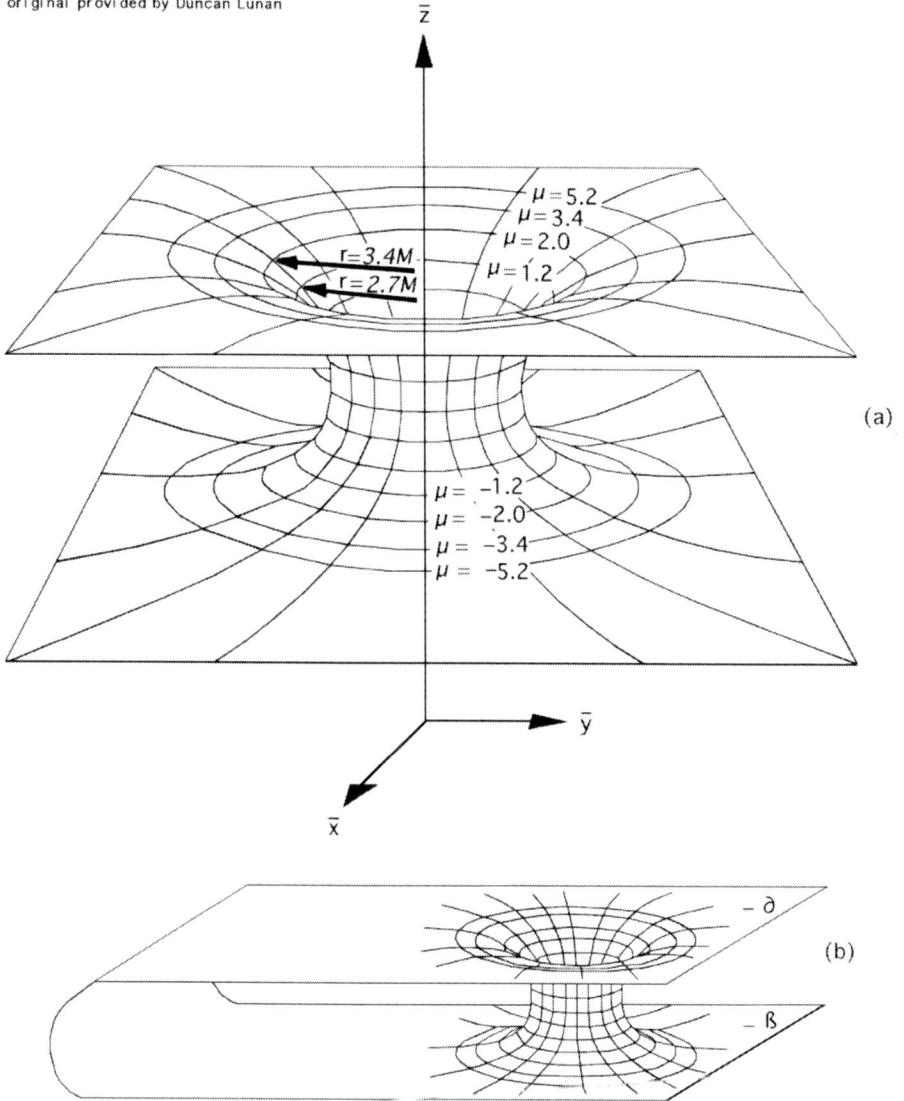

Figs. 18.1 (a) and (b).

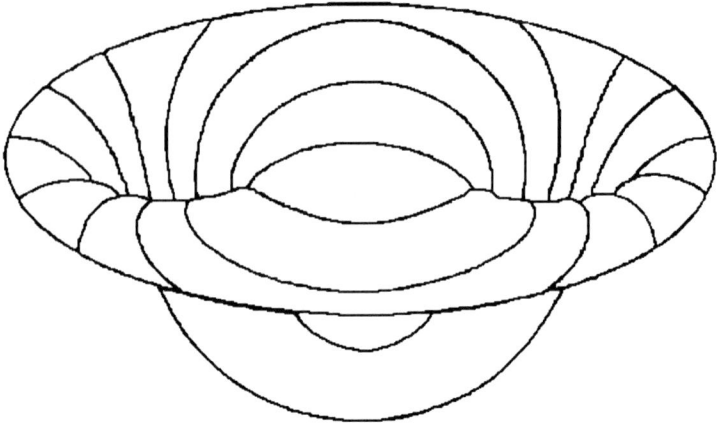

Figs. 18.1 (a), (b) and (c). Wormhole drawings by Nick Portwin, after Misner, Thorne and Wheeler, "Gravitation", W.H. Freeman, 1973.

Morris, Thorne and Yurtsever calculated that a wormhole could be kept open if there was a spherical, superconducting charged plate on each side,[14] but there would be no connecting tunnel: the two 'ends' would actually be spherical volumes. With one of them accelerated to near lightspeed, the wormhole could be a time machine, like the paired black holes above. It might take huge energy to create, but once created it might be controlled by a small further change - as we can tap the output of a nuclear power station by flicking a switch. It still seems near-impossible to get solid matter through such a portal, but we'll come back to that.

Matter transmission could be simulated, though limited to the speed of light. A technique called Solid Free-form Fabrication has amazing possibilities, using 'laser sintering' to manufacture objects from a solution of raw material, demonstrated at the Science Museum in 2009. So far it's been done only with inert objects, but in future such 'Makeboxes' may construct clothing, books, "even our food, medicines, or replacement organs".[15] If so, they could duplicate bodies. Advocates of 'nanotechnology', engineering at molecular scale, claim their future systems could do the same.[16] Probably the necessary 'blueprint' couldn't be obtained without destroying the original body, so it would be equivalent to matter transmission, not duplication.

Without knowing then what the system might be, John Kelk of ASTRA calculated that if the 'blueprint' was sent over interstellar distances by two routes, to check for errors on receipt, it could cross the Galaxy in just three leaps - though more than 100,000 years would pass meantime. Of course, a system like that couldn't be miniaturised to operate in a water-filled pit on a farm - could it? In theory, the energy could be available: appropriately nurtured, the common algae in a small pond could generate enough hydrogen to meet the continuing fuel needs of a dozen cars.[17] But, the late Paul Grant pointed out, if you can manufacture cattle, you don't have to teleport many to build up herds on a colony planet: just enough for a breeding pool, with blue-prints for copies as required. The same applies to any livestock, including people - and almost the only other word which William and Ralph both use, in their two versions of the green children story, is *pecora*, for animals, so general that it can mean people in the sense of 'the common herd'.

If we're duplicating, rather than transmitting people, that raises the question of personality, especially if the scanning process destroys the original. However, as Gregory Benford writes, "people cooled down to a state of clinical death on operating tables, for brain surgery, revive with their sense of self intact..." So with lightning strikes and other electric shocks which interrupt brain processes; only short term recall is affected. It suggests that copying the brain would also copy the personality.[18]

Could awareness and memory be transferred in some paranormal way? Easier still if we could 'teleport' minds AND bodies, by the power of thought... Enough odd things have happened to me, to convince me that there is a paranormal stratum of experience in life, but it seems to me like the remnant of a highly developed set of instincts, rather than a conscious, rational process which could be controlled and developed. Speech, and technology, have removed the evolutionary need for those abilities except in the occasional bizarre event or emergency. The point was elegantly made by Georgina Howell, interviewing the dramatist David Mamet, when he treated her to an apparent demonstration of telepathy. "I don't know what this proves," wrote Howell, "except... another way that he can communicate his message unforgettably. And we already know he can do that."[19] Just so; and as Mamet's plays and films make his points more effectively to many more people than one-to-one telepathy, so 'Trains and Boats and Planes' are more useful than individual teleportation - especially to move large numbers of people or objects.

My one possible brush with it was in an 'emergency'. During the Fire Service strike of 1977, I had to seek someone in a house fire. It was an 18th-century house with thick interior walls, which contained the fire to the kitchen; but it seemed I had to get in there, and the heat kept driving me back. I was nerving myself for a fourth try when suddenly I found myself in the midst of the fire, with no idea how I got there. As there was no-one there after all, I removed myself smartly by conventional means.

The obvious explanation is that under stress, my brain didn't register those few steps. We've all driven down a familiar road, finding suddenly that we don't remember the last few blocks, but in that case, the brain hasn't re-memorised the route because nothing happened there. By contrast, this experience was one of acute observation and slowed-down time: I vividly remember colours, sounds and smells, and subjectively it seemed to last half an hour, though it took less than four minutes. Why should the one thing blanked be the piece of self-knowledge I'd most like to have, 'How did I get myself to do that?' (Sir Laurence Olivier lost his temper after a great performance because he didn't know how he'd done it, so he couldn't do it again.) "Suddenly, as if placed in some loss of mind" exactly describes how I found myself in that kitchen.

Subsequent reactions to this are in interesting contrast to Alfred Bester's SF novel, *Tiger! Tiger!* On its first page, a researcher teleports out of a laboratory fire. "This was the first time it had ever taken place before professional observers... He made his will and said farewell to his friends. Jaunte knew he was going to die because his fellow researchers were determined to kill him. There was no doubt about that." And indeed they try, making him teleport again and again, until they learn how it's done.[20]

Without any death wish, I've mentioned my experience to scientists and paranormal investigators, without arousing interest. I've learned from members of the Skeptics that no demonstration, before trained observers or not, would verify it to their satisfaction. Observers can be bribed. Visual records? Special effects. Instrumentation? Hackers. But I'm not sure that scientific investigation is appropriate: for properties of the mind, investigation by philosophers might be more interesting.

Matter *can* disappear from one place to reappear in another , by 'quantum tunnelling'. Sub-atomic particles do it, typically taking 10^{-15} of a second to escape from containment which should be secure.[21] But it gets more difficult with increasing mass, and supposedly *only* sub-atomic particles can do it in reality.[22] But that used to be said about matter transmission though black holes; and after *Man and the Planets* I corresponded with a Russian student, Natasha Leonov, who believed that quantum tunnelling might be achieved on a macroscopic scale, by manipulating probability. Unlike 'gates' in regions of high space-time curvature such as black holes, Natasha's idea could be tested in low-curvature, 'flat' spacetime between the stars; but once perfected, might work within a gravitational field, especially in Bob Forward's 'flattened space-time' above. Frankly, Natasha's maths were beyond me, and I haven't heard from her since she returned to Russia; but unlike the other ideas above, hers would allow accidents like the one (apparently) in which the children appeared at Woolpit.

However, their experience doesn't sound like purely mental teleportation. They'd have to be taught to do it, but involuntarily, hypnotically conditioned to respond to a sound. The sound of bells here didn't do it, however desperately they wished to get back. Andy Nimmo suggested there might also have been some visual trigger, such as a hypno-disc, not needed when they were startled by the 'great sound', and they couldn't duplicate it here. It ties in with being in their father's fields at the wrong time, but not with much of the rest. What clues we have suggest that if this story involves matter-transmission, it's a physical process rather than a mental one.

Going back to 'makeboxes', nanotechnology etc., an even more exotic possibility is that a destructively scanned object could be recreated, atom by atom, from coherent streams released by the new form of matter called 'Bose-Einstein concentrates'.[23] Re-creation would be slow, needing the resources of an ultramodern physics laboratory - not a system which could operate inconspicuously in a mediaeval pit. The limitation of such concepts is that we're trying to put Humpty Dumpty together out of a new set of atoms at a new location. For true matter transmission, we need to persuade a set of atoms to cease to exist at one place and reappear in the same arrangement at another.

In the December 1993 *Analog*, John G. Cramer described the elaborate possibilities of 'quantum entanglement' and the transmission of 'quantum state vectors'.[24] Trying to describe it in words is like describing a spiral staircase without moving one's hands, but to make what follows understandable, I'll have to try.

Consider a beam of light. Sir Isaac Newton would think of it as a stream of particles (photons), and phenomena like the photo-electric effect, where photons dislodge electrons from a metal surface, fit Newton's description. But if you pass a beam of light through a slit in a screen, then through two slits in a second screen, the pattern cast on a third screen is what you would expect from a wave passing similar obstacles in air or water. Repeat the experiment with a beam of electrons, which are particles in the ordinary sense, and you get the same result. But Heisenberg's Uncertainty Principle, one of the basic rules of quantum physics, tells us that in dealing with objects as small as the electron, we can never measure the position and the velocity of the particle at the same time. Since we know the velocity of the particle beam, the positions of the individual electrons must be uncertain, and the pattern they cast on the third screen represents the different probabilities that they will occupy each position on it. And the same applies to the photons in the previous experiment.

The much more complex assembly of particles which makes up a solid object - even a person - could be described as a wave function, in these terms. It's nearly 100 per cent certain that in the next moment after reading this you will still be where you are now, but there is a possibility, however small, that you might instead be on the other side of the street or on a planet orbiting Alpha Centauri. And since matter and energy are equivalent, as Einstein established, it would be possible in theory to scan your body in such a way that all its particles were converted into energy without losing the pattern which constitutes 'you'. By ceasing your physical existence here, that process would generate an expanding wavefront of probability that you would exist somewhere else. When that wavefront reached some location where conditions made it more probable that you would exist there, rather than elsewhere, you could duly come back into existence at that point. As above, in October

1998 it was announced in the press that the feat had been achieved, but it was 'only' transmission of photon quantum states.   In 2001 a Danish team showed in theory that atoms could be transmitted, and in 2002 an Australian team teleported a laser beam carrying a message.[25]

In theory, such a process could give us a kind of matter-transmission: it could allow an object which has been destructively scanned *here* to be recreated *there*, but carrying the information at the speed of light or less, it's a slow and difficult way of travelling to the stars; and it needs a receiving station at the far end, tuned to the transmitter.   It's hardly likely to happen by accident, which we need, to account for the children's misfortune.   My guess is still that they were with their father's flock or herd, when they shouldn't have been because there was a livestock transfer scheduled from East Anglia; that they had with them some kind of locating device or communicator, and the system locked on to it and returned them to Earth, perhaps not to the transmitter site but at least to the same region on this planet.   I considered borrowing a term from Nigel Kneale's *Quatermass II* and calling such accidents 'overshoots', but Robert Burton has given us an even better word.   Though initially in this chapter I used it in his sense, a summary of everything which might be relevant, surely the best word for a matter-transmitter accident is a 'digression'.

I took my accumulated list of possible cases, 'digressions' and all, to Andy Paterson of ASTRA, who was a physics student before health reasons forced him to put that on hold and become a very talented space artist instead.   "If you know what happens when it goes wrong," Andy commented, "it's much easier to figure out how it works."   In his view, a combined system of quantum scanning and a wormhole stargate could fit the bill.   But to understand why it might begin to malfunction in the later years of the 12th century, we have to look at possible conditions at the other end of the link.

Chapter Nineteen - A LAND WITHOUT SUN

"If the heavens then be permeable, as these men deliver, and no lets, it were not amiss in this aerial progress to make wings and fly up, which that Turk in Busbequius made his fellow-citizens in Constantinople believe he would perform: and some new-fangled wits, methinks, should some time or other find out: or if that may not be, yet with a Galileo's glass, or Icaromenippus' wings in Lucian, command the spheres and heavens, and see what is done amongst them."

~ Robert Burton, *The Anatomy of Melancholy*, 1621

When I write science fiction, it's mostly 'hard SF' - consistent with present scientific knowledge, if possible. One frequent practise in hard SF is 'world building': we can't just put people anywhere - a planet must have a size, an age, chemical composition, internal structure, and a star of set type at specified distance; consistent with those, an atmosphere, surface gravity, climatic zones; appropriate life-forms, with history, languages, political systems if intelligent... and gimlet-eyed editors and eagle-eyed readers are watching for any slip-up. With friends in ASTRA and elsewhere, the aim here and in Chap.22 was to 'build' a world which fits the green children's description. William of Newburgh left out details he thought 'tedious', since they had no religious significance, but we may be able to surmise them from the few we've been given.

"...asked who and from whence they were, they are said to have replied: 'People of the land of Saint Martin... Asked whether the Sun rose [there], 'But the sun', they said, 'of our countries does not rise; and our country is little lit by its rays, but is satisfied with that measure of light, which with you precedes sunrise or follows sunset. Moreover/far off a certain bright land is seen not far from our land, with a very broad river dividing the two'. These and many other things, which it would be tedious to retell, they are said to have replied to those struck inquisitively." (WN)

"Asked often about the people of her country, she swore on oath that as many as all the inhabitants and all things/plants that were held in that land/world were dyed with the colour green, and that they saw no sun, but were pleased with a certain light, as if happened after sunset... When they emerged from the pit, as if astonished and made breathless with fear by the excessive brightness of the sun and the unaccustomed temperature of the air, they stayed for a long time over the rim of the cavern." (RC)

Ralph's first word for 'country' is *regio*, region, though from there as in William's account it's *terra*, 'continent' or even 'world'. In *The Girl Green as Elderflower*, Randolph Stow's monks suggest to the girl in Latin that she's from Mars - 'Martini' and 'Martiani' are very similar - but immediately drop the notion. He also toys with the mediaeval idea that the world might be a flat plate, never lit by the Sun on the underside.[1] But neither William nor Ralph mentions that, and Gervaise of Tilbury knew the Earth was round and the Sun shone on both sides of it (Chap.5).

In the 1960s the late Jean Sendy, who believed the Old Testament was a literal history of extraterrestrial Contact,[2] noted that Lunar Orbiter spacecraft had found a negative mascon under Sinus Iridum (the Bay of Rainbows), a lava-flooded crater on the northern rim of Mare Imbrium, the left 'eye' (as we see it) of the Man in the Moon.[3] Mascons ('mass concentrations') are areas of high density below the lunar crust, revealed by their pull on spacecraft overhead. Although below the largest impact basins (the Moon's dark 'seas'), mascons aren't thought to be the impacting bodies, but material raised from the lunar interior; so it's not obvious why any should be less dense than the crust. Jean suggested a vast cavern had been mined out below the Bay, perhaps given an atmosphere and made habitable. His biblical interpretation required arcane knowledge (literally) to be encoded in the Bay's name: the rainbow is *l'arc-en-ciel*, which he related to Jewish traditions linking the Moon with Noah's Ark and the Ark of the Covenant.[4] To quote Dudley Moore, "A colourful reading, but perhaps not entirely accurate..."[5]

Such caverns are standard planetary engineering proposals for small, airless worlds.[6] Humans could fly there, because the low gravity would let our arms support wings. Had Sir Herbert Read mentioned that, the cavern might fit the description of the green children's environment in his 1930's novel.[7] But gravity proves they weren't from Jean Sendy's cavern: if acclimatised to lunar gravity, on Earth they couldn't stand, much less run. And continued mapping found more negative mascons, many under highland regions, but some under basins such as Mare Tranquillitatis and Mare Vaporum.[8] John Braithwaite suggested that the upwelling material there had a high gaseous content; gaseous outbreaks are reportedly seen on the lunar maria and in larger craters, even today.   So Jean Sendy's cavern looks a lot less likely.

In *Habitable Planets for Man*, Stephen H. Dole examined the range of conditions for human survival.[9]   The allowable mass range for habitable planets was 0.4 to 2.35 times the mass of the Earth: the lower limit set by the need to retain a breathable atmosphere, the upper one for surface gravity no more than 1.5 times Earth's.   Mountaineering experience set the lower limit of atmospheric pressure, deep-sea diving the upper limit, with partial pressures of oxygen and other gases adjusted accordingly.   The temperature range had to permit water as solid, liquid and gas, putting the planet within a band of distance from its star termed the *ecosphere*... and even then, the rotation period should not be longer than 96 hours (4 Earth days).

But to fit the children's account we need an earthlike world, with a trapped rotation, keeping the same side always to its sun as the Moon does to the Earth.   (Even today, many people think the Moon keeps the same face towards the Sun, and say 'the dark side of the Moon' when they mean the side facing away from Earth.)   Astronomers used to think the planet Mercury had a trapped rotation, but radar proved the truth was more complicated: Mercury's rotation is Sun-locked, but in a 2:1 ratio.   It turns three times on its axis, with respect to the stars, in two orbital revolutions about the Sun; from a solar or planetary viewpoint, it makes half a turn in each Hermian year, so there are opposite 'heat poles' on the equator taking turns to receive the worst heat.

As a result surface features are sometimes visible from Earth, sometimes not, but when they are, they're always in the same places - hence the belief that Mercury had not only a trapped rotation but also an atmosphere, with clouds, so life might exist in the twilight zone   (the origin of the expression made famous by Rod Serling.)   V.A. Firsoff found that in theory Mercury could even have ice-caps.[10]   There are areas of permanent shadow near the poles, and radar scanning shows that apparently there *is* ice at the north pole.[11]   Presumably the water vapour was released from cometary impacts, like the ice in 'cold trap' craters at our own Moon's poles (Chap.12).

After analysis of their light, stars are grouped by spectral type.   The types were labelled before nuclear fusion was understood;   rearranged by surface temperature, the sequence from blue to red now runs O, B, A, F, G, K, M, R, N, S ('Oh be a fine girl, kiss me right now sweetie').   The Hertzsprung-Russell diagram (Fig. 19.1) plots stars by their light output (absolute magnitude) and surface temperature.   The hottest, brightest stars (class O and B), are found at top left;   the faint red dwarfs (class M and below) at bottom right.   Between them runs a diagonal band, the Main Sequence, on which all stable stars fall: our Sun is near the centre of the graph, classed G0 or G2.   Stable stars are fusing hydrogen to helium in their cores;   when the hydrogen is exhausted they move off the Main Sequence to upper right, becoming orange and red giants, increasingly unstable.   The more massive stars go on to more violent fusion reactions;   some explode as supernovae, synthesising the heavy elements which form planets like ours;   the most massive collapse into black holes.

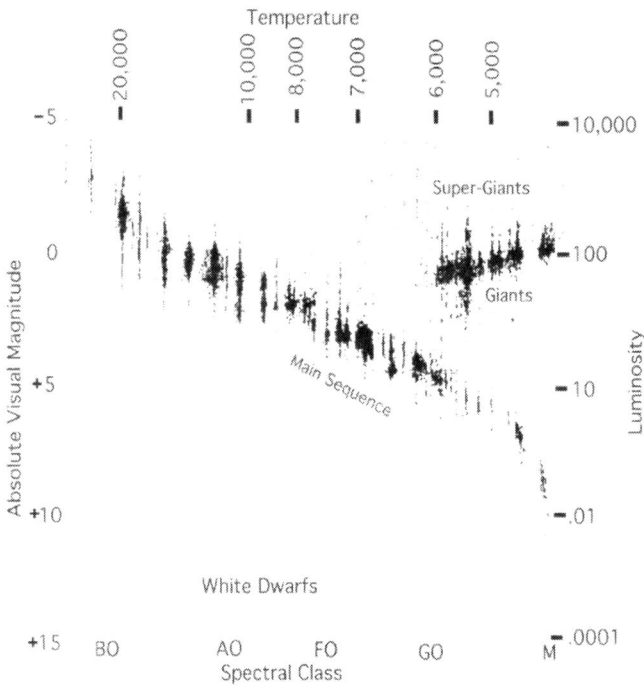

Fig. 19.1. Hertzsprung-Russell diagram.
Drawing by Nick Portwin, after W. Gillenberg, in Otto Struve, Beverley Lynds and Helen Pillans, "Elementary Astronomy", Oxford University Press, 1969.

In our Solar System, the ecosphere extends roughly from the orbit of Venus to the orbit of Mars, though Mars is too small to be habitable and Venus rotates too slowly. Venus may have had oceans in its early history, but its day is longer than its year, and the seas boiled on the side facing the Sun. The greenhouse effect of water vapour is much stronger than carbon dioxide's, and on Venus it melted the crust of the planet, triggering violent chemical reactions which created the hostile conditions there today.

Around a red dwarf star, much smaller than our Sun, the ecosphere would be so much closer that tidal forces would slow a planet's rotation until its day matched its year.[12] Even if the planet was originally earthlike, it was thought that oceans on the sunward face would boil, and over time the volatiles would all freeze on the nightside. If the children's world was like that, perhaps it had since been terraformed: made earthlike, with a breathable atmosphere and terrestrial life planted in the twilight zone.

Against that the late Chris Boyce cited Michael Hart's 1979 paper, 'Habitable Zones around Main Sequence Stars'. Hart estimated that if Earth had been only 5% nearer the Sun, it would have reached a runaway greenhouse condition four billion years ago as the Sun grew warmer; just 1% further away, it would have frozen completely in its first two billion years. That was a much narrower ecosphere for our Sun, and for less massive stars it would be narrower still, disappearing at type K1, three-quarters the mass of the Sun.[13] But for the ecosphere to be in the zone where a planet's rotation would be trapped, the star's mass would be a third less again, spectral class M.

Hart's paper was influential: T.A. Heppenheimer's *Toward Distant Suns* assumed that habitable planets could only be found about stars between F6 and G7.[14] It much reduced the likely number of habitable planets in the Galaxy. But now we know Mars and probably Venus had oceans in their early history, then had Venus rotated faster, and Mars been more massive, they might be earthlike today. Martyn Fogg thought planets could be habitable around type M stars,[15] and simulations at NASA's Ames Research Centre found that if such planets with trapped rotations have even 15% of Earth's atmosphere, circulation will keep temperatures below 50° C, even at the sub-solar point, and above –50°, even at the dark side centre.[16] Oceans would freeze there but there could be life under the ice, in geothermal vents. In the twilight zone the range would be from 10° above zero to 10° below. But that assumes the planet is a perfect sphere, and altering the topography could make a big difference, as we'll see.

Not all red dwarfs would qualify, even with earth-sized planets at the right distance. Particle streams from our Sun can overload Earth's magnetic field, causing aurora and disrupting communications (Chap.20), but some red dwarfs have much bigger flares, relative to their radiation output. Gas prominences are much bigger, relative to the star's diameter, than those of our Sun.[17] Sunspots can also be very large, reducing the star's output by up to 40% for months at a time.[16] But stable red dwarfs are common: most stars within 22 light-years of our Sun are that type,[9] and many could have planets with the right size and orbit for terraforming or for life of their own. However, the children didn't describe any difference in colours - quite the reverse, they said that 'all the inhabitants and all plants that were held in that land/world were dyed with the colour green', evidently much the same as they had here.

Chris O'Kane showed me an exhibit at Glasgow Science Centre with coloured silhouettes, lit with white light, red and purple. Coincidentally, or perhaps not, the green figure was a girl. In red light, she looked a darker red; in purple, she was black to me, but Chris saw her as grey. In purple *and* white, I saw her as grey. It's hard to work out how things would look under the full-spectrum light of another sun: we might not even be aware of the colour difference, only that the yellow light to which our eyes are most sensitive was brighter or dimmer.[16] Sydney Jordan's colour paintings (Figs. 19.2, 19.3, 22.6) assumed a star yellower than the Sun, perhaps type K, but not as dim as a red dwarf. On a planet close enough for its rotation to be trapped, sunward conditions would be more extreme than the Ames model, and for life in the twilight zone, terraforming would probably be needed: full-scale 'planetary engineering' - large-scale adaptation of conditions on other planets.

The planet has roughly Earth's mass, if internal composition and structure are similar, because the children weren't troubled by our gravity: when they made a break across the fields they were able to run If it was an otherwise Earth-like world, too close to its star for life to evolve, the creators of the colony could have given it a trapped rotation, to terraform the twilight zone. Freeman Dyson suggested speeding up a planet's rotation with an electrically conducting surface grid and a network of solar-powered satellites generating magnetic fields; the same method could slow it down.[18]   Saul J. Adelman considered spinning Venus up to a 24-hour day by asteroid impacts, but all the asteroids in the Solar System would not be enough;[19] the colony world's system might have more.   But Adelman also wanted to use impacts to change Venus's carbon dioxide atmosphere, which has sulphuric acid smog, surface temperature four times the boiling point of water, surface pressure equivalent to nearly a mile under water on Earth, and almost no water.   Adelman's bombardment would strip away the surplus atmosphere, but outgassing from the craters might leave things as bad as before.

Changing the atmosphere more gently, biologically, would take a very long time - three million years for ASTRA's Venus proposal - so unless the builders terraform suitable worlds on spec., they'd need to change the atmosphere much faster.   With matter transmitters, they could do that - and ship the surplus gases to a Mars-like world to terraform that as well.   But biological transformation could leave the planet with higher surface air pressure than Earth's.   Coming here instantaneously would risk embolism or 'the bends' - serious dangers for divers surfacing rapidly - but the children had no such problems, so the pressure differential may be slight.   The winds blasting out of the Peak Cavern in the 12th century may indicate higher pressure, but don't necessarily tell us about the colony world (see Chap. 23).

The bends are caused by dissolved nitrogen in the blood, forming bubbles when the external pressure is suddenly released; but we need an inert component in the atmosphere.   Human beings can live in pure oxygen, at much lower pressure than we're used to: early US spacecraft used it at 5 pounds per square inch, reducing structural loads on the hull, the weight, and the danger if the cabin decompressed.   But in the 1967 Apollo 1 fire, in pure oxygen at 15 psi, the accident was just waiting for a spark to make it happen.   Earth's air is balanced between having too little oxygen for animal metabolism, and having - things become super-inflammable.   Air bubbles formed in amber, shortly before the impact off Chicxulub in Mexico which wiped out the dinosaurs, show a high oxygen content.   It enabled the pterosaurs to fly despite their huge wingspans, giving them a high metabolic rate, but the iridium layer in geological strata, world-wide, at the Cretaceous-Tertiary boundary, contains a micro-thin layer of carbon: the impact was followed by fires over huge areas. A similar event 135 million years ago may have given flowering plants their first advantage over ferns.[20]

What saves us is that 80% of our atmosphere is nitrogen, from volcanic activity. Nitrogen-bearing ammonia is found in the gas giant planets, and free nitrogen in the atmosphere of Saturn's moon Titan. Nitrogen compounds are found in some asteroids, and in comets, so the gas can be used in space settlements. Whether there'll be enough for terraforming is another matter. Even for space settlements simulating earthlike conditions, great quantities of nitrogen are needed to fill the space. In *The Greening of Mars* James Lovelock and Michael Allaby suggested using carbon dioxide instead,[21] but that's a waste product of animal metabolism, and we can stand it only in very low concentrations.[22] Anything much over 3% of carbon dioxide in the atmosphere produces severe effects on human performance.[23]

On the other hand, at least two of Earth's Great Dyings or 'megadeaths' were due to oxygen shortage. 251 million years ago at the Permian-Triassic boundary, a sudden drop in sea level catastrophically exposed sea-bed over large areas to oxidation.[24] Sea-levels were higher in the Devonian period, 400-350 million years ago, but the explosive rise of conifers on land caused algal and bacterial blooms offshore, severely depleting oxygen in the oceans.[25] In our twilight zone, even if the "very broad river" runs round the world from pole to pole, the area for biological productivity is relatively small. To maintain breathable atmosphere it must be intensively forested, or much of it shallow sea, but with just one active band of longitude, lacking full sunlight, it's unlikely that the colony world could achieve the self-regulating stability which Lovelock postulates for Earth's atmosphere and biosphere in his 'Gaia hypothesis'.[26] To make up the difference might need industrial production, like the 'atmosphere plant of Barsoom' in Edgar Rice Burroughs's *A Princess of Mars*,[27] but in *Man and the Planets* we thought it could be done to counteract the losses if Earth's Moon were terraformed.

An 'atmosphere plant' on the planet's sunlit face would have continuous energy, and plenty of what Jean Sendy called 'oxygen-ore', i.e. rock.[2] Nobody's exposed to direct sunlight in the twilight zone, but the planet would have no magnetic field (Chap.20), and would need an ozone layer to prevent the atmosphere being stripped off by the solar wind, as happens over Mars.[27] It could be a rough ride for a John Carter to reach the factory and save the world, if he had to cross the 'brightside' unprotected.

But without sunward oceans, would the world become uninhabitable as water vapour froze out on the dark side? The US 'Contact' discussion group envisaged a dark side completely covered in ice, with glaciers thawing as they crept into the twilight zone.[28] It might have a water layer below, like the ancient lakes which are still liquid, below the Antarctic ice-cap.[29] However, it needs so much more water cover than Earth's that its oceans would be fresh for lack of continental mineral runoff.[28] The 'very broad river' might be part of an artificial control system: details William found tedious might include mountain barriers separating the twilight zone from the dark, generating rainfall for the inhabited strip. Glaciers in high latitudes would feed the river, carrying water back to the daylit hemisphere where it evaporates.

Containing the atmosphere to the sunlit face of the planet and twilight zone would cut the quantities needed by nearly half. If we could restrict it to the twilight zone *only*...

The 1994 impacts of Comet Shoemaker-Levy 9 on Jupiter renewed interest in the overlapping crater chains on Ganymede and Callisto (Fig 12.2). The biggest is 620 kilometres long, with 25 craters roughly 25 km. across, formed by bodies less than 4 km. across.[30] The asteroid which killed the dinosaurs was about 16 km (10 miles) across and its crater ten times that size (100 miles). In 1998 it was discovered that the mass extinction at the end of the Triassic period, 214 million years ago, coincided with five impacts in the Ukraine, France, Minnesota and Canada - North America was joined to Europe then. They could have taken as little as four hours, or been spread over several days, in which case there might be more on the sea floor.[31] The largest formed the Manicougan impact structure, over 100 kilometres in diameter and spectacularly visible from orbit.[32] More recently, seven or more impacts may have occurred around 7640 BC, interrupting the glacier melting at the end of the Ice Age.[33]

Artificially controlled, chains could be close enough together to merge into a groove on the planet's surface (Figs. 19.2, 19.3): it's happened on a small scale with secondary crater chains on Phobos, the inner moon of Mars. A 100-mile wide trench round an earth-sized planet from pole to pole would require 250 ten-mile objects, a possible number in a planetary system. If the planet was initially earthlike, and all the volatiles ended up frozen on the darkside as above, there could be a huge icecap from which to regenerate the atmosphere (Fig. 19.3). Ices could be mined and brought to the valley, or the cap could be heated using orbiting mirrors ('solettas') or an artificial ring. But if there was a runaway greenhouse effect on the sunward face many volatiles could react with molten rock, as apparently they did on Venus, so they'd be bound up in rocks on the sunward side and much harder to liberate. Importing fresh ones is probably the answer: a comet nucleus has about one-tenth the mass of a nickel-iron asteroid of the same size, so 2500 comets would create a channel as wide as the Mississippi along the centre of the valley. It's calculated that a cometary body 80 km. in diameter could provide a breathable atmosphere for our Moon, with one-sixteenth of the Earth's surface area:[34] that would correspond to 8000 Shoemaker-Levy fragments, the breakup of 400 large cometary nuclei. 2500 such fragments would give an atmosphere over one-fiftieth of the surface of an earthlike world. A 100-mile-wide strip ringing the planet has one-eightieth of the Earth's surface area, so there's plenty of water left to fill the river.

If only one hemisphere's twilight zone was terraformed, the number of impacts needed would be halved again, and that might well apply. On the Moon, Mars and Mercury there's 'chaotic terrain' opposite the big impact basins - very rough country broken up by the focussed shockwaves from the far side of the planet. Mars has a solid core, Mercury's is liquid, and though the Moon's is semi-liquid it's much smaller, proportionately, than Earth's, and the Moon's crust is very rigid, so perhaps the valley could be on both sides of the planet - but we'll only see evidence for one, and the model I'm putting forward requires a very rigid crust. Does the valley even run from pole to pole: how long does a habitable twilight zone need to be?

If direct sunlight never enters the inhabited side of the valley, the planet's orbit must be virtually circular, like Venus's. Otherwise, the rotation would go out of synchronisation when the planet was moving faster at its closest to the sun: as Mercury approaches perihelion, at the terminator our Sun comes back up where it previously set, even larger than before. Similarly, unless the children live on the equator, the axis of rotation must be perpendicular to the orbital plane; so there would be no seasons, and their first autumn and winter might have come as a shock - perhaps contributing to the depression which brought the boy's death. Even the alternation of day and night might be too much to take - some people can't cope even with the one-hour shift from Solar Time to Daylight Saving.[35]

Fig. 19.2.   Formation of the colony valley.
Painting by Sydney Jordan.

Fig. 19.3. Colony world from space.
Painting by Sydney Jordan.

If it was done by cratering and the craters are 20 miles deep, that tells us about the planet's interior.   A simple crater 100 miles across is 20-50 miles deep at first, an inverted hemisphere.   But on Earth, that punches through to the magma, and molten material fills the hole - another reason why large impact basins like the Manicougan Ring are often first identified from space.   At sea infilling is even more effective, because water pressure outside pushes the semi-solid walls into the crater, and then it's covered with sediment: that's why the Chicxulub feature off Mexico was so hard to find.   The impact occurred at an angle and although the crater was initially 125 miles across, it was only 7 ½ miles deep and quickly filled up from below.   In fact, liquefaction of rock surrounding the Chicxulub crater was so complete that it's not obvious why it didn't smooth out flat.[37]   Even If the craters weren't filled from below, Earth's crust isn't strong enough to sustain craters 20 miles deep.   The deepest point on the Earth's surface, in the Marianas Trench, is only seven miles below sea-level; the cleft of the Dead Sea stretches more than nine miles

309

from the hilltops overlooking it to the base, but the bottom seven miles are filled with sediment.[38]

The Venus crust is 60 miles thick, yet impact craters are shallow, as on the moons of Jupiter, perhaps due to 'crustal rebound': at the Chicxulub centre the crust rebounded upwards by eleven miles.[37]   Rebound could also create double rings: Lake Acraman, an impact basin 600 million years old in Australia, has an outer ring segment, Lake Gairdner, suggesting that a central mountain splashed up and then down again.[39]   So on the colony world there might not have to be a second series of impacts to create the river bed; but they'd still probably be needed to form the atmosphere, unless the right volatiles outgassed enough after the first impacts.

Jupiter's moons' crusts are relatively plastic, because of their ice content, and the big basins there used to be deeper.   On our Moon they filled up with lava, a billion years after the impacts.   The Moon's crust is more rigid than Earth's - hence its remarkable seismic properties, 'ringing like a bell' - and even today, the Aitken basin near the Moon's south pole is 12 km deep.[40]   On Mars, the Hellas basin is 10 km deep.[41]   On the asteroid Vesta there's a crater nearly 13 km deep, and fragments from it are found throughout the Asteroid Belt and reach Earth as meteorites.[42]   But that crater is 480 km across, Hellas is 2400 km , Aitken 2500 km;[43]   the nearest approach to the proportions we want is on Mimas, one of Saturn's ice moons, with a crater 130 km across and 10 km deep - provisionally named Arthur,[44] but now known as Herschel.[45]

Even if our planet has a rigid crust like the Moon's, as thick as Venus's, to create lasting, deep craters it might be necessary to freeze the material rising from below.   The planet's going to need nitrogen imports, so perhaps it's delivered in liquid form to stop the rising magma.   We'll come back to conditions there in Chap.22, but after discussing its core, it's time to look at the astronomical events of the late 12th century.   They illustrate the biggest difference between the colony planet and our own, and suggest what might go wrong with a matter transmitter operating between them.

310

Chapter Twenty - A FIRE IN THE SKY

"Every observer sees his own aurora as certainly as he sees his own rainbow."

~ Alexander von Humboldt, "Cosmos: Sketch of a Physical Description of the Universe", paraphrased in Sir John Herschel, 'Humboldt's Kosmos'[1]

1. His Own Aurora

Lord Lyttelton's life of Henry II adds "some events appertaining to natural history during that period... in the words of the ancient English historians, by whom they are related." He tries to keep to recognisable phenomena, but he knows less astronomy than he thinks. Of a spectacular example from 1173, that crucial year in our story, "It is hardly possible to give a more exact description... of an *aurora borealis*; a phenomenon then unusual in these parts of the globe, but of late much more frequent."[2]

Aurorae and magnetic storms on Earth are caused by the particle streams of 'coronal mass ejections' (CMEs) from the Sun.   It was thought that when they hit the Earth's magnetic field, they were diverted into the Van Allen Belts of trapped radiation, overloading them.   It now seems that backlash waves in the Earth's magnetic 'tail' enter the upper atmosphere along the 'rings of fire' surrounding the magnetic poles, forming rippling arcs, sheets and curtains of ionised gas - usually white, but higher energies generate the green light of ionised oxygen.   More intense radiation generates a red glow higher in the sky (Fig. 20.1), again due to oxygen, and still deeper penetration ionises nitrogen, which glows red in the lower parts of auroral arcs (Fig. 20.2).[3]

The dying geomagnetic storms interrupt communications and disrupt power supplies; one caused an 18-hour power cut in Quebec, in 1989.[5]   Recent evidence suggests that volcanic activity can also be affected.   The mechanism for that isn't obvious, though continent-building episodes in the distant past were correlated with resonances in the Earth's outer core caused by the interacting gravitational pulls of the Sun and Moon.[6]

Fig. 20.1. Auroral arcs of ionised oxygen.
Painting by Sydney Jordan.

Fig. 20.2.   Auroral 'dragon', with ionised oxygen above and nitrogen below.
Painting by Sydney Jordan.

Both flares and aurorae usually follow the 11-year cycle of sunspot activity, but 1645 to 1715 saw the 'Maunder Minimum', with 'only a sprinkling' of sunspots in the whole period.[7]   During it the Earth's northern hemisphere had a mini-ice-age, with winter ice fairs on the Thames; between 1400 and 1450 there was a similar drop, 'the Spörer Minimum', during which the Viking colonies in Greenland were wiped out and the Inuit had to abandon a 4000-year old colony on Ellesmere Island, northern Canada, first established from Mongolia.[8]   Between roughly 1250 and 1350 the 'Wolf Minimum' coincides with a lull in our story - after all the activity of both kinds between 1095 and 1250, nothing much of either happened until the Sun reawakened.

Carbon-14 deposition in tree rings increased between 1640 and 1720, so we can use earlier tree rings to chart the Sun's previous activity[9] (Fig. 20.3), and the record now goes back about 7000 years.   The rise in the 20th century corresponds to a marked increase in the numbers of solar flares up to 1970,[10] after which it flattened out - in the run-up to the 2001 peak, sunspots in 1999 were well below predicted levels,[11] and the rise in 2011 was two years late. Lyttelton's wrong about the 12th century: the most intense solar activity since the Bronze Age was from 1150-1200 AD, peaking in the 1170s with particularly warm weather (Fig. 20.3). In 1186, for example, astrologers predicted storms and pestilence because of a planetary conjunction in Libra, "the season proving, in a more than usual degree, serene and benignant".[2]   But in North America, the solar activity went with a temperature rise and drought which forced the Anasazi people to abandon their rock dwellings in the Grand Canyon.[12]

The extremely powerful aurora of 1117 lies on a peak of solar activity in Fig. 20.3, and the major ones before, during and after the First Crusade occurred during the previous rise.   53 aurorae were recorded that century, compared with 23 in the 9th, 27 in the 10th, 21 in the 11th... 16 in the 13th, 21 in the 14th and only seven in the 15th century, as the Maunder Minimum approached.[7] After a dip before 1000 AD, by 1150 solar activity had gone past average and was climbing steeply: red aurora all over the sky that year was followed by a very hard winter, but an excellent summer began the following May.[13]   The 12th century aurorae were the brightest in recorded history.

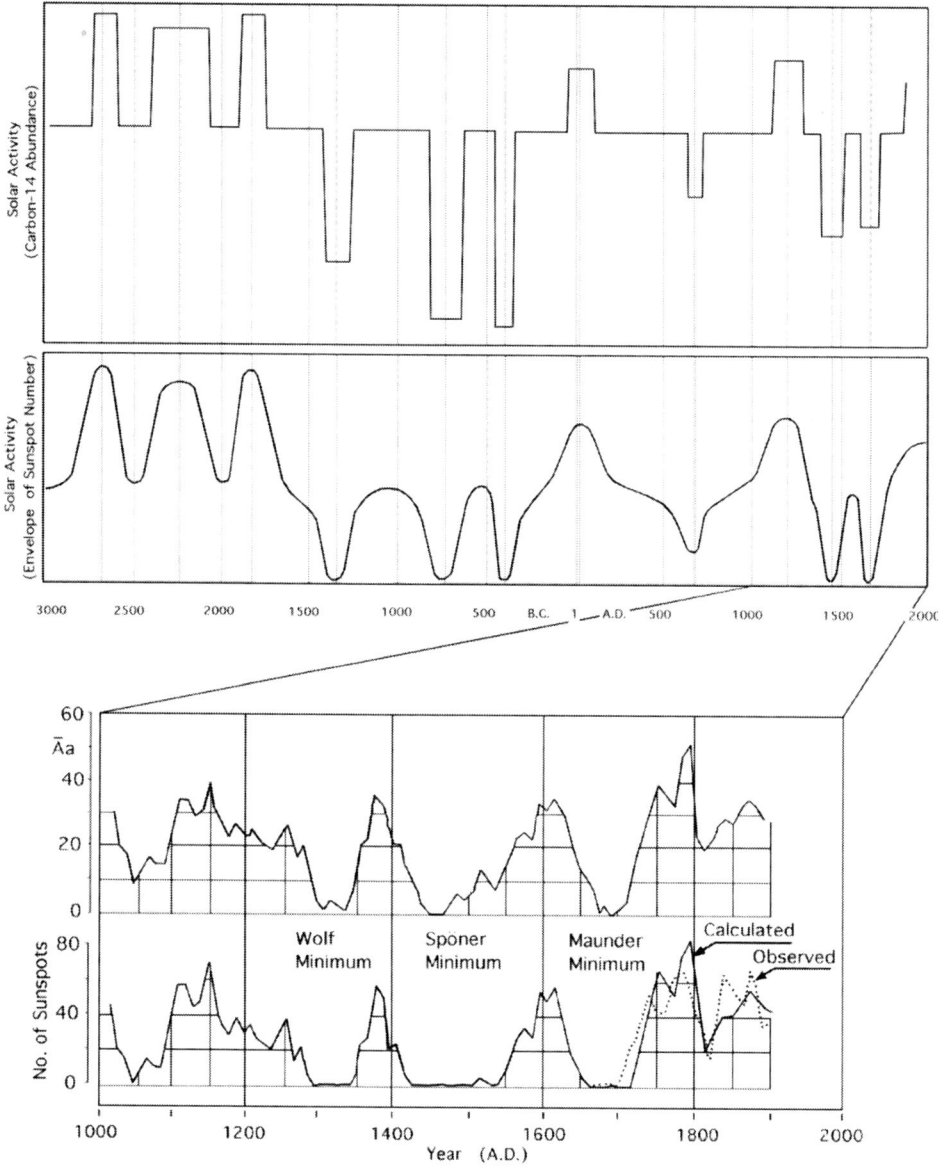

Fig. 20.3. Solar activity chart 3000 BC to present.
Drawing by Nick Portwin after John A. Eddy, Giovanni P. Gregori.

Japanese, Chinese and Korean astronomers recorded naked-eye sunspots (perhaps through cloud or haze) at roughly 11-year intervals through the century.[14] Sightings around 1171-72, and around 1185, coincide with peaks of solar and geomagnetic activity deduced from tree rings.[7] 1173 had a particularly sharp 'spike' of activity (Fig. 20.3 insert). Early that year, Gervase of Canterbury writes, "On February 10th a wonderful sign appeared in the sky, in more [hours] than the middle of the night. For a certain redness was seen in the air, between east and west, in the northern region. Moreover there were white rays crossing through that redness, which now slender in the form of lances, now truly broad in the form of sheets, and now here, now there, as if raised upwards from the earth to heaven. There were the foresaid white rays, as the rays of the Sun pierce the thickest cloud..."[10] Red aurora shows higher-energy particles entering the atmosphere, and it's unusual as far south as Canterbury, but this display was recorded at Magdeburg and Pohlde in Germany,[16] and another in France the following night.[17] Other than that, so far, Lyttelton's comment above was apt. But then something different happened: "Following was a brilliant light, similar to the summer sun rise, as it fully breaks into day: afterwards the most dense blackish cloud, in the same region, was raised as if from the earth, which gradually growing up overshadowed that day."

Things like that don't normally happen during aurora. It sounds like an impact, equivalent to a nuclear explosion: a fireball, rising over the horizon, followed by black cloud spreading southwards (which could have been coming anyway). For comparison, between 500 and a thousand years ago a 'football-field-size' meteorite in Nebraska created a depression a mile across, originally 500 feet deep and even now 70 feet below the local surface. According to a Kansas University palaeontologist, "if you were in the vicinity and looked at it, you'd be blinded. And there would be a tremendous roll of thunder followed by a shock wave."[18] Heat would ignite anything for a 20-mile radius. The giant Tunguska meteor in 1908 exploded in the air over Siberia, without forming a crater on the ground.

The 1173 event was higher, and seen from below. "Murray O' Coffey, bishop of Derry... resigned his spirit to heaven in the black abbey-church of Columb-kille [St. Columba] on the 4th of the Ides of February (Feb. 10th.) Great miracles were wrought in the night on which he died: the night was illumined from nocturns until cock-crow, and the ground was all in flames; and a large mass of fire ascended over the town, and proceeded towards the south-east; and all persons arose from their beds, imagining that it was day; and it was thus as far as the horizon, as they thought."[19]

That 'mass of fire' was the 'brilliant light' on the northern horizon at Canterbury, though not due north. The *Annals of the Kingdom of Ireland* describe it as a globe of fire, and the display "also thus on the eastern side of the sea", extending over the Scottish mainland, where 'streaks of fire' were recorded.[20] Yet there's no sound in the Irish records, so the 'explosion' may be part of the auroral display; though if so, its scale is beyond any modern ones. And it's not the only such event over Derry. In AD 597, on the night that St. Columba died on the island of Iona, monks and fishermen in Donegal saw a rising fiery column over Derry, "seen by us to light up the whole world, just like the summer midday Sun, and after that column pierced the sky, darkness followed as if after sunset".[15] It's just as well that the 1173 fireball was confirmed at Canterbury, otherwise one might think that the Irish always saw flares over Derry when their holy men died.

On December 5, 1737, red aurora across much of Europe, from Italy to Scotland, was coronal at Kilkenny, appearing directly overhead. "This same Phaenomenon was of great Extent in the Northern Parts of Europe; and at Kilkenny in Ireland, was seen somewhat like a Globe of Fire suspended in the Air for near space of an Hour; which then bursting, spread Flames around on every Side."[22] During a display at Greenwich in 1882, Maunder reported, "A great circular disc of greenish light suddenly appeared low down in the East-North-East, as though it had just risen, and moved across the sky, as smoothly and steadily as the Sun, Moon, stars and planets move, but nearly a thousand times as quickly. The circularity of its shape was merely the effect of foreshortening, for as it moved it lengthened out, and when it crossed the meridian and passed just above the Moon its form was almost that of a very elongated ellipse, and various observers spoke of it as 'cigar-shaped', 'like a torpedo'..."[23]

For the 1173 one to resemble the rising midsummer Sun, or a mass of fire, it would have to be brighter still. But the movements of the two masses were similar, presumably followed the lines of force of the Earth's magnetic field. During his troubled stay on the Mir space station in 1997, Commander Vasily Tsibliyev saw a glowing mass near the Earth's south magnetic pole, passing down from the height of the space station all the way into the clouds.

Although it behaved like a plasmoid, it must have been very bright to be visible in sunlight.[24]

In 1159, in the Irish annals, "a great mass of fire was seen in the firmament... bigger than St. Patrick's Mount... it dispersed in several showers of small sparkling fire, without doing any harm."[20] That's more like a fireball meteor, burning out in the upper atmosphere, which can light up the landscape like day - I've seen it! But if the 'mass of fire' in 1173 was one, as Alan Chapman suggested in our meeting during the *National Geographic Ancient X-Files* filming, the Derry inhabitants would have to rise quickly from their beds to see it. After the events which we've seen in 1195 and 1253, the 1173 and possibly the 1159 one, could be similar ones at high altitude.   But for the 1173 one to happen during an auroral display may be a major clue.

An auroral storm couldn't happen on the children's colony planet, with its trapped rotation. The minor Coriolis forces acting on the river would be even less effective within the core, and currents within the Earth's core generate our magnetic field.   Mars has no magnetic field because it solidified before crust, mantle and core had fully separated.   The Moon has none, because its small, semi-liquid core is non-conducting, and its rotation is slow (14 Earth days). Venus has a nickel-iron core like Earth's but rotates very slowly indeed (243 days) - no magnetic field; Mercury with its 176-day rotation has a liquid core, and only a small magnetic field.

So the children's planet won't have one.   As with Venus, the solar wind from its star will impinge directly on the upper atmosphere, generating a bow shock, and perhaps some phenomena on the dark side: Venus has one called the 'Ashen Light',   reported by amateur astronomers and argued about by professionals.   But not aurorae as we know them, the legendary spirits of dead warriors dancing in the northern sky, much less what Gervase describes on 29th November, 1177... "That same year, during the vigil of St. Andrew the apostle, nor as yet at the first hour, there appeared in Kent a certain red light as if a burning flame, flying by the impulse of the wind which was blowing. Indeed some strongly swore to have seen a fiery dragon with a jagged head manifesting itself at the same hour.   Very many said this sign had appeared throughout all England, either of the dragon or of the flame or of the red light."[10]

("Every observer sees his own aurora as certainly as he sees his own rainbow." For the same event, in the Annals of Margan, "an aurora was created in the twilight between night and day, before dawn, a wonderful coruscation of the air throughout all the land",[25] but imagination can make an auroral arc into a dragon   (Fig.20.2).   An 1188 aurora was compared to a flying dragon (Chap.13), and other chronicles refer to 'dragons seen in England in 1177.   In 1165 "a dragon of wonderful size was seen at St. Osyth [near the mouth of the Colne]   carried through the air so close to the earth that by its fire certain houses were consumed"[26] - presumably by coincidence…)

… not to mention what Ralph Diceto describes on November 4th, 1174: "The day before the nones of December, around the middle of the night, for the space of one hour and more than that, all the face of the sky from the northern part was seen to be blood-red and suffused with red light…"[27]   (also seen in Brittany[28]),

… let alone what Bravonius Wigorniensis has for 1172: "In the night of the Lord's birth, a thunderclap was heard in England, in Ireland, and in the whole kingdom of France, sudden and horrible, and the blood of St. Thomas was clearly seen with a roaring/rumbling call to the Lord,"[29] partly confirmed by Matthew Paris: "In the year of our Lord 1172, on the Natal night of the Lord, thunders were widely heard, specifically in England, Ireland and France, such as nobody could remember to have heard before."[30]   Later writers repeat this entry, simply copying.[31]   It's six weeks before the 'mass of fire', and like that, it's not what normally happens during an auroral display.   To be heard over so large an area, that thunderclap and the following rumble must have been an air-burst with a sonic boom, like the Tunguska event.

Some put it at the beginning of 1172, Christmas 1171 in our calendar, and the Guildford chronicle errs the other way, giving Christmas 1173 and February 1174: "On the night of the Lord's birth a light like day's sprang around the people going to vigils, and on Sexagesima Sunday to vespers, until the middle of the night horrible red colours were seen in the sky, and a light like dawn, as if in the middle of summer.   And without delay, followed war between the sons of the king and their father." (Quoting that, Blomefield wrote, "…so that our *aurorae boreales* are no new phenomena, as some modern philosophers would pretend".[32]   Neither he nor Lyttelton knew about the Maunder Minimum.)   C.E. Britton comes down in favour of 1171, but doesn't take the aurora into account.[28]   Henry II was at war with his sons in 1173 and 1174 (Chap. 9), but the Guildford chronicle relates to the onset of the war, Christmas 1172, because Sexagesima (second Sunday before Lent) was February 10th in 1173.

2. Somewhere over the Rainbow

All this suggests a possible cause of 'digressions', and Andrew Paterson came up with a matter-transmitter concept to fit the bill.   As he remarked when I issued the challenge (Chap.18), if the system is going wrong, and you know what makes it go wrong, it's much easier to figure out how it works properly. As he visualised it, the quantum scanning device in Chap.18 could be made to set up "a time-dependent spherical probability wave that could only collapse using a receiver, i.e. a machine specially designed to 'capture' the signal..." by transmitting the output signal through a wormhole.

As normally visualised (Fig. 18.1), a wormhole's other end could be anywhere in the Universe.   But that topographical model is in asymptotically flat space-time, linking points far out in space, away from concentrations of mass,[33] or else in Forward's 'flattened spacetime' (Chap.18).   In a revised version of his 1981 paper on black holes as stargates, John Fadum suggested that if the transmitting end of the system had a gravitational potential energy, e.g. it was near a star, then a spacecraft going through would materialise at a correspond-ing distance from the mass of the target star.[34]

Andrew suggested that initial conditions for a much smaller wormhole could be set to generate an overwhelming probability that it would materialise at the Earth's surface, 'bringing with it' the object which has been destructively scanned.   The wormhole and the object would both be given gravitational potential energy equal to what they'd have on the Earth's surface at the target point, correcting for any difference between gravitational fields at the two ends of the link.   Perhaps the generating system is in a spaceship or space station, so potential energy in the transmitting field can be 'trimmed' by varying acceleration or the rotation rate.   (One fundamental of relativity theory is that gravitational effects can't be distinguished from acceleration by tests conduct-ed within a system.)   Or in 'flattened spacetime', the controlling masses could be repositioned to match successively the surface gravities on the two worlds.

In a later letter, Andrew suggested such 'tuning' might not be necessary: the differences in gravitational potential between the planets' surfaces could be insignificant relative to the overall field of the Galaxy. The colony world and control centre have to be somewhere in the Milky Way's spiral arms, since potentials nearer the Galactic Centre would be too great to match out here. He put an inner limit for them at 17,700 light-years from the Galactic Centre, but we wouldn't expect earthlike, life-supporting planets closer to it than that: stars in the galactic nucleus are older than the disc's, and lack the heavier elements to form solid planets. There may be new stars there by now, but it's a violent environment - there's evidence of multiple explosions in the galactic core over its history.

Using gravitational potential alone, the transmitted object would be 'every-where and nowhere' on Earth, until something fixes its location, so a receiving device on Earth is required. As well as gravitational potential, the transmitting end of the wormhole is given an electrostatic one, i.e. a positive or negative charge. The homing device on Earth then generates an electric field corresponding to the one at the transmitting end, creating a match for conditions there and making the wormhole's probability wave collapse. The transmitted object then materialises here. (Though I've invoked Frank Herbert's *Dune* in Chap.23, it's tempting to do it differently here and call the process 'summoning a worm'.) Andy Paterson calls the activating devices 'keys'.

On most theoretical accounts, matter going through a wormhole would be destroyed so thoroughly that it couldn't be reassembled at the far end - so preserving causality. But by combining the wormhole with the 'quantum scanner', then "assuming the boundary conditions are right, there is a finite chance that the wave function will be non-zero across the wormhole and this would get round the speed of light limitation, and not violate causality because matter and energy haven't been transmitted as such."

Information is transmitted, so it might seem causality is violated, but Andrew disagreed, "Violations can only occur when a field or particle travels across spacetime faster-than-light. However, nothing is said about what happens when space itself is compressed or stretched. If something passes through a wormhole slower than light in that wormhole, causality is preserved no matter how far apart the hole throats are. Imagine the Earth last century when travel was restricted to a few miles per hour. To travel from Europe to Australia, you would have to navigate all the way down the African coast and then round the Cape into the Indian Ocean. This was the speed limit at the time. However, when the Suez Canal opened, the distance was cut between the continents but the ships still sailed at the same speed. There was a new causal link and the same is true for a wormhole: it is a causal link between distant points. The old causal link still exists but has been superseded by the shorter one."

The children described no scanning device in their father's field, as far as we know, and the quantum mechanical component of the combined system requires physical, destructive scanning of the object to be transmitted. But, Andy Nimmo pointed out, when the scanner is used in combination with a wormhole, all the outlets are the same outlet, so only one machine is needed, the one in mission control. Another way to put it is that they're all virtual, equivalent outlets. On a sub-microscopic scale, space itself can be considered a sea of multiply-connected wormholes and virtual particles: in 1963, Prof. John Wheeler suggested that was needed to account for the phenomenon of electricity.[35] Morris, Thorne and Yurtsever suggested that an advanced civilisation could create a navigable wormhole by pulling one out of the quantum foam and enlarging it to 'classical size'.[36] In Andrew's version, the number of possible outlets is limited only by the number of 'keys' in circulation, which explains how transmission can occur between points on the same planet, as apparently happened on Earth in Chaps.7, 11 and 16: the scanner can be on a different one, since it operates through the wormhole, which exists within it, with its beam of energy passing back and forth.

But the locating devices must get here in the first place. If one per planet is enough, the carrier vehicle could be as inconspicuous as Robert Forward's 'Starwisp', an interstellar probe only a foot across, visible in space only when illuminated by a super-power laser which propels it to a high fraction of lightspeed.[37] If one fell on Earth, carrying a relay device, thereafter the portal could be opened at will; but our chances of finding it are very small, unless it's been deliberately preserved.

That would be a slow way to spread relays, perhaps taking millions of years to locate inhabited worlds. But if the system's relatively insensitive to gravity variations, as above, the wormhole's electrostatic charge could be set to match random, natural events, such as lightning or auroral storms on destination planets. When a 'portal' opened, randomly, an explorer (probably a robot) would go through to see what had been found, and re-open the gateway after a prearranged interval. One by one, links could be made to every earthlike world in the Galaxy.

The potential link would remain locked to Earth, following it through space. Andrew worried about temperature and radiation at the portal mouth, but calculated that space temperature at the mouth of a five-metre wormhole would be only fractions of a degree above ambient. If there's a homing device already in place, the rotation of the Earth isn't a problem, so there's no need for a coordinate system, because the incoming wormhole automatically 'finds its own level'. Many of the possible cases involve moats, pits, or caves: perhaps to minimise atmospheric vortices generated by a wormhole, but perhaps also to reduce the hazard if the tuning isn't always accurate.

"In the night of the Lord's birth, a thunderclap was heard in England, in Ireland, and in the whole kingdom of France, sudden and horrible..." If that *was* a sonic boom, whatever or worse still *whoever* it was, certainly wasn't synchronised with the rotation of the Earth. But while some chronicles repeat 'sudden and horrible', others refer only to thunderclaps, without giving details. "AD 1172 on Christmas night there was thunder heard throughout England... also beyond the sea, and particularly in Ireland. For not only that night, but the whole of Christmas day, that storm continued, so people were so fearful that they were in all despair of their lives." The Chronicle describes several deaths by lightning, as does another wrongly giving the year as 1176.[26]

But when Ralph of Coggeshall describes the children's experience, the exact translation is that it happened "because the animals were being followed". The verb is the passive *sequerentur*, whose most straightforward meaning is that the children were following animals, but if so, it means the animals went down first into the 'cave'. That verb is definitely 'went *down*'. Perhaps the animals (or people) were being followed by someone or something else, and took cover in a cave or pit. In a poem by Steve Sneyd, the children attract the attention of a starving green cat - size unspecified.[38] Was the 'woolpit' so called because wolves came out of it - green wolves, which lost their colour as they consumed terrestrial prey? It would suggest that the children were unintended victims of a cull on the colony world. Or if we translate *sequerent-*

ur as 'tracked', perhaps the children were carrying a locating device, and the sound warned that the matter-transmitter had locked on to it. Ralph implies an element of authority or compulsion - 'Summoned by Bells', to quote Sir John Betjeman.

William has *sonitum quendam magnum audivimus, qualem nunc apud sanctum Edmundum cum signa concrepare dicuntur, audire solemus*: "we heard a certain great sound which now we are accustomed to hear at St. Edmund's when they say the bells are ringing". Old editions say *apud sanctum Albanum*, 'at St. Albans', but the British Library and Cambridge manuscripts have *sanctum Edmundum*; the Liberty of St. Edmund was nearly a third of Suffolk, so *apud sanctum Edmundum* may not even mean the town but just 'on land of...' The Abbey's great tenor bell was the largest in England when purchased, between 1107 and 1112,[39] and still the largest in the 16th century,[40] to be heard at a distance, so workers in the fields could cross themselves when mass was sung in church. But the key point is that the sound the children heard was *like* the bells of Bury, not the Bury bells themselves as Paul Harris says (Chap.8).

Magnus sonitus had a special meaning at Bury. Samson's successor, Hugh of Northwold, was awarded one on the anniversary of his death in 1211.[41] It wasn't change ringing as we know it: the first account in 1668 describes that as an innovation of the previous fifty to sixty years.[42] Before that bells were rung in a 'clocher'. The ringer leaned over the bell and pulled on the stock: dangerous, resulting in deafness and frequently in broken collar bones.[43] Bury St. Edmunds still had a clocher of four great bells at the Reformation, when they were broken up for scrap.[44] The best translation is 'a God-almighty din'.[43] The Bury monks could make one: the north tower of the Abbey fell in 1210 and wasn't rebuilt for a century, and the western tower fell in 1430, after which both were demolished, due to poor maintenance and excessive bell-ringing.[45] At the end of each day's chapter-house meeting, the subsacrist would formally announce to the prior and convent that there would be a single, double or triple *sonitus*. "For whom?", he would be asked, and would reply with a list of benefactors to be commemorated.[46] Did Richard de Calna have one, for sponsoring the stained-glass with the astronomical theme?

In some places, bells were rung for the arrival of an important visitor - visiting London in 1431, the Abbot of Canterbury "did not only look and wait for the ringing of bells, for a triumph of his coming, but took great snuff, and did suspend all the churches in London... so many as did not receive his coming with the noise of bells."[42] It would be interesting if the children's arrival was anticipated to the extent that the Bury bells were sounded for it, but it didn't always happen even there: Richard II gave orders against it when he visited in 1383.[47] But whatever the children's 'great sound' was, it was at the other end, not here. The children arrived in daylight, and the reapers would have been in the fields from first light - yet nobody heard anything or knew the children were there until they made a break for it.

Signa concrepare was a mediaeval Latin metaphor for ringing bells. But it means 'flags waving violently'; perhaps the snapping sound of electrical discharges. Another possible meaning is 'constellations moving violently'. On a planet with trapped rotation the stars would normally move very slowly, and in the twilight zone the brighter ones would always be visible. So it could mean "the great sound (like we now hear in the land of St. Edmund) when they say that the stars move", i.e. when space is distorted by the wormhole field. Other idiomatic meanings could be "when they say the red flags are flying" or "when they say the alarm bells are ringing"... or "the noise we're accustomed to hear at St. Edmund's where people say the stars move (though we know they don't)". Signa can also mean 'signs in the heavens', and there were plenty of those: indeed 'whirling draperies' are a common auroral form.

I think it's much more likely that the sound really was of bells, and I'll come back to that. I haven't found any reference to *signa concrepare* as auroral displays - dragons are much more common - though a display in 1355 was described as two banners, red and blue, fighting in the sky.[28] But if it *was* aurorae, it would suggest Agnes understood what had happened to her, in Andrew's interpretation.

Stray electric fields are generated when Earth's magnetic field is disturbed - aurorae disrupt power supplies and communications today, especially in high latitudes like Alaska and Scandinavia's. So if matter-transmitter links were set up when our Sun was quiet, and then the magnetic field was disturbed - more so than any time in the previous three thousand years, and with auroral storms reaching much further south than usual - then wormhole links could be triggered either by accident or by stray signals in the 'keys'. It would cause events like the Peak swineherd's and the green children's, alerting king Henry to strangers within his realm, if he didn't already know.

It may also explain the Templars' raid on Coggeshall Abbey, in Chap.12. If there was a meeting between Richard de Hastings and Gilbert Foliot, in which the bishop mentioned that the boy was buried in the clothes he arrived in, including a strange necklace, badge or bracelet - and de Hastings maintained his cool at that point, he deserved his post as Master of his Order in England: with the devices subject to random activation during the unexpectedly fierce aurorae, burying one was most dangerous After all the help the Templars had from Bernard de Clairvaux, would you want to explain to his successor that your equipment had just blown one of his newest abbeys into the strato- sphere? Immediate retrieval would have the highest priority.

The best chance to do it unnoticed would be at the dinner hour - it was Cister- cian practise to eat only once a day. If a locating device could be concealed within the Abbey, it would be easier to get into the grounds unobserved. The de Calnas could plant it in the guest house on one of their frequent visits: perhaps the same device the girl was carrying when she arrived. But that does raise another question.

Why didn't the children just go straight home? If the locating devices generate an electric field, presumably they'd be discharged in the transfer and weren't usable again before the children were caught. In Sue Jones's drawing which I mentioned in Chap. 8, the girl wears a medallion and the boy a jewelled breastplate; but when they were stripped to reveal they were green all over, any 'jewellery' would be confiscated as well. If the devices were solar powered, and believed to be heathen and locked away, they'd never recharge; but solar-power wouldn't be very effective in permanent twilight. If they had an inbuilt power source such as a radioactive isotope, they would rebuild their charge over time and become dangerous.

They'd be dangerous if tampered with, as well. Does that explain the lightning bolts from a clear sky which stopped Henry II's meeting with Philip (Chap.13)? Even if the devices had our trefoil radiation symbol, it would mean nothing to Henry II - even a skull-and-crossbones might only arouse his curiosity, especially if it was a Templar symbol (Chap.23). Andrew Paterson suggested that low-frequency sound in the portals might have a cumulative, harmful effect; Henry II, Richard de Calna and Geoffrey Ridell all died in the same year, 1189. Some deaths are associated with hair and nails falling out - Richard I lost his hair within days of reaching the Holy Land in 1191, though that's attributed to a malarial fever which swept through his camp.[48]   Richard de Clare's hair and nails fell out after the first poisoning attempt on him, but well it might, since the second one killed him.   If "others of note" hadn't died with him we might wonder about radiation nevertheless.   At the time, de Clare's steward and another man were arrested for the deed, and summarily convicted.[49]

But Walter de Coutances went with Richard I to the crusade, and returned in 1191 to become Chief Justiciar, head of the government, until 1193.   He quarrelled with Richard over a castle in the Vexin, and put the whole of Normandy under interdict.[50]   When John was king, de Coutances made him Duke of Normandy, before the French conquest of Normandy in 1204... to sum up, he lived on, unscathed.   So did Richard Barre; and particularly John of Oxford.

With all *his* connections, it's surprising that he hasn't played a more active part in our story.   He's associated with Richard Barre from the outset, and whenever Ridell or de Coutances appears as a witness to a charter, almost always John of Oxford is there too.   Keith Llewellyn of ASTRA suggested that the king's men had only one 'key' between them, of which John of Oxford was custodian.   He died in 1200, so perhaps he didn't use it much himself, or learned from what happened to previous 'keyholders'.

But it makes the 1195 event over his London town-house more interesting: condensation, electrical charges, a hole in the sky - could it have been a wormhole in that strange cloud, and if so, was that our Sun shining through it? The late A.T. Lawton concluded (from the inverse-square law) that from any habitable planet, the disc of its sun should look the same size regardless of spectral type and actual distance from it.[43]   But in the 1253 event over Derby, the star 'shining like the Sun' was just a point of light - perhaps our Sun, or some brighter star, from a more distant viewpoint.   The lesser red stars 'attacking' it, alternately attracted and repelled, sound electrostatic.   Ball lightning is the most likely explanation, and for 'I know not what' which descended in London, though the conical effect doesn't match usual descriptions.

What best fits is that the 'key' needs an external power source to charge it up: even in the 12th century there were several ways to do that.   The charter by which Sibylla de Calna sold Wykes included a water-mill in the middle of their land,[52] and there was a windmill in the area, so the de Calnas had sources of electric power, if they'd known how to use them. Even a mediaeval water-mill could have generated a kilowatt of electricity, so it could easily charge a capacitor during its everyday work. Windmills were relatively new technology in the 12th century, like the horse-plough;[53] they were introduced into Europe *by the Templars* and to England by 1137, with the major innovation that they were horizontal, not vertical, and could turn to face the wind.[54] So if there were unfamiliar additions to the one at Wykes, they could be brushed off, like the more recent photo-reconnaissance nose-cone on the Soviet Tu-104 airliner: "it's a design feature - the machine won't work without it." Was that why Sibylla's partnership in the Winkeneye mill was a secret (Chap.17)?

Ralph says that the children hid in the pit for some time, before they made a run for it across the fields. So, Jane Greatorex asked, why run out at all? Why not wait for twilight, which they were used to, or darkness? If they were from a twilight world, they may not have realised that either was coming, but it still leaves us asking why they ran when they did. Jane guessed they were startled by an earth tremor: though Lyttelton was dreaming when he thought we had volcanoes, in the 12th century the UK had several major earthquakes, though not at the right time, if it was the children's arrival which caused Henry II's dash to England in July 1173. Earthquakes commonly set church bells ringing, but there's no record of that when the children arrived. Had that been accompanied by bells ringing here, or by an earthquake, it's hard to imagine William of Newburgh finding it 'tedious' even if he set it in the wrong reign.

Perhaps they were frightened by a burst of sound suggesting that the wormhole was opening again. Andy Paterson pointed out that if the matter-transmitter was used to transmit livestock (in Chap.16, apparently, knights on horseback!) that limits the sounds the wormhole can generate: specifically, no ultrasonics. Andrew calculated that the wormhole might generate infrasound, below human hearing, but that too must avoid frequencies associated with earthquakes, of which animals often give warning by their behaviour. Mind you, if dogs in the area mysteriously started howling when the wormhole was activated, it would help to keep the peasants indoors...

The children might be conditioned to run from subsonic sound - though if so they weren't fast enough, on their home world.   But if there wasn't an earthquake, and nothing which had been following the animals came through, then the irony might be that they ran from an attempt to retrieve them.   As there are no sounds reported in the other incidents, it's still likely that the bells the children heard the first time were a warning - something on the locator which could be turned off when not wanted.

Do human beings have an innate ability to sense and orient ourselves by the Earth's magnetic field, deadened in the modern world by the electric circuitry which surrounds us?   Our brains contain magnetic sensors like other species including pigeons, salmon, whales, turtles, and even monarch butterflies and bacteria,[55] but whether still potentially active, is another question.   Isaac Asimov related how sad he was as a child when his family moved out of a slum apartment with had gas lights and a wood-burning stove: electricity had no magic - but he didn't become disoriented indoors, or lose his sense of direction in the street.[56]   If we have such a sense, deadened by overload, could the children - after a generation or more on a world without a magnetic field - have heightened sensitivity?   Did a fresh surge in the Earth's field impel them to flee from the pit?   Which way they ran, when they did, would be interesting.

3. De minimis non curat lex

Given the previous peaks of solar activity, in 2800, 2250 and 1800 BC (Fig. 20.3), it's remarkable that the Double Kettle at Darlington formed then, according to the 5000 year-old pollen found there (Chap.12).   So does the matter-transmitter only work when the Sun is disturbed, despite the problems that causes, or does its use in the Solar System upset the Sun?   What about the Maunder Minimum, Spörer Minimum, and other times when the solar activity was apparently below normal?

Andrew suggested that sunspot numbers - even the big naked-eye ones of the 12th century   might not truly indicate the state of the Sun.   The Maunder interpretation has been challenged, with obscure records suggesting that sunspot frequency was more normal than alleged, and the SOHO space probe has shown that when there are no sunspots, the Sun is fully as active in other respects.[57]   The apparent maxima and minima in Fig. 20.3 might be only variations of the Earth's magnetic field - natural, or some effect of the matter-transmitter on space-time; but the recent matches of carbon-14 readings with sunspot numbers, in the inset, suggest that at the peak times the overall solar activity really was disturbed.   The cessation of events during the Wolf Minimum, and the apparent resumption between it and the Spörer one (Chap.24), suggest to me that solar activity enables the gateways to open, rather than vice versa.

The de Calnas came from the parish next to Avebury, the greatest of all the English stone circle complexes, in the longest of the three 'corridors' I pointed out in Chap.17.   Work at Avebury began around 2700 BC, near the peak of solar activity, when the Double Kettle formed.   Matt Ewart of ASTRA claimed the Templars often built over megalithic sites: I haven't found evidence of that.   But in Aghaboe the Normans built on a neolithic site, at the Mote of Skirk, as did Roger le Poer at Salisbury; those might be two among many.   There definitely is a connection with megalithic sites to explore.

Chapter Twenty-one – THE CENTRE OF THE WORLD

We know by the Moon that we are not too soon,
We know by the sky that we are not too high,
We know by the stars that we are not too far,
And we know by the ground, *that we are within sound*…

~ *Gower Wassail* (traditional).[1]

1. Epsilon Boötis and the Galaxy

In March 1973 the late Kenneth Gatland published my article 'Space Probe from Epsilon Boötis' in the British Interplanetary Society's magazine *Spaceflight*, and a more popular version appeared in the January 1974 *Analog*[2] - causing some problems due to errors in copying my diagrams.   The two plus *Man and the Stars* caused such a stir that I'm still asked about it every time I appear in *Analog*, and it can be hard to get US radio interviewers to talk about anything else.

The 'space probe affair' centred on long-delayed radio 'echoes' (LDE's), first reported in the 1920's, and actually too powerful to be simple reflections of signals from Earth.   Experimenters studying round-the-world propagation of radio waves found their outgoing pulses being returned to them with a delay of three seconds, as if they were being amplified and returned by something at the distance of the Moon - but not the Moon itself.   In later experiments the delay times began to vary upwards from three seconds, in increasingly complicated sequences, but with no variation in intensity - still indicating a single source amplifying and returning the pulses.

Prof. Ron Bracewell of Stanford suggested in 1960 that they might have been rebroadcast by an unmanned probe from another civilisation, trying to attract our attention, and in 1972 I worked out a 'translation' of the 1920's echo patterns.[3]   The variations of delay times appeared random; but Prof. Bracewell himself had suggested the first signal from such a probe might be a star map, and the stars are spaced at random in the sky.   I tried plotting the delay times against the order in which the echoes were received, and at only the second attempt I found what looked like a star map - in which it appeared that the probe had come from the double star Epsilon Boötis, in the constellation Boötes, the Herdsman.   Arcturus, the brightest star in the constellation, seemed to be out of place in the map; but on checking, was shown at its place about 13,000 years ago.

Other parts of the supposed message seemed to give the scale of their planetary system, orbiting Epsilon Boötis A, and seemed at first to make sense. Epsilon Boötis A is an orange giant star, and the translation indicated that the probe makers had evolved on its second planet, emigrating to the sixth when their sun began to expand.   But the companion star (Epsilon B) was bright blue, apparently a short-lived sun of spectral type A2.   The distance given for the star in most reference books was too low, and at the true distance of 203 light-years, Epsilon B really was an A2 star and the orange giant Epsilon A had been an A0, like Sirius - too massive and with too high a radiation output to sustain habitable planets, too short-lived for life to have evolved there. More accurate 1920's records ruled out most of the 'star map' translations - not the 'Epsilon Boötis' one, but it too had to be treated as suspect.   I withdrew the entire translation,[4] but now it seems I may have gone too far.

After *Man and the Stars* came out,[5] I was contacted by Alan Evans, then a Captain in British Military Intelligence.   He liked the analysis I'd made of claimed past Contacts, concluding that Earth had not been visited more than four times, at most.   Alan suggested we jointly attempt something still more systematic: if the Earth had ever been visited, our aim would be to find proof. His was purely a personal interest, which had to remain confidential, but since he's left the Army that no longer applies.

In *Intelligent Life in the Universe*, Carl Sagan and I.S. Shklovskii suggested three criteria for past Contact: "(1) the account is committed to written record soon after the event;   (2) a major change is effected in the contacted society by the encounter;   and (3) no attempt is made by the contacting civilisation to disguise its exogenous nature."[6]   I suggested these were too stringent in some ways   (what if the visitors went out of their way not to affect the society contacted?)   and too lenient in others (from a future viewpoint, UFO's would pass these tests, but it's unlikely that they're true Contact).   I proposed (1) recognisable principles of technology, (2) rational purposes for the supposed Contact, (3) information freely given, and (4) leads for further investigation which could prove or disprove the suggested Contact.

Alan and I tightened up my approach into four categories of possible evidence, listed in my guest chapter for Chris Boyce's book *Extraterrestrial Encounter.*[7] (Noting the resistance in parts of the scientific world to the idea of Past Contact, Chris titled my chapter 'Past Contact and the Moving Caravan', as in the Arab proverb 'the dogs bark, but the caravan moves on' - hence my title for Chap.24.)   Category A would be our objective, an artefact of unquestionably extraterrestrial origin.   Category B would be optical or electromagnetic anomalies pinpointing such an object   (like the Tycho monolith in *2001*); Category D would be the 'von Däniken material' of legends, drawings etc., useful only in suggesting areas to search for other evidence.   The green children story is in Category D, but it meets Sagan & Shklovskii's criteria (1) & (3), and my (1) & (2), while in (4) the number of leads has been spectacular, even if they haven't turned up a definite proof yet.   As for (3), information may have been freely given to some people, but if so, the recipients kept it to themselves.

Alan proposed a new category C, of astronomical alignments in man-made structures, revealing knowledge which the builders shouldn't have had.   On high-resolution photographs of Stonehenge, he had identified markings which coincide with galactic alignments. If not coincidence, it's extraordinary. The Galactic Centre is 27,000 or 30,000 light-years from us, hidden behind dust clouds in the inner regions of the Milky Way, so it can't be pinpointed visually and it was first done by radiotelescope.   Until you know exactly where the Centre is, you can't determine the true plane of the Galactic Equator and the true positions of the Galactic Poles; apparently the Stonehenge builders knew exactly where they were, or took their cue from something or somebody or who did.   But in interstellar navigation, that's the only coordinate system which we would have in common with visitors.

Imagine a spacecraft travelling between the stars.   Its attitude sensing platform might be oriented to its home world (its own Right Ascension and declination)   or its home planetary system (its own Ecliptic coordinates). But neither will be relevant when it enters our Solar System: the only coordinate system common to its home system and ours is the galactic one. Landing here, it would be natural to use galactic coordinates: on a latitude equal to the declination of the galactic pole, once a day the azimuth and altitude of any star, measured from the rising point of the Galactic Centre, would correspond to its galactic coordinates, like B's in Fig. 21.1. If the attitude-sensing platform was fixed, it would still be correctly lined up with the sky once a day.

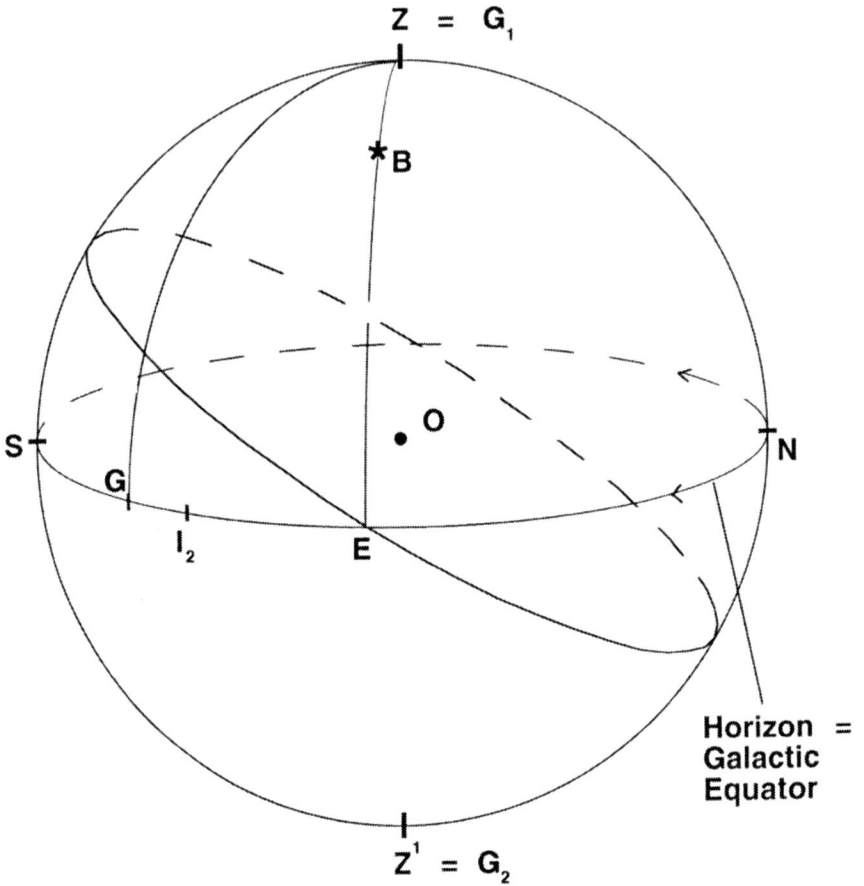

Fig. 21.1. Galactic coordinates at Stonehenge.
G = Galactic Centre; G1 = North Galactic Pole;
I_2 = southern node of the galactic equator with the Ecliptic, (the plane of the Earth's orbit).
Drawing by Nick Portwin.

What would annoy archaeologists, many of whom don't even admit 'conventional' archaeoastronomy, is the suggestion that the Stonehenge orientation is galactic at all. I looked for an optical marker, something which would have let the builders create Stonehenge without knowing about galactic coordinates or even without a spacecraft necessarily being there. I found one, but it didn't exactly make the alignments less controversial. In 2800 BC the star which had the same declination as the North Galactic Pole, equal to the latitude of Stonehenge, was Epsilon Boötis itself.

It was so hard to believe, when I'd abandoned the Epsilon Boötis 'translation' of the radio patterns, that I had to see it for myself - twice in the planetarium of the Jewel & Esk College in Musselburgh, then all over again at the much larger one in Armagh; and I've repeated it since at Glasgow Science Centre and elsewhere (see below). It feels extraordinary to see such findings, worked out with pages of calculations, simulated on the planetarium 'sky' overhead. With the date set to c.2800 BC, at the Stonehenge latitude, the Milky Way really does line up with the horizon once a day and Epsilon Boötis really goes through the zenith as well, earlier each day. The exact date when they coincide is 2582 BC - the midpoint of building the great pyramids in Egypt - and we found the same alignments at the first version of Stonehenge, and in the first and last of the great Pyramids, built 250-400 year later.[8]

The Great Pyramid is very accurately aligned to the cardinal points, north, south, east and west, and the argument about star alignments has gone on for at least a century. The southern 'star-shaft' of the King's Chamber of the Great Pyramid marks the declination of the star Alnitak in Orion's Belt c.2500 BC, crossing the meridian at an altitude of 45°, as Robert Bauval stressed in his book *The Orion Mystery*. But Alan Evans discovered that it was also about a degree from the declination of the Galactic Centre, lining up with it exactly in 2258 BC, in the time-frame of Stonehenge III; and the I_2 alignment of Fig. 21.1 is also marked by the north face of the Step Pyramid of Djoser (Fig. 21.2), which may originally have been filled and plated with limestone.[9]

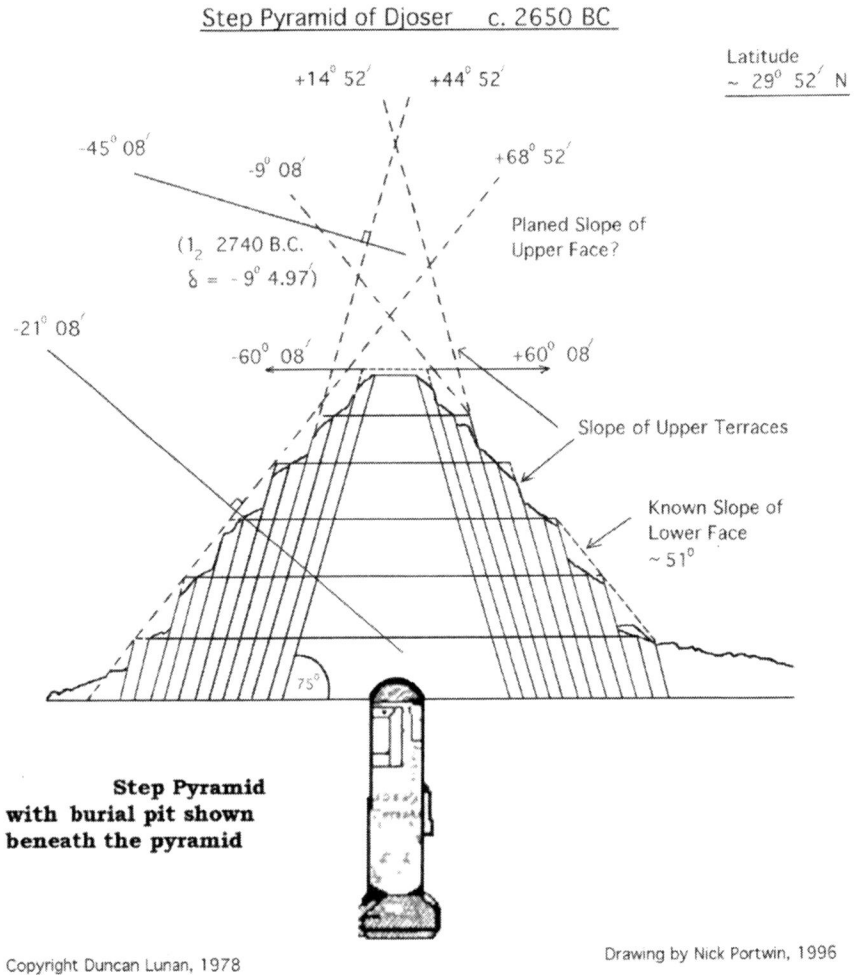

Fig. 21.2. Step Pyramid of Djoser.
Drawing by Nick Portwin (original by Duncan Lunan).

In *The Orion Mystery*, Robert Bauval suggested that the three giant pyramids of Giza not only marked star alignments in their 'air-shafts', or 'star-shafts' as he calls them, but also represented the stars of Orion's Belt mapped on to the landscape.[9]   In *Keeper of Genesis*, he and Graham Hancock claimed that the Pyramids' orientation to the Nile corresponds to the Belt stars' in relation to the Milky Way - not when they were built, but 8000 years before, due to Precession of the Equinoxes[10] (the 26,000-year wobble of the Earth's axis due to the pull of Sun and Moon on Earth's equatorial bulge). In reply Ian Lawton and Chris Ogilvie-Herald argued that the best match with the pyramids would be in 12,500 BC,[11] two thousand years earlier than Robert and Graham's 'First Time' - but still within the 'date range' of the 1928 'Boötes map'. If that map meant anything, it would be as a time marker, not navigational as I'd thought.

In 1996 I organised a seminar, 'Heresies in Archaeoastronomy', at the Edinburgh International Science Festival, chaired by Prof. Archie Roy, with other speakers including Robert Bauval, Alan Evans, and John Braithwaite, representing Matt Ewart. Graham Hancock couldn't attend the Edinburgh seminar, but he and Robert were both in Glasgow three weeks later for the launch of *Keeper of Genesis* and I arranged a meeting at the planetarium in the College of Nautical Studies. First I asked the operator to set the date to 2700 BC, as a mean date for Stonehenge I and the Pyramids, and I showed Robert and Graham the galactic orientation which Alan Evans and I had discovered. Robert Bauval made an extraordinary remark in response - see below.

Then, holding the date c.2700 BC, we shifted to the latitude of Giza, and verified Robert's calculations for *The Orion Mystery*, showing that the southern shaft of the King's Chamber did indeed mark the declination of Alnitak then, when Thuban in Draco was the Pole Star and marked by the northern one. It had never occurred to Robert to confirm it that way, and he was as moved as I'd been at seeing the ancient skies for himself - especially since his calculations were confirmed, as mine and Alan's had been. So too were the *Keeper* calculations for 10,500 BC, respecting Leo, Orion and the Sphinx, when we moved the setting back to that date. When the Sun rose below Leo at the Vernal Equinox c.10,500 BC, Orion was on the meridian, and the orientation of the Belt stars to the Milky Way resembled that of the Giza pyramids to the Nile 8,000 years later, even if not the closest possible match.

But when I showed the galactic orientation of Stonehenge I and explained what it might mean, Robert's show-stopping remark was, "It's the same at Giza in 10,500 BC, we just didn't know what it meant." If true, it would be true once a day, every day, at that latitude and date. So, just by letting the stars wheel on, we verified it at once. At Giza c.10,500 BC, due to the effect of precession, the same galactic relationship existed as at Stonehenge c.2840. Once a day, the sky took up the same Fig. 21.1 configuration, with the galactic

337

pole in the zenith and the plane of the Milky Way coinciding with the horizon. The relationship was exact in c.10,465 BC, Alan Evans later determined. But at the planetarium we saw it for ourselves: like a galactic 'compass rose' at each location, but the two instances separated by eight millennia of time.

But in that case, what was happening then at Stonehenge? We kept the date c.10,500 BC, and the custodian took the planetarium 'back up' to the latitude of Stonehenge. Having no idea what to look for, once again we just let the stars wheel freely around, through a normal day. And Epsilon Boötis went through the zenith! It was doing that daily c.10,500 BC, when the galactic alignments were in effect at Giza, and the effect of precession on it, over the next 8000 years, was to bring it *back* to the Stonehenge zenith, as an optical marker for the same galactic alignments at Stonehenge itself when Stonehenge I was created. Furthermore, as Epsilon Boötis passed over Stonehenge c.2550 BC, the Galactic Centre was within a degree of its transit of the King's Chamber star-shaft at Giza.

It still isn't Category A evidence, the artefact of indisputably extraterrestrial origin, nor the Category B anomaly that leads us to it. In this context, if A stands for 'artefact' and B stands for 'beacon', then Category C might stand for 'circumstantial'. But I can't believe that all those circumstances are coincidental; these multiple high-tech astronomical alignments are, in my opinion, the best evidence for Past Contact ever put forward. The synergistic combination of our research with Bauval and Hancock's has convinced me that we're on the track of something big. (Graham Hancock disagrees, because he has no belief in extraterrestrial Contact, but there we agree to differ.).

I wrote that up in a new article for *Analog*,[8] adding, 'what about the green children?', I said that only apparent connection was the three peaks of solar activity between 2700 and 1800 BC (Fig. 20.3). After returning the article proofs, back on the Ayrshire coast where I grew up, I was turning over the article in my mind when I realised what I had missed. If the Stonehenge/Pyramids and 12th century events are linked by unusual solar phenomena, then we should look for galactic alignments at the 12th century sites. I rang Alan Evans giving him the latitudes and longitudes of Woolpit, Darlington, etc., and asked him to check for galactic alignments around 1150 AD.

It didn't take him long to reply. The key date was 1146, to be precise, just before the Second Crusade. And the site where the Galactic Pole was overhead, as the Galactic Centre rose and the Galactic Equator coincided with the horizon - just as previously at Giza and Stonehenge - was Jerusalem itself.

Alan's discovery radically changed my perception of Past Contact research. My work with him had been a detective story, like the green children enquiry, but slow and dispassionate: long pages of abstract calculations of star alignments, following many false trails before reaching a fairly straightforward hypothesis. The planetarium sessions confirming it were dramatic, but came late in the day. The one with Bauval and Hancock had been amazing, and finally made it seem good enough to publish, but even then the excitement was intellectual, despite the revelation that the 1920s Boötes map apparently was real after all.

By contrast, the green children enquiry had been into local history, national politics, family trees, religion and the complexity of the mediaeval world. There might be extraterrestrial Contact, or 'just' one more mediaeval conspiracy, as James Bentley insisted, but it was intensely human, centred on the lives of the de Calnas, Richard Barre and Agnes. Now it seemed that the three enquiries were the *same* enquiry: if there was anything to them, there really was Contact in neolithic times, again in the 12th and 13th centuries, and a message from 1928. It required a change of emphasis throughout this book: and I had to start my account almost a century sooner, with the Norman Conquest (Chap. 3), to turn the spotlight on Jerusalem now.

2. Jerusalem and Beyond the Infinite

Obviously, now, the lightning strikes on the Dome of the Rock and the Church of the Holy Sepulchre, in 1146, look more significant. And when I checked out Jerusalem's twelfth-century galactic relationships after that, I found that the effect of precession was, temporarily, to move the galactic and celestial poles along parallel arcs in the sky. The galactic pole continued to pass through the Jerusalem zenith until 1187, the year the city fell to Saladin, and both Richard de Hastings and Richard de Calna may have been there, both times (Chaps.4 & 13).

In my second *Analog* article,[8] I talked about the galactic alignments in terms of spaceship landings, but now we're putting them in the mediaeval context of a matter-transmitter system. Andrew Paterson's two possible explanations are energy transfers, or information transfers. The 'keys' might draw energy from the massive black hole at the Galactic Centre - Alan Evans favoured that possibility - or from some intergalactic field, least affected by absorption in the Milky Way when the galactic pole was overhead. Andrew liked that best, though the nature of the field was unknown.

The other possibility, which appeals to me, is that the key needs to 'know' its orientation with respect to the control centre, which is oriented meaningfully to the magnetic and gravitational fields of the Galaxy. If that's on a rotating space station (Chap.18), presumably its axis is perpendicular to the Galactic Equator, and on a contacted planet, the main relay has to be where the galactic pole passes overhead, periodically moved to correct for Precession of the Equinoxes. Model aircraft autopilots determine their attitude using magnetic inductance coils, similarly to the magnetic sense of homing pigeons; the nearer to the equator, the better it works. Built into the matter-transmitter 'keys', the coils would read position and orientation relative to the master unit in Jerusalem. But, of course, they too would be disturbed by unexpected solar activity.

In Jerusalem near midnight at the spring equinox, March 21st 1146, the galactic pole was in the zenith and the Galactic Centre was rising with an azimuth of 124°. It's no surprise, then, that from the Church of the Holy Sepulchre that azimuth runs through the corner of the Templars' HQ in the Palace of Solomon, now the Aqsa Mosque, then out between the Mount of Olives and the Mount of Offence (Fig.21.3).[12]

The foot of the Southern Cross is on the Galactic Equator, and in all three epochs, when the galactic alignments were activated at the key sites, it was upright on the horizon, with Alpha and Beta Centauri, the Guardians of the Cross, just risen. In Jerusalem, 1146 AD, at midnight on March 21st, they stood virtually due south. Presumably that had no significance in 10,500 and 2900-2500 BC (unless the builders of the Sphinx already had the ankh motif), but during the Crusader occupation of Jerusalem, it should have been a

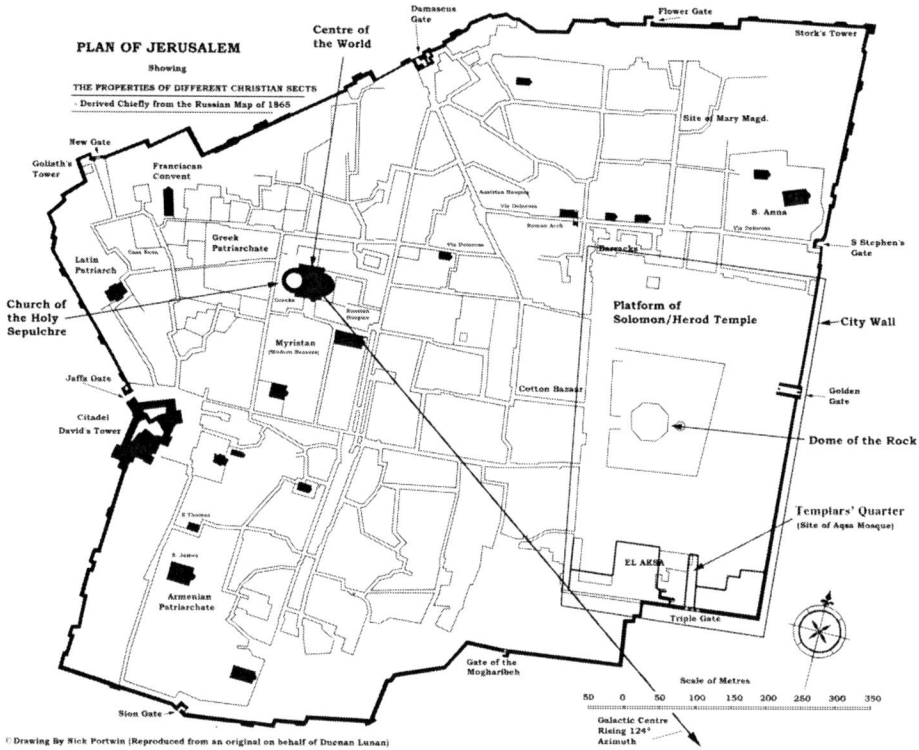

Fig. 21.3. Mediaeval Jerusalem.
Drawing by Nick Portwin, from a 19th century plan.

powerful symbol of divine will.   Yet there isn't a word about it anywhere - as
if the chroniclers went out of their way *not* to point out the city's orientation to
the sky.   The obvious answer would be that the Cross was obscured by hills,
but the southern skyline is clear:[13] Alpha Centauri and the bottom of the Cross
were below the true horizon, but atmospheric refraction would make them
both visible.

The Gospels place Golgotha and the Sepulchre outside the city walls - between the second city wall, constructed by Herod, and the later third one.[14]
Originally the rock tomb of the Sepulchre stood in a former quarry site, much
used for burials.   In 136 AD the Emperor Hadrian built a twenty-foot wall
round the tomb, filled in with rubble and concrete to support a temple of
Venus/Astarte, which was demolished by the Emperor Constantine in 326.[15]

341

Did Sibylla de Calna know that, when she was depicted wearing Ishtar's emblems (Figs. 15.1 & 2)?

A temple around the Sepulchre was completed in 335, according to legend. The monument was similar to the 'Tomb of Absalom' in the Valley of Jehosophat, a masonry pyramid on a cubical hewn rock base, open to the sky and surrounded by a circle of columns. In the 7th century the Edicule ('Little House') was built over it and successively enlarged later. [16] Meanwhile, the Dome of the Rock was erected in 687-91, on the site of the former Temple destroyed by the Romans. [17] The first Aqsa Mosque was built in 709-15, extended in 770, [18] but wrecked by an earthquake in 771. [19]

The Crusaders took over in 1099 under Geoffrey de Bouillon, who styled himself 'Guardian of the Holy Sepulchre'. [20] He died in 1100, and Baldwin I was crowned king of Jerusalem on Christmas Day. Baldwin died in 1118, which might be why the new Templar Order took responsibility for protecting the Sepulchre that year. A new building by Fulk of Anjou was dedicated in 1149, after the Second Crusade; Eleanor of Aquitaine, then married to Louis of France, was present. The dome was now supported by sixteen columns, eight round and eight square, with features copied from Cluny, from the 1090s Church of St. Sernin in Toulouse, [21] the early 12th century one of St. James in Compostela, [22] and the Church of St. Martin in Tours (interesting because of the woman in Chap.10 who allegedly could be in Tours and Derry on the same day, and the 1173 explosion over Derry). The first ground plan (Fig. 21.4) resembled the Compostela church's top end but the later plan was very different.

The new Sepulchre Church was under the Augustinian Order - Ralph of Coggeshall's, before he moved there, and William of Newburgh's, later - who shared property in Jerusalem with the Templars. Pope Celestine II found it necessary to rebuke them both in 1148, because an argument of some kind was threatening the arrangement. [25]

The Augustinian Rule was almost identical to the Benedictines', whose monastery stood southeast of the Anastasis. Further southeast, across the city, the Dome of the Rock was now 'The Temple of the Lord'. South of it stood the Aqsa, now called the palace of Solomon, where the Knights Templar first took up residence, [24] and it was under there that they apparently carved out their mysterious 'silos' (Chap.3) – which brings us to the miracle of the Holy Fire at the Church of the Holy Sepulchre.

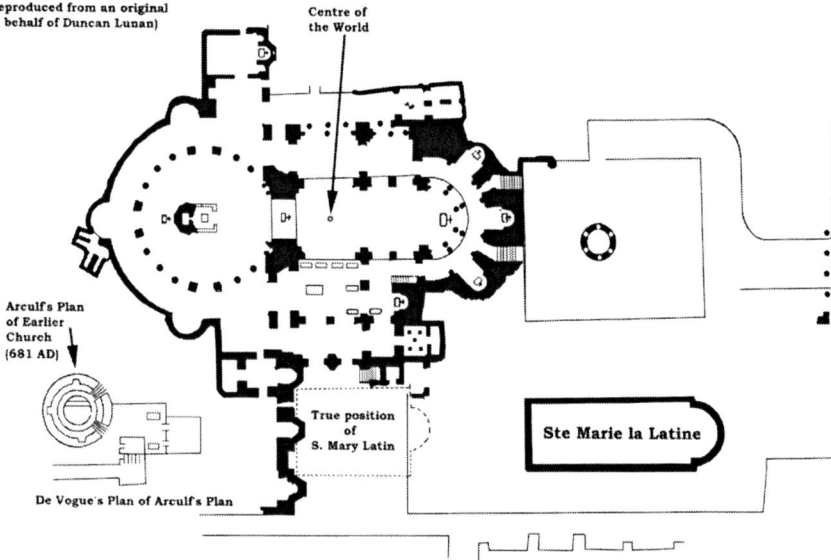

Plan of the Holy Sepulchre Church by Jeffrey, correcting De Vogue Plan of 1860

Fig. 21.4. Early plans of the Holy Sepulchre.
Drawing by Nick Portwin, after Jeffery, 1919.

The modern ceremony is symbolic: before a large crowd the Greek Orthodox patriarch of Jerusalem and an Armenian bishop emerge from the shrine with lighted candles, and the fire passes from hand to hand until everyone's candle is lit.[25] Health and safety factors were never predominant, and in the 19th century commentators described the struggle to get the Fire as "a burlesque".[12] In 1834, between three and five hundred people were asphyxiated, trampled or killed in mass hysteria and fighting. But the original version was more interesting: every year, says William of Malmesbury, on the Sabbath night before Easter Sunday, the lamps in the church lit by themselves, and had done since the 9th century - or 947 AD at least[26] The fire appeared first within the tomb, then the lamps in the rest of the Temple lit spontaneously even with no oil in them. To 'prove' it was miraculous, beforehand the wicks were replaced with copper wire. In 1009 a Syrian writer described its flame as of 're-

343

markable whiteness and brilliance', staged by coating the wire supporting the lamps in oil and kindling the flames on the roof.[27]   The copper wire sounds like a catalyst, because there were no green flames, though in 1106 Abbot Daniel said they were red, the colour of cinnamon.   When the miracle failed in 1101 the patriarch cleared the building, because the Lord couldn't stand any-one contaminated with sin, but it sounds more like an evacuation - especially because after a night of lamentation, the first lamp ignited, the patriarch rushed in with a taper, and the other lamps then lit in sequence.[26]

It all made me wonder if the miracle was gas-fired.   A silo - like those the Templars allegedly excavated - is the optimum shape for a methane generator, digesting either plant or animal waste, depending on the bacteria used.   The major construction phase above ground at the Aqsa was in 1172, interestingly enough, just before the arrival of the children in England.   The ground below the Temple Mount "is perfectly honeycombed with a network of rock-hewn cisterns", interconnected by overflow drains leading finally to the brook of Khedron.[14]   Even in the 19th century excavating and exploring within the wall was a sensitive issue, and consequently "the vast substructures of the Aqsa have never been very fully explored" in modern times.[21]   There were numerous cisterns under the Holy Sepulchre, either for rainwater or sources of quarried stone, and still more under the Hospital of St. John nearby. There could have been connections to the Templar silos as well: the 500-yard tunnel from near the Temple Mount, which caused riots in 1996 when the Israeli authorities opened a new tourist entrance to it on the Via Dolorosa, follows the line of an old water-course.[28]

Was the underground complex of the Aqsa the network of caves through which the children wandered, in Ralph's account - were they transported first to Jerusalem, and then to Woolpit?   According to one account, the Stables of Solomon below the Aqsa Mosque are large enough, for two thousand horses or 1500 camels!   Another says they could hold 10,000 horses, with their grooms;[29] not all under the Temple platform, if so, because those there today would hold 500 horses and grooms at most.   The modern ones are at least partly a reconstruction, incorporating stones from the old city wall,[14] but there are holes in the rock "through every 'coign of vantage'" for tethering animals.[30] However many knights there were, there seem to have been plenty of horses, perhaps to provide dung and used straw for a methane generator, an energy source on the Rock, where water-power wasn't available and a windmill would be inappropriate?   After 65 years of UFOs, it's particularly appealing to imagine the Templars using windpower, waterpower and methane digesters running on horse-dung, to charge up devices which let them walk between worlds - to go anywhere in the Galaxy that similar devices existed, without using spaceships at all - their sergeants ordering the servants to clean out the stables early because the Grand Master had to be on a planet of Tau Ceti by Vespers.

3. The Centre of the World

Outside the original Church of the Holy Sepulchre, seen by Bishop Arculf (Fig. 21.4 inset), stood the rock on which the body of Jesus supposedly was laid out and washed (the true Stone of Unction was elsewhere).   To Arculf and to Abbot Daniel of Russia, who described the Holy Fire in 1125, the rock was known as 'the Compass'.   Bernard the Wise, a century after Arculf, described four churches surrounding it and linked to it by chains.   By Abbot Daniel's time it was enclosed in a small domed building, adorned with mosaic, and when the Compass was enclosed in the Chorus Dominorum, as the church was extended to the east, the dome erected over it was the largest of its kind in Palestine (Fig. 21.5).   A vase-shaped altar was set up on it, described in the Cartulary of the Holy Sepulchre in 1169.   It was later replaced by a small open altar, with a cross inscribed in a circle on its floor, still later by a stone pillar.

In those phases, it was called "The Centre of the World".   Around 1150 John of Warzburg described it as a structure of marble slabs on an open ironwork lattice.[31]   When the Choir was extended to enclose it, and the Hospitallers' church moved out of the way by the formidable Dame Agnes, the new church built on the north had a porch, facing the Choir, whose outer arch was carved with the signs of the Zodiac![30]   The signs weren't those we know, but represented the months of the farming year: February as a pruner, July as a reaper, August as a thresher, September as a grape-gatherer -   like the window installed later at Bury St. Edmunds under Abbot Samson (Chaps.10 & 15). The Sun and Moon were in the middle of the arch, and a corniche above had figures of lions and other animals.[12]

Jerusalem was supposedly the centre of the world from the 4th century, at least, as the burial place of Adam. Golgotha, 'the place of the skull', was where Adam's head was believed to be interred. (Moslems hold that Adam's tomb and therefore the Centre are at the Mosque of El-Khayf near Mecca.) So to Abbot Daniel the Compass was also 'the Navel of the World', and Pope Urban II used both in his 1095 call for the First Crusade[10] (Chap.3). In *Foucault's Pendulum* Umberto Eco has the Templars looking for the Navel of the World as the source of 'telluric energy', whatever that might be, but as guardians of the Holy Sepulchre they were custodians of the Compass all along and any energy tapped there presumably was celestial.

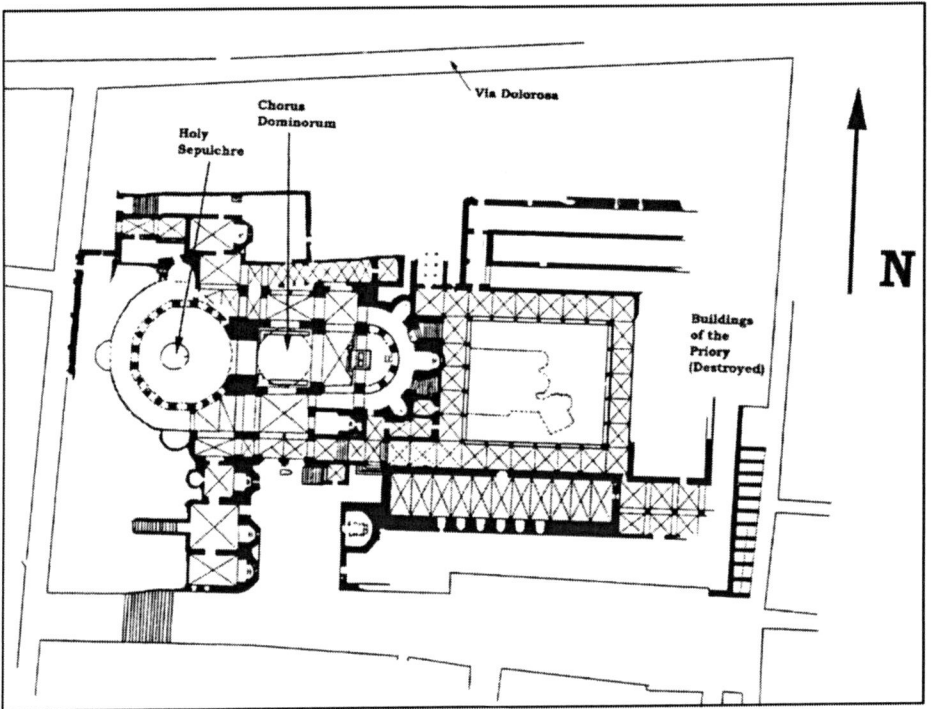

Fig. 21.5. Reconstruction of the Church of the Holy Sepulchre and Augustinian Convent as built in 1150.
Plan from George Jeffery, "A Brief Description of the Holy Sepulchre", 1919, processed by Nick Portwin.

Older Jewish traditions place Adam's tomb and the Centre of the World at the slab under the Dome of the Rock, sacred as the resting-place of the Ark of the Covenant, and to Moslems as the spot from which Mohammed ascended to Heaven on his 'Night Journey'. In some traditions it's said to have fallen from Heaven itself, although it's actually bedrock. Others say a network of tunnels there was carved out by Solomon to conceal the Ark, because he saw prophetically that the city would fall. The Dome, too, was called the navel of the world, and outside it, when back in Moslem hands, there was a sundial known as a compass. The story that Adam's tomb was at Golgotha, instead, appears to date from 221 AD; but still older tradition places Adam's tomb at Hebron, 20 miles southwest of Jerusalem.[19]

Although the unknown Richard (possibly de Calna) described the stripping of the Sepulchre church of its treasures after the fall of Jerusalem in 1187,[32] other accounts say Saladin left it untouched. (The task of keeping the gates of the church has been handed down through the centuries within the same family appointed by Saladin.)[33] Gibbon, quoting other Christian and Arabic sources, says that the patriarch of Jerusalem had gathered up the treasures into four ivory chests, which were seized by Saladin, deposited with the prince of Antioch and later redeemed by Richard I. Still another version is that the patriarch fled to the coast with the treasures after buying himself out, basely refusing to save anyone else.[34]

Saladin allowed the Hospitallers to remain in the city, to care for pilgrims and the sick.[20] The Templars might have hoped to use the matter-transmitter in a surprise attack, perhaps when Richard I's crusaders were at the walls; Richard was in effect an honorary Templar, and he relied on them for protection from his German and Italian 'allies'.[35] But if that was the plan, it never came to fruition: though the Sun was still disturbed when Richard was in the Holy Land, he had to sign a truce with Saladin in 1192 without ever gaining sight of the city, though pilgrim access to Jerusalem was restored. The Templars' modifications to the Aqsa were ripped out, and when Frederick II negotiated the return of the city to the Christians for ten years, 1229-39, the Temple area, including the Dome of the Rock and the Aqsa Mosque, remained in Moslem hands. Some parts of the Aqsa were reused when it was rebuilt in 1303,[30] while the Sepulchre was entrusted to Greek and Eastern Christians.[19]

Frederick II went to Jerusalem with Philip d'Aubigni, a signatory of the Magna Carta and Henry III's tutor, who died there in 1236. The same year, Henry III had the walls of Westminster Palace and Winchester Great Hall painted with a new type of map, the *mappa mundi*, depicting Jerusalem as the centre of the world. They were drawn on calfskin, with ink from oak galls, plus gold leaf, lapis lazuli and malachite for blue and green, and vegetable 'dragon's blood' for red. The Psalter Map, accompanying a book of psalms about 1250, is one of the earliest and may be a miniature copy of the Westminster map.[36] It's interesting that this new form of map coincides with the 1236 events at Roche Abbey and in Ireland, now that the Sun had calmed down.

The Templars weren't allowed personal jewellery, so any 'keys' they had must pass as something they were allowed. The red crosses on their cloaks might conceal them, if really small, maybe activated by touch, like the communicator badges in *Star Trek, Next Generation*. But I doubt that small devices could handle the energies we've been considering in previous chapters, discharges comparable to lightning bolts, or to the auroral fluxes which nowadays burn out the transformers of power stations - at least without injuring the wearers. Such 'keys' could be charged up with a glass rod and a piece of silk, and a matter-transmitter which could be accidentally activated by nylon underwear (even if there wasn't any at the time) is too sensitive to be practicable. Templar keys might instead be in the handles of swords, or daggers, and the emblems on de Calna's funeral tile may tell us that quite explicitly (Fig. 13.1). A storage device in the handle of a sword has interesting possibilities, given the powers which mythology and chivalric legends attach to swords - though Andy Paterson looked into it and concluded if the electric charge on a sword was more dangerous than the blade itself, the capacitor must be very powerful to fit inside the handle.

But if the 'key' simply 'summons a worm' (Chap.20), what determines the emergence point is a locator device at the other end - be it Woolpit, Peak Cavern, or the colony world. For each of those devices there has to be a 'keyhole' here, locked to it. I've no evidence for the next four paragraphs, but this is how I'd do it in science-fiction:

The controllers of the keys would be ellipsoidal, for reasons below, and the ellipses of different sizes because they would be slices out of an ellipsoidal solid, with a three-dimensional printed circuit embedded in it, perhaps cast in zero-gravity. I visualise its non-conducting substrate as obsidian (volcanic glass), but the m-t ellipsoid could as easily be clear lucite, like the Nebula Award of the Science Fiction Writers of America. Like the Nebula Award, it could have an image of a spiral galaxy embedded in it; only this would be an accurate map of our Galaxy, the Milky Way. It would be on the central plane of the ellipsoid, the slice which remains in mission control, while all the lesser slices 'remember' their orientation to it.

In 1808, 'The Centre of the World' was the only altar in the Church of the Holy Sepulchre to be reconstituted after a disastrous fire there. The restoration was otherwise heavily criticised for removing virtually all relics of Crusader times.[30] Detailed measurements of the restored monument were taken in 1888: a vase, 1 foot 9¼ inches high, of reddish Jerusalem stone, topped by a ball of whiter stone with stripes of black stone embedded in it to mark the cardinal points[37] - like the orb held by Abbot Samson on his seal for the charter of St. Saviour's Hospital (Fig. 6.3), with the duck's head and the fleur-de-lis, perhaps linking him to Sibylla de Calna and Agnes (Chap. 14). Did the cross surmounting it represent the Southern Cross, by any chance?

However, in the vase the ball representing the world wasn't a sphere. If it was a planet, it was markedly flattened at the poles, like Jupiter (Fig. 21.6). It can't be a model of the colony planet, because that rotates so slowly it presumably has no polar flattening. But that ball in Jerusalem, the 'centre of the world' in plain view, would be a copy of the device which was cut into elliptical slices, perpendicular to the Galactic Equator, as controllers for the 'keys'. If they were affixed to *mappae mundi*, users could see at a glance which was tuned to which destination. Pressing the pommel of your dagger (with the charged key hidden within) to the ellipse on the destination desired, would take you where you wanted to go. Or the ovals could be carried in compartments within signet-rings or personal seals like Abbot Samson's (Chap.24) and Sibylla de Calna's - making the theft of Geoffrey Ridell's ring from his tomb (Chap.14) particularly interesting.

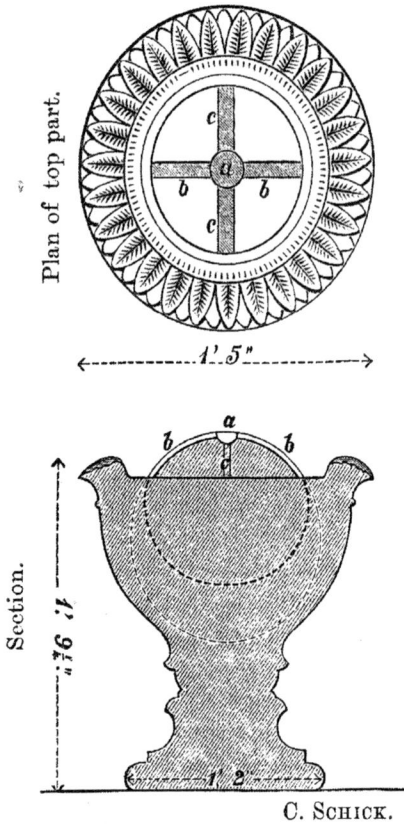

Plan of top part.

1'.5"

Section.

1'.9¾"

1'.2"

C. Schick.

a. Seems to be the pole.
b b. The Equator.
c c. The Meridian.

Fig. 21.6. 'The Middle of the World, in the Holy Sepulchre'.[37]

For transfers within Britain, a map like Matthew Paris's would serve - is it coincidence that he produced it about this time? A map of Suffolk produced between 1173 and 1200 was the first known British map to show a road, from Grimsby to the strategic new castle at Orford. Only Bury St. Edmunds and Thetford are shown in the centre of the county.[38] For interstellar transfers perhaps there would be ellipses fixed to a star map: we don't have any mediaeval ones, but there's no reason to think they didn't exist. But presumably each slice passes through the Galactic Centre and Pole as seen from here, the local prime galactic meridian. From mission control and other destination star

350

systems, bearings to the Galactic Centre would be different. The galactic meridians of those aren't parallel but radiating from the Centre; so if one ellipsoid had been sliced to allow terrestrial transfers to prearranged points like Woolpit or Cressing Temple, then for interstellar transfers there had to be another one, still intact, from which the keys elsewhere on Earth took their bearings. That ties in with Andy Paterson's comments in Chap.20 on how the matter-transmitters are affected by the gravitational field of the Galaxy. And the device would be at Jerusalem in 1146 and for some years afterward. I wonder where it might be now? The Galactic Pole is now overhead on latitude 27° North, which passes south of Kennedy Space Centre and through the islands of Japan, raising interesting thoughts about Carl Sagan's *Contact*; but it isn't over the Cape and it's at the wrong end of Japan to make the book and film come true. The two major construction projects on that latitude, now, are Libya's Great Man-Made River and China's Three Gorges Dam.

Jerusalem was seized in 1239 by David of Kerak, after which all Christian Palestine was put under the Templars and Hospitallers. Retrieved in 1243, the city was finally lost in 1244, when monks and priests were massacred in the Holy Sepulchre buildings.[30] The dates may be coincidental, but it's curious that the city should fall the year after we last hear of Agnes, and fall again in the year when we last hear of Sibylla. In October 1244 the Templars in the Holy Land were wiped out.[26] The Franciscans, put in charge of the Sepulchre under Frederick II, were allowed to remain after 1244, after which the Holy Fire ceremony was repudiated by the Pope,[16] and they restored the Church in 1535 or 1555,[19] after which in 1611 there was only a small pit at the Compass.[37]

4. London and Paris

"Traditions teach us that the first thing the Templars did, whenever they began a new establishment, was to put into their church an altar or a chapel which reminded them of the Tomb of Christ at Jerusalem..."[39] The New Temple in London was copied from the one in Paris, which in turn was copied from the Church of the Holy Sepulchre. The chapels were called 'caveaux', representing the Sepulchre itself. But many circular churches attributed to the Templars were much older, e.g. the round churches of Northampton and

**Eglise
Du
Temple
De paris
restituee par
Henri
de Curzon
1886**

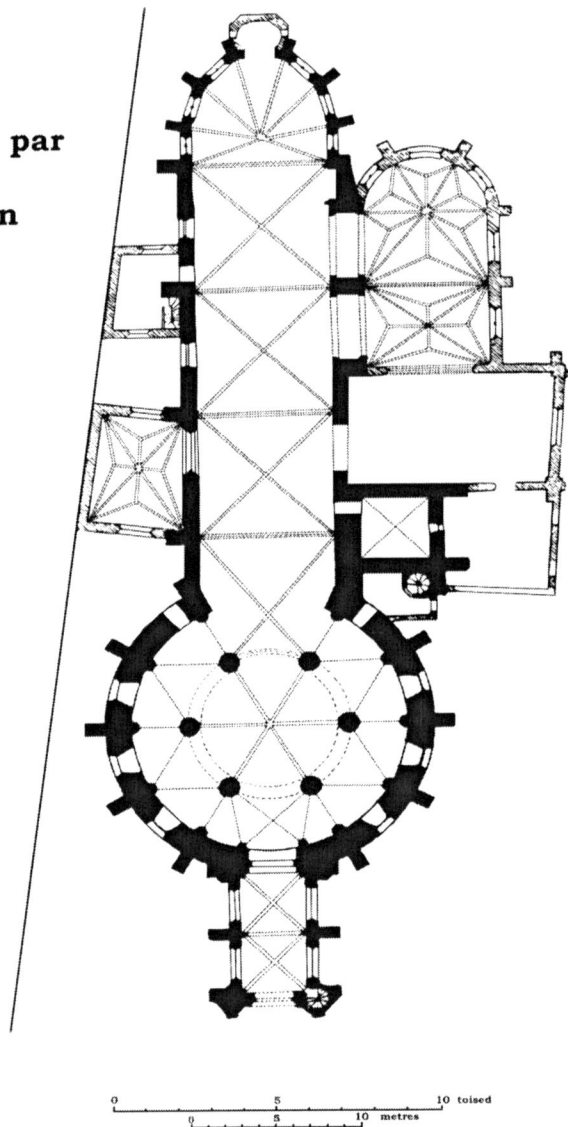

0   5   10 toised
0   5   10   metres

Figs. 21.7 & 21.8. Layout of The Church of the Paris Temple, 1860 (from Henri de Curzon, "La Maison du Temple de Paris", 1889)[39], and the Temple Church, London (from Robert Billings, "Illustrations and Account of the Temple Church", 1838)[41], processed by Nick Portwin.

352

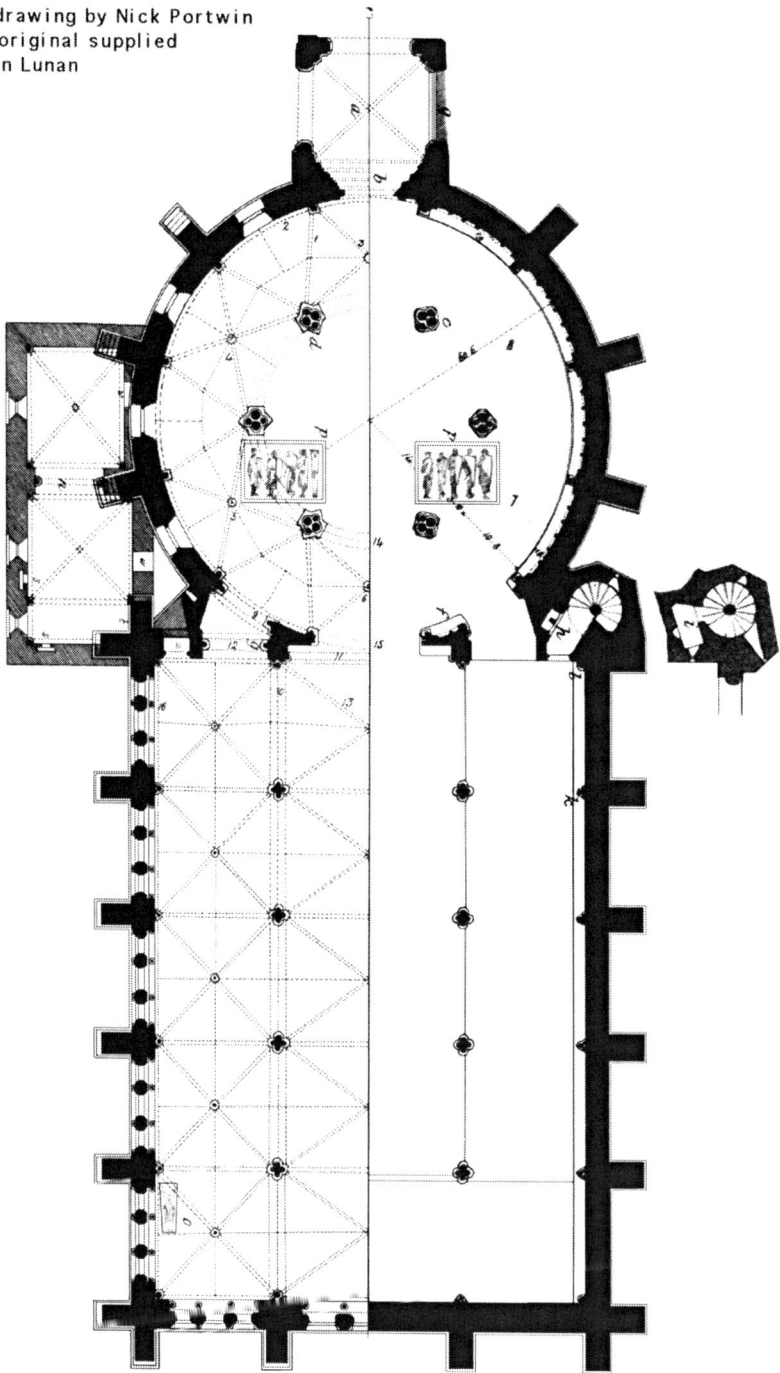

Cambridge, or much younger, e.g. the 'Chapel des Templiers' at Eunote on the pilgrim road to Compostela, which dates from the sixteenth century.[40]

In Florence, an exact copy of the Sepulchre was built into the San Pancrazio church in the 15th century, and the Medicean Grand Dukes formed a plan to move the real Sepulchre to Florence in the 16th. A replica of the Holy Fire ceremony was performed there until the 20th century, when it was replaced by a firework display.[30]

Curiously, though, nothing corresponds to 'the Centre of the World' in the plan of the Paris Temple church (Fig. 21.7), nor the Temple Church in London (Fig. 21.8). It features in copies of the Church of the Holy Sepulchre elsewhere in Europe, such as the 'New Jerusalem' Church of San Stefano in Bologna, where it's represented by an alms-disc on a vase of stone, attributed in a carving to a 'Liuprante' for whom there are two candidates, in the eighth and tenth centuries.[30] But in London and in Paris at corresponding points in the Choirs there's only empty space - though a crucial space in the geometry of the London building, as analysed in one 19th century essay[41] (Fig. 21.9). In fact the present enlarged Choir (Fig. 21.11) wasn't built on to the London Temple until 1240,[35] nor the Paris one till the end of the 13th century,[16] to match the extended Choir of the Holy Sepulchre. A reconstruction of it before the extension shows that the Compass offset from the geometrical focus of the building (Fig. 21. 10).[43] To me that suggests that even if the 'Centre of the World' provided the orientation for 'beaming out' of Jerusalem, plenty of room was needed for safety at the point of arrival.

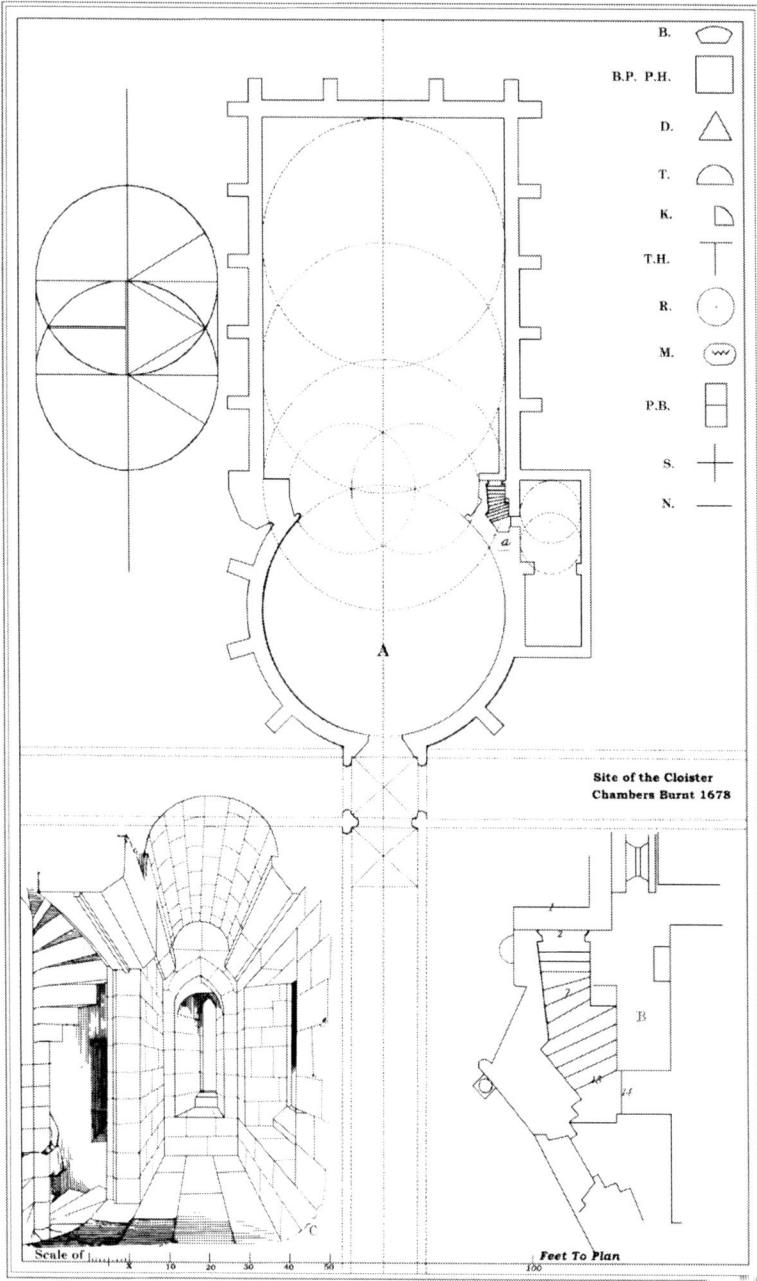

B.
B.P. P.H.
D.
T.
K.
T.H.
R.
M.
P.B.
S.
N.

Site of the Cloister
Chambers Burnt 1678

A

a

B

C

Scale of
X   10   20   30   40   50

Feet To Plan
100

Temple Church, London

Fig. 21.9.

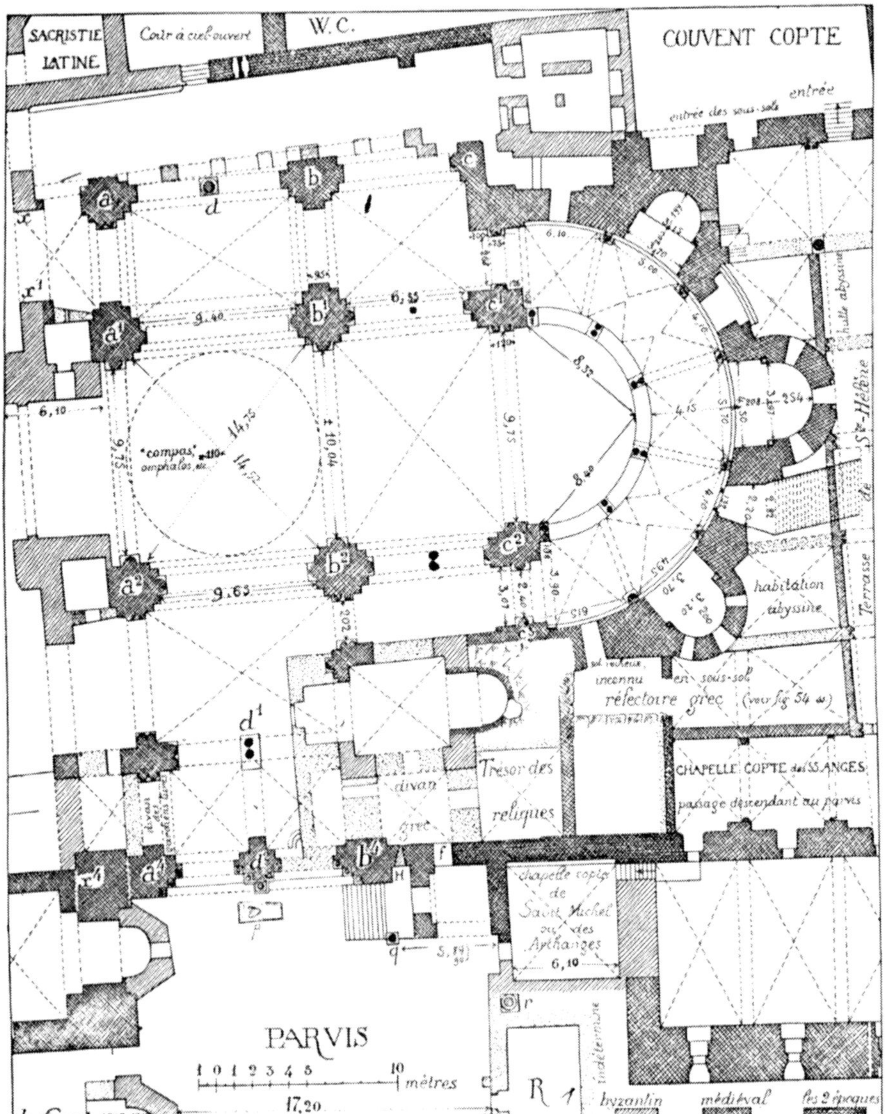

Figs. 21.9 & 21.10. Internal geometry of the Temple Church (from Robert Billings, above); Paris Church of the Holy Sepulchre before extending the Choir (H. Vincent, 1892-1102)[39], processed by Nick Portwin.

Fig. 21.11(a) and (b). The Temple Church, London, from Robert Billings, "Illustrations and Account of the Temple Church", 1838; photo by Duncan Lunan, 2000.

5. "I beseech it, that you beware in this transfer."

John Braithwaite suggested the reason might be the gravitational pull of the Moon. The colony planet couldn't have one of any size: a large moon orbiting a world with a trapped rotation would either pull the planet's rotation out of sun-lock, or be perturbed in its orbit until it was expelled or collided with the planet.

Objects are lighter when the Moon's overhead than when it's on the horizon. Could the Moon be a 'fine tuner', so the exact gravitational value required would only occur at certain times of the month - certain phases of the Moon? The Moon's pull at the Earth's surface is only 1:5000 of Earth's own. The ratio between the lunar and solar pulls is 2.17:1, on average, so the Sun's is only 1:11,000 of the Earth's. Even in concert, at the spring tides, their combined pull is only 1:3500 of Earth's, and in opposition at the neap tides the ratio is 1:9200. The colony planet isn't likely to be so perfect a twin of the Earth that so small a difference would be significant. But, Andy Paterson replied, what matters is the total energy at the transmission and reception points. While the colony world's orbit around its star is virtually circular, Earth's slightly elliptical orbit varies the solar factor in the total energy by one part in 30, relative to the mean value, between perihelion (the nearest point to the Sun) on January 3rd and aphelion on 3rd July. That doesn't affect the system, because combined potential and kinetic energy (relative to the Sun and the Galaxy) remains constant.

Nevertheless, as the Earth and Moon orbit around the barycentre (their common centre of mass), the Moon does cause a cyclic change in the position which an observer on the Earth's surface would otherwise occupy with respect to the Sun. The exact energy value for the matter-transmitter might be attained when the Moon and Sun were pulling together, at New Moon, or in opposition at Full Moon; or twice a month, at First and Third Quarter, when the lunar effect would be neutral. It would provide a clock for return to central control at prearranged times, if the energy level at that end varied on a fixed schedule; was that why Stephan de Tournai urged Richard Barre to keep track of the true motions of the Moon? Otherwise for each planet, separate wormhole pairs would be needed to allow two-way traffic at all times.

Andrew calculated that the position, at which an incoming object materialised, would vary by about one metre up or down, depending on the phase of the Moon at the time. That could explain why reception sites for incoming interstellar transfers might be water-filled pits or moats: your arrival might be an undignified splashdown, but it would be better than materialising in solid ground, or a metre above it for a bone-breaking fall. The possible cases in caves or buildings all seem to be from one place to another on Earth, so the lunar factor wouldn't apply. Animals wouldn't like a sudden drop into water, which suggests that the events of 1170 and 1236 were from place to place on Earth, but livestock transfers into the fields of the colony would need careful timing. Is that why, in both William of Newburgh and Ralph of Coggeshall's versions of the story, the children emphasised that their transfer to Earth happened because their father's beasts were being followed, herded or added to *on a certain day*? It again suggests that Agnes partly understood what had happened to her.

At that point Jane Greatorex raised a deceptively simple question. If the pit at Woolpit or Roche Abbey had fulfilled its secondary function, what if you beamed into it and there was a wolf waiting for you? The way to avoid it is to have a safety factor: before you transport yourself, you shift a corresponding volume - all being well, simply of air - in the opposite direction. If a wolf or something equally unwanted comes through, you stun it, kill it and/or send it back; anyway, now you know the pit at the other end is safe. So, presumably, at Woolpit a pig or a sheep or a cow was tethered in the pit, waiting to be transferred: and because the children were in the right place at the wrong time, that was how they came to be transferred here.

In Earth transfers, the Moon on the horizon, rising or setting, might similarly move the emergence point by a metre horizontally, and that might explain why there was no monument corresponding to the Compass in the London or Paris churches. If you were beside the one in Jerusalem, about to make an instantaneous transfer to either European capital, it would be reassuring to know that your emergence point wouldn't coincide with a similarly carved piece of rock.

It's not clear how much the matter-transmitters could move at a time - nine or more knights at Coggeshall, perhaps, but without horses, and unknown numbers in Yorkshire and Ireland, but still not whole armies at a time. (The

Templars might have had fewer defeats in the Holy Land, otherwise.) Large, enclosed volumes like the Peak Cavern might set the upper size limit for transfers at the planetary surface, perhaps with a much larger terminal somewhere nearby in space - see Chap.24.

It's a great pity that neither William nor Ralph tell us how the children reacted to the Moon.   In Glyn Maxwell's *Wolfpit* they respond only with childish delight that it turns their skin silver.   In our Solar System, the combination of Earth and Moon is in many ways unique, and can be better described as a double planet, rather than a planet and satellite combination.[44]   It's now widely believed that the Moon formed from the crustal material left over when a proto-planet the size of Mars collided with the proto-Earth.[45]   It's hard to assess how likely such events would be elsewhere in the Galaxy, or the effect on the evolution of life.   Would life have moved from the sea to the land, for example, but for the tides?   The Sun does raise tides too, but much lesser ones, as above.   For a while it was thought that there could be no life without such a Moon, but now it seems that's putting it too strongly.[46]

Although the colony planet would have no large moon, it might have a ring - its reflected light would help conversion of the atmosphere (Chap.19) - but if the children had mentioned anything so extraordinary, surely William and Ralph wouldn't leave *that* out.   Any intact moon the planet had would be much smaller and less spectacular than ours, and not likely to resemble a human face;   indeed, a project to carve a face on a moon elsewhere is the theme of a powerful novel by Jack Vance.[47]   So if I'm right, the children should have reacted to the Moon in a big way - even if they recognised it only from descriptions by their elders.   If they weren't surprised at all, it would be proof that they came from somewhere else on Earth.

At any rate, we now have a speculative explanation of where the children came from and how they got here.   If we look in more detail at possible conditions there, it may help us to guess what the overall situation might have been.

Chapter Twenty-two - BIOSPHERES WITHOUT WALLS

"All right!   Then a story you will have!   But let me warn you - what you are going to see will be VAST!   No trifling with the Universe here..."

~ 'Jeff Hawke' by Sydney Jordan, *Daily Express*, 1966

1. "Always Take the Weather With You"

Now we have an idea how the children's world could be created, and how it could be linked to Earth, we can look in more detail at what that world might be like.   In the process, perhaps we can begin to guess at what the purpose of creating it might be.

If the river bed was formed by a second series of cometary impacts, (Chap.19), the atmosphere over it would be carbon dioxide and water vapour, with some methane and ammonia.   Solar radiation would break down the ammonia, releasing nitrogen and hydrogen, as it has done on Saturn's giant moon, Titan; and the hydrogen would escape into space, as it has over Titan.   To generate breathable atmosphere would need the action of life, as on Earth, though here it took billions of years.   Simple forms of life, algae and lichen, would absorb carbon dioxide and release oxygen, reacting with the methane to release more water vapour and carbon dioxide.   Proportions would depend on the composition of the impacting ice, but for balance with breathable oxygen (Chap.19), extra nitrogen might have to be imported - perhaps in bulk, by matter-transmission, from a lifeless world with a nitrogen atmosphere, like Titan or Mars, or as ammonia from a giant planet like Jupiter.

It's hard to say how long it would take to form a breathable atmosphere, because almost all terraforming studies concern Venus and Mars, where conditions are very different from 'our' world's.   On Mars, if a carbon dioxide atmosphere with Earth-surface pressure could be generated, and a quarter of the surface coated with mats of blue-green algae, with Mars's low temperatures and seasonal variations it would take 7500 years to make the air breathable.[1]   One quarter of the Mars surface is equivalent to one-sixteenth of Earth's, and since the river valley's area is one-eightieth of Earth's, one-fifth of the Martian algae would fully cover the colony valley, cutting the conversion time to 1,875 years.

But those algae would be biologically active for only a quarter of the Martian year. On the colony planet sunlight would be continuous, and, on average, stronger: perhaps too strong in the sunlit half of the valley, and in the twilight half perhaps too low, but orbiting mirrors or a temporary ring could adjust that. With continuous generation, a breathable atmosphere might be produced in 500 years at most. But it would take very fine tuning to give it the same composition and surface pressure as Earth's, if a precise match was wanted. The layout of the valley could make it unnecessary, because if pressure is higher than Earth's (or any other world's) at the valley floor, a match can be found higher up the wall.

Asked whether the winds from the Peak Cavern might indicate a higher air-pressure on the colony world, Andrew Paterson calculated that with density approximately the same as ours, and a wormhole five metres across, a differential of 50 millibars (too small to cause the bends) would generate a wind of 87 metres per second, 195 miles per hour. The wind reported at Peak Cavern could be explained by the 450 m. (approx. 1500 feet) difference in altitude between it and Woolpit, supporting the idea that in the Peveril swineherd's 'digression' he went to Woolpit, triggering Henry II's annexation of the village. The recurring winds could have been generated simply by moving air, to build up fear and keep people out. But in expanding they would drop in temperature, perhaps enough to cause icing - the *hymalia*, 'winter things', which the swineherd saw on the way back.

As the river runs from pole to pole, along the terminator, one might think the twilight zone would stretch from it to the nightside ringwalls, in a band 50 miles wide. But the walls need to be as high as possible, to make the air trap effective, and Sydney Jordan gave us, literally, a new picture (Fig. 22.1). Sunlight would strike the inner face of the ringwall and be reflected, placing the twilight zone in the shadow of the sunward wall. Similarly in craters on our Moon, at low Sun angles the shadow of the central peak points towards the Sun.

Where the sunlit mountains become visible from the floor depends on their height above it, but even if the crater rims weren't raised above the mean planetary surface, if they stood twenty miles above the valley floor they should be visible all the way to the far walls. The brightly lit country, just across the river, would receive the full force of the reflected light. But there's scope here for more fine tuning: if the valley runs from pole to pole on only one side of the planet, its meridian doesn't have to be precisely on the terminator. Its longitude could be chosen to allow progressively more light and heat to enter the bowls as they approach the equator, or less light and heat, as the precise situation required; in which case the 'chaotic terrain' opposite would either be in permanent darkness, or permanent intense sunlight. Nevertheless, since it would include a random pattern of deep chasms, perhaps life would spread over the poles to colonise it.

Fig. 22.1. Colony valley from low orbit.
Drawing by Sydney Jordan.

The children didn't say colours were different here, not even their own, which suggests a light level not far below ours. Conditions in the twilight zone could be like Scotland after sunset, in June and July. We don't lose colours in the landscape until around 10 p.m. (GMT), when the sky overhead is still deep blue and only the first stars are showing. In the colony the sky would always

363

be that shade and the brighter stars would always be visible, drifting east to west, not with passing hours, but from month to month.

Although green and red are complementary colours, the children's account doesn't support the idea that their planet orbits a red star. If the light reflecting into the valley was predominantly red, green plants and people would appear black. The upper ringwalls are too high for sunlight to be reddened passing through the atmosphere, so if the children recognised colours here, the colour of their star can't be too different from our own's.

Above the sunward horizon, there could be high-altitude noctilucent clouds - but no aurorae, as we've seen. The mountains might be snow-capped even at the equator, like Mt. Kilimanjaro in Africa, their glaciers feeding tributary rivers or calving into the main one up near the poles, but they couldn't be scaled without spacesuits if the valley's 20 miles deep. Even the Bifrost-like bridge in Sydney Jordan's illustration could be beyond reach of 'the people that were held in that land', higher above them than the summit of Everest is to us - a useful viewpoint, perhaps, for the creators of the experiment to watch from out of reach. With a height of five miles and a span of a hundred the bridge might *look* impossible, and Sydney introduced it only to give perspective. But when he proposed to remove it, the ASTRA discussion group had already worked out a way to build it and thought of more ways to use it - see below.

If incoming solar illumination is higher than on Earth, even its reflection might create a desert on that side of the valley - until life adapted to conditions over there, like the crossing of the Jordan in Biblical art, though at the actual point the Jordan is just ten metres wide.[2] But there could be different forms of life over there - perhaps the builders themselves, isolated from the colony by the river and the desert. With every vertical surface in strong sunlight, and very low temperatures on the outer walls, there would be plenty of power for an industrialised settlement - wind, solar, hydro-electric, and thermoelectric power exploiting the temperature gradient.

Gordon Ross compared it to Germany's Mosel Valley, on a giant scale. 500 feet deep and 1-2 miles wide, that has vineyards on its steep northern slopes, which are very hot in summer. Southern slopes are forested; winds are channelled along the valley. Historically transport was by river, overlooked by castles placed strategically every few miles. On the colony world necks between bowls would be similarly important, especially if separating sections of different height, with portage or locks at the falls.

If the river bed was flat, Coriolis forces in the river would be weak, because of the planet's slow rotation, but water would drift towards the poles and eventually be locked up there as ice. To prevent that the cometary impacts would be graded by latitude, to create a gravity flow towards the equator, for evaporation to generate clouds. Each bowl would have its own air-circulation, forming ventricular clouds in the centres, tending towards the shadowed wall (Fig. 22.2): Gordon compared it to "a cyclone stood on end", travelling down the shadowed wall, across the floor, back up and across (Fig. 22.3). Unlike on most planets, the atmosphere circulates from day to twilight and back, never in true darkness, while features on the surface are fixed in one or the other. But Coriolis forces would move the higher clouds north and south in the valley, perpetuating the cycle as they rained on the mountains near the poles.

Aircraft could glide on the uplift at the sunlit wall. With pressurised cockpits or suits, very high-lift ones like the U-2 spy plane (now used by NASA for upper atmosphere research), could even soar out of the valley and ride along it on the standing wave and spill over at the top. But crossing from bowl to bowl would be perilous because of reduced lift, and they'd risk being carried into the nightside. If the creators of the valley refused to share their technology with humans (and any other occupants), then on the crater slopes aircraft might rapidly be developed, providing a way for rebels to escape the shadowed sides of the impact basins. But aircraft launched into the downdraughts on the shadowed side of the valley would need a lot of power to stay aloft till they reached the sunlit side of the river. The air circulation would reduce loss of volatiles to the dark side of the planet; but the upended cyclones pose another danger. Even on Earth, mountains can interact with the high-altitude, high-speed winds of the jetstream to generate invisible 'horizontal tornadoes',[3] one form of the clear-air turbulence which still occasionally destroys aircraft, despite radar warnings.[4]

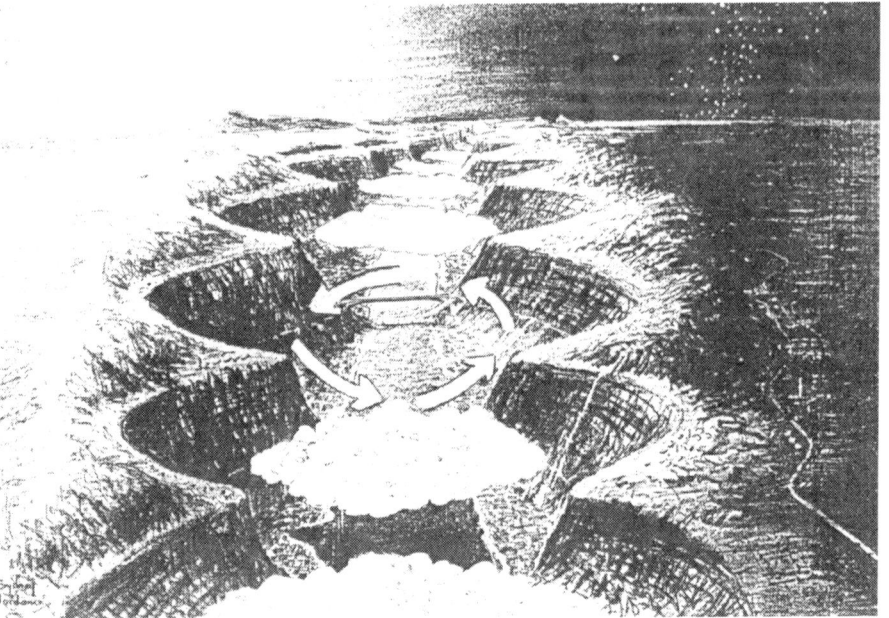

Figs. 22.2 & 22.3. Colony valley with low-level clouds - drawing by Sydney Jordan, and circulation in colony valley bowls - sketch by Gordon Ross and Duncan Lunan on Sydney Jordan background.

In lower latitudes on the colony world, with steady input of sunlight on one side, winds could reach hundreds of miles per hour. Solar energy absorbed by airborne dust drives the great storms on Mars, and in combination, the upended cyclones and the north-south flow of the valley could generate vicious erosion. From above it would look like a horizontal tornado, sandstorm or drill bit, boring away from the equator to straighten and widen the valley. Windpower generators, even big ones, would scarcely diminish its effect. Conditions in each bay would have to be stabilised for settlement; Sydney's artwork assumes that happens early, or settlements are at high latitudes. But it might not be possible to extend the valley into the equatorial zone at all.

Frank Herbert's 'Dune' novels have their Sandworms,[5] but this is a worm made of sand, or a Windworm, if you prefer. Imagine seeing it spinning over the river at the south end of your bowl, knowing that if it broke through the gap, or widened it sufficiently, it would be amongst you. What would it sound like? On Earth, relatively minor sandstorms are described as howling or screaming, driving people mad. Think how it would be feared if even occasionally a wormlet slid past the barrier, and what a weapon it would be for political and military control. ("Close your doors - Big Sandy's coming!") Maybe that huge bridge is a support, above the main body of the atmosphere, for lasers or mirrors which heat up the air on the shadowed side of the bays and keep the power of the worm in check. But the imagined rebel aircraft could fly unseen through the worm's central mouth, if they dared.

As erosion worked on them, the sunlit walls might become fluted like the great Martian rift valley, Valles Marineris (Fig. 22.4). And in the Valles the Viking probes photographed huge landslides, spilling half-way across the floor; another factor which might keep the sunlit half of the valley sterile, if that's how the makers wanted it. On Earth, this is more of an underwater phenomenon. Between 50 and 30,000 BC, and twice more around 6,200 BC, there were catastrophic slides of mud down the edge of the continental shelf off Norway, forming the 'Storegga Slides' of 1500 feet thick debris over 500 miles of deep sea floor and causing tsunamis all round Europe.[6] Similarly about 20,000 BC, in the last Ice Age, 600 billion cubic yards of mud from the Rhone river fan cascaded on to the seafloor off Sardinia, creating the Sardino-Balearic Abyssal Plain and causing tsunamis along Mediterranean coasts.[7] Wind erosion on the sunlit side of the valley would generate bad enough landslides,

Fig. 22.4. View across colony valley on low approach to rim.
Drawing by Sydney Jordan.

if unchecked, but on the shadowed side, rain would build dangerous slurry on upper slopes. To save the twilight zone from much bigger disasters than Aberfan, or the huge mudslide of the 1970 Peruvian earthquake, there would have to be drainage, bringing down new soil into highly fertile alluvial fans on the plains. Higher still, buildup of ice and snow could be equally dangerous, making avalanches in Switzerland trivial by comparison. Even if the soil at high altitudes became bonded by permafrost, a thaw triggered by a change in the weather pattern could lead to a collapse.

At the necks where bays meet, air pressure would be lower. Instead of biological containment using higher pressure as a barrier, organisms would be drawn into the next enclave - as if the valley was designed to speed up the mixing, though screens suspended from Sydney's bridges could hold it in check - see below. But the greater the pressure differential, the more rapidly the necks will erode, opening out the valley into a continuous strip like Philip Jose Farmer's 'Riverworld'.[8] Subsequent erosion could leave the sunward-facing wall sheer, as in Valles Marineris, or progressively more gentle, building dune-fields below.   Near the equator conditions would become less extreme, but air pressure in the valley would drop overall, unless replenished by out-gassing from the planet's interior, or fresh cometary input.   All these processes would conceal the valley's impact origin, as happens on Earth: Gosse's Bluff in Australia, a large impact ring near Alice Springs, has smoothed out so much in 142-143 million years that it was first spotted from orbit.

Andrew Paterson asked, if the sun is just below the horizon everywhere in the twilight zone, why should the poles be colder than the equator?   On further thought, he realised that even if the valley is twenty miles deep, the atmo-sphere will extend above it, round the planet.   So there will be climate zones, especially if the upper atmosphere rotates more rapidly than the planet: on Venus, which takes 243 days to rotate on its axis, the upper atmosphere goes round in only four.   And if the valley's longitude is not exactly on the terminator, but slightly to sunward on that side of the planet, then temper-atures will certainly drop nearer the poles.

Twenty miles up, Earth's atmospheric pressure is the same as at the surface of Mars, the value at the true surface of the colony planet - comparable to C.S. Lewis's Mars, in *Out of the Silent Planet*, where the 'canals' were artificial valleys to provide habitation as the overall atmosphere grew thinner - one of the few descriptions of the canals to give them a realistic width, to be visible from Earth.[9] Thin as the Martian atmosphere is, it carries water vapour and clouds of ice crystals; and it sustains violent dust storms, when Mars is nearest to the Sun.   The colony planet wouldn't have seasonal variations or even diurnal ones, because of its trapped rotation and zero axial tilt, and as temperature changes shatter rock, it might not build up dust as Mars has: there would be wind erosion, but not the planet-wide dust storms which develop on Mars.

If they did start, they could be difficult to contain: there would be a high-pressure sub-solar area   (as Venus has), pushing storms towards the twilight zone.   Ringwalls on the sunward side might be high enough to stop them spill-ing into the valley.   But a very large sunshade, at the 'L1 point' between sun and planet, would create a shadowed, low-pressure zone at the sub-solar point, drawing storms towards it.

Gases would still freeze out on the dark side, and have to be compensated for. Ozone forming on the day side, at ground level, would be another drain: highly reactive, it would combine with anything which could be oxidised - once suggested as a reason for the iron oxide in the crust of Mars.[10] An ozone layer is needed to prevent the atmosphere being stripped by solar wind (Chap.19), so oxygen would have to be replaced, at least until there was nothing left on the sunlit side to be oxidised. Even at orbital altitude over Earth erosion by oxygen is a problem, attacking spacecraft surfaces;[11] so it would affect the makers' operations by outside the valley.

Sydney next drew a diagonal view from orbit, with cumulus clouds over the sunlit ringwall. Lightning struck the dark land beyond, while rain fed waterfalls visible from orbit, cascading into the valley. Dramatic as it was, if the valley was 20 miles deep those cloud tops would be as high again and the lightning bolts ten miles long. With air of Martian density outside the valley, thunderheads are impossible, and had to go, but the mistake let Gordon Ross think about the circulation in more detail. It would be simple, overall, as on Venus: an equatorial jetstream, in the direction of rotation, from sunlight across the valley to the darkside. Surrounding it would be large convection cells in each half-hemisphere, light and dark (four cells in all) feeding air into the valley near the poles, and into the sub-solar area to expand and go round again. In the jetstream there might be wave clouds and thin cirrus, as on Mars.

Entering the valley, at the rim of the twilight zone, the stream would be drawn downwards. Frondy clouds would form, like a lace collar, or pleated, like an Elizabethan ruff turned upside-down, generating high-altitude snow or hail ("ruff weather up there today"). Further down, there would be strong turbulent winds where the airstreams swept down the lower slopes and across the twilit plain to the river. On the sunlit side, as they swept up the cliffs there, they would separate in two directions: one arcing back towards the twilight zone, the other rising to create the 'glider superhighway' at the cliff rims, linking into higher-altitude jetstreams and passing on nightwards. There would be rising cirrus there, feeding lenticular clouds extending into the nightside, looking from below like hummocks, the same shapes as the impact bowls, but inverted. Further downwind these would break up into wave clouds, croissant or banana-shaped, disappearing into the night. Similar patterns would repeat, less violently, in bowls north or south of the equator (Fig. 22.5).

Fig. 22.5. Colony valley with high-altitude clouds.
Drawing by Sydney Jordan.

On the twilit side, terrestrial plants would experience new, unchanging conditions. As Pete Manly has pointed out, on a trapped-rotation world, "plants would develop to catch energy on only one side of their leaves, having a 'dark side' which probably would conserve heat (or in more tropical climates be specially evolved to dissipate heat). At any rate, with the sun unmoving in the sky, plants could become much more specialised." The same would happen in the valley, except that the plants would be facing the sunlit mountains, with their backs towards the unseen sun. In twilight, they would evolve dark blue-green colours, to maximise the light absorbed.[12]

371

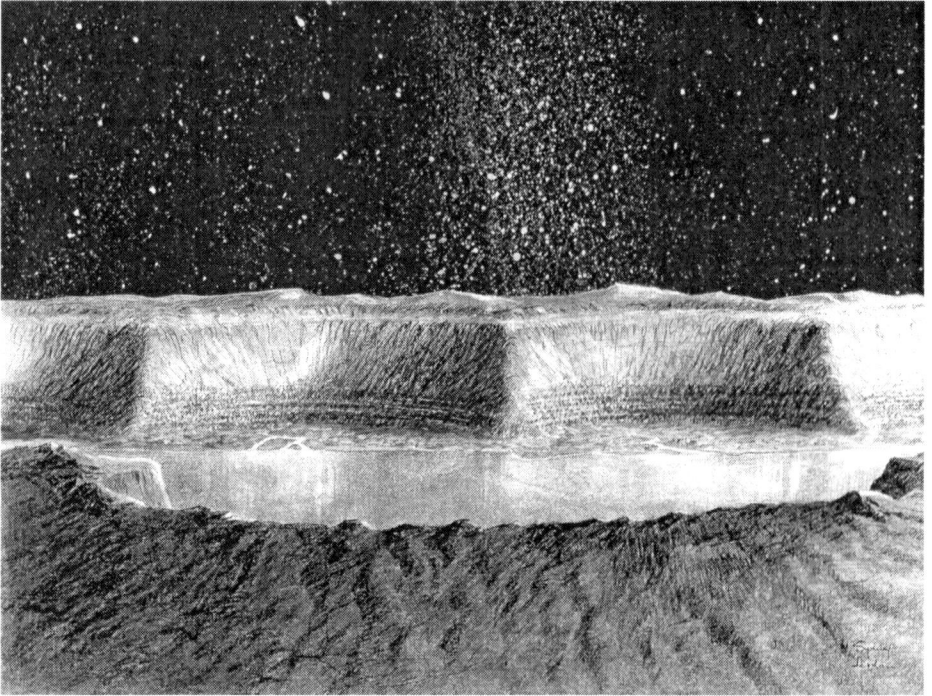

Fig. 22.6. Colony valley with plant cover.
Painting by Sydney Jordan.

Forest cover on the sunlit slopes would reduce erosion and trap moisture before it goes over the rim (Fig. 22.6). Genetic engineering would be needed to extend it to the rim, but Freeman Dyson has suggested that trees could be adapted even to live on comets, in vacuum and at much lower light levels than the colony world's.[13] The higher that sunlit tree belt grew, the more sunlight would be absorbed instead of reflecting destructively into the valley. It would damp the whole system, literally, trapping rain and draining it into Sydney's tall waterfalls, creating flood plains on the sunlit side, perhaps making it uninhabitable even if the light and heat would otherwise be tolerable. But even if they're too strong in the open, as the children implied, cultivation by humans might be possible on terraces shaded by the forest canopy. Andy Paterson pointed out that without terracing, waterfalls miles in height - from even higher than the treeline, if they came from the bases of the glaciers - could inject unwanted quantities of water vapour into the lower atmosphere. They could create rainforest on the plains, but it would need fine-tuning, otherwise they could generate permanent fog or even permanent cloud, perhaps with uncontrollable storms below.

The type, colour, thickness and vertical extent of the vegetation on each bowl's sunlit wall would have to balance three climatic requirements: retaining water and limiting erosion, regulating heat reflected into the valley, yet allowing enough light and heat for the twilight zone opposite. Needs could vary from bowl to bowl, if life was transplanted to the valley from more than one world, so the sunlit plant cover might have to be in place beforehand. Plants on the other side of the valley could be as alien to us as the Red Weed in Wells's *War of the Worlds*, and research by Tikhov, a Soviet pioneer of astrobotany, showed that if adapted to continuous strong sunlight it would indeed be red or orange,[12] as Sydney painted some of it (Fig. 22.6). If seeds from it came on the wind to take root in twilight, children might be conditioned not to eat anything not the right colour. Perhaps their insistence on the exact shade was an over-reaction to a strange environment with unfamiliar food - more on this below.

Fig. 22.7. Thunderheads in colony valley.
Drawing by Sydney Jordan.

Within the valley, there would be thunderheads at the tops of the atmosphere cells over the river (Fig. 22.7), coming back into the twilight, and clear zones in the centres of those cells, like the mouth of the sandworm visualised above. On the valley floor, the driest places might be at the necks between bowls - likely places for cities, especially if there's trade between bowls. In time, perhaps each neck between bowls would be bridged, and unless the aircraft were seaplanes, the safest places to land might be on the bridges themselves.

Conditions on Earth are regulated by much longer-term factors, Nick Portwin pointed out. Carbon and calcium, locked up in bodies, skeletons and shells of marine organisms, take carbon dioxide out of the atmosphere and form chalk beds. Over even longer periods, those are subducted at the edges of the continental shelves, into the interior of the Earth, and come back up as ash and gases from volcanoes. The colony world doesn't have the ocean area, the geologic processes or the timescale for such long, stable cycles. Losses to the river floor would be minor; but there would be a steady leaching of calcium and other trace elements towards the equator, and likewise, if the problem went unchecked, diminishing carbon dioxide to sustain the plants. If basins near the equator were water-filled, to boost oxygen production, they could hold coral reefs, mined to replace calcium losses at higher latitudes. Using sunlight energy, the water could be filtered and residues pyrolised to release carbon dioxide. Coriolis winds would return it to higher latitudes, and the ash would be used as fertiliser.

Carbon dioxide could be imported from a world like Venus, and the colony's atmosphere could even be cycled to and from the Earth, to let our extensive biosphere cope with any imbalances; but if there are non-terrestrial life-forms there, the air passing through would have to be sterilised. The late Paul Grant suggested that if nitrogen was being injected into Earth's middle atmosphere, circulating to and from the colony world, that could enhance the red colour of the auroral displays.

Gordon remarked that other terraforming studies paint with a broad brush, envisaging a single ocean over the northern hemisphere of Mars, or virtually all of Venus, because that's how the existing terrain lies. The valley world is more a designer exercise: its simple overall weather pattern allows accurate baseline predictions. Features can then be added or subtracted, fine-tuning to create individual micro-climates.   That brings us to the kind of life which the children and others could lead there.

2. What Could Turn People Green?

"...for several days they were kept without access to food.   When therefore they had almost expired of fasting, nevertheless they would not consider any food which was offered; by chance it came to pass that beans were brought in from the fields; seizing upon which from that place, they sought the bean itself in the stalks;   and finding nothing in the hollow of the stalks, they wept bitterly.   Then one of those present held out to them the beans removed from the pods, which at once they accepted and ate up freely.   They were fed by this food for several months, until they changed to the use of bread.   At length with the nature of our foods prevailing, their own colour gradually changing, they were even 'completed' like us..." (WN)

"Bread and other common foods were offered to them, but they did not wish to be nourished by any food which was brought to them, so for a long time they were tormented by great hunger, because they believed all the food of that place to be 'undigestible', as the girl later formally stated.   At length when beans with newly cut stalks were brought into the house, they signed with great avidity for those beans to be given to them.   When these were freely brought to them, they opened the stalks, not the pods of the bean-plants, thinking that the beans were contained in the stalks.   But finding no beans in the stalks, again they began to weep.   When the bystanders realised this, they opened the pods, showing the beans uncovered; these were eaten with great joy, and for a long time they would take absolutely no other food.   Truly the boy, always seeming brought down by exhaustion/depression, died after a short time.   Truly the girl enjoying a full recovery, and become accustomed to all kinds of food, put off that completely leek-green colour, and gradually regained a sanguine condition of the whole body..." (RC)

Why would the children think they could eat only food the same colour as themselves?   They didn't recognise the bean-plants - they didn't even know which part was edible, but they thought they knew, wrongly, which implies they were used to a leek-green plant with food in the stalk.   They did know that the colour was crucial.   It's not that every living thing in their homeland is that colour, just everything that's safe to eat - not a deficiency but an additive.

Ralph specifically uses the word 'dyed' for plants and people in the settlement, perhaps a marker identifying terrestrial life. Bill Ramsay suggested that colour-coding might be a key to the transport system, so weaning the children on to terrestrial food would trap them here - an inversion of many stories about Fairyland and the Underworld. If the children knew that, it might explain why they refused food that wasn't their colour. Or the green colour could exclude people from the system in normal circumstances, since the children's delivery to Earth seems to have been an accident. In 14th and 15th century incidents some people apparently had strange colours (Chap. 24); yet in the other 12th and 13th century ones, the people looked normal.

Algae feature in terraforming, and I was told they can turn people green. Spirulina alga, eaten around Lake Chad and exported for health-food products, is bright green before the chlorophyll is extracted, as is chlorella from South East Asia and Australia.[14] But at the Edinburgh International Science Festival Prof. Harold Baum directed me to the edible algae programme in Israel, aiming to meet market demand as Lake Chad becomes shrunken and polluted. Its Director, Prof. Shoshona Arad, replied that he hadn't heard of algae, or any other food, turning people green.[15]

As he and many others mentioned, too many carrots or too much carrot-juice can turn people yellow or orange,[16] and in strong sunlight carrots can cause a skin rash if picked with bare hands,[17] but the children were clear that they'd seen no Sun until they came out of the pit. In 2009 a man turned orange after drinking seven pints of cider daily for five years;[18] in the city of Tver north of Moscow, a couple who drank lacquer polish with a base of methylated spirits were saved by doctors, but ended up dyed purple.[19] But I haven't come across any food or drink which definitely turns people green, despite the Milarepa story (Chap.8).

James Bentley suggested that the twilight could be a factor. Light treatment has been used to alleviate jet-lag,[20] and bright lights help babies born with jaundice to recover;[21] this revives a traditional technique, because jaundice used to be treated by reflecting sunlight into the face from burnished metal.[22] Prof. Baum agreed that retention of bile products, in low light levels, with an unusual diet, might account for the colour. However, we've seen that apparently the children were used to light levels not too different from ours. Chris Coutts, a homeopathic doctor, once treated a baby with a bile defect who'd turned dark green with what he described as 'super-jaundice'. But he didn't see her until conventional treatment failed and her life was despaired of, and as I keep stressing, the green children were otherwise in good health. That also rules out the hormone deficiency, Addison's Disease, though Jane Austen, on her deathbed, described herself as "black and white and every wrong colour". She couldn't have been saved without hormone replacement therapy, and neither could the children if that was their problem. Chromohydrosis (coloured sweat) can occur, due to high concentrations of a pigment called lipofuscin, but doesn't affect skin colour.[23]

A surprising number of people suggested symbiosis with algae as a way to turn green. Sea-anemones and sea-slugs are green because they've achieved symbiotic partnership with algae, as plants did earlier with the organisms which became their energy-absorbing chloroplasts.[24] One such 'planimal' is Elysia chlorotica, a 'lurid green' sea slug found on the US Atlantic seaboard. The skin of the worm *Convoluta roscoffensis*, found on beaches of the French coast and the Channel Islands, contains algal cells of genus *Tetraselmis*, usually *Tetraselmis convolutae*, giving it a deep green colour. It reproduces sexually, so it's born without the algae but eats them after birth. The relationship is so finely tuned that if the worms don't absorb algae, they die without maturing. Adult worms don't need to eat because the algae supply their host with glucose, oxygen, fatty acids and steroids, while recycling nitrogen from the host's uric acid waste and supplying it back in amino acids. Their numbers turn the beaches green, but they retreat as people walk on them and the sandy colour returns.[25]

It would be little use to humans (despite tales that the US military is trying to develop a chlorophyll-based system to let US Marines, Navy SEALS etc., live on sunlight). Effective though symbiosis is for small organisms like sand-dwelling worms, it needs large surface area in relation to the volume of flesh it sustains. A treetrunk with the mass of a human being requires a large area of leafage, and as the proverb says, it can only climb a hill by dropping a seed up-slope. Solar energy on skin couldn't supply the energy for a typically demanding human day, where the first evolutionary requirement was to outrun both predators and prey on the open savannah of Africa, *by outlasting -*

stamina was the key, not the carnivore or herbivore's quick dash.[26] As Napoleon said, an army marches on its stomach; if it fed on sunlight the witches' warning to Macbeth would be literal - no danger till Birnam Wood comes to Dunsinane.

Frogs are green due to optically interacting blue and yellow pigment cells in their skins, but there are no green mammals:[25] getting an exact colour match with living plants would probably need genetic engineering. If both plants and humans were genetically modified, people might produce a pigment in response to the plants' chemical trigger; which brings us to bioluminescence. It's found in at least 40 different orders of animals, at least two groups of plants, some bacteria (which can make meat luminous); some insects, such as fireflies and their larvae, glow-worms; some fungi, which can make wood luminous (fox-fire); and numerous marine creatures including microscopic dinoflagellates, larger bottom-dwellers on the continental shelf and free-swimmers in the ocean depths. Blue or green light is emitted during a reaction of two compounds, *luciferin* and *luciferase*, produced by the organisms concerned.

Green canary and budgerigar breeders periodically introduce wild birds into the bloodlines, otherwise the colour is lost - so Agnes's descendants might not carry the greenness gene, and their DNA might be normal. That could be why no green people have cropped up among them, even if exposed by chance to the trigger compound.

But in 1997, at the Osaka University Microbiological Disease Research Institute in Japan, a gene from the Pacific *Aequoria Victoria* jellyfish was introduced into laboratory mice, to manufacture the luminous green protein *aequoria*.[27] The purpose was to track cells in ultraviolet, without using radioactive isotopes, and it gained the team the Nobel Prize for Chemistry in 2008.[28] A Cambridge scientist said in 1997 that we could already breed green people, if we chose.[29] At first the light produced was dim, and the mouse was white in ordinary light.[28] The protein would disappear from the skin as the tagged cells died, so the colour faded, as it did on the green children, if it wasn't replenished with more tagging molecules. For permanence the gene is inserted *in vitro* into fertilised eggs, so all cells in the body carry it and it could in theory be passed on to offspring. The experiment failed with monkeys, in Oregon: "These are not Day-Glo monkeys," said the research team head[30] -

but was successful in Taiwan, first with fish and then with pigs, but still only under ultraviolet light.[31]   By 2007, however, permanent GloFish were on sale in the USA, and the technique was used 'routinely' as a way of tagging other genetic transfers.[32]

More drastically, could genetic engineering replace haemoglobin, the oxygen carrier which gives blood its red colour?   It's one of the *chromoproteins*, incorporating heavy metal ions.   Haemoglobin uses iron; when deoxygenated it's blue, and the 'blue people', of Troublesome Creek, Kentucky, were afflicted for 140 years before their enzyme deficiency was identified and cured in 1964. Arthropods, including crabs, spiders, insects and some snails, use copper, forming haemocyanin, which is blue.   Vanadium in blue, green or orange aggregates is used by marine organisms classed as tunicates.   With magnesium the product is chlorophyll, the green agent of photosynthesis in plants, but the molecular form is different, with a porphyrin ring.

Some plants use haemoglobin, and some animals use chlorophyll, so might a crossover be possible?[33]   A magnesium-based molecule couldn't bind and transport oxygen in a human-type bloodstream; and haemoglobin isn't a major factor in skin colour, as witness the range that melanin pigment gives people on Earth.   Excessive sulphur can turn blood green, but not skin.[34]   Even in *Star Trek*, Leonard Nimoy's makeup has only a hint of green, though Spock's skin turns darker green at the site of a blow.   (Since he shows no emotions, he doesn't blush green where we would red.)

If people could be modified to use chlorophyll, it would be very hard to switch back.   It recalls the Irish joke about changing to driving on the right: to make the transition easier, they'd begin with heavy lorries.   The relatively minor operation of tagging skin cells seems a much better bet.   But if the children could be modified or given implants to manufacture both green and red blood cells, running two metabolic systems in parallel - why prohibit them from eating non-green food?   The prohibition was so strong that James Bentley suggested it involved aversion therapy.   "...they did not *wish* to be nourished by any food which was brought to them [my emphasis], so for a long time they were tormented by great hunger, because they believed all the food of that place to be 'undigestible', as the girl later formally stated."(RC)   I coined the word 'undigestible', because 'inedible' or 'indigestible' weren't exact translations.   The word is *incomestibilia*, 'things which are not to be consumed for nourishment' - not 'poisonous'. It hints at other chemistry which the human system can't absorb.

Life on Earth uses a limited range of amino acids and proteins, so on other earthlike worlds every living thing could be poisonous to us. And life here is based on left-handed versions of organic compounds, using right-handed sugars, whereas in meteorites, carbon compounds formed without life are left- or right-handed in equal numbers. Life which was a mirror image of ours at the molecular level, could be inert to our biochemistry: however fertile the environment, in terms of nourishment it could be a desert to us. Louis Pasteur found that living creatures could digest one form of tartaric acid but not the other. In some cases, the only difference is in flavouring, in others one form is poisonous. The anaesthetic Bupivacaine has an isomer which causes heart damage, so is restricted to epidural injections. Thalidomide is a useful tranquilliser in one form, but causes birth defects in the other.[35]

Even if life had the same 'handedness' as ours, and used the same amino acids, even if its evolution had converged with ours to the extent that we could survive in the same atmosphere, that same evolution could give it a very different protein structure - as some life on Earth uses proteins which are poisonous to animals or insects. One interesting point in David Attenborough's documentary was that many creatures use bioluminescence to warn off predators: they also manufacture unpleasant-tasting steroids, not themselves luminous. He showed cases, on land and in the sea, where the predators all too obviously didn't care; but maybe the green people have been tagged to mimic something which predators don't eat on their world.

That suggests a much simpler possibility. Genetic engineering didn't explain why the plants were the *same* colour as the people - and the word Ralph of Coggeshall quoted was definitely 'dyed'. He also says 'leek-green', but he may just mean bright green, rather than the precise shade, between viridian green and cadmium yellow, which it denotes on a modern artist's palette (and there's also the association of leeks with lightning - Chap.8). The Latin words are *asserebat quod omnes habitatores et omnia quae in regione illa habebantur viridi tingerentur colore* - she said that all the people and things that were held in that land were dyed with the same leek-green colour. I've been reading that as 'all plants', thinking of Ovid's poem in praise of spring: *Omnia tunc florent, tunc est novis temporis aestas* – "all things then are blossoming, it's the time of a new season". *Tingerentur* is in reported speech, so it might just be Ralph's manner of speaking, as he might have referred to a Moor as 'dyed black' - though I haven't found a case where he did. If I'm right, *omnia* doesn't cover the animals. If they *were* the same colour, most of the mechanisms above would need their true skin colour to be close to ours - see below.

In *River Out of Eden*, Richard Dawkins describes the specialisms and inadequacies of predator eyesight[36] - often evolved to detect certain colours, certain shapes or patterns of movement, often in specific conditions - certain times of day, seasons, and in general certain *light levels*. Was a predator loose in the colony - following the animals, in that reading of Ralph of Coggeshall - not good in twilight at seeing people dyed green from the plants? Perhaps, if they kept still, the predator saw them as *being* plants - especially if it saw them all as grey or black (Chap.19). Steve Sneyd imagined a green cat hunting the children, but 'at night all cats are grey' and maybe, to the predator, so are the people.

Makeup isn't enough: James Bentley pointed out that on the pilgrim route the villagers would be familiar with travelling players, and would soon notice if the colour didn't cover the inside of mouth, eyes and ears, more intimately the vagina and the cleft of the buttocks. Someone would have checked, and the children were "green of the *entire* body" [my emphasis]. But persistent, water-resistant colour (Gordon predicted heavy rainfall) would fade with shedding skin cells, and as the children adapted to terrestrial food, witnesses would assume the processes were connected.

Animals, undyed, wouldn't know to stand still, if the threat was unfamiliar. As Charles Darwin wrote, "Comparatively few young birds, in any one year, have been injured by man in England; yet almost all, even nestlings, are afraid of him. Many individuals, on the other hand, both at the Galapagos and at the Falklands, have been pursued and injured by man, but yet have not learned a salutary dread of him. We may infer from these facts what havoc the introduction of any new beast of prey must cause in a country, before the instincts of the indigenous [animal] inhabitants have become adapted to the stranger's craft or power."[37] Human inhabitants, with more to rely on than instinct, can react much faster. Take the sheep, not me!

3. Biospheres without Walls

The Biosphere II project in Arizona contained various interactive 'habitats', a microcosm of the Earth's living environment (Biosphere I). The twilight zone of the children's planet could be a similar experiment, to study the compatibility of terrestrial life with other forms - biospheres without walls. Partial walls at first, each group in its embayed enclave, but the different complexes of living creatures would meet as they expanded along the river valley.

Into this setting, the makers could gather life-forms from many earthlike worlds – perhaps all of them, if life is rare in the Galaxy. Up to two hundred worlds might be represented, each with its own enclave but destined to mingle. The valley system promotes that: first micro-organisms through the low-pressure zones between the bowls, then wind-borne spores, seeds, insects, spiders with airborne webs. Birds or the equivalent pass through by air, fish, reptiles and mammals by water, and corpses down-river: a steady mixing, upstream and down, at rates which the makers may have calculated but got interestingly wrong. Earth has algal blooms and 'red tides' when environmental factors go out of balance: colony enclaves could have water-borne invasions, like Wells's Red Weed, which local bacteria couldn't contain. Airborne invasions could be as severe as the 'Threadfalls' in Anne McCaffrey's 'Pern' novels.[38]

'Sydney's bridges' are under upward tension (see below), so they could support membranous barriers, to separate different atmospheres or different levels of salinity in the river, like the dam across Great Salt Lake in Utah which makes half of it usable for irrigation. Such barriers could enforce separation between really different biospheres, or similar ones subject to different influences from north and south. How far does mixing go, we might ask, or is there no attempt to control it - how ruthless is the experiment? In "The Garden of Rama" by Arthur C. Clarke and Gentry Lee, the creators of a similar one allow life-forms to interact as destructively as they please.[39] The colour-coding and food taboos in the children's society suggest that mixing has been allowed to go a long way. To what end? To decide where Contact would be safe, where exchanges would be productive, where settlements could be established - or with some longer-term goal?

In 1979, an 'engineer's approach to evolution' was outlined by Alan Bond,[40] later the originator of the HOTOL spaceplane concept. His rule of thumb assessed the degree of an organism's evolutionary advance by the number of proteins it utilised (a more sophisticated model used genome size[41]), starting with bacteria, then blue-green algae, and so on up to intelligent mammals such as ourselves. At each rising level fewer individual species were found on Earth, and Alan suggested that this would correspond to the distribution of life-forms in the Galaxy: bacteria on virtually every earthlike world, a much smaller number with algae, and so on. Integrating this idea with an estimate that there would be about 36 million such worlds in the Galaxy,[42] he concluded that there would be one or at most two intelligent species - and since Earth had both humans and cetaceans, that might exhaust the possibilities.

I pointed out that the biggest evolutionary leap on Alan's chart was the first one, from bacteria to blue-green algae - then the oldest form of life identified on Earth. Our Solar System is 4.6 billion years old, but there are stars like our Sun in the galactic disc up to twice that age - the nearest star system to us, Alpha Centauri, for example. It would therefore have been possible for a star-faring race to have evolved billions of years ago, found they were alone in the Galaxy, and seeded *all* the earthlike worlds with blue-green algae - in which case they now might all have intelligent life at the same level as ourselves. The idea that Earth may have been seeded from space has a venerable history, termed 'panspermia' if it happened in the course of nature and 'directed panspermia' if by intelligent life.

In the 1980s fossilised microscopic organisms were discovered in 3,500-million-year-old rocks from the Apex Chert of Western Australia: 'cyanobacteria' (blue-green algae) which live in large communities and produce layered sediment-clogged structures called 'stromatolites', still found on the Australian coasts in a few locations. The earliest marine reefs were made of stromatolites, dominant in the seas until animals appeared that could graze on those tempting mats of bacterial slime. Traces have been found of 'archaeobacteria' dating back 3.9 billion years, so soon after the final bombardment phase in the formation of the planets that the first living organisms may have come in on comets. Those single-celled organisms were here before the algae, but were definitely the ancestors of almost all life on Earth today. That doesn't completely rule out my idea, since the Earth hosts an entirely different family, the eubacteria, which seem to have originated on

Earth at the same time as the archaeobacteria and might represent a native form which the archaeobacteria supplanted.[44]

If that event was due to directed panspermia, then presumably there was a second episode several hundred million years later, in which the algae were seeded here. It puts the scale of the operation into perspective. In human affairs, we look for a return on business investment in three months, and few governments will back projects which will outlast their own span of four or five years. A billion years is more than five thousand times longer than *homo sapiens* has existed at all, and the panspermia project would still have at least three billion more to run. It would be easier with matter-transmitters than with interstellar probes, but the 'gardeners' must really want somebody to talk to, with whom to share the Galaxy in due course.

It could mean that life-forms on all earthlike worlds have common ancestors, and, perhaps, that they could prey on one another if gathered in one place. Without those ancestors, the usual science-fiction interactions between Earth life and aliens would be impossible. If we established colonies on planets with life incompatible with ours, T.A. Heppenheimer wrote, "...there would be no chance of devastation of indigenous species. A stock animal that wandered into the forest would not run wild and tear up young seedlings. Instead, it would be found dead of indigestion."[45]

'Stock animals' has an ominous ring, if people have been transplanted. Over a long time, predators would develop enzymes to cope with the other group's biochemistry, while the prey developed countermeasures. Genetic engineering could speed up the process... perhaps the aim is to develop a universal predator, able to achieve dominance on any inhabited world. We must be cautious about 'their' apparent interest in the compatibility of our life-forms with theirs, or others to which they have access.

However, I don't think we need be alarmed, at this stage. Having looked at what it would take to make a habitable valley on a trapped rotation world, what else could be going on to justify that effort? Industrial operations in permanent sunlight or darkness could be on such a scale that a biological project in the twilight zone would be only a spinoff, or even a hobby. That gives a perspective on what beings millions or even billions of years ahead of us might get from an enterprise like this. As Iain M. Banks once remarked, their test for what's worth doing will not be 'Is it profitable?', 'Is it scientific?' or even 'Is it dangerous?', but 'Is it *entertaining*?'

James Bentley suggested the colony might be a zoo, with any scientific function secondary; and conservationists might force a close-down, returning the inhabitants to their origin worlds. He also suggested that the colony might not be on another world at all, but underground somewhere on Earth. No problems then about air pressure, or gravity, during transfers... but why not just put it on an island, or in an isolated meteorite crater in the Australian desert? Perhaps extraterrestrial life in the experiment can't take the light levels we're used to; worrying, because it suggests the priority was to protect their biosphere, not ours, and the long-term aim was to transfer us to theirs, for whatever reasons. On the other hand, if they set up an underground experiment on Earth meantime, they might genuinely be concerned about what would happen to us if shipped off-planet - incongruous, but it could fit a zoo-keeper mentality.

4. Pecora, What Pecora?

Mentioning zoos brings up the livestock which the children were looking after, adding to or following. Both William and Ralph used the word *pecora*, almost the only word their texts have in common apart from *quia*. *Pecora* is one of the most general words for living creatures in Latin: it can be used collectively of pigs, sheep, cattle, horses, lions, seals, fowls, hens, fish, bees or even people in the sense of 'the common herd'. Unless that's what William and Ralph were implying, it's striking that both accounts use this very general word, without specifying herds of *what*. If the children described an animal for which there was no word in English or Latin, again we're up against William's lack of interest in the details.

Was the colony stocked from Europe at all? It could be from East Anglia itself: during the civil war it would have been easy to remove population and livestock unnoticed. The Bury St. Edmunds area was ravaged at least twice and for a time Essex was virtually depopulated, which must have some bearing on the time it took to complete Coggeshall Abbey. But on so short a timescale, the children should still speak English, unless they'd learned the speech of their captors, or fellow abductees.

385

The Coggeshall monks introduced sheep into Essex, starting the wool trade.[46] Rabbits were brought into England by 12th century Normans, as an early kind of 'factory farming', and one ancient warren (owned by the Earls of Leicester) is a listed ancient monument.[47] In the 13th century rabbits were still such a speciality that hunting rights in general were called 'Free Warren'. So the *pecora* weren't necessarily exotic. Maybe, now conditions were more settled, William and Ralph thought it wise not to specify what was being exported - though that would imply that they knew about it.

In the Peak Cavern one side passage was the 'Swine Hole' because the rope-works cottagers used it as a pigsty, periodically cleaned by the river. Not far down it daylight is lost, so how much sign was there was of pigs, if the swineherd pressed on into darkness, there or in the main cavern? No doubt a lot, if regularly used for livestock transfers; but then, why didn't William and Ralph just say *pigs*, instead of the mysterious pecora? The tooth of a woolly rhinoceros was found at the mouth of the cave,[48] and we're not told how fresh it was... Gerald of Wales said Fairyland had very small horses, but as we saw in Chap.8, that story has no connection with ours.

James Bentley pressed me to think again whether the setting might be in the southern hemisphere. He suggested the bright green food that the children were looking for could be the Australian bush banana,[49] and Jane Greatorex added that plantains, one of the many variants of banana in southeast Asia, are roasted and eaten when their skins are green. Should the reference to the Antipodes in the Peveril swineherd story be taken literally? I did turn up one possible link: St. Virgil of Aghaboe, 'Virgil the Geometer', no less. In 745AD he went to Europe, where he was put on trial for maintaining "against God and his own soul" that there was another world, and other peoples, under the Earth.[50,51] James suggested that it could be in New Zealand, destroyed when no longer needed, in the meteorite air-burst, circa 1200 AD, postulated by Dr. Steel (Chap.16). If so, they made a thorough job of it, not to say overkill, wiping out the moa (another candidate for pecora?).

Not so far south, the pecora might be llamas; there was no word for them in 12th century Europe, obviously, or for long time afterwards: even in the 18th century, in *Candide* Voltaire calls them *moutons rouges*, 'red sheep'. In a strange tie-in with current news, after trials in the USA against coyotes and wild dogs, llamas are being introduced into English flocks to protect lambs from foxes.[52]

If there were wolves in the colony as I suggested (Chap.20), perhaps the general 'pecora' implied *mixed* livestock. But it was also around 1200 AD that the Inca dynasty was founded in Peru. The legend is that Manco Capac, his brothers, sisters and followers emerged from three caves called Tampu-Tocco, 'Tavern Hole', at Paccari Tampu, 'Dawn Tavern', 18 miles south-east of Cuzco. (*Tocco* can also mean 'window', and some writers identify the scene with a wall at Macchu Picchu.) There were eight family and ten followers, each of whom was to start an Inca clan. But the brothers quarrelled, and one with a sling hurled stones from a hill with such force that they tore ravines in the landscape. Manco Capac sent him into the cave to fetch 'the sacred llama', had it walled up, and turned the other two brothers to stone.[53]

If the Incas and their livestock came from the colony planet, emerging in the high Andes suggests lower air pressure than here, on average. So when the green children appeared at Woolpit they would escape embolism or the bends, and the high winds at Peak Cavern could still be due to the altitude difference with East Anglia. The rocks which tore great ravines in the terrain are interesting: there are no impacts in Peru then that I know of, but the one in Nebraska around that time has only just been discovered.[54] Perhaps the battle with the rocks relates to the 1178 impacts on the Moon, or to the formation of the colony valley. If that 1173 'star' with its attendants is accurately described, in the western sky by day and night (Chap.9), it was either floating in the atmosphere, like the ships in *Independence Day*, or in geosynchronous orbit and closer to South America than to Europe.

Wherever he came from, Manco Capac was able to capitalise on the legend of Viracocha, 'sea-foam', whose people founded the pre-Inca civilisation of Tiahuanaco after crossing the sea and sailing down the west coast in reed boats.[55] Thor Heyerdahl's 'Ra expeditions' were intended to demonstrate that Viracocha and his followers, and the Maya counterpart, Quetzalcoatl, could have come from North Africa. Like many North Africans, they were fair-skinned and yellow-haired, and to pose as their heirs maybe Manco Capac and his followers also had a 'European' appearance. Perhaps they came from Europe, by way of the colony planet. But then, the green children spoke no known language... If the children were Viracochas, after their green colour faded they would appear normal in England, and maybe what the children spoke at first was a version of Quechua, used by the Incas' descendants to this day. But the girl didn't suffer, or bring with her, the shattering ailments which normally accompany contact between cultures.   With all respect to Richard de Calna, even if he was a doctor that's unlikely to be due to his 12th century skills, unless he knew where the children were from, and knew how to treat them once found - which doesn't fit with their starvation and the boy's death.

Agnes could be of recent English stock (she looked normal, once she'd lost her green colour); or there was enough contact between the colony and East Anglia to introduce new strains and keep up immunities (deliberately or by chance exposure).   Or she might have biological implants which could handle the problem.   In that case her 'wantonness and lasciviousness' might just be the 12th century view of a woman from a more sophisticated culture, someone we'd describe as liberated.   Otherwise, her group's separation from Europe has to be recent.

Nothing about the Incas suggests ET Contact, apart from the story of their origin.   Other versions of their arrival are interesting, but perhaps borrowed from the earlier pre-Inca Viracochas.[55]   If there was a conflict, with rocks which tore holes in the landscape, it left the Incas without European technology, not even writing or the wheel, so it might be the end of Contact as far as they were concerned.

5. Held in that Land

It's a pity that neither chronicle tells us how the children reacted to the Moon (Chap. 22), and we'd also like to know how they coped with sunburn.   If it wasn't a problem, maybe they were raised on Earth; or the green pigment protected from ultraviolet radiation; or they lived within sight of the mountains (or an orbiting ring) and significant ultraviolet was reflected into the valley.   It seems they had some natural or artificial protection, for if they'd been badly burned in the late summer of 1173, you would think that would be strange enough for William or Ralph to mention it.

If the land isn't on Earth, we can estimate the size of the colony.   In *Man and the Stars*, we tried to plan a feasible mission to establish one on an Earth-type world.   A group of 100 people would need intensive high-technology support.   Even then, mating would have to be strictly controlled: as recessive genes

388

surfaced, in so small a population, they would go through a bottleneck after three or four generations, where only a few couples could be allowed to breed. The group would be so vulnerable to accident or disease over that period that its chances of survival would be small.[56]   A thousand people would have a better chance, but would still need support; a mediaeval, rural group would need less than we would, because they'd have more of the necessary skills. Even so, in the strange environment of a new world they'd need a lot of help and heavy losses could be expected.   They could easily be wiped out, espec- ially in its early years, by a bad harvest, a pest invasion, a volcanic eruption, or a climate change like the 'Spörer Minimum' which ended Viking settlement in Greenland.[57]

The operation could perhaps be supported by a few powerful families here, with the resources of large mediaeval manors to call upon, when numbers were low.   The most realistic model builds up population to 10,000, plus new people, livestock and plants thereafter according to need, or as it becomes clear how the situation could be improved, and in Chaps.23 & 24 I'll suggest an operation on that large a scale.

James Bentley suggested the children might be sent to Earth to see what would happen, perhaps before returning a larger group.   They might be less at risk than adolescents or adults, more likely to be accepted as 'fairies' or 'godly messengers'.   In Murray Leinster's *Four from Planet Five*,[58] children are sent to Earth in advance of a main party, but in a case where it's more dangerous to remain.   Sending these children first would be relatively callous, perhaps to the extent of colouring them green to make them conspicuous - though they testified that everyone in the colony was the same colour.   Linda Lunan suggested that although they were returned here by accident, they weren't retrieved because someone wanted to see what would happen.   It would imply that what happened to them was monitored, unless they didn't come through where the experimenters intended.

But who were *they*?   For "the people that were held in that land" Ralph uses the passive *habebantur*, 'held' in the sense of being owned.   It might be feudal usage: in those days everybody was owned in some sense.   But if 'held' is what she said and she wasn't from a feudal culture, it may be a glimpse of the powers behind this affair.   As Charles Fort said, "I think we're property... I think we're fished for."[59]   How they went about it, and what could go wrong, are subjects for the next two chapters.

But in all the books alleging Past Contact, at many different times in human history, no convincing extraterrestrial has turned up - not even in the 12th century (Chap.8).   Drawings and statues are all of human beings, even if in 'spacesuits', usually found to be suits of armour.   Until H.G. Wells imagined truly nonhuman Martians and Selenites for *The War of the Worlds* and *The First Men in the Moon*, imagination didn't go in this direction: mediaeval bestiaries filled unexplored parts of the world with creatures, but they were cut-and-paste jobs from known life-forms.[51]   No-one in Europe imagined kangaroos before explorers reached Australia, and in the 1970's a 'Kangaroo Club' was formed in the Soviet Union, to investigate past Contact.   They looked for entities so strange that, before science-fiction, no-one could have imagined them, much odder than the humanoid aliens of UFO reports; and they didn't find any.

In the whole series of events, there's only one possible sighting of an extraterrestrial, and that's the one Ralph gives in 1205, found after the most violent thunderclap during a nation-wide electrical storm.   "A certain monster… struck by lightning… the head pertaining to an ass, a human belly, and other monstrous limbs truly dissimilar from any kind of animal; to which very black corpse one could scarcely approach nearer, than the burning's smoke, because of the intolerable odour."   The 'certain' is interesting: it's almost as if Ralph knew what this creature was.   He might have given us a clue with Jerome's *Ethics*, but in St. Jerome's complete works there's no surviving one of that title,[60] and he has no record as a demonologist – nor do ass-headed beings feature in most catalogues of demons,[61] or even modern zoological fakes.[62]   In the 19th century Collin de Plancy catalogued the Lechies, a 'demon of the woods' with long horns, donkey-like head, human torso and goat-like lower limbs; but his work is "of dubious scholarly value".[61] The next and last incarnation of Vishnu is to be a horse-headed giant called 'Kalkin', and there are minor horse-headed divinities in China;[63] Christians in ancient Rome were ridiculed with claims that they worshipped an ass-headed god,[64] but those too are no help.

The White Goddess by Robert Graves has a further range of horse deities, including a mare-headed version of Demeter, worshipped at Troy and in

390

Western Arcadia, who was overcome by Poseidon in his rôle as horse-tamer. But the ass-god is the Egyptian Set, corresponding to Greek Dionysus. Set was ass-eared; Sirius and the two Asses (in the constellation Cancer) ruled the hottest days of the year, and the Pharaohs carried ass-eared reed sceptres. The Scythians worshipped an ass-unicorn, the beast of Set, whose horn (says Herodotus) was 'exalted at midsummer'. "One must not be misled by... the extraordinary mythographic jumble in Shakespeare's *A Midsummer Night's Dream*, where Theseus appears as a witty Elizabethan gallant... and, most monstrous of all, the Wild Ass Set-Dionysus and the star-diademed Queen Of Heaven as ass-eared Bottom and tinselled Titania."[65]

There's still nothing about extraordinary limbs, which makes the monster more interesting. Dr. Jack Cohen, a 'reproductive biologist' who designs extraterrestrials for science-fiction writers, pointed out in 1991 that the true inadequacy of the UFO aliens (and those of media SF) is their knees and elbows.[66] The six broad divisions of animal life on Earth, including vertebrates like us, insects and fish, share the same genes for appendages such as legs, arms, claws, fins and antennae. They originated with a worm-like creature called *Urbilateria*, 600-700 million years ago, the common ancestor of all those forms.[67] All four-legged creatures with pentadactyl limbs like ours are descended from a fish that left the sea in the Devonian period: *Gogonassus*, the 'Gogo fish', whose 370-million year old remains are found in Australia[48] - just as all land plants derive from a variety of freshwater algae 450 million years ago.[69] Our knees and elbows are where they are because they correspond to the fin joints of the Gogo fish; that's what allows a human in costume to act a great ape or a dinosaur, or even two humans in costume to play a recognisable caricature of a cow or a horse.

The noxious smoke from the Maidenhead monster might imply a different chemistry from ours, but the most interesting things are the extraordinary limbs. If not one of the masters of the colony world, it might at least be a non-human occupant – intelligent or otherwise. Monsters, as truly non-human beings, are rare in mediaeval chronicles. Allegedly there was one near Kilkenny, at a cave now called 'Dunmore', more famous for the ossified remains of Viking attack victims. This creature, Luchtigern, 'The Lord of the Mice', was trampled to death by a female warrior called Aithbel, and is presumably mere legend. Curiously, the older name of the cave is Dearc-fearna, the Cave of the Alders,[70] from which green dye was made (Chap.8).

But Maidstone isn't in any of the three north-south 'corridors' of Contact sites in Fig. 17.3. That may not be significant, but even when I'd only noticed the one in East Anglia, Andy Nimmo suggested that it represented the north-south spread of human settlements along the shadowed side of the river, on the floor of one bowl of the colony world. Presumably it wouldn't have to be that way, since our world rotates with respect to its Sun, but Andy suggested there might be a psychological tendency to align Contact sites north-south, to match the layout back home.

Then the altitude of the Peak Cavern, west of the 'corridor' but only a little north, might correspond to a site on the sloping wall - perhaps a cave or a terrace. If so, and it's on the shadowed side of the valley, then the children lived in the northern hemisphere of their planet, defined by anticlockwise rotation and revolution about its sun; and on the trailing hemisphere of that world, at what would be the sunset line if it rotated more rapidly. So in trying to map sites in our world on to theirs, we can use our compass directions: the sunlit half-bowl is on the east side of the river, the twilight zone on the west, and perhaps they live on a latitude corresponding to Woolpit's.

Maybe the origin of the apparent high-altitude explosion of February 1173 was on top of the ringwall (giving a new meaning to "We'll guard old Derry's walls"), or on Sydney Jordan's imagined Bifrost-bridge. (Should it be shown broken?) And it wasn't the only such case: as we saw in Chap.20, on the night that St. Columba died in AD 597 on the island of Iona, monks and fishermen in Donegal saw a rising fiery column over Derry, "seen by us to light up the whole world, just like the summer midday Sun, and after that column pierced the sky, darkness followed as if after sunset".[71]

There's one class of natural phenomenon which might explain the 597 event, at least, in theory. Since the 1950's high-altitude pilots have reported seeing lightning strike vertically upwards from the tops of thunderstorms.[72] As previously happened with meteorites, 'Moon glows', ball lightning and other rare phenomena, scientists refused to accept their existence until the evidence became irrefutable - the upward bolts are now called *sprites*, and they reach the upper levels of the atmosphere. Their green and red colours are like auroral arcs.[73] But because they're from the tops of storms, sprites are seldom seen from the ground, and don't light it up like the midsummer Sun.

Trying to make one circle fit all the 'corridor' sites, with radii of 60 miles, 155 or 172, some sites can be made to fit each pattern but others are left out. But for comparison, the Bay of Rainbows on the Moon (Chap.19) is 100 miles across, and as the Sun rises on its ringwall, its floor remains in darkness. The Moon is smaller than an earthlike planet, with no atmosphere to diffuse twilight, and the colony craters are deeper than the Bay, to hold their atmosphere; but even so, if much larger than the Bay they wouldn't be half-lit by reflected sunlight from across the river. Other variations look even less convincing, with bowls approaching the size of the lunar maria.

So Darlington, Peveril Castle and Roche Abbey, Little Barre, and Calne, forming a corridor 225 miles long and 25 miles wide, would take in at least two bowls on the colony world. Darlington is at sea level, but Salisbury Plain, averaging 300 feet above sea-level, puts Calne in the foothills of a ringwall, perhaps on a debris fan, despite the risk of further landslides. It makes it more likely that the Calnas in Wiltshire was involved in what was happening, making the link with Kilkenny and County Leix stronger still. And Avebury (begun in 2700 BC) is in the parish next to Calne, and Stonehenge (begun 2840 BC) is due south of Avebury.

6. Bridge over Troubled Waters

With its five-mile height and fifty-mile span, 'the Sydney bridge' might seem impossible, but now we have several uses for it and there is a way to build it. If you put a piece of string round the equator of the Earth, with the ends touching, and then raised it one foot from the ground all round the planet, how far apart would the ends be? The answer is: 3.142 feet (check it for yourself). But suppose instead you have an airtight hollow tube, with expansion joints and with the air pumped out. Into it you inject iron filings, accelerate them electromagnetically along the tube, and keep going till you have a continuous current of them circling the planet, magnetically suspended and not touching the inner wall.

When circulating speed exceeds 18,000 mph, orbital velocity at the Earth's surface, the tube will be subject to a net outward thrust greater than the pull of Earth's gravity, and will rise and expand. At first you tether it with cables, but as it rises you insert segment after segment of very high towers, whose weight is sustained by the upward force acting on the ring, not by the ground below. When the ring's expanded by 150 miles, the towers are 150 miles high, projecting out of the atmosphere, and you can carry freight up them to be launched electromagnetically, along the ring, to geosynchronous orbit, to the Moon or the planets.[74] It's called 'the orbital ring', but that's misleading: the filings are in *forced* orbit, at more than orbital velocity, and the ring itself is stationary with respect to the ground. Unlike 'space elevators' where the tower would be suspended from a massive satellite in geosynchronous orbit, the orbital ring could be built with existing materials because the structural and dynamic loads on its components are much lower. But there is a way to do it on a smaller scale.

Begin instead with a tube like the storage ring of a supercollider, lying on the ground in some large, flat open area, with iron filings or an iron ribbon circulating inside instead of subatomic particles. Part is free to move and the rest held down by staples like huge croquet hoops, on mobile platforms instead of thrust into the ground. Now, as the iron gains speed, only the free section will rise and the anchored ones will draw closer together. Again you stabilise it with suspended towers, but this time only two are needed, and the section between them will be parallel to the Earth's surface and approached by inclined ramps to the tower tops. The segment between the towers is a 'partial orbital ring' and overall the structure is a 'launch loop'. As before, vehicles can be accelerated electromagnetically to high speeds on the section parallel to the Earth's surface, for launch to higher orbits, to the Moon or beyond.[75] On the planet, instead of lying flat the grounded segment of the loop would pass under the river and up the crater walls, solidly bedded in the rock, structurally more solid than the terrestrial version, with the 'supports' carrying the tube and the inclined ramps for ascending it (Fig. 23.8). It might be even higher up than Sydney's drawn it, giving weather-control lasers greater range, but too high to support biological screens to isolate one bowl from another - maybe impractical, or not desired (see below).

In space elevators, 'beanstalks',[76] the structure extends to the ground from a satellite in geosynchronous orbit, and requires a very large counterweight to balance it. At present there's no suitable material for its construction, though there are hopes for 'nanotubes' woven from the extraordinary carbon molecules known as 'buckyballs'. Martian and lunar tethers are possible with known composites such as Kevlar. For our colony world, a synchronous tether is impracticable because its centre of mass would have to be at either the sun-planet L1 or L2 point, much too far from the planet itself.

Again, there's a smaller-scale way to do it: a rotating tether, 8000 km. long, best pictured as a rimless wheel with two diametrically opposite spokes - also known as a 'skyhook'. As it orbited end-over-end around Earth the tips would dip alternately into the atmosphere every twenty minutes, seeming to come momentarily to rest before lifting away again. The designer, Hans Moravec, visualised the tips bottoming out at 50 km so that ramjet aircraft could rendezvous with them.[77] Over the colony, a cable's rotation could be timed for 'touch and go' on the bridge. For continuous solar power it could be in 'Sun-synchronous' orbit, passing up or down the valley - perhaps touching several bridges on the way - over the pole and back by way of the chaotic terrain on the other side of the planet. It would take coordination to step on and off, since the cable moves at right-angles to the planet's rotation: slow though that is, if its year is as long as Earth's it will be moving at three miles per hour on the equator, a fair pace. Get the timing wrong, and it's a long way down...

The tether could transfer cargoes from bridge to bridge (up to 1000 tons, for the dimensions given above), or aircraft from bowl to bowl, and launch spacecraft into transfers to higher orbit. All could be accomplished by matter transmitter, but another of the rotating tether's properties could be very useful, making local transport ancillary.

As it rotates end-over-end, the tether generates an outward g-pull, varying from nothing at the centre to a highest value at the tips. With the dimensions above, the rotational pull is 1.4 g at the tips. Consequently, when the tether is vertical and the planet's gravity is acting along it, the pull along it varies cyclically between 0.4 and 2.4 g, with intermediate values along its length,[77] bracketing the range for possible habitable planets (Chap.19). 'Mission control' for the matter-transmitter could be in zero-g at its hub (Chap.20); but at a tether tip, it can successively open gates to the range of habitable worlds in the Galaxy, and many with higher or lower gravities. From the other end, you don't have to synchronise transfers: if you activate your key at the wrong point of the cycle, it will just delay your arrival by a few minutes.

Fig. 22.8. Detail of 'the Sydney bridge'.

Finally we should think about the long-term future of the valley. As erosion brought down scree and landslides, the floor would rise, spilling air over the edges, while the river cut deeper. The Colorado has taken five million years to carve the Grand Canyon, but what's the timescale of this experiment? Hundreds of years, hundreds of thousands, more - enough to evolve new life, adaptable to all worlds? If the crater chain triggered plate tectonics, could the river become an ocean, like the Atlantic, with a rising central ridge? Or they could close the valley, ending the experiment when it became less interesting, or the results became dangerous to the makers. As we'll see, they may have underestimated the timescale on which that could happen.

Chapter Twenty-three - THE GUARDIANS OF THE PORTALS

"Quis custodiet ipsos custodes - who will guard the guardians themselves?"

~ Juvenal, *The Satires*

1. "I think we're fished for"

We still don't have an overall scenario; we have limited sources from which to derive one, but we can't leave the story without trying to find 'rational purposes for the supposed Contact', however hypothetical.

In Chap.24 I'm going to suggest that the colony valley was created around 2800 BC. Geological activity would have to stabilise before the river could be created by cometary impacts; perhaps that corresponds to the peak of solar activity in 2250. The primary atmosphere and climate would have to settle down before algae could be introduced to start biological terraforming, and that might correspond to the 1800 BC peak. It might take several attempts to get started, re-tuning environmental factors after each failure, (with corresponding bio-engineering on the algae, perhaps) until one of the algal blooms 'took' and the buildup of a breathable atmosphere began. Later, more advanced life could be introduced by transplanting the ecology of major terrestrial rivers, perhaps even turning some impact basins into land-locked seas. That might tie in with the other historical peak of solar activity, 350 BC - 450 AD.[1]   If all went well, then on the timescale discussed in Chap.23 for making the atmosphere breathable, a bowl could be ready for human settlement by (say) 1100 AD.

The colony would need food, raw materials and products from Earth, till it became self-supporting. That would need an international organisation, self-contained for secrecy, running a network of farms and factories, with its own transport system, regularly moving personnel and equipment on such a scale that the percentage which didn't go to the official destination wouldn't be conspicuous. It sounds like the Templars; Matt Ewart suggested that might have been the true purpose of the Order, with all their other activity a cover for supporting the colony.

As we saw in Chap.3, when they first came into being, before they began recruiting and instead of their official task to protect pilgrims between Ascalon and Jerusalem, supposedly they spent their first nine years excavating large storage chambers under the Dome of the Rock. At the very least, they were confident of growth soon to come. Once they began patrolling pilgrim routes, they'd have plenty of opportunity to recruit or even abduct people without arousing suspicion: Malcolm Barber's *The New Knighthood* quotes vividly the dangers on the Holy Land roads at the time.[2]

Following Charles Fort,[3] it would be a big operation to fish for 10,000 people, but the wars in England would have allowed it to pass unnoticed: Essex was virtually depopulated by the war between Stephen and Matilda, likewise the north of England in 1173. The Crusades could have provided still more opportunity: Peter the Hermit's abortive, civilian crusade, with all its astronomical harbingers, took an estimated 300,000 people off to the Holy Land. "It was not only individual peasants who took the road, but entire villages."[4] None of them arrived, and there are no figures for those who straggled home or were never seen again. It's been estimated that 600,000 soldiers embarked for the official First Crusade soon afterwards; recent estimates are lower, between 100,000 and 136,000, and 50,000 at most were at the taking of Jerusalem in 1099. But it's thought more than 200,000 monks, clerks, women and children followed them to the Holy Land, and there were 100,000 casualties in a backup Crusade of 1101 which most histories don't even mention.[5] Edward Gibbon estimated that more than a million people were involved in the Second Crusade;[4] 30,000 of the German army died of starvation or Turkish arrows without even getting there. The Third Crusade began in 1189-90 with 100,000, (600,000 according to Gibbon), already down to 40,000 by the death of Frederick Barbarossa.[5] The remainder were divided into four groups, one of which was wiped out by sickness, one was imprisoned at Aleppo, one diverted to Bogras and only 5000 reached the Holy Land. Among losses like these, there would be scope for mass abductions on a scale far beyond anything suggested by 20th century Ufologists.

St. Bernard's tour on behalf of the Templars, and the whole support network which arose, might be part of a conspiracy to use extraterrestrial technology – presumably for political and religious gain, resumed in the 13th century when the solar activity returned to normal. Their network of farms, from the west coast of Ireland to Croatia and Slovenia,[6] could be used to sustain the colony.

Instead of a few families quietly supplying it from their manors, as I've been suggesting, we'd have a support organisation extending across Europe with the approval of the nobility, the Vatican, the rulers of Europe and of the Holy Land. The Crusades gained control of the key site in Jerusalem, but could also provide cover for the mass abductions needed to populate the colony and the Templar network needed initially to support it. It may not be the main reason for the Crusades, but those reasons were many and complex and there's room even for one as far-out as this. It would be particularly ironic if the Crusades and the Templar Order were ostensibly to protect pilgrims, but were used to cover a new hazard to them - being shanghaied to an interstellar colony. At least some of the political and religious leaders of the time would have to be aware of what was happening; as I said in Chap.1, *"The X-Files* are set in the wrong century".

I can't stress too much that Contact on this scale is a hypothesis, not a "claim that I have proof". I'm not saying that this did happen; only that it *might* have happened, and wouldn't it be interesting if it did. I did say earlier it was only half-serious; but it's what my initial aim to write an article about the green children has led to. Rick Standley, a musician friend, foresaw where the enquiry was leading and predicted I'd be scared out of my mind by the scenario when I found it; but I don't scare that easily. Probably I ought to be more scared of the academic reaction to it.

In the early 13th century, there was more opportunity to 'fish' for humans, if more recruits were needed - especially if children were wanted as more adapt-able. The Children's Crusade of 1212 showed nothing was learned from the disaster of Peter the Hermit's. Led by a French shepherd boy named Stephen and a boy from Cologne called Nicolas, around 100,000 children marched towards Italy, to sail to the Holy Land, but due to starvation, disease and enforced prostitution, less than a third came home, probably having dropped out early. 7,000 who reached Italy drowned at sea later; Stephen's 'army' was sold into slavery in Egypt; just 18 children reached the Holy Land, to be executed by the Saracens. The Pied Piper story, supposedly in 1284, may be a memory of it, and it would be easy to spirit large numbers away during it.

Perhaps instead there was trouble on the colony world, in which the Templars tried to intervene, or in which they were called on as guardians of the portals. Or did they try to take on the creators of the experiment, rebelling against the

Fortean status of 'property'? If the Matthew Paris incidents are genuine, it would mean rather startlingly that the Templars had access to the technology for a hundred years or more, and perhaps they'd come to think of it as their own, or decided to try for ownership. (Since they called the Holy Land *Outremer*, beyond-the-sea, the word for the colony planet could be *Outré*.) The Paris entries led John Braithwaite, James Bentley and me all to suggest that the Templars might have tried to take over the matter-transmitter system. If all portals were in effect one portal, with one control point, it might seem easy.

In Poul Anderson's novel *The High Crusade*, a spaceship from a military empire lands in a mediaeval village and the occupants try to overawe the people. But local knights have taken the Cross and mustered for the Holy Land, so they charge the ship, take it over, and order the surviving alien to fly them to the relief of king Richard. Instead, he sets the controls for home... so by the time the USA invents the interstellar drive, the Galaxy is under English domination.[7] *The High Crusade* is great fun, partly because the characters take themselves so seriously: I've seen a report on a slapstick film version, which looks disastrous. But whatever the knights at Roche Abbey were practising for, disaster was the result, according to Matthew Paris's margin notes: it didn't succeed, or if it did, the losses were heavy.

When the Abbot of Bury St. Edmunds submitted that old list of knights' fees to the treasury (Chap.4) - also in 1236, interestingly - that concealed de Sherdilowe's occupancy of Wykes and anything unusual he was up to. In 1238, moreover, he and his brother lost control of their lands until their debts were settled. It's not said that they were at the hearing. Robert continued his distinguished career as a king's justiciar, but Hugh makes no further appearance at Wykes[8] or anywhere else that I can find. John Braithwaite remarked, "Did they tell him about the monster in the basement?" If he disappeared, some statutory time had to elapse before the manor was resold. So what happened to Hugh - did he know what he was buying into, and did he survive it?

But for some incidents in mid-14th century (Chap.24), one might think the Templars' participation in the Contact ended with 1236, whatever *that* was. Some very odd things happened to the Order thereafter, but not the kind of oddness we're looking for - likewise what more has been alleged in modern times (Chap.3).

After mistakenly ascribing the *Chronicle of the Holy Land* to Ralph of Coggeshall, Beatrice M. Rose tells an odd story. Ralph, she says, was "carried away" by "the subtle wisdom of the East... He threw himself into the study of black magic and necromancy. He took part in forbidden rites. He knew he had done wrong. He had sinned, had blasphemed. He had committed heresy. He would write a book about it all to show that he repented... When the work was finished he reread the parchment. He sat quiet. It was like reading the life of another man. Suddenly he stood up and told the monk to bring the parchment to the warming room. 'Burn,' he said. The lay brother, a poor tool of a man who did not understand what he wrote, trembled at the loss of so much labour. 'Burn,' said Ralph, and with his old hands seized the roll and cast it into the huge log fire blazing in the centre of the room. The parchment sizzled while the smoke curled up through the roof."[9]

After which, supposedly, he retired - so he'd been practising forbidden rites etc. in Coggeshall for the best part of thirty years, without the rest of the convent (who resisted his retirement) catching on? Ms. Rose says, "This is a story which never was written". I'd class it with the report that the bells of the Abbey can still be heard chiming at midnight,[10] except that I can't shake the idea that I've read it somewhere before, and Abbot Ralph's supposed sins correspond to the accusations made against the Templars, when the Order was brought to an end.

2. The End of an Era

At their height the Templars had an annual income in Europe estimated at six million pounds, from more than nine thousand farms and manors - half to two-thirds that of the Cistercians,[11] who were so far ahead in some respects that in the wool trade, for instance, their clips were committed for years ahead.[12] But the Templars' riches aroused the envy of Philippe the Fair, king of France. In addition, the Templars, the Hospitallers and the Pope were all opposed to his policy for the Holy Land, which involved merging the two wealthy, militant Orders for a new crusade to be led by his son.[13] Getting nowhere with that, in 1308 he arrested the French Templars *en masse*, obtained various confessions by torture and bullied the Pope into ordering similar action throughout Christendom.

The Holy Land was now fully in Moslem hands: the last stronghold, Acre, fell in 1291. The Templars held out for three days after the rest of the city, making their last stand at the round church, by the end of which only ten of the 500-strong garrison survived.[4] The ostensible reasons for the Order's existence no longer applied, but even so response to Philippe's action was patchy, except in states under French control such as Naples and Lombardy. In Germany the prosecution collapsed, in Cyprus it was inconclusive;[13] in Ireland fifteen Templars were tried, with no result.[12]

There were only 144 full Templars in England then: 15-20 knights, 8-16 priests, 108-121 sergeants and serving brothers. The English response to the papal commands was a wonderful forerunner of more recent events: having delayed the problem by commissioning a report, Edward II was ordered in 1310 to extract confessions by torture. He replied that he would like to oblige, but due to recent financial cuts, England had a shortage of torturers.[12]

That was less of a problem elsewhere. The Inquisition to seek out heretics was formalised by 1233 and assigned to the Dominicans and Franciscans by Pope Gregory IX (1227-41). The ironically named Innocent IV added the use of torture in 1252.[14] In 1308 there were experts on tap, but even then it was said that many interrogators of the Templars were drunk and called in local children as assistants. Frying the feet in oil or batter was one of the favourite techniques.

Altogether, about 900 Templar depositions survive to the present.[11] But even where the victims were willing to 'confess', men who could live happily under the Rule of the Templars lacked the imagination to invent any interesting sins, even to save themselves from torture. Instead they confessed in hapless repetition to a banal list of crimes drafted by king Philippe and his chief minister, Guillaume de Nogaret: these featured minor acts of homosexuality, such as kissing the navel of the brother admitting one to the Order.

More seriously, the brothers were accused of spitting on a cross and denying the divinity of Christ, again during the initiation ceremony. It's generally supposed that if it had any truth, this was a distorted version of an obedience test, but in *The Holy Blood and the Holy Grail* Baigent, Leigh and Lincoln suggest that the Templars were set up to handle the discovery, in Jerusalem, of evidence that Christ's death on the cross was faked, and that he had a son by

Mary Magdalene whose blood-line descended through the Germanic Merovingian kings (the ones who officially claimed descent from a four-horned sea creature.)[15] 'Let each man say of this what he will', but to me it seems at odds with what the Templars were doing for the rest of their two centuries in the Holy Land. "And it's one, two, three, four, what are we fighting for...?"

The only significant confessions concerning the Order's day-to-day activities involved worshipping an idol. Here too the imaginations of the victims failed, most describing it simply as like a human head or a cat. Where given a name it was called 'Baphomet', or in some cases not attempting even that elementary disguise, 'Mahomet'.[13] Marion Melville says that the name was first used by a victim giving evidence in the Provençal *langue d'oc*, in which the 'M' was transformed to a 'B' - also in Scots, as it happens. Still another version makes it an idol of a demon called *un maufé*.[5] But if the accusers claimed it was Mohammedan that was nonsense, because the Moslem faith bars all representational art, let alone idolatry.

One or two with more education described the head as a product of necrophilia, thrown into the Gulf of Satalia, where it consumed fish and caused whirlpools and storms, like the head of the Gorgon Medusa - a classical story, retold by Roger de Hoveden and reinforced by an encounter between the king of France's ship and a waterspout on his way back from the Holy Land in 1191.[16] The dead woman in the horror story was called Yse, whom Gérard de Sède identifies with Isis,[17] suggesting the original story was *much* older.

Ishtar/Astarte is much more likely in this context. Satalia in Crusading times was ancient Adalia/Attaleia, modern Antalya, the largest seaport on the south coast of Turkey: Saint Paul sailed from there to Antioch, Louis VII's fleet sailed to Syria from there in the Second Crusade, and in the Third Richard I gathered his fleet there before taking Cyprus. It faces straight across to Paphos on Cyprus. Old Paphos dates from 1200 BC at least, possibly 1800 BC at the end of the Trojan War. New Paphos, ten miles west, was destroyed by the Saracens in 960 AD, but it dated from Roman times and is also known as Paphu or Baffo, or, in French, Bapho.[14] It was the centre of the cult of Aphrodite, formerly Ishtar and later Astarte, worshipped there as sea-foam (from which she was born) and also in the form of a black conical stone.

(Presumably like the *Omphalos* stone at Delphi, and similar ones at shrines of Zeus and Apollo. Although called 'the navel of the world', it belonged to a different mythology from the Jewish and Moslem 'navels' at the birthplace of Adam – though Fig. 21.10 marks the Compass as 'Omphalos'.) So 'Baphomet' *could* relate to Sibylla de Calna's crescent and star on her personal seal (Chap. 15), and Stephan de Tournai's reference to "the planet of the Cyprian" (Chap. 14).

Another charge sheet referred to worship of 'weird women' who appeared and disappeared in the vicinity of the idols, none which were ever found.[13] There are only three descriptions of the head. Étienne de Troyes described it as very bluish, with dog-like hair, and a black-and-white beard like some Templars', wearing a jewelled collar. This was one of the most detailed, given by a man who had left the Order, and didn't claim he had been tortured. His description suggests a reliquary - a holder for the bones of a saint or, in this case, perhaps of Hugues de Payens, the founder of the Order;[14] in fact, one defendant swore in front of the Pope that it was just that.[11] The colour was probably the result of poor embalming. One Bartholomew Bochier gave a similar description, saying it wore a cap - like the Templars themselves - and had a long grey beard.[14] Andreas Armanni, a *frère marié* who had been in the Order only eight or nine months, said the idol was a cubit high with three heads.[11] A major search for a suitable head, at the Templar stronghold in Paris, found only a silver-gilt reliquary, containing the skull of a small woman. Baphomet - Bapho - Paphos - Astarte - Aphrodite - Ishtar... could the head possibly have been Agnes's, or Sibylla de Calna's? It has an interesting tale attached to it, but that's a very different story.

In France, the leaders of the Order withdrew their confessions and were burned at the stake. Elsewhere the consequences were milder. In Spain the Templars were absorbed into the Orders of St. James (who were allowed to marry) or of Calatrava; king Denis of Portugal refused the papal order to suppress the Templars and created the Order of Christ for them, under which they played a major rôle in prince Henry's 15th century exploration of the African coast.[5] In Scotland all but two Templars escaped, and their trial in Dublin was inconclusive: folklore has it that the rest joined the guerrillas of Robert the Bruce, to play a major part at Bannockburn in 1314.[18]

The Bruce never ratified the Scottish Templars' dissolution, and Masonic tradition says he admitted all Templars to the Royal Order of Scotland the same year.[19] His heart was taken to the Holy Land by William de St. Clair, Master of the Templars in Scotland; he later brought back the heart and remains of four knights, whose short coffins have led to suggestions that their bones were buried in the shape of the skull and crossbones.[20] It was a Templar emblem, carved for example into the base of their tower in Hackney,[21] and a recent burglary in Australia has brought to light that human skulls-and-crossbones are used in some Masonic rites as a *memento mori*,[22] so perhaps that's the explanation for the idol-worship accusations. James Bentley suggested that the raid on Coggeshall Abbey cemetery was to obtain bones, for a secret initiation ceremony in the Guest House. But to justify desecration of a Cistercian cemetery it would need very high priority, especially if done with the knowledge of the Abbot.

William de la More, the last Master in England, died in prison,[23] still maintaining his innocence. Many English Templars were 'retired' to monasteries, including Roche Abbey,[24] where they weren't always welcome. The Order's properties were assigned to the Hospitallers, and quite a lot were handed over, once stripped of their assets; in France, especially, former Templar properties were unprofitable long after.[25]

If the Templars asked for extraterrestrial help in 1308, then publicly, at least, they didn't get it. Unlike 1178, which needed only some celestial fireworks to awe king Henry, to prevent the arrests and trials across Christendom would require major intervention, perhaps more than the visitors could permit themselves (Chap.24). The only marvel was in Ireland, apparently 'Moon-dogs' caused by high-altitude ice crystals, and did the Templars no good at all. "Also on the morrow of St. Luce the Virgin, the third year of the reign of Edward, there were six moons, which was marvelled much of. They were of diverse colours, whereby it was judged and thought that the Order of the Templars should be suppressed and done away for ever."[25]

Around 1318, a supernova should have been visible in the south-east of the constellation Vela.[26] 1295 AD is an alternative date. Nearly as far south as the Southern Cross, it wasn't visible from Europe, but it should have been seen from Jerusalem and Egypt, Morocco and points south. But there are no known records of it, although at a distance of 500-600 light-years, it could have been brighter than the Full Moon.[27]

3. I See No Ships

The disposal of the Templar fleet remains a mystery. As we saw in Chap.3, in 1139 Eleanor of Aquitaine allowed them a 'freeport' in La Rochelle for their Atlantic trade. The port refused to support Richard in the rebellion of 1173,[28] and Henry III lost it in 1224,[29] because he couldn't spare troops from the siege of Bedford (Chap.24).   Bordeaux, Nantes, Bristol and Dover were also Templar ports,[2] and one major export from Bristol was wool from their own farms.   Horses were shipped in great numbers, and Moslem slaves brought back.   The first known ship of their own is at Constantinople in 1207, but it seems there was a big expansion in Templar shipping by 1216, after which many ships are named.   The Order had unrestricted sailings from Marseilles then, in great convoys for protection against pirates, but the competition annoyed local shippers and by 1233 they and the Hospitallers were restricted to two sailings per year each to the Holy Land from there:[5] *Passagium Martis* and *Passagium Sancti Johannis*,[23] at the spring equinox and summer solstice respectively - interesting dates, given what we've seen in Chap. 21.   They also had regular sailings from Spain.[5]   At Acre, the principal destination, they maintained a permanent fleet and a large complex of buildings in the southwest quarter.[30]

The ships were *esnecciae*, smacks, with sail power alone; galleys with two tiers of oars, based on Norse 'Drakhars'[15] and Roman designs; and transports, 'busses' in northern Europe, 'dromonds' in the Mediterranean and Levant. They were seaworthy in the Atlantic, so it remains odd that Richard I, warned of likely arrest at Toulouse, chose to go up the Adriatic and try to get home overland instead of just sailing past Gibraltar.[31] Large numbers of people and enormous quantities of goods were transported by the Templars: 6000 pilgrims a year just within the Mediterranean, from Spain, France and Italy.[2] Because of the restrictions at Marseilles their ships carried as many as 1500 people; few names have come down to us, but *La Templere* and *Le Buscard' de Templo* are on record in 1230/ 31, probably out of service by 1308.[32]   *La Blanche Garde* was a later one, named for a great Templar castle in the Holy Land, and *The Falcon*, purchased from the Genoese in 1291 and used in the

406

final evacuation of Acre, was reputedly the largest ship to date.[2] *La Maîtresse* was a floating bank, with a safe deposit, a *huche*, for treasure entrusted to her.[25] So where did they all go?

The colony has a large river flowing through it, so it would be easy for 'special' ships to detach from the fleet, and rejoin the convoy on its way back; or to rendezvous with ships from the colony, transfer human or material cargoes, and later blame pirates or slavers if questions were asked. Do such transfers explain the mystery ships, with weapons and supplies for an army, off Berwick (Chap.17)? They weren't any of the seagoing types above, and they were forced ashore by high winds - perhaps because they were primarily for river operations.

I even found a possible instance, in the evacuation of Acre in 1291. Gustave Schlumberger tells us, "The fantastic account of Ludolf de Suchem [who visited Acre and wrote it up in 1335] of the five hundred ladies and young women of quality, running to the port, offering their jewels and even their hand in marriage to anyone who could save them, then suddenly and happily conducted to Cyprus by a mysterious sea-captain who disappeared immediately afterwards, is certainly nothing but a legend."[28] He may well be right... but still...

Bad weather could cover transfers: despite Richard I's efforts to prevent it, knowing how often it happened, 25 ships were separated from his fleet on the way to the Holy Land in 1191. Two were wrecked on Cyprus, others re-located and some rescued, but some were never seen again.[31] If there was regular traffic to and from the colony, under cover of sailings to the Holy Land, perhaps this explains the de Calnas' acquisition of a ship (from La Rochelle) in 1225, just after they reclaimed Wykes (Chap. 15); and also the disappearance of the fleet in 1308. The bigger the ship, the safer a transfer would be: in Chap.22, Andrew Paterson calculated that the emergence point could vary up and down by a metre over the lunar month. If a rowing-boat materialised a metre down it would be swamped, and from a metre up it would come down very hard, but a big ship would just rise or settle to its natural buoyancy level.

Moving the Templar fleet to the colony world, in 1308, would allow a rescue on the scale of Dunkirk. The total of Templars brought to trial was far below the full complement of the Order: 900 that we know of, from an estimated 5-20,000 throughout Europe. When the 546 members of the Order imprisoned in France were collected together in Paris, only 18 of them were knights.[33] The knights tortured and burned, or retired after 'confessing', might have missed the boat, literally, or volunteered to stay, to cover the escape of the rest.

At the destination, hundreds of ships in a bowl 100 miles across would give them control of the river or an inland sea, a more effective takeover than an attack on the ground (if that is what they attempted in 1236). If Sydney Jordan's right about the grading in the river bed creating waterfalls at the 'steps' between bowls, they would need locks or portage to get into the next bowls up or down - or shipyards, if wood was available - if there was no higher-tech opposition. But if the divisions between bowls were no obstacles, the Templar fleet could take control a long way up and down-river. *The High Crusade* might not be far off the mark, after all.

Chapter Twenty-four - PAST CONTACT AND THE MOVING GOALPOSTS

Bethan   But the moon smiles on them always,
                    The moon smiles back at them.
Sara   All of the world
                    Calls that a smile.   I call it a frightened stare
                    At something crawling up behind us.

~ Glyn Maxwell, *Wolfpit*

1. Castles in the Air

Between the 1250s and the 1360s, for the duration of the Wolf Minimum, there were no spectacular events in the sky and no strange ones on the ground. 'Absence of evidence is not evidence of absence', and I mightn't suggest the correlation was significant, were it not that both types of event began again as soon as the Wolf Minimum ended.   It may be a foretaste that in 1227, Henry III directed Robert de Sherdilowe (whose brother bought Wykes, eight years later) to retrieve 11,000 marks from the Master of the Templars in England, by order of the Pope, in settlement of a debt concerning Bedford Castle.[1]   The earl of Bedford was William Beauchamp, who had been trying to get the castle back since 1217, and when the holders refused, in one of a series of challenges to Henry III, the castle was taken by siege in 1224 and largely destroyed; the rebel garrison was hanged and Beauchamp took over.

William de Cantilupe was another dissident, and Calne was one of the first places seized - but at Bedford de Cantilupe sided with the king, and got his Wiltshire property back in hereditary right.[2]   There was something strange about the affair:[3] there was no obvious reason to bring matters to a head at that time, and diverting resources to it had severe consequences elsewhere, including the loss of La Rochelle (Chap.23).   But this restored earl of Bedford was the same William Beauchamp poisoned with Richard de Clare in 1262; and 137 years later again, even stranger things were happening at Bedford.

"In the year of grace 1399, and the 22nd year of king Richard, on the day of the Lord's Circumcision [January 1st], near Bedford, a very deep water, which ran between the villages of Suelleston and Harewood, suddenly stopped and divided itself, so that for three miles it remained dry, presenting dry access to anyone.   This prodigy was seen by many to signify the division of the kingdom, and the departure of the king; which happened that year."[4] Probably a natural event (though not the first we've had on January 1st), although the only similar ones I've found involved tidal rivers, the Medway and the Thames, when low tides coincided with drought in 1114.[5]   But if it wasn't natural, it had nothing to do with Richard II's forced abdication.   In 1402:

"In this summer, even, fast by the towns of Bedford and Biggleswade, appeared certain men of divers colours, running out of woods, and fighting horribly.   This was seen on mornings and at midday; and when men followed to look what it was, they could see 'right nothing'."[6]   This comes from John Capgrave, 1393-1464, provincial head of the Augustinians in England and (probably) Prior of Lynn.   The 19th century editor dismisses it with the word 'Legend'; should we do the same?   Bedford isn't in the 'corridors' of Chap.17, but the 'very deep water' was the Ouse, which links Bedford to Ely and King's Lynn,[7] and Bedford was where Sibylla and Agnes laid claim to Aston (Chap.14).

The same dismissal ('Legend') appears on an earlier entry, for 1361: "Both in England and in France also appeared castles in certain forests, and in desert places, out of which castles went two hosts, one white, the other black; and sometimes the white had the victory, when they fought, and sometimes the black had the victory; and suddenly the castle and the hosts vanished and were not seen."

Thomas Walsingham gives details.   "And in the summer time of this year, in England and in France, in places unoccupied and flat, two castles were often seen by many suddenly to appear, from which two armies of armed men came forth; of whom one was decorated with the symbol of knights, the other indeed showed a black colour: and when they came together, the knights conquered the blacks.   At another time, the blacks overcame the knights, and returning into the castles everything disappeared."[4]

As with the green children, when an unusual event is in more than one chronicle, and in different words, it encourages us to take it seriously. "Desert places... unoccupied and flat" ring true: northern France was depopulated by the Hundred Years' War and the Black Death, which struck for the third time in 1361.[8] But the castles and mock battles aren't in the very detailed 14th century chronicle by John Froissart.[9]

Motte-and-bailly castles could rapidly be put up and torn down. But as Bill Ramsay pointed out, any large structure which wasn't a church would be 'a castle', especially if it had a monolithic appearance, because there were no other large buildings. Like the 'phantoms' of Chap.7, the armies appeared and disappeared at will; perhaps in 1192, 1236 and 1366, they were in training. 1192 was the year that Richard I marched on Jerusalem, and parties of crusaders were permitted to visit sacred sites including the Holy Sepulchre; was there a Trojan Horse among them, planning to retake the city from within (Chap.14)? There's a reference in 1330-31 to a mobile 'castle' in a tournament at Valenciennes,[10] and the 1366 black armies matched against white sound like 'living chess'. But the Templar banner, the 'Beauseant', was half black, half white: the Order had been destroyed in 1308, but was it as dead as it was supposed to be, and if not, what were they training for?

In 1402, 'divers colours' - including green? - were fighting 'horribly', but apparently with mediaeval weapons and hand-to-hand; not too scary to approach, unlike the knights at Roche Abbey. Extraterrestrials breed human warriors in science fiction: rearing groups of different skin colours, and encouraging competition between them, could be part of the process. Using Earth itself for training exercises would be risky, especially with the Black Death in 1361. But it's remarkable that 'appearing and disappearing' events restart then, only thirteen years after John Bardwell acquired rights in Wykes and probably in Woolpit, apparently having married a descendant of Richard and Agnes (Chap.17). John's son William was nearly adult by 1361 and his rights in Bardwell probably included Wykes.[11] Regaining Wykes was important to Sibylla and her husband, and bearing in mind what happened when Sibylla gave it up, we should look closely at the 1360s.

In 1359 the Normans lost Aghaboe to the Irish Fitz-Patricks,[12] and it remained 'beyond the pale' for centuries. In 1360, according to several sources, a Franciscan friar, mathematician and astronomer of Oxford named

Nicholas of Lynn voyaged to Norway, and travelled all the way *a gradu 54 usque ad polum* [from 54 degrees to the Pole], alone, making observations with an astrolabe.[13] His book *A Fortunate Invention*, including an account of the Maelstrom, was presented to Edward III and described by John Dee, who thought Nicholas had also visited Iceland on his five voyages. (Edward III gave the fishermen of Lynn extensive privileges of trade with Iceland, which Dee said could be reached by a fortnight's sailing in good weather.)

Nicholas of Lynn might be descended from Richard de Calna (Chap.13). That and the loss of Aghaboe may be coincidental; and that when the intriguingly named John de Aston was abbot of Roche between 1358 and 1396, the advowson of the Abbey passed from a John Levet to Richard Barry, citizen and merchant of London,[14] who may or may not be the Richard Barre recorded in Staffordshire in the mid-fourteenth century; but even if these changes at Aghaboe and Roche aren't linked to the 1360s incidents, if they might be 'digressions', we should look at the state of the Sun.

2. Uneasy Skies Once More

Although quiet by comparison with the 1170s, solar activity was on the rise from 1361 to 1402, with naked-eye sightings of sunspots again, and a corresponding rise in carbon-14 ratios at the end of the 'Wolf Minimum' (Fig. 20.3). In 1192 the Sun was again very active, as we saw in Chap.14. And sure enough, under 1361 or 1362 we find, recorded by "a certain monk of Malmesbury" and copied by other chronicles:

"In this year on the 25th day of the month of February in the middle of the night there appeared from thin air a certain glowing cloud like a fire, by which men could see small stones and grains of sand at their feet, and they could thread a needle at midnight because the light was so great; which cloud caused great fear to the beholders."[17]

In 1366, on 12th January, John of Reading recorded, "after sundown till it rose again, a great redness covering the whole firmament; now bloody, now fiery white, beams were emitted backwards from it, illuminating the earth and its buildings just as if day were dawning. In which the stars twinkled more than usual…"[5]

Later that year, however, the lid came off - a metaphor the Malmesbury monk would probably have used if he knew it. "In this year, on the 22nd day of the month of October, with Dawn appearing and the Moon shining as if Full, burning torches were seen in the firmament, more of the colour of blood than of fire, descending from the globe of the Moon, extending to the west where the Full Winter Moon is usually found, emitting burning flames here and there in opposite directions, hurling burning darts to the North and northern regions. Also more than a hundred stars were seen to fall from the sky although no star in the heavens appeared to be missing. This was seen in Oxfordshire, in Gloucestershire, in Wiltshire by more than three hundred people."[15]

The Earth encounters fifty or so meteor showers every year. When a comet passes close to the Sun, dust particles are driven off, sometimes forming a separate 'dust tail', because dust grains move slower than gaseous ions under sunlight pressure. Diffracted sunlight can make dust tails appear red, and as relative motions often put a curve on a comet's tail, it didn't take much mediaeval imagination to see a bloody scimitar in the sky and predict disaster for Christians in the Holy Land.

Dust spreads along the comet's orbit, and if the Earth's orbit intersects it, there's a meteor shower. The meteors are on parallel tracks, but perspective makes them seem to come from a single point in the sky called the *radiant*. The constellation containing the radiant gives the shower its name: meteors from Comet Tempel-Tuttle are called the Leonids, and they now come in November, due to planetary perturbations and to changes in the calendar – but in mediaeval times, they were in October.

A meteor shower might share the sky with an aurora, but if it keeps happening, that's more remarkable. The *Gesta Stephani* records simultaneous meteors and aurora in 1138, confirmed by John of Worcester, and that too was in October – and just after king Stephen had besieged and taken Bedford, as it happens.[5] The meteors were almost certainly Leonids:[16] techniques developed by Drs. David Asher and Robert McNaught now allow Leonid storms to be predicted very accurately, and the 1138 event was probably on October 13th - although, oddly, the known meteor stream would have struck at 11 a.m. and not been visible in Britain.[17]

The Leonids travel in narrow streams close to the comet and major displays occur at 33-year intervals when Tempel-Tuttle swings past the Sun.[18]   In 1966 there were displays over the USA before dawn, though nothing was seen in Britain.   There were signs that the next 33-year peak would be big - in November 1997 several satellites suffered minor damage [19] - and in 1998 there was a major storm over Britain, a year and a day ahead of schedule.   But on November 17th, 1999, from Dumfriesshire, I counted 226 meteors in an hour. On November 18th, 2000, when the Moon's position virtually coincided with the Leonid radiant, conditions in Scotland were cloudy, but any meteors would have seemed to be coming from the Moon,[20] like the 1366 ones. There's small chance of that at the same time as an auroral display, unless the Sun is very active at the time.

In October 1366, the 'burning torches' were "descending from the globe of the Moon, extending to the west where the Full Winter Moon is usually found". In the Julian calendar then in use, the Full Moon was on October 19th.[21]   So it would have been on the wane by the 22nd, and in the west at dawn, as described.   The date is early for the Leonids, but the Taurid meteors also occur during October, especially in the first two weeks.   They come from the short-period Comet Encke, possibly a survivor from the break-up of a super-comet around 3000 BC (see below).   They're not currently associated with major displays, keeping up "a drizzle through most of the month"[22] - though from time to time that includes bright fireballs - but when the Earth crosses the dust stream from it again in June, that shower is much more intense (Chap.12), and may have included the multiple fragments which hit the lunar Farside in 1178.   So a big Taurid display in October 1366 is possible.

But "emitting burning flames here and there in opposite directions, hurling burning darts to the North and northern regions. *Also* more than a hundred stars were seen to fall from the sky..." (my emphasis)?   Auroral displays are centred on magnetic north, normally.   The Moon has no magnetic field of its own, but this description reads as if the Moon had temporarily acquired a magnetic field much more intense than the Earth's, or that a very highly charged, conducting stream of particles was being projected from the Moon towards the Earth.   It couldn't be coming from the Sun past the Moon, because they were on opposite sides of the sky.

"In the same year on the 8th day of the month of October, at daybreak, burning torches were seen to flock together in the firmament, travelling here and there, extending from the lunar globe to the Earth, one as thick as a human arm and up to three cubits long, one up to six, one up to twelve, with very sharp spikes at their upper tips, thickening all the way to the bases, made in the form of wax tapers, but a hundred times thicker, showing proportionate length. For this vision lasted for two full hours, as was related to us by two brother monks who were travelling at that time, nor can this be called what the astronomers call a lunar eclipse, because in no part was [the Moon] damaged nor its light obscured, but by its clear light stars were seen to fall, although in all the sky no star appeared missing; however that was seen by many to light up the void below the firmament as much as if someone was searching with a burning torch inside a dome or hollow place, looking through windows or chinks, so from within there appeared such great burning beams with very sharp upper tips, more extended in many fine points, gradually diminishing until consumed from the South and West to the North and East crossing by slow steps."[15]

Unable to measure degrees and minutes of arc, the unknown monk ties himself in knots trying to give a full account (William of Newburgh, are your ears burning?) In the 14th century 'tapers' were very large candles, weighing 24 pounds or more.[23] Again it sounds like plumes of dust and ionised gas from the Moon, like the onset of the divine plague on Egypt in *The Ten Commandments*, causing aurorae and meteor showers as they hit Earth's atmosphere, and shifting around the rim of the lunar disc (Fig. 25.2). The 1998 Leonid peak was at New Moon, and a 'tail' of sodium atoms was blasted off the lunar surface towards the Earth, propelled by sunlight and the solar wind.[24] Transient lunar events caused by impacts were seen again in 1999;[25] but the 1366 accounts seem as if the Farside was shielding Earth from the worst of intense particle beams, like the exhaust of an antimatter-powered photon drive.

Fig. 25.2. 1366 'flares'.
Drawing by Sydney Jordan.

The meteors were natural, though there's at least one mistake in the chronicle. The Moon was full on October 19th, 1366, so it couldn't have "no part damaged nor its light obscured" on the 8th, when it would be a crescent in the evening sky and not visible at daybreak at all.   It's more likely that the date, given as *octavo die mensis Octobris*, should be *vicesimo octavo*, the 28th, as the 22nd is written *vicesimo secundo*. That would put the Moon east of south at daybreak, even though the effect was "gradually diminishing until consumed from the South and West to the North and East crossing by slow steps", which sounds more like the event of the 22nd.   Moving the second one to the 28th would explain why it's chronicled after the one of the 22nd.

So the 28th meteors *were* Leonids, with Leo in the morning sky.   Planetary perturbations have now moved the peak to November 17th, but in the 10th century, Leonid showers would be on October 20th.   In the mid-1300s they'd be expected on November 5th, but the calendar hadn't yet been reformed, so they'd be recorded on October 28th. That fits the second display to perfection; the year might seem wrong, but the comet's period isn't exactly 33 years, and a Chinese sighting of it in 1366 was used by Joachim Schubart to calculate it precisely and locate the comet on its brief appearance in 1965.[26]   Another method of calculation gives October 22nd, which would fit the first one,[21] but not both - especially if both were centred on the Moon, in which case the first stream would have to be Taurids.   So the meteor events were probably on the 22nd and 28th, Taurids and Leonids respectively; but what about 'thick tapers', 'burning beams', and the shifting rayed effect like torchlight through windows?

Consecutive showers during aurorae would be surprising, since ordinarily there's no link between the two: aurorae occur at much higher levels, in much more tenuous atmosphere, than the burn-out of a meteor.   To make both displays entirely natural, we'd have to assume a Moon in Taurus during an auroral storm which happened to occur during a Taurid meteor peak, followed less than a week later by a Moon in Leo during an auroral storm which happened to occur during a Leonid peak.   Other accounts indicate storms on the 21st and 23rd as well as the 22nd,[16] and still another describes falling stars, which supposedly burned the clothes of people struck by them,[5] on October 31st - with no mention of the Moon, which would be disappearing into the dawn by then.   Perhaps all five are inaccurate accounts of the same event and the simultaneous auroral display wasn't really centred on the Moon, as David

Asher suggested.[17] But since the Moon's placing in the Malmesbury accounts is apparently accurate, showing the chronicler's taken pains to give a detailed description, he's unlikely to have got that wrong. The 'moving spear' effect which he noted was remarked on by Edmund Halley in 1716, when he collated accounts for the Royal Society of the rare, intensive type of auroral storm which Halley dubbed 'coronal'. But in coronal aurora the distinctive feature is that the arcs appear to be centred on the observer's zenith (Chap.3): some 18th century accounts compare the effect to a Maltese Cross suspended overhead.[27] If the 1366 observers had seen anything like that, they would surely have described it, rather than saying the effect was centred on the Moon which was low in the sky.

A magnetic field centred on the Moon, powerful enough to distort the Earth's field and generate an auroral storm, might be a side-effect of a protective system for installations exposed to the meteor showers on the lunar Farside. There could be a portal at the L2 point, in line with the centres of Earth and Moon, unseen from here and 150, 000 miles behind the Moon. A body orbiting the Earth at that distance would make an apparent orbit around L2, coming into view over the rim of the Moon. Recurring plane-change manoeuvres ('phase jumps') could keep it permanently in view in 'halo orbit',[28] or, with more expenditure of mass and energy, keep it out of sight. One solution could be to anchor it to the centre of the Farside with a space elevator (Chap.23) linking the portal to the lunar surface.[29] Perhaps from there some kind of protective shield could be deployed over the Farside, with a magnetic field whose bow shock in the Solar Wind streamed back and impinged on the Earth's.

"The Moon's had a glut of strangers", says one of Glyn Maxwell's characters in *Wolfpit*.[30] Were the events on Earth part of a real war, or were they and the lunar ones just a game? Remember the Iain M. Banks quotation in Chap.22: for these beings, the question isn't, 'Is it profitable?', 'Is it wasteful?' but ultimately 'Is it entertaining?' One would like to think that the actions of a culture so far ahead of us in technology and presumably in evolution would be 'environmentally and ethically positive', but there's no guarantee of that. At his untimely death, the late Chris Boyce was working on a book to be titled *ET Presence*, in which he was going to argue that by our standards, advanced societies might be very unethical indeed.

Perhaps I'm being unjust to the visitors. If they were performing some peaceful task behind the Moon so that it couldn't harm the Earth, perhaps the fighting on-planet was the equivalent of a 'friendly' between works football teams. If a Contact situation existed and its creators were as far ahead of us in technology as I've supposed, it would be surprising if we could deduce all their purposes and methods from glimpses in mediaeval chronicles. And it would be surprising if their attitude to us wasn't sometimes casual, seen from our viewpoint.

But greater physical power doesn't mean we should concede them moral superiority. I'm with those who believe, with Immanuel Kant, that ethics are intimately related to logic, and both are universal and binding on all rational agents.[31] If so, there is no such thing as the SF cliché, 'a higher order of logic', and still less could there be a higher or even a different order of ethics. As a much younger Bill Ramsay put it in the *Man and the Stars* discussions, cutting that Gordian Knot very neatly, "If their ethics are different from ours, we're not going to get on very well with them, are we?"[32] No indeed; and since that's what ethics are *for*, they should be universal and in Contact situations we should accept no substitutes. The correlation of such great events in the sky with apparently trivial skirmishing on the ground makes one decidedly uneasy. On that count, what are we to make of the previous lunar event, the formation of the Giordano crater in 1178?

Perhaps it was a natural, multiple impact, which the visitors directed to the Moon rather than the Earth - a diversion, not a digression. There are several ways to deflect an incoming comet or asteroid: most involve nuclear weapons, but Gordon Ross and I proposed a 'comet-chaser' with a parabolic solar sail and an adaptive optic system, to burn 'hot spots' on the nucleus, forming controllable jets by which to steer it.[33] To prevent a Shoemaker-Levy event would take a small fleet of these craft, but they could be manufactured cheaply and easily in space, if there was time available.

But if the visitors can stage multiple impacts with hundreds of asteroids and thousands of comets ranged in order of size, forming the colony valley, then staging one such event would be trivial - our 'comet-chasers' would be low-tech by comparison. Why not make the 1178 threat miss the Earth-Moon system altogether? Maybe they wanted us to realise, 800 years later, that they were here: an interesting way of doing it without generating the culture shock of full Contact. But if it began as a natural event, isn't it extraordinary that such a threat to Earth should arise in just the period when they happened to be here?

After the birth of Richard, later de Rushell/Rulegh, illegitimate son of Agnes, was the display of violence on the Moon a warning to Henry to leave the family alone in future? Perhaps it was in response to wider pressure from Henry II. If *he* wanted control of operations, perhaps he thought it was time to make his play. He'd seen the French expulsion of the Templars in 1160, and he could threaten their holdings in England. That, and an assault on Agnes, might have been part of pressure he exerted on Richard de Calna, and/or Richard de Hastings, when he was at Wykes at the end of April 1177 and in Bury St. Edmunds at Easter.

A comet could have been hurled past Jupiter in (say) 1176, soon after the Templars were identified at Coggeshall, perhaps, to break up and cause multiple impacts on the Moon in 1178. But even that implies 'storing' comets in the matter-transmitter system, as uncollapsed probability waves (Chap.20), ready for materialisation at will. So no Jupiter flyby was needed, and the impacts could be in response to threats from Henry only days or weeks before, and so have much more effect. The visitors would have had the drop on us, literally, all along, and their emissaries could make that point to Henry with some force. The explosions of 1172, 1173 and December 1178 could have been 'digressions' from that armoury, and the June '78 event could be a similar accident. But in the context of the Templars' raid on Coggeshall and Henry's likely reaction to it, the 1178 one looks more purposeful and more frightening. James Bentley suggested that instead it might be unrelated to events on Earth: a final discharge of energy which would seal off the matter-transmitter portal for good. But the lunar installation would have to be very large if it took twelve explosions that size to destroy it. The builders might instead have been creating a facility, since the 1360s events suggest that operations continued behind the Moon for 190 years.

But why create a new crater, rather than use an existing one? Outgassing in that 1178 event was very powerful, if the observed darkening of the Moon was due to a temporary atmosphere, and if the newly formed crater could be capped in time, it would be relatively easy to pressurise the dome and make its atmosphere breathable. When it was over the lunar enclave could be destroyed simply by removing its cover and decompressing it; that might account for the 1366 event, when the Moon was in the morning sky and sunlight pressure would blow the escaping dust and gas towards Earth. But if that was the end of the Contact, it leaves the 1402 fighting men of 'divers colours' outside the frame.

In *Man and the Stars*, I suggested that past Contact in recorded history hadn't happened more than four times, of which the 3500-2500 BC slot could be one;[32] further research with Alan Evans, prior to this book, made me narrow it down to just that one, and to 2900-2500 BC. Now we have another in the 12th century AD, and the Chap. 21 revelations have made me add still another c.10,500 BC, but there's no indication of Contact, that I know of, between 2500 BC and the 12th century, and it's unlikely that the human colony I've envisaged on the children's world could be in existence, in isolation, all that time. If it were, I'd expect major epidemics when Contact was resumed - but the Black Death and the Plague weren't till much later.

3. 1402 to the Present

With the onset of the Spörer Minimum immediately after 1400, sunspots and aurorae ceased for a time, and looking for events since then which might fit into the Contact scenario, I found virtually nothing. In 1544 the manor of North Fambridge was taken over by the new earls of Essex - the Devereux family,[34] by now descended fully from Richard Barre and Agnes[35] (Chap.17). In 1547, the end of the Spörer Minimum was shown by a three-day obscuration of the Sun in which stars were visible in daylight and spots could be seen on the Sun's disc.[36] The solar cycles which followed were of normal intensity (Fig. 20.3), but there was a major auroral display in 1564, following prolonged meteor showers the previous winter.[37] John Stow recorded an exceptional aurora in 1566: "...at night from seven of the clock till nine was seen in the element as though the same had opened the breadth of a great sheet and showed a great flame of fire and then closed again, and as it were at every minute of an hour to open and close again, the which I being at the Barrs without Aldgate saw plain east as it were over the church called Whitechapel." ('Barrs', promising as it sounds, doesn't refer to the family but to the 'bars' or barriers which marked the limits of the city's jurisdiction, where tolls were levied – such as Holborn Bar and Temple Bar, mentioned in earlier chapters.)

He saw another big aurora in 1574, on 14th November, coming from a black cloud in the north like the 1173 event.[38] It was followed next night by a major coronal display.

At Aldeburgh in Suffolk, north of Orford, in 1642: "A sign from Heaven, or a Fearful and Terrible Noise was Heard in the Ayre at Aldborow in the County of Suffolk, on Thursday the Fourth Day of August, at five of the clocke in the afternoone - wherein was heard the beating of Drums, the discharging of Muskets and great Ordanance, for the space of an howre or more... with a stone that fell from the sky in that storme or noise farther, which is here to be seen in Towne [London, eight days later], being of great weight."[39] Probably it was a natural meteorite fall accompanied by sonic booms, in which case the 'howre or more' is perhaps exaggerated; or a fall during a natural storm, which would be coincidence.

Galileo observed sunspots in 1609, two years before aurorae were reported by Jesuits in North America,[40] but the Maunder Minimum began c.1630 and continued till 1750, at least. Forty years later, Stonehenge was owned briefly by descendants of Richard and Agnes Barre. John Aubrey, the 17th century diarist and courtier, was the first to describe the 'Aubrey Holes' in his account of Avebury and Stonehenge. His *Monumenta Britannica* describes Stonehenge as lying within the farm of West Amesbury, "part of the inheritance of the wife of Lord Ferrers of Chertley, who was the daughter and heir of Laurence Washington Esq."[35] This was Sir Robert Shirley, who became the first of the new earls Ferrers in 1711, when the title was recreated. He was christened in 1650 and married Elizabeth Washington in 1671;[41] her grandfather, Sir Laurence, had bought West Amesbury manor sometime between 1615 and 1643 and passed it to his son of the same name, who died in 1661. Elizabeth and Robert sold the manor in 1677 to a Thomas Heywood, and it passed through many other hands before Stonehenge itself was bought and presented to the nation in 1915.[42]

The next event is in East Anglia, back in the 'corridor', and less than four years later in May 1646. "Betwixt Newmarket and the town of Thetford in the aforesaid County, there was observed a pillar of Cloud to ascend from the earth, with the bright hilts of a sword towards the bottom of it, which pillar did ascend in pyramidal form, and fashion itself into the form of a Spire or broad steeple, and there descended also out of the sky, the form of a pike or lance, with a very sharp head or point to encounter with it. Also at a distance, there appeared another Spear or Lance, with a very acute point out of the Sky likewise, which was ready to interpose, but did not engage itself.

"The first Spear which came down from heaven point blanck was after a while elevated higher, and that Spire or Spear which went up from the earth, ascended after it, to encounter with it the second time."[43]

The pamphlet was reprinted in 1969 by the *Eastern Daily Press*, and Cyril Blount, then Secretary of the Norwich Astronomical Society, suggested it was a meteorite. The Society organised a search, starting at the Devil's Punchbowl,[44] north of Thetford and eight miles northwest of Knettishall - a very weird place, rather like the Hells Kettles. It's one of a number of meres in the area, mostly inaccessible on army ranges, but it's perfectly circular and apparently a sinkhole.

However, nothing was found. At first one might think this was another underground explosion like the one at the Hells Kettles, but the funnel cloud coming down to meet the pyramid, and the other in the middle distance, suggest an atmospheric/electrical phenomenon. That's supported by a report of ball lightning in Cambridgeshire the same year, and a very similar pyramidal cloud effect, again with electrical discharges, at Swaffham Prior there between 1633 and 1661.[43]

Supposedly, a grounded UFO was seen at RAF Woodbridge airfield near Ipswich, in December 1980. One witness reported a pyramidal object, 2-3 metres on a side, floating or on legs.[45] Others said the lighted 'object' repeatedly changed colour, apparent texture and shape while sitting in a field where it left scorch marks, and at least one shape was pyramidal.[46] (Ufologists often cite 'impossible' changes of shape or direction, but won't concede that the 'objects' might not be solid.) My friend Ian Ridpath suggests that the sighting was actually a space debris re-entry (there was one that night, a Soviet spy satellite according to ufologist Jenny Randles) combined with a misidentification, through the trees, of the beams from the Orford Ness lighthouse - the local Police put that forward The witnesses disagree on the size of the marks on the ground, which Ian says could just be rabbit scrapings.[47]

The grounded pyramid in the Woodbridge event sounds to me like a night sighting of the Thetford and Swaffham electrical phenomena, and it's interesting that it's in 'our' area. Although these resemble the conical effect over the bishop of Norwich's London house in 1195 (Chap.14), they don't mean that a matter-transmitter still exists in East Anglia. The previous 'odd events' were tightly grouped within decades of unusually high solar activity, and mostly at sites with family, church and political connections, whereas these are centuries apart, when the Sun was very quiet or normal, and nothing else seems to be happening.

4. The Final Conjecture

As we saw in Chaps. 20 & 21, the solar-terrestrial magnetic disturbances just before the Bronze Age were the biggest in recorded history, even more violent than the late 12th century's. The 3500-2500 period may also have seen a wave of impact events. Drs. Victor Clube and Bill Napier suggest that a 'super-comet', perhaps a hundred miles across - four times the size of Comet Hale-Bopp in 1997- broke up in the inner Solar System then. [48] The asteroid Chiron, between Saturn and Uranus, and Phoebe, the outermost moon of Saturn, may be such objects, captured. The event would generate comets, meteor showers, impacts, perhaps extending the Zodiacal Light (normally seen over sunset and sunrise) into a continuous glowing band circling the Ecliptic;[49] present-day 'Earth-grazing' asteroids and meteor showers may be debris of the object, including the Tunguska object, the 1178 ones and the Taurid meteors, above.

If it was large enough to be differentiated by internal heating, fragments from its core could have struck the Earth as stony or even metallic meteorites. The Henbury craters in Australia were formed by iron meteorites around 2700 BC,[50] corresponding to the origin of the Geminid meteor shower from the asteroid Phaethon,[51] which has a high metallic content. The original Flood, in Sumerian mythology, could have been generated by one of those impacts, in the Persian Gulf or more probably in the Tigris marshes: in 2354-45 BC there was an abrupt turndown in global climate,[52] and the oldest and most detailed accounts of the Flood, which appear to describe an impact, date from c. 2250 BC.[53] Remarkably, one 19th century estimate put the Biblical Deluge at 2349 BC, though that's probably a coincidence because other Bible studies, then, put it much further back.[54]   Around 2000 BC a so-called 'bouncing asteroid' (probably twinned, as many asteroids are) created a double crater at Campo Cielo in Argentina; this was the largest impact of modern times, with an energy release of about 300 megatons.[55]

But the raw materials needed for the creation of the colony valley could have been supplied by the break-up of such a 'super-comet'.   The Flood event could have been an accident, a fragment which went out of control. If the rest of it was directed, the builders would have to stake out our Solar System a lot earlier to have access to its resources at that crucial time.

At the end of it all, the scenario (the part of it we can see, at least) looks like this:

c.10,500 BC:	gateway opens, possible First Contact.
3000-2500 BC:	inner Solar System 'mined' for comets to create the colony valley?
c.2300 BC:	first terraforming attempt?
c.1800 BC:	second terraforming attempt, or phase two?
1095-1250 AD:	human settlement of 'terrestrial' bowls, under cover of the Crusades, English Civil War, Templar farms and shipping? Lunar base established?
1250-1360 AD:	Contact interrupted by Wolf Minimum?
1360-1410 AD:	lunar base destroyed; Contact terminated?
c1410 AD:	onset of Spörer Minimum; gateway closes.

For us, who think thousands of years a long time, it's hard to appreciate such long-term planning: to them 80% of written human history may be no more than an eye-blink.   But I'm drawn to the idea that in Galactic terms they too are relative newcomers.   They've found a way to beat the vast interstellar distances, but with random access, initially.   When a portal opens, they establish a presence in that area of the Galaxy; but they don't take over other people's planets, they terraform sites elsewhere, even if it's rough on individual life-forms moved around.

They aren't gods: they make mistakes.   They can be thrown by unexpected interaction between the matter-transmitters, the magnetic field of the Contacted planet and the sunspot cycle of an unexpectedly variable star.

Their miscalculations can result in something as human as two lost children in East Anglia, blowing their cover with the girl's 'wilfulness and independence', or, in the other meaning of *lasciva et petulans*, her sexual drives.

Great though their powers were, we could relate to them. There is only one order of logic and we could talk to these beings: if the opportunity arose, those would be 'interesting times'. And although that was a curse in ancient China, as regressive elements in our own times never cease to remind us, in Russia it's said to be a privilege.[56]

There's a famous comment on Contact from the early 1960's. "Anthropological files contain many examples of societies, sure of their place in the universe, which have disintegrated when they had to associate with previously unfamiliar societies espousing different ideas and different life ways; others that survived such an experience usually did so by paying the price of changes in values and attitudes and behaviour."[57] In a well-known interview, Stanley Kubrick linked it to a quotation from Jung: "the reins would be torn from our hands and we would, as a tearful old medicine man once said to me, be left 'without dreams'... we would find our intellectual and spiritual aspirations so outmoded as to leave us completely paralyzed".[58] Later the original compiler was dismayed to find it quoted as a justification for shutting down NASA's Search for Extraterrestrial Intelligence, and said it was an old report, best forgotten.

But the point remains, and says something about the visitors, if they exist. By breaking off Contact when they apparently did, they left us free to continue our own development, perhaps along lines very different to theirs. In my *Interface* stories (Chap. 18), I invented a race who invented 'conventional' matter-transmission because they had a pathological fear of flying. They weren't very nice people: jealous guardians of their technology, they used it to exploit other intelligences and particularly the resources of their planets. With matter-transmitters, that temptation would be there, and with our shortcomings, our romantic and even idealistic involvement with the spaceship may be the better way to go. Whoever the visitors may have been, whatever their own purposes were, they were good enough to leave us with our dreams.

I discovered the green children mystery in 1967, when I was a student. I traced William of Newburgh's version in Glasgow University Library in 1972,

426

when researching "Man and the Stars", and I put the quotation in a chapter heading, to see what reaction it would get (none!). In 1989 I located Ralph of Coggeshall's account in the National Library of Scotland, and in 1993, when covering a conference in London for the Glasgow *Herald*, I went to Woolpit to gather some local colour for an article. But beforehand I got together with Bill Ramsay, who's a history graduate, and we worked out a list of questions. I was made very welcome in Woolpit, but I kept being told, "You'll have to go to the County Records Office for that".

In Bury St. Edmunds, I joined the County Archives Research Network, and was directed to the card index. Five hours later, exhausted, starving and dehydrated, I left convinced that I was on to something big; and eighteen years later, ten years of it full-time work, I can scarcely believe what I'm looking at. Mass abductions by extraterrestrials, for experimental purposes, with the knowledge, connivance and even support of some of the authorities of the day - *The X-Files*, in the 12th century! At the end of it, I can't better the last words of William of Newburgh, at the end of his Chapter 27:

"Let each one say what he wishes, and account for these things as best he can; but it does not grieve me to have set forth this strange and wonderful event."

ONLY THOSE MARKED '?' ARE CONJECTURAL.
UNUSUAL EVENTS ITALICISED.

1066: Norman Conquest; William the Conqueror gives Calne and other lands to Nigel the Doctor.

1095-8: Auroral and meteor storms.

1096: Peter the Hermit's crusade.

1099: First Crusade takes Jerusalem.

1118: Founding of the Knights Templar; 'Hugh Bar' of England in Holy Land.

c.1120: Adam de Calna acting bishop of Norwich; Everard de Calna elected.

1133: Nigel de Calna elected bishop of Ely.

1135: Richard de Calna owner of Wykes & Knettishall Manors, Suffolk.

1140: Cistercian Abbey of Coggeshall, Essex, founded by king Stephen and queen Matilda.

1146: Galactic alignments at Jerusalem; Dome of the Rock and Church of the Holy Sepulchre struck by lightning.

1147-50: Birth of Richard Barre; Richard de Calna godfather?

1147: Electrically charged vortex over Crusader fleet carrying parties from Hastings and East Anglia.

1148: Second Crusade.

1150: Auroral display; start of 50-year peak of solar activity, highest in

1173: northern hemisphere warming.

1154: Death of Stephen; poisoning of the Earl of Chester; Henry II becomes king.

Pre-1155: Peveril swineherd incident.

1155: Henry takes control of Peveril Castle, Derbyshire.

- Richard de Hastings becomes Provincial Master of the Knights Templar in England.

1157: April-May, Henry in Norwich, Thetford, & crowned at Bury St. Edmunds.

- July, Henry at Northampton, then Peveril Castle; receives report of Peveril swineherd incident?

1158-9: Richard de Calna excused payment of taxes by royal mandate.

1160: May, Richard de Hastings with Henry in Normandy.

- Henry annexes Woolpit. Samson goes to Rome about it.

- Henry puts Geoffrey Ridell in charge of Woolpit.
- Richard de Hastings and Tostes de St. Omer expelled from France over the handover of castles in the Vexin.

1161: Samson returns with Pope Alexander's letter, is imprisoned and exiled to Acre (or Castle-Acre?).

1162: Thomas à Becket becomes Archbishop of Canterbury.

1163: Henry takes control of Hagenet Castle, near Woolpit.
- Knights Templar given permission to appoint own chaplains.

1164: Henry issues Constitutions of Clarendon. Becket accused of high treason; flees to France.
- Samson returns to England?

1165/6: Samson takes holy orders.

1167: Coggeshall Abbey buildings completed and high altar dedicated by Gilbert Foliot, Bishop of London.
- Richard Barre becomes ambassador under John of Oxford; sponsored by Richard de Calna?

1169: Death of Nigel de Calna, bishop of Ely.

1169-71: Robert Fitz Stephen, under Dermot of Leinster, leads invasion of Ireland.
- Richard Barre ambassador to the Pope.

1170-2: Richard de Clare (Strongbow), earl of Pembroke, joins invasion of Ireland. Strongbow assigns Gowran in Ossory to Theobald fitz Walter; Templar preceptory established later.

1170: Dec., Becket killed by Henry's knights at Canterbury.

Late 1170: 'phantom army' in Ossory (at Aghaboe?) defied by Robert du Barry.

1171: Richard Barre ambassador to the Pope at Frascati.

1172: Dec. 24[b], apparent airburst explosion or sonic boom during auroral storm.

1173: Templars' power to appoint own chaplains confirmed; members exhorted to confess to them only.
- Richard Strongbow gives Aghaboe to Adam de Hereford.
- Very high peak of solar activity.
- *Feb. 18: upper atmosphere explosion over Derry during auroral storm.*
- Thomas à Becket canonised by the Pope.
- March, rebellion of princes Henry, Richard, Geoffrey fomented by Henry II's queen, Eleanor of Aquitaine.
- Richard Barre and William Blundus leave prince Henry's service.

- May, Geoffrey Ridell becomes Bishop of Ely. Richard Barre temporarily in charge of Woolpit? Pope orders return of Woolpit to Abbey; Samson 'exiled' again.
- *Summer, mystery 'stars' stationary in west.*
- *July, green children arrive?* Henry II rushes to East Anglia.
- Sept., special forces (mercenaries or Templars?) at Hagenet Castle, by Woolpit, under Ranulph de Broc, and at Peveril Castle. Building work to strengthen Peveril Castle begun (completed 1179).
- Oct., Earl of Leicester invades Suffolk, takes Hagenet Castle troops in full for ransom, and is defeated by combined English forces near Bury St. Edmunds, backed by Irish troops from Wexford.

1174: Henry II does penance at Canterbury for murder of Becket.
- King of Scots captured; rebellion in England collapses.
- Green children christened by Gilbert Foliot? Boy dies; buried at Coggeshall Abbey?
- by then or soon afterwards: Richard Barre becomes archdeacon of Lisieux.
- Henry assigns Woolpit to Walter de Coutances.
- Nov. 4th, auroral storm.

1175: John of Oxford becomes bishop of Norwich.
c. 1175: Ralph of Coggeshall canon at Barnwell, Cambridge, later moving to Coggeshall itself, authorised by Geoffrey Ridell.
1176-79: Templars search Coggeshall Abbey cemetery; report to Henry?
1177-78: Birth of Richard de Rushell, natural son of Richard Barre and Agnes.
1177: Nov. 29th, auroral storm.
1178. *June, monks at Canterbury see the flares from impacts on the far side of the Moon; fall of stones in England.*
- Henry II pilgrimage to shrine of Becket.
- *Dec. 25th [again], underground explosion at Darlington.*
1179: Henry repeats pilgrimage during lunar eclipse.
1180: Jerpoint Abbey founded in Kilkenny.
- Richard Barre marries Agnes?
- Birth of William Barre (legitimate).
- Birth of Sibylla de Calna, granddaughter of Richard de Calna. Agnes surrogate mother to Sibylla?
1180's: Ralph of Coggeshall a monk there; Richard de Calna's visits to him. Green girl (Agnes?) 'in ministerio' on de Calna's staff.

1182: Walter de Coutances becomes Bishop of Lincoln. Henry allows ownership of Woolpit to revert to Bury St. Edmunds Abbey, and allows Samson to become Abbot.

By 1185: Richard de Hastings retires as English Master of the Templars.

1185: Death of Richard de Calna's son Walter. Sibylla de Calna orphaned at five years old, made royal ward with arranged marriage to John Fitz-Bernard.

- Death of Robert du Barry in Ireland.

- Adam de Hereford, now of Aghaboe, marries Damietta, widow of Ranulph de Broc.

1187: Defeat of Knights Templar at Hattin; Richard de Calna at fall of Jerusalem? Third crusade planned; Richard Barre ambassador to Germany, Hungary and Constantinople.

By 1189: Death of Richard de Calna.

1189: Richard Barre becomes archdeacon of Ely.

- *Death of Henry II after freak lightning strikes*; Geoffrey Ridell dies soon after.

1190: Richard Barre becomes royal justice.

1191: Richard Barre in Holy Land; visits Jerusalem?

1195: William of Newburgh begins "Historia Rerum Anglicarum", describes green children's arrival.

- *Mystery event at London house of John of Oxford.*

1196: First records of Castleton village; because wind from Devil's Cavern had ceased?

1197: Agnes Barre and Sibylla de Calna jointly claim property at Aston in Staffordshire, near Little Barre, inherited from Walter de Calna.

1198: Death of William of Newburgh.

c.1200: *Emergence of first Incas near Cuzco, Peru.*

1205: *Monster in electrical storm at Maidstone.*

1207: Ralph of Coggeshall becomes sixth Abbot.

1209: Death of Richard Barre.

1214: John Fitz-Bernard, husband of Sibylla de Calna, reclaims Wykes & Knettishall manors.

1217: Earl of Derby (descendant of William Peverell) gains Peveril Castle.

1218: Ralph of Coggeshall resigns abbacy due to ill-health.

1222: Court case reveals Richard de Rowley (Rushell) to be the illegitimate older brother of William Barre.

- William de Cantilupe in charge of Calne.

1224: Death of Richard de Rowley (Rushell).

\- Siege and destruction of Bedford Castle, remains returned to William Beauchamp.

\- Henry III loses La Rochelle to France.

1225: Younger Richard de Calna seizes ship at La Rochelle.

1228 or 1230: Death of Ralph of Coggeshall.

1230: Death of John Fitz-Bernard.

\- Sibylla de Calna reclaims North Fambridge and Reed.

1234: Richard, Earl Marshal, murdered in the Curragh at Irish peace conference organised by the Templars.

1235: Henry III at Peveril Castle.

\- Ralph de Southwark made Master of the Templars in Ireland and promptly quits the order, succeeded by Roger le Waleis.

\- Sibylla de Calna & her son Walter Fitz-Bernard sell Wykes and Knettishall to Hugh de Sherdilowe.

1236: Hugh de Sherdilowe refuses tenant access to Wykes.

\- *Knights (clues suggest Templars) materialise to hold practise battles near Roche Abbey, Yorkshire.*

\- *Similar knights materialise wounded, retreating, in Ireland (at Aghaboe?).*

\- Disappearance of Hugh de Sherdilowe?

1238-9: Last trace of Agnes; Henry III at Erdington, part of Aston.

1244: Sibylla de Calna and Walter de Horkesley win legal action at Thursford.

c.1247: Richard de Clare, earl of Gloucester, inherits Kilkenny in the dissolution of Leinster; Eve de Braose, later married to William de Cantilupe aka de Calna, inherits Aghaboe.

c.1250: Onset of Wolf Minimum.

1250: Matthew Paris begins "Historia Anglorum", later adds Richard de Clare's testimony on 1236 Irish knights in margin, and similarly in the "Chronica Majora".

1253: *early March, Supposedly the New Moon seen three days early.*

\- *March 18th, red obscuration of the sky, in which the Sun, Moon and stars were immersed in a kind of mist or smoke.*

\- *9th October, bells supposedly heard in the air in two places at the time of Robert Grosseteste's death.*

\- *15th October, thick cloud with bright star shining like the Sun, 'attacked' by two sparkling red stars over many hours.*

\- December 14th, heavy snow and 'unnatural' thunder.

1254:	*January Ist, 'wondrous fantastic apparition' of 'a certain large ship' in the air at St. Albans.*

1254: *January Ist, 'wondrous fantastic apparition' of 'a certain large ship' in the air at St. Albans.*

\- Continual storms from May to November.

\- *February 8th, furious winds, mystery ships put in at Berwick.*

1255: Death of William de Barre.

1258: Walter Fitz-Bernard leases North Fambridge manor to Richard de Clare.

1262: Richard de Clare and William Beauchamp die by poison.

1308: Destruction of the Knights Templar begun by Philippe the Fair and Guillaume Nogaret.

\- Edward II marries Isabella, daughter of Philippe the Fair.

\- Piers Gaveston marries Margaret de Clare, given Peveril Castle.

1309: Gaveston exchanges Peveril Castle for earldom of Cornwall.

1314: Scots Templars possibly help in defeat of Edward II's army by Robert the Bruce at Bannockburn.

1348: John Bardwell marries descendant of Richard and Agnes Barre.

1351: Anne Barre marries Sir William Devereux; late 20th century descendants include Bill Washington and the Earl Ferrars.

1359: Normans lose control of Aghaboe.

c.1360: End of Wolf Minimum.

1361: Auroral and meteor storm.

\- *Castles and armies allegedly appear and disappear, in England and France.*

c.1362: Young Sir William Bardwell acquires rights at Bardwell, Thorp, possibly Wykes and Woolpit.

1366: *October, two auroral and meteor storms centred on the Moon.*

1399: 'Disappearance' of river Ouse near Bedford.

1402: *Fighting bands of men 'of divers colours' appear and disappear between Bedford and Biggleswade.*

c.1410: Onset of Spörer Minimum.

1544: Devereux family, descended from Richard and Agnes Barre, take over North Fambridge as new Earls of Essex.

1547: Three-day solar obscuration with sunspots in Germany; end of Spörer Minimum.

1646: Pyramidal electrical cloud near Knettishall; same decade, another at Swaffam Prior.

1671-7: Lord Ferrars, descended from Richard and Agnes Barre, holds Stonehenge by marriage; lowest years of the Maunder Minimum.

REFERENCES

"Some modern writers have composed general histories, in which this period is comprehended; but, without derogating from the merit of any of these, it must be acknowledged, that, in works of so vast an extent, there cannot be such a full detail of particulars, nor so much exactness and accuracy, as in those which are confined to narrower limits. It is only in the latter, that the several steps and preparatory measures, by which great actions are conducted, and great events are brought on, can be shown with any clearness."

~ George Lord Lyttelton, "The History of the Life of King Henry the Second, and of the age in which he lived, in Five Books", J. Dodsley, London, 1769.

Most mediaeval sources quoted are in 19th and 20th century editions which are indexed, so I mostly haven't supplied page numbers in these references. For sources like the Curia Rolls below, cited many times in some chapters, it wouldn't be practicable to give every page reference, and in others like the "Monasticon Anglicanum" below, there are different editions with different pagination or even different volume numbers, so precise page numbers would be unhelpful.

Chapter One - ABOUT THE GREEN CHILDREN

1.   Mabillon quoted in G.G. Coulton, preface to H.S. Bennett, "Life on the English Manor", Oxford University Press, 1948.
2.   Bohr quoted in Michio Kaku, "Hyperspace", Oxford University Press, 1994.
3.   Robert Burton, "The Anatomy of Melancholy", vols.1-3, Everyman's Library, J.M. Dent & Sons, 1932 ('Digression of the Air' in Vol. 2).
4.   Marjorie Hope Nicolson, "Voyages to the Moon", Macmillan, 1960 (inc flying Turk);   Francis Godwin, "The Strange Voyages and Adventures of Domingo Gonsales, to the world in the moon", J. Lever, London, 1768, Duke University Libraries, Utopian Literature Archive, internet 2011.   For heavenly spheres and 'fifth essence' see Chap. 6, and for Lucian see Chap. 8.
5.   R. Howlett, ed., William of Newburgh, "De Rerum Anglicarum", in "Chronicles of the Reigns of Stephen, Henry II and Richard I", Rolls Series No.82, Longman & Co., London, 1884; ed. P.G. Walsh, M.J. Kennedy, Aris & Phillips Ltd., 1988; ed. Picard, Paris, 1610; ed. T. Hearne, Oxford, 1719.

6. Giles Milton, 'Arthur Doesn't Live Here Any More', *Daily Telegraph*, March 27th, 1999.

7. Christopher Howe, 'Green Men Cut in Church Stonework', *Daily Telegraph*, 2nd May 2009; Kathleen Basford, "The Green Man", D.S. Brewer, Cambridge, 1978; Christopher Somerville, 'Someone to Watch over You', *Daily Telegraph*, March 25th, 2000.

8. Marion Melville, "La Vie des Templiers", Gallimard, Paris, 1951.

9. J. Stephenson, ed., Ralph of Coggeshall, "Chronicon Anglicanum", Rolls Series No.66, Longman & Co., London, 1875.

Chapter Two - THE VISITATION OF WOOLPIT

1. (Anon), "Walk Around Woolpit Village, No.1", Woolpit Bygones Museum, undated.

2. (Anon), "Woolpit in a Nutshell", Woolpit Historical Society, undated.

3. Richard Yates, "History and Antiquities of the Abbey of St. Edmund's, Bury", London, 1843.

4. Francis Blomefield, "An Essay towards a Topographical History of the County of Norfolk", 11 vols., William Miller, London, 1805-10.

5. Walter W. Skeat, 'The Place-Names of Suffolk', Cambridge Antiquarian Society, Vol. 46, 1913.

6. (Anon), 'Walk Around Woolpit, No.2: St. Mary Church', Woolpit Bygones Museum, undated.

7. Paul Harris, 'The Green Children of Woolpit', *Fortean Times*, 57, 39, 41, (Spring 1991).

8. William Page, ed., "Victoria History of the Counties of England: Suffolk, Vol.1", Constable, 1911.

9. Steve Harvey, 'Woolpit', personal communication, 1997.

10. Marianne Hulland, 'The Legend of Bury's Caves', Bury Free Press, July 18th, 1997.

11. W.A. Copinger, "County of Suffolk... materials for the History of Suffolk", 5 vols., Henry Sotheran & Co., London, 1904.

12. Glyn Maxwell, "Wolfpit", Arc Publications, 1996.

CHAPTER THREE: 1066 AND AFTER

1. W.C. Sellar and R.J. Yeatman, "1066 and All That", Methuen, 1930.

2. Reginald L. Poole, 'The Beginning of the Year in the Middle Ages', *Proceedings of the British Academy*, X, 113-137 (1921-23).

3. Georg Heinrich Pertz, 'Annales Dunelmensis', in "Monumenta Germanica Historica", Vol. XVIII, Hanover 1866.

4. W.P. Blair, 'Peering into the Heart of the Crab Nebula', *Astronomy & Space*, August 2000.

5. C.L. Wrenn, "The English Language", Methuen, 1952; Otto Jespersen, "Growth and Structure of the English Language", Blackwell, 1962.

6. D.C. Douglas, ed., "Feudal Documents from the Abbey of Bury St. Edmunds", British Academy Records of Social and Economic History, Oxford University Press, 1932.

7. Gérard Serbanesco, "Histoire de l'Ordre des Templiers et les Croisades", Byblos, Paris, 1969; Sean Martin, "The Knights Templar, The History and Myths of the Legendary Military Order", Pocket Essentials, 2009.

8. John Morris, general editor, "The Domesday Book", 38 vols., Phillimore, 1970s-1980s. The Domesday listings can also be found county by county in the Victoria History of the Counties of England, often cited below.

9. George Jefferey, "A Brief Description of the Holy Sepulchre, Jerusalem, and Other Christian Churches in the Holy City", Cambridge University Press, 1919; Joshua Prawer, "Crusader Institutions", Oxford University Press, 1980;

10. Mike Baillie, "Exodus to Arthur, Catastrophic Encounters with Comets", revised, Batsford, 2000.

11. Stephen Howarth, "The Knights Templar", Collins, 1982; Jean Flori, "Pierre l'Ermite et la Première Croisade", Fayard, 1999. For accounts of the same meteors, auroral displays etc., but some of them a year different in date, see Heinrich Hagenmeyer, ed., "Ekkehardi Uraugiensis Abbatis Hiero-solymita", Verlag und Druck von Franz Fues, Tübingen, 1877, and "Fulcheri Canotensis Historia Hierosolymitana (1095-1127)", Carl Winters Universitätsbuchhandlung, Heidelberg, 1913.

12. Benjamin Thorpe, ed., "The Anglo-Saxon Chronicle, according to the Several Original Authorities", Rolls Series No.23, Longman, Green, Longman & Roberts, 1861.

13. Robert Levine, ed., Guibert de Nogent, "The Deeds of God through the Franks", Boydell Press, 1997; John Glover, ed., "Le Livere de Reis de Brittanie", Rolls Series No. 42, Longman, Green, Reader & Dyer, 1865; Paul Alphandéry, Alphonse Dupront, "La Chrétienté et l'Idée de Croisade", Editions Albin Michel, Paris, 1954.

14. Edward A. Bond, ed., "Chronica Monasterii de Melsa", Rolls Series No.43, Longmans, Green, Reader & Dyer, 1866.

15. Thomas Arnold, ed., "The History of the English, by Henry, Archdeacon of Huntingdon, from A.D. 55 to A.D. 1154", Rolls Series No. 74, Longman & Co., 1879; H.A.R. Gibb, ed., Ibn Al-Qalanisi, "The Damascus Chronicle of the Crusade", Luzac & Co, London, 1932.

16. Jane Greatorex, personal communication, January 1998.

17. "Chronicle of St. Evrault", quoted in Thomas Forester, ed., "The Ecclesiastical History of England and Normandy, Vol.4", Henry Bohn, London, 1854; C.E. Britton, 'A Meteorological Chronology to AD 1450', *Geophysical Memoirs*, 70, VIII, Meteorological Office, 1937.

18. Geoffrey Regan, "Saladin and the Fall of Jerusalem", Croon Helm, 1987.

19. F.E. Peters, "Jerusalem: the Holy City in the Eyes of Chroniclers, Visitors, Pilgrims and Prophets from the Days of Abraham to the Beginnings of Modern Times", Princeton University Press, 1985.

20. Richard Fariña, sleeve notes, 'The Falcon' on Mimi and Richard Fariña, "Celebrations for a Grey Day", Fontana TFL6060, 1965. "The hawks and harriers of Point Lobos had a serenity and freedom that seemed to vanish in the spectre of the Birchers who took to Santa Lucia on weekends, bivouacking, practising armed manoeuvres, and preparing for a foreign invasion. Goldwater was about to win the California primary and the skies were somewhat uneasy."

21. Rev. John Williams ab Ithel, ed., "Brut Y Twysogion, or the Chronicle of the Princes", Rolls Series No. 17, Longman, Green, Longman and Roberts, 1860.

22. J.E. Gore, "The Worlds of Space", Innes, London, 1894.

23. J. Stephenson, ed., Ralph of Coggeshall, "Chronicon Anglicanum", op cit.

24. Keith Hindley, 'The Stars Fell Like Rain', *New Scientist*, 13.10.77, pp.78-80.

25. Bravonius (Florentius) Wigorniensis, "Chronicon ex Chronicis", Typis Wechaliensis apud Claudium, Frankfort, 1601.

26. François Arago, "Popular Astronomy", Longman, Brown, Green, Longman & Roberts, 1858.

27. Nancy Atkinson, 'Evidence of Supernovae Found in Ice Core Sample', *Universe Today*, February 23rd, 2009.

28. Geoffrey Bosanquet, ed., "Eadmer's History of Recent Events in England", Cresset Press, London, 1964.

29. G.F. Chambers, "The Story of Eclipses", George Newnes, London, 1899.

30. D.E.R. Watt, ed., Walter Bower, "Scotichronicon", Vol. 5, Aberdeen University Press, 1995, has aurora on December 20th, 1117, and violent electrical storms in January, July and August 1118.

31. Mark Peplow, 'John of Worcester Spot on with His 1128 Sun Diagram', *Daily Telegraph*, 17th July.2001.

32. Michael Baigent, Richard Leigh, Henry Lincoln, "The Holy Blood and the Holy Grail", Jonathan Cape, 1982.

33. Joshua Prawer, 'Social Conditions in the Crusader States: the "Minorities"', in Kenneth M. Setten, ed., "A History of the Crusades, Vol. V", University of Wisconsin Press, 1985.

34. Richard Andrews, "Blood on the Mountain, a History of the Temple Mount from the Ark to the Third Millennium", Weidenfeld & Nicolson, 1999.

35. Col. Sir Charles W. Wilson, "Jerusalem, the Holy City", J.S. Virtue & Co., London, 1888; Malcolm Barber, 'The Origins of the Order of the Temple', in his "Crusaders and Heretics, 12-14th Centuries", Variorum, 1995.

36. Malcolm Barber, "The New Knighthood", Cambridge University Press, 1994.

37. 'History Zone: Mazes and Labyrinths', BBC-2, 19th June 1999; Sarah Foot, 'Happy to Lose Himself in Those Long and Winding Mysteries', *Daily Telegraph*, August 27th, 1994, and George Terence Meaden, "The Goddess of the Stones", Souvenir Press, 1991.

38. Leonard Cottrell, "The Mountains of Pharaoh", Robert Hale, 1956.

39. Robert William Hamilton, "A Short History of the Aqsa Mosque", Oxford University Press, 1949.

40. Martin Hugh, 'The Crusaders' Strategy against Fatimid Ascalon and the "Fatimid Project" of the Second Crusade', in Michael Gervers, ed., "The Second Crusade and the Cistercians", St. Martin's Press, N.Y., 1992.

41. J.M. Upton-Ward, "The Rule of the Templars", Boydell Press, 1992.

42. G.C. Addison, "The Temple Church", Longman, Brown, Green and Longmans, 1843.

43. Peter Portner, "The Murdered Magicians", Oxford University Press, 1981.

44. Marion Melville, "La Vie des Templiers", Gallimard, Paris, 1951.

45. Gérard de Sède, "Les Templiers Sont Parmi Nous", J'Ai Lu, Paris, 1962.

46. C.G. Addison, "The Knights Templar", Longman Brown, 1842.

47. Edouard Champion, ed., "Cartulaire Général de l'Ordre de Temple. 1119?-1150", Librairie Ancienne, Paris, 1913.

48. Malcolm Barber, "The Trial of the Templars", Cambridge University Press, 1978.

49. G.C. Bosset, trans., "The Templars", Anthroposophical Publishing Co., Montrose, 1960.

50. Malcolm Barber, 'The Templars and the Turin Shroud', in Malcolm Barber, "Crusaders and Heretics", op cit.

51. Michael Bentine, "The Templar", Bantam, 1988.

52. Herbert Wood, "The Templars in Ireland", *Proceedings of the Royal Irish Academy*, XXVI, 327-377 (1907).

53. Desmond Seward, "The Monks of War", Eyre Methuen, 1972.

54. Marie Luise Bulst-Thiele, 'The Influence of St. Bernard of Clairvaux on the Formation of the Order of the Knights Templar', in M. Gervers, ed., "The Second Crusade and the Cistercians", op cit.

55. Edith Swann, "The Piebald Standard, a History of the Knights Templar", Cassell, 1959.

56. Thomas M. Parker, "The Knights Templar in England", University of Arizona Press, 1963.

57. Helen Nicholson, "The Knights Templar, A New History", Sutton, 2001.

CHAPTER FOUR: 'OF LORD RICHARD DE CALNA'

1. (Anon), 'Honours Plan Puts Knights to Sword', *The West Australian*, supplied by James Bentley.

2. Christopher Dyer, "Standards of Living in Medieval England", Cambridge University Press, 1989. 3. Antonia Gransden, "Historical Writing in England", vol.1, Routledge & Kegan Paul, 1982.

4. P.H. Reaney, "The Place-Names of Essex", Cambridge University Press, 1935.

5. Z.N. Brooke, Dom. Adrian Morey, C.N.L. Brooke, eds., "The Letters and Charters of Gilbert Foliot", Cambridge University Press, 1967.

6. (Anon) 'A Brief History of Wakes Colne', in "Wakes Colne & Chappel Flower Festival Programme", 16/17 June, 1984.

7. Christopher Harper-Bill, ed., "English Episcopal Acta VI: Norwich 1970-1214", OUP, 1990.

8. John Caley, Sir Henry Ellis, Rev. Bulkeley Bandinel, eds., Sir William Dugdale, "Monasticon Anglicanum", James Bohn, London, 1846 (8 vols.), first published in 6 vols., in Latin, in the 1660s. The 1846 edition, in Glasgow's Mitchell Library and Glasgow University Library, translates the

main text with much additional material, mostly in Latin.   Vol. VI was extended to 'Parts 1, 2 & 3', each book length, bound in the Mitchell Library as Vols. VI, VII & VIII.   So the 1846 page numbers and some volume numbers don't match earlier editions.   It's best to use the Index, at the end of Vol. 6.3 in that edition (Vol. VIII in the Mitchell).

9. Norman Scarfe, "Suffolk in the Middle Ages", Boydell Press, 1986.

10. Francis Blomefield, "An Essay towards a Topographical History of the County of Norfolk", op cit.

11. D.C. Douglas, ed., "Feudal Documents from the Abbey of Bury St. Edmunds", op cit.

12. Richard Newcourt, "Reportorium Ecclesiasticum Parochiale Londiniense (An Ecclesiastical Pastoral History of the Diocese of London)", London, 1708; for Geoffrey Calna see (Anon) "Registrum Cartarum Prioratus de Binham in agro Norfolcienibus", British Library Cotton Claudius MS D.XIII..

13. J.H. Round, "Geoffrey de Mandeville, a Study of the Anarchy", Longmans, Green & Co., 1892.

14. Robert Uhlig, '"Error" Led to Myth of Ancestors' Short Lives', *Daily Telegraph*, 11th March, 1999.

15. A.E.W. Marsh, "A History of the Borough and Town of Calne", Castle, Lamb & Storr, 1904.

16. R. Gough, ed., William Camden, "Britannia, or a Chorographical Description", 4 vols., John Stockdale, London, 1806.

17. Deputy Keeper of the Records, ed., "Curia Regis Rolls of the Reign of Richard I and John, Preserved in the Public Record Office", HMSO, 1922. The series goes on to the reign of Henry III and runs to 17 volumes, as held by Glasgow University Library; the last two have separate editors, below.   William de Cantilupe III appears as "Sir William de Kalna alias Cantilupo" in Vol.1 of "Calendar of Inquisitions Post Mortem and other analogous documents", HMSO, 1904.

18. Charles Roberts, ed., "Calendarium Genealogicum - Henry III and Edward I", (2 vols.), Longmans, Green & Co., 1865.

19. Caroline & Frank Thorn, eds., "The Domesday Book, Vol.6: Wiltshire", Phillimore, 1979.

20. C.H. Talbot, "Medicine in Medieval England", Oldbourne, 1967.

21. See the relevant volumes county by county of John Morris, ed., "The Domesday Book", op cit.

22. M. Brett, "The English Church under Henry I", Oxford University Press, 1975.

23. Edward J. Kealey, "Roger of Salisbury, Viceroy of England", University of California Press, 1972.

24. William of Newburgh, op cit.

25. Ralph V. Turner, 'The *Miles Literatus* in Twelfth- and Thirteenth-Century England: How Rare a Phenomenon?', in Ralph V. Turner, "Judges, Administrators and the Common Law in Angevin England", Hambledon Press, London, 1994.

26. John McNeill, "Old Sarum", English Heritage, 2006; William Dodsworth, "An Historical Account of the Episcopal See, and Cathedral Church of Salisbury", Wilkie, London, 1814.

27. K.R. Potter, ed., "(Anon) Gesta Stephani, the Deeds of Stephen", Nelson, 1955.

28. Arthur Hughes, C.G. Crump, C. Johnson, eds., "Richard Fitz-Neal, De Necessariis Observantiis Scacarii Dialogus (Dialogus de Scacario)", Oxford University Press, 1902.

29. Diana E. Greenway, ed., John Le Neve, "Fasti Ecclesiae Anglicanae 1066-1300, Vol. I, St. Paul's, London", University of London Institute of Historical Research, Athlone Press, 1968.

30. John Le Neve, "Fasti Ecclesiae Anglicanae, or a Calendar of the Principal Episcopal Dignatories of England and Wales... from the earliest times to the year M.DCC.XV", Oxford University Press, 1854.

31. Sir Walter Besant, "The Survey of London: Mediaeval London, Vol.2 - Ecclesiastical", Adam & Charles Black, 1906.

32. Sir William Dugdale, "History of St. Paul's Cathedral", Longman, 1818.

33. William Maitland, "The History and Survey of London from its Foundation to the Present Time, Vol. 2", T. Osborne, London, 1760.

34. Charles Johnson, H.A. Cronne, eds., "Regesta Regum Anglo-Normannum 1066-1154, Vol. III: Regesta Regis Stephanis ac Mathildis Imperatricis ac Galfridi et Henrici Ducum Normannorum 1135-54", O.U.P., 1868. For Cripplegate, Aldersgate, and Templar & Hospitaller headquarters, John Strype, "Survey of London", London, 1720, revised edition of John Stow's 16th century "Survey of London".

35. Zev Vilney, "The Sacred Land: Vol.1, Legends of Jerusalem", Jewish Publications Society of America, 1973.

36. Herbert Wood, "The Templars in Ireland", op cit.

37. Joseph O'Connor, "Star of the Sea", Secker & Warburg, 2002.

38. John L. Fisher, Avril & Raymond Powell, eds., "A Medieval Farming Glossary of Latin and English Words, taken mainly from the Essex records", 2nd edition, Essex Record Office, 1997.

39. Henry B. Wheatley, "The Story of London", J.M. Dent, Mediaeval Towns Series, 1922; Paul Devereux, "Haunted Land", Piatkus, 2001.

40. David M. Smith, ed., "English Episcopal Acta, Vol. I: Lincoln 1067-1185", Oxford University Press, 1980; Diana E. Greenway, ed., "John Le Neve, "Fasti Ecclesiae Anglicanae Vol. III: Lincoln", University of London Institute of Historical Research, 1977.

41. Jim Bradbury, "Stephen and Matilda, the Civil War of 1139-53", Alan Sutton, 1996.

42. Elizabeth Critall, ed., "The Victoria History of the Counties of England: Wiltshire, Vol. 8", Oxford University Press, 1965.

43. D.A. Crowley, ed., "Victoria History of the Counties of England: Wilts., Vol. 11", O.U.P., 1980.

44. J.H. Round, ed., "Calendar of Documents Preserved in France Illustrative of the History of Great Britain, Vol. 1, 918-1206", Eyre & Spottiswoode, 1899.

45. M.J. Franklin, ed., "English Episcopal Acta VIII: Winchester 1070-1204", O.U.P., 1993.

46. Anon, ed., "The Pipe Rolls of 31 Henry I, Michaelmas 1130", facsimile reprint, His Majesty's Stationery Office, 1929.   Pipe Rolls publication began as a government project; after two vols. the Pipe Roll Society took over: their Vol. 3 Introduction has a glossary of mediaeval Latin terms and shorthand. The first series covers the reign of Henry II year by year, and HMSO reproduced the first two vols. in the same format, as above.   The New Series (PRNS below) covering Richard I, king John and Henry III, has individual editors and more specialist single volumes, so references are more specific.

47. William Henry Jones, ed., "Fasti Ecclesiae Sarisberiensis, or a Calendar of the Bishops, Deans, Archdeacons and Members of the Cathedral Body of Salisbury", Simkin, Marshall & Co., 1879.

48. 'Tewars', 'Everard Bishop of Norwich', *Notes and Queries*, 4th Series Vol. X, 26-27 (1872).

49. William Farrer, "An Outline Itinerary of King Henry the First", English Historical Review, XXXIV, (July, Oct. 1919), reprinted Frederick Hall, Oxford, undated.

50.   Geoffrey Bosanquet, ed., "Eadmer's History of Recent Events in England", op cit.;   Martin Rule, ed., "Eadmeri Historia Novorum in Anglia", Lib. V, Rolls Series No.81, Longman & Co., 1884.

51.   Rev. W. Rich Jones, Rev. W. Dunn Macray, eds., "Charters and Documents Illustrating the History of the Cathedral, City and Diocese of Salisbury in the 12th and 13th Centuries", Rolls Series No.97, Eyre & Spottiswoode, 1891.

52.   James Bentham, "The History and Antiquities of the Conventual and Cathedral Church of Ely", Cambridge University Press, 1771.

53.   Ian Atherton, Eric Fernie, Christopher Harper-Bill & Hassell Smith, eds., "Norwich Cathedral, Church, City and Diocese", Hambledon Press, 1996.

54.   L. Landon, 'Everard Bishop of Norwich', *Proc. Suff. Inst. of Archaeology & Nat. History*, XXVI, 186-198 (1920).

55.   William Stubbs, ed., "Willelmi Malmesbiriensis Monachi de Gestis Regnum Anglorum", 2 vols., Rolls Series no.52, Eyre & Spottiswoode, 1889.

56.   Edward Meyrick Goulburn & Henry Symonds, eds., "The Life, Letters and Sermons of Bishop Herbertus de Losinga", James Parker & Co., 1878; Patricia M. Barnes, C.F. Slade, eds., "A Mediaeval Miscellany for Doris M. Stenton", Pipe Rolls Society New Series (PRNS) Vol.36, J.W. Ruddock, Lincoln, 1962.

57.   Thomas Arnold, ed., "The History of the English, by Henry, Archdeacon of Huntingdon", op cit.

58.   M. Brett, "The English Church under Henry I", Oxford University Press, 1975.

59.   Deputy Keeper of the Records, ed., "A Descriptive Catalogue of Ancient Deeds Held in the Public Records Office", HMSO, 1890-1915.

60.   Frank Barlow, ed., "Letters of Arnulf of Lisieux", Camden Society Third Series vol. LXI, 1939.

61.   H.W. Saunders, ed., "The First Registry of Norwich Cathedral Priory", Norfolk Record Society, Vol. XI, 1939.

62.   Barbara Dodwell, ed., "The Charters of Norwich Priory, Part 1", PRNS 40, Ruddock, 1974; "...Part 2", Vol. 46, 1985.

63.   William Stubbs, Introduction to Ralph de Diceto, in Arthur Hassall, ed., "Historical Introductions to the Rolls Series", Longmans, Green & Co., 1902.

64   Henry Richards Luard, ed., Bartholomew Cotton, "Liber de Archiepiscopis et Episcopis Angliae", in "Historia Anglicana", Rolls Series No. 16, op cit.

65. A. Thomson, "The British History of Geoffrey of Monmouth", James Bohn, London, 1842.

66. J.S.P. Tatlock, "The Legendary History of Britain", University of California Press, 1950.

67. Michael J. Curley, "Geoffrey of Monmouth", Maxwell Macmillan International, 1994.

68. Rev. H.E. Salter, ed., "Cartulary of Oseney Abbey", 5 vols., Oxford Historical Society, 1929.

69. Eleanor Rathbone, 'Roman Law in the Anglo-Norman Realm', *Studia Gratiana*, XI, p.260, (1967).

70. Ralph V. Turner, 'Richard Barre and Michael Belet: Two Angevin Civil Servants', reprinted in Ralph V. Turner, "Judges, Administrators and the Common Law in Angevin England", op cit.

71. Pipe Roll Society, Vol.5, "The Great Roll of the Pipe for the Eighth Year of King Henry II AD 1161-62", 1884, continuing through the first Series and New Series to 1221.

72. David Crouch, "The Beaumont Twins, the Roots and Branches of Power in the Twelfth Century", Cambridge University Press, 1986; Michael Baigent, Richard Leigh & Henry Lincoln, "The Holy Blood and the Holy Grail", op cit.

73. William Page, ed., "The Victoria History of the Counties of England: Buckinghamshire, Vol. Three", St. Catherine Press, 1925.

74. Charles Travis Clay and David C. Douglas, ed., Lewis C. Lloyd, "The Origins of Some Anglo-Norman Families", Harleian Society Vol. 103, Leeds, 1951; James Cruikshank Dansey, "The English Crusaders", Dickinson & Co., 1849. Dansey states his source documents are in the British Museum (now British Library) and Bibliothèque Royale (now Bibliothèque Nationale) manuscript collections, but he's extracted the most important information, here and in chap. 14, from 'the Courtois collection', which is unknown to either – personal communications, Michael St. John, British Library, Jean-François Chanal, Bibliothèque Nationale, 3rd April, 2001.

75. John G. Jenkins, ed., "The Cartulary of Missenden Abbey", Part 1, Records Branch, Buckinghamshire Archaeological Society, 1938; Part 2, 1955; Part 3, HMSO, 1962.

76. Christopher Tyerman, 'Who Went on Crusade to the Holy Land?', in Benjamin Z. Kedar, ed., "The Horns of Hattin", Variorum, 1992; Jonathon Riley-Smith, "The Crusades, a short history", Athlone Press, 1987.

77.   Henrietta Leyser, "Medieval Women, A Social History of Women in England 450-1500", Weidenfeld & Nicolson, 1995, and Nicholas Orme, "The Mediaeval Child", Yale U.P., 2001.

78.   R.C. van Caenegem, ed., "English Lawsuits from Wm. I to Richard I", Vol. I, Selden Soc., 1990.

79.   Pipe Roll Society, Vol.1, "The Great Roll of the Pipe, for the fifth year of the reign of King Henry the Second, AD 1158-1159", et seq, (38 vols.), Wyman & Sons, London, 1884.

80.   Dr. Thomas Tanner, "Noticia Monastica, or an Account of All the Abbeys, Priories and Houses of Friers [sic], formerly in England and Wales", Cambridge University Press, 1787.

81.   Anon, "Binham Priory", Norfolk Records Office MC 619/1/782 x 6.

82.   Revs. W. Rich Jones, W. Dunn Macray, eds., "Charters and Documents Illustrating the History of the Cathedral, City and Diocese of Salisbury in the 12th and 13th Centuries", Rolls Series 97, op cit.

83.   Doris M. Stenton, ed., "The Great Roll of the Pipe for the Second Year of the Reign of King Richard the First", PRNS 1, Ruddock, 1925;   Deputy Keeper of the Records, ed., "Patent Rolls of the Reign of Henry III, preserved in the Public Records Office, AD 1216-1266" (first of 5 vols.), HMSO, 1901, "Close Rolls of the Reign of Henry III", AD 1227 et seq, HMSO, 1902.

84.   Numerous charters witnessed by lord Reginald and lord William de Calna after 1200 are in William T. Reedy, ed., "Bassett Charters c. 1120 to 1250", PRNS 50, Ruddock, 1995.   For lord William and his son the scribe see Historical Manuscripts Commission, "Report on the Manuscripts of the Late Reginald Rawdon Hastings Esq. of The Manor House, Ashby de la Zouche, Vol. 1", HMSO, 1928.

85.   John T. Appleby, "The Troubled Reign of King Stephen", G. Bell, London, 1969.

86.   James Bentham, "The History and Antiquities of the Conventual and Cathedral Church of Ely", op cit.

87.   Joseph Stevenson, ed., "Chronicon Ricardi Diviensis de Rebus Gestis Ricardi Primi Regis Angliae", English Historical Society, 1838.

88.   G.C. Coulton, "Mediaeval Panorama, The English Scene from Conquest to Reformation", Cambridge University Press, 1938.

89   Glyn Maxwell, "Wolfpit", op cit.

90.   E.O. Blake, ed., "Liber Eliensis", Camden Society Third Series Vol. XCII, Royal Historical Society, London, 1962.

91. John Beeler, "Warfare in England 1066-1189", Cornell University Press, 1966.

92. F.R. Chapman, "Sacrist Rolls of Ely", Cambridge University Press, 1907.

93. Leopold Delisle, "Recueil des Actes de Henry II", Imprimerie Nationale, Paris, 1908.

94. Joseph Hunter, ed., "Magnum Rotulum Scaccarii, vel Magnum Rotulum Pipae, de Anno Tricesimo-Primo Regni Henrici Primi (ut videtur) quam plurimi hactenus laudarunt pro Rotulo Quinta Anno Stephani Regis", Commissioners on the Public Records of the Kingdom, 1833.

95. W.R. Powell, ed., "The Victoria History of the Counties of England: Essex, Vol. IV: Ongar Hundred", Oxford University Press, 1956.

96. Arthur Doubleday and William Page, eds., "The Victoria History of the Counties of England: Essex, Vol.1", Oxford University Press, 1903.

97. Anon, ed., "The Great Roll of the Pipe for the Second, Third and Fourth Years of King Henry II", HMSO, 1930.

98. W.R. Powell, ed., "The Victoria History of the Counties of England: Essex, vol. VIII", Oxford University Press, 1983.

99. W.R. Powell, ed., "The Victoria History of the Counties of England: Essex, Vol. IV", op cit.

100. R.H.C. Davis, ed., "The Kalendar of Abbot Samson", Roy. Hist. Soc. Camden Third Series vol. Lxxiv, 1954.

101. Walter W. Skeat, "The Place-Names of Suffolk", op cit.

102. "William White's History, Gazeteer and Directory of Suffolk", R. Leader, Sheffield, 1844.

103. H.E. Butler, ed., "The Chronicle of Jocelin of Brakelond", Nelson's Mediaeval Texts, 1949.

104. W.A. Copinger, "The Manors of Suffolk", T. Fisher Unwin, 1905.

105. Ralph V. Turner, 'The Curiales and the Conservative Critics', in Ralph V. Turner, "Judges, Administrators and the Common Law in Angevin England", op cit.

106. Guillaume de Poitiers, in Raymonde Foreville, ed., "Histoire de Guillaume le Conquérant", Paris, 1952.

107. Alex Rumble, ed., "The Domesday Book: Suffolk", Vol. 34 - (1) & (2), Phillimore, 1986.

108. J. Caley & W. Illingworth, eds., "Testa de Nevill sive liber feodorum in curia scacarii, temp. Hen. III et Edw. I", the Record Commission, 1807; Deputy Keeper of Records, ed., "Liber Feodorum, the Book of Fees,

commonly called Testa de Nevill, reformed from the earliest MSS.   Part I, AD 1198-1242", His Majesty's Stationery Office, 1920.

109.   David C. Douglas, George W. Greenaway, eds., "English Historical Documents 1042-1189", Eyre Methuen, 1981.

110.   Randolph Quirk & C.L. Wrenn, "An Old English Grammar", 2nd edition, Methuen, 1957.

111.   M.P. Statham, 'Bardwell Manors' (note correcting Copinger ref. Wykes), Bardwell file, Suffolk County Records Office, 16th September 1965.

112.   Christopher Dyer, "Everyday Life in Medieval England", Hambledon Press, 1994.

113.   George Cooper Homans, "English Villagers of the Thirteenth Century", Harvard University Press, 1942.

114.   Pipe Rolls Society, Vol.1, "The Great Roll of the Pipe, for the fifth year of the reign of King Henry the Second, A.D. 1158-59", Wyman & Sons, 1884.

115.   Pipe Roll Society, Vol.2, "The Great Roll of the Pipe for the 6th Year of King Henry II ", Wyman, 1884.

116.   Charlotte A. Newman, "The Anglo-Norman Nobility in the Reign of Henry I", University of Pennsylvania Press, 1988.

117.   W.H. Rich Jones, ed., "The Register of St. Osmund", Rolls Series No.78, Longman, 1883.

118.   William Henry Jones, "Fasti Ecclesiae Sarisberiensis, or a Calendar of the Bishops, Deans, Archdeacons, and Members of the Cathedral Body at Salisbury, from the earliest times to the present", Brown & Co., Salisbury, 1879.

119.   Emilie Amt, "The Accession of Henry II in England: Royal Government Restored, 1149-59", Boydell Press, 1993.

120.   L.F. Salzmann, "Henry II", Constable, 1917; see also Pipe Rolls, 2-9 Henry II.

121.   Diana E. Greenway, ed., "Fasti Ecclesiae Anglicanae, Vol.2: Monastic Cathedrals", University of London Institute of Historical Research, Athlone Press, 1971.

122.   Joseph Warichez, "Étienne de Tournai et Son Temps", Annales de la Société Royale d'Histoire et de l'Archéologie de Tournai, New Series Vol.20, Tournai, 1936.

123   Hubert Hall, ed., "The Red Book of the Exchequer", Rolls Series No. 99, (3 vols.), Eyre & Spottiswoode, 1896.

124.   M.R. James, "Suffolk and Norfolk", J.M. Dent, 1930.

125. Pipe Roll Society, Vol. 17, "Feet of Fines of the Reign of Henry II and the First Seven Years of Richard I, AD 1182 to AD 1196", Wyman, 1894.

126. Pipe Roll Society, Vol. 38, "The Great Roll of the Pipe for the 34th Year of King Henry II", Hereford Times Ltd., 1925.

127. John H. Mundy, "Europe in the High Middle Ages, 1150-1309", Longman, 1973; H.S. Bennett, "Life on the English Manor", op cit.

128. 'Phillippa of Brookhaven', 'Gods, Doctors and Philosophers, Herbalists through the Ages', *Tournaments Illuminated*, XVIII, no.70, 20-22 (Spring 1983).

129. Beatrice Adelaide Lees, "Records of the Templars", British Academy Records Series, 1935.

130. Malcolm Barber, 'The Social Context of the Templars', in Malcolm Barber, "Crusaders and Heretics", op cit.

131. G.C. Addison, "The Temple Church", op cit.

132. Robert William Hamilton, "A Short History of the Aqsa Mosque", Oxford University Press, 1949.

133. George Jefferey, "A Brief Description of the Holy Sepulchre, Jerusalem, and Other Christian Churches in the Holy City", op cit.

134. Benjamin Thorpe, ed., "The Anglo-Saxon Chronicle", op cit.

135. George Lord Lyttelton, "The History of the Life of King Henry the Second", op cit. This work has two Indices, at the ends of Book III (vol. 4, as bound by Glasgow Uni Library) and Book VI.

136. G.F. Chambers, "The Story of Eclipses", op cit.

137. Dr. Thomas Short, "A General Chronological History of the Air, Weather, Seasons, Meteors, Etcetera, in Sundry Places and at Different Times", 2 volumes, Longman, 1749.

138. Ralph of Coggeshall, op cit.

139. Roberta J.M. Olson, 'Giotto's Portrait of Halley's Comet, *Scientific American*, July 1979, reprinted in John C. Brandt, ed., "Comets", W.H. Freeman, 1981; William Stubbs, ed., "The Historical Works of Master Ralph Diceto, Deacon of London", Rolls Series (2 vols.), Longman & Co., 1876.

140. Gérard Serbanesco, "Histoire de l'Ordre des Templiers et les Croisades", op cit; Marion Melville, "La Vie des Templiers", op cit.

141. Hans-Dietrich Kohl, 'Crusade Eschatology as Seen by St. Bernard in the Years 1146 to 1148', in Michael Gervers, ed., "The Second Crusade and the Cistercians", op cit.

142. Amnon Linder, 'An Unpublished Charter of Geoffrey, Abbot of the Temple in Jerusalem', in Benjamin Z. Kedar, H.E. Meyer & R.C. Smail, eds.,

"Outremer, Studies in the History of the Crusading Kingdom of Jerusalem", Izhak Ben-Zari Institute, Jerusalem, 1982.

143. G. Constable, 'A Note on the Route of the Anglo-French Crusaders of 1147', *Speculum*, 28, 525-526, 1928.

144. Malcolm Barber, "The New Knighthood", op cit.

145. William Stubbs, ed., 'Osbernus de Expugnatione Lyxbonensi', in "Itinerarium Peregrinorum et Gesta Regis Ricardi", Rolls Series 38, Longman, Green, Longman, Roberts and Green, 1864.

146. Harold Livermore, '*The Conquest of Lisbon* and its Author', *Portuguese Studies*, 6 (1990), 1-16.

147. Jonathan P. Phillips, ed., "The Second Crusade, Scope and Consequences", Manchester University Press, 2001.

148. Jonathan P. Phillips, "The Second Crusade, Extending the Frontiers of Christianity, Yale, 2008.

149. David Nicholle, "The Second Crusade 1148, Disaster outside Damascus", Osprey, 2009.

150. Jonathon Riley-Smith, 'Family Traditions and Participation in the Second Crusade', in Michael Gervers, ed., "The Second Crusade and the Cistercians", op cit.

151. Caroline D. Eckhardt, ed., "Castleford's Chronicle, or the Boke of Brut", Vol.2, Early English Text Society, Oxford University Press, 1996; Mike Baillie, "Exodus to Arthur", op cit.

152. J.H. Wiffen , 'English nobility and gentry', appendix to his translation of Tasso, "Jerusalem Liberated", Henry G. Bohn, London, 1854. Elizabeth Siberry, "The New Crusaders", Ashgate, 2000, lists the names in alphabetical order, whereas Wiffen divides them up by the reigns of the kings. Dansey in ref. 74 above is more comprehensive. 'Werris de Valoign' is in Pipe Roll Society, "Feet of Fines for the Tenth Year of King Richard the First", Vol.24, Love & Wyman, 1900, and John de Valences in Eugène de Rozière, "Cartulaire de l'Église du Saint Sépulcre de Jérusalem", Imprimerie Nationale, Paris, 1849, as well as ref. 132.

153. Stephen Howarth, "The Knights Templar", op cit; René Grousset, "Histoire des Croisades et de Royaume Franc de Jérusalem", Librairie Plon, Paris, 1935; Sir E.A. Wallis Budge, "St. George of Lydda", Luzac & Co. Semitic Text and Translation Series, London, 1930, quoting William of Malmesbury.

154. William Stubbs, ed., "Ymagines Historiarum", in "Ralph de Diceto, Dean of London", op cit.

155. William Stubbs, Introduction to "The Chronicle of the Reigns of Henry II and Richard I A.D. 1169-92, known commonly under the name of Benedict of Peterborough", Rolls series No.49, Longman, Green, Reader & Dyer, 1867.

Chapter Five - THE 'ANTIPODES' INCIDENT

1. J. Stephenson, Preface to Ralph of Coggeshall, "Chronicon Anglicanum", op cit.
2. W.M. Loftie, "A History of London", Stanford, London, 1883.
3. Christopher N.L. Brooke, "London 800-1216: the Shaping of a City", Secker & Warburg, 1975.
4. Alfred John Kempe, "Historical Notices of the Collegiate Church or Royal Free Chapel and Sanctuary of St. Martin-le-Grand", Longman, 1825.
5. D.C. Douglas, "Feudal Documents from the Abbey of Bury St. Edmunds", op cit.
6. John Willis Clark, ed., "Liber Memorandum Ecclesia de Bernewelle", op cit.
7. William Camden, "Britannia", op cit.
8. Sir William Dugdale, "The Baronage of England, or a Historical Account of the Lives & Most Memorable Actions of Our English Nobility", Newcomb, London, 1675.
9. Richard Newcourt, "Repertorium Ecclesiasticum Parochiale Londiniense", op cit.
10. Edward Freeman, "The History of the Norman Conquest of England", Clarendon Press, Oxford, 1871.
11. W.A. Copinger, "The Manors of Suffolk", op cit.
12. Rev. Samuel Pegge, "Sketch of the History of Bolsover and Peak Castles in the County of Derby", J. Nichols, London, 1785.
13. J.H. Round, "Geoffrey de Mandeville", op cit. William Peverell had two manors in Essex, in Domesday; he's credited with more in G. Martin, ed., Philip Morant, "The History and Antiquities of the County of Essex", (2 Vols.), EP Publishing, 1978, but that's corrected in H. Arthur Doubleday & William Page, eds., "The Victoria History of the Counties of England, Essex: Vol.1", op cit.
14. Celia Parker, Sara Wood, eds., "The Domesday Book, Vol.28: Nottinghamshire", Phillimore, Chichester, 1977.
15. Thomas Forester, ed., "The Ecclesiastical History of England and Normandy", op cit.

450

16. William Farrer, "An Outline Itinerary of King Henry the First", op cit.

17. D.F. Renn, "Norman Castles in Britain", John Baker, London, 1968.

18. Philip Morgan, ed., "The Domesday Book, vol.27: Derbyshire", Phillimore, Chichester, 1978.

19. Sir William Dugdale, "Monasticon Anglicanum", op cit.

20. Richard Yates, "History and Antiquities of the Abbey of St. Edmund's, Bury", op cit.

21. George Lord Lyttelton, "The History of the Life of King Henry the Second", op cit.

22. George Burton Adams, "The History of England", Longmans, 1905.

23. Rev. Peter Whalley, ed., "The History and Antiquities of Northamptonshire, compiled from the manuscript collections of the late learned antiquary John Bridges", J. Cooke, Oxford, 1791.

24. J.R. Planché, "The Conqueror and His Companions", Tinsley Brothers, London, 1874.

25. Charles Johnson, H.A. Cross, eds., "Regesta Regum Anglo Normannum 1066-1154 Vol. II: Regesta Henrici Primi 1100-1135", Oxford University Press, 1956.

26. H.G. Richardson, 'Gervase of Tilbury', *History, Journal of the History Association*, XLVI, 1961.

27. Charles H. Harteshorne, 'Peverell's Castle in the Peak', *Archaeological Journal*, 5, 207-216 (1848).

28. Beric Morley, "Peveril Castle", English Heritage, 1990.

29. Annie Duchesne, "Gervais de Tilbury", Les Belles Lettres, Paris, 1992. Ms. Duchesne cites no source for the dates she gives for Robert's time as Prior of Kenilworth. However, he's a witness to a charter between 1152 and 1167, in John Horace Round, ed., "Ancient Charters Royal and Private prior to AD 1200, Part 1", Pipe Roll Society, First Series, Vol.10, Wyman, 1888.

30. J.H. Round, ed., "Calendar of Documents Preserved in France Illustrative of the History of Great Britain", op cit.

31. David M. Smith, ed., "English Episcopal Acta, Vol. I: Lincoln 1067-1185", op cit.

32. Jeff Torrington, "Swing Hammer Swing!", Secker & Warburg, 1992.

33. S.E. Banks, J.W. Binns, eds., "Otia Imperialia, Recreation for an Emperor", Clarendon Press, 2002; Angela Hall, trans., Rudolf Simek, "Heaven and Earth in the Middle Ages, the Physical World before Columbus", Boydell Press, 1992.

34. Glossary, William Dunn McRae, ed., "Chronicon Abbatiae de Evesham", Rolls Series No.29, Longman, Green, Longman, Roberts and Green, 1863.

35. John Lennon, 'The Wrestling Dog', in "John Lennon in His Own Write", Jonathon Cape, 1964.

36.   Charles Johnson, H.A. Cronne, eds., "Regesta Regum Anglo Normannorum 1066-1154, Vol. III", op cit.

37. Edward King, 'An Account of the Great Seal of Randulph of Chester and of Two Ancient Inscriptions Found in the Ruins of Saint Edmund's Abbey', *Archaeologia* IV, 119-131 (1886).

38. K.R. Potter, ed., "Anon, Gesta Stephani, the Deeds of Stephen", op cit.

39. William Stubbs, ed., Gervase of Canterbury, "The Chronicle of the Reigns of Stephen, Henry II and Richard I", Rolls Series No.73, Longman & Co., 1879.

40. Henry Richards Luard, ed., "Chronica Majora" of Roger de Wendover & Matthew Paris, (7 vols.), Rolls Series No.57, Longmans & Co., 1883.

41. William Andrews, ed., "Bygone Derbyshire", Frank Murray, Derby, 1892.

42. John Leyland, "The Peak of Derbyshire", Seeley & Co., London, 1891.

43. B.H. St. J. O'Neil, "Peveril Castle, Derbyshire", H.M. Office of Works, 1934.

44. (Anon), 'Peverel of the Peak', *Derbyshire Countryside*, 25, 4, 17 (June-July 1960).

45. W. Adam, "The Gem of the Peak", Longman & Co., 1843.

46. John Middleton & Tony Waltham, "The Underground Atlas, a gazetteer of the world's cave regions", Hale, 1986.

47.   Richard Howlett, ed., "The Chronicle of Richard of Torigni", in "Chronicles of the Reigns of Stephen, Henry II and Richard I", op cit, vol.4.

48.   William Stubbs, ed., "The Historical Works of Master Ralph Diceto, Deacon of London", op cit.

49. Thomas Arnold, ed., Henry of Huntingdon, op cit.

50. Sir Walter Scott, "Peveril of the Peak", Adam & Charles Black, 1899.

51. Brian Christie, 'Great Scott Clean-up Spells More Sex', *The Scotsman*, 16th Aug. 1993.

52. Stephen Glover, "The Peak Guide", Henry Mozley & Son, Derby, 1830.

53. Dr. Thomas Short, "The Natural, Experimental and Medicinal History of the Mineral Waters of Derbyshire, Lancashire and Yorkshire", F. Gyles, 1734.

54. Sir Arthur Conan Doyle, 'The Terror of Blue John Gap', *The Strand Magazine*, 1910, reprinted in "The Collected Short Stories of Sir Arthur Conan

Doyle" and in Peter Haining, ed., "The Ancient Mysteries Reader", Gollancz, 1976.

55. J.A. MacCulloch, "Mediaeval Faith and Fable", Harrap, 1932.

56. Brian Woodall, "Peak Cavern", J.W. Northend, Sheffield, 1979.

57. Sir George Head, "A Home Tour through the Manufacturing Districts of England in the Summer of 1835", John Murray, London, 1836.

58. William of Newburgh, op cit.

59. Rev. R.W. Eyton, "Court, Household and Itinerary of King Henry II, noting also the chief agents and adversaries of the king in his government, diplomacy and strategy", Taylor & Co., London, 1878.

60. W.H. St. John Hope, 'The Castle of the Peak, and the Pipe Rolls', *The Reliquary*, New Series 2, 33-37 (1888).

61.   G.V. Scammell, "Hugh du Puiset, Bishop of Durham", Cambridge University Press, 1956.

Chapter Six - CONCERNING SAMSON DE BOTINGTON

1.   George Lord Lyttelton, "The History of the Life of King Henry the Second", op cit.

2. Thomas Arnold, ed., "Memorials of St. Edmund's Abbey", (3 vols.), Rolls Series No.96, Eyre & Spottiswoode, 1890.

3. H.E. Butler, ed., "The Chronicle of Jocelin of Brakelond", op cit.

4. Brian Patrick McGuire, 'The Collapse of a Monastic Friendship: the Case of Jocelin and Samson of Bury', Journal of Mediaeval History, 4, 347-368 (1978).

6. James Bentley, personal communication, 7th March 1999.

7. Henry Shaw, FSA, "Dress and Decoration of the Middle Ages", 1840, First Glance Books, 1998.

8. John Telfer Dunbar, "Highland Costume", The Mercat Press, Edinburgh, 1983.

9.   Ralph V. Turner, "The English Justiciary in the Age of Glanvill and Bracton, c.1176-1239", Cambridge University Press, 1985.

10. Edward J. Kealey, "Roger of Salisbury, Viceroy of England", op cit.

11.   Francis J. West, "The Justiciarship in England 1066-1232", Cambridge University Press, 1966

12. C. Johnson, H.A. Cronne, "Regesta Regum Anglo Normannorum 1066-1154, Vol. III", op cit.

13. J.H. Round, ed., "Documents Preserved in France Illustrative of the History of Great Britain", op cit; Frank Barlow, "Thomas Becket and His Clerks", Friends of Canterbury Cathedral, 1987.

14. Henry Wharton, ed., "Anglia Sacra sive Collectio Historiarum, de Archiepiscopis et Episcopis Angliae, a prima fidei Christianae susceptione ad annum MDXL", Richard Chiswell, London, 1591.

15. Beatrice Adelaide Lees, "Records of the Templars", op cit.

16. John H. Mundy, "Europe in the High Middle Ages, 1150-1309", op cit.

17. R. Howlett, ed., "The Chronicle of Robert of Torigni", op cit.

18. J. Stephenson, ed., Ralph of Coggeshall, "Chronicon Anglicanum", op cit.

19. R. Howlett, ed., Stephani Rothomagensis, "Draco Normannis", in "Chronicles of the Reigns of Stephen, Henry II and Richard I", op cit.

20. Francis Blomefield, "An Essay towards a Topographical History of the County of Norfolk", op cit.

21. N. Makhouly, C.N. Johns, "Guide to Acre", Government of Palestine Department of Antiquities, 2nd edition, 1946.

22. Richard Vaughan, ed., "The Illustrated Chronicles of Matthew Paris", Alan Sutton Publishing, 1993, includes a stylised map of Acre as a detail from Paris's 13th century map of the Holy Land. Most of its features can be identified on a plan of Acre dated 1291, in Edith Swann, "The Piebald Standard", op cit. It shows a castle within the walls, by St. Anthony's Gate, but doesn't attribute it to anybody, unlike the 'Tower of the Countess of Blois', 'Tower of King Hugh' and 'Tower of King Henry II'. Paris marks Swann's unnamed one as 'castle of the king of Acre'. The other castles within the walls belonged to the Knights Hospitallers, the Knights Templar and the Teutonic Knights.

23. Two of those are also shown on a mid-century plan in Malcolm Barber, "The New Knighthood", op cit, on which it seems that the unnamed castle in Swann's plan is Venetian. Nor is there any record of a de Warenne castle in detailed descriptions of Acre and its crusader suburb Montmusard - David Jacoby, 'Crusader Acre in the Thirteenth Century: Urban Layout and Topography' (with map, and a black-and-white reproduction of the Matthew Paris map), 'Montmusard, Suburb of Crusader Acre: the First Stage of its Development', both in David Jacoby, "Studies on the Crusader States and on Venetian Expansion", Variorum, Northampton, 1989; nor in the letters of Jacques de Vitry, bishop of Acre 1216-1225, R.B.C. Huyens, ed., "Lettres de Jacques de Vitry (1160/70-1240), évêque de Saint-Jean d'Acre", E.J. Brill, Leiden, 1960; nor in a detailed account of the fall of Acre, Gustave

Schlumberger, 'Prise de Saint-Jean-d'Acre en l'An 1291 par l'Armée de Soudan d'Égypte', in Gustave Schlumberger, "Byzance et Croisades, Pages Médiévales", Librairie Orientaliste Paul Guenthner, Paris, 1927.

24. Rev. R.W. Eyton, "Court, Household and Itinerary of King Henry II", op cit.

25. Sir William Dugdale, "The Baronage of England", op cit.

26. Christopher Harper-Bill, "English Episcopal Acta VI: Norwich", op cit.

27. Ralph V. Turner, "King John", Longman, 1994.

28. Herbert Wood, 'The Templars in Ireland', op cit.

29. Gérard de Sède, "Les Templiers Sont Parmi Nous", op cit.

30. For the seals of bishops and abbots see James Aveling, "The History of Roche Abbey from its Founding to its Dissolution", Robert White, Worksop, 1870. Through Jane Greatorex, Canterbury Cathedral supplied a very dramatic photograph of Samson's seal, but unfortunately the shadows conceal the wording. John Gage Rokewood, ed., "Chronica Jocelini de Brakelonda, de Rebus Gestis Samsonis Abbatis Monasterii Sancti Edmundi", Camden Society, 1840, gives a clear reproduction of both sides of Samson's seal as a frontispiece. It's described in Richard Yates, "History and Antiquities of the Abbey of St. Edmund's, Bury", op cit, which also reproduces Samson's other seal with the orb, plain cross and fleur-de-lis, from the founding charter of St. Saviour's Hospital. Yates dates it to 1200, but Christopher Harper-Bill, "Suffolk Charters: Charters of the Mediaeval Hospitals of Bury St. Edmunds", Suffolk Records Society, 1994, gives the founding as 1197 at the latest. In the copy of Yates held by the National Library of Scotland that plate is missing (if it's been stolen, it's been done very neatly, because it looks as if it was never there), but the Suffolk County Records Office copy has it. The seal impression is held by the British Library Manuscripts Department as 'lxxi.90'; see entry no. 2796 in Walter de Grace Birch, ed., "Catalogue of Seals in the Department of Manuscripts in the British Museum", [as it then was], Longmans, 1887.

31. For the terminology of different designs of cross see John Ellison Kohn, ed., "Reader's Digest Reverse Dictionary", Reader's Digest Association Limited, 1989.

32. J. Bruce Williamson, "The History of the Temple, London", Murray, 1924

33. G. Nahon, trans., Joshua Prawer, "Histoire du Royaume Latin de Jérusalem", Éditions du Centre de la Research Scientifique, Paris, 1969.

34. F.A. Inderwick, Introduction to "The Inner Temple, Its Early History as Illustrated by Its Records", Henry Sotheran & Co., London, 1896

35. Rokewood above reproduces the Banner of St. Edmund drawn by John Lydgate, whose "Life and Miracles of Saint Edmund" is held in the British Library as Harleian MS. 2278.   Lydgate's tomb was discovered at the same time as the earl of Chester's seal (see Chap. 5); for his epitaph see Edward King, 'An Account of the Great Seal of Randulph of Chester and of Two Ancient Inscriptions Found in the Ruins of Saint Edmund's Abbey', op cit.

36. H.R. Barker, "West Suffolk Illustrated", F.G. Pawsey, Bury St. Edmunds, 1907.

37.   Helen Nicholson, "The Knights Templar, a New History", op.cit; Wm. Page, ed., "Victoria History of the Counties of England: Suffolk, Vol. II", Constable, 1907.

38. D.F. Renn, "Norman Castles in England", op cit.

39. W.H. St. John Hope, 'The Castle of the Peak, and the Pipe Rolls', op cit.

40. Michael David Knowles, "The Monastic Orders in England", Cambridge University Press, 1941.

41.   John Leland, ed., "Antiquarii de Rebus Britannicis Collectaneorum", 6 vols., Gul. et Jo. Richardson, London, 1770.

42. Matthew Paris, "Chronica Majora", op cit.

43.   William Dodsworth, "An Historical Account of the Episcopal See, and Cathedral Church of Salisbury", op cit.

44.   James Craigie Robertson, ed., "Materials for the History of Thomas Becket, Archbishop of Canterbury", Rolls Series No.67 (7 vols.), Longman & Co., 1876.

45.   Henry T. Riley, ed., "The Annals of Roger de Hoveden", H.G. Bohn, London, 1853 (also Rolls Series No.51).

46. Stephen Howarth, "The Knights Templar", Marion Melville, "La Vie des Templiers", op cit.

47. G. Martin, ed., Philip Morant, "The History and Antiquities of the County of Essex", op cit.

48. Lilian J. Redstone, 'The Liberty of St. Edmund', *Proceedings of the Suffolk Institute of Archaeology*, XV, 207-209, 1915.

49.   Antonius Hall, ed., "Nicolai Triveti, Dominicani, Annales Sex Regum Angliae", E. Theatro Sheldoniano, Oxford, 1729; Arthur Hassall, ed., William Stubbs, Introduction to Walter of Coventry, in "Historical Introductions to the Rolls Series by William Stubbs, DD", op cit.

50. David M. Smith, ed., "English Episcopal Acta I: Lincoln 1067-1185", op cit.

51. L.F. Salzman, ed., "The Victoria History of the Counties of England: Warwickshire, Vol. VI - Knightlow Hundred", Oxford University Press, 1951.

52. Hubert Hall, ed., "The Red Book of the Exchequer", op cit.

53. Ralph V. Turner, 'Richard Barre and Michael Belet', op cit.

54. Eleanor Rathbone, 'Roman Law in the Anglo-Norman Realm', op cit.

55. Joseph Warichez, "Étienne de Tournai et Son Temps", op cit.   James A. Brundage, "Medieval Canon Law", Longman, 1995, gives a later date for Stephan's birth and 1191 for his Tournai appointment, but Canon Warichez's biography of him seems authoritative.

56. H.G. Richardson, 'Gervase of Tilbury', *History, the Journal of the Historical Association*, XLVI, Routledge & Kegan Paul, 1961; G.C. Coulton, "Mediaeval Panorama, The English Scene from Conquest to Reformation", op cit.; J.M. Upton-Ward, "The Rule of the Templars", op.cit.

57. Anon, "Summa de multiplici iuris divisione", reprinted in Richard M. Fraher, 'The Becket Dispute and Two Decretist Traditions: the Bolognese Masters Revisited and Some New Anglo-Norman Texts', *Journal of Mediaeval History*, 4, 347-368

58. Miller, Butler and Brooke, eds., "The Letters of John of Salisbury", Vol.1, Nelson Mediaeval Texts, 1955; Vol.2, Oxford Mediaeval Texts, 1979.

59. Rev. R.W. Eyton, "Antiquities of Shropshire", Vol. I, John Russell Smith, 1854.

60. R. Howlett, ed., Stephani Rothomagensis, "Draco Normannis", in "Chronicles of the Reigns of Stephen, Henry II and Richard I", op cit.

61. Benedict of Peterborough, op cit.

62. Zachary Nugent Brooke, 'The Register of Magister David of London and the Part He Played in the Becket Crisis', in H.W.C. Davis, ed., "Essays in History Presented to Reginald Lane Poole", Oxford University Press, 1927.

Chapter Seven - GHOSTS IN THE NIGHT

1. James F. Dimock, ed., "Giraldus Cambrensis Opera, Vol. V", Rolls Series No.21, Longman, Green, Reader & Dyer, 1868; James Henthorn Todd, ed., "The Irish Version of the Historia Britonum of Nennius", Irish Archaeological Society, Dublin, 1848.

2. John O'Donovan, ed., "The Annals of the Kingdom of Ireland, by the Four Masters, from the earliest period to the year 1616", Hodges, Smith & Co., Dublin, 1856.

3. Thomas Moore, "The Cabinet Cyclopaedia: Ireland, Vol. II", Longmans, Brown, Green & Longmans, 1846.

4. Mary Hayden, George A. Moonan, "A Short History of the Irish People, from the earliest times to 1920", Longmans, Green & Co., 1921.

5. Rev. J.F. Shearman, 'The Early Kings of Ossory', *Journal of the Kilkenny Archaeological Society/ Royal Society of Antiquarians of Ireland*, 4th Series, no.4, 1876-78, 336-408.

6. Marion Melville, "La Vie des Templiers", op cit.

7. Walter Harris, ed., Sir James Ware, "The History and Antiquities of Ireland... with the History of the Writers of Ireland, in Two Books", Robert Bell, Dublin, 1764.

8. Walter Harris, "Hibernica, or Some Pieces Relating to Ireland", John Milliken, Dublin, 1770.

9. Rev. William Carrigan, "The History and Antiquities of the Diocese of Ossory", Sealy, Bryers & Walker, Dublin, 1905.

10. Rev. Edward Ledwich, "Antiquities of Ireland", Arthur Gruebar, Dublin, 1790.

11. Goddard H. Orpen, 'Motes and Norman Castles in Ossory', *Royal Society of Antiquaries of Ireland Journal*, Series 5, XIX, 312-42 (1909).

12. Hilary D. Walsh, "Borris-in-Ossory, Co. Laois, an Irish rural parish and its people", Kilkenny Journal Ltd..

13. R.A.S. Macalister, "Corpus Inscriptionum Insularum Celticarum", Dublin Stationery Office, 1945.

14. Rev. Edward Ledwich, "A Statistical Account of the Parish of Aghaboe", Bonham, Dublin, 1796.

15. W.G. Hanson, "The Early Monastic Schools of Ireland", W. Heffer, Cambridge, 1927.

16. Rev. John Lanigan, "An Ecclesiastical History of Ireland", (4 parts in 3 vols.), Grainberry, Dublin, 1822; Aubrey Gwynn, R. Neville Hadcock, "Mediaeval Religious Houses in Ireland", Longman, 1970.

17. Eric St. John Brooks, ed., "Knights' Fees in Counties Wexford, Carlow and Kilkenny (13th-15th Century)", Dublin Stationery Office, 1950.

1. Dr. John Wilson, introduction to J.A. Kane, "The Ancient Building Science", Edwards Bros. Inc., 1940; quoted in Robert Bauval & Adrian Gilbert, "The Orion Mystery", Heinemann, 1994.

2. H.G. Richardson, 'Gervase of Tilbury', op cit.

3. H.E. Butler, ed., "The Chronicle of Jocelin of Brakelond", op cit.

4. John H. Mundy, "Europe in the High Middle Ages, 1150-1309", op cit.

5. Lilian J. Redstone, 'The Liberty of St. Edmund', op cit.

6. 'Beaumont', "Coggeshall, a Savigny-Cistercian Monastery", Essex Archaeological Society, 1960; Beatrice M. Rose, "The Story of King Stephen and Queen Maud and the Abbey They Founded at Coggeshall in Essex", 1952 (held at Essex County Records Office, Chelmsford).

7. Alfred John Dunkin, ed., "Radolphi Abbatis de Coggeshall Works", private edition, (25 copies), 1852; held at Essex County Records Office. That Ralph was first a canon at Barnwell appears in Thomas Tanner, "Bibliotheca Britannico-Hibernica", Gulielmus Bower, London, 1748, quoted in Thos. Duffus Hardy, ed., "Descriptive Catalogue of Materials Relating to the History of Great Britain and Ireland", Rolls Series No. 26, Longman, Green, Longman, Roberts & Green, 1865.

8. William Stubbs, ed., Benedict of Peterborough, op cit.

9. John Willis Clark, ed., "Liber Memorandum Ecclesia de Bernewelle", Cambridge U.P., 1907.

10. Paul Harris, 'The Green Children of Woolpit', op cit.

11. W.R. Hensyll, ed., "Stedman's Medical Dictionary", 25th edition, Williams & Wilkins, 1990; J.W. Wyngaarden, L.H. Smith, J.C. Bennett, eds., "Cecil's Textbook of Medicine", 19th edition, W.B. Saunders, 1992.

12. Glyn Maxwell, "Wolfpit", op cit.

13. (Anon), 'Children Lost in Andes for Three Weeks', *The West Australian*, 4th December, 1994.

14. Carl Sagan, "The Demon-Haunted World: Science as a Candle in the Dark", Headline Book Publishing, 1996.

15. W.R. Ross, ed., E.S. Forster, trans., 'The Coloration of the Flesh', in "The Works of Aristotle, Vol. VII, Problematica", Oxford University Press, 1927.

16. Margaret Humphreys, 'Chlorosis, the Virgin's Disease', in Kenneth F. Kiple, "Plague, Pox and Pestilence, Disease in History", Weidenfeld & Nicolson, 1997.

17. Kenneth F. Kiple, "Plague, Pox and Pestilence, Disease in History", op cit.

18. Francis Blomefield, "An Essay towards a Topographical History of the County of Norfolk", op cit.

19. J. Reid Moir, "Grime's Graves, Weeting, Norfolk", Ministry of Works, His Majesty's Stationery Office, 1936.

20. Christopher Howse, 'A Flinty Treat in Southwold', *Daily Telegraph*, August 2nd, 2008.

21. Brian Branston, "The Lost Gods of England", Thames & Hudson, 1957; Ralph Whitlock, "In Search of Lost Gods, a Guide to British Folklore", Phaidon, Oxford, 1979.

22. Joseph Stevenson, ed., "Chronicon Ricardi Diviensis de Rebus Gestis Ricardi Primi Regis Angliae", English Historical Society, 1838.

23. Ian Atherton et al, eds., "Norwich Cathedral, Church, City and Diocese", op cit.

24. Dr. Karl Shuker, "The Unexplained - an Illustrated Guide to the World's Natural and Paranormal Mysteries", Carlton, 1996.

25. 'Chemical Elements', New Encyclopedia Britannica, 15th edition, Macropaedia, Vol.15.

26. Sam Kean, "The Disappearing Spoon", Little, Brown & Co., 2010; Jane Greatorex, personal communication, March 10th 1998.

27. Fred Pearce, 'Arsenic in the Water', *The Guardian*, February 19th, 1998.

28. Fred Pearce, personal communication, March 17th, 1998.

29. Paul Harris, 'The Green Children of Woolpit: a 12th Century Mystery and its Possible Solution', personal communication, 1997.

30. Garma C.C. Chang, "The Hundred Thousand Songs of Milarepa", 2 vols., University Books, New York, 1962.

31. Richard Simpson, 'Great Drives', *The Daily Telegraph - Motoring*, February 24th, 2001.

32. Elisabeth Crawfoot, Frances Pritchard, Kay Stanilaw, eds., "Mediaeval Finds from Excavations in London: 4, Textiles and Clothing", HMSO, 1992.

33. J.J. Bagley, "Life in Mediaeval England", Batsford, 1960.

34. Roger Highfield, 'Priory Seeds Burst into Life after 400 Years', *Daily Telegraph*, June 26th 1999.

35. H.V. Morton, "In Search of Ireland", Methuen, 1930.

36. Robert Graves, "The White Goddess", Faber 1948.

37. Vanessa Parker, "The Making of King's Lynn", Phillimore, 1971; Henry J. Hillen, "History of the Borough of King's Lynn", self-published, Norwich, 1907, reprinted EP Publishing Ltd., 1978.

38. J. Arnold Fleming, "Flemish Influence in Britain", Vol.1, Wylie, 1930, quoted by Harris in ref.26.

39. Helen Clarke, Alan Carter, eds., "Excavations in King's Lynn, 1963-70", Society of Mediaeval Archaeology, Monograph Series 7, 1977.

40. Gerry Kennedy & Rob Churchill, "The Voynich Manuscript", Orion Books, 2004.

41. Elspeth Thompson, 'Urban Gardener: Elderberries', *Daily Telegraph Gardening*, 9th Oct. 2005.

42. John Strype, "Survey of London", op cit.

43. Hakluyt under 'Greenwood' in "The Compact Edition of the Oxford English Dictionary", Oxford University Press, 1971.

44. Ian Mortimer, "The Time-Traveller's Guide to Medieval England", Vintage Books, 2009.

45. Sue Jones, personal communication, 15th May 2000.

46. Montse Stanley, 'Two 13th Century Knitted Cushions from the Castilian Royal Tombs at the Monastery of Las Huelgas, Burgos, Spain', 'Unravelling the Evidence' conference of the Early Knitting History Group in conjunction with the Medieval Dress and Textile Society, London, 8th March 1997.

47. William Melczer, "The Pilgrim's Guide to Compostela", Italica Press, New York, 1993; Barry Cunliffe, "Facing the Ocean, the Atlantic and its Peoples 8000 BC – AD 1500", Oxford U.P., 2001.

48. Adam Hopkins, 'Pray for Me - and My Feet', *Daily Telegraph*, 21st June 1997; Derek Bishton, 'Pilgrim's Spain: Back from the Future', 22nd April 2000.

49. Madelaine Pelner Cosman, "Mediaeval Holidays and Festivals", Piatkus Books, 1984.

50. Paul Harris, 'St. Martin's Land, an Alternative Possibility', personal communication, 1997.

51. A.B. Whittingham, "Bury St. Edmunds Abbey", *Archaeological Journal*, CVIII, 1951; reprinted HMSO, 1971, English Heritage, 1992.

52. Nick Milles, "The Gough Map: the Earliest Road Map of Great Britain", Oxford, 2007.

53. G.C. Coulton, "Mediaeval Panorama, The English Scene from Conquest to Reformation", op cit.

54   Arthur Hassall, ed., "Historical Introductions to the Rolls Series by William Stubbs, D.D.", op cit.

55. Gillian Hutchinson, "Mediaeval Ships and Shipping", Leicester University Press, Cassell, 1994.

56. William Camden, "Britannia", op cit; Francis Hickes, trans., Lucian of Samothrace, "The True History", 1634; excerpt, 'How Lucian of Samothrace Voyaged to the Moon and How He Was Afterwards Swallowed by a Whale', in H.M. Tomlinson, ed., "Great Sea Stories of All Nations", Harrap, 1930; Marjorie Hope Nicolson, "Voyages to the Moon", op cit.

57. Judith Stinton, "Tom's Tale", Walker Books, 1990.

58. Kevin Crossley-Holland, Alan Marks, "The Green Children", Oxford University Press, 1994.

59. Kevin Crossley-Holland, Nicola LeFanu, "The Green Children", Novello, 1991 [for their opera about the wild man of Orford, discussed in Chap. 5, see Michael Kennedy, 'A Revelation on a Lousy Night', *Sunday Telegraph*, (*Review* section, p.8], 18th June, 1995); Susanna Clapp, Richard Maybe, 'The Green Children of Woolpit', BBC Radio 4, 8th June 2010.

60. Ellen Phillips, Robin Richman, eds., "The Enchanted World - Fabled Lands", Time-Life Books, 1986.

61. James F. Dimock, ed., "Giraldus Cambrensis Opera, Vol. VI", op cit.

62. Herbert Read, "The Green Child, a romance", Heinemann, 1935.

63. J.G. Ballard, "The Crystal World", Jonathon Cape, 1966.

64. Simon Cox, 'Appendix 4: A Sanctuary for Sohar', quoting Sir James Fraser, "The Golden Bough", in Robert Bauval, "Secret Chamber, the Quest for the Hall of Records", Arrow Books, 2000.

65. Randolph Stow, "The Girl Green as Elderflower", Secker & Warburg, 1980.

66. John Crowley, 'The Green Child', in Terri Windling & Mark Alan Arnold, eds., "Elsewhere", Ace Books, 1981; Gary K. Wolfe, review of John Crowley, "Antiquities", (Incunabula, Seattle, limited edition, 1993), *Locus* 31, 6, 21 (Dec. 1993).

67. Peter Kolosimo, "Not of This World", Sugar Editore, Milan, 1969; trans. Souvenir Press, 1970.

68. (Anon, ed.), "The Unexplained, mysteries of mind, space and time", Orbis Publishing, 1992.

69. Desmond Leslie & George Adamski, "Flying Saucers Have Landed", Werner Laurie, 1953; Harold T. Wilkins, "Flying Saucers on the Attack", 1954; Ace Books, 1967.

70. (Anon, ed.), "Folklore, Myths and Legends of Britain", Reader's Digest Association, 1977.

71. Carroll C. Calkins, ed., "Mysteries of the Unexplained", Reader's Digest association, 1982.

72. C. Leonard Wooley, "Ur of the Chaldees", Ernest Benn, 1929.

73. Farouk El-Baz, 'Finding a Pharaoh's Funeral Bark', *National Geographic Magazine*, 173, 4, 513-550 (April 1988).

74. Michael Bentine, "The Templar", op cit.

75. Marion Melville, "La Vie des Templiers", op cit.

76. A.T. Hatto, trans., "Wolfram von Eschenbach, Parzival", Penguin, 1980. The Parzival version of the Holy Grail is a Heavenly stone which can provide any food or drink on demand, like the devices of Philip Jose Farmer's *Riverworld* novels (Chap. 22 refs.).   Aptly, my pen ran out of ink as I took notes on it.

77. Andrew Sinclair, "The Discovery of the Grail", Century, 1998.

78. H.V. Morton, "In the Steps of the Master", Rich and Cannon, 1934.

79. Kathy Brewis, 'The Flying Squad', *Sunday Times Magazine*, 12th November, 2000; Mike Baillie, "Exodus to Arthur", op cit; Francesco Gabrieli, ed., "Arab Historians of the Crusades", Routledge & Kegan Paul, 1969; Zev Vilney, "The Sacred Land: Vol.1, Legends of Jerusalem", Jewish Publications Society of America, 1973;   Benjamin Z. Kedar, H.E. Meyer & R.C. Smail, eds., "Outremer, Studies in the History of the Crusading Kingdom of Jerusalem", op cit.

80. For the destruction of the church of St. Mary the Green in 934 AD see J. Katchikovsky, A. Vasiliev, 'Histoire de Yahya ibn Sa'id d'Antioche', Patrologia Orientalis, Paris, 1924.   The other source cited, (Joshua Prawer, 'The Town and County of Ascalon during the Crusades') apparently is available only in Hebrew.

81. Noel Malcolm review, Kris Lane, "The Colour of Paradise: Colombian Emeralds in the Age of Gunpowder Empires", *Sunday Telegraph 'Seven'*, 18th April, 2010.

82. Idries Shah, "The Way of the Sufi", Cape, 1968; Sir E.A. Wallis Budge, "St. George of Lydda", op cit.

83. F.E. Peters, "Jerusalem", op cit.

84. C.S. Lewis, "Out of the Silent Planet", John Lane the Bodley Head, 1938; "Perelandra", aka "Voyage to Venus", 1943.

85. Peter Dronke, "Fabula: Explorations into the Uses of Myth in Medieval Platonism", E.J. Brill, Leiden, 1974.

86 Winthrop Wetherbee, ed., "The Cosmographia of Bernardus Silvestris" (English trans.), Columbia University Press, 1973.

87. Peter Dronke, ed., "Bernardus Silvestris Cosmographia" (Latin text), E.J. Brill, 1978.

88. Harry Sperling & Maurice Simon, eds., "The Zohar", Soncino Press, London, 1931.

89. For example S.L. MacGregor Mathers, "The Kabbalah Unveiled", Kegan Paul, Trench, Trubner & Co., 1926; Moshe Idel, "Kabbalah, New Perspectives", Yale University Press, 1988.

90. Angelo S. Rappoport, "Myth and Legend of Ancient Israel", 3 vols., Gresham Publishing Co., London, 1928.

91. David Goldstein, "Jewish Mythology", Hamlyn 1987.

92. Rev. Oswald Cockayne, "Leechdoms, Wortcunning and Starcraft of Early England, Vol. 3", Rolls Series 35, Longmans, Green, Reader & Dyer, 1866.

93. Taken seriously in Erich von Däniken, "Return to the Stars", Souvenir Press, 1970.

94. Model by Peter Rush, photograph by John Marmarus, 'Is There Anyone Up There Like Us?', *Daily Telegraph Magazine*, no.383, March 3rd, 1972.

95. Fred Hoyle and N.C. Wickramasinghe, "Lifecloud, the Origin of Life in the Universe", Dent, 1978; "Evolution from Space", Dent, 1981.

96. Edgar Rice Burroughs, "A Princess of Mars", Methuen, 1919; "The Gods of Mars", Methuen, 1920.

97. Carl Sagan, Gifford Lectures, Glasgow University, 1985.

Chapter Nine - THE OVERTHROW OF LEICESTER

1. Palgrave quoted in William Stubbs, Introduction to Benedict of Peterborough, op cit; also in Arthur Hassall, ed., "Historical Introductions to the Rolls series, by William Stubbs, D.D.", op cit.

2. Rev. John Williams ab Ithel, ed., "Brut y Tywysogion; or, the Chronicle of the Princes", op cit.

3. John Bellenden, trans., "The History and Chronicles of Scotland: written in Latin by Hector Boece, canon of Aberdeen", Vol. II, W. & C. Tait, Edinburgh, 1821.

4. Thomas Stapledon, ed., "Chronicon Petroburgense", Camden Society, Vol. XLVII, 1849.

5. Rev. R.W. Eyton, "Court, Household and Itinerary of King Henry II", op cit.

6. Rodney M. Thomson, ed., "The Archives of the Abbey of Bury St. Edmunds", Suffolk Records Society Vol. XXI, Boydell Press, 1980.

7. George Lord Lyttelton, "The History of the Life of King Henry the Second", op cit.

8. Joseph Warichez, "Étienne de Tournai et Son Temps", op cit.

9. Pipe Roll Society, "The Great Roll of the Pipe for the 16th Year of King Henry the Second, AD 1169-70", Vol.15, 1892.

10. Rev. John Lingard, "A History of England from the First Invasion of the Romans to the Accession of Henry III", 3 vols., J. Mawman, London, 1819. The struggle to move the see of Norfolk from Thetford to Bury St. Edmunds is detailed in Richard Yates, "History and Antiquities of the Abbey of St. Edmund's, Bury", op cit.

11. Jim Wilson, ed., "900 Years, Norwich Cathedral and Diocese", Jarrold Publishing, 1996.

12. Thomas Arnold, ed., "Memorials of St. Edmund's Abbey", op cit; H.E. Butler, ed., "The Chronicle of Jocelin of Brakelond", op cit..

13. William Farrer, ed., "Early Yorkshire Charters", Ballantine, Hanson & Co., Edinburgh, 1914.

14. William Stubbs, ed., Benedict of Peterborough, op cit; Ralph V. Turner, 'Richard Barre and Michael Belet', op cit. Prince Henry's seal is reproduced in L.F. Salzmann, "Henry II", op cit.

15. Deputy Keeper of the Records, ed., "A Descriptive Catalogue of Ancient Deeds Held in the Public Records Office", op cit.

16. George Caspar Homans, "English Villagers of the Thirteenth Century", op cit.

17. G.V. Scammell, "Hugh du Puiset", op cit.

18. Francis Blomefield, "An Essay towards a Topographical History of the County of Norfolk", op cit.

19. David J. Cathcart King, "The Castle in England and Wales", Routledge, 1988.

20. David J. Cathcart King, "Castellarum Anglicanum, an index and bibliography of the castles in England, Wales and the Islands", Kraus International Publications, 1983; Vincent Redstone, "Memorials of Old Suffolk", Bernrose & Sons, 1908.

21. B.H. St. J. O'Neil, "Castles", HMSO, 1954.

22. William Page, ed., "Victoria Historia of the Counties of England: Hampshire and the Isle of Wight, Vol. 4", Constable, 1911.

23. Rev. R.W. Eyton, "Antiquities of Shropshire", op cit.

24. William Stubbs, ed., "The Historical Works of Master Ralph de Diceto", op cit.

25. William A. Dutt, "Highways and Byways of East Anglia", Macmillan, 1914.

26. Richard Howlett, ed., Jordan Fantosme, "Chronicle of the War between the English and the Scotch in 1173 and 1174", in "Chronicles of the Reigns of Stephen, Henry II and Richard I", op cit.

27. Matthew Paris, "Chronica Majora", op cit.

28. Henry T. Riley, ed., "The Annals of Roger de Hoveden", op cit.

29. William Stubbs, ed., "The Chronicle of the Reigns of Stephen, Henry II and Richard I, by Gervase the Monk of Canterbury", op cit.

30. John Gage Rokewood, ed., "Chronica Jocelini de Brakelondi", op cit.

31. Hon. H.C. Neville, "The Romance of the Ring, or the History and Antiquity of Finger Rings", Literary Society of Saffron Walden, 1856, in Glasgow University Library Special Collections, "Archaeological Tracts", Vol.1.

32. Richard Howlett, ed., "The Chronicle of Richard of Torigni", op cit.

33. Richard Yates, "History and Antiquities of the Abbey of St. Edmund's, Bury", op cit.

34. Thomas Wright, ed., "Historical Works of Giraldus Cambrensis", H.G. Bohn, London, 1863.

35. Thomas Moore, "The Cabinet Cyclopaedia: Ireland, Vol. II", Longman, Brown, Green & Longmans, 1846.

36. Herbert Wood, 'The Templars in Ireland', op cit.

37. Michael Baigent and Richard Leigh, "The Temple and the Lodge", Jonathon Cape, 1989.

38. Charles H. Harteshorne, 'Peverell's Castle in the Peak', Archaeological Journal, 5, 207-210 (1848).

39. D.F. Renn, "Norman Castles in England", op cit.

40. William Andrews, ed., "Bygone Derbyshire", op cit.

41. Stephen Glover, "The Peak Guide", op cit.

42. Tom Austen, 'Charting the Channel', *The West Australian*, 4th October, 2003.

43. Gérard Serbanesco, "Histoire de l'Ordre des Templiers", op cit.

44. William Camden, "Britannia", op cit.

45. Henry Wharton, ed., "Anglia Sacra", op cit.

46. J.H. Round, ed., "Calendar of Documents Preserved in France Illustrative of the History of Great Britain", op cit.

47. D.C. Douglas, ed., "Feudal Documents Relating to Bury St. Edmunds", op cit.

1. Malcolm Barber, "The Trial of the Templars", op cit.

2. William Farrer, ed., "Early Yorkshire Charters", op cit.

3. James Bentham, "History and Antiquities of the... Church of Ely", op cit, shows Ridell's arms in black-and-white, supposedly from H. Wharton, ed., "Anglia Sacra sive Collectio Historiarum", op cit, but they're not there.

4. Dom. Martin Bosquet, Vols. 1-2 of 24, "Recueil des Historiens des Gaulles et de la France", Libraires Associés, Paris, 1738-1904.

5. Jacques Fontaine, ed., Sulspice Sévère, "Vie de Saint Martin", Sources Chrétiennes no. 133, Éditions du Cerf, Paris, 1967.

6. M.R. James, 'On the Abbey of St. Edmund at Bury', Cambridge Antiquarian Society Vol. XXVIII, Macmillan 1895.

7. John Mabillon, ed., "Vetera Analecta, sive Collectio Veterum Aliquot Operum", Montallant, Paris, 1723, includes a dialogue between two mediaeval bishops on the subject, which may be the Bury text.

8. James Henthorn Todd, ed., "The Irish Version of the Historia Britonum of Nennius", op cit.

9. A.B. Whittingham, "Bury St. Edmunds Abbey", op cit.

10. Jo Marchant, "Decoding the Heavens", Heinemann, 2008.

11. Beatrice Adelaide Lees, "Records of the Templars in England in the 12th Century", op cit.

12. D.D. Andrews, ed., "Cressing Temple, a Templar and Hospitaller Manor in Essex", Essex County Planning Department, 1993.

13. Timothy Baker, "Mediaeval London", Cassell, 1970; Alfred John Kempe, "Historical Notices of the Collegiate Church or Royal Free Chapel and Sanctuary of St. Martin-le-Grand", op cit.

14. John Morris, gen. editor, "The Domesday Book", vol.32, "Essex", Phillimore, Chichester, 1966-92.

15. Walter Besant, "London", Chatto & Windus, 1892; William Maitland, "History and Survey of London", op cit.

16. Glyn Maxwell, "Wolfpit", op cit.

17. James Cruikshank Dansey, "The English Crusaders", op cit.

18. George Lord Lyttelton, "The History of the Life of King Henry the Second", op cit.

19. Rev. R.W. Eyton, "Court, Household and Itinerary of King Henry II", op cit.

20. Sir Frederic Madden, ed., Matthew Paris, "Historia Anglorum", Rolls Series No.44, Longmans, Green, Reader & Dyer, 1866.

21. Edward J. Kealey, "Roger of Salisbury, Viceroy of England", op cit.

22. A.J. Kempe, "Historical Notices of the Collegiate Church of St. Martin-le-Grand, London", op cit.

23. Ralph Turner, 'Who Was the Author of Glanvill?', in "Judges, Administrators and the Common Law in Angevin England", op cit.

24. John T. Appleby, "The Troubled Reign of King Stephen", op cit.

25. David C. Douglas, G.W. Greenaway, eds., "English Historical Documents 1042-1189", op cit.

26. J.S. Godwin, report on Coggeshall Abbey Gatehouse Chapel, February 5, 1961, Essex County Records Office.

27. J.S. Gardner, 'Coggeshall Abbey and its Early Brickwork', *Journal of the British Archaeological Association*, XVIII, 19-32, Plates V-XIV (1955).

28. George F. Beaumont, "A History of Coggeshall in Essex", Marshall Bros., London, 1890, Beatrice M. Rose, "The Story of King Stephen and Queen Maud and the Abbey They Founded at Coggeshall in Essex", op cit.

29. Jane Greatorex, "Coggeshall Abbey and Abbey Mill", Manors, Mills & Manuscripts Series, 1999.

30. James Aveling, "The History of Roche Abbey from its Founding to its Dissolution", op cit.

31. Paul Harris, 'St. Martin's Land, an Alternative Possibility', op cit.

32. C.R. Cheney, Bridgette A. Jones, eds., "English Episcopal Acta II: Canterbury", Oxford University Press, 1986.

33. Henri de Curzon, "La Maison du Temple de Paris", Librairie Hachette, Paris, 1889.

34. Jean Gimpel, "The Medieval Machine", Gollancz, 1977.

35. Elisabeth Crawfoot, Frances Pritchard, Kay Staviland, "Mediaeval Finds from Excavations in London: 4, Textiles and Clothing", op cit.

36. Ronark Program Co., "The Lion in Winter, an Avco Embassy Film", James Kantor & Associates, London, 1968.

37. Dr. Sarah Brewer, 'Keeping Your Head for Drink', *Daily Telegraph*, December 8th, 1999.

38. Jeremy Cherfas, 'A Taste for Danger', *Kew*, Autumn 1995, 33-34.

39. Kate Mertes, "The English Noble Household, 1250-1600, Good Governance and Politic Rule", Basil Blackwell, 1988.

40. Gérard Serbanesco, "Histoire de l'Ordre des Templiers et les Croisades", op cit; A.T. Hatto, Foreword to "Wolfram von Eschenbach, Parzival", op cit.

41. Peter Coss, "The Knight in Mediaeval England, 1000-1400", Alan Sutton, 1993.

42. George Lord Lyttelton, "The History of the Life of King Henry the Second", op cit.

43. Joseph Hunter, ed., "Fines, sive Pedes Finium: sive finales concordiae in curia dominici Regis A.D. 1195 - A.D. 1214", Commissioners on the Public Records of the Kingdom, 1835; John Horace Round, ed., "Rotuli de Dominibus et Pueris et Puellis de XII Comitatibus", Pipe Roll Society, vol.35, St. Catherine Press, 1913.

44. R.E.G. Kirk, ed., "Feet of Fines for Essex" (3 vols.), Colchester Castle Museum Society, 1899-1910.

45. Herbert Read, "The Green Child, a romance", op cit.

46. Randolph Stow, "The Girl Green as Elderflower", op cit.

47. Deputy Keeper of the Records, ed., "A Descriptive Catalogue of Ancient Deeds Held in the Public Records Office", op cit.

48. Nicholas Orme, "The Medieval Child", op cit.

49. "Suffolk Charters", Vols. I-XIV (various eds.), Suffolk Records Society, Boydell Press, 1979 - 94.

50. Vivien Brown, ed., "Suffolk Charters: Eye Priory Cartulary and Charters", Suffolk Record Society, Boydell Press, 1992.

51. H.W. Saunders, ed., "The First Registry of Norwich Cathedral Priory", op cit.

52. Hubert Hall, ed., "The Red Book of the Exchequer", op cit.

53. Charles Roberts, ed., "Excerpta è Rotulis Finium in Turri Londiniensi Asservatis, Henrico Tertio Rege, AD 1216-1272", Commissioners on the Public Records of the Kingdom, 1835.

54. For the rules of inheritance by daughters see J.J. Bayley, "Life in Mediaeval England", op cit.

55. *Encyclopedia Britannica* and Henry Shaw, FSA, "Dress and Decoration of the Middle Ages", 1840, op cit, with a 15th century painting of St. Agnes, plus John Lanchester, 'Listen to the Building', *Daily Telegraph – Arts & Books*, 24th February, 2001.

56. William Stubbs, Introduction to Roger de Hoveden, in Arthur Hassall, ed., "Historical Introductions to the Rolls Series", op cit; Marion Melville, "La Vie des Templiers", op cit.

57. A. Mary Kirkus, ed., "The Great Roll of the Pipe for the Ninth Year of King John, Michaelmas 1207", PRNS 22, Ruddock, 1946.

58. Pipe Roll Society, Vol. 23, "Feet of Fines, in the Public Record Office, of the Ninth Year of King Richard the First, A.D. 1197 - A.D. 1198", Love & Wyman, 1898.

59. William Page, ed., "The Victoria History of the Counties of England: Buckinghamshire, Vol. Two", Constable, 1908.

60. H. Arthur Doubleday & William Page, eds., "The Victoria History of the Counties of England: Warwickshire, Vol. One", Constable, 1904.

61. Ralph V. Turner, 'Richard Barre and Michael Belet', op cit; Michael Baigent, Richard Leigh & Henry Lincoln, "The Holy Blood and the Holy Grail", op cit; Marion Melville, "La Vie des Templiers", op cit.

62. R.B. Pugh, ed., "The Victoria History of the Counties of England: Warwickshire, Vol. Seven", Oxford University Press, 1964.

63. John Morris, ed., "The Domesday Book: vol.24, Staffordshire", Phillimore, 1976.

64. Rev. R.W. Eyton, 'Staffordshire Pipe Rolls of 31 Henry I, 1-35 Henry II', Collections for the History of Staffordshire, Vol.1, William Salt Archaeological Society, 1880.

65. James F. Dimock, ed., "Giraldus Cambrensis Opera", op cit, Vol. V".

66. P.H. Reaney, "A Dictionary of British Place-Names", Routledge & Kegan Paul, 1958; Eilent Ekwall, "The Concise Oxford Dictionary of English Place-Names", 4th ed., Oxford U.P., 1960.

67. John Le Neve, "Fasti", op cit.

68. Arthur Maule Oliver, ed., 'Early Deeds relating to Newcastle upon Tyne', Surtees Society, Vol. 137, 1924.

69. Pipe Roll Society, Vol. 29, "The Great Roll of the Pipe for the Twenty-sixth Year of King Henry the Second", St. Catherine Press, 1908.

70. Miss E. Street, Archivist, Staffordshire Archive Service, personal communication, 10th August 1995; citing their reference 3005/1.

71. The Very Rev. H.E. Savage, 'Shenstone Charters', Collections for the History of Staffordshire (New Series), 1923.

72. Major-General George Wrottesley, 'Curia Regis Rolls of the Reign of Richard I and King John', *Collections for the History of Staffordshire*, Vol. 3, 1882.

73. Anon, *'Bush Telegraph* on England's Three Lions', *Daily Telegraph*, 25th June, 1966.

74. Walter de Grace Birch, ed., "Catalogue of Seals in the Department of Manuscripts in the British Museum", op cit; "Seals", Methuen, 1907. John de Grey's seal, British Library XL-7, is entry 2019.

75. John Ellison Kohn, ed., "Reader's Digest Reverse Dictionary", op cit.

76. John Lydgate, "Life of St. Edmund", British Library Harleian MS 2278; banner tracing in John Gage Rokewood, ed., "Chronica Jocelini de Brakelondi", op cit.

77. Henry J. Hillen, "History of the Borough of King's Lynn", op cit.

78. Frank Barlow, ed., "The Letters of Arnulf of Lisieux", op cit.

79. Z.N. Brooke et al, eds., "The Letters and Charters of Gilbert Foliot", op cit.

80. Frank Barlow, ed., "English Episcopal Acta, XI: Exeter 1046-1184", Oxford U.P., 1996.

81. Mary G. Cheney, "Roger, Bishop of Worcester 1164-1179", Oxford University Press, 1980.

22. Revs. W. Rich Jones, W. Dunn Macray, eds., "Charters and Documents Illustrating the History of the Cathedral, City and Diocese of Salisbury in the Twelfth and Thirteenth Centuries", Rolls Series Vol.97, op cit.

CHAPTER ELEVEN - THE SEARCH PARTY

1. 'Beaumont', "Coggeshall, a Savigny-Cistercian Monastery", op cit.

2. George F. Beaumont, "A History of Coggeshall in Essex", op cit.

3. Ralph of Coggeshall, "Chronicon Anglicanum", op cit.

4. J.S. Gardner, 'Coggeshall Abbey and its Early Brickwork', op cit.

5. Jane Greatorex, "Coggeshall Abbey and Abbey Mill", op cit.

6. Plan of 'Little Coggeshall, The Abbey of St. Mary the Virgin', "Royal Commission on Historical Monuments, Vol.3, the monuments of north-east Essex", p.166, 1922.

7. J.M. Upton-Ward, "The Rule of the Templars", op cit.

8. Thomas M. Parker, "The Knights Templar in England", op cit.

9. Christopher Brooke and Wim Swann, "The Monastic World 1000-1300", Elek, 1974.

10. J.T. Fowler, ed., "Cistercian Statutes 1256-7, Supplementary Statutes of the Order", 1890.

11. (Anon), 'Bones Clear Columbus', Sally Pook, 'Pox-Ridden Monks Disprove Columbus Theory of Syphilis', *Daily Telegraph*, 30th May & 24th July 2002.

12. Michael David Knowles, "The Monastic Orders in England", op cit.

13. C.G. Addison, "The Knights Templar", op cit.

14. Peter Portner, "The Murdered Magicians", op cit.

15. Malcolm Barber, "The Trial of the Templars", op cit.

16. Gérard Serbanesco, "Histoire de l'Ordre des Templiers", op cit.

17. Gérard de Sède, "Les Templiers Sont Parmi Nous", op cit.

18. G.V. Scammell, "Hugh du Puiset", op cit.

19. Rev. R.W. Eyton, "Court, Household and Itinerary of King Henry II", op cit.

20. Leopold Delisle, "Recueil des Actes de Henry II", op cit.

21. Sir William Dugdale, "Monasticon Anglicanum", op cit.

22. Ralph V. Turner, 'Richard Barre and Michael Belet', op cit.

23. Rev. W. Rich Jones, Rev. W. Dunn Macray, eds., "Charters... of Salisbury", Rolls Series No. 97, op cit.

24. Mary G. Cheney, "Roger, Bishop of Worcester 1164-1179", op cit.

25. H. Arthur Doubleday, ed., "The Victoria History of the Counties of England: Hampshire and the Isle of Wight, Vols. 1 & 2", Constable, 1900/1903.

26. William Page, ed., "The Victoria History of the Counties of England: Hampshire and the Isle of Wight, Vol. 4", op cit.

27. William Page, ed., "The Victoria History of the Counties of England: Hampshire, Vol. 3", Constable, 1908.

28. John Le Neve "Fasti", op cit.

29. Pipe Roll Society, "The Great Roll of the Pipe for the Twentyfifth Year of King Henry the Second, AD 1176-1177", Vol.28, Doubleday, 1907.

30. "Rufford Charters Vol.1", Thoroton Society Record Series vol. XXIX, Derry & Sons, Nottingham, 1972.

31. Historical Manuscripts Commission, "Report on the Manuscripts of Lord Middleton at Wollaton Hall, Nottinghamshire", His Majesty's Stationery Office, 1911.

32. George Caspar Homans, "English Villagers of the Thirteenth Century", op cit.

33. Elisabeth Crawfoot, Frances Pritchard, Kay Staviland, "Mediaeval Finds from Excavations in London: 4, Textiles and Clothing c.1150 - c.1450", op cit; Barry Cunliffe, "Facing the Ocean", op cit.

34. Joseph Warichez, "Étienne de Tournai et Son Temps", op cit.

35. A.T. Hatto, trans., "Wolfram von Eschenbach, Parzival", op cit.

36. J.H. Wiffen, trans., Tasso, "Jerusalem Liberated", op cit; Marion Melville, "La Vie des Templiers", op cit; Gérard de Sède, "Les Templiers Sont Parmi Nous", op cit.

37. William Stubbs, Introductions to Benedict of Peterborough and to 'Memorials of the Reign of Richard I', in Arthur Hassall, ed., "Historical Introductions to the Rolls Series", op cit.

38. Gwen Benwell & Arthur Waugh, "Sea Enchantress, The Tale of the Mermaid and her Kin", Hutchinson, 1961.

39. Michael Baigent, Richard Leigh & Henry Lincoln, "The Holy Blood and the Holy Grail", op cit.

40. Amélie Bosquet, "La Normandie Romanesque et Merveilleuse", J. Tachener, Paris, 1845.

41. Geoffrey Ashe, "King Arthur's Avalon, the Story of Glastonbury", Fontana, 1973.

42. George Lord Lyttelton, "Life of King Henry the Second", op cit.

43. 'Carta Ricardi Barre Eliensis Archidiacon.' in "Registerium Monasterii S. Crucis de Waltham", Mus. Brit. Bibl. Cotton Tiberius, Vol. CIX, ff. 152-152v, in British Library; Z.N. Brooke, C.N.L. Brooke, 'Notes and Communications: 1. Hereford Cathedral Dignitaries in the Twelfth Century - Supplement', *Cambridge Historical Journal*, VIII, 179-184 (1944-46) No.3.

44. Julia Barrow, ed., "English Episcopal Acta VII: Hereford 1079-1234", Oxford University Press, 1993.

45. Thomas Stapleton, ed., "Magni Rotuli Scacarii Normanniae sub Regibus Angliae, Vol. I", Society of Antiquaries of London, 1840.

46. Beatrice M. Rose, "The Story of King Stephen and Queen Maud and the Abbey They Founded at Coggeshall in Essex", op cit.

Chapter Twelve - MAKING AN IMPACT WITH KING HENRY

1. Carl Sagan, "Cosmos", Macdonald Futura, 1980.

2. William Stubbs, ed., "Gervase of Canterbury", op cit.

3. Derral Mulholland, Odile Calame, 'Lunar Crater Giordano Bruno', *Science* 199, 875-877 (24th Feb. 1978).

4. Paul Withers, 'Meteor storm evidence against the recent formation of lunar crater Giordano Bruno', *Meteoritics and Planetary Science*, 36, 525-529 (2001).

5. Graeme Waddington, letters, 'The Date of Gervase's "Wonderful Sign in 1178'; 'The Date of Gervase's Event of June 1178', *Cambridge Conference Net*, 28th March 2001.

6. Joseph Stevenson, ed., "Chronica de Mailros e Codice Uno", Edinburgh Printing Company, 1835.

7. William Stubbs, ed., "The Historical Works of Master Ralph de Diceto", op cit.

8. Robert Russell Newton, "Medieval Chronicles and the Rotation of the Earth", John Hopkins University Press, Baltimore, 1972; "Ancient Astronomical Observations and the Accelerations of the Earth and Moon", John Hopkins, 1970.

9. John North, "The Fontana History of Astronomy and Cosmology", Harper-Collins, 1994.

10. Dr. Thomas Short, "A General Chronological History of the Air, Weather, Seasons, Meteors Etc. in Sundry Places and at Different Times", op cit.

11. Jack B. Hartung, 'Was the Formation of a 20-KM-Diameter Impact Crater on the Moon Observed on June 18, 1178?', *Meteoritics*, 11, 3, 187-194 (Sept. 30, 1976).

12. Paul M. Schenk, 'Comet to Hit Jupiter', *Lunar and Planetary Information Bulletin*, 69, 3-5 (November 1993); Michael Hanlon, "The Worlds of Galileo", Constable, 2001..

13. Harold Masursky, G.W. Colton, Farouk El-Baz, eds., "Apollo Over the Moon, A View from Orbit", NASA SP-362, US Govt. Printing Office, 1978.

14. Robert G. Musgrove, ed., "Lunar Photographs from Apollos 8, 10 and 11", NASA SP-246, US Govt. Printing Office, 1971.

15. Patrick Moore, 'What We Know About the Moon' (with tentative Farside map), in L.J. Carter, ed., "Realities of Space Travel", Putnam, 1957.

16. N.P. Barabashov, A.A. Mikhailov, Yu. N. Lipskiy, eds., "Atlas of the Other Side of the Moon", Pergamon, 1961.

17. E.A. Whitaker, 'Discussion of Named Features: Provisionally Approved Nomenclature', in "Analysis of Apollo 8 Photography and Visual Observations", NASA SP-201, US Govt. Printing Office, 1969.

18. Frances A. Yates, "Giordano Bruno and the Hermetic Tradition", Routledge & Kegan Paul, 1964.

19. Derral Mulholland, 'How High the Moon: a Decade of Laser Ranging', *Sky & Telescope*, 60, 4, 274-279 (Oct. 1980).

20. François Arago, "Popular Astronomy", op cit.

21. James E. Oberg, "New Earths", Stackpole Books, 1981.

22. V.S. Safronov, Y.L. Rushkol, "History of the Lunar Atmosphere and the Possibility of Ice and Organic Compounds Existing on the Moon", *Vosprosy Kosmogonii*, 9 (1963), NASA Technical Translation TT F-232, U.S. Government Printing Office, September 1964.

23. Jeff Gillis, 'Inside the Batcave: the Clementine 1 Mission', *Lunar and Planetary Information Bulletin*, 71, 2-5 (May 1994), (Anon), 'Clementine's Lunar Mapping Mission: an Overview of the Science Results', ibid, 72, 16-17 (August 1994).

24. Peter Bond, 'Prospector Finds Ten Times More Ice', *Astronomy Now*, 12, 10, 51-52 (Oct. 1998); Brian Berger, 'Scientists: Moon Contains More Ice', *Space News*, 9, 34, 10 (September 7-13, 1998).

25. Frank Morning Jr., 'Images Appear to Show Water Ice on Moon', *Aviation Week*, July 28th, 2010; Nancy Atkinson, 'Radar Images Reveal Tons of Water Likely at the Lunar Poles', *Universe Today*, August 2nd, 2010.

26. Linda M.V. Martel, 'How Young Is the Lunar Crater Giordano Bruno?', *Planetary Science Research Discoveries*, February 17th 2010.

27. Ralph of Coggeshall, "Chronicon Anglicanum", op cit.

28. Robert Uhlig, 'Chunk of Moon Rock Seen Orbiting the Sun', *Daily Telegraph*, 25th February 1999.

29. (Anon), 'Nebraska Crater Only a Pup', *Astronomy Now*, 8, 2, 13 (Feb. 1994).

30. Duncan Steel & Peter Snow, 'The Tapanui Region of New Zealand: Site of a 'Tunguska' Around 800 Years Ago?', in A. Harris & E. Bowell, eds., "Asteroids, Comets, Meteors 1991", Lunar & Planetary Institute, Houston, Texas, 1992.

31. William Henry Jones, "Fasti Ecclesiae Sarisberiensis, or a Calendar of the Bishops, Deans, Archdeacons, and Members of the Cathedral Body at Salisbury, from the earliest times to the present", Brown & Co., Salisbury, 1879.

32. Mike Baillie, "Exodus to Arthur", op cit.

33. Duncan Lunan, "Man and the Stars", Souvenir Press, 1974; US edition "Interstellar Contact", Henry Regnery Co., 1975.

34. Alastair McBeath, Göran Johansson, letters, Cambridge Conference Network, Internet, 3rd December 2001.

35. John McNeill, "Old Sarum", op cit; George Lord Lyttelton, op cit. Rev. R.W. Eyton, op cit, gives 15th July for Henry's sailing, 18th July at Canterbury.

36. Ralph V. Turner, 'The Miles Literatus in Twelfth- and Thirteenth-Century England: How Rare a Phenomenon?', op cit.

37. Johannes Brompton, "Chronicon ab anno Domini 588, quo St. Augustinus venit in angliam usque mortem regis Ricardi I scilicet annum

Domini 1198", in "Historiae Anglicanae Scriptores, ex vestibus manuscriptis, nunc primum in lucem editi", Jacob Flesher, Cornelius Bee, London, 1652.

38. Red Harrison, 'Overture to Courage and Death (review of Robin Prior & Trevor Wilson, "Passchendale: The Untold Story", Yale University Press, 1996)', *The Australian*, 24th September, 1996.

39. Prof. Steve Jones, 'When Geologists Were Sent to the Front', *Daily Telegraph*, 27th August, 1997.

40. George Lord Lyttelton, "The History of the Life of King Henry the Second", op cit.

41. alburt plethora, 'Venjinss', in Duncan Lunan, ed., "Starfield, Science Fiction by Scottish Writers", Orkney Press, 1989.

42. E.C. Waterscheid, 'Plowshare Today', *Analog Science Fiction/Science Fact*, LXXIII, 4, 8-16, 81-84 (June 1964).

43. James LeFanu, 'Doctor's Diary', *Daily Telegraph*, 6th October 2008.

44. James Clephan, 'The Hell Kettles', 'North-Country Lore & Legend', *Monthly Chronicle*, October 1887, 353-356.

45. William Page, ed., "Victoria Hist. of the Counties of England: Durham, Vol.1", Constable, 1905.

46. (Anon), 'At Hell Kettles', typescript, Darlington Branch Library, Durham County Council, undated; 'The Hell Kettles', typescript, Darlington Branch Library, undated.

47. Alan & Ann Fell, 'Hell Kettles: the facts', letter, *Darlington & Stockton Times*, 11th March, 1980.

48. W.H.D. Longstaffe, "The History and Antiquities of the Parish of Darlington in the Bishoprick", Darlington, 1854.

49. (Anon), 'The Hell Kettles', *Monthly Chronicle*, October 1887 (Darlington Library Cuttings Book p.34); J.W. Hudson, K.J. Crompton, B.A. Whitton, 'Ecology of Hell Kettles, 2: The Ponds', *Vasculum*, LVI, 3, 38-45 (October 1971).

50. (Anon), 'Frogmen "Take Lid Off" Kettles Legends', *Northern Despatch*, 1st December, 1958.

51. 'E', 'The Hell Kettles', 'North-Country Lore & Legend', *Monthly Chronicle*, November 1887; B.D. Wheeler, B.A. Whitton, 'Ecology of Hell Kettles, 1: Terrestrial and Sub-aquatic Vegetation', *Vasculum*, LVI, 3, 25-37 (1971); Colin Sargent, Prof. Neil R. Goulty, 'Seismic Reflection Survey for Invest-igation of Dissolution and Subsidence at Hells Kettles, Darlington, UK', *Quarterly Journal of Engineering Geology and Hydrogeology*, 42, 31-38, DOI 10.1144/1470-9236/07-071..

52. (Anon) 'The "Hell Kettles" of the Tees', *Newcastle Weekly Chronicle*, Darlington Library Cuttings Book, p.34.

53. Michael Worth Davison, ed., "Everyday Life through the Ages", Reader's Digest Assoc., 1992.

54. Colin Gleadell, 'Rare Sights at Auction', *Daily Telegraph*, May 21st, 2001; Ted Nield, "Incoming! Or Why We Should Stop Worrying and Learn to Love the Meteorite",Granta, 2011.

55. W.H.D. Longstaffe, 'On Bishop Pudsey's Buildings in the Present City of Durham', *Transactions of the Architectural and Archaeological Soc. of Durham and Northumberland*, MDCCCLXII, 1-8, 1862.

56. 'Tewars', 'Everard Bishop of Norwich', op cit.

57. G.V. Scammell, "Hugh du Puiset"; James Cruikshank Dansey, "The English Crusaders", op cit.

58. William Farrer, ed., "Early Yorkshire Charters", op cit.

59. Rev. William Greenwell, ed., "Boldon Buke, a Survey of the Possessions of the See of Durham, made by order of Bishop Hugh Pudsey, in the year MCLXXXIII", Surtees Society, Vol. 25, 1853.

60. 'J.F.F.', 'Rites of Durham', Surtees Society Vol. 107, 1902.

61. 'Mr. Stevenson', ed., 'Libellus de Vita et Miraculis de S. Godrici, Hermitae de Finchale', Surtees Society, Vol. 20, 1845.

62. T.S.R. Boase, "English Art 1100-1216", Oxford University Press, 1953.

63. George Caspar Homans, "English Villagers of the Thirteenth Century", op cit.

64. Edward Miller, "Domesday Book and Beyond, Three Essays in the Early History of England", Cambridge University Press, 1895.

65. William Camden, "Britannia", op cit.

66. "The Annales or General Chronicle of England, begun first by maister John Stow, and after him continued and augmented with matters forreyne, and domestique, auncient and moderne, unto the end of this present yeere 1614, by Edmond Howes, gentleman", Thomas Adams, London, 1615.

67. John Chandler, ed., "John Leland's Itinerary: travels in Tudor England", Alan Sutton, Stroud, 1993.

68. Gladys Hinde, ed., 'Registers of Cuthbert Tunstall, bishop of Durham 1530-59', Surtees Society Vol. 137, 1946.

69, (Anon). 'The Hole Thing', *Young Telegraph*, 27th August 1994.

70. Paul Stokes, '120 ft Hole Opens Next to Family's Front Door', *Daily Telegraph*, April 25th, 1997; Robert Uhlig, 'Down-to-earth Story behind Alice's Tumble', *Daily Telegraph*, September 15th, 1999.

71. John G. Jenkins, "The Cartulary of Missenden Abbey", op cit.

72. John Hooker, ed., Raphaell Holinshed, "Chronicles of England, Scotland and Ireland", vol.2 of six, J. Johnson, London, 1807.

Chapter Thirteen - 1180's: IN MINISTERIO

1. Joseph Warichez, "Étienne de Tournai et Son Temps", op cit.

2. Frank Barlow, ed., "The Letters of Arnulf of Lisieux", op cit.

3. J.H. Round, ed., "Calendar of Documents Preserved in France Illustrative of the History of Great Britain", op cit.

4. Ralph V. Turner, 'Richard Barre and Michael Belet', op cit.   Turner gives full references for various obscure events in Richard Barre's life as archdeacon of Lisieux between 1179 and 1187, and where I've gained access to them I've given the references below.   But I've verified the others because the list was originally supplied to Ralph Turner by Prof. David S. Spear of Furman University, South Carolina, who very kindly sent me his notes on them all, compiled for his book "The Personnel of the Norman Cathedrals, 911-1204".

5. William Stubbs, ed., Benedict of Peterborough, op cit; Roger de Hoveden, op cit; Percy Dearmer, "Highways and Byways in Normandy", Macmillan, 1910.

6. James Bentham, "History and Antiquities of the Conventual and Cathedral Church of Ely", op cit.

7. William Farrer, ed., "Early Yorkshire Charters", op cit.

8. Jim Wilson, ed., "900 Years, Norwich Cathedral and Diocese", Jarrold Publishing, 1996.

9. Gillian Hutchinson, "Mediaeval Ships and Shipping", op cit.

10. Christopher Harper-Bill, ed., "English Episcopal Acta 6: Norwich", op cit.

11. Dorothy M. Owen, "The Making of King's Lynn", Oxford University Press, 1984.

12. Vanessa Parker, "The Making of King's Lynn", op cit.

13. Rev. R.W. Eyton, "Itinerary of King Henry II", op cit; George Lord Lyttelton, op cit.   A portrait of William Longespée as Earl of Salisbury is reproduced in Henry Shaw, FSA, "Dress and Decoration of the Middle Ages", op cit.

14. Kate Mertes, "The English Noble Household, 1250-1600", op cit.

15. W. Richards, "The History of Lynn", W.G. Whittingham, King's Lynn, 1812.

16. Christopher Harper-Bill and Richard Mortimer, eds., "Suffolk Charters Vol.4: Stoke by Clare Cartulary, Part 2", Suffolk Records Society, 1983; Pipe Roll Society, "The Great Roll of the Pipe for the Thirtyfirst Year of King Henry II", Vol.34, St. Catherine Press, 1913.

17. Francis Blomefield, "An Essay towards a Topographical History of the County of Norfolk", op cit.

18. Henry J. Hillen, "History of the Borough of King's Lynn", op cit.

19. Helen Clarke, Alan Carter, "Excavations in King's Lynn 1963-70", op cit. Stockfish definition from "The Compact Edition of the Oxford English Dictionary", op cit.

20. "Binham Priory", op cit.

21. Richard Newcourt, "Repertorium Pariochiale Londiniense", op cit.

22. Vivien Brown, ed., "Suffolk Charters: Eye Priory Cartulary and Charters", Suffolk Record Society, Boydell Press, 1992.

23. A.B. Emden, "A Bibliographical Register of the University of Oxford to AD 1500, Vol.1", Oxford University Press, 1957.

24. Christopher Harper-Bill, "Suffolk Charters: Charters of the Mediaeval Hospitals of Bury St. Edmunds", Suffolk Records Society, 1994.

25. "English Episcopal Acta II: Canterbury", op cit.

26. Henry Richards, ed., "Chronica Majora" of Roger de Wendover & Matthew Paris, op cit; Henry Thomas Riley, ed., "Gesta Abbatum Monasterii Sancti Albani, a Thoma Walsingham, regnante Ricardo Secundo, ejusdem ecclesiae praecentore, compilata; Vol.1, AD 793-1290", Rolls Series No.28, Longmans, Green, Reader & Dyer, 1867.

27. Glyn Maxwell, "Wolfpit", op cit.

28. Pipe Roll Soc., "Great Roll of the Pipe for the Thirtyfirst Year of King Henry the Second", op cit.

29. William Henry Jones, "Fasti Ecclesiae Sarisberiensis", op cit.

30. W.H. Rich Jones, ed., "The Register of St. Osmund", op cit.

31. Rev. W. Richard Jones, ed., "Charters and Documents Illustrating the History of the Cathedral City and Diocese of Salisbury", Rolls Series No.97, op cit.

32. John T. Gilbert, ed., "Chartularies of St. Mary's Abbey, Dublin", Rolls Series No.80, Longman & Co., 1884.

33. D. Mackerell, "The History and Antiquities of the Flourishing Corporation of King's Lynn in the County of Norfolk", E. Cave, London, 1738.

34. Sidney Painter, 'Norwich's Three Geoffreys', *Speculum*, 28, 808-813 (1953).

35. S.A. Moore, ed., "Cartularium Monasterii Sancti Johannis Baptiste de Colecestria", Vol.1, Roxburghe Club, 1897.

36. Thomas Arnold, ed., "Memorials of St. Edmund's Abbey", op cit.

37. H.E. Butler, ed., "The Chronicle of Jocelin of Brakelond", op cit.

38. T.S.R. Boase, "English Art 1100-1216", Oxford University Press, 1953.

39. M.J. Franklin, ed., "English Episcopal Acta 17: Coventry and Lichfield, 1183-1208, British Academy, Oxford University Press, 1998; W. Wattenbach, S. Loewenfeld, F. Kaltenbrunner, P. Ewald, eds., P. Jaffé, "Regesta Ponticum Romanorum ad annum 1198", Leipzig, 1885-8.

40. John G. Jenkins, ed., "The Cartulary of Missenden Abbey", op cit.

41. W. Dunn Macray, ed., "Chronicon Abbatiae Rameseiensis, a saec. X. unque ad an. circiter 1200: in quatuor partibus", Rolls Series No.64, Longman & Co., 1886.

42. Pipe Roll Society, Vol.38, op cit.

43. John Horace Round, ed., "Rotuli de Dominibus et Pueris et Puellis de XII Comitatibus", op cit.

44. Anon, Part 1, Thomas of Ely, Part 2, "Historia Ecclesiae Eliensis", in Vol.2, "Rerum Anglicarum Scriptorum Veterum", E. Theatro Sheldoniano, 1684.

45. Philip Morant, "The History and Antiquities of the County of Essex", op cit; James Nasmyth, ed., Dr. Thomas Tanner, "Novitia Monastica", op cit; Arthur Doubleday & William Page, eds., "The Victoria History of the Counties of England: Essex", Vol. I, op cit; R.B. Pugh, ed., Vol. III, University of London, 1963.

46. Sir William Dugdale, "Monasticon Anglicanum", op cit.

47. Major Alfred Heales, ed., "Records of Merton Priory", Henry Frowde, London, 1898.

48. C.R. Cheney, Eric John, eds., "English Episcopal Acta III: Canterbury 1193-1205", Oxford University Press, 1986.

49. Prof. Dom. David Knowles, Prof. C.N.L. Brooke, Vera London, eds., "The Heads of Religious Houses in England and Wales 940-1216", Cambridge University Press, 1972.

50. Thomas Moore, "The Cabinet Cyclopaedia: Ireland, Vol. II", op cit.

51. "Catalogue of Ancient Deeds", op cit.

52. Sir Henry Ellis, ed., "Chronica Johannis de Oxeneden", Rolls Series No.13, Longman, Brown, Green, Longmans & Roberts, 1859.

53. Robert William Billings, "Architectural Illustrations and Account of the Temple Church", Boone & Billings, 1838; for details of the Old Temple see John Strype, "Survey of London", op cit.

54. Henri de Curzon, "La Maison du Temple de Paris", op cit; Norman Hammond, 'City Find Is Knights Templars' Oldest London Church', The Times, 27th August, 2002.

55. William Stubbs, Introduction to 'Memorials of the Reign of Richard I', in Arthur Hassall, ed., "Historical Introductions to the Rolls Series", op cit.

56. Thomas M. Parker, "The Knights Templar in England", op cit.   Other sources including the *Encyclopedia Britannica* say Gerard de Ridefort had already been appointed Grand Master in 1184.

57. C. Addison, "The Knights Templar", op cit; Jonathan Phillips, "The Second Crusade, Scope and Consequences', op cit..

58. J.H. Wiffen, trans., Tasso, "Jerusalem Liberated", op cit; Marion Melville, "La Vie des Templiers", op cit; Gérard de Sède, "Les Templiers Sont Parmi Nous", op cit.

59. Beatrice Adelaide Lees, "Records of the Templars", op cit.

60. Mary Hayden, George A. Moonan, "A Short History of the Irish People, from the earliest times to 1920", op cit; A.G. Richey, "Lectures on the History of Ireland Down to AD 1534", E. Ponsonby, Dublin, 1869.   Robert Fitz-Stephen may have been with the Irish force at Fornham St. Genevieve, because the *Britannica* says that he 'gave good service' to Henry II in the crisis.

61. George Lord Lyttelton, "Life of King Henry the Second", op cit; Régine Peroud, "Les Croisades", René Julliard, Paris, 1960; Stanley Lane-Poole, "Saladin and the Fall of the Kingdom of Jerusalem", Putnams, 1901.

62. Francesco Gabrieli, ed., "Arab Historians of the Crusades", op cit; Geoffrey Regan, "Saladin and the Fall of Jerusalem", op cit.

63. Richard Hinckley Allen, "Star Names, Their Lore and Meaning", Dover, 1963; Camille Flammarion, "Les Étoiles", Paris, 1881.

64. Dave Goulder, 'The Raven and the Crow', in "The January Man, a Dave Goulder Songbook", Machair Books, Lewis, 1987; Dave Goulder & Liz Dyer, "The Raven and the Crow", Argo, 1971, reissued Vinyl Japan JASKCD164, www.davegoulder.co.uk

65. C.W. Wilson, C. Warren, "The Recovery of Jerusalem: a Narrative of Exploration and Discovery in the City and the Holy Land", Richard Bentley, London, 1871; Benjamin Z. Kedar, 'The Horns of Hattin Revisited', in Benjamin Z. Kedar, ed., "The Horns of Hattin", op cit, and in Benjamin Z. Kedar, ed., "The Franks in the Levant, 11th to 14th Centuries", Variorum, 1993.

66. Malcolm Barber, "The New Knighthood", op cit.

67. Janet Shirley, trans., Jean Richard, "The Latin Kingdom of Jerusalem", North-Holland Publishing Company, 1979; Marshall Whithed Baldwin, "Raymond III of Tripolis and the Fall of Jerusalem", Adolf M. Hakkert, Amsterdam, 1969.

68. Gérard Dédéyan, ed., "La Chronique Attribuée au Connétable Smbat", Librairie Orientaliste, Paris, 1980.

69. Stanley Lane-Poole, "Saladin and the Fall of the Kingdom of Jerusalem", Geoffrey Regan, "Saladin and the Fall of Jerusalem", in ref. 65 above; Hans E. Meyer, 'Henry II of England and the Holy Land', in Hans E. Meyer, "Kings and Lords in the Latin Kingdom of Jerusalem", Variorum, 1994. Dr. Thomas Short, "General Chronol. Hist. of the Air, Weather, Seasons, Meteors, Etc.", op cit, gives the UK and Verona eclipse but wrongly gives the date as September 8th.

70. Joseph Stevenson, ed., "Chronicon Sanctae Terrae", op cit.

71. J.S. Gardner, 'Coggeshall Abbey and its Early Brickwork', op cit.

72. Michael Baigent & Richard Leigh, "The Temple and the Lodge", op cit.

73. Jane Greatorex, "Coggeshall Abbey and Abbey Mill", op cit.

74. Régine Pernoud, "Dans les Pas des Croisés, Librairie Hachette, 1959.

75. A.C.D. Crommelin, 'Comets', in "Hutchinson's Splendour of the Heavens", Hutchinson, c.1930.

76. Henry Shaw, FSA, "Dress and Decoration of the Middle Ages", op cit. The *Encyclopedia Britannica* confirms that, though contradicted by Alfred Duggan, "The Story of the Crusades 1097-1291", Faber, 1963, which states that the custom dates from the early 1100's.

77. Joshua Prawer, "The World of the Crusades", Weidenfeld & Nicolson, 1972.

78. Adam Hopkins, 'Pray for Me - and My Feet'; Derek Bishton, 'Pilgrim's Spain: Back from the Future', op cit.

79. Anon, 'Pilgrim's Progress a Painful Affair', Daily Telegraph, 7th September, 1994.

80. Roger Highfield, 'Battered Face of Soldier from Wars of the Roses Stares Across the Centuries', *Daily Telegraph*, June 28th, 1999.

81. Pipe Roll Society, "The Great Roll of the Pipe for the Thirtythird Year of King Henry the Second", Vol.37, St. Catherine Press, 1915; Ralph V. Turner, "The English Justiciary in the Age of Glanvill and Bracton", Cambridge University Press, 1985.

82. Jane Greatorex, personal communication, 1st March 1998.

83. Joseph Warichez, "Étienne de Tournai et Son Temps", op cit.

84. Ferdinand Opll, "Das Itinerar Kaiser Frederich Barbarossus (1152-1190)", Hermann Böhlaus Nachf., 1978.

85. Jules Zeller, "Histoire d' Allemagne", vol.4, "L'Empire Germanique sous les Hohenstauffen", Librairie Académique, Paris, 1881.

86. Geoffrey Regan, "Saladin and the Fall of Jerusalem", op cit.

87. George Lord Lyttelton, "Life of King Henry the Second", op cit.

88. Henry Richards Luard, ed., 'Annales de Margan', in "Annales Monastici", Rolls Series No.36, Longman, Green, Longman, Roberts & Green, 1864; 'Annales de Wintonia', in "Annales Monastici", vol.2; Arthur Hassall, ed., William Stubbs, Introduction to Gervase of Canterbury, in "Historical Introductions to the Rolls Series", op cit.

89. Dr. Thomas Short, "General Chronol. Hist. of the Air, Weather, Seasons, Meteors, Etc.", op cit.

90. L.F. Salzmann, "Henry II", op cit.

91. John Speed, "Historie of Great Britaine, from the time of the Romans to king James", 3rd edition, Book V, London, 1640 (though in the copy held by Glasgow University Library Special Collections, the date had been scored through and '1632 ?' added in pencil).

92. Henry T. Riley, ed., "The Annals of Roger de Hoveden", op cit.

93. D.E.R. Watt, ed., Walter Bower, "Scotichronicon", op cit.

Chapter Fourteen - THE 1190'S: LADY OF THE MANOR

1. Kate Norgate, "Richard the Lion Heart", Macmillan, 1924.

2. Christopher Harper-Bill, "English Episcopal Acta VI: Norwich", op cit.

3. G.C. Coulton, "Mediaeval Panorama, The English Scene from Conquest to Reformation", op cit.

4. David Keene, 'Mediaeval London and its Region', The London Journal, 14, 2, 99-111 (1989); Henry J. Hillen, "History of the Borough of King's Lynn", op cit.

5. Joseph Warichez, "Les Disputations de Simon de Tournai", Spicilegium Sacrum Lovoniense, Louvain, 1932.

6. John Gilissen, "Introduction Historique au Droit", Établissements Émile Bruylant, Brussels, 1979.

7. Stephen Kuttner, "Gratian and the Schools of Law", Variosum Reprints, London, 1983.

8.   Michael Bertram Crowe, "The Changing Profile of the Natural Law", Martinus Nijhoff, The Hague, 1977.

9.   Joseph Warichez, "Étienne de Tournai et Son Temps", op cit.

10.   L'Abbé Jules Desilve, ed., "Lettres de'Étienne de Tournai", Alphonse Picard, Paris, 1893.

11.   Ralph V. Turner, 'Richard Barre and Michael Belet', op cit.

12.   Eleanor Rathbone, 'Roman Law in the Anglo-Norman Realm', op cit.

13.   Richard Aldington & Delano Ames, trans., Felix Guirand, ed., "Larousse Encyclopedia of Mythology", Batchworth Press, 1959.

14.   Frances A. Yates, "Giordano Bruno and the Hermetic Tradition", op cit.

15.   Angela Hall, trans., Rudolf Simek, "Heaven and Earth in the Middle Ages", the Physical World before Columbus", op cit.

16.   David Ewing Duncan, 'Millennium Time-Warp', *Sunday Telegraph Review*, December 27th 1998; Anthony Wood, 'Life of Roger Bacon' in J.S. Brewer, ed., "Fr. Rogeri Bacon, Opera Quaedam Hactenus Inedita, Vol. 1", Rolls Series 15, Longman, Green, Longman and Roberts, 1859.

17.   Rev. C.L. Feltoe, Ellais H. Minns, 'Vetus Liber Archidiaconi Eliensis', *Cambs. Hist. Soc.* 48, 1917.

18.   Diceto, "Ymagines Historiarum", op cit.

19.   Rev. W. Rich Jones, Rev. W. Dunn Macray, eds., "Charters and Documents Illustrating the History of the Cathedral, City and Diocese of Salisbury", op cit.

20.   D.C. Douglas, "Feudal Documents from the Abbey of Bury St. Edmunds", op cit;. Ralph V. Turner, 'Who Was the Author of Glanvill?', in "Judges, Administrators and the Common Law in Angevin England", op cit.

21.   M.J. Franklin, "English Episcopal Acta VIII: Winchester 1070-1204", Oxford U. P., 1993.

22.   Joseph Stevenson, ed., "Chronicon Ricardi Diviensis de Rebus Gestis Ricardi Primi Regis Angliae", English Historical Society, 1838; J.A. Giles, "The Chronicle of Richard of Devizes concerning the deeds of Richard the First, king of England", James Bohn, London, 1861; John T. Appleby, ed., "The Chronicle of Richard of Devizes of the Time of King Richard the First", Nelson, 1963.

23.   Giraldus Cambrensis, op cit.

24.   Pipe Roll Society, "Feet of Fines of the Reign of Henry II and the First Seven Years of Richard I, AD 1182 to AD 1196", Vol.17, op cit; "Feet of Fines of the Ninth Year of King Richard I, AD 1197 to AD 1198", PRNS 23, Ruddock, 1947.

25. A.B. Whittingham, "Bury St. Edmunds Abbey, Suffolk", op cit.

26. Sir William Dugdale, "Monasticon Anglicanum", op cit.

27. William Stubbs, ed., Benedict of Peterborough, op cit.

28. Ralph V. Turner, 'The Reputation of Royal Judges under the Angevin Kings', in Ralph V. Turner, "Judges, Administrators and the Common Law in Angevin England", op cit.

29. Francis West, "The Justiciarship in England 1066-1232", Cambridge University Press, 1966.

30. J.H. Round, ed., "Calendar of Documents Preserved in France Illustrative of the History of Great Britain", op cit.

31. Doris M. Stenton, ed., "The Great Roll of the Pipe for the Third and Fourth Years of King Richard the First, Michaelmas 1191, 1192", PRNS 2, Ruddock, 1926.

32. James Cruikshank Dansey, "The English Crusaders", op cit.

33. Norbert Ohler, "The Medieval Traveller", op cit.

34. Lionel Landon, ed., "The Carta Antiquae Rolls 1-10", PRNS 17, Ruddock, 1939.

35. Arthur Hassall, ed., William Stubbs, "Historical Introductions to the Rolls Series", op cit.

36. Doris M. Stenton, ed., "The Great Roll of the Pipe for the Fifth Year of King Richard I, Michaelmas 1193", PRNS 3, Ruddock, 1927.

37. G.V. Scammell, "Hugh du Puiset", op cit.

38. Kate Norgate, "John Lackland", Macmillan, 1902.

39. Ralph V. Turner, "Men Raised from the Dust: Administrative Service and Upward Mobility in Angevin England", University of Pennsylvania Press, 1988.

40. R.H.C. Davis, ed., "The Kalendar of Abbot Sampson", op cit.

41. Barbara Dodwell, ed., "The Charters of Norwich Cathedral Priory", op cit.

42. Deputy Keeper of the Records, ed., "A Descriptive Catalogue of Ancient Deeds Held in the Public Records Office", op cit. Charters witnessed by Walter de Calna senior and junior also appear in "Suffolk Charters", Vols. I-XIV (various editors), Suffolk Records Society, Boydell Press, 1979-1994.

43. Diane Greenway, ed., "Fasti, Vol.3: Lincoln", op cit.

44 Christopher Harper-Dill, ed., "Suffolk Charters: Blythbury Abbey Cartulary, part 1", Suffolk. Records Society, 1980.

45. Vivien Brown, ed., "Suffolk Charters: Eye Priory Cartulary and Charters", op cit.

46. Richard Mortimer, ed., "Suffolk Charters Vol.1: Leiston Abbey Cartulary and Butley Priory Charters", Suffolk Records Society, 1979.

47. A.B. Emden, "A Bibliographical Register of the University of Oxford to AD 1500, Vol.1", Oxford University Press, 1957.

48. Deputy Keeper of the Records, ed., "Calendar of the Liberate Rolls... Henry III AD 1226-1245", (2 vols.), HMSO, 1916.

49. Deputy Keeper of the Records, ed., "Curia Regis Rolls of the Reign of Richard I and John", op cit.

50. H.G. Richardson, ed., "The Memoranda Rolls for the Michaelmas Term of the First Year of the Reign of King John, 1199-1200", PRNS 21, J.W. Ruddock, 1943; "Placitorum in Domo Capitulari Westmonasteriensi Asservatorum Abbrevatio, temporibus regum Ric. I Johann. Henr. III Edw. I Edw. II", Commissioners on the Public Records of the Kingdom, 1811.

51. Deputy Keeper of the Records, ed., "Patent Rolls of the Reign of Henry III, preserved in the Public Records Office, AD 1216-1266", op cit.

52. Barbara Dodwell, ed., "Feet of Fines for the County of Norfolk for the Reign of King John, 1201-1215; for the County of Suffolk, 1199-1214", PRNS 32, J.W. Ruddock, 1925.

53. William Henry Hart, ed., "Historia et Cartularium Monasterii Sancti Petri Gloucestriae", Rolls Series No.33, Longman, Green, Longman, Roberts & Green, 1863.

54. Major-General the Honourable George Wrottesley, 'Staffordshire Suits Extracted from the Plea Rolls, temp. Richard I and King John', *Collections for the History of Staffordshire*, III, 1882.

55. Lionel Landon, ed., "The Itinerary of King Richard the First", PRNS 13, Ruddock, 1935.

56. Doris M. Stenton, ed., "The Great Roll of the Pipe for the Sixth Year of King Richard the First, Michaelmas 1194", PRNS 5, Ruddock, 1928.

57. Doris M. Stenton, ed., "The Chancellor's Roll of the Ninth Year of the Reign of King Richard the First, Michaelmas 1196", PRNS 7, Ruddock 1930; also PRNS 17, op cit.

58. - , "The Great Roll of the Pipe for the Seventh Year of King Richard the First, Michaelmas 1195", PRNS 6, Ruddock, 1929.

59. - , "The Great Roll of the Pipe for the Second Year of the Reign of King John, Michaelmas 1200", PRNS 12, Ruddock, 1934.

60. - , "Pleas before the King or His Justices 1198-1202, Vol.2", Selden Society Vol.68, 1952; also PRNS 32, op cit.

61. Details of the problem are given in James Bentham, "The History and Antiquities of the Conventual and Cathedral Church of Ely", op cit.

62. Doris M. Stenton, ed., "The Great Roll of the Pipe, for the Tenth Year of King Richard the First, Michaelmas 1198", PRNS 9, Ruddock, 1932.

63. W. Farrer, ed., "The Lancashire Pipe Rolls and Early Lancashire Charters", Henry Young & Sons, Liverpool, 1902.

64. Hubert Hall, ed., "The Red Book of the Exchequer", op cit.

65. C.R. Cheney, Eric John, eds., "English Episcopal Acta III: Canterbury 1193-1205", op cit.

66. Dorothy M. Stenton, ed., "The Great Roll of the Pipe for the Ninth Year of King Richard the First", PRNS 8, J.W. Ruddock, 1931.

67. Anon, "Introduction to the Study of the Pipe Rolls", Pipe Roll Society Vol.3, 1884.

68. William Page, ed., "Victoria History of the Counties of England: Bucks., Vol. 2", op cit.

69. Anon, ed., "The Pipe Rolls of 31 Henry I, Michaelmas 1130", op cit.

70. William Page, ed., "The Victoria History of the Counties of England: Buckinghamshire, Vol. 1", James Street, 1905.

71. W.A. Copinger, "The Manors of Suffolk", op cit.

72. R.B. Pugh, ed., "Victoria History of the Counties of England: Warwickshire, Vol. VII", op cit.

73. William Dugdale, "The Antiquities of Warwickshire", T. Warren, London, 1661.

74. Will Bennett, 'Buyer Pays £2.7 m. for Crusader's Prayer Book', *Daily Telegraph*, 24th June 1998.

75. Charity Cannon Willard, trans., Madeleine Pelner Cosman, ed., Christine de Pisan, "A Medieval Woman's Mirror of Honour: The Treasury of the City of Ladies", Bard Hall Press & Persca Books, 1989. I've also drawn on the French text in C.C. Willard & Eric Hicks, "Christine de Pizan, Le Livre des Trois Vertus, Édition Critique", Librairie Honore Champion, Paris, 1989. A 15th century painting of Christine by Lucas van Leyden is reproduced in Henry Shaw, "Dress and Decoration of the Middle Ages", op cit, with a two-page account of her life.

76. George Caspar Homans, "English Villagers of the Thirteenth Century", op cit. G.C. Coulton, "Mediaeval Panorama, The English Scene from Conquest to Reformation", op cit.

77. Madelaine Pelner Cosman, "Mediaeval Holidays and Festivals", op cit.

78. Margaret Collins, personal communication, 6th July, 1999.

79. M.J. Franklin, ed., "English Episc. Acta XVII: Coventry and Lichfield, 1183-1208", OUP, 1998.

80. William Yates, 'A Map of the County of Staffordshire, from an Actual Survey, Begun in the Year 1769, and Finished in 1775", reprinted as *Collections for the History of Staffordshire*, Series 4, Vol.12. NB. In Glasgow University Library the reproduction map was not filed with the rest of *Collections...* on Level 8. It was in the map section on Level 7, filed under 'Maps c17: 55 101'.

81. "The Victoria History of the Counties of England: Warwickshire, Vol. VI", op cit.

82. W.M. Greenslade, G.C. Burgh, 'Stebbing Shaw and the History of Staffordshire', *Collections for a History of Staffordshire*, 4th Series, No.6, Staffordshire Records Society, 1970.

83. William Stubbs, ed., Gervase of Canterbury, "The Chronicle of the Reigns of Stephen, Henry II and Richard I", op cit.

84. William Maitland, "The History and Survey of London, Vol.2", op cit.

85. Richard Barre, "Compendium Veteri et Novi Testamente", Harleian MS 3255, British Library Manuscript Collection.

86. Ralph V. Turner, "The English Justiciary in the Age of Glanville and Bracton", op cit.

87. M.R. James, catalogue of Lambeth Palace mediaeval MSS, quoted in R.J. Palmer, Librarian, personal communication, 12th July, 1990.

88. Lambeth Palace MS 105, "Liber Ricardi Barre super bibliam".

89. Dr. M.C. Breay, British Library Dept. of Manuscripts, personal communications, 25th & 31st August, 1999.

90. William Stubbs, Introduction to Roger de Hoveden, op cit.

91. H.G. Richardson, 'Gervase of Tilbury', op cit.

Chapter Fifteen - 1200's: SIBYLLA AND AGNES

1. Doris M. Stenton, ed., "Pleas before the King or His Justices 1198-1202, Vol.2", op cit.

2. Ralph V. Turner, 'Richard Barre and Michael Belet', op cit.

3. Doris M. Stenton, ed., "The Great Roll of the Pipe for the Fifth Year of the Reign of King John, Michaelmas 1203", PRNS 16, Ruddock, 1938.

4. Deputy Keeper of the Records, ed., "Curia Regis Rolls of the Reign of Richard I and John", op cit, Vols. 1-5.

5. Doris M. Stenton, ed., "The Great Roll of the Pipe for the Sixth Year of the Reign of King John, Michaelmas 1204", PRNS 18, Ruddock, 1940.

6. R. Allen Brown, ed., "The Great Roll of the Pipe for the Tenth Year of the Reign of King John, 1207-1208", PRNS 31, Ruddock, 1957.

7. Sir William Dugdale, "Monasticon Anglicanum", op cit.

8. J.C. Holt, ed., "Pipe Rolls 17 John and Praestita Rolls 14-18 John", PRNS 37, Ruddock, 1964.

9. J. Caley & W. Illingworth, eds., "Testa de Nevill", op cit, Deputy Keeper of Records, ed., "Liber Feodorum", op cit.

10. J.H. Round, ed., "Calendar of Documents Preserved in France Illustrative of the History of Great Britain", op cit.

11. Pipe Roll Society, "The Great Roll of the Pipe for Twentyseventh Year of the Reign of King Henry the Second", Vol.30, St. Catherine Press, 1909.

12. D.M. Stenton, ed., "The Great Roll of the Pipe for the Seventh Year of Richard the First", op cit.

13. Ralph V. Turner, 'The Exercise of the King's Will in the Inheritance of Baronies', in Ralph V. Turner, "Judges, Administrators and the Common Law in Angevin England", op cit.

14. R.B. Pugh & Elizabeth Crittall, eds., "Victoria History of the Counties of England: Wiltshire, Vol. Five", Oxford University Press, 1957.

15. Matthew Paris, "Chronica Majora"; J.H. Wiffen, trans., Tasso, "Jerusalem Liberated", op cit.

16. Lionel Landon, ed., "The Carta Antiquae Rolls 1-10", PRNS 17, op cit.

17. Eric St. John Brooks, ed., "Knights' Fees in Counties Wexford, Carlow and Kilkenny (13th-15th Century)"; W.R. Powell, ed., "Victoria History of the Counties of England: Essex, Vol. IV", op cit.

18. Matthew Paris, "Chronica Majora" and "Historia Anglorum", op cit, apparently listed for 1204 and 1205 by Dr. Thomas Short, "History of the Air, etc...', op cit.

19. D.M. Stenton, ed., "The Great Roll of the Pipe for the Eleventh Year of King John, Michaelmas 1209", PRNS 24, Ruddock, 1949. For the return of Barre lands to the de Siffrevasts see Buckingham Record Society, 4 (1), 36, (1940), held by Glasgow University Library on microfiche.

20. Curia Rolls Vol.5.

21. Curia Rolls Vol. 6; 'W' doesn't even appear in Le Neve's "Fasti".

22. Rev. W. Rich Jones, Rev. W. Dunn Macray, eds., "Charters and Documents Illustrating the History of the Cathedral, City and Diocese of Salisbury in the 12th and 13th Centuries", op cit.

23. "English Episcopal Acta VI", op cit.

24. T. Duffus Hardy, ed., "Rotuli de Liberate ac de Misis et Praestitis, Regnente Johanne", Eyre & Spottiswoode, 1844.

25. Barbara Dodwell, ed., "Feet of Fines for the County of Norfolk for the Reign of King John, 1201-1215; for the County of Suffolk, 1199-1214", PRNS 32, op cit.

26. Edward A. Bond, ed., "Chronicle of the Abbey de Melsa, Vol.1", op cit.

27. Curia Rolls, op cit, Vol. I; 'Curia Regis Rolls', *Collections for a History of Staffordshire*, III, 1882.

28. Joseph Hunter, ed., "Fines, sive Pedes Finium", op cit.

29. Nicholas Barrett, ed., "Receipt Rolls for the Fourth, Fifth and Sixth Years of the Reign of King Henry III, Easter 1220, 1221, 1222", PRNS 52, 2003.

30. Curia Rolls, op cit, Vol. X; confirmed in L.C. Hector, ed., "Curia Rolls Vol. XVI, 21-26 Henry III (1237-1242)", HMSO, 1979.

31. Doris M. Stenton, ed., "The Great Roll of the Pipe for the Sixth Year of King Richard the First", PRNS 5, op cit, & "The Great Roll of the Pipe for the Seventh Year of King Richard the First, Michaelmas 1195", PRNS 6, op cit.

32. George Caspar Homans, "English Villagers of the Thirteenth Century", op cit.

33. Doris M. Stenton, ed., "The Great Roll of the Pipe for the Third Year of King John, Michaelmas 1201", PRNS 14; entries continued in Vols. 15 & 16; Ruddock, 1936.

34. Doris M. Stenton, ed., "The Great Roll of the Pipe for the Fourteenth Year of King John, Michaelmas 1212", PRNS 30, Ruddock, 1955.

35. R.A. Brown, ed., "Pipe Roll 17 John"; J.C. Holt, ed., "Praestita Roll 14-18 John", PRNS 37, op cit.

36. E. Pauline Ebdon, "The Great Roll of the Pipe for the Second Year of King Henry the Third, Michaelmas 1218", PRNS 39, J.W. Ruddock, 1972.

37. Charles Roberts, ed., "Excerpta e Rotulis Finium in Turri Londiniensi Asservatis, Henrico Tertio Rege, A.D. 1216-1272", op cit.

38. Deputy Keeper of the Records, ed., "Patent Rolls of the Reign of Henry III, preserved in the Public Records Office, AD 1216-1266", op cit.

39. Deputy Keeper of the Records, ed., "Close Rolls of the Reign of Henry III", op cit.

40. D.A. Carpenter, "The Minority of Henry III", Methuen, 1990.

41. William Page, ed., "The Victoria History of the Counties of England: Warwickshire, Vol. Two, Constable, 1908.

42. L.F. Salzman & Philip Styles, eds., "The Victoria History of the Counties of England: Warwickshire, Vol. III", Oxford University Press, 1945.

43. Sir William Dugdale, "The Baronage of England", op cit, Vol.1.

44. H.S. Sweetman, ed., "Calendar of Documents relating to Ireland preserved in Her Majesty's Public Record Office, London, 1171-1251", Longman & Co., 1875.

45. John T. Gilbert, ed., "Chartularies of St. Mary's Abbey, Dublin", Rolls Series No.80, Longman & Co., 1884.

46. Fred & Annarie Cazel, eds., "'Rolls of the Fifteenth' of the Ninth Year of King Henry III", PRNS 45, Ruddock, 1983.

47. R.E.G. Kirk, ed., "Feet of Fines for Essex", Vol.1, op cit.

48. Chalfont Robinson, ed., "The Great Roll of the Pipe for the Fourteenth Year of King Henry III", PRNS 4, University of Princeton Press, 1927.

49. W.A. Copinger, "The Manors of Suffolk", op cit.

50. G. Martin, ed., "The History and Antiquities of the County of Essex" by Philip Morant, op cit.

51. R. Allen Brown, ed., "Memoranda Rolls 16-17 Henry III Preserved in the Public Records Office", HMSO, 1991.

52. Michael Baigent, Richard Leigh, Henry Lincoln, "The Holy Blood and the Holy Grail", op cit.

53. James Le Fanu, 'Doctor's Diary', Auslan Cramb, 'Is Santa Flying High on Magic Mushrooms?', *Daily Telegraph*, 27th July 1999 and 14th December, 2001.

54. C.W. Wilson, C. Warren, "The Discovery of Jerusalem: a Narrative of Exploration and Discovery in the City and the Holy Land", Richard Bentley, London, 1871.

55. Sibylla de Calna seal imprint, Harl. Ch. 52.C.48, British Library.

56. Sibylla de Calna seal imprint, Harl. Ch. 47.H.37.

57. W. de G. Birch, "Catalogue of Seals in the Dept. of Manuscripts in the British Museum", op cit.

58. Sibylla de Calna master seal D.C. E287, British Library.

59. Arthur Guirdham, "The Great Heresy", Neville Spearman, 1977; Michael Baigent, Richard Leigh and Henry Lincoln, "The Holy Blood and the Holy Grail", op cit.

60. Henrietta Heald, ed., "Chronicle of Great Britain and Ireland", Chronicle Communications, 1992.

61. Zev Vilney, "The Sacred Land: Vol. 1, Legends of Jerusalem", op cit.

62. Richard Andrews, "Blood on the Mountain", op cit; Sam Kiley, 'The Righteous Will Survive and the Rest Will Perish', *The Times*, December 13th, 1999.

63. H. Frankfort, "Cylinder Seals", Macmillan, 1939; (anon), 'Professor Oliver Gurney, the world authority on the extraordinary civilisation of the Hittites', *Daily Telegraph, Obituaries*, 23rd Jan. 2001.

64. Robert Bauval, "Secret Chamber", op cit.

65. "Larousse Encyclopedia of Mythology", op cit.

66. H.V. Morton, "The Heart of London", in "H.V. Morton's London", op cit.

67. Richard Hinckley Allen, "Star Names, their Lore and Meaning", op cit.

68. Esther Casier Quinn, "The Quest of Seth", University of Chicago Press, 1962.

69. Michael Baigent and Richard Leigh, "The Temple and the Lodge", op cit.

70. Robert Graves, "The White Goddess", op cit; "The Temple and the Lodge", op cit.

71. Robert Graves, "The Greek Myths: 2", revised edition, Penguin, 1960.

72. Gwen Benwell & Arthur Waugh, "Sea Enchantress", op cit, cites "The White Goddess" but only on the mermaid's mirror representing the Moon; curiously, Mary of Egypt isn't mentioned - and I haven't found her in the "Larousse Encyclopedia of Mythology" or others except for "The Greek Myths".

73. A.L. Lloyd, "Folk Song in England", Panther Arts, 1969. *Hunting the Wren* is on "Steeleye Span - Live at Last", Chrysalis Records CHR 1199, 1978, and as *The Cutty Wren* on Steeleye Span, "Time", Park Records PRK MC34, 1996; as an instrumental, on Andy Cronshaw, "Earthed in Cloud Valley", Trailer LER 2104, Transatlantic Records, 1977. The words are in Arnold Wesker, "Chips with Everything" (see for example Eluned Brown, "York Notes: Arnold Wesker, 'Chips With Everything'", Longman York Press, 1982) and an orchestral arrangement of the tune is incorporated in George Butterworth's *The Banks of Green Willow*. It was a rallying song in the Peasants' Revolt in 1381, when Wat Tyler stormed the London Temple and burned the English records of the Order along with the law-books; details are in G.C. Addison, "The Temple Church", op cit. An Irish song on the same theme is featured in the medley, *The Wren! The Wren!* on The Chieftains, "The Bells of Dublin", RCA Victor LC 0316, 1991.

74. Christopher Howse, 'May Day Is for Merry Men', *Daily Telegraph*, 1st May 2000.

75. '"Meet the Ancestors" Special', BBC-2, 15th January, 2000.

76. Henry J. Hillen, "History of the Borough of King's Lynn", op cit.

77. Thomas Keneally, "The Great Shame, A Story of the Irish in the Old World and the New", Vintage, 1999.

78. W.H. Rich Jones, ed., "The Register of St. Osmund", op cit.

79. Pipe Roll Society, "Feet of Fines for the Tenth Year of King Richard the First", op cit.

80. A.E.W. Marsh, "A History of the Borough and Town of Calne", op cit.

81. Personal communications, Adrian Ailes, National Archives Public Record Office, 2nd and 17th May, 2000.

82. William de Cantilupe seal 'Cart. Harl. 47.G.35', British Library.

83. Historical Manuscripts Commission, "Report on Manuscripts in Various Collections", Vol.4, HMSO, 1907.

84. Leslie Stephen, ed., "Directory of National Bibliography, Vol. VIII, Burton-Cantwell", Smith, Elder & Co., 1886.

85. Peter Blenensis, "Continuatio ad Historiam Ingulphi", in Vol.1, "Rerum Anglicarum Scriptorum Veterum", op cit.

86. R.C. van Caenegem, ed., "English Lawsuits from William I to Richard I", op cit.

87. Leopold Delisle, "Recueil des Actes de Henry II", op cit.

88. Historical Manuscripts Commission, "Manuscripts of the Late Reginald Rawdon Hastings Esq.", op cit.

89. Patricia Barnes, ed., "Great Rolls of the Pipe for the Sixteenth Year of King John, Michaelmas 1214", PRNS 35, Ruddock, 1962.

90. L.C. Hector, ed., "Curia Regis Rolls... (Vol.16) 21 to 26 Henry III (1237-1242)", 1979.

91. Curia Regis Rolls, op cit, Vol.15.

92. John H. Mundy, "Europe in the High Middle Ages, 1150-1309", op cit.

93. Anon, "Binham Priory", op cit.

94. The British Library, Additional Charter 15520, purchased from A.F. Bernard, 27th July 1861; Richard Newcourt, "Repertorium", op cit.

95. Deputy Keeper of the Records, ed., "A Descriptive Catalogue of Ancient Deeds Held in the Public Records Office", op cit.

96. Clive Aslet, 'Village Voice', *Daily Telegraph*, 30th June 2007.

97. James Bohn, "Charter Notes for the County of Suffolk, 1635-1655", British Library, Additional Manuscript 15520. Avoid confusing this with Additional Charter 15520, above - useful though this one was for details of the de Sherdilowes, when I accidentally requested it.

98. Ralph V. Turner, "The English Justiciary in the Age of Glanvill and Bracton", op cit.

99. Deputy Keeper of the Records, ed., "Calendar of the Liberate Rolls... Henry III AD 1226-1245", op cit.

100. Adrian Henstock, Principal Archivist, Nottinghamshire County Council, personal communication to Jane Greatorex, 19th January, 1998.
101. "Rufford Charters, Vol.1", op cit.

Chapter Sixteen - 1236: YORKSHIRE AND IRELAND

1. William Stubbs, ed., "The Historical Collections of Walter of Coventry", Rolls Series No. 58, Longman & Co., 1873.
2. William Andrews, ed., "Bygone Derbyshire", op cit.
3. Stephen Glover, "The Peak Guide", op cit; Camden, "Britannia", op cit.
4. Peter Coss, "The Knight in Mediaeval England, 1000-1400", op cit.
5. B.H. St. John O'Neil, "Peveril Castle, Derbyshire", op cit.
6. Henry Richards Luard, ed., "Chronica Majora" of Roger de Wendover & Matthew Paris, op cit. Richard Vaughan, editor of "The Illustrated Chronicles of Matthew Paris", op cit, considers that Paris also wrote the "Flores Historiarum" and that the first part of the "Chronica Majora" is based on de Wendover's work, not simply incorporating it.
7. Matthew Paris, "Historia Anglorum", op cit.
8. Richard Andrews, "Blood on the Mountain, a History of the Temple Mount from the Ark to the Third Millennium", op cit.
9. Manuel Komroff, ed., "The Apocrypha", Tudor Publishing Co., New York, 1937.
10. John Irvine Whitty, "Water Supply of Jerusalem Ancient and Modern", Williams & Norgate, 1864.
11. Edith Swann, "The Piebald Standard", op cit; Marion Melville, "La Vie des Templiers", op cit.
12. Paris's map of Britain is reproduced in colour in Henrietta Heald, ed., "Chronicle of Great Britain and Ireland", op cit. A clearer version, but incomplete, is in Richard Vaughan, ed., "The Illustrated Chronicles of Matthew Paris", op cit. The 1950 edition of the *Encyclopedia Britannica*, vol.14, p.840, reproduces under 'Map' a black-and-white tracing on which place-names are easier to read, but detailed text is missing.
13. Sir William Dugdale, "Monasticon Anglicanum", op cit.
14. Alexander Hamilton Thompson, "Roche Abbey, Yorkshire", Her Majesty's Stationery Office, 1935 (reprinted 1936 & 1954).
15. Oliver Rackham, "Trees and Woodland in the British Landscape", Dent, 1976.

16. James Aveling, "The History of Roche Abbey from its Founding to its Dissolution", op cit.

17. Glyn Coppack, "The English Heritage Book of Castles and Priories", Batsford, 1990.

18. Kate Norgate, "Richard the Lion Heart", op cit.

19. Richard Barber, Juliet Barker, "Tournaments: Jousts, Chivalry and Pageants in the Middle Ages", Woodbridge, 1989.

20. William Page, ed., "The Victoria History of the Counties of England: Yorkshire, Vol. III", Constable, 1913.

21. Christopher Knight, Robert Lomas, "Uriel's Machine, the Prehistoric Technology that Survived the Flood", Century, 1999.

22. Seal 3918 of W. de G. Birch, ed., "Catalogue of Seals in the Department of Manuscripts in the British Museum", op cit, reference no. LXXII.99 – but that seal doesn't match Aveling's version.

23. Thomas M. Parker, "The Knights Templar in England", op cit.

24. Richard Vaughan, "The Illustrated Matthew Paris", op cit.

25. Aristotle's "Book of Meteors" is identified in C.E. Britton, "A Meteorological Chronology to AD 1450", op cit.

26. John O'Donovan, ed., "The Annals of the Kingdom of Ireland", op cit.

27. 'W.S.B.', 'The Spectre Horsemen of Southerfell', *Notes & Queries*, lst. Series, VII, 178, 304 (Mar.26, 1853); 'Buriensis', 'Spectral Coach and Horses', lst. Series, V, 129, 365 (April 17, 1852). NB: Aveling ("The History of Roche Abbey", above) mistakenly gives the issue number as 186. *Notes and Queries* is confusingly numbered, in 'Series' within each of which Vol.1, 2 etc. start again from scratch. Curiously, there are no index entries for the stories repeated by Aveling, although they are both in 1st Series Vol. V, as above.

28. Sir William Dugdale, "The Baronage of England", op cit.

29. Deputy Keeper of the Records, ed., "Close Rolls of the Reign of Henry III, A.D. 1234-37", HMSO, 1908.

30. Henrietta Heald, ed., "Chronicle of Great Britain and Ireland", op cit.

31. Stephen Gwynn, "The History of Ireland", Macmillan, 1924.

32. Malcolm Barber, "The New Knighthood", op cit.

33. Goddard Henry Orpen, "Ireland under the Normans", 6 vols., Clarendon Press, 1911; Hilary D. Walsh, "Borris-in-Ossory, Co. Laois," op cit.

34. Herbert Wood, 'The Templars in Ireland', op cit.

35. Commissioners for the Records of the Kingdom, "Calendarium Rotulorum Patentium in Turri Londiniensi", House of Commons, 1802.

36. For example René Grousset, "Histoire des Croisades et de Royaume Franc de Jérusalem", op cit.

37. Rev. William Healy, "History and Antiquities of Kilkenny (County and City)", vol. 1, P.M. Egon, Kilkenny, 1893.

38. Miss May Sparks, 'Gowran', *Old Kilkenny Review*, 3, 43-46 (1950).

39. H.S. Sweetman, ed., "Calendar of Documents relating to Ireland preserved in Her Majesty's Public Record Office", op cit.

40. A.E.W. Marsh, "A History of the Borough and Town of Calne", op cit.

41. Rev. J.F. Shearman, 'The Early Kings of Ossory', op cit.

41. Maureen Hegarty, 'Jerpoint', Old Kilkenny Review, 4-14 (1972).

43. Charles H. Harteshorne, 'Peverell's Castle in the Peak', op cit.

44. Rev. R.W. Eyton, "Court, Household and Itinerary of King Henry II", op cit.

Chapter Seventeen - 1240'S AND AFTER: SIBYLLA AND AGNES

1. T.S. Eliot, "Murder in the Cathedral", Faber & Faber, 1935.

2. R.E.G. Kirk, ed., "Feet of Fines for Essex", Vol.1, op cit.

3. Dr. Thomas Short, "General Chronol. History of the Air, Weather, Seasons, Meteors Etc...", op cit.

4. For the de Calna/Bernay charters see "Registrum Cartarum Prioratus de Binham", op cit.

5. Francis Blomefield, "An Essay towards a Topographical History of the County of Norfolk", op cit.

6. Matthew Paris, "Chronica Majora", op cit.

7. "Faden's Map of Norfolk", boxed set, sheet 2, Norfolk Record Society Vol.42 (undated).

8. Brian Cushion, Norfolk Landscape Archaeology Dept., Norwich Museums Service, surveys of Fulmedeston moated complexes, Barney.

9. Deputy Keeper of the Records, ed., "Patent Rolls of the Reign of Henry III", op cit, AD 1225-1232.

10. "Calendar of Charter Rolls, Vol. I: Henry III AD 1226-1257", HMSO, 1903.

11. Deputy Keeper of the Records, ed., "Close Rolls of the Reign of Henry III", op cit.

12. "Patent Rolls of the Reign of Henry III", op cit, AD 1247-1258.

13. Tony Ryan, 'Moon Shadow, Eclipses in the Ancient Annals, Part 2', *Astron. & Space*, July 1999.

14. C.E. Britton, 'A Meteorological Chronology to AD 1450', op cit.

15. Conrad Lycosthenes, "Prodigia ac ostentorum chronicon", Henricus Petri, Basel, 1557, and Jeremy Hodges, 'Somewhere Out in Space There Is an Asteroid...', *The Scotsman*, 17th November, 1998.

16. J.J. Bagley, "Life in Mediaeval England"; Jean Gimpel, "The Medieval Machine", op cit.

17. Mike Baillie, "Exodus to Arthur", op cit.

18. Henry Richards Luard, ed., "Annales de Burton, AD 1004-1263", in "Annales Monastici", op cit, Vol.1.

19. Mark Baily, 'Per Impetum Maris: Natural Disasters in East Anglia 1275-1350', in Bruce M.S. Campbell, ed., "Before the Black Death: Studies in the 'Crisis' of the Early Fourteenth Century", Oxford University Press, 1992.

20. Jean Gimpel, "The Medieval Machine", op cit; 'The Day the World Took Off: the Medieval Machine', Channel 4, 18th June 2000.

21. Michael Baigent & Richard Leigh, "The Temple and the Lodge", op cit.

22. Sir William Dugdale, "The Baronage of England", op cit; Roger de Wendover, "Flores Historiarum", op cit.

23. Richard Vaughan, ed., "The Illustrated Chronicles of Matthew Paris", op cit.

24. W.A. Copinger, "The Manors of Suffolk", op cit.

25. Henry Richards Luard, ed., 'Annales de Dunstaphlia', in "Annales Monastici", op cit, vol. 3.

26. Commissioners for George III, "Calendarium Inquisitorium Post Mortem and Esceatum, Vol. I, Temporibus Regum Hen. III, Ed. I and Ed. II", 1806.

27. G. Martin, ed., Philip Morant, "The History and Antiquities of the County of Essex", op cit.

28. Richard Newcourt, "Repertorium Ecclesiasticum Parochiale Londiniense", op cit.

29. J. Caley & W. Illingworth, eds., "Testa de Nevill sive liber feodorum in curia sacarii, temp. Hen. III et Edw. I", op cit.

30. Deputy Keeper of the Records, ed., "Calendar of Inquisitions Miscellaneous (Chancery) Preserved in the Public Record Office", HMSO, 1916.

31. Anon, "Binham Priory", op cit.

32. Sir William Dugdale, "Monasticon Anglicanum", op cit.

33. Maj.-Gen. Hon. George Wrottesley, ed., 'Staffordshire Suits, extracted from the Plea Rolls temp Richard I and King John', *Collections for a History of Staffordshire*, III, 1-106, 1882.

34. Charles Roberts, ed., "Excerpta e Rotulis Finium", op cit.

35. John Horace Round, ed., "Rotuli de Dominibus et Pueris...", op cit.

36. Commissioners for the Public Records, "Placitorum Abbrevatio in Domo Capitulari Westmonasteriensi Asservatorum Abbrevatio", House of Commons, 1811.

37. Curia Rolls, Vol. XVI, op cit.

38. Doris M. Stenton, ed., "The Great Roll of the Pipe for the Third Year of King John, Michaelmas 1201", PRNS 14, op cit.

39. Major-General Hon. George Wrottesley, 'Plea Rolls of the Reign of Henry III' & 'Final Concords or Pedes Finium, Staffordshire, temp. Henry III', *Coll. Hist. Staffs.*, Second Series, Vol.4, William Salt Archaeological Society, 1883.

40. Ms. Philippa Bassett, Senior Archivist, Birmingham Central Library, personal communication, 11th Sept. 1995.

41. Ethel Stokes & Frederick C. Wellstood, eds., "Warwickshire Feet of Fines, Vol. I, 7 Ric. I (1195) - 12 Ed. I (1284)", Dugdale Society (Oxford University Press), 1932; R.B. Pugh, ed., "The Victoria History of the Counties of England: Warwickshire, Vol. VII", op cit.

42. Hon. & Rev. Canon Bridgeman, 'An Account of the Family of Swynnerton', *Coll. Hist. Staffs.*, Vol. VII, part 2, 1886; Rev. Charles Swynnerton, 'The Earlier Swynnertons of Eccleshall', *Coll. Hist. Staffs.*, New Series, Vol.3, 1900.

43. Anon, 'Military Service Performed by Staffordshire Tenants', *Coll. Hist. Staffs.*, Vol. VIII, 1887.

44. Anon, 'Inquisitions Post-Mortem etc., 1327-66', *Coll. Hist. Staffs.*, New Series, 1913.

45. 'Reviews', *Coll. Hist. Staffs.*, 1921.

46. Major-General George Wrottesley, 'Extracts from the Plea Rolls for the Reign of Edward III and Richard II', *Coll. Hist. Staffs.*, Vol. XIII, 1892.

47. Anon, 'Inquisitions "Post Mortem", "Ad Quod Damnum", etc. Staffordshire, 1223-1327', *Coll. Hist. Staffs.*, 1911.

48. Anon, 'Liberate Rolls of Henry III and Final Concords Edward I - Edward II, Inquisitions, etc., Relating to Staffordshire', *Coll. Hist. Staffs.*, Vol. VI, 1885; see also ref. 44.

49. Major-General the Hon. George Wrottesley, 'Extracts from the Plea Rolls, AD 1272 to AD 1294', *Coll. Hist. Staffs.*, Vol. VI, 1885; anon., ed., 'The Subsidy Roll of AD 1327', ibid, Vol. VII, 1886.

50.   Very Rev. H.E. Savage, 'The Great Register of Lichfield Cathedral, known as Magnum Registrum Album', *Coll. Hist. Staffs.*, 1924.

51.   Anon, ed., 'Pleas of the Forest, Staffordshire', *Coll. Hist. Staffs.*, Vol. V, 1884.

52.   *Coll. Hist. Staffs.*, Vol. VI, op cit.

53.   *Coll. Hist. Staffs.*, Vol. I & Vol. VI, op cit.

54.   Major-General the Hon. George Wrottesley, 'Extracts from the Plea Rolls Temp. E III', *Coll. Hist. Staffs.*, Vol. XI, 1890;   'Extracts from the Plea Rolls of the Reign of Edward III', ibid., Vol. XII, 1891.

55.   Anon, 'Extracts from the Plea Rolls of Edward II, 1307-1327'/'The Barons of Dudley', *Coll. Hist. Staffs.*, Vol. IX, 1889.

56.   Josiah C. Wedgewood, 'Staffordshire Parliamentary History from the Earliest Times to the Present Day', *Coll. Hist. Staffs.*, 1917.

57.   Anon, 'The Subsidy Rolls of 1327', *Coll. Hist. Staffs.*, Vol. VII, 1886.

58.   W.B. Stephens, ed., "The Victoria History of the Counties of England: Staffordshire, Vol. VII, The City of Birmingham", Oxford University Press, 1964.

59.   Major-General the Hon. George Wrottesley, 'The Staffordshire Hundred Rolls', *Coll. Hist. Staffs.*, Vol. V, 1884.

60.   W.B. Stephens, ed., "The Victoria History of the Counties of England: Staffordshire, Vol. VIII, City of Coventry and Borough of Warwick", Oxford University Press, 1969.

61.   "A Descriptive Catalogue of Ancient Deeds", op cit.

62.   M.E. Cornford, E.B. Miller, 'Calendar of the Salt MSS', *Coll. Hist. Staffs.*, 1921.

63.   I.H. Jeayes, 'Staffordshire Charters in the Possession of the Marquis of Anglesey', *Coll. Hist. Staffs.*, 1939.

64.   Thomas Rymer & Robert Sanderson, eds., "Foedera, Conventiones, Litterae et cujuscunque generis Acta Publica, inter Reges Angliae et alios quosvis Imperatores, Reges, Pontifices, Principes, vel Communitates, ab Ingressu Gulielmi I in Angliam, A.D. 1066, ad Nostra usque Tempora", Vol.3.2, London 1816.

65.   Anon, 'Plea Rolls of the Reign of Edward I', *Coll. Hist. Staffs.*, Vol. VII, 1886.

66. Duncan Lunan, 'Children from the Sky', *Analog*, September 1996; Evelyn P. Shirley, "Stemmata Shirleiana, or the Annals of the Shirley Family", Nichols & Sons, 1873.   For the history of the Devereux family see Walter Bourchier Devereux, "Lives and Letters of the Devereux, Earls of Essex, in

the Reigns of Elizabeth, James I, and Charles I" (2 vols.), John Murray, 1853.

67. For example in the Patent Rolls, op cit, 1218, after Thomas de Erdington's death.

68. *Coll. Hist. Staffs.*, Vols. I & V, Vol. IX Part 2; Major-General George Wrottesley, 'Military Service Performed by Staffordshire Tenants in the 13th and 14th Centuries', Vol. VIII, 1887; ibid, 'Fines of Mixed Counties which Include Manors and Tenancies in Staffordshire', Vol. XII; ibid, 'Crécy and Calais', Vol. XVIII.

69. Avrom Saltman, ed., 'The Cartulary of Tutbury Priory', *Coll. Hist. Staffs.*, 4th Series, Vol.4, 1962.

70. Anon, 'Staffordshire Quarter Sessions Rolls Temp. Elizabeth and James I', *Coll. Hist. Staffs.*, 1934, Part 2.

71. Peter Coss, "The Knight in Medieval England 1000-1400", op cit.

72. *Coll. Hist. Staffs.*, Vol. XII, op cit.

73. Major-General the Honourable George Wrottesley, 'Extracts from the Plea Rolls of the Reign of Edward III', *Coll. Hist. Staffs.*, Vol. XIV, 1893.

74. Jim Wilson, ed., "900 Years, Norwich Cathedral and Diocese", op cit.

75. "Who's Who 1997", A.C. Black, London, 1997.

76. Michael Tierney, 'Tory Minister's Ancestor from Another Planet', *Saturday (Evening) Times*, 26th April 1997; Sarah Lonsdale, 'Unsurpassed in Englishness', *Daily Telegraph*, November 23rd, 2002. 77. Jon Stock, 'Inside Story: Cell Park', *Daily Telegraph*, Property section, 16th September, 2000.

78. Camden, "Britannia", op cit; Ralph V. Turner, 'The Exercise of the King's Will in the Inheritance of Baronies', op cit.

79. John Crowley, 'The Green Child', op cit.

80. Deputy Keeper of the Records, ed., "A Descriptive Catalogue of Ancient Deeds", op cit.

81. W.H. St. John Hope, 'The Castle of the Peak and the Pipe Rolls', op cit.

82. "The Minority of Henry III", op cit.

83. John Burton, "Monasticon Eboracense, and the Ecclesiastical History of Yorkshire", N. Nicholson, York, in the Coffee-Yard, 1758.

84. Rev. R.W. Eyton, "Court, Household and Itinerary of King Henry II", op cit.

85. Georges Bordonove, "Les Templiers", Fayard, 1977.

86. Rev. William Hudson, 'Three Manorial Extracts of the 13th Century', (publication unnamed), XN, 2-56. Copy held by Suffolk County Records Office.

87. W.A. Copinger, "County of Suffolk... materials for the History of Suffolk", op cit.

Chapter Eighteen - A DIGRESSION OF MATTER TRANSMITTERS

1. Glyn Maxwell, "Wolfpit", op cit.
2. Stephen E. Whitfield, Gene Roddenberry, "The Making of Star Trek", Ballantine Books, 1968.
3. James Blish, "Spock Must Die!", Bantam, 1970.
4. Duncan Lunan, 'The Moon of Thin Reality', *Galaxy*, July 1970; 'Here Comes the Sun', 'Liaison Assignment', 'Falling through the World', 'The Galilean Problem', March, April, May-June, Sept. 1971.
5. Arthur C. Clarke, 'The Sun', in "The Challenge of the Spaceship", Ballantine Books, 1961; quoted in Duncan Lunan, "Man and the Stars", op cit.
6. Adrian Berry, "The Iron Sun, Crossing the Universe through Black Holes", Cape, 1977.
7. Duncan Lunan, "Man and the Planets", Ashgrove Press, 1983; US import by Salem House.
8. John H. Fadum, 'Black Holes, Stargates and Starships', ASTRA *Spacereport* 4, 1, 14-19 and insert (Sept. 1981).
9. Robert L. Forward, 'Flattening Spacetime near the Earth', *Physical Review* D, 26, 4, 735-744 (15th August 1982); 'Flattening Spacetime', *Analog*, CIII, 3, 58-73 (March 1983).
10. John G. Cramer, 'Wormholes and Time Machines', *Analog* CIX, 6, 124-128 (June 1989); 'More About Wormholes - To the Stars in No Time', CX, 6, 99-103 (May 1990).
11. Thomas Donaldson, 'The Holes of Space-Time', *Analog*, CXIII, 8 & 9, 122-135 (July 1993).
12. R.W. Fuller & John A. Wheeler, 'Causality and Multiply-Connected Space-Time', *Physical Review*, 128, 2, 919-929 (15th Oct., 1962); John C. Graves & Dieter R. Brill, 'Oscillatory Character of Reissner-Nordstrom Metric for an Ideal Charged Wormhole', ibid. 120, 4, 1507-1513 (15th Nov., 1960). 1507 (1960).
13. Carl Sagan, "Contact", Simon & Schuster, 1986.
14. Michael Morris, Kip Thorne, Ulvi Yurtsever, *Physical Review Letters*, 61, 13, 1446-1449 (26th September, 1988); John Gribbin, 'Time Machines,

Wormholes and the Casimir Effect', *New Scientist*, 120, 1634, 31 (15th October, 1988).

15. Arlan Andrews, 'Manufacturing Magic', *Analog* CXII, 11, 60-72 (Sept. 1992); '3D Printer Could Shape the Future', *Daily Telegraph*, 26th August 2009.

16. Robert A. Freitas, Jr., 'The Future of Computers', *Analog* CXVI, 4, 57-73 (March 1996).

17. James Chapman, 'Pond Life Could Soon Be Powering Our Cars', *Daily Mail*; Roger Highfield, 'Pond Algae Can Make Energy Gas', *Daily Telegraph*, both 22nd February, 2000.

18. Gregory Benford, 'A Scientist's Notebook: Calculating the Future', *Fantasy & Science Fiction*, 85, 3, 78-87 (Sept. 1993).

19. Georgina Howell, 'David Mamet, Voice of America', *Telegraph Magazine*, 18th June 1994, 16-22.

20. Alfred Bester, "Tiger! Tiger!" (aka "The Stars My Destination"), Sidgwick & Jackson, 1956.

21. John G. Cramer, 'The Alternate View: Tunnelling through the Light Barrier', *Analog* CXV, 14, 93-97 (December 1995).

21. Peter Conveney & Roger Highfield, "The Arrow of Time", W.H. Allen, 1990.

22. John G. Cramer, 'The Atom Laser', *Analog* CXVII, 7/8, 182-185 (July/August 1997).

23. John G. Cramer, 'The Quantum Physics of Teleportation', *Analog* CXIII, 14, 111-115 (Dec. 1993).

24. A. Furusawa, J.L. Sorensen, et al, 'Unconditional Quantum Teleportation', *Science* 282, 706-709, 23rd October, 1998; John Kerin, 'Science Beyond the Laser's Edge', *The Australian*, June 18th 2002.

Chapter Nineteen - A LAND WITHOUT SUN

1. Randolph Stow, "The Girl Green as Elderflower", op cit.

2. Jean Sendy, "L'Ére du Verseau, Fin de l'Illusion Humaniste", Robert Laffont, Paris, 1970.

3. Harold C. Urey, 'Origin and History of the Moon', *Bulletin of the Atomic Scientists*, September 1969, reprinted in Eugene Rabinowitch & Richard S. Lewis, eds., "Men in Space", Medical & Technical Publishing Co., Oxford, 1970.

4. Harry Sperling & Maurice Simon, eds., "The Zohar", op cit.

5. Peter Cook & Dudley Moore, 'Bo Dudley', Decca Record Co., 1966.

6. Duncan Lunan, "Man and the Planets", op cit.

7. Sir Herbert Read, "The Green Child", op cit.

8. Grant H. Heiken, David I. Vaniman, Bevan M. French, eds., "Lunar Sourcebook, a user's guide to the Moon", Cambridge U.P., 1991.   On a similar map in Gene Simmons, "On the Moon with Apollo 16, a Guidebook to the Descartes Region", NASA EP-95, US Govt. Printing Office, April 1972, the quality of reproduction is poor.   In the companion volume, "On the Moon with Apollo 17", the gravimetric readings are illegible.

9. Stephen H. Dole, "Habitable Planets for Man", Blaisdell, 1964.

10. V.A. Firsoff, 'Could Mercury Have Ice-Caps?', *The Observatory*, April 1971.

11. Simon Mitton, 'Mercury's Icy North Pole', *Astronomy Now*, 6, 2, 8 (Feb. 1992).

12. Carl Sagan & I.S. Shklovskii, "Intelligent Life in the Universe", Holden-Day, 1966.

13. Michael Hart, 'Habitable Zones about Main Sequence Stars', *Icarus* 37, 351-357 (1979).

14. T.A. Heppenheimer, "Toward Distant Suns", Stackpole Books, 1979.

15. Martyn J. Fogg, 'Terraforming, as Part of a Strategy for Interstellar Colonisation', *J. Brit. Interplan. Soc.*, 44, 183-192 (1991); 'A Planet Dweller's Dreams', *Analog* CXII, 12, 60-77 (Oct.1992).

16. Ken Crosswell, 'Red, Willing and Able', *New Scientist*, 169, 2275, 28-31 (27th January, 2001); Stephen L. Gillett, 'Retirement Homes of the Gods', *Analog*, CXXV, 11, 50-58 (November 2005).

17. 'Extreme Ultraviolet Explorer Yields Clues on Stars', *Space News*, 5, 3, 13 (Jan. 17-23, 1994).

18. Freeman J. Dyson, 'The Search for Extraterrestrial Technology', in "Perspectives in Modern Physics", R.E. Marshak, ed., Interscience Publishers, 1966.

19. S.J. Adelman, 'Can Venus Be Transformed into an Earth-like Planet?', *JBIS* 35, 1, 3-8 (Jan.1982).

20. John G. Cramer, 'The Alternate View: Dinosaur Breath', *Analog* CVIII, 7, 140-143 (July 1988); Richard Gray, 'Gardeners' Debt to the Fires that Once Swept Earth', *Sunday Telegraph*, 19th Dec.2010.

21. Michael Allaby & James Lovelock, "The Greening of Mars", André Deutsch, 1984.

22. David G. Simons, Don A. Schanche, "Man High: 24 Hours on the Edge of Space", Sidgwick & Jackson, 1960.

23. Henry S.F. Cooper, Jnr., "13: The Flight that Failed", Angus & Robertson, 1973.

24. Paul Wignall, 'The Day the World Nearly Died', New Scientist, 133, 1805, 51-55 (25 Jan. 1992.)

25. Adrian Berry, 'How Trees Tried to Kill Off Life on Earth', *Sunday Telegraph*, 23rd April 1995.

26. James E. Lovelock, "Gaia: a New Look at Life on Earth", Oxford University Press, 1979.

27. 'The Solar Wind at Mars', NASA Science News, 31st January, 2001.

28. Edgar Rice Burroughs, "A Princess of Mars", Methuen, 1919.

29. Elizabeth Ann Viau, G.D. Nordley, 'Contact' group discussion, 24th January - 1st April, 1997.

30. (Anon) 'Cracking the Ice', *Daily Telegraph*, 25th May, 1995; Roger Highfield, 'Ice Lake "A Huge Time Capsule"', 20th June, 1996.

31. (Anon) 'Hubble Takes a Closer Look at Shoemaker-Levy', op cit.

32. Diana Steele, 'Crater Chain on Two Continents Points to Impact from Fragmented Comet', University of Chicago News Office, 24th March 1998.

33. M.R. Dence, 'The Manicougan Impact Structure Observed from Skylab', in "Skylab Explores the Earth", NASA SP-380, US Govt. Printing Office, 1977; Nicholas M. Short, Paul D. Lowman, Stanley C. Freden, William A. Finch, "Mission to Earth: Landsat Views the World", NASA SP-360, 1976.

34. Christopher Knight, Robert Lomas, "Uriel's Machine", op cit.

35. James E. Oberg, "New Earths: Transforming Other Planets for Humanity", Stackpole, 1981.

36. Helen Croydon, 'Does British Summer Time Damage Your Health?', *Daily Tel.*, March 29th, 2010.

37. Walter Alvarez, "T. Rex and the Crater of Doom", Princeton U.P., 1997; (anon), 'Computer Modelling Offers New Insight Into The Formation Of the Chicxulub Crater in Mexico', Imperial College News Release, 14th November 2000; Mary Lenz, 'New Geophysical Data Link Yucatan Crater To Mass Extinction Of Dinosaurs', Office of Public Affairs, Univ. of Texas-Austin, 22nd Dec 2000.

38. 'Naked Planet: the Dead Sea', Channel 4, 20th September, 1999.

39. Priscilla Stone & Frederick Engle, "Looking at Earth", Turner, 1996.

40. Jeff Gillis, 'The Clementine 1 Mission', *Lunar & Plan. Information Bulletin*, 71, 1-5 (May 1994).

41. Paul Reger, 'Highs and Lows of Mars', *West Australian*, 7th June, 1999; Duncan Steel, "Target Earth", Time-Life, 2000; Gregory Beekman, 'Origin of Meteorites', ASTRA *Spacereport*, Aug. 1993.

42. John Gribbin, Simon Goodwin, "Origins, Our Place in Hubble's Universe", Constable, 1997.

43. David Morrison, "Voyages to Saturn", NASA SP-451, U.S. Govt. Printing Office, 1982.

44. Jay L. Inge et al, 'Preliminary Pictorial Map of Mimas', U.S. Geological Survey Sm 5M 2AN, 1982; earlier version and photograph in Carl Sagan, "Pale Blue Dot, A Vision of the Human Future in Space", Headline, 1995.

Chapter Twenty - A FIRE IN THE SKY

1. Alexander von Humboldt, "Cosmos: Sketch of a Physical Description of the Universe", Longman, Brown, Green & Longman, 1846; paraphrased in 'Humboldt's Kosmos', in Sir John Herschel, "Essays from the Edinburgh and Quarterly Reviews" by Longman, Brown, Green, Longmans & Roberts, 1857.

2. George Lord Lyttelton, "The History of the Life of King Henry the Second", op cit.

3. Thomas Duffus Hardy, ed., "Descriptive Catalogue of Materials relating to the history of Great Britain and Ireland", op cit; William Stubbs, ed., "The Chronicle of the Reigns of Henry II and Richard I, (Benedict of Peterborough), op cit.

4. (Anon), 'Satellite Sees New Northern Light Source', *Spaceport News*, John F. Kennedy Space Centre, June 19, 1987; Carl Størmer, "The Polar Aurora", Oxford University Press, 1955.

5. Warren Febster, 'Experts Disagree on Severity of Next Solar Storm', *Space News*, 20-26th Jan. 1997.

6. Giovanni P. Gregori, 'Satellites, Volcanoes and Global Change', *Earth Space Review*, 5, 1, 17-26 (Jan-March 1996); Roger Highfield, 'Sun and Moon "Set Off" Volcanoes', *Daily Telegraph*, 27th November 1999.

7. John A. Eddy, 'The Maunder Minimum', *Science*, 192, 4245, 1189-1202 (18th June, 1976.)

8. Adrian Berry, 'Arctic Search for a Race that Vanished', *Daily Telegraph*, 3rd May, 1982.

9. John A. Eddy, 'The Case of the Missing Sunspots', *Scientific American*, 236, 5, 80-88 & 92, May 1977.

10. Bevan M. French, 'The Once and Future Moon', in Owen Davies, ed., "The Omni Book of Space", Zebra Books, 1981.

11. Carmelo Amalfi, 'Warm Seas Hail Wet Outlook; Solar Cycles, Rainfall Linked', *The West Australian*, January 17th, 2000; (Anon), 'Sun Turns on Cosmic Fireworks', February 22nd, 2000.

12. 'Naked Planet: Grand Canyon', Channel 4, 4th October 1999.

13. Caroline D. Eckhardt, ed., "Castleford's Chronicle or the Boke of Brut", op cit.

14. Sigeru Kanda, 'Ancient Records of Sunspots and Auroras in the Far East and the Variation of the Period of Solar Activity', *Proceedings of the Imperial Academy (Tokyo)*, 9, 293-296 (1933).

15. William Stubbs, ed., Gervase of Canterbury, op cit.

16. Robert Russell Newton, "Medieval Chronicles and the Rotation of the Earth", op cit.

17. D.E.R. Watt, ed., Walter Bower, "Scotichronicon", Vol. 5, op cit, pp. 311 & 513.

18. (Anon), 'Nebraska Crater Only a Pup', op cit.

19. William H. Hennessy, ed., "The Annals of Loch Cé, a chronicle of Irish affairs 1014-1590", vol.1, Longman & Trubner, London, 1871 (also Rolls Series No.54).

20. John O'Donovan, ed., "The Annals of the Kingdom of Ireland," op cit; D.E.R. Watt, ed., "Scotichronicon", op cit.

21. J.T. Fowler, ed., "Adamnani Vita S. Columbae", Clarendon Press, Oxford, 1920.

22. Thomas Stack, 'An account of a book intitled, Observationes de Aere & Morbis Epidemicis....', *Philosophical Transactions of the Royal Society of London*, 40, 429-440 (December 1738, n.451); 'A collection of the observations of the remarkable red light seen in the air on Dec. 5, 1737, sent from different places to the Royal Society', *Phil. Trans. Roy. Soc.*, London, 41, 583-606 (January-March 1741; n.459).

23. Arthur C. Clarke, 'Things in the Sky', in "The Challenge of the Spaceship", op cit.

24. Colin Foale, "Waystation to the Stars, The Story of Mir, Michael and Me", Headline Book Publishing, 1999.

25. Henry Richards Luard, ed., 'Annales de Margan', op cit.

26. Edward A. Bond, ed., "Chronica Monasterii de Melsa", op cit.

27. William Stubbs, ed., "Works of Master Ralph Diceto", op cit; H.W. Newton, "The Face of the Sun", Penguin Books, 1958.

28. John Glover, ed., "La Livere de Reis de Britannie", op cit; C.E. Britton, 'A Meteorological Chronology to AD 1450', op cit.

29. Bravonius (Florentius) Wigorniensis, "Chronicon ex Chronicis", op cit.

30. Sir Frederic Madden, ed., Matthew Paris, "Historia Anglorum", op cit.

31. Sir Henry Ellis, ed., "Chronica Johannis de Oxeneden", op cit; Henry Richards Luard, ed., "Bartholomaei de Cotton, Historia Anglicana", op cit.

32. Francis Blomefield, "An Essay towards a Topographical History of the County of Norfolk", op cit.

33. Ian Stewart, 'The Real Physics of Time Travel', *Analog* CXIV, 1 & 2, 106-130 (Jan. 1994).

34. John H. Fadum, 'Starflight', private communication, 12th Aug. 1989.

35. John A. Wheeler & Seymour Tilson, 'The Dynamics of Space-Time', in Robert Colborn, Chief Editor, & the Editors of International Science & Technology, eds., "Modern Science and Technology", Van Nostrand Company, 1965.

36. Michael Morris, Kip Thorne, Ulvi Yurtsever, *Physical Review Letters*, op cit; John Gribbin, 'Time Machines, Wormholes and the Casimir Effect', op cit.

37. Robert L. Forward, 'Laser Weapon Target Practise with Gee-Whiz Targets', Laser Propulsion Workshop, Lawrence Livermore Laboratory, 7-18 July 1986.

38. Steve Sneyd, 'The Green Cat', *Ocular*, 14, 22.

39. Letters, 'The Bells at Bury St. Edmunds', *Notes and Queries*, 6th series, I, 193, 303; II, 97 (1886).

40. M.R. James, "Suffolk and Norfolk", op cit.

41. R.M. Thomson, "The Chronicle of the Election of Hugh, Abbot of Bury St. Edmunds and Later Bishop of Ely", Oxford University Press, 1974.

42. Ernest Morris, "The History and Art of Change Ringing", Chapman & Hall, 1931.

43. Jane Greatorex, personal communication, 30th January, 1998.

44. James Gairdner, ed., "Letters and Papers, Foreign and Domestic, of the Reign of King Henry VIII", Vol.13 Part 2, HMSO, 1893; Kraus Reprint Ltd, Vaduz, 1965.

45. H.R. Barker, "West Suffolk Illustrated", op cit.

46. M.R. James, 'On the Abbey of St. Edmund at Bury', op cit.

47. William Page, ed., "The Victoria History of the Counties of England: Suffolk, Vol. II", op cit.

48. Kate Norgate, "Richard the Lion-Heart", op cit; C.H. Talbot, "Medicine in Medieval England", op cit.

49. Henry Richards Luard, ed., "Flores Historiarum" of Roger de Wendover, Rolls series No.95, Eyre & Spottiswoode, 1890.

50. "Encyclopedia Britannica", 1950 edition, Vol.6, p.614.

51. A.T. Lawton, 'Star Trekking: Whose Sun Are You?', *Spaceflight*, 16, 7, 255-257, 280 (July 1974).

52. Additional Charter 15520, British Library, op cit.

53. Donald Hill, "A History of Engineering in Classical and Mediaeval Times", Routledge, 1996; John H. Mundy, "Europe in the High Middle Ages," op cit.

54. Peter James & Nick Thorpe, "Ancient Inventions", Michael O'Mara Books, 1995.

55. Thomas M. Haugh, 'Scientists Find Magnets inside Human Brains', *The West Australian*, June 8th 1992; (Anon), 'Magnetic Turtles', *Daily Telegraph*, 1st May, 1996; Aisling Irwin, 'Turtle Highway: Animal Magnetism Keeps Them in Line', 13th March 1998; Roger Highfield, 'Migrating Monarch Butterflies Use a Magnetic Compass', 23rd November, 1999.

56. Isaac Asimov, 'The Fire of Life', *Fantasy & Science Fiction*, 75, 2, 128-137 (August 1988).

57. Roger Highfield, 'Space Probe Shows Sun's Violent Side', *Daily Telegraph*, May 4th, 1996.

Chapter Twenty-one - EPSILON BOÖTIS REVISITED

1. A.L. Lloyd, "Folk Song in England", op cit; Steeleye Span, "Ten Man Mop, or Mr. Reservoir Butler Rides Again", Pegasus Records PEG 9,1971 .

2. Duncan Lunan, 'Space Probe from Epsilon Boötis', *Spaceflight*, 15, 4, 122-131, April 1973; 'Space Probe from Epsilon Boötis?', *Analog*, XCII, 5, 66-84, January 1974.

3. Ronald N. Bracewell, 'Communications from Superior Galactic Communities', *Nature*, 186, 670 (1960).

4. Duncan Lunan, 'Long-Delayed Echoes and the Extraterrestrial Hypothesis', *Journal of the Society of Electronic and Radio Technicians*, 10, 8, 180-182, September 1976.

5. Duncan Lunan, "Man and the Stars", op cit.

6. Carl Sagan and I.S. Shklovskii, "Intelligent Life in the Universe", op cit.

7. Duncan Lunan, 'Past Contact and the Moving Caravan' (guest chapter), in Chris Boyce, "Extraterrestrial Encounter, a Personal Perspective", David & Charles, 1979.

8. Duncan Lunan, 'Epsilon Boötis Revisited', *Analog* CXVIII, 3, 52-68 (March 1998).

9. Robert Bauval & Adrian Gilbert, "The Orion Mystery", Heinemann, 1994; I.E.S. Edwards, "The Pyramids of Egypt", Penguin, 1947.

10. Robert Bauval & Graham Hancock, "Keeper of Genesis", Heinemann, 1996.

11. Ian Lawton and Chris Ogilvie-Herald, "Giza, The Truth", Virgin, 1999.

12. Col. Sir Charles W. Wilson, "Jerusalem, the Holy City", op cit.

13. H.V. Morton, "In the Steps of St. Paul", Rich & Cowan, 1936.

14. C.W. Wilson, C. Warren, "The Discovery of Jerusalem: a Narrative of Exploration and Discovery in the City and the Holy Land", op cit.

15. Jan Selignan, Jerusalem District Archaeologist, interviewed in "The Tomb of Christ", Channel 4, 17th April, 2000; Eusebius Pomphilus, "The Life of the Blessed Emperor Constantine", Samuel Bagster, London, 1845.

16. William Harvey, "Church of the Holy Sepulchre, Jerusalem, Structural Survey Final Report", Oxford University Press, 1935.

17. Denis Meehan, "Adamnan's De Locis Sanctis", Dublin Institute for Advanced Studies, 1958.

18. Robert William Hamilton, "A Short History of the Aqsa Mosque", op cit.

19. F.E. Peters, "Jerusalem", op cit.

20. Gérard Serbanesco, "Histoire de L'Ordre des Templiers", op cit.

21. George Jefferey, "A Brief Description of the Holy Sepulchre, Jerusalem, and Other Churches in the Holy City", op cit; Thomas W. Lyman, 'The Counts of Toulouse, the Reformed Canons and the Holy Sepulchre', in Benjamin Z. Kedar, ed., "The Horns of Hattin", op cit, & R.C. Smail, "The Crusaders in Syria and the Holy Land", Thames & Hudson, 1973.

22. Compostela plan in Tim Wallace-Murphy, Marilyn Hopkins, "Rosslyn, guardian of the secrets of the Holy Grail", Element Books, 1999.

23. Eugène de Rozière, "Cartulaire de l'Église du Saint Sépulcre de Jérusalem", op cit.

24. Marie Luise Bulst-Thiele, 'The Influence of St. Bernard de Clairvaux on the Formation of the Order of the Knights Templar', op cit.

25. Victoria Clark, 'Holy Fire Sets Orthodox Rivalry Ablaze in Jerusalem', *Daily Telegraph*, April 26th, 2003.

26. William Stubbs, ed., "Willelmi Malmesbiriensis Monachi de Gestis Regnum Anglorum", op cit.

27. Thomas Keightley, "The Crusaders, or Scenes, Events and Characters for the Time of the Crusades", John W. Parker, 1847.

28. Anon, 'Premier Appeals to Arabs for Calm as Bloodshed Mars Netanyahu's First 100 Days', Glasgow *Herald*, 26th September, 1996.

29. Malcolm Barber, "The New Knighthood", op cit.

30. Jefferey, op cit, quoting Macbeth Act 1 scene 6 line 7.

31. James R. MacPherson, trans., "Fetellus (circa 1130 AD)", Palestine Pilgrims' Text Society, 1896.

32. Joseph Stevenson, ed., "De Expugnatione Terrae Sancti", in Ralph of Coggeshall, op cit.

33. H.V. Morton, "In the Steps of the Master", op cit.

34. Edward Gibbon, "The Decline and Fall of the Roman Empire, Vol.4", Gibbings, London, 1890; Alfred Duggan, "The Story of the Crusades 1097-1291", op cit.

35. Michael Baigent, Richard Leigh, "The Temple and the Lodge", op cit; Kate Norgate, "Richard the Lion-Heart", op cit.

36. Peter Whitfield, "The Image of the World, 20 Centuries of World Maps", British Library, 1994.

37. William Simpson, 'The Middle of the World, in the Holy Sepulchre', Palestine Exploration Fund Quarterly Statement for 1888, 260-263.

38. Lilian J. Redstone, "Suffolk", Alfred A. Knopf, 1930.

39. Henri de Curzon, "La Maison du Temple de Paris", op cit.

40. Élie Lambert, "L'Architecture des Templiers", A. & J. Picard, Paris 1955.

41. Essay by Edward Clarkson, Esq., cited in Robert William Billings, "Architic Illustrations and Account of the Temple Church", Boone & Billings, London, 1838.

42. William Burge, "The Temple Church, an Account of its Restoration and Repairs", William Pickering, London, 1843, bound into *Archaeological Tracts*, Vol.1, Special Collections, Glasgow University Library; G.C. Addison, "The Temple Church", op cit; Rev. Canon Joseph Robinson, 'Temple Church', Pitkin Guides, 1997. The earlier Choir was demolished and the much larger present one was added because Henry III wanted to be buried there, though he later changed his mind in favour of Westminster Abbey.

43. Plan from L.H. Vincent and F.M. Abel, 'Jérusalem: recherches de topographie, d'archéologie et d'histoire, 2: Jérusalem nouvelle', reproduced in Thomas W. Lyman, 'The Counts of Toulouse, the Reformed Canons and the Holy Sepulchre', op cit.

44. V.A. Firsoff, "Strange World of the Moon", Hutchinson, 1959.

45. P.D. Spadis et al, "Status and Future of Lunar Geoscience", NASA SP-484, US Government Printing Office, 1986.

46.   David Shiga, 'Aliens don't need a moon like ours', *New Scientist*, 13th November 2011.

47.   Jack Vance, "The Face", Dobson Books, 1980.

Chapter Twenty-two - BIOSPHERES WITHOUT WALLS

1. M.M. Averner, R.D. MacElroy, "On the Habitability of Mars, an approach to planetary ecosynthesis", NASA SP-414, National Technical Information Service, 1976.

2.   Magnus Magnusson, "BC, the Archaeology of the Bible Lands", The Bodley Head, 1977.

3. Robert Cooke, 'Fright Flights', *The West Australian*, November 20th, 2000.

4.   Stan Miller, 'Air Turbulence Warning Now Possible', NASA Ames Research Centre release 76-80, 11th November, 1976.

5. Frank Herbert, "The Great Dune Trilogy", Gollancz, 1982.

6. Prof. David Smith, 'Orkney's Killer Waves BC', Orkney Science Festival, September 1991.

7. Robert Matthews, 'The Hidden Waves of Destruction', *Daily Telegraph*, 13th May, 1998.

8.   Philip Jose Farmer, "To Your Scattered Bodies Go", Berkley Medallion Books, 1971; "The Fabulous Riverboat", Berkley Medallion, 1973; "The Dark Design", Granada, 1979;   "The Magic Labyrinth", Berkley Publishing Corporation, 1980.

9. C.S. Lewis, "Out of the Silent Planet", op cit.

10. Willy Ley, 'Mars: Red Soil and Ozone', in "Satellites, Rockets and Outer Space", Signet Key Books, 1958.

11. Donald E. Hunton, 'Shuttle Glow', *Scientific American*, 261, 5, 70-77 (Nov. 1989).

12. G. Tikhov, "Reaching for the Stars", op cit; Pete Manly, 'World Building Questions', Internet, 24 January 1997.

13. Freeman Dyson, "Disturbing the Universe", Harper & Row, 1979.

14. Marshall T. Savage, "The Millennial Project", Little, Brown & Co., 1994; Victoria Lambert, 'Green Shoots of Recovery Emerge from the Far East', *Daily Telegraph*, August 17th, 2009.

15.   Prof. Shoshona Arad, Institutes for Applied Research, Ben-Gurion University of the Negev, personal communication, August 6th , 1997.

16.   'Ten Most Common Old Wives' Tales, 3: Carrots', *Sunday Times (Australia)*, May 29th, 1994.

17. Jenny Jarvie, 'Health Warning over Harvesting Carrots in Sun', *D. Telegraph*, October 26th, 1999.

18. 'In Brief: Man Turns Orange after Cider Binge', *Daily Telegraph*, October 29th, 2008.

19. (Anon), 'Hangover in Colour', It's a Wacky World, *The West Australian*, Tues. Oct. 19th 1993.

20. Roger Highfield, 'Spotlight on the Knee May Cure Jet Lag', Ricard Dawood, 'Can Boeing Make Light Work of Jet Lag?', *Daily Telegraph*, 16th January1999, 19th March 2005.

21. Marnie McKimmie, 'Light Way to Better Health', *The West Australian*, February 19th 1994.

22. Harry Sperling & Maurice Simon, eds., "The Zohar", op cit, 1931.

23. Pepita Smyth, 'Creeping Disease Can Change Your Colour', *The West Australian*, June 21st, 1999.

24. Prof. Steve Jones, 'Little Green Slaves Are Working Overtime at the Bottom of My Garden', *Daily Telegraph*, April 21st, 2004.

25. D.C. Smith, A.E. Douglas, "The Biology of Symbiosis", Edward Arnold, 1987; Molly Oldfield, John Mitchison, 'QI Turns Green', *Daily Telegraph*, 6th November 2011;   Paul J. McAuley, 'Slaves', in Paul J. McAuley, "Invisible Country", Gollancz, 1966.

26. Rick Cook, 'The Long Stern Chase: a Speculative Exercise', *Analog*, CVI, 7, 32-43 (July 1986).

27. Helene Feger, 'Jellyfish May Shine Light on a Cancer Cure', *The Express*, December 12th 1996.

28. David Attenborough, 'Nature's Neons', BBC-2, 16th July 1998; Richard Alleyne, 'Glowing Praise: Jellyfish Trick Earns Scientists Nobel Prize', *Daily Telegraph*, 9th October, 2008.

29. Bryan Christie, 'Five Green Mice, See How They Glow', *The Scotsman*, 13th June 1997.

30. Roger Highfield, 'Scientists Create First Genetically Modified Monkey', *Daily Telegraph*, 12th Jan. 2001, p.1; '244 Eggs, 40 Embryos, One Genetic Monkey', ibid, p.6.

31. (anon), 'Taiwan Glows with Tail of First Green Pigs', *West Australian*, 17th January 2006.

32. Jonathon Leake, '617 Hens Lay Eggs to Fight Cancer', *Sunday Times*, 14th January, 2007; Roger Highfield, 'We Could Grow Our Own Fairy Tree Lights', *Daily Telegraph*, 21st December 2011.

33. V.A. Firsoff, "Life Among the Stars", Wingate, London, 1974.

34. Anon, 'Op Patient Sheds Green Blood', *The Herald*, 8th June 2007.

35. Robert Matthews, 'Drugs with Two Faces', *Sunday Telegraph*, 9th. January 1994.

36. Richard Dawkins, "River Out of Eden, a Darwinian View of Life", Weidenfeld & Nicolson, 1995.

37. Charles Darwin, "Journey of a Voyage Round the World", Nelson, 1893.

38. Anne McCaffrey, "Dragonflight", Rapp & Whiting, 1969, "Dragonquest", Ballantine Books, 1975.

39. Arthur C. Clarke, Gentry Lee, "The Garden of Rama", Gollancz, 1991.

40. Alan Bond, British Interplanetary Society Interstellar Studies Conference, 1979.

41. Alan Bond, 'On the Improbability of Intelligent Extraterrestrials', *JBIS* 35, 5, 195-207 (May 1982).

42. Alan Bond, Anthony R. Martin, 'A Conservative Estimate of the Number of Habitable Planets in the Galaxy', *JBIS*, 31, 11, 411-415 (November 1978); Part 2, *JBIS*, 33, 3, 101-106 (March 1980).

43. Ken Croswell, "Planet Quest, The Epic Discovery of Alien Solar Systems", O.U.P., 1997.

44. Simon Jarman, 'Dividing the Old from the Eu', *Daily Telegraph*, 15th June, 1994.

45. T.A. Heppenheimer, "Toward Distant Suns", op cit.

46. 'Beaumont', "Coggeshall, a Savigny-Cistercian Monastery", op cit.

47. Maurice Weaver, 'Rabbit Warren Could Become a Listed Monument', *Daily Telegraph*, 20th April 1998.

48. C.H.D. Cullingford, ed., "British Caving", Routledge & Kegan Paul, 1953.

49. Les Higgins, 'Bush Tucker Man: John McDowall Stuart',1996, Channel 4, UK, 19th June 2000.

50. W.G. Hanson, "The Early Monastic Schools of Ireland", op cit.

51. Angela Hall, trans., Rudolf Simek, "Heaven and Earth in the Middle Ages", op cit.

52. Christian Dymond, 'A Llama Called in to Raise the Alarm', *Daily Telegraph*, 1st April, 1995; David Brown, Agriculture Editor, 'Llamas Save Lambs from Fox Attacks', 7th April, 1999.

53. J. Alden Mason, "The Ancient Civilizations of Peru", Penguin Books, 1969.

54. 'Nebraska Crater Only a Pup', op cit.

55. Thor Heyerdahl, "The Ra Expeditions", Penguin, 1972; "American Indians in the Pacific", Allen & Unwin, 1952.

56. Duncan Lunan, "Man and the Stars", op cit.

57. Giovanni P. Gregori, 'Satellites, Volcanoes and Global Change', op cit; Isaac Asimov, "The Sun Shines Bright", Grafton, 1984.

58. Murray Leinster, "Four from Planet Five", Gold Medal Books, 1959.

59. Charles Fort, "The Book of the Damned", in "The Books of Charles Fort", Henry Holt, 1941.

60. Marianus Victorius, ed., St. Jerome, "Opera Omnia", Bibliopolae urbis Parisiensis Consortes, Paris, 1609.

61. Fred Gettings, "Dictionary of Demons", Guild Publishing, 1988.

62. Peter Dance, "Animal Fakes & Frauds", Sampson Low, 1976.

63. Felix Guirand, ed., "Larousse Encyclopedia of Mythology", op cit.

64. Christopher Howse, ed., 'AD: 2000 Years of Christianity, Part 1', *Daily Telegraph Magazine*, Supplement, 24th April, 1999.

65. Robert Graves, "The White Goddess", op cit.

66. Jack Cohen, 'The Possibility of Life on Other Planets', *Biologist*, 38, 1, 7-9 (1991).

67. Roger Highfield, 'Naomi's Debt to a Body-Building Worm', *Daily Telegraph*, August 20th, 1997.

68. Elisia Bennett, 'Fishing for Fossils'; Joe Poprzeczny, 'WA's Fossil Fish Is on the Go Go', *The Sunday Times (Australia)*, February 9th, 1997, May 18th, 1997, respectively.

69. Roger Highfield, 'Plant Life Stems from a Single Eve', *Daily Telegraph*, August 5th, 1999.

70. N.J. Dunnington, J.C. Coleman, 'Dunmore Cave, Co. Kilkenny', *Proceedings of the Royal Irish Academy*, LIII, 15-24 (January 1950); Arthur Wynne, 'An Account of a Visit to the Cave of Dunmore, Co. Kilkenny, with Some Remarks on Human Remains Found Therein', *Royal Society of Antiquaries of Ireland*, New Series, 1, 65-94 (1870-71).

71. J.T. Fowler, ed., "Adamnani Vita S. Columbae", Clarendon Press, Oxford, 1920.

72. Lt. Col. David G. Simons, "Man High, 24 Hours on the Edge of Space", op cit.

73. (Anon), 'Mystery Sprites Crackle and Pop', *The West Australian*, December 10th, 1994); Roger Highfield, 'Scientists Shed Light on Sprite Mystery', *The Daily Telegraph*, 13th November, 1995; 'Savage skies: Riders on the Storm', Scottish Television, 26th March 1996; colour photograph, *West Australian*, 1st February, 1999.

51. P. Birch, 'Orbital Ring Systems and Jacob's Ladders - 1', *Journal of the British Interplanetary Society*, 35, 11, 475-497 (November 1982); '... - 2', *JBIS*, 36, 3, 115-128 (March 1983); '... - 3', *JBIS*, 36, 5, 231-238 (May 1983).

52. Keith H. Lofstrom, 'The Launch Loop', *Analog*, CIII, 13, 67-80 (December 1983).

53. Duncan Lunan, "Man and the Planets", op cit.

54. Hans Moravec, 'Cable Cars in the Sky', in J.E. Pournelle, ed., "The Endless Frontier", Ace, 1979.

Chapter Twenty-three - THE GUARDIANS OF THE PORTALS

1. Roger Highfield, 'Signs of Global Warming Existed 2,000 Years Ago', *Daily Telegraph*, 14th August 1998.

2. Malcolm Barber, "The New Knighthood", op cit; Michael Baigent, Richard Leigh, "The Temple and the Lodge", op cit.

3. Charles Fort, "The Book of the Damned", op cit.

4. Edward Gibbon, "Decline and Fall of the Roman Empire", op cit, Vol.4; G. Nahon, "Histoire du Royaume Latin de Jérusalem", op cit; G.C. Addison, "The Temple Church", op cit.

5. Gérard Serbanesco, "Histoire de l'Ordre des Templiers", op cit; Marion Melville, "La Vie des Templiers", op cit;   Jonathon Riley-Smith, "The Crusades, a short history", op cit; Malcolm Barber, 'The Templars and the Turin Shroud', and 'Supplying the Crusader States: the Role of the Templars', both in Malcolm Barber, "Crusaders and Heretics", op cit, the latter also in Benjamin Z. Kedar, ed., "The Horns of Hattin", op cit.

6. Stephen Howarth, "The Knights Templar", op cit.

7. Poul Anderson, "The High Crusade", Macfadden-Bartell, 1964.

8. Deputy Keeper of the Records, ed., "Close Rolls of the Reign of Henry III", op cit.

9. Beatrice M. Rose, "The Story of King Stephen and Queen Maud and the Abbey They Founded at Coggeshall in Essex", op cit.

10. E. Austen, "The Hooded Monk", Ardleigh, Colchester, undated (held at Essex County Records Office).

11. Anne Gilmour-Bryson, "The Trial of the Templars in the Papal States", Bibliteca Apostolica Vaticana, 1982.

12. Thomas M. Parker, "The Knights Templar in England", op cit.

13. Peter Portner, "The Murdered Magicians", op cit.

14. Malcolm Barber, "The Trial of the Templars", op cit.

15. Michael Baigent, Richard Leigh & Henry Lincoln, "The Holy Blood and the Holy Grail", op cit.

16. Roger de Hoveden, op cit.

17. Gérard de Sède, "Les Templiers Sont Parmi Nous", op cit.

18. Desmond Seward, "The Monks of War", op cit.

19. Robert Freke Gould, "The History of Freemasonry", Thomas C. Jack, London, 1886.

20. Andrew Sinclair, "The Discovery of the Grail", op cit.

21. James Bentley, 'Hackney from the Romans to the Knights Templar', personal communication, 1st January 1995.

22. (Anon), 'Pirate Bones Puzzle Police'; Mairi Barton, 'Freemason Ritual Linked to Bone Find'; (Anon), 'Ritual Bones Return'; Marie Barton, 'Bones Find Still Puzzles'; (Anon), 'Police Research Law on Newman Masonic Skull'; Anne Buggins, 'Aboriginal Bones Shed New Light on Masonic Rites', 'Former Mason Isaacs Shocked by Bone Rite', *The West Australian*, Feb. 9th, 10th, 12th & 18th, March 4th, 22nd and 23rd July 1999, respectively.

23. James Aveling, "The History of Roche Abbey", op cit.

24. Henri de Curzon, "La Maison du Temple de Paris", op cit.

25. Herbert Wood, 'The Templars in Ireland', op cit.

26. Aisling Irwin, '14th-Century Star Gazers Left in Dark', *Daily Telegraph*, 2nd April 1998.

27. (Anon), 'Sky Lit Up, Nobody Homed In', *West Australian*, 12th April 1999.

28. Gustave Schlumberger, 'Prise de Saint-Jean-d'Acre en l'An 1291 par l'Armée de Soudan d'Égypte', op cit; D.A. Carpenter, "The Minority of Henry III", op cit.

29. G.C. Addison, "The Knights Templar", op cit.

30. N. Makhouly, C.N. Johns, "Guide to Acre", op cit.

31. Kate Norgate, "Richard the Lion Heart", op cit.

32. Templar ships in the 1230s named in "Close Rolls", op cit, Vol. I.

33. Marie-Luise Bulst-Thiele, 'The Influence of St. Bernard of Clairvaux on the Formation of the Order of the Knights Templar', in Michael Greaves, ed., "The Second Crusade and the Cistercians", op cit.

1. Rev. Walter Waddington Shirley, ed., "Royal and Other Historical Letters Illustrative of the Reign of Henry III, Vol. I, A.D. 1216-1235", Rolls Series No.27, Longman, Green, Longman & Roberts, 1862.
2. "Close Rolls of the Reign of Henry III", op cit, 1231-34".
3. D.A. Carpenter, "The Minority of Henry III", op cit.
4. Henry Thomas Riley, ed., "Thomae Walsingham, Quondam Monachi S. Albani, Historia Anglicani, Vol. II, A.D. 1381-1422", Rolls Series No.28, Longman, Green etc., 1864.
5. C.E. Britton, 'A Meteorological Chronology to AD 1450', op cit; K.R. Potter, ed., "Gesta Stephani", op cit.
6. Rev. Francis Charles Higeston, ed., John Capgrave, "The Chronicle of England", Rolls Series No.1, Longman, Brown, Green, Longmans & Roberts, 1858.
7. W. Richards, "The History of Lynn", op cit.
8. Barry Cunliffe, "Facing the Ocean", op cit.
9. John Froissart, "The Chronicles of England, France, Spain, etc., 1338? to 1410?", reprinted as George T. Diller, ed., "Froissart Chroniques", (5 vols.), Librairie Droz, Geneva, 1991-98;   M. le baron Kervyn de Lettenhove, "Oeuvres de Froissart", reimpression of 1867-77 edition, Biblio-Verlag, Osnabrück, 1967.
10. R. Barber, J. Barker, "Tournaments: Jousts, Chivalry and Pageants in the Middle Ages", op cit.
11. W.A. Copinger, "The Manors of Suffolk", op cit.
12. Hilary D. Walsh, "Borris-in-Ossory, Co. Laois," op cit.
13. Richard Hakluyt, ed., "The Principal Navigations, Voiages, Traffiques and Discoveries of the English Nation", op cit, Vol. 1 p.121-2.
14. James Aveling, "The History of Roche Abbey from its Founding to its Dissolution", op cit.
15. Frank Scott Hayden, ed., "Eulogium (Historiarum Sive Temporis)", op cit.
16. Umberto Dall'olmo, 'Meteors, Meteor Showers and Meteorites in the Middle Ages: from European Medieval Sources', *Journal for the History of Astronomy*, 9, 123-134 (1978).
17. Dr. David Asher, Armagh Observatory, personal communication, 4th April, 2001.

18. Neil Bone, 'Waiting for the Lion's Roar', *Astronomy Now*, 9, 11, 15-16 (November 1995).

19. Leonard David, 'Leonids Trigger Satellite Worries', *Space News*, 8, 46, 3 & 20, Dec. 1-7, 1997.

20. NASA Science News, 'The Moonlit Leonids 2000', Internet, 16th October 2000.

21. Mark McAuley, Public Relations Officer, Royal Observatory, Edinburgh, personal communication, 21st March 1995.

22. E.C. Krupp, 'Hard Rain', *Sky & Telescope*, 100, 5, 93-95 (November 2000).

23. Barbara Harvey, "Living and Dying in England, 1150-1540, The Monastic Experience", Clarendon Press, 1993.

24. Shauna LaFauci, 'Boston University Center for Space Physics Discovers Lunar Sodium Tail', Jet Propulsion Laboratory Stardust website, June 3rd, 1999; (Anon), 'The Moon's "Leonid" Tail', *Sky & Telescope News Bulletin*, Internet, 11th June 1999.

25. Peter Bond, 'A Leonid on the Moon?', *Astronomy Now*, 14, 1, 6 (January 2000).

26. Dr. David Asher, 'Leonids 2000, Encounters with Cometary Dust Trails: How to Predict Meteor Storms', *Astronomy & Space*, December 2000, pp. 18-21.

27. H.W. Newton, "The Face of the Sun", op cit.

28. R.W. Farquhar, "The Control and Use of Libration-Point Satellites", NASA TR R-346, US Govt. Printing Office, Sept. 1970.

29. Jerome Pearson, 'The Orbital Tower: a Spacecraft Launcher Using the Earth's Rotational Energy', *Acta Astronautica*, 2, 9-10, 785-799 (Sept./Oct. 1975); 'Anchored Lunar Halo Satellites for Cislunar Transportation and Communication', L5 Society (Western Europe) Conference, London, 1977.

30. Glyn Maxwell, "Wolfpit", op cit.

31. H.J. Paton, ed., Immanuel Kant, "Groundwork of the Metaphysic of Morals", Harper & Row, 1964.

32. Duncan Lunan, "Man and the Stars", op cit.

33. Duncan Lunan, 'Keep Watching the Skies!', op cit.

34. Richard Newcourt, "Repertorium", op cit.

35. "Stemmata Shirleiana", op cit.

36. Alexander von Humboldt, "Cosmos: Sketch of a Physical Description of the Universe, Vol.1", op cit; Duncan Lunan, 'A Dust Cloud Orbiting the Sun?', op cit. According to Harold T. Wilkins, "Flying Saucers on the At-

tack", op cit (a very unreliable source, as noted in Chap.8), allegedly this event, discussed by Humboldt, is reported in "Thanner Kronic des Klosters in Klass", Deutsche kronic bis 1077 zu 1742; "Chronica Magdeburg", 1584; "Braunschweigische und Lunnenburgische Chronica"; and Paulus Crusius, "De Epochis seu Aeris Temporum et Imperiorum", Basel, 1578. I haven't been able to get access to the German sources; but the Paulus Crusius volume is held by the British Library, and by Glasgow University Library Special Collections. It's devoted to matching up various calendars including the Christian ones reckoning from the birth of Christ (*Anno Domini*) or from the date of the Passion; the Moslem Calendar (*Anno Hegirae*); and the Roman one (*Anno Urbis Conditae*). Astronomical events such as eclipses are mentioned as guides, but there's no mention of the 1547 obscuration and the year appears only as a worked example in converting A.H. dates to A.D..

37. Thomas Short, "A General Chronological History of the Air, etc.", op cit.

38. James Gairdner, ed., 'Stowe's Memoranda', in "Three Fifteenth Century Chronicles with Historical Memoranda by John Stow, the Antiquary", Camden Society, 1880.

39. William A. Dutt, "Highways and Byways of East Anglia", op cit.

40. Anon, 'News Update: In Brief', *Astronomy Now*, August 2005.

41. John Fowles, ed., John Aubrey, "Monumenta Britannica", Dorset Publishing Company, 1980.

42. D.A. Crowley, ed., "The Victoria History of the Counties of England: Wiltshire, Vol. 15", Oxford University Press, 1995.

43. Cyril D. Blount, 'British Meteorites', *Cygnus*, 4/89, 9-14, Norwich Astronomical Society, 1989.

44. Leslie Able, 'Hunt for Meteorite "from God" Planned', *Daily Telegraph*, 1975.

45. Timothy Good, "Above Top Secret", Sidgwick & Jackson, 1987.

46. Lawrence Moore, 'Network First: UFO', Independent Television, Tuesday 10th Jan., 1995.

47. Ian Ridpath interview, 'Strange but True', ITN, June 1997.

48. Victor Clube & Bill Napier, "The Cosmic Serpent", op cit.

49. Duncan Steel, "Rogue Asteroids and Doomsday Comets", op cit.

50. Duncan Steel & Peter Snow, 'The Tapanui Region of New Zealand: Site of a 'Tunguska' Around 800 Years Ago?', op cit.

51. (Anon) 'Age of the Geminid Meteor Stream', *Sky & Telescope*, 56, 3, 211 (September 1978).

52. (Anon), 'Comet Hit Earth Claim', *Evening Times*, 25th May 1998; Mike Baillie, "Exodus to Arthur: Catastrophic Encounters with Comets", op cit.

53. James B. Pritchard, ed., "Ancient Near Eastern Texts Relating to the Old Testament", 2nd edition, revised and enlarged, Princeton University Press, 1955.

54. Admiral W.H. Smyth, Robert Grant, ed., François Arago, "Popular Astronomy", op cit.

55. Jeremy Hodges, 'Somewhere Out in Space There Is an Asteroid...', op cit.

56. Duncan Lunan, 'Science Revisited', *New Moon*, 1, 40-43 (September 1991).

57. Donald N. Michael, ed., the Brookings Institute, "Proposed Studies on the Implications of Peaceful Space Activities for Human Affairs", US Govt. Printing Office, 1961.

58. '*Playboy* Interview: Stanley Kubrick', reprinted in Jerome Agel, ed., "The Making of Kubrick's *2001*", New American Library, 1970.

ACKNOWLEDGEMENTS

All quotations from Glyn Maxwell's play "Wolfpit" appear by kind permission of the author. The script is included in "Plays One: The Lifeblood, Wolfpit, The Only Girl in the World" by Glyn Maxwell, Oberon Modern Playwrights, 2006.

Chapter Three: The quotations from "Jerusalem: the Holy City in the Eyes of Chroniclers, Visitors, Pilgrims and Prophets from the Days of Abraham to the Beginnings of Modern Times", by F.E. Peters, copyright © Princeton University Press, 1985, appear by permission of the publishers.

Chapter Five: The quotation from "Swing Hammer Swing" by Jeff Torrington, published by Secker & Warburg, is reprinted by permission of The Random House Group Limited.

Chapter 11: The quotation from "Foucault's Pendulum" by Umberto Eco appears by permission of Random House.

Chapter 12: The Galileo spacecraft image of Enki Catena crater chain on Ganymede appears by courtesy of NASA, and the Kayuga-Selene image of lunar crater Giordano Bruno by courtesy of the Japanese space agency, JAXA.

Chapter 17: The quotation from "Murder in the Cathedral" by T.S. Eliot appears by permission of Faber & Faber.

I must acknowledge the vast body of work over the last 200 years by editors and publishers of chronicles, court cases and property records of the mediaeval period, plus the many historians whose books and papers I've consulted. All these are credited in the References, and many in the text.

I have to thank Ian Stratford, local expert in Wakes Colne; John Gunson and later Stuart Banks, of the Grange Barn Museum at Coggeshall;. Terry and Sheila Waring of Thurston; Mark Hayward of the Whistlebinkies; Mrs. Brew and more recently Roger Hadlee, of Coggeshall Abbey Farm; Alan and Ann Fell of Oxen-le-Fields; John Wiley of Woolpit Museum and his predecessors; John Clark, Curator Emeritus, Department of Archaeological Collections and Archives, Museum of London; the curators of Cressing Temple and Peak Cavern; the Durham, Essex, Gloucestershire, Staffordshire, Suffolk and Wiltshire County Records Offices, Birmingham Central Library, the Staffordshire Archive Service; Dr. Pendleton of Suffolk County Archaeology Department; Dr. Jane Freeman of the Victoria History of Wiltshire; Adrian Ailes of the National Archives Public Record Office at Kew, staff at the British Library, Lambeth Palace Library, the Parker Library of Corpus Christi, Cambridge; the National Library of Scotland, Glasgow University Library, Durham University Library, and the Mitchell Library in Glasgow; the reference libraries of the *Herald* (Glasgow), the *Scotsman* and the *Daily Telegraph*; the Doncaster, Matlock, Barnsley and Trowbridge Libraries; Kilkenny Archaeological Society, and Declan Macauley of Kilkenny County Library; in my family, my mother Gwen Lunan, cousins Jill Bowyer, Tony Brown, also Dave Goulder and my sister Mary Goulder;   for photographs, Lyndesay Birkmyre, John Braithwaite, Tony Brown, Matt Ewart, Jane Greatorex, Linda Lunan, Nick Portwin; and of course, Dave Allen, Sydney Jordan, Andy Nimmo, Nick Portwin and Larry Tyler for the other illustrations.

I take sole responsibility for the controversial content of this book and for any errors.   But in hammering out these ideas, I have to acknowledge the participation of Dave Allen, Gregory Beekman, James Bentley, Craig Binns, John Braithwaite, Jim Campbell, Mike Gallagher, Mark Hayward, John Kelk, Keith Llewellyn, George McCue, Jamie McLean, Andy Nimmo, Chris O'Kane, Andrew Paterson, Nick Portwin, Bill Ramsay, Rick Rodriguez, Gordon Ross, Prof. Archie Roy, John Stark, Ann Steel; the late Chris Boyce, Roddy Chisholm, Matt Ewart, John Fadum, Paul Grant, Danny Kane and Oscar Schwiglhofer - all of ASTRA, the Association in Scotland to Research into Astronautics – and of Veronica Colin, Barry Condon, Elsie Donald, Hal Duncan, Irene Gordon and other members of the Glasgow Science Fiction Writers' Circle.   Other writers include Tony Crerar, Paul Devereux, Dr. Owen Dudley Edwards, Brian Finch, Tony Frewin, Jane Greatorex, Rudolph Kenna, Dr. Francis Lambert, Louise Wildman, Angus McAllister, Tom McArthur, Paul J. McCauley, Ian Ridpath, Montserrat Stanley, Robert Temple, Gerald Warner, the late Martin Caidin and the artist Sue Jones. Members of other organisations included Prof. Shoshona Arad of the Institute for Applied Research, Ben-Gurion University of the Negev; Dr. David Asher of Armagh Observatory; Desi Atkinson of the Glasgow Branch of the Fortean Society; Dr. David Clark of Glasgow University Observatory; Bruce Durie and Julian Smith of the Edinburgh International Science Festival; Dr. David Gregory of the Science Line, and through him the Royal Greenwich Observatory;   Mark Macaulay of the Royal Observatory, Edinburgh;   Dr.

John Major of the University of Durham; and Robert Teague of 'The News from Boötes' website.

Mediaeval history experts who answered queries included Dr. M.C. Breay, Department of Manuscripts, British Library; Prof. Christopher Harper-Bill, Centre of East Anglian Studies, University of East Anglia; Dr. Dorothy Owen; Prof. David Spear, Furman University, South Carolina; in regard to Woolpit and the green children, Paul Harris, Ron Jones and Steve Harvey. Individuals who helped or made suggestions include Chris Coutts, Joe Irvine and Rick Standley, all of Glasgow, Marise Chapman of High Wycombe and Margaret Collins of Great Barr. For practical help, thanks to Richard and Jayce Foss of the Science Fiction Writers of America; Joe and Cindy Lazzaro; Richard Kealey of International Correspondence Schools; Stanley Schmidt, editor of *Analog*; David Smith of Dave's Disk Doctor Service Ltd.; Billy Blackwood, Gina Cullen, Kerr Armstrong and Suzanne of Working Links.

Finally, substantial parts of this book were thought out and even written in jazz sessions: the Bobby Wishart band at the Halt Bar; the Tap Trio (and friends) at the Brewery Tap; the late Ricky Fernandez at La Taverna; Laura MacDonald's Band at Blackfriars; George Penman at the Curlers; Bobby Deans at the Curlers, Michael Deans at Cottier's, and many others, especially at the Glasgow Jazz Festivals. After I moved to Glasgow, live jazz became my substitute for the inspiration I used to find on the Ayrshire beaches, but even that still works - the breakthrough which led to the third of the book's six drafts came on the beach between Prestwick and Troon, on a trip back to old haunts.

Poscript: filming and more research in 2011-2012 have created a need for still more thanks: to Val and Trevor Howling at the Bull in Woolpit; the Parker Library at Corpus Christi College, Cambridge; Norwich Records Office; John Wiley at the Woolpit Museum; Isobel Tang, Rebecca Burrell, Steve, Billy and the team at WAG TV; Filip Coppens and Kathleen McGowan; Dr. Allan Chapman of Oxford; Prof. Helen King of the Open University; Dr. John Clark of the Museum of London; Mark Harding of the GSFWC (see above); Sean Martin of Mutus Liber, and many more including the young people who took part in the *National Geographic* reconstructions. The story's not over yet and the list will undoubtedly keep growing.

INDEX

Barre, Robert and Petronilla, 146, 222, 225.
Barre, William, 167, 187-188, 196, 204, 222, 225, 228-229, 236-238, 270, 430-431.
Beans, 5, 7, 8, 9, 55, 109-111, 120, 140, 141, 375.
Bedford, 144, 186, 269, 406, 409-413, 432-433.
Bells, 6, 8, 69, 133, 266, 287-288, 295, 324-329, 331-332, 401, 432.
Beltane, see May Day.
Bentley, James, 77, 139, 143, 157, 165, 218, 268, 288, 339, 376, 379, 381, 385, 389, 400, 405, 420.
Berwick, 268, 283, 407, 433.
Bigot, Hugh, earl of Norfolk & Suffolk, 121, 125.
Binham Priory and Bernay, Norfolk, 34, 50, 57, 186-188, 236-237, 241, 251, 264-270, 279, 285.
Bioluminescence, 378-380.
Biospheres, 361, 380.
Black holes, 289-290, 292, 295, 301, 320, 340.
Blundus, family, 23, 51, 58, 67, 88-89, 119-120, 194, 429.
Bologna, 58, 67, 88-89, 138, 204, 209-211, 354.
Boyce, Chris, 302, 333, 418.
Braithwaite, John, 64, 75, 97-98, 132, 161, 178, 299, 337, 358, 400.
Bristol, slave trade, 48, 92, 127-128, 268, 406.
Bruno, Giordano, 1, 172-177, 212.
Burroughs, Edgar Rice, *A Princess of Mars*, 116, 305.
Burton, Robert, 1, 10, 99, 104, 110, 172, 266, 285, 297-298.
Bury St. Edmunds, 3, 6, 12, 13, 15, 34, 40, 50-51, 55, 58, 65, 67, 69, 74-75, 78, 80, 83-85, 86, 100, 102-103, 105, 119, 124, 131, 134, 135, 137, 150, 167, 186-191, 209, 220-221, 236, 240, 251, 260, 269, 282, 284, 285, 324, 345, 350, 385, 400, 420, 427-431.
Byron, Lord, 72-73.
Cabbala, 114-115.
Calne, Wiltshire, 35, 36, 38, 45-48, 149, 175, 188-189, 200, 234, 239, 247-249, 262, 285, 393, 409, 428, 431.
Camden, William, *Britannia*, 110, 177, 181.
Canons, prebendary, 37-38, 42, 46, 56-57, 89, 139, 147-149, 162-163, 168, 188, 191, 217, 248.
Canterbury, 3, 39, 46, 58, 63, 78, 84, 89, 90, 109, 117, 125, 129, 130, 137, 139, 162, 169, 171, 176, 183-185, 233-234, 236, 241, 316-317, 324, 429-430.
Carroll, Lewis, 143, 181.
Castle-Acre, see Acre.
Castles, appear and disappear, 410 412, 433.
Castleton, Derbyshire, 66, 68, 73, 283, 431.
Cathars, 100, 213, 243.

Meteors, meteorites, 22, 23-24, 26,27, 32, 87, 170, 174-175, 180, 235, 260, 265-267, 281, 283, 310, 312-313, 318, 321, 380, 385-386, 391-393, 402, 413-424, 428, 433, 435.

Milarepa, nettles, 106, 376.

Minima, solar: Wolf Minimum, 265, 267, 314, 330, 409, 412, 425, 432-433; Spörer Minimum, 314, 339, 389, 421, 425, 433; Maunder Minimum, 314, 319, 329, 422, 433.

Mills, 29, 41, 180, 181, 217, 228, 254, 328, 345.

Monmouth, Geoffrey of, 3, 43, 44.

Monster, Maidstone, 235-239, 282-286, 390-396, 431.

Moon, 2, 10, 23, 26, 117, 135, 169-170, 172-176, 181-182, 212, 243-247, 263, 270-271, 282, 285, 299-300, 305, 307, 310, 313-314, 317, 321, 334, 349, 358-362, 388-394, 397-399, 406, 409, 410, 413, 415-426, 430, 432-433.

Mote of Skirk, 94-98, 122, 161, 262, 284-285, 330.

Newburgh, William of, 2-6, 11, 36, 43, 55, 99, 112, 113, 135, 143, 185, 187, 217, 228, 287-290, 293, 301-302, 309, 328, 346, 359-364, 390, 393, 415, 426-427, 431-434.

Nogent-le-Rotrou, 206, 208, 283.

Norman Conquest, 13, 19, 22, 33, 51, 277, 339, 428.

Normandy, 22, 36, 39, 43, 74, 78, 88, 117-118, 176-180, 189, 202, 214, 219, 327, 428.

North Fambridge, Essex, 143, 192-193, 237, 240-241, 243, 264, 268-269, 279, 283, 285, 421, 432-433.

Northampton, 67, 120, 186-190, 216, 219, 233, 239, 351, 428.

Norwich, 3, 33, 39-40, 51, 105, 118, 134, 138, 144, 162, 182, 186-191, 194, 215-219, 227-232, 423-424, 428, 430.

Obscuration of the sky, 117, 265-266, 282, 432.

Orford, Essex, 8, 98, 99, 103, 105, 350, 422, 423.

Ossory, 92-93, 98, 146, 194, 234, 239, 261-262, 265, 281, 285, 429.

Oxford, 39, 42, 47, 67, 100, 148, 165, 416.

Oxford, John of, 85, 87, 89, 131, 135, 148, 161-162, 185, 186-192, 195, 202, 212, 215, 217, 228-229, 267, 282, 327, 429-431.

Paranormal, 293-294.

Paris, France, 24, 29, 40, 58, 75, 88-89, 104, 118, 138, 140, 189, 203-204, 209, 211, 213, 216, 412.

Paris, Matthew, 65, 70, 109, 125, 171, 192, 234, 253, 254-255, 260, 262, 264, 267, 269, 281, 319, 350, 400, 432.

Peak Cavern, 71-73, 281, 304, 348, 360, 362, 386-387, 392, 433, 436.

Peter the Hermit, 24, 26, 282, 398-399, 428.

Peverell, William the younger, 66 71, 128, 225, 253, 265, 278, 281, 431.

Peverell, William, 22, 65, 228, 281.

Peveril Castle, Derbyshire, 66-68, 71, 74, 84, 93, 128, 207, 216-220, 233, 236, 252-253, 256, 263, 267, 278-279, 282, 283, 285, 361, 393, 428, 430-433.

About the Author

Duncan Lunan was born in Edinburgh and grew up in Troon, Ayrshire, attending Marr College and Glasgow University. He is an M.A. with Honours in English and Philosophy with Physics, Astronomy and French as supporting subjects, and has a postgraduate Diploma in Education. He is a full-time author with emphasis on astronomy, spaceflight and science fiction, but undertakes a wide range of other writing and speaking as a researcher, tutor, critic, editor, lecturer and broadcaster. His publications include four previous books, over 700 articles and 32 short stories including ten for the comic strip 'Lance McLane' created by Sydney Jordan (see below). He was science fiction critic of the *Glasgow Herald* 1971-92 and as Manager of the Glasgow Parks Dept. Astronomy Project, 1978-79, he designed and built the first astronomically aligned stone circle in Britain for over 3000 years.

Duncan is a Director of the educational company Astronomers of the Future. From 1963 to 2010 he was a Council Member of ASTRA, the Association in Scotland to Research into Astronautics, Curator of Airdrie Public Observatory 1980-81, 1987-97 and 2005-2008, and in 2006-2009 ran an educational outreach project from the Observatory to schools, funded by the National Lottery. His other interests include ancient and mediaeval history, jazz, folk music and hillwalking.

BOOKS BY DUNCAN LUNAN:
Man and the Stars
New Worlds for Old
Man and the Planets
(Edited) Starfield, science fiction by Scottish writers.
With Time Comes Concord and Other Stories
(In press) The Stones and the Stars, a New Stone Circle for Scotland.
(In press) Incoming Asteroid!

About the Artist

Sydney Jordan was born in Dundee and in 1954 created 'Jeff Hawke', the world's longest-running science fiction strip cartoon, for *The Daily Express* and *Scottish Daily News*, followed by 'Lance McLane' for *The Daily Record*; both were syndicated in Europe and three collections of Jeff Hawke stories have been published by Titan Books. 'Jeff Hawke' has been available in book form in Europe for many years, and there is now a Jeff Hawke Club reprinting the stories in magazine and book form in the UK, for which Duncan Lunan writes the accompanying 'Hawke's Notes'.

Sydney frequently illustrated articles in *The Daily Express* and his work has appeared in many newspapers and magazines including *New Worlds*, *Starburst* and *New Scientist*. He has illustrated articles and stories by Duncan Lunan in *World Magazine*, *The Journal of Practical Applications in Space*, *Asgard*, *Nuclear Free Scotland* and *Analog Science Fiction/Science Fact*, and created the cover painting for "Starfield: science fiction by Scottish writers", edited by Duncan Lunan for Orkney Press. In recent years he has worked in advertising and the film industry and his credits include some of the story-boards for *Independence Day*.

Lightning Source UK Ltd.
Milton Keynes UK
UKOW030831131212

203586UK00002B/15/P